D1555910

THE LAW OF FEDERAL INCOME TAXATION

By

Joshua D. Rosenberg

Professor of Law, University of San Francisco

and

Dominic L. Daher

Director of Internal Audit and Tax Compliance, University of San Francisco
Adjunct Professor of Law, University of San Francisco
Adjunct Professor of Accounting, University of San Francisco

HORNBOOK SERIES®

Mat #40369177

Hornbook Series, *Westlaw*, and West Group are trademarks registered in the U.S. Patent and Trademark Office.

© 2008 Thomson/West
      610 Opperman Drive
      P.O. Box 64526
      St. Paul, MN 55164–0526
      1–800–313–9378
Printed in the United States of America

ISBN: 978–0–314–16133–8

TEXT IS PRINTED ON 10% POST CONSUMER RECYCLED PAPER

Dedications

I dedicate this book to my wonderful friends and colleagues at the University of San Francisco School of Law. I cannot imagine a better place to be or better people to be with anywhere.

-Josh Rosenberg

I dedicate this book to: my wife, Stacy, and my parents, Charles and Patricia, who love and support me; the faculty at New York University School of Law who taught me so much about federal tax law; the University of San Francisco which employs me and fosters a culture of academic excellence; and the Society of Jesus which helps make the world a better place through its efforts to educate individuals in the Jesuit Catholic tradition and serve as a voice for those without one.

-Dom Daher

*

Preface

This is the successor to the Hornbook on *Federal Income Taxation* written by the late John C. Chommie of the University of Miami School of Law and Michael D. Rose of Ohio State University School of Law. We thank Professors Chommie and Rose for their fine work on the former editions of the Hornbook on *Federal Income Taxation*.

The Hornbook on *The Law of Federal Income Taxation* is a capstone treatise which provides expert guidance to law students and practitioners alike on this increasingly complex area of the law. The Hornbook on *The Law of Federal Income Taxation* provides up-to-date comprehensive coverage of pertinent provisions of the Internal Revenue Code, relevant administrative guidance, and appropriate caselaw. Above all, the Hornbook on *The Law of Federal Income Taxation* provides a unique blend of the theoretical and practical aspects of federal income taxation. Herein we bring to life one of the most challenging areas of the law with expert analysis. This treatise is a necessity for anyone hoping to gain a better understanding of federal income taxation.

We have written this Hornbook on the *Law of Federal Income Taxation* with the intention that it serve as a capstone treatise for law students, practitioners, and the judiciary. Hereafter, this Hornbook will be updated from time to time, and new editions will be produced as significant changes in the tax law warrant.

We hope the Hornbook on the *Law of Federal Income Taxation* will serve as your trusted reference guide when researching federal income tax law.

JOSHUA D. ROSENBERG
and
DOMINIC L. DAHER

San Francisco, CA
December 2007

*

WESTLAW® Overview

The Law of Federal Income Taxation offers a detailed and comprehensive treatment of the basic rules, principles, and issues relating to federal income taxation law. To supplement the information contained in this book, you can access Westlaw, West's computer-assisted legal research service. Westlaw contains a broad array of legal resources, including case law, statutes, expert commentary, current developments, and various other types of information.

Learning how to use these materials effectively will enhance your legal research abilities. To help you coordinate the information in the book with your Westlaw research, this volume contains an appendix listing Westlaw databases, search techniques, and sample problems.

The instructions and features described in this Westlaw overview are based on accessing Westlaw via westlaw.com® at **www.westlaw.com**.

THE PUBLISHER

*

Summary of Contents

Page

Table of Contents

_____

THE LAW OF FEDERAL
INCOME TAXATION

*

Chapter 1

INTRODUCTION

Table of Sections

---

§ 1.01 OVERTURE

It was Benjamin Franklin who suggested "[i]n this world nothing can be said to be certain, except death and taxes."[1] Every form of civilized society requires the rule of law, and such civilized societies require some form of government to enforce the law. As a result, even a

§ 1.01

1. Benjamin Franklin, *Letter to Jean Baptiste Le Roy* (1789).

1

society that appears to spend nothing for the common good or for its own defense must at least compensate those who govern. In the history of the world, there has never been an organized civilization completely free from taxation in one form or another.

The similarity of taxes to death goes beyond their mutual inevitability; they are, and have always been, almost equally unpopular. Throughout history, as governments have grown, so have taxes, and as taxes have grown, so has resistance to those taxes.

§ 1.02 "THE PRICE WE PAY FOR A CIVILIZED SOCIETY"[1]

Most Americans readily acknowledge the complexity of federal income tax law. Among all kinds of legislative and judicial decision making, only tax laws seem capable of engendering nearly universal anger, anxiety, paranoia and outright hatred. Millions of otherwise law-abiding citizens cheat on their taxes (and even boast about it to others),[2] and millions more would join them if only they were more confident they could get away with it.[3] Economists have estimated that the amount of tax revenue fraudulently withheld from the government is over $100,000,000,000 per year, or roughly enough to balance the federal budget.[4]

The fact that many people do not comply with tax laws does not lessen their hatred of those laws. For most Americans, any tax is a bad tax, regardless of its actual economic or social consequences. Even those whose own taxes would be unaffected (or reduced) are more likely than not to be against any proposed "tax increases."[5] Candidates for political

---

§ 1.02

1. Compania General de Tabacos de Filipinas v. Collector, 275 U.S. 87, 100, 48 S.Ct. 100, 72 L.Ed. 177 (1927).

2. See generally, Tax Cheats Called Out of Control, N.Y. Times, August 1, 2006, page C1; James L. Wittenbach, IRS Launches Assault on Frivolous Tax Evasion Schemes, 73 Prac. Tax Strategies 359, 2004 WL 2801162 (W.G. & .L.).

3. See Eric M. Rice, The Corporate Tax Gap: Evidence on Tax Compliance by Small Corporations, in Why People Pay Taxes 125 (Joel S. Slemrod ed., 1992). About two thirds of corporations fail to fully comply with the tax laws. Id. at 132–33. Among individuals who have the opportunity to avoid taxes, noncompliance is also substantial. John S. Carroll, How Taxpayers Think about Their Taxes: Frames and Values, in Why People Pay Taxes 43, 45 (Joel S. Slemrod, ed. 1992) (discussing the use of tax law to influence behavior). Compliance is typically higher only among wage earners whose taxes are withheld at the source, and

whose opportunities for noncompliance are scarce. Id. When a taxpayer's receipts are not reported by someone else (e.g., an employer or other payor) they are often not likely to be reported at all. Id. Surprisingly, our self-assessment system works well beyond what one would predict based solely on the possibility of detection and prosecution. Id. For the most part, however, this is due to the fact that many people misunderstand how unlikely it is that their tax fraud will be found and/or punished. Indeed, there is substantial evidence that once people have been audited and learn that the process is not nearly as disastrous as they had believed, they may become more likely to cheat than they had been prior to the audit. Carroll, *supra* at 47.

4. Joel S. Slemrod, Why People Pay Taxes: Introduction, in Why People Pay Taxes 1, 1 (Joel S. Slemrod ed., 1992).

5. See Edward J. McCaffery, Cognitive Theory and Tax, 41 UCLA L. Rev. 1861, 1880 (1994). See also Russell B. Korobkin and Thomas S. Ulen, Law and Behavioral Science: Removing the Rationality Assump-

office do not run on themes such as "no new torts" or "no new contract laws," but they win when they run on themes such as "no new taxes." Even Populists who promise to make the "fat cats" pay will rapidly lose their appeal among the middle class and the poor when they begin to propose tax increases, even if those increases apply only to the wealthiest taxpayers.[6]

Our dislike of taxes is so pervasive that "Tax Freedom Day"[7] seems to be evolving into a national holiday. No one has yet suggested "tort freedom day" or "contract law freedom day," or even "occupational safety freedom day," despite the fact that the timing of such days could easily be determined, and might even come up around the same time as Tax Freedom Day.

Hatred of taxes is not a novel idea; nor is it limited to America. Nevertheless, in a country whose citizens are more and more frequently in search of some common ground, perhaps the only thing that truly unites all Americans is a common perception of the Internal Revenue Service as the enemy.

Despite, and in part because of, this hatred of taxation, individuals dedicate an inordinate amount of time and attention to taxes. Personal conversation, political debate, and millions of practitioners are focused on tax issues. Moreover, the legislative process that surrounds tax is qualitatively different from, and significantly more public than, the process that surrounds other legislation.[8]

As Oliver Wendel Holmes so aptly put it, taxes are the "price we pay for a civilized society."[9] Nonetheless, most Americans do not pay nearly as much attention to the "civilized society" that we have acquired with our tax revenue as we do to what we see as the exorbitant "price we pay" through our taxes. Basically, Americans understand that taxes are what we pay[10] (and what the government takes), and the enactment and

tion from Law and Economics, 88 Calif. L. Rev. 1051 (2000).

6. See Edward J. McCaffery, Cognitive Theory and Tax, 41 UCLA L. Rev. 1861, 1887 (1994).

7. If all earnings went to pay the year's taxes until all taxes were paid, and no one could take home any earnings until all taxes were paid, "Tax Freedom Day" would be the day on which taxes were paid in full and the rest of the year's earnings could be kept rather than paid to the government. This day usually occurs sometime in April. See, e.g., GOP Senators Attach Comments on Tax Freedom Day to Policy Committee Release, Tax Notes Today, 96 TNT 96–35 (May 15, 1996); Curtis S. Dubay and Scott A. Hodge, America Celebrates Tax Freedom Day, Tax Foundation Special Report No. 152, http://www.taxfoundation.org/publications/show/93.html.

8. Cf. Stanley S. Surrey, The Congress and the Tax Lobbyist—How Special Tax Provisions Get Enacted, 70 Harv. L. Rev. 1145, 1164–65 (1957). Several former government officials intimately involved in the legislative process have written that "[f]ederal tax statutes and the legislative process that produces them differ from other legislation in such degree that the difference is tantamount to a difference in kind." Bradford L. Ferguson et al., Reexamining the Nature and Role of Tax Legislative History in Light of the Changing Realities of the Process, 67 Taxes 804, 806 (1989). To some extent, of course, tax laws have been subject to certain restrictions ever since the first drafting of the Constitution. U.S. Const. art. I, § 2, cl. 3.

9. Compania General de Tabacos de Filipinas v. Collector, 275 U.S. 87, 100, 48 S.Ct. 100, 72 L.Ed. 177 (1927).

10. Unlike other laws, tax laws were explicitly intended to be descriptive (e.g., from whom the government can get money) rather than normative, and they are de-

enforcement of all nontax laws is what we get (and what the government gives). "Taking" is what we assume tax laws are all about in this country. When we think about taxes we tend to focus on the extent, and the victims (ourselves), of that taking.

Because we focus so fixedly on taxes as the instrument of governmental taking, that taking is almost all we see when we look at taxes. This is in many ways a self-fulfilling prophecy.[11] In the classroom, when professors are told that some students are "trouble-makers" and that others are "high achievers," the professors tend to focus on the trouble-making behaviors of the first group and on the achieving behaviors of the second group.[12] Even when both groups of students exhibit virtually identical amounts of troublesome behaviors and achieving behaviors, professors almost always incorrectly conclude that those labeled "troublemakers" cause more trouble and those labeled "high achievers" show more achievements; they focus on those expected behaviors, pay more attention to them, and they unconsciously encourage more of them.[13] In the realm of laws, taxes are the usual suspects for making trouble and achieving little.

When laws other than tax laws are analyzed, they are evaluated primarily by deciding whether the laws' commands correspond with accepted standards of behavior. For example, most Americans believe that laws against murder are good because murder is morally wrong.

When people evaluate tax laws, though, the primary considerations quickly become almost anything *other* than morality. Instead, tax laws are judged primarily by their *economic* impact:[14] how many members of which economic class will pay how much more tax, and how many members of the same economic strata will pay how much less tax?[15]

---

signed to have as little impact as possible on anyone's conduct or moral attitude. Professor Andrews suggested that tax laws at best do nothing more than uniformly and neutrally convert private good to public good. William D. Andrews, Personal Deductions In An Ideal Income Tax, 86 Harv. L. Rev. 309, 325–26 (1972). Indeed, tax theory rests on the assumption that the "best" tax is a "neutral" tax: one that allows the free market to take its course, and that leaves to other kinds of laws the role of improving or regulating human conduct. Id. at 326. Tax laws have frequently been used to influence behavior through the use of tax incentives or tax expenditures. See, e.g., §§ 103, 168. But when this happens it is typically viewed as a "tax preference" deviation from "pure" tax laws and as the intrusion of tax laws into territory generally reserved for other areas of law.

11. Joshua D. Rosenberg, The Psychology of Mediation, The Recorder ADR Special Supplement, Spring 1994, at 11. See also Hans H. Strupp and Jeffrey L. Binder, Psychotherapy in a New Key, A Guide to

Time–Limited Dynamic Psychotherapy 38, 76 (1984) (discussing expectations concerning self-image and other's reactions to it).

12. Interview with Professor Stephen Zlutnick, University of San Francisco School of Education, San Francisco, CA (Oct. 17, 1994).

13. Interview with Professor Stephen Zlutnick, University of San Francisco School of Education, San Francisco, CA (Oct. 17, 1994). See also John C. Masters, et al., Behavior Therapy 245–46 (3d ed. 1987).

14. Michael J. Graetz, Paint-by-Numbers Tax Lawmaking, 95 Colum. L. Rev. 609, 612–13 (1995). See also Cheryl D. Block, Pathologies at the Intersection of the Budget and Tax Legislative Processes, 43 B.C. L. Rev. 863 (2002).

15. Michael J. Graetz, Paint-by-Numbers Tax Lawmaking, 95 Colum. L. Rev. 609, 621 (1995). See also Cheryl D. Block, Pathologies at the Intersection of the Budget and Tax Legislative Processes, 43 B.C. L. Rev. 863 (2002).

Unlike legislative proposals in other areas, proposed changes in tax law are always accompanied by, and often driven by, revenue estimates and tables illustrating the projected distribution of economic burdens among different classes of incomes and wealth.[16] This constant analysis of and attention to the economic burdens imposed by taxes reinforces the perception of taxes primarily as the instrument of governmental taking, and it reinforces our belief that taxes take more and give less than other types of laws.

In fact, tax laws are not so different from any other laws. Every law "takes" from some group within society and "gives" to others. Indeed, were legislatures to prepare distributional tables for property laws and for criminal laws relating to property, as they do for all federal income tax laws, it would likely become evident that property laws and laws against conversion of property keep money out of the hands of the poor and in the hands of the rich.[17] Undoubtedly the activities which have been criminalized are primarily activities the poor would be more likely to engage in than the rich, but by incarcerating convicted criminals (who are primarily poor), freedom is taken from the poor to a much more significant extent than from the rich. Additionally, further study of nontax laws would likely reveal significant racial and gender biases in the impact of these laws.[18] Indeed, if nontax laws underwent the same level of scrutiny and analysis, Americans would find many to be completely unacceptable.

People often judge the *equity* of tax laws by standards very different from those applied to nontax laws; not surprisingly, people often use

16. Id. at 612. A good example of this phenomenon occurred in the 1993 tax legislation. In order to balance the distributional impact of the legislation and in order to be able to project desired revenue, Congress enacted tax rates that imposed a substantial "marriage penalty." Many people took this as a sign that Congress was "anti-family;" it was instead only a sign that when Congress enacts tax legislation, social policy can become irrelevant, and economic concerns can take control.

17. Dave Palermo, Assault on Crime Criticized, Las Vegas Rev.-J., Oct. 13, 1996, at 1B. Some have suggested a tax-type analysis of the taking done by at least some of the criminal laws. Noting the high percentage of African–American males between the ages of 18 and 25 who have been sentenced to prison, primarily for crack cocaine, some commentators have pointed out the fact that the sentences for possession of crack cocaine, which is used more by African–Americans, are more harsh than the sentences for other cocaine, used predominantly by white Americans. The result is that the criminal sentencing laws take substantially more from the nonwhite drug users than they do from white drug users. See Carole Wolff Barnes & Rodney Kingsnorth, Race, Drug and Criminal Sentencing: Hidden Effects of the Criminal Law, 24 J. Crim. Just., 39, 39–55; Harvey Berkman, Congress Keeps Tough Crack Penalty, Nat'l L.J., Nov. 6, 1995, at A14; House Clears Bill to Keep Stiff Sentences for Crack Cocaine, Congressional Quarterly Weekly Reporter, Oct. 21, 1995, at 3212. Others have determined that "three strikes" laws are applied to African Americans about 1300% more frequently than they are applied to white males, Christopher Davis et al., "Three Strikes:" The New Apartheid, Report by the Center on Juvenile Crime and Justice 2 (Mar. 1996).

18. Drew S. Days III, Race and the Federal Criminal Justice System: A Look at the Issue of Selective Prosecution, 48 Me. L. Rev. 179, 183–89 (1996). See also Elizabeth Tison, Amending the Sentencing Guidelines for Cocaine Offenses: The 100–to–1 Ratio is not as "Cracked" up as Some Suggest, 27 S. Ill. U. L.J. 413 (2003); Steven L. Chanenson, Booker on Crack: Sentencing's Latest Gordian Knot, 15 Cornell J.L. & Pub. Pol'y 551 (2006).

very different standards to judge the *efficiency* of the two kinds of laws. When people judge the efficiency of nontax laws, they generally look at the extent to which such laws succeed at getting people to change their behaviors. When people analyze the efficiency of tax laws, they focus primarily on how likely the laws will be able to raise the "hoped-for" revenues *without* unduly impacting the behavior of those from whom they take. As a general proposition, the effect of taxes on behavior is either ignored or viewed as an unfortunate but necessary inefficiency.

To see the impact of this focus, consider the history of the initial proposals for mandatory seatbelt laws. Proponents argued such laws would save lives and save medical costs, and most people agreed they were an effective way to improve public safety.[19] Opposition to seatbelt laws was based on ideas of freedom: the government had no business telling people they could buy only cars that had seatbelts, or telling people they could not drive without having their seatbelts fastened.[20] The debate focused almost exclusively on the issue of freedom from governmental intrusion versus the governmental interest in preventing serious injuries.[21]

Rather than requiring manufacturers to install seatbelts, Congress could have imposed a sizeable tax on cars manufactured and sold without seatbelts. Aside from the facts that a seatbelt tax would have left a few people with unsafe cars and less money, such a tax would have allowed individuals to pay for the privilege of purchasing an unsafe car, rather than revoking that privilege altogether. The tax would have generated some revenue for the public treasury, and the law would have had an impact similar to that of the mandatory seatbelt laws that were in fact enacted.

Analysis and debate of the *tax* proposal would have looked much different from the analysis and debate surrounding the actual mandatory seatbelt requirement. Congress would have focused immediately on the economic impact of the tax both on the public treasury and on different income classes. In fact, at least three different congressional and administrative committees would have been required to prepare detailed graphs showing the distribution of the tax burden among income classes.[22] Because, at that time, high-priced cars typically came equipped with seatbelts as standard equipment and low-priced cars did not, a "no seatbelt" tax would have impacted much more heavily on low-income individuals, and people would have focused on the regressive nature of the tax. Undoubtedly commentators would have pointed out that the

19. Gary C. Fredenburg, Legal Issues Presented by Motor Vehicle Restraint Systems, 17 Akron L. Rev. 781, 787–88 (1984).

20. Id. at 787.

21. See, e.g., Linda Geller Dubinsky, The Minnesota Mandatory Seat Belt Law: No Right to be Reckless?, 10 Hamline L. Rev. 229, 229 (1987); Jeffery Thomas, Freedom to be Foolish? L.B. 496: The Mandatory Seatbelt Law, 19 Creighton L. Rev. 743,

743 (1986); Anthony P. Polito, Constitutional Law: Seatbelt Laws and the Right to Privacy, 10 Harv. J.L. & Pub. Pol'y 752, 757 (1987).

22. Graetz, *supra* note 15, at 614–15 (noting these committees include the Joint Committee on Taxation, the Congressional Budget Office, and the Treasury's Office of Tax Analysis).

addition of seatbelts in low-priced cars costs as much as their addition to high-priced cars, thereby resulting in a greater proportionate price increase in low-priced cars, and they would have argued that a "no seatbelt" tax would increase the price of cars in the same way as would a sales tax, which is inherently regressive with respect to income simply because the poor are forced to spend a greater percentage of their income on taxable purchases.

Congress would also have paid close attention to the revenue raised by the proposed tax. Some politicians would have explained that they would tolerate no net tax increase, so that if a "no seatbelt" tax were to be enacted, some other tax would have to be correspondingly decreased. Other politicians would have suggested not only that some other tax would have to be decreased, but that a tax decrease would have to impact the same income classes who would be impacted most significantly by the new tax; hence, the ultimate impact of the tax legislation would be neutral across income classes.[23]

Because the actual legislation was framed as a public safety law rather than a tax law, people tended to overlook the fact that the law had a harsher economic impact on the poor than it did on the wealthy in both relative and absolute terms.[24] Legislators discussed the fact that requiring manufacturers to install seatbelts would increase the prices of cars, but neither Congress nor the general public focused on whether the price increase would have a disproportionate impact on one income class as opposed to another income class.[25] Instead, the populace debated whether or not the law was fair to those who disliked seatbelts, regardless of income class. Because the law was framed as a public safety law, people saw the fact that a high percentage of wealthy automobile owners already had seatbelts in their cars as an indication that poor people ought to be entitled to the same protection that the rich already enjoyed, rather than as evidence the law would be more costly to low-income individuals.

Framing the law as a public safety issue led people to ignore what are essentially economic issues. If the law had been framed as a tax, people would have ignored significant safety issues, such as the fact that the tax would have done more to protect the poor than to protect the wealthy, both because the economic burden would be more likely to convince the poor to purchase safe cars and because the poor tended to have less safe cars initially than the wealthy. Had Congress decided that only luxury cars and cars driven by the wealthy had to be guaranteed the

23. Graetz, *supra* note 15, at 617–20.

24. A higher percentage of low-income people were hit by the new requirement because many high-priced cars were already equipped with seatbelts as standard equipment, so that the cost of those high-price cars, unlike the cost of less expensive models, would not be increased because no new equipment had to be added; the additional expense of seatbelts was higher for low-

income persons relative to both the price of their cars and their net income.

25. Lloyd N. Cutler, Book Review: Regulatory Mismatch and its Cure, 96 Harv. L. Rev. 545, 550–51 (1982) (reviewing Stephen Breyer). See also Thomas A. Murawski and Steven L. Schooner, Communicating Governance: Will Plain English Drafting Improve Regulation?, 70 Geo. Wash. L. Rev. 163 (2002).

safety of seatbelts (and that cars purchased and driven by poor people could continue to be as dangerous as before), it is likely that advocates of the poor would have been less than thrilled. On the other hand, had Congress decided to impose a no-seatbelt tax only on purchases of high-priced cars that came without seatbelts, those same advocates for the poor would likely have been delighted Congress had imposed a higher economic burden on the wealthy than on the poor.

Although, as suggested above, most people associate moral imperatives with criminal or tort laws, it is likely that tax laws could do a significantly *better* job of changing people's behavior than criminal, tort or contract laws. When governments want to change the way people act, they tend to issue commands ("do this," or "do not do that"). When the commands are not followed, the government is likely to attempt to punish the wrongdoer. In fact, commands followed by punishments are relatively ineffective at bringing about desired behavior changes.

People are significantly more likely to actually adopt desired behaviors in response to a system that: (1) uses rewards for correct behaviors in addition to, and, where possible, in place of, punishments for wrong behaviors; and (2) ensures that both rewards and punishments are administered swiftly[26] and consistently. In both of these respects, tax laws can be significantly more effective than other laws in bringing about desired behaviors. Unlike criminal and other civil laws, only tax laws allow not just for punishments (in the form of increased tax liability) for individuals who do not follow the law, but also for rewards, by means of tax deductions or credits, for those who engage in the desired behaviors. In addition, the huge sanctions of the criminal law (and the less severe sanctions of contract law and tort law) are applied only infrequently,[27] and often after the lapse of significant time. As a result, these sanctions are relatively ineffective at bringing about behavior change.[28] Tax laws alone are enforced at least quarterly, or, in the case of wage withholding, once every pay period.

---

26. A swift system of rewarding desired behavior has been found most effective. John M. Ivancevich & Michael T. Matteson, Organizational Behavior and Management 200–01 (3d ed. 1993). Tax lawyers can probably understand better than anyone else the "time value" of reinforcement, irrespective of whether the reinforcement mechanism involves money. Much of the work of tax lawyers is devoted to delaying the "punishment" of taxation and accelerating the "rewards" that accompany current tax deductions. A significant difference between the "time value of money" and the "time value" of rewards and punishments is that compound interest principles result in the value of an investment increasing more rapidly in later years than in early years, while the impact of rewards and pun-ishments decreases most dramatically in the time periods closest to the behavior.

27. Criminal laws are applied slowly and infrequently because of numerous limitations and delays in the criminal justice system. Other civil laws are applied infrequently because violators are not punished unless the victim is injured, knows about her remedies, and decides to bring an action. As a result, negligent behavior that causes no injury is subject to no punishment.

28. The sanctions of criminal law do, of course, isolate the criminal from society for a period of time, which does have an immediate impact on the criminal's behavior.

§ 1.03 A BRIEF HISTORY OF AMERICAN TAXATION

The federal income tax has not always dominated the federal government's revenue raising activities. Although an income tax was proposed as early as 1815, perhaps influenced by the English income tax first levied during the Napoleonic Wars, the federal government did not resort to an income tax until 1862, when revenue was needed to finance the Civil War. The Act of 1862 had tax rates ranging from 1.5% to 5%; income tax contained prototypes of a number of salient features of the present structure such as graduated rates, tax withholding, and returns filed under penalties of perjury. However, this first individual income tax was retained for only a decade, and from 1872 to 1913 the federal government limited its taxing measures largely to excise duties, primarily on liquor and tobacco, and customs receipts. These were the traditional means of raising revenues.

The elimination of the Civil War income tax in 1872 was hardly met with widespread approval. The issue of the desirability of an income tax remained a topic of heated political controversy. The income tax became a major plank in the platforms of such political groups as the Greenback, Anti–Monopoly, and Populist parties. The controversy cut across the lines of the Democratic and Republican parties, and Congress divided largely on a sectional basis. The representatives of the agricultural West and South pressed for reenactment while those representing the industrial East were opposed. Economic groups were also divided. The banking and manufacturing interests who favored continued protective tariff legislation were opposed to the income tax, while importers and merchants favored it as a revenue device in lieu of high customs duties.

The controversy reached a climax in 1894 with the enactment of a new income tax that imposed a flat rate 2% tax on individual and corporate income. Although the Civil War Act had withstood attacks of unconstitutionality,[1] in an immediate test of the 1894 Act a sharply divided Supreme Court in Pollock v. Farmers' Loan & Trust Co.[2] struck down the new law as unconstitutional. The Court held that an income tax was a direct tax, which under the Constitution was required to be apportioned among the states on the basis of population.[3]

Despite the apportionment requirement, the proponents of an income tax were not dissuaded. By 1909 they had gained sufficient strength to bring about the enactment of a 1% excise tax on corporations and the passage of a joint resolution of Congress that ultimately became the Sixteenth Amendment to the Constitution. The Sixteenth Amendment provides as follows: "The Congress shall have power to lay and collect taxes on incomes, from whatever source derived, without appor-

---

§ 1.03

1. Springer v. United States, 102 U.S. (12 Otto) 586, 26 L.Ed. 253 (1880).

2. 157 U.S. 429, 15 S.Ct. 673, 39 L.Ed. 759 (1895).

3. This tax was upheld against attack on constitutional grounds on the theory that it was not a direct tax but an excise tax on the privilege of doing business in the corporate form. Flint v. Stone Tracy Co., 220 U.S. 107, 31 S.Ct. 342, 55 L.Ed. 389 (1911).

tionment among the several States, and without regard to any census or enumeration."

By 1913 a sufficient number of states had ratified the proposed amendment, and it became part of the supreme law of the land. In the same year Congress enacted the first income tax under the new amendment as part of the Tariff Act of 1913. Unlike the ill-fated 1894 Act which imposed a flat-rate tax, the 1913 Act imposed rates on individuals on a graduated basis starting at 1% on the first $20,000 of net income. The top rate was 7% on income over $500,000. Exemptions were allowed of $3,000 for single persons and $4,000 for married persons. Corporations were taxed at a flat rate of 1% under the 1913 Act, and the 1909 excise tax was repealed.

The exemptions and the graduated rates were attacked on constitutional grounds for alleged denial of due process of law under the Fifth Amendment. In 1916 the Supreme Court upheld the validity of the law in Brushaber v. Union Pacific Railroad Co.[4] Since that time a federal tax on income has never been seriously contested on constitutional grounds, and only in a few instances has the Court struck down the application of particular provisions for failure to comport with the power granted Congress under the Sixteenth Amendment. In short, the legal problems since the first revenue acts under the amendment have been problems of statutory construction rather than problems of constitutional law.

The claims brought in the 1960s on the basis of conscientious objection to United States involvement in Vietnam serve as good examples of modern judicial treatment of taxpayers' constitutional arguments. In Autenrieth v. Cullen[5] the 124 plaintiffs sought refunds of the percentage of their taxes spent on the military; they argued that the First and Fourteenth Amendments prevented the government from forcing them to finance the war. In rejecting the First Amendment freedom of religion argument, the Ninth Circuit held that Congress constitutionally could tax anyone, regardless of religion, "for support of the general government." The court noted the difficulty of running a government if a prorated refund of the type sought by the plaintiffs were permitted. Such a response is typical of the tendency of courts to cast taxpayers' claims in terms of property rights rather than in terms of fundamental individual rights or liberties.

During the years since the enactment of the 1913 Act, much has happened to both the form and content of the statute prescribing the rules governing the imposition of the federal income tax. The form of the federal income tax has changed considerably. The 1913 Act was sixteen pages of section II of the Tariff Act of 1913. While separation from the usual biannual consideration of the tariff was effected early, until 1939 each revenue act was self-contained, and the preceding revenue act was superseded entirely. Of course, much of each succeeding act was a

---

4. 240 U.S. 1, 36 S.Ct. 236, 60 L.Ed. 493 (1916).

5. 418 F.2d 586 (9th Cir. 1969), cert. denied, 397 U.S. 1036, 90 S.Ct. 1353, 25 L.Ed.2d 647 (1970).

verbatim copy of the act that came before, the only differences being the amendments announced by the superseding act. This procedure of complete reenactment was unnecessary and needlessly complex from the point of view of statutory referencing. To correct these difficulties Congress enacted the Internal Revenue Code of 1939 and revised the Code in 1954 and 1986. Since 1939 new legislation has been cast as amendments to the 1939 Code, 1954 Code, or 1986 Code. The present provisions of the federal tax law are found in the Internal Revenue Code of 1986, as amended.

While Congress has amended the Code almost every year, from a historical perspective, the present Internal Revenue Code of 1986 remains largely a product of evolutionary growth rather than the revolutionary product of a particular Congress.

§ 1.04   TAX RATES AND BURDENS

Section 1 sets forth the rates for six categories of taxpayers: (1) married persons filing joint returns and certain surviving spouses; (2) heads of households; (3) unmarried persons; (4) married persons filing separate returns; (5) children under age 18 who have unearned income; and (6) estates and trusts. Why are there six different categories in section 1? The answer to this question, like the answers to many federal income tax enigmas, is found in the legislative history and the political compromises made by Congress.

Section 11 sets forth the rates for corporations. However, as a general rule, under section 1363 an S corporation, as defined in section 1361, is generally not subject to taxation.

§ 1.05   OVERVIEW OF VARIOUS TAX PROCESSES

[1]   TAX LAWMAKING

Two features of the Constitution lie at the heart of the tax law-making process.[1] The first is the division of power between the branches of government; the second is the right of the people to petition for redress of grievances. However, in 1790 when the first Congress acceded to Treasury Secretary Alexander Hamilton's fiscal plan for funding the federal debt, it could hardly have anticipated that the need would develop for Congress to rely upon an extensive bureaucracy to administer its revenue raising efforts. Nor could the first Congress have foreseen

§ 1.05

1. See Reese, The Politics of Taxation (1980); Gallagher, The Tax Legislative Process, 3 Rev. Tax'n Individuals 203 (1979); Ferguson, Hickman & Lubick, Reexamining the Nature and Role of Tax Legislative History in Light of the Changing Realities of the Process, 67 Taxes 804, 808–12 (1989).

See also Pechman, Federal Tax Policy 37–51 (4th ed. 1983); Evans, The Condition of the Tax Legislative Process, 39 Tax Notes 151 (1988); Leonard, Perspectives on the Tax Legislative Process, 38 Tax Notes 969 (1988); McDaniel, Federal Income Tax Simplification: The Political Process, 34 Tax L. Rev. 27 (1977).

that the right to petition would result in the development of private interest groups that lobby both the executive and the legislative branches of government. Today it is in these complex relationships between Congress, the executive branch, and special interest groups that an understanding of the tax law-making process is found.

In the Department of the Treasury the administration's proposals are formulated by the Assistant Secretary of the Treasury for Tax Policy. The Assistant Secretary is assisted by three staffs: (1) the Office of Tax Legislative Counsel, consisting of lawyers who analyze issues and prepare legislation; (2) the Office of Tax Analysis, a group of economists and statisticians who estimate the revenue effects of proposals; and (3) the Office of International Tax Counsel, a group of attorneys responsible for foreign source income and foreign citizens. Of course, this is only part of the formal organizational structure, and it does not reveal the pressures that are brought to bear on the administration from a variety of constituents.

The role of the Treasury does not mean that Congress functions as a rubber stamp in the tax law-making process. Quite the contrary, the House Ways and Means Committee and Senate Finance Committee have critical and powerful roles, and the views of their members must be taken into account by the Treasury in formulating its proposals. Indeed, Congress may take the initiative in preparing tax legislation.

If a tax bill has its origins in the Treasury Department, congressional consideration provides a new stage for various interests to exert their influence. The relationships here can be quite complex. For example, if the Treasury's proposal is designed to change certain provisions of the Internal Revenue Code relating to particular business deductions, the tax-writing committee members may find themselves caught between the administration and the potentially impacted private parties. On the other hand, If the bill reflects the policies of a tax-concession oriented administration, the tax committee members may find themselves contending with the Treasury and the potentially impacted private parties. Ultimately, compromise is the likely result of this complex political process.

Under the Constitution all tax legislation must originate in the House.[2] Proposed tax legislation is handled by the House Ways and Means Committee, which is composed of members of both political parties. The Ways and Means Committee ordinarily holds public hearings. These hearings have aspects of both a fact-finding inquiry and an adversary proceeding between the Treasury and the potentially impacted private parties. Testimony is taken from representatives of the Treasury and from representatives of various constituencies.

Hearings on proposed tax legislation frequently reveal the various constituencies affected by the proposed legislation. Although the role

---

2. U.S. Const. art. I, § 7, requires: "All Bills for raising Revenue shall originate in the House of Representatives; but the Senate may propose or concur with Amendments as on other Bills."

hearings play in the final legislative product may not be clear, the exposure of interests, which may itself provide a sufficient justification for hearings, often signals the political strength of various constituencies. There is little evidence that the hearing process itself provides needed technical data to properly evaluate the positions of governmental and private interests. In fact, most lobbyists seek preferential treatment for their constituents, but at the same time they attempt to find a way to convince lawmakers that the issue at hand is really one which of great importance for some other reason—such as national security, national fiscal policy, etc.

After concluding its hearings the Ways and Means Committee engages in mark-up sessions in which the tax legislation is prepared. After the House's Legislative Counsel completes preparation of the bill, it is reported back to the House accompanied by a printed Committee Report justifying and explaining the provisions of the legislation.

Although Article I, Section 7, of the Constitution states that all revenue bills shall originate in the House, in recent years the Senate has occasionally proceeded on its own initiative and attached tax legislation onto other House bills.

In the Senate the process described for the House is repeated. The Senate Finance Committee holds hearings, prepares legislation, and reports back to the Senate.

After Senate passage, differences between the House and Senate versions are worked out in a Conference Committee, which is composed of members of both the House Ways and Means Committee and the Senate Finance Committee. From the Conference Committee comes a reconciled bill and conference report. If passed by both houses of Congress, this version is sent to the White House. The President then has 10 days to sign the bill.

Besides the law itself, the legislative process produces the basic documents of the legislative history, which are used in interpreting the law. These documents consist primarily of the testimony and supporting documents taken at the public hearings and the Committee Reports. These reports describe the proposed legislation's provisions and the laws impacted (and not impacted) by the proposed legislation. Thus, in addition to indicating rationale, Committee Reports deal with the technical aspects of the law; also, they provide a framework for drafting regulations.

[2] THE ADMINISTRATIVE PROCESS

The Code is administered by the Internal Revenue Service, the largest unit in the Department of the Treasury. The Service has its headquarters in Washington, D.C. The Commissioner of Internal Revenue is appointed by the President.[3] The Commissioner works in the National Office along with Associate and Assistant Commissioners.

---

3. § 7803(a)(1)(A).

These principal officers of the Service provide the general policy making and management functions for the enforcement of the Internal Revenue Code and the Treasury Regulations promulgated thereunder.

The Service has more than 115,000 employees in district and local offices, service centers, and regional offices.[4] The 58 districts, which are headed by District Directors, are grouped into 7 regions, each headed by a Regional Commissioner who supervises the work of the District Directors. The field organization also includes 10 service centers, each headed by a Director reporting to a Regional Commissioner. These centers process tax returns, perform certain accounting functions, and otherwise service the districts in the performance of their basic activities of auditing, investigating, and collecting.

In broad outline, the Service may be viewed as having two basic goals. The primary objective of the IRS is the collection of revenue; in 2004, the IRS collected in excess of \$2 trillion in revenue through the processing of more than 224 million tax returns.[5] A secondary objective of the IRS is ensuring that taxpayers have satisfied their responsibilities, a mission that includes an interpretation function.

The collection process nominally starts with tax withholding and taxpayer returns. As wages and salaries are earned, the income tax is withheld by employers and paid to the government for each employee.[6] Tax is collected on other income through quarterly installment payments by individual taxpayers on the estimated amount of anticipated income tax liability for the year.[7] Corporations are also required to file declarations of estimated tax and make installment payments.[8] In this manner most taxpayers keep current in their annual income tax obligations.

A final self-assessment of tax is made on the annual return. The return must generally be filed with the taxpayer's service center within 3½ months after the close of the tax year.[9] Hence, the filing date is April 15 for an individual using a calendar year.[10] Failure to file, late filing, and failure to make payments as due subject the taxpayer to penalties.[11]

Returns are processed at the service centers. Initially, they are checked for mathematical and other errors. Later they are processed to select a limited number for possible audit. Those selected are sent to field offices where audits are conducted.

Discrepancies revealed during an audit are usually resolved through administrative procedures. If the taxpayer cannot settle with the examining agent, the taxpayer may have a formal conference with an appeals officer. During this process an attorney or accountant may represent the taxpayer before the IRS.

---

4. Reforming the IRS, 143 Cong. Rec. S10205–01.

5. http://www.irs.gov/irs/article/0,,id=98141,00.html.

6. See Treas. Reg. § 31.3402(a)–1(b).

7. See § 6654.

8. See § 6655.

9. See § 6072(a).

10. Id.

11. See § 6651.

The Service's general interpretive authority is based on section 7805 of the Code, which authorizes the government "to prescribe all needful rules and regulations for the enforcement" of the Code. Also, authority and direction to issue regulations is prescribed by a number of Code provisions dealing with particular areas and transactions.[12]

The Service issues various types of interpretations of the Code. The highest order of these consist of Treasury Decisions, which are published in the Federal Register on the signature of the Commissioner of Internal Revenue and approved by the Assistant Secretary of the Treasury for Tax Policy.[13] Generally, Treasury Decisions consist of final regulations or amendments to them. Regulations first appear in proposed form in the Federal Register as required by the Administrative Procedure Act.[14] Publication permits interested persons to comment. Consideration is given to the comments before proposed regulations are adopted in final form. Along the way, public hearings on proposed regulations are held upon request.

Treasury regulations carry a presumption of correctness, and the courts seldom invalidate them.[15] Legislative regulations (those issued pursuant to specific authority granted in the Code) are regarded as having the status of law, while interpretative regulations (those issued under the general authority of section 7805(a)) as well as any consistent prior administrative and judicial interpretations may acquire the status of law through the reenactment doctrine.[16] Under this doctrine Congress is regarded as having approved consistent and long-standing administrative and judicial interpretations by reenacting a provision without change.[17]

Less important interpretations include revenue rulings and private letter rulings. Revenue rulings are first published in the Internal Revenue Bulletin, a weekly publication of the Service, and are later compiled in the Cumulative Bulletin, a semi-annual publication.[18] Private letter rulings are provided for particular taxpayers in response to their requests for opinions on past or prospective transactions.[19] Private rulings are of two basic types: "letter rulings"[20] issued by the National Office in Washington and "determination letters"[21] issued by a District Director.

12. See e.g., § 351(g)(4) which provides: "The Secretary may prescribe such regulations as may be necessary or appropriate to carry out the purposes of this subsection and sections 354(a)(2)(C), 355(a)(3)(D), and 356(e). The Secretary may also prescribe regulations, consistent with the treatment under this subsection and such sections, for the treatment of nonqualified preferred stock under other provisions of this title."

13. See Treas. Reg. § 601.601(a)(1).

14. 5 U.S.C.A. § 551 et seq.

15. Chevron U.S.A., Inc. v. Natural Resources Defense Council, Inc., 467 U.S. 837, 104 S.Ct. 2778, 81 L.Ed.2d 694 (1984). See

also Sidell v. Commissioner, 225 F.3d 103 (1st Cir. 2000).

16. See National Muffler Dealers Ass'n v. United States, 440 U.S. 472, 477, 99 S.Ct. 1304, 59 L.Ed.2d 519 (1979). See also Commissioner v. Engle, 464 U.S. 206, 224, 104 S.Ct. 597, 78 L.Ed.2d 420 (1984).

17. Id.

18. See Treas. Reg. § 601.601(d)(2)(v)(a).

19. See Treas. Reg. § 601.201(a)(1).

20. See Treas. Reg. § 601.201(b).

21. See Treas. Reg. § 601.201(c).

The majority of determination letters relate to pension and profit-sharing plans and exempt-organization status.

The Service regards its practice of issuing private rulings, which was established in the early 1940s, as a public service since there is no legislative requirement that it issue them. Certain transactions are made subject to a favorable ruling, particularly when the tax costs of improper planning may be high, such as for a corporate reorganization or the sale of a business with highly-appreciated assets. Although the Service cannot be estopped on the basis of its opinions expressed in rulings, if the transaction turns out to be as represented in the request, a ruling will not be revoked or modified retroactively with respect to the taxpayer to whom it was issued or one whose tax liability was directly involved (except in rare or unusual circumstances).

The Service will not rule on all matters.[22] In general, rulings will not be issued on such factual issues as whether compensation is reasonable, or on issues involving subjective tests such as whether an amount paid is a nontaxable gift rather than taxable compensation, or whether the purpose of the acquisition of a corporation constitutes tax evasion or tax avoidance.

[3] SURVEY OF JUDICIAL REVIEW

If no agreement between the taxpayer and the Service has been reached during the administrative process, the taxpayer may obtain judicial review by acting on the deficiency notice received from the Service in one of two ways. The taxpayer may pay the deficiency and sue for refund in federal district court or in the United States Court of Federal Claims. This procedure is also available if the taxpayer discovers an error in the taxpayer's favor before the statute of limitations has run on the return. If the taxpayer recovers he is entitled to interest on the amount determined to be due.

Instead of paying the deficiency, the taxpayer may file a petition in the United States Tax Court, a court of record established under Article I of the Constitution.[23] The Tax Court has 19 regular judges, several ''senior judges'' (those recalled by the Chief Judge of the court), and special trial judges.[24] The jurisdiction of the Tax Court is limited to hearing deficiencies asserted by the Service. It cannot act on refund claims other than when a refund is determined to be due a taxpayer in the course of an action on an asserted deficiency. Unlike a district court, a jury trial is not available in the Tax Court. Tax Court proceedings are generally conducted by a single judge. The Chief Judge then determines whether the case will be reviewed (without a further hearing) by the entire court of regular judges. The decision of the entire Tax Court carries greater weight than an unreviewed decision.

---

22. Treas. Reg. § 601.201(b)(1).

23. See § 7441 *et. seq.*

24. See §§ 7443; 7443a; 7447.

Section 7463 authorizes special proceedings in "small" Tax Court cases. According to the court's rules, proceedings under section 7463 are simplified and conducted informally without briefs (unless permitted by the court) or oral arguments. These proceedings are available at the taxpayer's option if the court concurs and the amount in controversy for any tax year does not exceed $50,000.[25] A decision entered under "small" case proceedings is not reviewable in any other court and cannot be treated as precedent for any other case.[26]

Either the taxpayer or the Service may take an appeal from the district court, United States Court of Federal Claims, or Tax Court to the appropriate United States court of appeals and from there, in rare cases, on writ of certiorari to the United States Supreme Court. The Supreme Court ordinarily accepts review only in the event of a conflict in law between two or more Courts of Appeals or when the issue is of particular importance.

Judicial review by the Courts of Appeal and the Supreme Court annually adds thousands of decisions to federal income tax caselaw. As the Supreme Court rarely opines on federal income tax matters, this leaves the decisions of the Courts of Appeals, with their sometimes conflicting views, as the main body of appellate tax law.[27]

The Tax Court will follow "a Court of Appeals decision which is squarely in point where appeal from our decision lies to that Court of Appeals and to that court alone."[28]

The Service adheres to the view that it must administer the federal income tax uniformly on a nationwide basis. Because there is no federal legislation requiring an administrative agency to treat judicial opinions as binding except as to the parties to the litigation, the Service is bound only by Supreme Court precedent. When the Service loses in the Tax Court, the Commissioner announces whether he will follow the decision in the future by indicating acquiescence or nonacquiescence. Similarly, in revenue rulings the IRS may indicate whether it will follow a court of appeals decision or continue to litigate the issue.

§ 1.06 FUNDAMENTAL ISSUES OF FEDERAL INCOME TAXATION

There are several fundamental issues that arise consistently and necessarily in any discussion of federal income taxation. Put simply, these issues raise questions about: (1) what to tax; (2) who to tax; (3) how much to tax; (4) when to tax; and (5) how and why to tax.

---

25. § 7463(a).

26. § 7463(b).

27. The holdings of the Supreme Court, of course, are binding on the lower courts and the Service. The United States district courts and the United States Court of Federal Claims must abide by the opinions of their courts of appeals.

28. Golsen v. Commissioner, 54 T.C. 742 (1970), aff'd on other issues, 445 F.2d 985 (10th Cir.1971), rev'g on this issue Lawrence v. Commissioner, 27 T.C. 713 (1957).

[1] WHAT TO TAX: THE TAX BASE

When the federal income tax was first enacted, those responsible gave little thought to the precise theoretical definition of "income." Tax rates were sufficiently low and machinations were sufficiently rare so that the basic common-sense notion that one has income when one makes money was all the definitional guidance needed. Since that time, the stakes have changed. Taxpayers have millions of dollars worth of reasons to argue that what they have is not "income" (and therefore not subject to taxation) and the IRS has an equally strong incentive to argue that it is income.[1]

Unless one is satisfied with defining "income" as anything that happens to be subject to the income tax, it is clear that tax is not imposed on all "income." Many types of common income are intentionally excluded from taxation;[2] many other kinds of income simply fall through the cracks; and many deductions are allowed which do not even profess to result in the accurate measurement of income.[3] In addition, there is no apparent consensus that a tax on "income," however defined, is superior to a tax on consumption, wealth, some combination of all of these; hence some argue that no purpose is served by even attempting to define "income" by reference to anything outside of the law that defines it.

[a] Fairness

Many people believe that it is important to have a guiding definition of "income" for at least two reasons: (1) fairness and (2) behavioral affects of taxation. Each of these merit some elaboration.

While a tax on "income" may not be the fairest of all possible taxes, most people believe that since that happens to be the kind of tax currently used, fairness suggests that, absent good reason for doing otherwise, the tax should be applied evenhandedly to all types of income rather than arbitrarily or simply in accordance with political power. For example, taxing earnings of plumbers, but not earnings of carpenters, would seem to many to be unfair and too arbitrary to be acceptable. Similarly, taxing interest earnings from bank accounts but not taxing rental earnings from real estate investments might also seem unfair.

In our tax system, it turns out that numerous distinctions *are* drawn between different kinds of income, some of which are subject to taxation and some of which are exempt from taxation. Sometimes the distinctions are based on other types of "fairness" concerns. Sometimes the distinctions are based on administrative convenience, administrative neglect, political power, or clever machinations conceived by tax lawyers. Having

§ 1.06

1. See § 61 stating, "Except as otherwise provided … gross income means all income from whatever source derived."

2. See e.g., § 104(a)(2) (excluding from the definition of gross income amounts received on account of personal physical injuries or physical sickness).

3. See e.g., § 151 (generally providing for personal and dependency exemption deductions in computing income).

some underlying agreement on what constitutes "income" in the first, albeit theoretical, instance, provides some baseline against which those deviations from "income" can be observed, measured and judged.

[b]   Behavioral Effects

Although the income tax is not intended to be a penalty, it, as any tax, nonetheless functions as one. A consumption tax discourages consumption by making it more costly. A wealth tax discourages accumulation of wealth by imposing additional costs on its accumulation. And, an income tax discourages (at least to some extent) the production of income.

However, more significantly a tax on less than all income discourages some forms of income and encourages others. Every time a person has "income" subject to tax, she must pay money to the government, and the more "income" she has, the more money she must pay. As a result, if an individual has a choice of two different activities which will provide relatively equal benefits to her, if given the choice, she will choose the non-taxed (or tax deductible activity). Hence, if one activity is subject to tax (because it results in "income" as defined by the law) and the another activity is tax-free (because the benefit it provides is not defined to be "income" subject to tax) or, better yet, provides tax deductions, the individual will likely choose the non-taxed (or tax deductible) activity.

Of course, Congress often *intentionally* uses the behavioral impact of taxation as a tool for economic or social policy by granting deductions for certain desired behaviors[4] or excluding from taxable income certain recoveries.[5] However, absent a comprehensive definition of "income" which includes as income *all* benefits a person may enjoy and which grants as deductions all costs of producing income, the tax system will also *unintentionally* and unknowingly encourage some activities (those which produce benefits not subject to tax) and discourage others (those which result in taxable benefits). Having a comprehensive definition of income that includes all benefits a person may enjoy at least allows Congress to act intentionally rather than arbitrarily or unconsciously in determining which activities to encourage and which to discourage.

[c]   What Is Income?

Fortunately, numerous economists and scholars have weighed in on the issue of exactly how to define "income." The notion of income is an economic concept, and there are a number of economic formulations of what constitutes income. The most widely accepted definitions of income are those of Professors Haig and Simons.[6] Haig and Simons defined

---

4. See e.g., §§ 161(a), (h)(2)(d) (which generally provides for a deduction of home mortgage interest).

5. See e.g., § 104(a)(2) (which generally excludes from gross income recoveries on account of personal physical injury or physical sickness).

6. See Henry C. Simons, Personal Income Taxation: The Definition of Income as a Problem of Fiscal Policy 50 (1938); Robert Murray Haig, The Concept of Income–Economic and Legal Aspects, in The Federal Income Tax 1, 7 (Robert Murray Haig ed., 1921).

income as "the money value of the net accretion to ones economic power between two points of time."[7] The basic concept underlying the Haig–Simons definition is that all "income" increases a person's economic power, and, correspondingly, that *any increase* in a person's economic power is, in turn, "income."[8]

One apparent problem with defining income as any "net accretion" to ones economic power is that such accretion may be difficult to measure. If a person retains all of her economic power during a period of time, then one can measure the net accretion to that economic power by simply determining the difference between her net worth at the beginning of any period and her net worth at the end of that period. If T has more economic power on the last day of the year than she had on the first day of the year, the value of that excess is her income for the year. Whether that increase in economic power arises from labor, from luck, from appreciation in T's assets, from T's exchange during the year of one form of wealth (for example, dollars) for some other form of wealth (for example, stocks or bonds or real estate), or from any other conceivable source is of no relevance. All that matter under the Haig–Simons model is that a determination of T's income is the difference in T's wealth between the two points in time. While this result is simple in theory, in reality it would be impossible to keep track of all accretions to ones economic power.

The problem is that *no* person actually retains all of her economic power over the course of a year (or even over the course of a day). Every person who *has* economic power will *exercise* some of that economic power. People *use* their economic power for consumption—to obtain food, shelter, and pleasure. A person's choice of how to *use* her economic power for consumption, and of how much of that power to use for consumption at any particular time, obviously has no effect on the net "accretions" to economic power. It reflects only what she *did* with some of her economic power rather than any accretions *to,* or depletions of, that economic power. Under the Haig–Simons model, one can *measure* a person's income (her net accretions to wealth) during any period by finding the "sum of: (1) the market value of rights *exercised in consumption* and (2) the change in value of the store of property rights between the beginning and end of the period in question."[9] In other words, all increases in income are necessarily either stored or used. The sum of the value of economic power used for consumption plus the increase (or minus the decrease) in ones retained economic power necessarily equals the net accretions to that power during any period.

A simple and complete "income" tax would be a tax imposed on all "income" as defined by the Haig–Simon model. Income subject to tax would include any increase in economic power that could be either stored or used. Purchases and sales of investments for their fair market value

---

7. Id.

8. Id.

9. See Bittker, A "Comprehensive Tax Base" as a Goal of Income Tax Reform, 80 Harv. L. Rev. 925, 932 (1967).

would not themselves generate income; for example, if T sells stock worth $10,000 for $10,000 that transaction would neither increase T's net worth nor provide T with consumption. Even so, increases in the value of assets would generate income regardless of whether those assets were sold, used, or saved. Under the Haig–Simons model increases in net worth, and running accounts of amounts spent on consumption, rather than receipts, would determine the amount of tax due from each taxpayer.

An understanding of the economic definition of income is essential for purposes of understanding our income tax and its unintended, as well as intended, consequences. Unfortunately, while the economic understanding of income has had some influence in the formulation of tax policy, its influence is at best indirect. It was not the driving force behind the development and refinement of the federal income tax, and it may often actually hinder an understanding of how the courts and the IRS approach tax issues. Arguably, the distinctions drawn historically between income and capital in more general economic theory.

The most basic problem with adapting the federal income tax to theories of economic income is that the economic concepts include *accretion* to, or increases in, ones economic power and consumption. The tax laws, on the other hand, apply to market *transactions* such as receipts or "realization events." The difference between the two measurement systems can be substantial.

For example, if T owns stock that is worth $10,000 at the beginning of the year and the stock is worth $100,000 at year's end, T has a $90,000 increase in economic power or wealth, and $90,000 of income under virtually any accepted economic definition of that term. On the other hand, under our federal income tax laws, T has no income at all unless and until she either sells the stock or at least receives a dividend. It is true that T will be taxed on all of her gain if and when she sells the stock, but as explained throughout this volume the timing of taxation can be as important as the amount on which the person is taxed or the tax rate imposed.

Another significant difference, aside from the "realization" issue, between our market transaction-based federal income tax laws and the economic definition of income arises from the treatment of a taxpayer's use of her own property.

If T owns and lives in a home worth $1,000,000 with an annual rental value of $36,000, an economist would suggest that T's ownership of property worth $1,000,000 represents economic power, and T is exercising the economic power of her ownership interest every day. The fact that she exercises that economic power by living nicely in the moment rather than by adding to her store of wealth by collecting and saving rents reflects her choice of what to *do* with her economic power, but it does not minimize the daily *accretions* to that power. Accordingly, each day her ownership interest provides T alone with the economic power to use the home. Over the course of the year, T's ownership of the property provides her with $36,000 worth of consumption, in the form of shelter and comfort. T's use of her home for a residence for the year thus results in "income" of $36,000 under the economic definition of income. Of course, T would have no taxable income for federal income tax purposes unless she rented the home to a third party and received rental payments.[10]

Similarly, the lawyer who does $100,000 worth of work and uses the proceeds to pay a contractor $100,000 to renovate her home has $100,000 of income under section 61(a)(1) upon receipt of payment for her services. On the other hand, a building contractor that puts $100,000 worth of her own labor into renovating her home, thereby increasing its value by $100,000 has no taxable income because she has no "receipt of income." Each has grown wealthier by $100,000 during the period in question, and each has $100,000 of "income" according to any economist (with the contractor's income being "imputed" to her), but only one is taxed under our current system of federal income taxation.

Other examples of items of economic income not subject to tax laws because they involve no obvious "receipt" or market transaction include the value of government benefits such as police protection of property and safety, fire protection, military protection of property and safety, and the value of free public education.

There are also many untaxed items of income that have escaped any serious attention from the tax laws despite the presence of obvious receipts and market transactions. Some common untaxed receipts include: amount paid on account of personal physical injury or physical sickness;[11] "property acquired by gift, bequest, devise, or inheritance;"[12] qualified scholarships;[13] and "meals or lodging furnished for the convenience of the employer."[14] Of course, this is by no means an all-inclusive list of items excludable from gross income.

Certain other items, such as long-term capital gains which are generally taxed at 15%,[15] are tax more favorably than others; moreover other transactions, such as transfers to controlled corporation[16] or qualified reorganizations[17] enjoy delayed taxation.

Although there may be a perfect system that imposes a tax on all income, that system is not anything similar to our federal income tax system, and it is not attainable anywhere but in the theoretical realm. Notwithstanding the foregoing, an understanding of the theoretical definition of income, and the ways in which the practical definitions of our tax laws differ from that theoretical perfection, is important.

---

10. See § 61(a)(5) (which generally includes in gross income amounts received as rents).

11. See § 104(a)(2).

12. § 102(a).

13. See § 117(a).

14. § 119.

15. § 1(h).

16. See § 351.

17. See § 354.

[2]   THE IMPACT OF INFLATION ON TAXATION

A hallmark of modern industrial society is inflation. To some extent, this may be because wages and prices are "sticky downward;" i.e., workers do not like to take pay cuts.

Whatever the reason inflation is a fact of life, and it impacts taxes. Among the many different ways that inflation impacts taxes are its impact on the cost and value of assets as illustrated in the following example. Assume that T purchases an asset for $10,000 in 1960, holds it in the hope of appreciation for 47 years and sells it for $15,000 in 2007. T has made a terrible investment. If her $10,000 1960 cost were to be translated into 2007 dollars, she invested the equivalent of about $100,000 for the property she has just sold for a $15,000. Because the tax system does not take inflation into account in determining the cost of property, however, T will be taxed on a $5,000 gain upon the sale of the property.[18]

Many people suggest that what is needed to deal with this problem is to give favorable tax treatment for capital gains. Indeed, our system does impose a lower tax on capital gains from sales of property than it does on other forms of income, such as salaries.[19] Unfortunately, rather than fixing the problem, this reduced long-term capital gain rate at the same time both *fails* to account for actual inflation that *has* occurred and often gives benefits to taxpayers when inflation has *not* occurred.

To return to the prior example, if T were taxed on her $5,000 capital gain at the favorable long-term capital gain rate of 15% rather than the otherwise applicable maximum ordinary income rate of 35%, T would pay a tax of $750 instead of $1,750. Since T has actually suffered a *loss* in purchasing power, and in actuality has no gain at all, taxing T at a reduced rate cannot solve the problem.

Even worse off than T, though, might be the taxpayer who simply puts her money in the bank and earns interest. Assume, as has at times been the case, that T puts $10,000 in the bank at 3% interest in the beginning of year one and leaves it there for a year. If there was inflation during the year of, say, 7%, then by the end of the year T has $10,300, but these dollars are each worth only 93% of what her dollars were worth at the beginning of the year. The total value of her $10,300, in terms of year one dollars, is only $9,579. Despite this loss, T has taxable income of $300, and, moreover, T is not entitled to the benefit of the reduced rates available on capital gains.

On the other hand, there are many places where inflation *is* taken into account in the Internal Revenue Code. Section 1 takes inflation into account in determining the exact dollar amount at which a taxpayer goes from a lower to a higher tax bracket, and numerous other limits on deductions and credits are adjusted annually to take into account the

---

18. See § 61(a)(3).

19. Compare § 1(h) (which generally provides for a favorable 15% tax rate on long-term capital gains) with § 1(a)-(e) which generally taxes ordinary income at a maximum of 35%).

effects of inflation.[20] The net result is a system that sometimes takes inflation into account and sometimes does not, without any particular method (other than to simply examine the Internal Revenue Code) to determine what result occurs when.

[3] WHO TO TAX: CHOICE OF THE TAXABLE UNIT

At first blush, it may seem intuitive, easy, fair, and accurate to simply tax each individual on his or her income each year; unfortunately, in reality only the "intuitive" portion of this list of adjectives holds true.

First, if only individuals were taxed on all their income, many well-advised individuals would see to it that the income that would eventually redound to their benefit was earned by trusts or other entities not subject to taxation; this issue would not be resolved simply by imposing an income tax on every entity similar to the one imposed on individuals.

To see the potential problems with this purported solution, assume that T is an individual in the 35% tax bracket. If T invests $1,000,000 and earns investment income of $100,000 per year, she will be required to pay tax of $35,000 on that $100,000 of income.

However, if T were well advised, she might instead transfer $10,000 to each of 100 newly created trusts. Each trust would then have a total income of only $1,000 and therefore pay no tax at all because each trust would have so little income.[21] Not surprisingly, the tax law does not permit such tax avoidance.[22] Instead, to ensure that the proper amount of tax is paid, there are numerous interrelated (and complicated) Code provisions governing the taxation of trusts, corporations, partnerships and other entities in order to attempt to ensure that income will be appropriately taxed, and it will be taxed at the proper rates, regardless of how individuals and entities may be arranged.

Beyond problems with the taxation of entities, taxing every individual separately generates very inaccurate results because taxable income does not include amounts received as gifts,[23] inheritance,[24] child support,[25] or the value of parenting. As a result, gross inaccuracies arise beginning at birth—when the truly rich child and the truly poor one pay identical taxes (of zero) on highly disparate real incomes. This result is possible because the lifestyle of the rich child will be financed exclusively by nontaxable receipts.

On the other hand, taxing families rather than individuals would create logistical nightmares. It would be impossible to determine when children became independent from their family of origin, how extended and complete the sharing of family wealth was, and exactly what

---

20. See e.g., Rev. Proc. 2006–53, 2006–48 I.R.B. 996.

21. A discussion of the taxation of trusts is outside the scope of this volume, but see John L. Peschel and Edward D. Spurgeon, Federal Taxation of Trusts, Grantors & Beneficiaries (RIA 2007) for a complete discussion of the taxation of trusts.

22. Id.

23. See § 102(a).

24. Id.

25. See § 71(c).

constitutes a "family," especially given the diverse kinds of relationships which that term is often used to describe in this country today.

While our current federal income tax system does not impose tax on the family unit as such,[26] it does utilize different tax rates for married couples than for unmarried individuals. Even this is problematic, however. To see how the problems arise, assume that T and W are individuals with taxable incomes of $500,000. If W marries H, who has no income, W and H, as a married couple, will be able to file a joint return, which is subject to lower tax rates (on the same income) than those imposed on an unmarried individual. As a result, W's marriage will reduce her tax liability, and W's tax liability will be less than that of T's, despite their equal income.

Assume instead, however, that W falls in love with and marries T rather than H. As before, W and T, as married persons, can file a joint return which is taxable at lower rates than individuals with the same income. Unfortunately, while the rates applied to married couples are lower than the rates applied to unmarried individuals *with the same income*, because T and W each have income of $500,000, their total income is no longer $500,000 each, but, instead, it is now a total of $1,000,000. Because of their higher total income, the tax rates imposed on both W and T will *increase* rather than decrease. It turns out that any progressive rate structure that is "fair" to married couples is necessarily "unfair" to at least some single taxpayers, and any system designed to be "fair" to single taxpayers will necessarily punish at least some married taxpayers.[27]

Section 1 sets forth tax rates for six categories of taxpayers (excluding corporations):[28] (1) married persons filing joint returns and certain surviving spouses; (2) heads of households; (3) unmarried persons; (4) married persons filing separate returns; (5) children under age 18 who have unearned income; and (6) estates and trusts. The presence of these six different categories of taxpayers represent the answer to the question of who *is* taxed, and at the same time these categories conveniently sidestep the issue of who *ought* to be taxed, or what is the appropriate taxable unit.

So, why are six different categories of taxpayers necessary? The answer to this question, like the answers to most federal income tax questions, is found in the history of the tax legislation and the political compromises made by Congress in resolving policy issues, rather than in any theoretical logical development of the law. Congress began by taxing individuals. The scale applicable to joint returns of married couples is

---

26. But see § 1(g)(2)(A) which generally taxes children's unearned income (over specified thresholds) at their parent's marginal tax rate.

27. This issue is one that would not arise if there were only a single tax rate on all income or if the base subject to tax were complete; i.e., if all elements of economic income were actually subjected to taxation this issue would not arise. Since neither of these is the case, however, the determination of who to tax can be significant.

28. Section 11 sets forth the tax rates for corporations. However, under section 1363 an S corporation, as defined in section 1361, is not subject to tax as a general rule.

the result of (failed) efforts made in 1948 to equate the tax burden on married persons living in common law states with the burden on married couples living in community property states. The scale applicable to heads of household was first prescribed in 1951 in recognition of the burdens of a taxpayer maintaining a household of dependents in a manner similar to that of a married couple. Single persons received a separate scale in 1969 after pressure was exerted on Congress to eliminate the alleged discrimination against them as evidenced by the treatment accorded married persons. Children under 18 were taxed on unearned income at their parents' rate as a result of 2006 tax legislation,[29] to counter attempts by well-advised parents to shift taxable income to their children in order to ensure that the income was taxed at the children's then lower rates.

[4] HOW MUCH TO TAX: TAX RATES

[a] Progressive or Flat Rate Structure

Another issue that will likely always be discussed and never resolved is the appropriate rate of tax to impose on income. There are thousands of pages of debate about whether everyone ought to be taxed at a single flat rate (for example, a 30% tax on all income), or whether those with higher incomes ought to be taxed at higher rates on their excess income (progressive rates). Those in favor of a flat rate believe that fairness requires taxing all income at the same rate. Those in favor of progressivity believe that fairness requires taxing those with excess income at higher rates because those with smaller incomes have more need for the little money they earn. Those in favor of flat rates argue that progressive rates encourage high-income individuals to try to shift their tax liabilities onto related parties (for example, children) in order to take advantage of those lower rates. Those in favor of progressivity argue that trying to avoid "cheating" by high-income earners may be a noble idea, but it should not be accomplished by simply levying such low taxes on high-income earners that they have no incentive to cheat.

[b] Marginal and Effective Rates

In addition to different views as to the fairness of progressive tax rates, it is also important to keep in mind some of the other impacts of the graduated rate structure. An important concept for tax planners to understand is the difference between "marginal" rates of tax and "the average, or effective," rate of tax that a person pays.

By way of example, assume an individual is subject to the following hypothetical income tax structure:

$0–$20,000...taxed at 15%

---

29. See § 1(g)(2)(A) (which generally taxes children's unearned income, over specified thresholds, at their parent's marginal tax rate) which was modified by § 510 of the Tax Increase Prevention and Reconciliation Act of 2005, Pub L No. 109–122 (May 17, 2006). This "kiddie tax" was first enacted as part of the Tax Reform Act of 1986, but at that time (and for many years thereafter) only applied to unearned income of children under 14.

$20,001–$50,000...taxed at 25%

$50,001 and above...taxed at 31%.

A taxpayer's "marginal" tax rate is the rate at which she will be taxed on the next dollar of additional taxable income she earns. In other words, in this example if T has taxable income of $70,000, she is in the 31% marginal tax bracket, because every dollar of taxable income she earns will generate 31 cents in additional federal income tax liability.

Because T's first $20,000 of income was taxed at the 15% rate, though, and because her next $30,000 of income (from $20,001 to $50,000) was taxed at 25%, her total tax liability is *not* 31%, but, instead, it is only $16,700 [($20,000 x 15%) + ($30,000 x 25% [$50,000–$20,000]) + ($20,000 x 31% [$70,000–$50,000]). T's average, or effective rate of tax, is thus only $16,700 (tax paid)/$70,000 (total taxable income), or 23.86%.

[c] Higher Rates Result in More Valuable Deductions

One of the most significant "side effects" of the progressive rate structure is that because high earners are in a higher marginal tax bracket, and pay more tax on additional income, those same high earners also get additional benefits from either excluding or deducting the same amount from income. For example, if R is in the 35% tax bracket and is allowed to exclude from income a $10,000 inheritance, R will thereby save $3,500 in taxes he would otherwise have had to pay. If P is in the 15% bracket and is allowed to exclude from income an equivalent $10,000 inheritance, P will reduce her taxes by only $1,500 rather than $3,500. Hence, the value of the exclusion varies directly with the taxpayer's marginal tax bracket.

Because the value of deductions and exclusions varies with the taxpayer's marginal tax bracket, many argue that tax benefits ought to take the form of tax "credits" rather than exclusions or deductions. Unlike a deduction or exclusion, a tax credit results in a direct dollar-for-dollar reduction of the amount of tax due. Regardless of the taxpayer's marginal or effective tax rate, a $200 credit reduces her tax liability by $200. Even so, there are some credits that impact high and low-bracket taxpayers differently.[30] These are credits that are either limited to those with incomes below a certain level or those that are "phased out" as the taxpayer's income increases.[31]

While it may sound counter-intuitive, some of the impacts of progressive rates would exist, albeit to a lesser extent, even if our tax system had a single flat rate. This is because as long as there are some people whose income is sufficiently low that they pay no tax, they are effectively in the zero percent bracket. Because they pay no tax, for

30. See for example § 32 which provides the earned income credit which is available to low-income tax payers only; i.e., the earned income credit is not available to high-income taxpayers.

31. Id.

example, spending money on a "deductible" expense gives them no tax benefit whatsoever.

[d]   What Rate?

In addition to the numerous implications of progressive rates, even those who favor a single tax rate disagree on the appropriate rate. Some suggest that the tax rate must be high enough to prevent huge government deficits, while others claim low rates will eventually force the government to cut its spending. Some argue that higher tax rates can finance an effective government, while others argue that money can be used more efficiently in the private sector than by government.

In addition to debating what rates to apply to what taxpayers, there will also likely always be debates about what rates to apply to different types of income. For decades many have argued that "capital gains" income ought to be taxed, if at all, at a rate lower than income from wages, because a reduced tax on realized capital gains might stimulate the economy. Others have argued that reducing the rate of tax on capital gains while maintaining a higher rate of tax on wages would mean taking more from the working class and even less from the wealthy, and it would also encourage people to minimize their taxes by simply designing clever schemes to have their income characterized as capital gain rather than ordinary income without actually changing the amount of income or the manner in which they earn it. As is the case in many tax debates, both sides are actually correct.

[5]   WHEN TO TAX

Each taxpayer must calculate tax his or her liability and pay tax annually. If someone works and receives compensation in the same year, then it is obvious that year is the year in which the taxpayer includes the compensation in income. If the work and the payment occur in different years, then which of those years determines the year of inclusion in taxable income depends on the taxpayer's accounting method—cash or accrual. Similar issues arise with respect to the timing of a payer's deduction, assuming that the payment is one that is otherwise deductible.

But this basic answer regarding when amounts are properly included or deducted does not really reach the difficult and ever-present issues of tax timing. Unfortunately, tax timing raises numerous problems for two basic reasons: (1) the impact of the timing of income and deductions can be very significant and (2) many items of income and deduction are not as simple as the receipt or payment of compensation. Each of these issues will be addressed in turn.

[a]   The Time Value of Money

The importance of timing in tax stems from the time value of money. Put simply, it is better to have any given amount of money now than it is to have the same amount of money in the future. The reason for this is that any money one has now can be invested, so by the time the "future" arrives there will be more of it. For example, if T has $10,000 now and the interest rate is 10%, T can simply leave that money in the bank for one year and at the end of that time T will have $11,000 before taxes.

To see how this relates to the timing of income and deductions for tax purposes, assume that T has income of $25,000 and she is in the 35% tax bracket. T will have to pay tax of $8,750. Knowing this, T sets aside $8,750 to pay the tax when it is due. If that $25,000 is includable in income now, T has to pay the $8,750 in tax now, but if the $25,000 is includable in income at some time in the future, T will have to pay no tax until that future time occurs. The longer T can postpone the payment of the tax, the longer T can continue to keep the money invested, and, and accordingly, the more money T will end up with in the final analysis. Correspondingly, the more quickly T is allowed to deduct expenses, the more quickly T can reduce her tax payments, and the more quickly T can have money to invest.

If T can postpone including the $25,000 in income for seven years, and thereby postpone her $8,750 tax payment for seven years, then T can leave that $8,7500 invested during the seven year period. At the end of seven years T will have $17,500 rather than $8,750. Of course, if T then has to pay her $8,750 in taxes, she will still have $8,750 left over to spend at her discretion.

Another way to look at this situation is to see that if T has $8,750 and she has to pay the entire tax liability now, she will have nothing left to invest. If T has $8,750 now and will have to pay $8,750 in seven years, then T can take $4,375 of the $8,750, invest it at 10%, and in seven years that $4,375 will turn into $8,750. T can use that $8,750 to pay her tax obligation when it comes due in seven years, and T can take the other $4,375 that T has now and use it at her discretion. By postponing payment of $8,750 for seven years, T has actually cut the "present value" of her tax liability in half.

What this means is that postponing the payment of taxes reduces the present value (or present cost, from the taxpayer's perspective) of this tax liability. This is the economic equivalent of reducing the tax rate by 50%, in this case from 35% (35% of $25,000=$8,750) to 17.5% (20% of $25,000=$4,375).

Obviously, the longer the taxpayer can defer making any particular payment, the longer the taxpayer can leave that money invested and earning more money. Similarly, the sooner the taxpayer can take deductions and reduce her tax liability (or get tax refunds) the more valuable those deductions are to the taxpayer. On the other side of the ledger, the more quickly the taxpayer has to pay a given tax liability, the worse off the taxpayer is in true economic present value terms.

The exact value of deferral depends on three factors: the interest rate, the compounding period, and the length of the deferral of the tax liability. Of these three factors, the first and third are intuitively obvious. A higher interest rate means that the taxpayer will make more money on her investment. That means that if the taxpayer deposits her $8,750 (or any other amount, of course) rather than paying it now, she will have more money later. Another way to look at it is to understand that a higher interest rate means that the taxpayer need to invest less money now to end up with the $8,750 she will need in the future; the money she invests now will grow more quickly than it would at a lower interest rate. Similarly, the longer the taxpayer can defer payment, the greater chance the money has to grow before the taxpayer needs to make that payment.

The compounding period is perhaps a little less intuitive, but, nevertheless, it is important. As long as the taxpayer leaves her initial $8,750 invested, she will of course earn interest on that amount. If the interest is "compounded," that means that in addition to earning interest on her $8,750 initial investment, she will also earn interest on the previously earned interest. If interest is compounded annually, that means that after one year, the taxpayer's account will be credited with the first year's interest of $875 (assuming a 10% rate). From that time on, the taxpayer will be earning interest not on just $8,750, but on $9,625 (the principal plus the compounded interest). If interest is compounded daily, then the taxpayer will start earning interest on her interest not after one year, but after only one day. Although the amount of interest credited to the taxpayer's account after a single day will not be large (1/365 x $875, or about $2.40), the mere fact that the taxpayer has started earning interest on her interest more quickly will substantially increase the rate at which her investment grows. Over time, the differences between daily, annual, and no compounding can be quite significant to the actual return generated by any investment.

The most important lesson to draw from all of this is simply that timing matters; taxpayers can benefit substantially by deferring taxation.

Of course, so long as tax measures a person's true economic income, the only way to defer taxation would be to not have any income, and that is not a choice most people would make on their own accord. Ultimately, it is preferable to make money and pay taxes rather than making no money at all.

On the other hand, in our tax system, the timing of taxation often differs from the actual accrual of income, and that changes things in several ways. First of all, taxpayers will have an incentive to invest in those investments where taxable income, and thus the tax liability, is deferred, or where deductions are accelerated. Rather than deciding among investments by judging only their economic merit, informed investors will take into account, and often treat as the determining factor in choosing investments, the way that particular investment choices are taxed.

Consider, for example, the following example: Taxpayer pays $100,000 for stock of Microsoft in January. By the end of the year, the stock is worth $110,000. Clearly Taxpayer is richer, but does he have a tax liability? Under our current tax system, Taxpayer will pay no tax unless or until there is some "realization event;"[32] i.e., unless or until he gets something different from the original Microsoft stock he is not taxed. This generally means that Taxpayer will pay tax on his gain only when he sells or exchanges the stock. So long as Taxpayer holds onto the stock, he will pay no tax regardless of how rich he becomes. As a result, investments in assets such as stock that appreciate over time are treated quite well by our tax system; Taxpayer can defer his tax liability indefinitely. One result of this may be to encourage investment in assets that are taxed in this fashion.

Of course, the manner in which our tax system taxes income from investments does not actually guarantee the taxpayer will pay no tax until he sells. If the taxpayer receives a dividend while he simply holds the stock, he will be taxed on that amount (although at a reduced rate)[33] even if his original $100,000 investment is worth the same or substantially less than that at the time the dividend is paid. This all may seem simple, but it also means that one investor who holds onto his original investment which pays no dividends may actually make millions and defer paying tax, while another who receives dividends on a losing investment may pay significant taxes currently despite his actual loss. Deferring payment of tax is equivalent, in present value terms, to reducing the amount and rate of tax paid; similarly, accelerating payment of tax is equivalent, in present value terms, to increasing the rate of tax. The consequences for investors can be significant.

In addition, to provide maximum benefits to their clients, tax lawyers will work to structure transactions and investments to defer taxation as long as possible. If a client wishes to invest in X, a good tax lawyer may be able to figure out a way to make that investment look and act like one that results in deferred rather than immediate taxation.

As a result, inaccurate timing of income will: (1) distort economic decision-making by encouraging taxpayers to earn money in ways that have tax benefits and not simply in the ways that would otherwise be most appealing, and (2) encourage taxpayers and their attorneys to structure transactions in ways that generate favorable tax results.

[6] HOW AND WHY WE TAX

One goal of the tax system is to collect tax dollars from those the lawmakers believe ought to pay. Of course, this goal likely raises more issues than it resolves, since different lawmakers have differing ideas about who ought to pay. Some think the rich should pay a majority of taxes. Others think everyone should be taxed on their economic income. Others think tax breaks should be given to those who are sick, have dependents who are sick, or who have suffered some unexpected harm. Others think income from labor (rather than capital) should be the

---

32. See § 1001 (which defines discusses the computation of gain or loss on the sale other disposition of assets).

33. See § 1(h)(11) (which provides for a preferred tax rate of 15% on qualified dividends).

primary tax base. And, still others have altogether different notions about what should be considered a "fair" allocation of the tax burden.

In any event, collection of revenue in a way that is fair is not the only goal of our tax system. Lawmakers are also concerned with the impact of taxes on people's behavior. Some lawmakers would like a tax system that manages to avoid influencing people's economic decisions. They would like people to choose among jobs and investments based on the economics of each, and they want a tax system that just does not get in the way of people making those decisions.

Others want to use the tax system not to simply allow taxpayers to make their own economic choices, but they also want to use it to *influence* those decisions. Our tax system encourages people to save for retirement,[34] and for their children's education.[35] Additionally, our tax system encourages employers to provide health insurance for their employees.[36] As a result, there are numerous provisions in the Code that either exclude or defer income, or grant or accelerate deductions precisely to encourage certain taxpayer behaviors.

Beyond being concerned about the fairness and the behavioral effects of the federal income tax, all lawmakers also want an income tax system that is administrable. Lawmakers want a tax system in which people can determine how much they owe with certainty, and the government wants to be able to verify the taxpayer's information and obtain all the revenue it is due. Ultimately, lawmakers want a tax system in which all questions have yes or no answers and are not subject to manipulation. Unfortunately, life is not black and white, and any good tax lawyer will tell you there are many shades of grey in between the black and white.

Tax laws (like all laws) are made by lawmakers subject to lobbying and other political pressures. The Code has its share of provisions that have resulted from these types of pressures, and it has also seen numerous other potential provisions edited out prior to (or in some cases after) enactment for these same reasons.

Another concern of tax lawmakers is that they do not want to be disruptive of whatever legitimate, non-tax motivated transactions are going on in the business world. As a result, many provisions of the Code are designed in order to avoid interfering with current business practices. Typically, the result of these kinds of provisions is that certain ongoing practices are exempted from the imposition of new taxes.

[7] SUBSTANCE VERSUS FORM AND OTHER JUDICIAL DOCTRINES

When tax laws were enacted not simply to collect revenue in a way lawmakers thought was fair, but also to change behavior, taxpayers

---

34. See e.g., § 401(k).

35. See e.g., § 529.

36. See § 162 (which generally provides a deduction for all ordinary and necessary business expenses, including the cost of health insurance).

generally reacted by changing their behavior. Taxpayers took the tax laws into account when they were supposed to, and they made appropriate economic choices.

It should not be surprising, of course, that tax lawyers do whatever they can to help their clients legally minimize their tax liabilities. And, given that tax attorneys are among the highest paid attorneys, at least on an hourly basis, it should not be surprising that over the years they have found many creative ways to assist their clients in minimizing their tax liabilities. Rather than just going about doing whatever they were going to do most of the time and changing their behavior only in the ways Congress meant to encourage, tax lawyers learned how to do just the opposite!

If the taxpayer, for her own economic reasons unrelated to tax, wanted to engage in transaction X, but transaction X was a taxable transaction, the tax lawyer learned how to structure the transaction to make it *look* like the transactions at issue were *not* taxable. The result was that the taxpayers did what they wanted, but they managed to avoid tax on transactions Congress had intended to be taxable.

On the other hand, when Congress enacted tax benefits to affirmatively encourage taxpayers to engage in specific behaviors and to invest in certain kinds of assets, taxpayers learned how to avoid making those desired investments while structuring transactions to make it appear that they had done so. The result was that taxpayers did *not* do what Congress wanted, but they nonetheless managed to claim the tax breaks that Congress had intended as encouragement for those investments that they never made.

All of this was possible for at least two reasons: (1) all the factors discussed above lead to a tax system that is complicated, and (2) while the tax laws are imposed by Congress on certain transactions, the transactions are structured not by Congress but by attorneys and taxpayers. Since the design and structure of these transactions, together with the precise information reported to the IRS, is in the control of the taxpayer, the IRS often finds itself confronted by transactions that appear to be something very different from what they might have looked like, had they not been designed to take advantage of tax "loopholes."

Examples of these kinds of transactions permeate the tax laws. Sales may be made to look like gifts; gifts may be made to look like sales; mere retained ownership may be made to look like a sale and leaseback; and loans may be made to look like compensation or vice versa.

In some cases, what the taxpayers are doing is nothing more, or less, than fraud. In these cases, the taxpayers may have documents that say X to the IRS, but they have no intention of abiding by those documents and have agreed among themselves to do Y.

In other cases, though, violation of the law is not as clear. Taxpayers may engage in transactions which have little or no independent economic substance and which are done solely for tax reasons, but which are nonetheless not necessarily fraudulent.

For example, assume that O is the owner of X, that O can receive tax benefits by selling X, and T can receive tax benefits by purchasing X. X and T may arrange a series of transactions that are not "fraudulent;" that can be reported to the IRS as a sale of X from O to T, and that nonetheless have no economic substance because O continues to possess X, to use X, and to bear any risk of loss or chance of gain on X; and T has no possession, use, risk of loss or chance of gain with respect to X.

One way these transactions were structured was to have T "purchase" X from O by paying $1 in cash and having O provide $10,000,000 financing on a nonrecourse basis (so that T has no personal liability to pay any of the obligation to O, and if T fails to pay, O's only recourse is to take back the property). In addition, T would "lease" X back to O for "rent" exactly equal to payments due on the purchase money debt (so that (1) O actually retained possession of X, (2) each year for the duration of the lease O must pay X $1,000,000 rent, and (3) each year, X must pay O $1,000,000 on the purchase money debt). Finally, O was granted an option to "repurchase" X at the termination of the lease for $1.

In turn, the judiciary has developed some weapons to help the IRS combat these techniques. The Service and the judiciary often refer to the doctrines of "substance versus form" or "business purpose," or the "step-transaction doctrine" to enable them to recharacterize these cleverly designed transactions and to treat them as they would have been taxed had they been designed in a straightforward manner without any attempt to minimize taxes in the first place.

Unfortunately, it is rarely if ever clear whether any of these doctrines will be applied in any particular case. The results are (1) an incredibly complex and technical Internal Revenue Code, (2) even more complex and complicated transactions designed to minimize taxes by taking advantage of some of these intricacies and technicalities, and (3) judicial doctrines which, when they apply, essentially allow the courts and the IRS to disregard the technical aspects of the Code and the transactions. But, it is next to impossible to know in advance whether or when these judicial doctrines will be applied; this, of course, can make for a very unpleasant surprise.

The uncertainty in application of the doctrines often arises from the fact that, as in most areas of law, tax laws need to be able to answer questions with either a clear "yes" answer or a clear "no" answer. These judicial doctrines all embrace some version of the idea that transactions will be taken at face value if engaged in for legitimate business purposes, but these same transactions will be disregarded if engaged in for tax avoidance purposes. The unfortunate truth is that almost all financial transactions engaged in by sophisticated individuals are in reality done *partly* for business reasons and *partly* for tax avoidance. Requiring all or nothing decisions with respect to activities that are really some of this and some of that inevitably leads to further confusion and complexity in the tax law.

This type of confusion arises not only in intentionally structured tax-minimization transactions, but it also arises in other areas as well. Taxpayers may object to being told that some amount is taxable, or that some other amount is not deductible, but somewhere, somehow, lines must be drawn. It will not do to explain that amounts are "sort of" taxable or deductible, and the tax laws do not allow for taxpayers to report amounts as "sort of" income. While it is true that disputes may ultimately be settled somewhere in between what the results would be if amounts were fully taxable and what the results would be if the amounts were not at all taxable, absent compromise resolution of specific disputes, it is not permissible for either party to initially take such a position. For example, a taxpayer may believe there is a 50% chance that the $1,000,000 she just received is taxable and a 50% chance the amount is not taxable, but she cannot then decide to simply report half of that amount in income and to exclude the other half from income.

This issue also often arises on the deduction side of the tax equation, when distinctions must be made between expenses that are nondeductible personal expenses and those that are deductible business expenses. Every expense must be identified as one or the other, but the truth is almost every expense is in reality part of each. Street clothes, deodorant, and toothpaste are generally treated as entirely personal,[37] although the truth is that without these things one would likely have a very difficult time getting and keeping a job or conducting any type of business. On the other hand, certain accommodations at work and while traveling in pursuit of business are treated as entirely deductible business expenses,[38] when in fact the taxpayer's personal preferences are really being satisfied.

§ 1.07 AN OVERVIEW OF THE TAX EQUATION

The remainder of this volume will discuss in lucid detail the many detailed components of the tax equations. Accordingly, an overview of the tax equation is warranted at the outset.

The Tax Equation

Income	$XXX,XXX
Less: Exclusions from Income	($XXX,XXX)
Gross Income	$XXX,XXX
Less: For AGI[1] Deductions	($XXX,XXX)
AGI	$XXX,XXX
Less: the Greater of the Standard Deduction or Itemized Deductions	($XXX,XXX)

37. See § 262 (which generally disallows deductions for personal expenditures).

38. See § 162 (which generally provides a deduction for all ordinary and necessary business expenses).

§ 1.07

1. AGI is used here and throughout to mean adjusted gross income. For a complete definition of AGI, see § 62.

Less: Personal and Dependency Exemptions   (\$XXX,XXX)

Taxable Income   \$XXX,XXX

In order to compute taxable income, a taxpayer must begin with income (both taxable and nontaxable). Income for this purpose is essentially equivalent to gross receipts less: (1) the amount of any borrowed funds, and (2) the amount of any return of capital.

From this initial income amount, certain types of recoveries are excluded in computing taxable income. Common examples of these exclusions, include, but are not limited to: (1) amounts received on account of personal physical injuries or physical sickness;[2] certain proceeds paid out under accident and health plans;[3] interest on state and local bonds;[4] life insurance proceeds paid on account of death;[5] gifts, bequests, and inheritances;[6] or meals or lodging furnished for the convenience of the employer.[7] Of course, the foregoing is by no means an all-inclusive list.[8]

Once the foregoing items (or other allowable exclusions) have been taken into account, the net result is gross income. Gross income is defined in section 61 as "income from whatever source derived," unless somehow otherwise excepted.[9]

Once a taxpayer has computed gross income, he is ready to take any applicable for-AGI deductions. Common examples of for-AGI deductions include: trade or business expenses;[10] alimony;[11] moving expenses;[12]interest on education loans;[13] and higher education expenses.[14] It is important to note that for-AGI deductions are deductible by all taxpayers, even if they choose to take the standard deduction rather than itemize their deductions.

Of course, once a taxpayer has taken any applicable for-AGI deductions, the result is simply AGI, which is nothing more than a subtotal in computing taxable income.[15] Even so, it is an important subtotal for the following reasons: (1) many phase-outs and deductions are tied to AGI,[16] and (2) for-AGI deductions help reduce AGI and therefore increase the amount of a taxpayer's itemized deductions.

2. See § 104(a)(2).

3. See § 105.

4. See § 103(a).

5. See § 101(a)(1).

6. See § 102(a).

7. See § 119.

8. For a more detailed discussion of exclusions from gross income, see Chapter 3.

9. For a more detailed discussion of gross income, see Chapter 2.

10. See § 62(a)(1).

11. See § 62(a)(10).

12. See § 62(a)(15).

13. See § 62(a)(17).

14. See § 62(a)(18).

15. For a more detailed discussion of AGI, see § 62.

16. See e.g., § 213(a) (which generally provides for a deduction for qualified medical expenses to the extent they exceed 7.5% of a AGI). See also § 165(h)(2)(A)(ii) (which generally provides for a deduction for personal casualty losses to the extent they exceed 10% of AGI); § 170(b)(1)(A)(flush language) (which generally provides for a deduction for personal charitable contributions to the extent such contributions do not exceed 50% of AGI).

After computing AGI the taxpayer must either subtract the greater of his itemized deductions or the standard deduction. Common examples of itemized deductions include: medical expenses;[17] home mortgage interest,[18] and charitable contributions.[19] If the taxpayer does not have enough itemized deductions he may simply subtract the standard deduction from AGI instead.

Lastly, in computing taxable income the taxpayer must subtract the amount of any applicable personal and dependency exemptions. Section 151(a) generally provides for one personal or dependency exemption per person; the amount of the personal and dependency exemption is adjusted annually by the IRS.[20]

This is the last step in computing taxable income.

17. See § 213.

18. See §§ 163(a), (h)(2)(D).

19. See § 170(a)(1).

20. § 152(d)(2) disallows personal and dependency exemptions for those taxpayers who are claimed as dependents by another taxpayer. Additionally, § 153(d)(3) provides for the phase-out of personal and dependency exemptions for certain high-income taxpayers.

Chapter 2

GROSS INCOME

Table of Sections

---

§ 2.01 INTRODUCTION TO GROSS INCOME

Except as specifically limited by statute or otherwise, the meaning of gross income is very broad.[1] Section 61 provides:

§ 2.01
1. See § 61(a).

(a) General definition.—Except as otherwise provided in this subtitle, gross income means all income from whatever source derived, including (but not limited to) the following items:

(1) Compensation for services, including fees, commissions, fringe benefits, and similar items;

(2) Gross income derived from business;

(3) Gains derived from dealings in property;

(4) Interest;

(5) Rents;

(6) Royalties;

(7) Dividends;

(8) Alimony and separate maintenance payments;

(9) Annuities;

(10) Income from life insurance and endowment contracts;

(11) Pensions;

(12) Income from discharge of indebtedness;

(13) Distributive share of partnership gross income;

(14) Income in respect of a decedent; and

(15) Income from an interest in an estate or trust.[2]

Additionally, Treasury Regulation section 1.61–1(a) provides in pertinent part, "Gross income means all income from whatever source derived, unless excluded by law. Gross income includes income realized in any form, whether in money, property, or services. Income may be realized, therefore, in the form of services, meals, accommodations, stock, or other property, as well as in cash."

Before delving into exactly what is meant by section 61's definition of gross income, it is important to understand the background behind the term gross income. Economists have for centuries provided us with a body scholarly work around the meaning of the term income. As discussed more completely in § 1.06[1][c], income in an economic sense is best understood as a person's net accretion to economic power during a given time period. Because any accretion to economic power in turn is either used to provide consumption or added to the person's store of wealth (saved or invested), income is best measured by taking the sum of a person's consumption for any period of time plus any increase (or minus any decrease) in her net worth during that period.

It is important to understand, though, that these kinds of theoretical definitions of "income" are *not* what Congress had in mind when it enacted this section 61. It is more accurate, and more productive to one seeking to understand federal income taxation, to simply know that

2. § 61.

Congress has not adopted *any* particular concept or theory of income for income tax purposes.[3]

When the predecessor to section 61 was first enacted, there were no tax shelters or other complex transactions being designed to avoid the federal income tax, and there was no perceived need for any theories or complicated definitions of income. Instead, Congress simply set forth the common sense understanding that, as a general rule, when someone gets something of value, he has income. Obvious examples are wages or interest earned on money deposited in a bank. The basic idea was no more than that whenever a taxpayer gets something of value he did not have before, he has income equal in value to whatever he received.

What the taxpayer gets that he must include in income may be cash, property, services, the use of property, or the elimination of an obligation (to pay money or provide property or services, etc.) he previously had.[4] In addition, the way he obtains income may be from hard work, investments, luck, theft, or almost any other way.[5] Finally, his receipt may be direct or indirect.[6] He may receive the income himself, or it may be paid on his behalf to someone else, or it may even be the result of something *done* on his behalf.[7]

What this means is that while not theoretically developed or fine-tuned, the definition of gross income in section 61 was intended to be very broad.

Of course, not all gross receipts represent income. The Code provides for the exclusion from income of a wide variety of economic benefits. These exclusions are discussed in detail in Chapter 3.

[1] SCOPE

Though the Supreme Court has attempted to articulate a definition of gross income, it has not developed an absolute definition. Instead, the Court has stated that "no single, conclusive criterion has yet been found to determine in all situations what is a sufficient gain to support the imposition of an income tax."[8]

[a] Windfalls

One of the Court's initial attempts to define the term "income" arose in Stratton's Independence, Ltd. v. Howbert,[9] which held that "income may be defined as the gain derived from capital, from labor, or from both combined."[10]

3. For a more complete discussion of the theoretical underpinnings of the definition of income, see § 1.06[1][c], *infra*.

4. See Treas. Reg. § 1.61–1(a).

5. See § 61(a). See also Treas. Regs. §§ 1.61–1 through 1.61–14.

6. See Treas. Reg. § 1.61–1(a).

7. Id.

8. Commissioner v. Wilcox, 327 U.S. 404, 66 S.Ct. 546, 90 L.Ed. 752 (1946).

9. 231 U.S. 399, 34 S.Ct. 136, 58 L.Ed. 285 (1913).

10. 231 U.S. 399, 415, 34 S.Ct. 136, 140.

In Commissioner v. Glenshaw Glass Co.,[11] the taxpayer had recovered treble damages in a private suit under the antitrust laws, and it contended that only the actual damages, and no part of the punitive damages, were income. Glenshaw Glass contended that punitive damages were "derived from neither capital nor labor" nor anything else attributable to the taxpayer, but, instead, they were simply the result of the defendant's bad acts. And as a result those damages were not income.

The Supreme Court, in reversing two lower courts, held that all of the damages, including the taxpayer's windfall gain, fell within the broad sweep of what is now section 61(a). Basically, the Court shifted from the "derived from" test enunciated it first articulated in Stratton's Independence, Ltd. v. Howbert,[12] to an "accession to wealth" test. The Court, in what is now often-quoted language, indicated "Here we have instances of undeniable accessions to wealth, clearly realized, and over which the taxpayers have complete dominion. The mere fact that the payments were extracted from the wrongdoers as punishment for unlawful conduct cannot detract from their character as taxable income to the recipients."[13]

In case this left any doubt, the Court went on to explain that in interpreting the language of what is now section 61(a), it "has given a liberal construction to this broad phraseology in recognition of the intention of Congress to tax *all gains* except those specifically exempted." Within the confines of the requirement that the taxpayer have an "accession" to wealth rather than an accretion to economic power, this definition is about as broad as possible, and it is the benchmark for analysis of what constitutes gross income.

Similarly, in General American Investors Co. v. Commissioner,[14] a companion case to Glenshaw Glass, the Court held that a corporate taxpayer realized income when it received $170,000 in disgorged "insider profits" that its executives were required to pay over under applicable provisions Securities Exchange Act. Simply put, there was an accession to wealth by the taxpayer (the corporation); there was no applicable exclusionary provision under the tax law which prevented this particular accession to wealth from being included in income; therefore, this accession to wealth was properly accounted for as income.

Moreover, the regulations have also long provided that "treasure trove" constitutes gross income "for the taxable year in which it is reduced to undisputed possession."[15] This notion was applied in Cesarini v. United States;[16] the court, in applying the regulation, held that $4,500

---

11. 348 U.S. 426, 75 S.Ct. 473, 99 L.Ed. 483 (1955).

12. 231 U.S. 399, 34 S.Ct. 136, 58 L.Ed. 285 (1913).

13. Commissioner v. Glenshaw Glass Co., 348 U.S. 426, 431, 75 S.Ct. 473, 477, 99 L.Ed. 483 (1955).

14. 348 U.S. 434, 75 S.Ct. 478, 99 L.Ed. 504 (1955). See also Liddane v. Commissioner, T.C. Memo. 1998–259.

15. Treas. Reg. § 1.61–14(a).

16. 296 F.Supp. 3 (N.D. Ohio 1969), aff'd per curiam, 428 F.2d 812 (6th Cir. 1970). See also Collins v. Commissioner, T.C. Memo. 1992–478.

in currency discovered in 1964 in a used piano purchased in 1957 constituted income in 1964 when it was first "reduced to undisputed possession." The court understood that the extent of the taxpayer's actual rights to the property and the exact time when the taxpayer's rights vested were determined under applicable state law. Even so, the court held the determination of exactly what rights were sufficient to constitute the kind of undisputed possession sufficient to require inclusion in income was solely a matter of interpretation of the Internal Revenue Code.[17]

In addition to their specific holdings and their statements with regard to the breadth of the definition of income, these cases demonstrate that income need not be earned, given freely, come from any particular source, or come for any particular reason. It is sufficient to show that one somehow acquired something or some benefit that he did not have prior to the event in question.

[b] Illegal Activities

"It had been a well-established principle . . . that unlawful, as well as lawful, gains are comprehended within the term 'gross income.' "[18]

For example, in United States v. Sullivan[19] the Supreme Court held that a bootlegger's income was subject to tax although derived from an illegal activity, and in Avery v. Commissioner[20] the taxpayer's income from illegal sales of heroin was subject to federal taxation.

Initially, the Supreme Court held gains from fraudulent activities were not subject to tax because the taxpayers had a legal obligation to make restitution. In Commissioner v. Wilcox[21] the Court held that embezzled funds did *not* constitute income, emphasizing the taxpayer's obligation to repay the illegally obtained funds. However, six years later in Rutkin v. United States[22] the Court held that an extortionist realized income; in its holding, the Court reasoned that embezzled funds could be distinguished on the dubious ground that a victim of extortion gives up the money willingly. The dichotomy between Wilcox and Rutkin was finally eliminated by the Supreme Court in James v. United States,[23] in which embezzled funds were held taxable and Wilcox was overruled. The Court in James held that even though the taxpayer was under a legal obligation to make restitution, such an obligation should be disregarded, and the transaction should not be considered as a loan because of the

---

17. See Cesarini v. United States, 296 F.Supp. 3, 5 (N.D. Ohio 1969).

18. James v. United States, 366 U.S. 213, 218, 81 S.Ct. 1052, 1055 (1961).

19. 274 U.S. 259, 47 S.Ct. 607, 71 L.Ed. 1037 (1927). See also United States v. Roush, 466 F.3d 380 (5th Cir. 2006); Taylor v. Commissioner, T.C. Memo. 2006–67; CCA 200547012, 2005 WL 3131996 (Nov. 25, 2005); Rev. Rul. 2005–19, 2005–14 I.R.B. 819.

20. 574 F.2d 467 (9th Cir. 1978). See also Urwyler v. United States, 125 F.3d 860 (9th Cir. 1997); Williams v. Commissioner, 999 F.2d 760 (4th Cir. 1993).

21. 327 U.S. 404, 66 S.Ct. 546, 90 L.Ed. 752 (1946).

22. 343 U.S. 130, 72 S.Ct. 571, 96 L.Ed. 833 (1952).

23. 366 U.S. 213, 81 S.Ct. 1052, 6 L.Ed.2d 246 (1961).

lack of a "consensual recognition" of the contemporaneous obligation to repay.

Amounts received do *not* constitute income when accompanied by consensual recognition of a contemporaneous obligation to repay. That recognition has been interpreted as existing in the context of illegally obtained amounts, though, only when the obligation to repay is characteristic of a loan arrangement between the taxpayer and the victim. Thus, in United States v. Rochelle[24] amounts obtained by a "confidence man" in the form of loans were held includible in gross income. The Fifth Circuit said that if it were "to hold otherwise, confidence men could avoid the tax consequences of their transactions by merely adding a false promise to repay to their other representations."[25]

In Buff v. Commissioner[26] the taxpayer, who was employed as a bookkeeper, embezzled approximately $22,000 from his employer. After the employer discovered the crime, the taxpayer confessed. At the employer's insistence the taxpayer signed an affidavit of confession of judgment for the embezzled amount, plus interest, and he agreed to continue his employment, and to repay $25 a week from his paycheck. The Second Circuit held that because there was no agreement by the victim to treat the embezzled amount as a loan, there was no contemporaneous obligation to repay and, therefore, the embezzled amount was subject to taxation.

In Quinn v. Commissioner,[27] the taxpayer executed and delivered a promissory note in the same year he had embezzled funds from a bank; the court held that because the bank had rejected the promissory note there was a lack of consensual agreement between the parties to treat the illegally obtained funds as a loan.

§ 2.02 FORM OF RECEIPT

[1] NONCASH RECEIPTS AND BARTER EXCHANGES

"Gross income means all income from whatever source derived, unless excluded by law. Gross income includes income realized in any form, whether in money, property, or services. Income may be realized, therefore, in the form of services, meals, accommodations, stock, or other property, as well as in cash...."[1] Hence, it has long been clear that income can take the form of *receipt* of assets, the *use* of assets, or the receipt of *services*, so long as what is received has an economic value.

---

24. 384 F.2d 748 (5th Cir. 1967), cert. denied, 390 U.S. 946, 88 S.Ct. 1032, 19 L.Ed.2d 1135 (1968). See also Aaron v. Commissioner, T.C. Memo. 2004–65; Diers v. Commissioner, T.C. Memo. 2003–229.

25. United States v. Rochelle, 384 F.2d 748, 752 (5th Cir. 1967).

26. 496 F.2d 847 (2d Cir. 1974). See also Collins v. Commissioner., 3 F.3d 625 (2d Cir. 1993); Ianniello v. Commissioner, 98 T.C. 165 (1992).

27. 524 F.2d 617 (7th Cir. 1975). See also Reser v. Commissioner, 112 F.3d 1258 (5th Cir. 1997); Montgomery v. Commissioner, 300 F.3d 866 (10th Cir. 1999); Vons Companies, Inc. v. United States, 51 Fed.Cl. 1 (2001).

§ 2.02

1. Treas. Reg. § 1.61–1(a).

In Dean v. Commissioner[2] the taxpayer and his wife were the sole shareholders in an investment company. Upon the insistence of a bank, a creditor of the corporation, the family residence was transferred to the corporation, but the family continued to live in it as it had prior to the transfer. The court upheld the Commissioner's treatment of the *rental value* of the house as additional income to the taxpayer after the transfer, presumably as a dividend or as compensation for services.

Additionally, taxpayers who enter into barter exchanges in which one person provides some service or property to another in exchange for the other's provision of some other service or property each have income equal to the *value of the services* or property received.[3]

[a] Indirect Benefits

The courts have held that a variety of indirect noncash benefits represent taxable income even beyond the receipt of property or the use of property or services. For example, in Old Colony Trust Co. v. Commissioner[4] the Supreme Court held that an employee had additional gross income when his employer paid his income taxes, even though the employee never received the funds which were paid directly to the IRS by the employer.

The Court held that "The discharge by a third person of an obligation to him is equivalent to receipt by the person taxed."[5] Without question, the employee's wealth was increased by his employer's payment of his federal income tax liability as a form of compensation for services rendered; accordingly the amount was properly includible in the employee's gross income. Today, Treasury Regulation section 1.62–14(a), adopts the result of Old Colony by explicitly providing, "Another person's payment of the taxpayer's income taxes constitutes gross income to the taxpayer."

While the facts of Old Colony were limited to payments made to discharge the taxpayer's actual existing debts, the idea behind the holding, and its consequences, are broader. If ones debt is discharged by a third person, she is wealthier. But a taxpayer is also wealthier if she has no debt to begin with and another makes a deposit to an account in her name (or a contribution of her behalf or any other payment) that increases the taxpayer's wealth or purchasing power.

Whether the payment discharges an existing debt or instead provides a future credit is not significant. What matters is only whether the payment is made for the taxpayer's benefit, past, present, or future.

---

2. 187 F.2d 1019 (3d Cir. 1951). See also Greenspun v. Commissioner, 72 T.C. 931 (1979); Arenstein v. Commissioioner, T.C. Memo. 1993–339.

3. Rev. Rul. 79–24, 1979–1 C.B. 60. See also Treas. Reg. § 1.61–2(d)(1) which states, "If services are paid for in exchange for other services, the fair market value of such other services taken in payment must be included in income as compensation."

4. 279 U.S. 716, 49 S.Ct. 499, 73 L.Ed. 918 (1929).

5. Old Colony Trust Co. v. Commissioner, 279 U.S. 716, 729, 49 S.Ct. 499, 504 (1929).

Although the transaction in Old Colony was in the nature of compensation for services, which is explicitly taxable under § 61(a)(1), the result would be the same even if that were not the case; of course, this assumes there is no explicit exclusion from income applicable to the particular direct or indirect receipt in question.

[b] Cancellation of Indebtedness

In United States v. Kirby Lumber Co.[6] the corporate taxpayer was found by the Supreme Court to have realized income through market purchases of its own bonds at a discount; the Court held that its increased net worth should be subject to tax as a result of the bond repurchase transaction that resulted in extinguishment of its debt. As in Old Colony, the reduction of the taxpayer's debt was a benefit clearly realized and therefore taxable. So long as the taxpayer realizes some clear economic benefit, whether the source of the benefit is a third party, or the creditor herself, or the result of the taxpayer's repurchase of its bonds does not change the fact that absent some specific exclusionary provision, the receipt of that economic benefit is taxable in an amount equal to the value of that benefit.

More specifically, section 61(a)(12) provides that income may be realized by a taxpayer who engages in a transaction whereby the taxpayer's indebtedness is settled for less than the amount owed. This is predicated on an increase in net worth notion (by being relieved of indebtedness a taxpayer's net worth is increased) with the increase being equivalent to realized income.

Despite the general rule of section 61(a)(12) that gross income includes income from discharge of indebtedness, section 108, provides that the amount of indebtedness discharged is not income if it occurs in a case under Title 11 of the United States Code, which pertains to bankruptcy, or it occurs when the taxpayer is insolvent.[7] For discharge in a Title 11 bankruptcy case or when the taxpayer is insolvent, the amount of discharged debt excluded from gross income is applied to reduce certain "tax attributes,"[8] such as net operating losses and the basis of property of the taxpayer.[9]

Under section 108(e)(5) if the seller of property reduces the debt of the purchaser and the reduction does not occur in a bankruptcy case or when the purchaser is insolvent, the reduction of the purchase money debt is treated as a price adjustment on the property. Consequently, in this case the purchaser does not have income, but it must reduce the cost basis of the property. And, assuming the property increases in value, the purchaser will later pay additional taxes upon the disposition of the property in a taxable transaction.[10]

---

6. 284 U.S. 1, 52 S.Ct. 4, 76 L.Ed. 131 (1931).

7. See § 108(a)(1)(A) and (B).

8. See § 108(b)(1).

9. See § 108(b)(2)(A)-(G). Note: Section 1017 provides mechanical rules for the reduction of basis in property required by section 108.

10. See § 1001(a) (which generally provides that gain or loss on the sale of

[c] Discounts

[i] Compensatory Discounts

If the taxpayer has derived any other kind of economic benefit from a transaction in a commercial context, the courts have held that she has income.[11] Thus, in Commissioner v. Minzer[12] the Fifth Circuit held that an insurance salesman realized taxable income when he purchased a policy on which the premium owed was reduced by the amount of commission he was entitled to receive. The court reasoned that the discount was compensation arising out of an employment relationship,[13] and, accordingly, the value of the discount was taxable income.[14]

[ii] Noncompensatory Bargains or Discounts

Discounts or bargain purchases from *unrelated* parties may represent accessions to wealth. Nonetheless, such discounts are *not* income for tax purposes. The reason for this is that the tax law presumes that if there is a sale of property (or services) between unrelated parties, they have adverse economic interests, and the amount paid is the actual fair market value of the property.[15]

For tax purposes, fair market value is defined as, "the price at which property would change hands in a transaction between a willing buyer and a willing seller, neither being under compulsion to buy or sell and both being reasonably informed as to all relevant facts."[16]

Thus, for example, assume that A, B, and C purchase identical new cars from the same dealer on the same day, and that A pays $20,000, B pays $22,500 and C pays $25,000. None of the buyers have any taxable income. A is presumed to have purchased a vehicle worth $20,000 (with a basis of $20,000); B is presumed to have purchased a vehicle worth $22,500 (with a basis of $22,500); and C is presumed to have purchased her vehicle worth $25,000 (with a basis of $25,000).[17]

property shall be computed by subtracting the basis of the property from any amount realized upon its disposition).

11. See e.g., Commissioner v. Minzer, 279 F.2d 338 (5th Cir. 1960); Faris v. Commissioner, 937 F.2d 616 (10th Cir. 1991); Wentz v. Commissioner, 105 T.C. 1 (1995); Shotts v. Commissioner, T.C. Memo. 1990–641; Rev. Rul. 92–96, 1992–45 I.R.B. 22.

12. 279 F.2d 338 (5th Cir. 1960). See also Faris v. Commissioner, 937 F.2d 616 (10th Cir. 1991); Wentz v. Commissioner, 105 T.C. 1 (1995); Shotts v. Commissioner, T.C. Memo. 1990–641; Rev. Rul. 92–96, 1992–45 I.R.B. 22.

13. See also Commissioner v. Daehler, 281 F.2d 823 (5th Cir. 1960) (realtor received commission on sale of land to self).

14. But see § 132(a)(2) (which specifically excludes from gross income "qualified employee discounts").

15. See Van Duzer v. Commissioner, T.C. Memo. 1991–249; Brannen v. Commissioner, 722 F.2d 695 (11th Cir. 1984).

16. United States v. Cartwright, 411 U.S. 546, 551, 93 S.Ct. 1713, 1716 (1973). See also A & A Tool & Supply Co. v. Commissioner, 182 F.2d 300 (10th Cir. 1950); Goldstein v. Commissioner, 298 F.2d 562 (9th Cir. 1962); Kalmon Shoe Mfg. Co. v. Commissioner, 321 F.2d 189 (8th Cir. 1963); Arc Realty Co. v. Commissioner, 295 F.2d 98 (8th Cir. 1961); Hamm v. Commissioner, 325 F.2d 934 (8th Cir. 1963); Estate of Fitts v. Commissioner, 237 F.2d 729 (8th Cir. 1956).

17. See § 1012 which provides "The basis of property shall be the cost of such property . . ."

This rule applies whenever there is a cash purchase from an unrelated party acting at arm's length. If there is an exchange of properties, services or anything other than a cash purchase, the same rule may be inapplicable. If neither asset exchanged is cash, then while it may nonetheless be true that the "amount paid" is the presumed fair market value of the property purchased, the "amount paid" may not be readily determinable.[18]

In addition, it is important to note that what is not income is the "bargain element" of a purchase at arm's length. The taxpayer who buys assets at arm's length at a good price is not taxed on the benefit of her bargain. If she has paid $20,000 for a car worth $25,000, she may have a clearly realized accession to wealth, but it is simply one that is not taxed. The strongest justification for this exclusion is that any other rule would be unenforceable and administratively impractical. The IRS is simply not about to investigate taxpayers' shopping habits in order to measure gross income; obviously, from a tax administration standpoint, this would be a nightmare.

If a taxpayer trades property, services or any other asset for some other property, then, the bargain element of her *acquisition* will theoretically not be taxed, but if the taxpayer acquires property in exchange for something other than cash, it will likely be impossible to determine whether any "good deal" the taxpayer received is a bargain element of her *acquisition* or a bargain element of her *disposition* of the property she is trading away. If the latter, she is taxed. If the determination of which party the benefit accompanies is not obvious, the Service will assume that the bargain represents a good deal on the disposition rather than acquisition, by determining the value of the property acquired by the taxpayer and taxing her on the extent to which that value exceeds her basis in the property disposed.[19]

To see how this situation may arise, recall that if T negotiates the arm's length purchase of a car for $20,000, T has no gross income, even if others pay $25,000 for its equivalent. If T and the car seller agree instead that T can pay for her car (for which others are paying $25,000) by transferring to the seller T's old truck for which T paid $10,000 and which T believes she could likely sell for about $20,000, T might argue that the cost of the car is still only $20,000, because $20,000 is the value of her old truck. The IRS, though, might well argue that the cost of the car was actually $25,000. This assertion would be based not on the Service's desire to tax T on her bargain with respect to the new car, but, instead, it would be based on its desire to tax T on her gain on the exchange of her old truck. T would likely have a difficult time trying to convince the IRS that the "bargain" was on the acquisition of the car rather than on the disposition of the truck. Accordingly, as a general

---

18. See Philadelphia Park Amusement Co. v. United States, 126 F.Supp. 184 (Ct. Cl. 1954).

19. Id.

proposition, unless the taxpayer's bargain purchase is made for cash, the rule excluding any bargain element of purchases is inapplicable.

[d]   Interest–Free and Below–Market Loans

In the past, some courts had held that interest-free loans did not give rise to taxable income, even though there is no doubt that the borrower received an economic benefit from the interest-free use of money.[20] In Dean v. Commissioner[21] the Tax Court held that no taxable gain was realized by the borrower on account of an interest-free loan. The holding created an illogical dichotomy between the rent-free use of property, which is subject to tax, and the uncompensated use of money. Congress rectified this issue in 1984 with the enactment of section 7872, which generally treats as income to the borrower of interest-free or below-market loans the spread between the amount of interest actually paid and the applicable federal rate.[22]

Prior to the Tax Reform Act of 1984 taxpayers used interest-free and below-market loans in a variety of ways to reduce taxes.[23] Such loans were used, for example, to shift income between family members. Loans between family members made to avoid the assignment of income rules and grantor trust rules generally involved a parent loaning money to a child, but without charging any interest. Income the child earned on the money would be taxed at the child's lower rate, resulting in a lower overall tax liability for the family.[24] Thus, an interest-free loan to a family member involved a gratuitous transfer of the right to use the amount borrowed until repayment. If the parent had merely assigned

20. See Dickman v. Commissioner, 465 U.S. 330, 104 S.Ct. 1086, 79 L.Ed.2d 343 (1984) (interest-free use of money held a property right subject to the gift tax).

21. 35 T.C. 1083 (1961), nonacq., 1973–2 Cum. Bull. 4.

22. § 7872(e) uses term "applicable federal rate," defined in § 7872(f)(2) as the rate in effect under § 1274(d).

23. Hurley, The Interest–Free Loan Is Free No More, 9 Rev. Tax'n Individuals 353 (1985); Hutton & Tucker, The Taxation of Below–Market and Interest–Free Family Loans: A Legislative and Judicial History, 19 Fam. L.Q. 297 (1985); Lieber, Interest–Free Loans, 23 Duq. L. Rev. 1019 (1985); Christopher T. Carlson, Personal and Business Planning: The Impact of a Low–Interest Loan, 44 N.Y.U. Inst. on Fed. Tax'n 35–1 (1986); Phillip J. Closius & Douglas K. Chapman, Below Market Loans: From Abuse to Misuse—A Sports Illustration, 37 Cas. W. Res. L. Rev. 484 (1986); Gregor S. Chvisuk, Taxation of Loans Having Below–Market Interest Rates, 21 Idaho L. Rev. 257 (1985); Mark D. Edwards, Interest–Free Loans Are Held To Be Gifts in Supreme Court's Recent Dickman Decision, 60 J.

Tax'n 266 (1984); Michael D. Hartigan, From Dean and Crown to the Tax Reform Act of 1984: Taxation of Interest–Free Loans, 60 Notre Dame L. Rev. 31, 53–57 (1984); S. Scott Massin & Charles R. McGuire, Death of a Loophole: Recent Legislation and Case Law Dealing with Taxation of Interest–Free and Low–Interest Loans, 24 Am. Bus. L.J. 105 (1986); Howard M. McCue III & Patricia Brosterhous, Interest–Free and Below–Market Loans After Dickman and the Tax Reform Act of 1984, 62 Taxes 1010 (1984); Lynn K. Pearle, Interest–Free and Below–Market Gift Loans, 26 Tax Mgmt. Mem. 3 (1985); Stephen L. Seftenberg, Kiss Your Crown (Loan) Goodbye: Below–Market Rate Loans After the Tax Reform Act of 1984, 74 Ill. B.J. 34 (1985); S.J. Willbanks, Interest–Free Loans Are No Longer Free: Tax Consequences of Gift Loans, 47 Mont. L. Rev. 39 (1986).

24. *Nota bene:* Even absent § 7872 this assignment of income would not be successfully today because of the "kiddie tax" found in § 1(g)(2)(A) which generally taxes children's unearned income, over specified thresholds, at their parent's marginal tax rate.

the income to the child, the parent would have been taxed under the assignment of income doctrine. Likewise, if the parent had made a transfer to a trust for the child that had a term of less than ten years or that was revocable at will, the income would have been taxed to the parent.

Prior to the Tax Reform Act of 1984 loans from corporations to shareholders were used in a similar fashion. Congress believed that an interest-free or a below-market loan from a corporation to a shareholder is the economic equivalent of a loan by the corporation to the shareholder that requires payment of interest at the market rate and a distribution by the corporation to the shareholder with respect to its stock. Hence, the borrower would have dividend income and an offsetting interest deduction, and the lender would have interest income. Prior to 1984, if the transaction was structured as an interest-free or below-market loan, the lender avoided including the interest in income. Consequently, the lender was in the same position as it would have been had it been able to deduct amounts distributed as dividends.

Prior to the Tax Reform Act of 1984 loans to persons providing services were used to circumvent rules requiring payment of employment taxes and rules restricting deductibility of interest in certain situations by the person providing the services. Congress viewed a below-market loan to a person providing services as the equivalent of a loan requiring the payment of interest at a market rate and payment in the nature of compensation equal to the amount of interest required to be paid under the terms of the loan. Before the enactment of section 7872, a transaction structured as a loan and a payment in the nature of compensation often did not result in any tax consequences for either the lender or the borrower because each would have offsetting income and deductions. There were, however, situations in which the payment of compensation and a loan requiring payment of interest at a market rate would not offset each other. For example, if a taxpayer used the proceeds of an arm's-length loan to invest in tax-exempt obligations, the deduction for interest paid on the loan would be disallowed under section 265(a)(2).[25]

Congress' rationale in enacting section 7872 was to recognize that the use of funds at below-market rates was the economic equivalent of a receipt of income in the amount of interest saved. Again, the lack of any identifiable object that was received, and the fact that the accession to wealth took the form of temporary use of another's money or property, does not prevent that accession to wealth from being included in income.

Section 7872 treats below-market loans as transactions in which the lender is deemed to have charged a statutorily established rate of interest and transferred some or all of that amount to the borrower. This transfer is treated as a gift, compensation, or a dividend that the borrower is deemed to have retransferred to the lender as interest.[26]

---

25. See § 265(a)(2) (which generally disallows any interest expense deduction for funds borrowed to purchase tax-exempt bonds).

26. See § 7872(a)(1)(A) and (B).

The following types of loans are subject to section 7872:[27]

(1) Gift loans. A gift loan is any interest-free or below-market loan in which the foregone interest is in the nature of a gift.[28] In general, there is a gift if property, including foregone interest, is transferred for less than full and adequate consideration under circumstances in which the transfer is a gift for gift tax purposes.[29]

(2) Compensation-related loans. A compensation-related loan is any interest-free or below-market loan made in connection with the performance of services directly or indirectly between an employer and an employee or an independent contractor and a person for whom such independent contractor provides services.[30]

(3) Corporation-shareholder loans. A corporation-shareholder loan is any interest-free or below-market loan made directly or indirectly between a corporation and one of its shareholders.[31]

(4) Tax avoidance loans. A tax avoidance loan is an interest-free or a below-market loan in which a principal purpose is the avoidance of federal taxation by either the lender or borrower.[32]

(5) Other below-market loans. This catch-all category includes interest-free or below-market loans in which the interest arrangement has a significant effect on the tax liability of the borrower or the lender.[33] Such arrangements result in the conversion of a nondeductible expense into the equivalent of a deductible expense. An example of this is a member of a club who makes a noninterest bearing refundable deposit to the club in lieu of part or all of the membership fee.

To apply section 7872, one must determine whether the transaction is a term loan or a demand loan. A demand loan is "any loan which is payable in full at any time on the demand of the lender."[34] Any other loan is considered a term loan.[35] To fall within the bailiwick of section 7872, the loan must be a below-market loan. This requirement is met in the case of a demand loan or term gift loan if the interest rate on the loan is lower than the applicable federal rate.[36] For a demand loan or a term gift loan the lender is treated as transferring to the borrower an amount equal to the foregone interest, compounded semiannually.[37] For a term loan, other than a term gift loan, the below-market rate requirement is met if the amount loaned exceeds the present value (calculated on the basis of the applicable federal rate) of all payments due on the loan.[38] For a term loan, other than a term gift loan, the lender is treated as transferring to the borrower an amount equal to the excess of the

27. See § 7872(c)(1)(A)-(E).
28. See § 7872(f)(3).
29. See § 7872(c)(1)(A).
30. See § 7872(c)(1)(B)(i) and (ii).
31. See § 7872(c)(1)(C).
32. See § 7872(c)(1)(D).
33. See § 7872(c)(1)(E).
34. § 7872(f)(5).
35. § 7872(f)(6).
36. § 7872(e) uses the term "applicable federal rate," defined in § 7872(f)(2) as the rate in effect under § 1274(d).
37. See § 7872(a)(1).
38. See § 7872(b)(1).

amount of the loan over the present value of all principal and interest payments due under the loan.[39] This transfer is treated as occurring on the date the loan is made.[40]

If the total of all the loans outstanding between the lender and the borrower is not greater than $10,000, two de minimis exceptions may be potentially applicable.[41] A compensation loan is exempted if a principal purpose was not to avoid paying taxes,[42] and a gift loan is exempted if the borrower did not buy income-producing assets with the amount borrowed.[43] There is a further exception if the aggregate amount outstanding on gift loans between individuals is not greater than $100,000.[44] In such a situation the amount treated as retransferred from the borrower to the lender at the end of the year will not exceed the net investment of the borrower.[45] If the net investment income is no more than $1,000, the amount treated as retransferred is zero.[46]

[e]   Valuation Issues

[i]   De Minimis Receipts

One issue that may arise when a taxpayer receives some benefit other than cash has to do with valuation. The first priority relating to valuation is to firmly establish that, for administrative and other reasons having nothing to do with the basic theoretical conceptualization of income, there are spoken and unspoken de minimis rules constantly at play.

It would be theoretically accurate to suggest that if Taxpayer One and Taxpayer Two are roommates, and they agree that One will wash the dishes and Two will take out the trash, each is receiving some service of value from the other. Each taxpayer therefore has income equal to the value of the service received. Similarly, one who finds a pretty rock on the sidewalk and takes it home theoretically has income equal to the value of that rock. Yet no one would imagine that the "income" received in either of these situations should actually be reported to the IRS. Sometimes de minimis rules are built into the Code.[47] Other times they are just a matter of common sense. In either event, they do not call on any taxpayer to be so *theoretically* pure to the concept of gross income as to be *practically* ridiculous.

[ii]   Other Valuation Issues

Even where the taxpayer receives some economic benefit that is not de minimis, valuation issues may well arise. Consider the taxpayer who either finds or otherwise receives, directly or indirectly, some object or benefit the value of which, though perhaps significant, is nonetheless not

---

39. Id.

40. Id.

41. See § 7872(c)(2) and (3).

42. § 7872(c)(3).

43. § 7872(c)(2)(A) and (B).

44. § 7872(d)(1).

45. § 7872(d)(1)(A).

46. § 7872(d)(1)(E)(ii).

47. See e.g., § 132(a)(4).

readily determinable. An example is a game show contestant who wins free nontransferable airfare to anywhere in the world. She may use her prize to obtain a ticket to an exotic location, worth as much as $10,000; instead she may choose to fly to some location within her same state ($99 ticket value); or she may be afraid of flying and simply not use the ticket at all. While it may be tempting to wait and see exactly what the winner does with her winnings, the tax system does not generally provide a way to include something in income currently but determine the appropriate amount of inclusion in income at some later time. Instead, since the contestant has income at the time of receipt, the amount of her income must be determined at that time.

If the taxpayer's taxable benefit can be sold, the determination of its value may be at least theoretically straightforward; for tax purposes, the fair market value of anything can be defined as "the price at which property would change hands in a transaction between a willing buyer and a willing seller, neither being under compulsion to buy or sell and both being reasonably informed as to all relevant facts."[48]

Indeed, if the seller wants, she can immediately sell whatever it is that she has received in an arm's length transaction. The amount the seller receives will not only give her the value of what it was she received, but it will also provide her the cash to pay whatever tax is due.

If the taxpayer's benefit is either not marketable or not transferable, valuation becomes more difficult on even the theoretical level. In Turner v. Commissioner,[49] the taxpayers won two round-trip nontransferable first-class steamship tickets, restricted as to transferability, to Buenos Aires, with a retail value of $2,220. The taxpayers exchanged the first-class tickets for four tourist-class tickets of almost the same value, which they then used. The taxpayers reported only $520 as income, explaining that although the tourist tickets would cost significantly more than that to someone who wanted them, they themselves were not particularly excited about their trip and would not have paid more than $520 for the tickets.

The government contended that the tickets should have been valued at their full retail value of $2,220. The Tax Court determined that the tickets were worth $1,400. The court said:

> "The winning of the tickets did not provide them with something which they needed in the ordinary course of their lives and for

48. United States v. Cartwright, 411 U.S. 546, 551, 93 S.Ct. 1713, 1716 (1973). See also A & A Tool & Supply Co. v. Commissioner, 182 F.2d 300 (10th Cir. 1950); Goldstein v. Commissioner, 298 F.2d 562 (9th Cir. 1962); Kalmon Shoe Mfg. Co. v. Commissioner, 321 F.2d 189 (8th Cir. 1963); Arc Realty Co. v. Commissioner, 295 F.2d 98 (8th Cir. 1961); Hamm v. Commissioner, 325 F.2d 934 (8th Cir. 1963); Estate of Fitts v. Commissioner, 237 F.2d 729 (8th Cir. 1956). *Nota bene:* While theoretically

straightforward, the practical issue of valuation is not solved by reference to a willing buyer and a willing seller. As a practical matter, valuation issues may be difficult to resolve.

49. T.C. Memo. 1954–38. See also Wade v. Commissioner, T.C. Memo. 1988–118; Brunskill v. Commissioner, T.C. Memo. 1982–645; James R. Repetti, Commentary It's All About Valuation, 53 Tax L. Rev. 607 (Summer 2000).

which they would have made an expenditure in any event, but merely gave them an opportunity to enjoy a luxury otherwise beyond their means. Their value to the petitioners was not equal to their retail cost." While one may note that the value placed on the prize by the court was essentially midway between the amounts argued for by the two parties, the court, while noting a significant problem with respect to valuation, gave no real indication of how that problem might be resolved, other than by determinations of the facts of each case by the relevant trier of fact.

§ 2.03 REALIZATION

Given the breadth of the definition of income in the Internal Revenue Code, one might ask whether in fact there are *any* inherent limitations in that definition. An accession to wealth may be received from any source, legal or not, or from no source at all (found property). The accession to wealth may be for any reason, or for no reason at all. The receipt may be direct or indirect (for example, a payment made to a third party on the taxpayer's behalf).[1] The "accession to wealth" that is received may be cash, property, services, or the temporary use of cash or property or services, or any other benefit.[2] So where are the limits?

The primary limit on the concept of income as used in the tax law lies in the all important concept of "realization." Unlike an "accretion" to wealth, which requires nothing more than an *increase* in a taxpayer's net worth (or consumption), an "accession" to wealth requires that the taxpayer *receive* something she did not have before. It seems fairly clear that one becomes more wealthy, and thus has income in an economic sense, when ones property increases in value.

If T has a net worth of $10,000 on January 1 of the current year and has a net worth of $100,000 on December 31 of the current year, few could deny that in any economic sense of the word T has income of at least $90,000 for the year, regardless of whether the growth in T's net worth is the result of T's labor, T's receipts, or the increase in value of T's property.

Even so, as a general proposition our federal income tax system imposes no tax without some receipt of something of value.[3] By and large, taxable income as our system knows it does not include appreciation in income until and unless the taxpayer receives something other than or in addition to his or her previously-held property.[4] Whether our federal income tax system *could* constitutionally include such appreciation in income is an open question.

§ 2.03

1. See e.g., Old Colony Trust Co. v. Commissioner, 301 U.S. 379, 57 S.Ct. 813, 81 L.Ed. 1169 (1937).

2. See Treas. Reg. § 1.61–1(a).

3. But see § 1272 (which generally mandates the current inclusion in gross income of any original issue discount) and § 1256 (which generally mandates the current inclusion in gross income of any annual unrealized gain relating to straddle positions).

4. Id.

Aside from the apparent lack of equity the realization requirement also distorts taxpayer behavior. For example, the wage earner who earns $100,000 and wants to be an investor must pay tax on all of her earnings; the investor whose stock increases in value from $100,000 to $500,000 has had a much better year financially than the wage earner, but yet she incurs no tax liability.

Investments that generate appreciation without being sold (or otherwise exchanged) go untaxed, while those that generate current income are taxed in full. The impact on investment behavior is significant. The impact of this problem on Congressional behavior (as Congress attempts to mend the economic impacts of the realization requirement) is often both astounding and confusing.

§ 2.04   IMPUTED INCOME

[1]   IMPUTED INCOME FROM PROPERTY

While a taxpayer who benefits from the use of another's property must include in income the value of that use, one who benefits from the use of her own property does not have income, regardless of the value of that use. For example, the Taxpayer whose employer allows her to use his house (with an annual fair rental value of $10,000) for a year has $10,000 of income (the fair rental value of the use the employee receives). Notwithstanding the foregoing, the taxpayer who allows herself to use her *own* house, also with an annual fair rental value of $10,000, has no income at all.

Admittedly, the notion that a person may have income from simply using her own home for a year may seem counterintuitive at any level, either practical or theoretical. As such, the notion is worth a bit more analysis.

Assume that as of the beginning of the year, A has exactly $1,000,000, and that the current pre-tax going rate of return is 6%. A can put her $1,000,000 in the bank at 6% interest, earn $60,000, and use that investment return to pay $5,000 per month for rent ($60,000 per year), which is the fair rental value of a $1,000,000 house.[1] If A does so, the $60,000 return on her investment she earns will be fully taxable, and the fact that she uses all of that income to pay rent has no further impact on her federal income tax liability.

If, instead, A uses her $1,000,000 to purchase real property which she leases out for $60,000 per year, she will again earn enough to pay the rent for her to live in a $1,000,000 home for a year. Once again, the full $60,000 she receives as rental income and then pays as the rent on her residence will be taxable.

----

§ 2.04

1. This assumes that the market is stable, so that the $1,000,000 value of the house is not expected to fluctuate.

If, alternatively, A invests the $1,000,000 in real property worth $1,000,000, she may simply live in that property herself.

In each of these three situations, A has used her $1,000,000 to provide housing for herself for a year, and at the end of the year A still has something (either cash, rental property or her own home) worth $1,000,000. But in only the last situation she escapes having a tax liability as a result of her actions.

The truth is that *all* assets have value because they are at least potentially productive; i.e., they are expected to produce something of value. Tangible assets may be used to produce rental income or employed in some other money-making activity. For example, equipment may be used in a business, or undeveloped land may be used in farming, mining, or any similar productive activity. Cash can be used to earn interest. Stocks and bonds can be used to earn dividends or interest. Any investments that produce nothing currently (for example, diamonds or gold held solely for investment) are expected to produce appreciation in value. Any asset that produces nothing of current utility but that nonetheless has value (in case anyone can imagine such an asset), can, if nothing else, be traded for some other asset that can be used, and, therefore, it too can be used to produce some current benefit.

What a house produces, at a basic level, is shelter and comfort. One might sell that current shelter and comfort (lease out the property) or one might consume that current utility (live in the property). Either way, ownership of real property worth $1,000,000 produces an amount of shelter and comfort worth approximately $60,000 per year. This assumes applicable interest rates are approximately 6%, and the property is not held exclusively for appreciation.[2] The important thing from a tax perspective is that if one *sells* the current utility, she will have a "receipt," and it will be taxed. If one simply keeps it for herself, she avoids tax completely. This result is achieved because the taxpayer who owns and uses her own property is not seen as receiving anything she did not already own; moreover, and perhaps more importantly, the taxpayer in these circumstances is not seen as having had a realization event which would justify taxation.

Imputed income from the use of ones own property is not unknown in tax systems of other countries, and economists have suggested the availability of such income as a means of expanding the base of the U.S. income tax.[3] Nevertheless imputed income is not included in gross

---

2. If one owns undeveloped land with a current value of $1,000,000, it is arguable that the land produces no current utility, since the land cannot be used as it is. Nonetheless, if the land is actually worth $1,000,000 on January 1 of year one in a setting where the pre-tax rate of return is 6%, the land is expected to produce current utility in the form of appreciation at a 6% rate. If currently unusable land is expected to be worth only $1,000,000 at the end of the year, it simply could not have a value of $1,000,000 at the beginning of the year. The unusable land at the beginning of the year could not be worth more than its expected future value at yearend discounted by the 6% rate of return.

3. One comprehensive base-broadening proposal would have included imputed rent on owner-occupied homes and a substantial portion of unrealized capital gain in the income for federal income tax purposes. The failure to include such income is probably a self-imposed limitation of the government, based upon historical, political, and administrative considerations, rather than upon legal[4] or economic ones.

[2] IMPUTED INCOME FROM SERVICES

Also related to the realization requirement is the imputed income that arises when rather than using their own property, individuals perform *work* for themselves. Thus, the carpenter who receives compensation for improving another's building may have income, but the carpenter who improves his own building has no income at all (until and unless he sells that house at a profit). Similarly, the farmer who grows and *sells* crops has income from the fruits (or grains, etc., as the case may be) of his labor, but the farmer who grows and *consumes* his crops has no income. Congress has not attempted to tax this imputed income, and the Service, mainly for reasons of perceived equity and actual administrative convenience, has not argued that such benefits constitute income even within the broad meaning of section 61.

While the federal income tax system's failure to tax imputed income from services one provides directly for herself seems reasonable, it can create some problems and resentment of taxes for certain taxpayers. For example, assume that A and B are a married couple. Further assume that B earns a substantial salary (which results in A and B being in the 35% marginal tax bracket), that A resides at home taking care of the house and garden and cooking meals for himself and B, and that A's household services are worth $25,000 per year. Of course, A and B must pay taxes on B's salary, but they are not taxed on the $25,000 value of A's services because there has been no "realization event." Neither A nor B would object to this result, nor would observers of their situation.

However, what happens if A seeks employment outside the home? Assume that A accepts a job that pays $30,000 per year. In order to maintain the same well-manicured home they have become accustomed to living in, A and B hire C to perform the services that had been performed by A prior to taking his new job. As noted earlier, the value of the household services previously performed by A were worth $25,000 per year; accordingly, A and B agree to pay C $25,000 per year in order to perform these same services. Taxes aside, A and B have increased their economic power by $5,000 per year. A will now earn $30,000 per year, and this amount exceeds the $25,000 value of his previously-performed household services by $5,000 on a pre-tax basis.

base of the income tax. See Attiat & Ott, Simulation of Revenue and Tax Structure in Studies in Substantive Tax Reform 25 (Willis ed. 1969).

4. In dictum, the Supreme Court observed that rental income imputed from the use of real property would not withstand attack on constitutional grounds because it did not constitute income within the meaning of the Sixteenth Amendment. Helvering v. Independent Life Ins. Co., 292 U.S. 371, 54 S.Ct. 758 (1934). See also the comment in Morris v. Commissioner, 9 B.T.A. 1273 (1928), that farm products consumed by a farmer and his family were comparable to the rental value of a private residence and neither were intended to be regarded as income by Congress.

Of course, when A worked at home the $25,000 per year value of his services was exempt from taxation. Under section 61(a)(1) the amount A receives as a salary when working outside the home is includable in gross income.

If A and B are in the 35% marginal tax bracket, A's $30,000 salary results in a $10,500 additional federal income tax liability. Hence, on an after-tax basis A and B loose $5,500 ($30,000 salary—$10,500 federal income tax liability-$25,000 salary paid to C) per year as a result of A working outside the home.

§ 2.05   TAXATION OF CAPITAL RECEIPTS

[1]   IN GENERAL

The Sixteenth Amendment provides: "The Congress shall have power to lay and collect taxes on incomes, from whatever source derived, without apportionment among the several States, and without regard to any census or enumeration." Nowhere in the foregoing grant of taxing authority is Congress given the power to tax capital receipts. Of course, the pertinent question here is what are capital receipts? This question may be encountered in a number of areas of the tax law.

In some areas of the tax law, capital receipts can be readily identified. For example, section 118(a) provides that gross income does not include "any contribution to the capital" of a corporation. Furthermore, there is no gross income which results from repaying the principal of a loan. Nevertheless, application of the concept of capital receipt has not been an easy matter. For example, in Clark v. Commissioner[1] the taxpayer's lawyer gave advice that resulted in additional tax liability of $19,000. The lawyer reimbursed the taxpayer this amount and the government contended that the taxpayer was in receipt of income. The Tax Court held that the amount was not income, but, instead, it was reimbursement for loss of capital.

[2]   SCOPE OF RECOVERY: CAPITAL OR EXPENSE

Probably the most common transaction in which the capital receipt or recovery concept is recognized is the sale of property. Section 1001(a) allows the taxpayer to receive the unrecovered cost of property tax free when it is sold. A similar result is obtained for a taxpayer who has an inventory of goods; the regulations indicate that the taxpayer's cost of goods sold is subtracted from the gross receipts.[2]

§ 2.05

1. 40 B.T.A. 333 (1939), acq., 1957–1 Cum. Bull. 4. See also Concord Instruments Corp. v. Commissioner, T.C. Memo. 1994–248; IRS CCA 200504001, 2005 WL 190296; Rev. Rul. 81–277, 1981–48 I.R.B. 5.

2. Treas. Reg. § 1.61–3(a) states that " 'gross income' means the total sales, less the cost of goods sold" in a manufacturing or merchandising business. See also Treas. Reg. § 1.446–1(a)(4)(i).

[3] SUBSIDIES

In Edwards v. Cuba Railroad Co.[3] the taxpayer built a railroad for the Cuban government under a contract calling for $1,700,000 worth of subsidies. These subsidies were used for capital expenditures, but no corresponding reductions were taken in the cost of the construction. Although the taxpayer had agreed to provide certain reduced rates and services to the Cuban government, the Supreme Court held that the subsidies were not income under the Sixteenth Amendment, but, instead, they were reimbursements for capital expenditures granted to induce land settlement and for other broad purposes rather than payments for future services.

A similar result was reached in Brown Shoe Co. v. Commissioner,[4] in which community contributions of cash and property to a corporation that were made to induce its location in the community were held to be contributions to capital rather than income. The rule of this case is now embedded in section 118. The exclusion provided by section 118 is subject to section 362(c), which by requiring the corporation to use a zero basis as its measure of investment has the effect of bringing the contributions into income over the life of the property since no deduction will be available for depreciation or cost recovery.[5] The Court in Brown Shoe held that the purpose of the payment by a nonstockholder to a corporation will be determinative of whether the payment is a contribution to capital. Thus, a payment intended as compensation for present or future services will be treated as taxable income.

In Teleservice Co. of Wyoming Valley v. Commissioner[6] payments made by homeowners for the construction of a community antennae system were found to be in exchange for the use of the system and held to constitute income. Similarly, in John B. White, Inc. v. Commissioner[7] the Tax Court held that the payment of $60,000 by an automobile manufacturer, a nonshareholder, to the taxpayer-dealer to induce it to move to a better location constituted taxable income rather than a contribution to capital under section 118; in this case the payment had a reasonable nexus with the taxpayer's business, the sale of the manufacturer's automobiles.

In Federated Department Stores, Inc. v. Commissioner[8] section 118 was held to apply to a contribution of 10 acres and $200,000 a year for

---

3. 268 U.S. 628, 45 S.Ct. 614, 69 L.Ed. 1124 (1925). See also EPCO, Inc. v. Commissioner, 104 F.3d 170 (8th Cir. 1997); United States v. Swan, 187 Fed.Appx. 21 (1st Cir. 2006).

4. 339 U.S. 583, 70 S.Ct. 820, 94 L.Ed. 1081 (1950). See also Rev. Rul. 2007–31, 2007–21 I.R.B. 1275; Rev. Rul. 2005–46, 2005–30 I.R.B. 120; TAM 200450035; TAM 200434019; TAM 200411008.

5. For the purpose of computing the deduction for depreciation or cost recovery under §§ 167 or 168, the basis of property is its cost as a general rule. See § 1012.

6. 254 F.2d 105 (3d Cir. 1958), cert. denied, 357 U.S. 919, 78 S.Ct. 1360, 2 L.Ed.2d 1364 (1958). See also TAM 200411008; EPCO, Inc. v. Commissioner, 104 F.3d 170 (8th Cir. 1997).

7. 55 T.C. 729 (1971), aff'd *per curiam*, 458 F.2d 989 (3d Cir. 1972). See also Brooks v. Commissioner, 89 T.C. 43 (1987); FSA 200227007.

8. 426 F.2d 417 (6th Cir. 1970). See also TAM 200310003; G.M. Trading Corp. v. Commissioner, 121 F.3d 977 (5th Cir. 1997); Convergent Technologies, Inc. v.

10 years by a realty company to an operator of retail department stores as an inducement to construct and operate a store in a shopping center. In upholding the Tax Court the Sixth Circuit reasoned that the benefit to the realty company was too remote and indirect to warrant treatment of the contributions as payments for future services. The Sixth Circuit concluded that the legislative history of section 118 indicated that it was not intended to be limited to contributions made by governmental units or civic groups, as the Commissioner contended, but, instead, it also applied to contributions made by "an association of individuals having no proprietary interest in the corporation."

In United States v. Chicago, Burlington & Quincy Railroad Co.[9] the Supreme Court enumerated several characteristics prerequisite to a nonstockholder contribution to capital under the Code. The factors were as follows:

> (1) The contribution "must become a permanent part of the transferee's working capital structure; (2) The contribution may not be compensation, such as a direct payment for a specific, quantifiable service provided for the transferor by the transferee; (3) The contribution must be part of a bargain; (4) The asset transferred foreseeably must result in benefit to the transferee in an amount commensurate with its value; and (5) The asset ordinarily, if not always, will be employed in or contribute to the production of additional income and its value assured in that respect."[10]

Accordingly, the Court found that the property constructed with state funds and later transferred to the railroad was not a contribution to capital.

§ 2.06 PRIZES AND AWARDS

Section 74(a) generally mandates that prizes and awards are includable in gross income.[1] There are three primary exceptions so the rule of section 74(a): (1) amounts which are subject to section 117 are by definition outside the bailiwick of section 74(a);[2] (2) certain employee achievement awards are excludable from gross income;[3] and (3) certain prizes and awards for "religious, charitable, scientific, educational, artistic, literary, or civic achievement" are excludable from gross income under certain circumstance.

The taxation of scholarships and fellowships is discussed in Chapter 3.

Commissioner, T.C. Memo. 1995–320; Chief Counsel Attorney Memorandum, 2007 WL 465835.

9. 412 U.S. 401, 93 S.Ct. 2169, 37 L.Ed.2d 30 (1973). See also Kohler Co. v. United States, 468 F.3d 1032 (7th Cir. 2006); H.J. Heinz Co. and Subsidiaries v. United States, 76 Fed.Cl. 570 (2007).

10. Id.

§ 2.06

1. See also Treas. Reg. § 1.74–1(a); Teschner v. Commissioner, 38 T.C. 1003 (1962).

2. See § 74(a). The taxation of scholarships and fellowships are discussed in Chapter 3.

3. See § 74(c).

As to the second exception from the general rule of section 74(a), section 74(c) provides an exclusion from gross income for employee achievement awards. Section 274(j) defines an "employee achievement award" as an item of *tangible* personal property transferred by an employer to an employee for length of service achievement or for safety achievement, but only if the item is awarded as part of a meaningful presentation and under circumstances that do not create a significant likelihood of the payment of disguised compensation.[4]

An award for length of service cannot qualify for exclusion if it is received during the employee's first five years of employment for the employer making the award, or if the employee has received a length of service achievement award (other than a de minimis fringe excludable under section 132(e)(1)) from the employer during the year or any of the preceding four years.[5] An award for safety achievement cannot qualify for the exclusion if made to an individual who is not an eligible employee, or if, during the taxable year, employee awards for safety achievement (other than awards excludable under section 132(e)(1)) have previously been awarded by the employer to more than 10% of the employer's eligible employees.[6]

An employee achievement award is excludable from gross income if the cost of all such awards provided the same employee during the taxable year do not exceed $400.[7] However, for one or more qualified plan awards made to the same employee during the taxable year, the amount may not exceed $1,600.[8] A "qualified plan award" is defined in section 274(j)(3)(B) as an employee achievement award provided under an established, written plan or program that does not discriminate in favor of highly compensated employees.

As to the third exception from the general rule of section 74(a), section 74(b) provides "gross income does not include amounts received as prizes and awards made primarily in recognition of religious, charitable, scientific, educational, artistic, literary, or civic achievement." In order for section 74(b) to be applicable: (1) the recipient must be selected without taking action to enter the contest at issue;[9] (2) the recipient cannot be required to perform

> "substantial future services as a condition to receiving the prize or award;[10] and (3) the prize or award must be transferred to a qualified tax-exempt organization or governmental unit.[11]

§ 2.07 UNEMPLOYMENT BENEFITS

Section 85 provides that unemployment benefits received under a federal or state program are includible in gross income.

4. § 274(j)(3).
5. § 274(j)(4)(B).
6. § 274(j)(4)(C).
7. § 274(j)(2)(A).
8. § 274(j)(2)(B).

9. § 74(b)(1).
10. § 74(b)(2).
11. § 74(b)(3).

§ 2.08 PENSIONS BENEFITS

Amounts received as a pension constitute gross income unless excluded by law.[1] If the recipient did not contribute to the cost of the pension and was not taxed on the employer's contributions, the full amount is includable in the recipient's gross income, subject to special Code provisions.[2] When amounts are received under other arrangements, a portion of the payments may be excluded from gross income.

§ 2.09 SOCIAL SECURITY BENEFITS

Section 86 includes in gross income a portion of Social Security benefits. Under section 86 a portion of Social Security benefits are included in the gross incomes of persons whose adjusted gross income (including tax-exempt interest) combined with 50% of their benefits exceed certain amounts. Ultimately, as much as 85% of an individual's Social Security benefits may be taxable.

The computation as to what portion of social security benefits are taxable is unnecessarily complex. In order to determine the taxable portion of social security benefits you must apply one of two different formulas provided for in section 86;[1] these formulas employ a special measure of income, modified adjusted gross income.[2]

Modified adjusted gross income is essentially the taxpayer's adjusted gross income (excluding social security benefits) increased by any tax-exempt interest income as well as any excluded foreign earned income.[3]

Through operation of the formulas articulated in section 86, a base amount[4] and adjusted base amount[5] are established. The base amount is $32,000 for married couples filing jointly,[6] $0 for married couples filing separately who do not live apart for the entire year,[7] and $25,000 for all other taxpayers.[8] The adjusted base amount is $44,000 for married couples filing jointly,[9] $0 for married couples filing separately who do not live apart for the entire year,[10] and $25,000 for all other taxpayers.[11]

If modified adjusted gross income plus 50% of Social Security benefits received during the tax year exceed the applicable base amount, but not the applicable adjusted base amount, the taxable portion of the Social Security benefits is the lesser of: (1) 50% x (Social Security benefits) or (2) 50% x [modified adjusted gross income + 50% (Social

§ 2.08

1. See § 61(a)(11).
2. See Treas. Reg. § 1.61–11.

§ 2.09

1. See § 86(a)(2)(A) and (B).
2. See § 86(b)(2).
3. See § 86(b)(2)(A) and (B).
4. § 86(c)(1).

5. § 86(c)(2).
6. § 86(c)(1)(B).
7. § 86(c)(1)(C)(i) and (ii).
8. § 86(c)(1)(A).
9. § 86(c)(2)(B).
10. § 86(c)(2)(C).
11. § 86(c)(2)(A).

Security benefits)—base amount].[12]

If modified adjusted gross income plus 50% of the Social Security benefits received during the tax year exceeds the applicable adjusted base amount, the taxable portion of Social Security benefits is the lesser of: (1) 85% x (Social Security benefits) or (2) the sum of 85% x [modified adjusted gross income + 50% (Social Security benefits)—adjusted base amount], and the lesser of (a) 85% (Social Security benefits) or $4,500 ($6,000 for married couples filing jointly).[13]

§ 2.10 ANNUITIES

Under § 72 gross income generally includes any amounts received under an "annuity, endowment, or life insurance contract."[1]

Notwithstanding the foregoing, "gross income does not include that part of any amount received as an annuity under an annuity, endowment, or life insurance contract which bears the same ratio to such amount as the investment in the contract (as of the annuity starting date) bears to the expected return under the contract (as of such date)."[2] This "exclusion ratio" is then applied to the payments received by the taxpayer to arrive at the amount excluded.[3]

For example, assume that the taxpayer's investment, the total premium, is $15,000 and that the expected return, based on life expectancy, is $20,000. The exclusion ratio is then 15,000/20,000 or 75%. If the taxpayer received twelve $100 monthly payments or $1,200 during the year, the amount excluded from income is $900 ($1,200 x 75%), and the $300 balance is taxable. When the taxpayer has recovered the $15,000 investment at the rate of $900 a year, it is logical to require the amounts received thereafter to be treated as taxable, and this is the rule under section 72(b)(2).

The general rule of section 72, which separates income from the return of capital, is subject to refinements, exceptions, and limitations that are contained in this lengthy Code section and countless pages of regulations.[4]

§ 2.11 GROUP–TERM LIFE INSURANCE

Section 79(a) includes in income any premiums paid by an employer for group term life insurance to the extent such premiums provide insurance in excess of $50,000 in death benefits. For each $1,000 in

---

12. § 86(a)(1)(A) and (B).
13. § 86(a)(2)(A) and (B).

§ 2.10

1. § 72(a).
2. § 72(b)(1).
3. Id.

4. These matters are beyond the scope of this volume and include amounts not received as annuities (section 72(e)) as well as special rules applicable to employee annuities and distributions under employee plans (section 72(m)).

insurance coverage provided by an employer to an employee[1] in excess of the $50,000 base amount, the employee must include a corresponding amount in gross income; this amount is determined in the regulations as follows:[2]

Five Year Age Bracket	Cost Per $1,000 of Protection for One Month
Under 25	$.05
25 to 29	$.06
30 to 34	$.08
35 to 39	$.09
40 to 44	$.10
45 to 49	$.15
50 to 54	$.23
55 to 59	$.43
60 to 64	$.66
65 to 69	$1.27
70 and above	$2.06

§ 2.11

1. *Nota bene:* for purposes of § 79(a) the term "employee" includes former employees. § 79(e).

2. See Treas. Reg. § 1.79–3(d)(2).

Chapter 3

EXCLUSIONS FROM GROSS INCOME

Table of Sections

§ 3.01   INTRODUCTION

This chapter discusses several specific exclusions from gross income. Each of these exclusions is justified by a variety of different arguments which are discussed below. Prior to looking at any specific exclusion, however, it is worth noting a few considerations that may help place these exclusionary provisions in context.

First, many people resent paying taxes. No one who receives a gift, or life insurance proceeds would argue that she ought to pay more taxes, and few others would point to that recipient and find fault with this exclusion from gross income. Of course, there may be some voices encouraging Congress to tax "the rich," but even many of those voices would likely be silenced if "rich" were defined broadly enough to include them. It is mostly "rich" people that benefit significantly from exclusions from gross income. Even so there is always the occasional "poor" person who is allowed to exclude some amount from gross income, and this exclusion becomes the strongest anecdotal evidence in favor of retaining the particular exclusion.

What this means is that there is no "special interest groups" supporting a broader tax base. No one argues to Congress that it ought to impose taxes on exclusions from gross income; this is because the only ones really interested in the exclusions are the ones who benefit from them. Although the tax rates imposed by our federal income tax system can be viewed as independent of the tax base, many who call for a "flat tax" have in mind as part of that "flat tax" an expanded tax base, which cuts back on some or all exclusions from income.

[1]   TAXATION AS A ZERO SUM GAME

To some extent, taxation is a zero sum game. Since excluding any receipt necessarily reduces the tax liability of the recipient, then to retain tax neutrality, typically someone else must pay *more* tax. Either some other taxpayer must include some amount that she otherwise would not, or the tax rates on everyone must be raised to maintain the same net revenue to the United States Treasury. If nobody's tax liability is correspondingly increased when another's tax liability is decreased (by allowing some receipt to go untaxed), the result is either an increased federal deficit or reduced government services.

Of course, taxes and economic productivity are not entirely independent, and not all tax provisions actually are zero sum in nature. Often exclusions are enacted not simply as a way to help those who receive a particular form of income, but, instead, some exclusions are enacted to encourage people to provide for or invest in assets that will produce those types of income. There may be times when excluding some item from the recipient's income will enable or encourage that person to become sufficiently more productive so as to produce societal benefits that will *more* than offset any lost governmental revenues. These societal benefits produced by tax provisions may take the form of increased economic activity; in turn this may produce more income for more people which generates tax revenue from other sources in excess of the revenue sacrificed by the particular exclusion. Alternatively, the societal benefits may take other forms, such as encouraging taxpayers to give funds directly to good causes or to engage personally in good works.

Ultimately, then, with respect to any receipt of economic income that is excluded from tax, one ought to ask: (1) whether it is likely that the exclusion will generate an amount of increased economic productivity sufficient to generate new taxpayer income in excess of the amount excluded; or (2) if not, whether it is likely the exclusion will encourage other taxpayer behaviors whose benefit to society will likely exceed the benefits that would be provided with the revenue left uncollected because of the exclusion. If such increased economic or behavioral productivity is not likely, the next appropriate question is who ought to bear the burden of the resulting *increase* in tax or *decrease* in government services made necessary by the exclusion.

[2] DIFFERENT VALUES FOR DIFFERENT TAXPAYERS FOR EXCLUSIONS

Because our federal income tax system has graduated tax rates, an exclusion of some receipt from gross income provides different amounts of benefit for different taxpayers. If T1 is in the 35% tax bracket, T2 is in the 15% tax bracket, and T3 has little enough income to put her in the 0% tax bracket, then the same exclusion from income of the same amount received will have very different tax consequences for the three taxpayers. The exclusion of $1,000 will save T1 the $350 tax she would otherwise have to pay on an extra $1,000 of income. It will save T2 the $150 she would otherwise have to pay on that extra $1,000 of income, and it will save T3 nothing, since T3 will pay no tax regardless of whether she is required to include the $1,000 receipt in income.

In the context of inheritance and life insurance, for example, assume that Mother Rich and Mother Poor both die. Child Rich, child of Mother Rich, is in the 35% tax bracket because she earns substantial income from ongoing investments. Child Poor is in the 10% tax bracket because she has no income at all. If each child inherits $10,000 and also is the beneficiary of a $10,000 life insurance policy on her mother, the exclusion of these items from income will save Child Rich approximately $7,000, the tax she would otherwise be required to pay on $20,000 of income. The same $20,000 exclusion would save Child Poor an amount closer to only $2,000, the tax she would otherwise have to pay on gross income of $20,000. It is true that the death of a parent is hardly a propitious time to impose tax, so there may be good reason to exclude inheritance and life insurance proceeds from income, but it is equally true that using an exclusion rather than some form of "death credit" provides significantly greater benefits to Child Rich than it does to Child Poor. In addition to providing greater tax relief to higher bracket taxpayers than it does to those in lower-brackets, an exclusion also provides a benefit only to those who have income of the particular type being excluded.

§ 3.02   GIFTS AND INHERITANCES

[1]   RATIONALE FOR EXCLUDING GIFTS AND INHERITANCES

Obviously, the receipt of gifts and inheritances represent accessions to wealth that are clearly realized, and would fit within any economist's definition of income. Nonetheless, section 102(a) generally provides for their exclusion from gross income.

The reasons for this exclusion have never been made entirely clear. It is well settled that if an individual finds money on the street it constitutes gross income.[1] Why then should the recipient of a gift be able to receive that gift tax free?

Some have suggested that while it would be appropriate to tax the recipient of a gift on income equal to the value of the gift, it would also be appropriate to grant a *deduction* to the donor, since the gift that *increases* the donee's net worth also *decreases* the donor's net worth by the same amount. If one were to conclude that *giving* a gift is itself something other than a (nondeductible) act of consumption,[2] then the argument would follow that by neither taxing the recipient of the gift nor granting a deduction to the donor, the income tax system takes into account the same net amount of income (zero) as if it both taxed the recipient and granted a deduction to the donor.

Of course, while these corresponding errors (no deduction for the donor, no income for the donee) may give rise to the correct net amount of income, they result in the wrong amount of income for each individual; i.e., the donee gets a tax benefit (no income), while the donor suffers a tax detriment (no deduction). In addition, because the donor and donee may be in different brackets, the same net amount of combined taxable income can result in very different amounts of actual tax liability. Indeed, since the typical donor is likely in a higher tax bracket than the typical donee, it is likely that the exclusion of gifts from income and the lack of a deduction for the donor generally works in favor of the IRS.

Since gifts and inheritances generally occur among family members, many people may think of these transfers as intra-family transfers, and

---

§ 3.02

1. Cesarini v. United States, 296 F.Supp. 3 (N.D. Ohio 1969), aff'd per curiam, 428 F.2d 812 (6th Cir. 1970).

2. The argument against this proposition would be based on the assumption that the person who gives a gift wants to do so and wants the donee to have the gifted property. If those assumptions are true (and if they are not, the transfer may well not be a gift for tax purposes), then one might argue that giving a gift to benefit another is not a mere reduction in ones wealth, but is itself an act of *consumption* of some part of that wealth. In other words, Person A might consume by going on vacations, and Person B might choose to consume by giving away property to loved ones. In that event, giving a gift ought to be no more deductible than is the cost of taking a vacation. Instead, it would represent both nondeductible consumption by the donor and income for the donee.

may see the relevant inquiry as one based on an understanding of the appropriate taxable unit. No one has proposed legislation that would tax minor children on the value of the goods and services provided to them by their parents on a daily basis, and many may see more extraordinary gifts or bequests as essentially akin to such transfers.

[2] DEFINITION OF THE TERM "GIFT"

Section 102(a) provides: "Gross income does not include the value of property acquired by gift, bequest, devise, or inheritance." A gift is defined as "The voluntary transfer of property to another without compensation."[3] The Supreme Court began to define the meaning of the term gift in Bogardus v. Commissioner, where it stated: "what controls is the intention with which payment, however voluntary, has been made."[4] The Supreme Court further defined the term gift in Robertson v. United States, and stated: "where the payment is in return for services rendered, it is irrelevant that the donor derives no economic benefit from it."[5] In Commissioner v. LoBue, the Supreme Court continued to enhance its interpretation of the term gift and proclaimed that a genuine gift is made in: "detached and disinterested generosity."[6]

In Commissioner v. Duberstein, the Supreme Court applied a comprehensive definition of the term gift, compiled from each of the aforementioned cases.[7] In Duberstein, the Court proffered that a genuine gift is one made out of "detached and disinterested generosity ... out of affection, respect, admiration, charity, or like impulses."[8] The Supreme Court, in Duberstein, held that an expensive luxury vehicle which was received from a business associate as a reward for past business favors was includible in the gross income of the donee, and that such a transaction did not meet the previously-defined[9] judicial interpretation of the term gift. Moreover, courts are generally suspicious of any transaction that is claimed to be gratuitous in nature when it occurs in the business context. Through the years, courts were forced to make this facts and circumstances differentiation on a number of occasions.

[3] EMPLOYER–EMPLOYEE RELATIONSHIPS

Section 102(c)(1), address the issue of whether a transfer from an employer to an employee could be considered gratuitous in nature. Section 102(c)(1), provides: "Subsection (a) [which provides a general exclusion from gross income for gifts] shall not exclude from gross income any amount transferred by or for an employer to, or for the benefit of, an employee." There are exceptions to the general rule of section 102(c)(1), which allow excludible transfers from employers to employees in two circumstances: (1) certain de minimis fringes excluded

3. Black's Law Dictionary (8th ed. 2004).

4. 302 U.S. 34, 45 (1937).

5. 343 U.S. 711, 714 (1952).

6. 351 U.S. 243, 246 (1956).

7. See 363 U.S. 278, 285 (1960).

8. 363 U.S. 278, 285 (1960).

9. LoBue, 351 U.S. at 246; Robertson, 343 U.S. at 714; Bogardus, 302 U.S. at 43.

from gross income governed by section 132(e);[10] and (2) certain employee achievement awards which are excluded from gross income by section 74(c).[11]

[4] SERVICE PROVIDERS

Section 102(c) does not apply outside of an employer/employee relationship, but the underlying idea, that transfers for past services rendered or for hoped for future services are not tax free gifts, is well ensconced in case law.[12] Payments pursuant to something other than a moral or legal obligation made to people other than employees, such as waiters, housecleaning workers, deliverers, etc. are clearly taxable income to the recipient, as are "tokes" given to casino workers by gamblers.[13]

[5] LABOR UNIONS AND STRIKE BENEFITS

The Supreme Court in United States v. Kaiser[14] found that in certain circumstances strike benefits are properly excludable from gross income. Deferring to the lower court's fact-finding, under the principles espoused in Duberstein, decided the same year, the Court found that the jury's determination that the payments were a gift was supported by the evidence, including the facts that the taxpayer was not a member of the union when he started to receive the payments, assistance was granted on a need basis, and picketing was expected but not required.

The Service, in an apparent attempt to limit the reach of Kaiser, has stated that in facts "substantially like those in the Kaiser case"[15] it will regard the payment as non-taxable gifts, but that "other cases will be scrutinized to determine whether the payments constitute gross income."[16]

[6] BUSINESS "GIFTS"

After Duberstein,[17] gratuitous transfers in the business context are almost never found to be excludable from gross income. Inevitably, the IRS and courts find some motive other than "detached disinterested generosity" underlying the transfer in question. The motive may be to compensate for past services, to attract future business, general public relations, favorable publicity, or something else, but rarely do those charged with determining the intent of the donor find it to be detached admiration in situations where business relationships are involved.

---

10. § 132(e) is discussed in detail, *infra*.

11. Employee achievement awards are discussed in detail in § 2.06.

12. See Commissioner v. Duberstein, 363 U.S. 278, 285, 80 S.Ct. 1190, 4 L.Ed.2d 1218 (1960).

13. See Olk v. United States, 536 F.2d 876, 879 (9th Cir.1976), cert. denied, 429 U.S. 920, 97 S.Ct. 317, 50 L.Ed.2d 287 (1976).

14. 363 U.S. 299, 80 S.Ct. 1204, 4 L.Ed.2d 1233 (1960).

15. Rev. Rul. 61–136, 1961–2 C.B. 20.

16. Id.

17. Commissioner v. Duberstein, 363 U.S. 278, 285 (1960).

[7] FAMILY–BUSINESS RELATIONSHIPS

When family members share an employer/employee relationship whether a transfer between the family members qualifies as a non-taxable gift under section 102(a) is essentially a question of fact. Hence if the transfer in question is one made out "detached and disinterested generosity" there may be a viable argument that the transfer should be treated as a gift. Of course, if instead the transfer is more akin to compensation for services, the transfer should be treated as gross income under section 61(a)(1). The real question here is whether the transfer is attributable to the familial relationship rather than the employment relationship.

[8] THE DONOR'S INTENT

In Duberstein the transferor of the property characterized the transfer as a deductible business expense. It is worth noting that even with this characterization by the transferor, the Court did *not* find as a fact that the transferor's motivation was something other than the kind of detached disinterested generosity that would make the transfer a gift. Although the Court upheld the trial court's non-gift determination, it is significant that the transferor's attempt to deduct the transfer was not conclusive evidence of the absence of the motivation that would make the transfer a gift. Instead, the Court referred to other evidence of intent and deferred to the trial court's findings.

This meant that in any quasi-business setting, it remained possible for the recipient to contend that the transfer was a nontaxable gift and for the transferor to contend that the transfer was a deductible business expense. Unfortunately for the government, neither the recipient nor the donor was bound by the other's representations. As a result, when faced with this situation, it was possible that the IRS might go after the transferor and assert that the transfer was a nondeductible gift. After losing, the IRS might then go after the recipient and argue that the transfer was not a gift and was therefore taxable on receipt. While the transferor's prior claims (that the transfer was business-motivated rather than a gift) would not be binding on the recipient, the recipient might well point to the position the IRS had taken (and lost) in the prior litigation (that is, that the transferor was a nontaxable gift). In short, it was not a pleasant situation for the IRS.

Section 274(b) provides relief for the Service in this context. Section 274(b) both clarifies the situation as far as deductibility to the transferor is concerned, and it provides some incentive for the transferor to characterize a transfer in the business setting as something other than a gift. Section 274(b) provides that no deduction is allowed for "gifts" to recipients in amounts of more than $25 annually.

[9] DE MINIMIS TRANSFERS

There are numerous situations where individuals receive transfers of property worth less than $25, where the transferor deducts its costs, and where the transferee does not report income, despite the fact that the payment is not a "gift." Receipt of free samples and other products pursuant to an advertising or public relations campaign go unreported each day. The reason the IRS typically pays no heed to these receipts, however, has nothing to do with section 102, since these receipts clearly do not qualify as gifts. It is instead due to the fact that the Service has no interest in quibbling about the de minimis amounts usually at issue. Indeed, when those amounts are substantial (for instance, if high-fashion boutiques were to provide high-priced designer gowns for free to a fashionable first lady so the designer would receive publicity), the Service's reaction might be substantial as well.

[10]   GIFTS OF SERVICES

Technically, section 102 excludes from income only the value of "property" acquired by gift, etc. There is no doubt, however, that the same principles apply to the transfer of services.[18] If a person does favors and provides services for a loved one, the recipient will not be taxed on the value of the services regardless of the fact that those services may not be "property" referred to in section 102.[19] So long as the services are provided as a result of detached and disinterested generosity and not as part of a business relationship (or as compensation for past or anticipated future services), the receipt of those services is tax free.[20] Along the same lines, if the donor's "gift" takes the form of cancelling an obligation owed to her by the donee, or benefiting the donee by assuming an obligation owed by the donee, the transaction is nonetheless a gift, and it is not taxable to the donee if it arises from the detached and disinterested generosity.

Correspondingly, if one receives something as a result of some business or employment relationship, and not as a result of detached disinterested generosity, the fact that what is received takes the form of services rather than property does not prevent the recipient from being taxed on the value of the services received.[21]

[11]   GIFTS OF INCOME FROM PROPERTY

If someone receives a simple gift of property, she thereafter owns the property, and, as any property owner, she is taxed on any income generated by that property.[22] The fact that she may have initially received the property as a gift obviously does not inoculate her from tax on her future income from that property.[23]

Section 102(b)(2) provides that where the gift, etc., "is of income from property," the donee may not exclude as a tax-free gift "the amount of such income." Section 102(b)(2) basically serves as a backstop to the assignment of income principals discussed in Chapter 6. As

---

18. See United States v. Harris, 942 F.2d 1125 (7th Cir. 1991).

19. Id.

20. Id.

21. See § 61(a)(1); Treas. Reg. § 1.61–1(a).

22. See § 102(b)(1).

23. See § 102(b)(2).

discussed in § 6.02 if a person retains ownership of an asset and transfers only rights to the income generated by that asset, then under generally accepted assignment of income principals, the property owner will be taxed on that income, and the transaction will be taxed to the donor not the donee.[24]

For example, if Dad owns stock in XYZ and makes a gift to Son of any dividends paid on the stock for the next 10 years, then whenever dividends are actually paid (presumably to Son), Dad will be taxed on the dividends paid, and both Dad and Son will be treated as if Dad then gave a gift to Son equal to the amount of the dividends actually paid to Son.

Under these principals, only the taxpayer who makes a gift of the income while retaining the property is taxed, and the person who divests himself entirely of the property is not taxed on any income generated by that property.[25] As this distinction became apparent, some clever taxpayers attempted to use it not simply to transfer a tax liability for current income, but to avoid it altogether. To do so, T divested herself of property by transferring the right to current income from property to one donee (for example, Child 1), and the remainder interest to another (Child 2). T would not be taxed on income generated by the property because she had divested herself of any interest in the property. Child 2 could not be taxed on income from the property because she never had any right to that income, and Child 1 excluded the current income as the "gift" she received tax free under section 102. Section 102(b)(2) now provides that in this and similar situations, Child 1 will be taxed on the income as she receives payments.[26]

[12] INHERITANCE

[a] In General

Property acquired by bequest, devise or inheritance is also excluded from income by section 102. As a general rule, heirs, unlike lifetime donees, generally need not make any showing with respect to the deceased's state of mind or motivation for making the transfer. Specifically, there is no need to establish that the transfer was made out of anything approaching detached and disinterested generosity. The primary reason for this is that section 102 excludes not only bequests and devises, but also inheritance under state law.

Despite the difference between inheritance, which may be statutorily mandated despite the wishes of the deceased, and gifts, not all transfers that take the form of a bequest, devise, or inheritance are excluded. While a transfer at death need not result from mere generosity to be excluded, it will nonetheless be subject to taxation if it is in fact disguised compensation.[27]

---

24. Helvering v. Horst, 311 U.S. 112, 61 S.Ct. 144, 85 L.Ed. 75 (1940).

25. Id.

26. § 102(b)(2).

27. See Wolder v. Commissioner, 493 F.2d 608 (2d Cir.1974), cert. denied 419 U.S. 828, 95 S.Ct. 49, 42 L.Ed.2d 53 (1974).

[b] Will Contests and Settlements

Because the testator's motivation is not relevant to the exclusion of bequests and inheritance other than to require the inclusion of amounts specifically intended as compensation, the exclusion granted by section 102 to inheritance is not conditioned on any indication that the deceased had any interest whatsoever in ensuring that her property was actually passed on to the heir who receives it. As a result, whether the heir receives the property smoothly and with little effort or instead her receipt is the result of a will contest has no impact on its excludability;[28] under either scenario the property is excludable from gross income through the application of section 102(a). As discussed more completely in Chapter 11, any litigation recovery or settlement should be taxed based on the origin of the claim.[29] Hence, in a will contest any recovery is excludable under section 102(a) just as it would be had the transfer of property to the heir gone smoothly, and the will contest were not necessary.

[c] Section 102(b)

Section 102(a) excludes from income any *property* received as a gift, bequest, devise, or inheritance; however, section 102(b) denies exclusion to any gift, bequest, devise, or inheritance of *income* from property. As a result, if Parent leaves to Child 1 a current income interest in property and leaves to Child 2 the remainder interest, Child 2 will include none of what she gets in gross income, and Child 1 will be required to pay tax on everything she gets.

§ 3.03   PROCEEDS FROM LIFE INSURANCE

Section 61 sets out the general rule that proceeds from life insurance contracts constitute gross income.[1] Notwithstanding the foregoing, section 101(a) provides for an exclusion from gross income where life insurance proceeds are paid on account of the death of the insured.

[1] EXCLUSION OF "MORTALITY GAINS"

The exclusion from income of the proceeds of life insurance paid by reason of death of the insured is of major importance to many taxpayers and to the insurance industry. Outside of the life insurance context, if T pays $1,000 for an opportunity to collect $100,000 on the happening of some unlikely event during the year (for example, if T places a $1,000 wager at 100 to one odds that his favorite team will win the Superbowl), and the event occurs and T wins, T will obviously be taxed on her net profit (in this case, $999,000). On the other hand, if the "wager" is made with respect to T's own death during the year (and is made as part of a

---

28. See Lyeth v. Hoey, 305 U.S. 188, 59 S.Ct. 155, 83 L.Ed. 119 (1938).

29. United States v. Gilmore, 372 U.S. 39, 83 S.Ct. 623, 9 L.Ed.2d 570 (1963).

§ 3.03

1. § 61(a)(10).

life insurance contract[2]) and T "wins" the wager by losing his life, the $999,000 profit goes completely untaxed under section 101(a).

On the other side of the life insurance equation is the fact that if L pays the same $1,000 for a year's life insurance and survives the year, he will get no deduction for his $1,000 cost.[3] From the perspective of the IRS, excluding from income the profit of the one in one hundred unlucky taxpayers who collects on life insurance by dying and prohibiting a deduction for the approximately 99 other taxpayers who survive the year and lose their $1,000 has approximately the same net result as taxing the profits and allowing the losses to be deducted. Even so, this result raises significantly less revenue than the alternative of taxing those who win the life insurance bet and *disallowing* deductions for individuals who purchase insurance and survive, but it is at least arguable that surviving taxpayers ought to be allowed to deduct the cost of their expired policies.[4]

Several other arguments have been put forth to justify the exclusion of life insurance proceeds payable by reason of the death of the insured. Perhaps most obvious among them is the fact that the death of the insured is a time of economic and emotional hardship for the family, and it is therefore not an appropriate time to levy a tax. Of course, this argument was not successful against some other taxes, including federal estate taxes, which are levied at the time of the death.

Additionally, the mortality gain proceeds are usually to replace the lost earnings of the insured. While those earnings would have been taxable income when earned, they would have been earned, and thus taxed, over a number of years. If the deceased had anything close to an average income, the earnings would be taxed at a relatively low rate each year. Even so, if a lump-sum insurance payment were received all in one year, it would likely be taxed a much higher marginal rate because the income is bunched in a single year rather than spread over several years.

2. Section 101(a) refers to amounts received "under a life insurance contract." For such a contract there must be an actuarial risk. On the one hand, the presence of such a risk is not always enough to convert a gamble into a life insurance contract. On the other hand, though, the absence of that risk may convert what otherwise appears to be a life insurance contract into something very different, at least for tax purposes. In Kess v. United States, 451 F.2d 1229 (6th Cir. 1971), the decedent purchased a life insurance contract that would not have been issued without the simultaneous purchase of an annuity contract. Because the risks of the two policies counteracted each other, the court held that the carrier did not assume an insurance risk, but only an investment risk. The proceeds were not excludable under section 101 because they were not amounts received "under a life insurance contract."

3. While investment losses are generally deductible, "gambling" losses are deductible only to the extent of income from gambling. § 165(d). Query whether life insurance is more or less of a gamble than other investments, or whether in fact most investments are as much of a gamble as an outing in Las Vegas. The other issue with respect to deductibility of expired life insurance policies would relate to whether the very existence of the policy coverage constituted consumption throughout the year to the taxpayer who had the comforting knowledge that, should she die during the year, her heirs would not be left penniless.

4. There are nonetheless some differences, in part because different taxpayers are in different tax brackets, and in part because not all of the payout from all life insurance contracts really represents gain from beating, or losing to, as the case might be, the odds.

Finally, perhaps the most telling argument is that society wishes to encourage the purchase of life insurance, to promote financial security. The favorable treatment of employee group-term life insurance suggests that policy.[5]

[2] BASIC TYPES OF LIFE INSURANCE

There are many different kinds of life insurance; this is in no small part a result of the tax exemption provided for by section 101(a) which has inspired many people to figure out ways to take advantage of it. Perhaps the most common type of life insurance other than simple term insurance is "whole life" insurance. This type of policy allows the insured to pay level premiums for life, or at least for as long as the policy is in effect. Typically, whole life policies also allow the insured to cash in the policy while alive for some guaranteed amount, or to borrow against the policy prior to death.

As an initial matter, it is important to understand that if one purchases successive $100,000 term life insurance policies, the premiums will necessarily rise each year as the insured ages. This is simply because (all other things being equal) the older one is, the more likely she is to die during the year. On the other hand, if an individual takes out a single $100,000 ordinary "whole life" policy, her premiums (and her coverage) will stay the same each year for as long as the policy is in effect. The reason that the premiums on whole life insurance do not rise is not that somehow the purchase of insurance changes the likelihood of death. Instead the early payments for whole life insurance are higher than they otherwise would be (if the insured were simply purchasing term insurance), and the later payments are lower than they would otherwise be had term insurance been purchased.

To see what happens, assume that T is 45 years old, and purchases a $100,000 whole life insurance policy that requires annual payments of $3,000. Also assume that a one year term insurance policy at that age would have cost $400. If T lives until age 65, his payments on his whole life policy will continue to be $3,000, even if a one year term policy at that age would (if available) cost him $6,000. The insurance company can continue to charge T only $3,000 per year for his whole life policy because it has essentially invested the "extra" $2,600 that T paid at age 45 (and all of the extra amounts T paid each year in the early years) on T's behalf, and it uses those early premiums and the interest earned on those premiums to finance some of the cost of insuring T's life for the current year. Similarly, if T chose to cash in his policy rather than to continue it, the proceeds available to him would represent in part the return of his initial "overpayments" for the term insurance benefit and in part the income earned on those early payments.

Note that without purchasing a whole life insurance policy, T could obtain essentially identical economic (but not tax) results beginning at age 45 by purchasing a one year term life insurance policy each year and

---

5. See 79(a). See also § 2.11 for a discussion of § 79(a).

simultaneously investing for his own account the difference between $3,000 and the cost of that policy. In other words, T could have purchased a one year term policy for $400 at age 45, and put the other $2,600 into an investment account. The next year, he might have been able to purchase a one year term life insurance policy for $450 and could have put the remaining $2,550 into his investment account, etc.

If T had purchased only term insurance and had invested the excess amounts each year, he would be taxed on his investment income.[6] By simply purchasing whole life insurance, though, T is able to exclude from income not only any mortality gain from the insurance, but also the investment income. Depending on what ultimately happens, some of that investment income may be used to subsidize some of the later annual premiums; it may be a part of the surrender value of the policy; or it may come back to T's estate as part of the payout upon death. Regardless of how that investment income is used on T's behalf or actually received by T, the tax implications of this are that section 101(a) excludes from gross income all of the investment income as well as any mortality gains so long as the funds are paid on account of the death of the insured.

The section 101(a) exclusion of the investment element on whole life insurance has provided some tax avoidance potential for the very wealthy. Taxpayers who had little or no actual need for whole life insurance protection (because their assets, even absent insurance, were more than sufficient to provide for their heirs) found it attractive to purchase substantial life insurance policies which provided only minimal potential mortality gain, but a very large element of savings and interest income. As a result, the amounts payable on the death of the insured on these "life insurance policies" would increase annually by a proportion similar to the going interest rate. The return on the investment might appear similar to interest, but since the ultimate payment on the policy occurred only on the death of the insured, and since there was some (even though not much) potential mortality gain, the payment was excluded under section 101(a). Taxpayers who might otherwise be taxed at the 35% rate on interest were able to avoid tax entirely on their investment income by characterizing their investments as life insurance.

Taxpayers' exploitation of this possibility through the use of so-called "universal life insurance" policies, offered by many insurance companies, led Congress to enact guidelines in this area. These guidelines specify the relative size of the premiums, cash surrender value and death benefits allowable for policies to qualify as life insurance the proceeds of which are excludable under section 101(a). These guidelines disallow the exclusion of section 101(a) with respect to policies that offer only minimal pure life insurance protection and that have a significant investment element.[7]

---

6. The timing and character of his investment income would depend on the specific investments, but one way or another, that income would be taxed. See § 61(a).

7. § 101(f).

[3] TAXABLE PAYMENTS AT DEATH: TRANSFERS OF THE POLICY FOR CONSIDERATION

At least one basis for the exclusion provided by section 101(a) is that those for whom the deceased would otherwise provide for ought not to bear a significant tax burden upon the death of the would-be provider. State and federal regulations of the insurance industry typically ensure that strangers do not essentially wager on the death of others by requiring that the purchaser of insurance have an "insurable interest" in the person covered by the policy. While those regulations may not prevent an insured from taking out a policy on herself and then selling that policy to another, section 101(a)(2) provides that the proceeds of an insurance policy that has been transferred for "valuable consideration" will be excluded from the income of the beneficiary only to the extent of the consideration paid plus any subsequent premiums and other amounts paid by the transferee. A "transfer for valuable consideration" that precludes exclusion does *not* include a transfer in which the transferee takes the transferor's basis (a substituted basis), such as with a gift or corporate merger. In addition, a transfer for valuable consideration does not include one to the insured, a partner of the insured, or a corporation in which the insured is a shareholder or an officer.[8]

[4] PAYMENT OTHER THAN BY REASON OF DEATH OF THE INSURED

Payments on account of ownership of a life insurance policy may be received either prior to the death of the insured or subsequent to the death. Either alternative is likely to at least raise concerns about taxability.

[a] Prior to Death

[i] Sale

Because section 101(a) excludes from income only amounts payable by reason of the death of the insured, the policy holder who sells a life insurance policy is taxed as she would be on the sale of any other asset.[9] This tax to the seller is, obviously, in addition to any tax the purchaser will have to pay on its gain, since, as discussed above, the exclusion of 101(a) does not generally apply to the purchaser of a life insurance policy (other than a purchase from the issuing insurance company, of course).

[ii] Terminally Ill Policy Holders

Congress decided to extend the benefit of the exclusion of life insurance payouts to those who, though not yet deceased, needed access to the policy benefits because of terminal (or in some cases chronic[10])

---

8. In Swanson v. Commissioner, 518 F.2d 59 (8th Cir. 1975), the court held that a transfer of an insurance policy to a trust controlled by the insured-grantor is a transfer to the insured for purposes of § 101(a)(2)(b).

9. See § 61(a)(3).

10.

The term "chronically ill individual" means any individual who has been cer-

illness.[11] This extension of the exclusion is embodied in section 101(g) which allows taxpayers to exclude from income payouts made under the life insurance policy itself, or payments made by viatical settlement providers in exchange for all or part of the death benefits of a life insurance policy. If the insured is chronically, but not terminally ill, the exclusion applies only to payments made for certain qualified long-term care services.[12]

[iii] Surrender for Cash Value

As is the case with a sale to any third party, the insured who surrenders a policy to the insurer for its cash value is taxed on the excess of any amount realized over the total amount she has paid for the policy.[13] Although the rule is straightforward, note that its application can be helpful for taxpayers who cash in (or sell) whole life insurance. Since at least a part of each premium paid is applied to each year's coverage, after even a single year the insured has already received at least some of the benefit (a year's term coverage) for which she has paid. Nonetheless, in determining her gain on disposition, she can use the entire amount she has paid for the policy to offset her amount realized.[14]

[iv] Borrowing Against the Policy

If the insured neither cashes in nor sells her life insurance policy, but instead borrows money from the insurer based on the value of the policy or pledges the policy as security for a loan, the insured will be taxed only if, and to the extent, that the loan proceeds exceed her entire cost of the policy.[15]

[b] Payments Received After Death

While the beneficiary of life insurance can generally exclude the insurance proceeds from income, section 101(a) does not permit her to exclude from income any interest or other amounts earned on those death benefits.[16] Pursuant to agreements with insurance companies,

---

tified by a licensed health care practitioner as—

(i) being unable to perform (without substantial assistance from another individual) at least 2 activities of daily living for a period of at least 90 days due to a loss of functional capacity,

(ii) having a level of disability similar (as determined under regulations prescribed by the Secretary in consultation with the Secretary of Health and Human Services) to the level of disability described in clause (i), or

(iii) requiring substantial supervision to protect such individual from threats to health and safety due to severe cognitive impairment.

§ 7702B(c)(2), as referenced by § 101(g)(4)(B).

11.

The term "terminally ill individual" means an individual who has been certified by a physician as having an illness or physical condition which can reasonably be expected to result in death in 24 months or less after the date of the certification. § 101(g)(4)(A).

12. See § 101(g)(3).

13. See § 1001(a).

14. See § 1012.

15. § 72(e)(4)(A); § 72(e)(5)(A), (C).

16. See § 101(c) and (d).

beneficiaries may choose to collect some or all of the proceeds from the insurance company at some time subsequent to the insured's death, and the insurance company may in turn pay some additional amounts to the beneficiary.[17] If that happens, any amounts collected in excess of: (1) the death benefit available at death and/or (2) the present value, at the death of the insured, of any other rights to future payments under the insurance contract,[18] will be taxable in full to the beneficiary.[19]

The timing of the beneficiary's income depends on the specific agreement between the beneficiary and the insurance company.[20] If the insurer simply holds the death benefit for some period of time under an agreement to pay simple interest until the benefit is paid out, the interest is taxable in full to the beneficiary when received.[21] If, instead, the beneficiary will receive periodic payments from the insurer, then a portion of each payment received will be treated as income and a portion will be treated as payment of the beneficiary's tax free benefits due under the contract.[22] In this scenario, the Code provides that the tax-free portion of each payment is determined by pro-rating the entire tax-free portion over the period during which payments are to be made (assuming that the annual payments to be made will be equal).[23]

If payments are to be made for the life of a beneficiary, then calculation of the excluded amount each year is determined based on the assumption that the payments will last for the duration of the beneficiary's predicted (according to the insurer's mortality tables) remaining life.[24] Once the calculation of the amount of each payment that is excluded has been determined, that percentage (of income versus return of tax-free death benefits) applies to any annual payments received, regardless of the beneficiary's actual life span.[25] As a result, the beneficiary who dies prior to the expiration of her predicted life span will have excluded less than the full amount of the (presumably tax free) death benefits, and the beneficiary who lives beyond her predicted life-span will be allowed to continue to exclude a portion of each payment received even after she has excluded an amount equal to the presumably excludable death benefits.

§ 3.04 DISCHARGE OF INDEBTEDNESS

[1] GENERAL RULE

Generally, in order to have income from discharge of indebtedness, a taxpayer must first have indebtedness; i.e., borrowing money is a necessary precipitating event to income from discharge of indebtedness. Even so, the mere act of borrowing does not give rise to income to the borrower, because the borrower who may receive cash is simultaneously

---

17. See § 101(d)(1).

18. § 101(d)(2).

19. § 101(d)(1).

20. See § 101(d)(1) and (2).

21. § 101(c).

22. See § 101(d)(1) and (2).

23. See § 101(d)(2).

24. Treas. Reg. § 1.101–4(c)

25. Id.

encumbered with the obligation to repay the borrowed funds. As a result, borrowing typically does not represent any current or previous accession to wealth.[1]

It is clear from Old Colony Trust v. Commissioner[2] that when a third party pays a taxpayer's obligations is a situation that is not a gift, the payment is gross income to the former obligor. Income from the cancellation of indebtedness typically arises when there is no third party involved, but where the obligee either cancels some or all of an outstanding debt, or the obligor pays off the debt, at less than face value.

Basically, a taxpayer who owes money with interest payable at a fixed rate becomes relatively wealthier whenever either the interest rate rises, there is inflation, or its credit rating changes in a way that makes its creditors willing to accept less than the full amount of the debt. As in United States v. Kirby Lumber Co.,[3] a rise in interest rates will lead creditors to accept less than the face amount of a debt otherwise payable only in the future at a fixed, lower, interest rate. Inflation basically means the borrower who pays back the same number of dollars will nonetheless have to part with less purchasing power than it initially received; this change in the taxpayer's wealth, however, is not typically accompanied by realization events. Even so, the explicit cancellation of some or all of the indebtedness is a realization event that gives rise to taxability.

The seminal case in the area of income from discharge of indebtedness is Kirby Lumber where the taxpayer corporation issued roughly $12M of bonds in exchange for its own preferred stock. Shortly thereafter, interest rates increased, and, as a result, the bonds previously issued by Kirby, which paid interest only at the lower rate in effect when the bonds were issued, became worth significantly less than their $12M face amount. Accordingly, Kirby Lumber was able to purchase back these bonds at a discount, and this discount was found to be gross income. After Kirby Lumber, section 61(a)(12) was added to the Internal Revenue Code, and it specifically provides that gross income includes income from discharge of indebtedness.[4]

Today a taxpayer who is excused from paying some or all of her debt, or who is permitted to purchase or otherwise extinguish her obligation at less than the face amount, is treated as if she received (from the creditor) cash equal to the amount of debt cancelled or avoided, and she used that cash to pay the debt. This treatment has

---

§ 3.04

1. It is at least arguable that borrowing funds on a nonrecourse basis secured by property with a basis lower than the amount of the debt which it secures does indeed represent the realization of a previously accrued accession to wealth. Nonetheless, even such borrowing is not included in income.

2. 279 U.S. 716, 49 S.Ct. 499, 73 L.Ed. 918 (1929). For a complete discussion of Old Colony Trust, see § 2.02[1][a].

3. 284 U.S. 1, 52 S.Ct. 4, 76 L.Ed. 131 (1931).

4. Notwithstanding the general rule of § 61(a)(12), a taxpayer may be able to escape income from discharge of indebtedness if it occurs in the context of bankruptcy or insolvency. See § 108(a).

several implications. If the creditor's direct transfer of cash (followed immediately by the debtor's use of that cash to pay the debt) would have been treated as a nontaxable gift (because made out of detached disinterested generosity) or a nontaxable bequest, then the former debtor will be treated as having received nontaxable proceeds and will not be taxed on income from the cancellation of indebtedness. Additionally, if the debtor's payment of the debt would have been deductible (for example, because the debt was a business expense incurred by the taxpayer), the transaction would be treated not only as income on the imputed receipt of cash but also as a deduction on the imputed use of that cash to pay the debt; this results in the income and deduction cancelling each other out and leaving no net tax consequences.[5]

If debt is not cancelled, but paid in whole or part by the debtor's transfer of property or services rather than money, then no income from the cancellation of indebtedness arises from the debtor's payment, but the payor may well have other forms of income. For example, if T owes Creditor $1,000 and performs $1,000 worth of services in satisfaction of the obligation, T will have $1,000 of *compensation* income (as if she received $1,000 for her services and used that amount to pay the debt) and no income from the cancellation of indebtedness.[6] Similarly, if T transfers to Creditor property worth $1,000 in satisfaction of the debt, she will be taxed as if she sold the property for $1,000 and used the proceeds to pay the debt.[7] The difference can be important because the type of income T is taxed on can impact both whether section 108 applies to exclude an amount from income entirely, and whether T, if taxed, may be taxed at lower capital gains rates.

If in the above examples T provided services or property worth some amount less than the full debt in partial satisfaction of her obligation, and the rest of her debt was cancelled, T may have both cancellation of indebtedness income and some other kind of gain or income. For example, if T owes Creditor $1,000 and performs $700 worth of services (or provides property worth $700) which Creditor accepts as payment in full payment of T's obligation, T will have $700 of compensation income (or be treated as having received $700 in exchange for the property, as the case may be) and will *also* be taxed on $300 income from the cancellation of indebtedness. In other words, any amount of the debt not paid off by T (via cash, services or property) will, if written-off by Creditor, generate income from the cancellation of indebtedness.[8]

[2] NONRECOURSE DEBT

If nonrecourse debt is *cancelled*, the result is cancellation of indebt-

---

5. See § 162(a) (which provides for the deduction for business expenses); § 61(a)(12) (which generally provides for the inclusion in gross income of income from discharge of indebtedness).

6. See § 61(a)(1); Treas. Reg. § 1.61–12(a).

7. See § 1001(a); Treas. Reg. § 1.1001–1(a).

8. See § 61(a)(12); Treas. Reg. § 1.61–12(a).

edness income to the debtor.[9] Moreover, there is a significant difference in the tax treatment of recourse and nonrecourse debt when the owner of property that secures the debt *transfers* that property still subject to the debt. Unless the debtor/owner amends the terms of the loan to remain personally liable on the underlying debt even after the transfer, the transfer of the property subject to the debt by operation of law releases the original owner/debtor from liability.[10] For tax purposes, the debt relief that comes automatically with the transfer of the property that secures nonrecourse debt is treated as part of the transferor's amount realized for the transferred property.[11] This is the case regardless of the actual value of the property.[12]

Thus, for example, if T owns land subject to a $10,000 nonrecourse debt and transfers that land subject to the debt for $8,000 cash, T's amount realized for the land is $18,000 ($8,000 cash plus $10,000 debt relief). If the land is worth only $4,000 and T's transfer of the land is due to the lender's foreclosure (because T realizes she is better off simply not paying the $10,000 debt to keep the $4,000 land), T's amount realized will be $10,000, the amount of the debt relief, despite the low value of the land subject to the debt.

The cancellation of indebtedness issue has also arisen with regard to child support payments. Some commentators have argued that a parent who fails to pay court-ordered child support payments should be taxed on discharge of indebtedness income. If the taxpayer had a legally binding obligation to make those payments, does not do so, and the obligation is never enforced, the taxpayer's benefit is clear. Under current law, the failure to pay child support does not result in gross income from cancellation of indebtedness.

Perhaps the most important question in the discharge of indebtedness area is whether there was an actual debt for which the taxpayer was liable that was discharged. Obviously, if there was no legally enforceable debt, there can be no income from the cancellation of indebtedness.[13]

[3]   SECTION 108

[a]   Insolvency and Bankruptcy

Once the idea that income is generated when the obligor discharges a debt at less than its face value became well established, it was not too long until Congress started curbing this rule. The primary problem, as

---

9. See § 61(a)(12). But see also § 108(a) (which generally provides for an exclusion from gross income in certain cases of insolvency or bankruptcy).

10. See Treas. Reg. § 1.1001–2(a).

11. Id.

12. See Treas. Reg. § 1.1001–2(b).

13. See Zarin v. Commissioner, 916 F.2d 110 (3d Cir. 1990). See also, Mark J. Marroni, Zarin v. Commissioner: Does a Gambler Have Income From the Cancellation of a Casino Debt, 27 New Eng. L. Rev. 993 (Summer 1993); Jon D. Rigney, Zarin v. Commissioner: The Continuing Validity of Case Law Exceptions to Discharge of Indebtedness Income, 28 San Diego L. Rev. 981 (1991); Theodore P. Seto, Inside Zarin, 59 SMU L. Rev. 1761 (2006).

Congress saw it, was that cancellation of indebtedness more often than not occurred when a taxpayer struggling along on the verge of collapse managed to pull off a deal to help itself a little (that is, by repaying or repurchasing its own obligations at less than face value). To impose tax liability on the taxpayer when it was the taxpayer's very financial distress that enabled the transaction in the first place just seemed too harsh.

This led to the passage of section 108, which provides, *inter alia*, that cancellation of debt income is excluded if the discharge occurs in a bankruptcy[14] or the taxpayer is insolvent.[15]

For purposes of section 108:

[T]he term 'insolvent' means the excess of liabilities over the fair market value of assets. With respect to any discharge, whether or not the taxpayer is insolvent, and the amount by which the taxpayer is insolvent, shall be determined on the basis of the taxpayer's assets and liabilities immediately before the discharge.

Section 108 is designed to give taxpayers assistance when they are in dire straits, but it also has built into it ways for the government to get back that assistance once the taxpayer has navigated through to more clear sailing. Accordingly, section 108(b) provides for a reduction of certain tax attributes.[16]

[b]   Section 108(e)(5): Purchase Money Debt

Section 108's exclusions of cancellation of indebtedness income are not strictly limited to bankruptcy or insolvency; a few other exclusions are also worth mentioning. Section 108(e)(5) provides that when the seller of property cancels debt of the purchaser that arose from the sale of the property, that transaction will not generate cancellation of indebtedness income. Instead, to the extent that purchase money debt to the seller is reduced, the purchaser/debtor is simply treated as if she agreed to purchase the property for a lower price; i.e., a price which does not include the purchase money debt. This exception applies only to the cancellation of purchase money debt owed by the purchaser *to* the seller. The reduction or elimination of debt owed to a separate lender does not qualify for exclusion under section 108(e)(5), regardless of whether the loan proceeds may have been used to purchase property.

[c]   Section 108(f)(3): Student Loans

In order to accommodate and encourage certain student loan forgiveness programs, section 108(f)(3) provides tax-free treatment for the forgiveness of certain student loans; this tax-free student loan forgiveness is generally available for certain individuals working for a period of years in a particular profession.

---

14.   § 108(a)(1)(A).

15.   § 108(a)(1)(B).

16.   § 108(b)(2)(A)–(G).

[d] Section 108(a)(1)(D): Qualified Real Property Business Indebtedness

Section 108(a)(1)(D) provides for the exclusion from income of the discharge of certain qualified real property business indebtedness. In order to qualify for treatment under section 108(a)(1)(D), the debt (either the original debt or refinanced debt, to the extent the amount refinanced is not in excess of the remaining purchase money debt at the time of the refinance) must have been incurred to acquire, construct, or improve property used in a trade or business (not held as either investment property or as the personal residence of the buyer).[17] In addition, this exclusion, which is elective on the taxpayer's part,[18] is limited to the amount by which the property's qualified acquisition indebtedness exceeds the fair market value of the property actually acquired with the loan proceeds; hence, the exception is available only if and when the qualified business property decreases in value below the amount of debt incurred to purchase that property.[19]

As explained earlier, the taxpayer whose debt is cancelled is generally treated as if she received (from the creditor) cash equal to the amount of debt cancelled or avoided and as if she used that cash to pay the debt. If the cancelled debt is one that would be deductible when paid, then the taxpayer is treated as if she received (in a taxable transaction) cash and then used that cash to pay a deductible expense. The net result would be: (1) income equal to the amount of the cancelled debt and (2) a deduction equal to the amount of the cancelled debt. The income and deduction would typically cancel each other out, leaving the taxpayer with zero net tax result. Section 108(e)(2) short circuits the need for these calculations by simply announcing that to the extent the payment of a debt would give rise to a deduction, its cancellation gives rise to no income.

[e] Section 103: Tax Exempt Interest

As a major refuge from the progressive rate structure for the high-income taxpayer, interest on most obligations of any state, territory or possession of the United States, or any political subdivision thereof, or of the District of Columbia is exempt from taxation.[20] This exemption for interest on government obligations has been in the tax law since the first federal income tax statute in 1913. It was originally thought to rest on constitutional grounds.[21] Although it is now clear that the provision is not constitutionally mandated,[22] there are many political interests who favor the exemption provided for by section 103(a). High-income taxpayers love section 103(a) because it allows them to earn income without paying federal income tax on those earnings. States and municipalities also love section 103(a) because it allows them to issue bonds at lower

17. § 108(c)(3).

18. § 108(c)(3)(C).

19. § 108(c)(2).

20. See § 103(a).

21. See e.g., H.R. Rept. 413, 91st Cong., 1st Sess. pt. 1 at 172–174, 1969.

22. See South Carolina v. Baker, 485 U.S. 505, 108 S.Ct. 1355, 99 L.Ed.2d 592 (1988).

interest rates. Hence it seems clear the exemption provided for by section 103(a) will remain part of federal income tax law for the foreseeable future.

The exemption of the interest on state and municipal bonds from taxation provided for by section 103(a) is not totally without justification, even absent constitutional concerns. Allowing states and municipalities to pay interest that the lender can exclude from tax enables those government entities to borrow money at reduced interest rates. To see why, it is important to note initially that most interest earned is taxable.[23]

As a result, a taxpayer (T1) in the 35% tax bracket who lends $100,000 to a corporation at a 10% rate of interest will receive $10,000 annual interest. Because that interest is subject to tax at T's 35% tax rate, T1 will be required to pay income tax of $3,500, leaving him, after-taxes, with net income of $6,500. If T1 could instead invest his $100,000 in a state or municipal tax-free bond at, for example, 6.1%, he would earn $6,100, pay no tax at all, and be better off, after-taxes, than he would have been with his 10% taxable corporate bond. Hence, states and municipalities can borrow money at significantly lower interest rates than can other borrowers with similar credit ratings. Ultimately, section 103 provides a *significant* benefit to states and municipalities. In fact, it is probably fair to say that some states and municipalities would have a difficult time surviving if they had to pay market rates in order to borrow money.

Nevertheless, some commentators do not care for section 103; they complain that one problem with section 103, as with any exclusion from income, is that the value of the benefit of the exclusion varies directly and proportionately with the investor's marginal tax rate. For example, if T2, who also has $100,000 to invest, is in the 28% tax bracket, then her investment in a 10% taxable corporate bond would yield a gross annual amount of $10,000, minus federal income tax due of $2,800, for a net profit of $7,200. On the other hand, an investment in a tax-exempt bond would yield, both before and after-tax, only $6,100 annually. Rather than saving money, T2 would lose money by investing in tax exempt bonds. Obviously, for taxpayers in lower-brackets, the loss from investing in tax-exempt bonds would be even greater.

Fortunately for lower-bracket taxpayers, they are not forced to invest in tax-exempt bonds, and they can simply invest in the 10% taxable corporate bond. Interestingly, while this is fortunate for those lower-bracket taxpayers, it turns out to be even more fortunate for the high-income taxpayers who do invest in tax-exempt bonds! Because tax exempt bonds have appeal for only a limited number of taxpayers, it turns out that in order for states and municipalities to sell their bonds they need to offer higher interest than one might otherwise imagine.

---

23. See § 61(a)(4) (which generally includes interest income as part of gross income).

Indeed, tax-exempt bonds typically pay interest at a rate fairly close to the taxable interest rate.

To continue the example above, the state that wishes to borrow $100,000 when the taxable interest rate is 10% would likely have to offer something more like 8.3% interest instead of 6.1%. Of course the state still saves money by paying interest at a rate 1.7% below that required from other borrowers (8.3% as opposed to 10%), but it soon becomes apparent the states are not the only ones deriving substantial benefits here. If T1 can earn $8,300 each year rather than $6,100 after-tax by investing in tax-exempt bonds, his after-tax benefit is $2,300 per year.

If section 103 did not exist, the state would be required to pay interest at the 10% rate, costing it an additional $1,700 per year ($10,000 instead of $8,300) in interest payments. At the same time, the federal government would receive the tax on the $10,000 interest paid (tax of $3,500), even though a state or local government was the borrower. In other words, in this example, section 103 costs the federal government $3,500 in lost revenues. To say the least, section 103 seems to be an inefficient way to assist states and municipalities with the costs associated with their borrowing of funds. It is important to note, however, that while this analysis is not incorrect, it is less than 100% accurate, as is almost any analysis of anything having to do with the federal income tax. Specifically, the example assumes that in the absence of section 103, T1, the 35% bracket taxpayer, would invest in taxable bonds. It is equally likely, however, that in the absence of section 103, T1 would simply find some other untaxed investment.

Another problem that some commentators have with section 103 is that the section only benefits states and municipalities that borrow money. The government that decides to live within its means and finances its expenditures with tax revenues is missing out on a huge benefit. The result is that the very existence of section 103 encourages those who qualify for it to maximize their benefits by borrowing as much as possible.

Rather than repealing section 103, Congress has enacted some provisions to attempt to cut down on some perceived abuses which the section had previously seemed to encourage.

The earliest and most typical "abuse" of section 103 was use of "arbitrage bonds." Simply put, once governments realized that they could borrow money at an interest rate less than the rate being paid by other borrowers, they borrowed substantial sums for the sole purpose of investing that money at higher rates. To use the numbers from the previous example, if a government can borrow at 8.3% and invest the funds at 10%, it can clear a risk-free and unlimited profit of $1,700 on every $10,000 it borrows, and section 103 becomes a virtual money-making machine.

Section 103(c) now provides that the interest on such arbitrage bonds is not tax-exempt, and arbitrage bonds are defined by section 148 as any bonds a portion of the proceeds of which are "reasonably expected" to be used directly or indirectly to either acquire or refinance higher yielding investments. A basic problem with this idea is that since money is fungible, if a government has any investments at all and borrows any money at all, it is impossible to know the relationship between the new borrowing and the continued investments. It is always possible that the government might have sold investments instead of borrowing money, but it is also possible that the two were considered entirely independently. The result of this dilemma is a lengthy statute and lengthy regulations which attempt to provide guidance and which are well beyond the scope of this work.[24]

§ 3.05 SECTION 104: CERTAIN LITIGATION RECOVERIES AND SETTLEMENTS

Certain litigation recoveries and settlements are excludable from gross income under section 104. Specifically, payments relating to personal physical injuries or physical sickness are generally excludable from gross income under section 104(a)(2). Tax issues related to litigation recoveries and settlement payments are discussed in detail in Chapter 11, *Tax Issues Related to Litigation Recoveries and Settlements.*

§ 3.06 EXCLUDABLE EDUCATIONAL BENEFITS

[1] QUALIFIED SCHOLARSHIPS AND FELLOWSHIPS

The Code contains numerous provisions designed either to assist students and their parents or to convince voters that members of Congress cared about students and their parents. Several of these benefits, including the exclusion of qualified scholarships,[1] qualified tuition reductions,[2] and educational assistance programs,[3] take the form of exclusions from gross income.

Section 117 generally excludes from gross income amounts received by a degree candidate as a scholarship or fellowship if used for tuition and course-required fees, books, supplies, or equipment.[4] Amounts received for room, board, or incidental expenses are not excludable under section 117.[5] The exclusion does not generally apply to a scholarship, fellowship, or tuition reduction that represents payment for teaching, research, or other services required of the student.[6]

---

24. For a discussion of regulations under § 148, see Steven D. Conlon and Alan L. Kennard, Final Regs. on Tax–Exempt Private Activity Bonds–Strict New Rules for Municipal Finance, 86 J. Tax'n 354 (June 1997).

§ 3.06
1. § 117(a), (b).

2. § 117(d).

3. § 127(a).

4. § 117(a) and (b).

5. See § 117(b) (2).

6. § 117(c)(1).

The regulations[7] promulgated under section 117 provide in pertinent part that amounts paid or allowed to, or on behalf of, an individual to enable him to pursue studies or research are amounts received as an excludable scholarship or fellowship "if the primary purpose of the studies or research is to further the education and training of the recipient in his individual capacity and the amount provided by the grantor for such purpose does not represent compensation or payment for ... services."[8] If the amount represents "compensation for past, present, or future employment services or represents payment for services which are subject to the direction or supervision of the grantor," it is not an excludable scholarship or fellowship.[9]

[2] QUALIFIED TUITION REDUCTIONS

Under Section 117(d)(1) a "qualified tuition reduction" is also excludable from gross income; the term is defined as the reduction in tuition accorded an employee of an educational institution, his or her spouse, or dependent children.[10] Section 117(d) does not apply to graduate level education.[11] Moreover, any tuition reduction under section 117 cannot discriminate in favor or "highly compensated employees."[12]

[3] SECTION 127: EDUCATIONAL ASSISTANCE PROGRAMS

Section 127 allows an employee to exclude from gross income up to $5,250 annually of certain qualifying educational assistance provided by her employer. For purposes of section 127, educational assistance includes courses, books and supplies furnished by the employer and the payment by the employer of expenses the employee incurs for tuition, books or supplies related to education.[13]

Section 127 has several limitations designed to ensure that it will allow exclusion only of what Congress believed to be "legitimate" educational expenses. To begin with, any education involving sports, games or hobbies is excluded from the definition of "educational assistance."[14] Additionally, the provision or reimbursement to the employee of the cost of tools or supplies, such as a computer, which may be retained by the employer after completion of the course of study does not qualify for exclusion under section 127.[15] Nor does payment for or provision of meals, lodging, or transportation.[16] Since the employee can exclude (or deduct, if she pays out of her own pocket) expenses relating to job-related education, travel expenses, and equipment under other provisions,[17] Congress saw no apparent need to allow for the exclusion of what might well be disguised personal expenses under section 127.

7. Treas. Reg. § 1.117–4.

8. Treas. Reg. § 1.117–4(c)(1)

9. Treas. Reg. § 1.117–4(c)(2).

10. § 117(d)(2).

11. Id.

12. § 117(d)(3).

13. § 127(c)(1).

14. § 127(c)(1)(B).

15. Id.

16. Id.

17. See Treas. Reg. § 1.162–5.

The most significant limitations on section 127 are those that require that in order to qualify for exclusion, the employer-provided benefits must be part of a written plan[18] that offers only these educational benefits (and does not offer these benefits as an alternative to any other kind[19] of benefits); pursuant to that plan must be made available to and made known to employees generally;[20] and must not be either only available to or only known about by only owner-employees or only highly compensated employees.[21] In general, this restriction on exclusion under section 127 is similar to the restrictions on exclusions under 132(a).[22]

[4]   SECTION 529 PLANS

Section 529 enables all taxpayers to avoid paying income tax on investment income so long as the income and the principal invested are: (1) invested in a qualified 529 plan and (2) used for "qualified higher education expenses" of a designated beneficiary.[23]

Qualified higher education expenses for purposes of section 529 include not only tuition, fees, books, supplies and equipment required for the enrollment or attendance at an "eligible educational institution," but also reasonable costs for room and board of the designated beneficiary while attending the institution.[24] The term "eligible educational institution" is defined in section 529(e)(5) by reference to section 481 of the Higher Education Act of 1965; it includes accredited post-secondary educational institutions offering credit toward a bachelors degree, an associates degree, a graduate level or professional degree, or other recognized post-secondary credential.[25]

In other words, for those who can afford to invest for their own or their children's college educations, section 529 provides a fairly simple way to ensure that all of the investment income will be excluded from gross income.[26] While the history of section 529 is somewhat complicated, its present incarnation is fairly simple for those who wish to take advantage of it. Section 529(a) provides tax-exempt status to the qualified plans themselves, to ensure the amounts invested will grow tax free.[27] Section 529(c) provides that neither current earnings nor any distributions from the plan shall be taxable to either the contributor or the beneficiary of such plan.

---

18.   Treas. Reg. § 1.127–2(b).

19.   Treas. Reg. § 1.127–2(c)(2).

20.   Treas. Reg. § 1.127–2(e)(1).

21.   § 127(b);   Treas.   Reg.   § 1.127–2(e)(1).

22.   For a complete discussion of § 132, see § 3.08, *infra*.

23.   See § 529(a).

24.   § 529(e)(3)(A) and (B).

25.   The term "eligible educational institution" also includes certain proprietary and post-secondary vocational institutions, as defined under 20 U.S.C. § 1088. § 529(e)(5). To be considered eligible, an educational institution must be qualified to participate in the Department of Education student aid programs. Id.

26.   See § 529(a).

27.   *Nota bene:* despite having tax-exempt status, § 529 plans are still subject to "section 511 (relating to imposition of tax on unrelated business income of charitable organizations)." § 529(a).

Every state has a "section 529 plan." Taxpayers may invest in their own state's plan, or they may invest in a plan administered by another state if the other state's plan is open to non-state residents. As a result, taxpayers may simply choose a section 529 plan based upon its available investment options, and those investment options are frequently quite broad.

There are some limits on the operation of section 529 plans, as well as on the use of funds withdrawn from those plans. The limits on the plans themselves are directed at the states (or institutions) that establish the plans, and they are intended to ensure the plans are established and run by states or their instrumentalities (or by educational institutions) in ways that will guarantee they will be used for appropriate educational expanses. Hence, section 529 plans must require, *inter alia*, that contributions must be made in cash;[28] the specific investment decisions cannot be made by the contributor or designated beneficiary[29] (although the contributor can choose from among a fairly wide array of investment options): the plan must provide adequate safeguards to prevent contributions from exceeding those necessary to provide for the beneficiary's qualified expenses;[30] and interests in the program cannot be pledged as security for loans.[31]

The limits on contributors to section 529 plans are also intended to guarantee that the amounts contributed and earned will be used for qualified educational expenses; accordingly, section 529(c)(3) provides that distributions from section 529 plans that are not paid directly by the plan for a qualified educational benefit[32] will be taxed to the distributee to the extent the distributions exceed the distributee's qualified educational expenses. Not surprisingly, the determination of the distributee's qualified educational expenses for this purpose consists of the actual qualified educational expenses reduced by those expenses paid directly by the plan,[33] as well as by any otherwise qualified educational expenses for which the Hope or Lifetime learning credit were taken.[34]

If the amount distributed exceeds the qualified educational expenses as so determined, a portion of the excess distribution will be taxed.[35] The

---

28. § 529(b)(2). This limit prevents taxpayers from contributing appreciated property and attempting to escape taxation on any pre-contribution appreciation.

29. § 529(b)(4).

30. § 529(b)(6). This limit is designed to ensure the contributed and earned amounts will actually be used for qualified educational expenses.

31. § 529(b)(5). This limit is intended to ensure that the contributed and earned amounts will continue to be available for qualified educational expenses, by ensuring they cannot be seized by a creditor prior to such use.

32. Expenses paid directly by the plan are excluded from gross income under § 529(c)(3)(B)(i).

33. These payments are excluded under section 529(c)(3)(B)(i), discussed *supra*.

34. § 529(c)(3)(B)(v). If the distributee was also the beneficiary of a Coverdell education savings account (see § 3.06[5], *infra*), then the statute requires that if the distributions from the § 529 plan and the Coverdell account together exceed the qualified educational expenses (as reduced above), then the taxpayer must allocate the qualified educational expenses among the distributions from each in order to determine the amount of such distributions that will be tax free. § 529(c)(3)(B)(vi).

35. See § 529(c)(3)(A).

portion of the excess distribution subjected to tax is equal to that percentage of the total distributions that represent gains or profit rather than mere return of contributed capital.[36] In addition, a 10% penalty is assessed on any excess distributions.[37]

In order to enable the taxpayer to avoid taxation and penalties that would otherwise arise as a result of the taxpayer's overestimation of expected educational expenses, section 529 allows the taxpayer to either roll the excess amounts in a plan to an existing plan for a different family member or to simply designate a different family member as the beneficiary of the amounts remaining in the account.[38] Eligible family members include the beneficiary's spouse, parents, children, siblings and first cousins.[39]

[5] SECTION 530: COVERDELL EDUCATION SAVINGS ACCOUNTS

Section 530 provides an alternative to investment in section 529 plans for some taxpayers.[40] Section 530 provides tax-free treatment to certain qualified trusts and distributees (to the extent of the distributee's qualified educational expenses) similar to that provided by section 529 for qualified plans and beneficiaries.[41]

Notwithstanding the foregoing, the benefits provided by section 530 are significantly more limited than those provided by section 529. Under section 530, contributions cannot exceed $2,000 in any year, and that amount is phased out (by 1% for every $150 of additional income) for single taxpayers with incomes in excess of $95,000 or (by 1% for every $300 of additional income) for a married couple filing a joint return with income in excess of $190,000.[42] As a result of the phaseouts, a single taxpayer with an income of $110,000 or more, and a married couple with an income of $220,000 or more, cannot contribute to a Coverdell account.[43]

One benefit permitted by section 530 that is not available under section 529 is that funds from the account may be used for private elementary and secondary schools in addition to higher education institutions.[44] Other than that, the basis rules with respect to distributions and their use described above with respect to section 529 plans apply as well to section 530 plans.[45]

[6] SECTION 135: EDUCATIONAL SAVINGS BONDS

Section 135 provides an additional exclusion related to education for certain low and middle income taxpayers. If a taxpayer who is at least

---

36. § 529(c)(3)(A).

37. § 529(c)(6); § 530(d)(4).

38. § 529(c)(3)(C).

39. § 529(e)(2).

40. No taxpayer can make a contribution to both a § 529 plan and a § 530 plan in the same year. § 529(c)(3)(B)(iv).

41. See § 530(a).

42. § 530(c).

43. See § 530(c).

44. Compare § 530(b)(3)(A)(i) and § 529(b)(1)(A).

45. See § 530(b)(1).

age 24[46] purchases Series EE or Series I US Savings Bonds,[47] she can exclude from her income the accrued but as yet untaxed interest in the year of redemption[48] to the extent the bond proceeds do not exceed the taxpayer's qualified educational expenses paid by the taxpayer for the taxable year.[49] Qualified educational expenses are educational expenses, defined by reference to section 529,[50] to the extent incurred by the taxpayer, her spouse or dependent, but the amount of such expenses is reduced by any expenses taken into account for purposes of sections 529, 530 or 25A.[51] To the extent the bond redemption proceeds exceed the qualified educational expenses paid by the taxpayer during the year, the portion of the excess that represents accrued interest (as opposed to amounts initially paid for the bond) is taxable.[52]

The most significant limitation on section 135's exclusion from gross income of bond proceeds is the fact that the exclusion is phased out.[53] Individual taxpayers with a modified adjusted gross income[54] of $40,000 or more lose 1% of the exclusion for every $150 by which their modified AGI exceeds $40,000;[55] hence, the entire exclusion is lost if their income equals or exceeds $55,000.[56] Married couples filing joint returns have the exclusion phased out at the rate of 1% for every $300 by which their modified AGI exceeds $60,000;[57] hence, the exclusion disappears at an income of $90,000.[58]

§ 3.07 TRANSFERS DURING MARRIAGE OR PURSUANT TO DIVORCE

[1] SEPARATION AND DIVORCE

When married taxpayers either divorce or formally separate, several different tax issues can arise: (1) there will likely be a change in the taxable unit(s) (that is, two separate individuals rather than a married couple filing either a joint return or two "married filing separate" returns); (2) there will likely be transfers of property between the divorcing or separating spouses; and (3) if children are involved, there will be a question as to which spouse will be entitled to the personal exemption for the children and child support. Each of these are discussed below.

[2] SECTION 1041: TRANSFERS BETWEEN SPOUSES OR IN-CIDENT TO DIVORCE

Section 1041(a) provides for nonrecognition of gain or loss on the transfer of property between spouses or between former spouses if

---

46. § 135(c)(1)(B).

47. § 135(c)(1)(C); 31 U.S.C. § 3105.

48. § 135(a).

49. § 135(b)(1).

50. § 135(c).

51. § 135(d)(2)(A) and (B).

52. § 135(b).

53. See § 135(b)(2).

54. § 135(c)(4).

55. This amount is adjusted for inflation. § 135(b)(2)(B).

56. § 135(b)(2).

57. This amount is adjusted for inflation. § 135(b)(2)(B).

58. Id.

incident to divorce. Under section 1041(c), a transfer between former spouses is treated as incident to divorce if it occurs within one year after, or is related to, the cessation of the marriage.

Section 1041(b)(2) provides that the transferee's basis in the property received is equal to the transferor's adjusted basis prior to the transfer. Hence, any property which falls within the bailiwick of section 1041 has a carryover basis, and, accordingly, and pre-transfer gain or loss in transferred with the property. For example assume H and W get divorced in the current year, and as part of the divorce W transfers to H a rare antique Ferrari with a basis of $10,000 and a FMV of $200,000. Assume further that two years later H sells the rare Ferrari to T (an unrelated third party) for $260,000. Under section 1001(a), H's gain is equal to his amount realized less his adjusted basis.[1] H's adjusted basis under section 1041(b)(2) is $10,000, and H's amount realized under section 1001(b) is $260,000. Accordingly, H's gain on the sale of the Ferrari is $250,000 [$260,000 amount realized—$10,000 adjusted basis].[2]

Congress enacted section 1041 for several reasons. Congress believed that to tax transfers between spouses is inappropriate since a husband and wife may be regarded as a single economic unit. Furthermore, the rules governing transfers of property between spouses or former spouses incident to divorce had resulted in intense controversy and litigation. Finally, in divorce situations the government was often whipsawed by the transferor neglecting to report gain on a transfer while the recipient, upon the subsequent sale of the property, computed gain by reference to a basis equal to the fair market value of the property at the time it was received.

Section 1041 is not limited to transfers of property incident to divorce; it applies to any transfer of property between spouses, regardless of whether the transfer is a gift or is a sale or exchange between spouses acting at arm's length. Moreover, even if the transfer is a bona fide sale, the transferor nonetheless recognizes no gain, and the transferee does not acquire a basis in the transferred property equal to the transferee's cost. Section 1041(b)(2) provides that the basis of the transferred property in the hands of the transferee is the adjusted basis of the property in the hands of the transferor, regardless of the value of the transferred property at the time of the transfer.

[3] ALIMONY AND SEPARATE MAINTENANCE

[a] In General

In 1917 the Supreme Court held that alimony paid to a divorced wife under a court decree did not fall within any of the terms employed by the Tax Act of 1913 to define "income." Twenty-five years after the Supreme Court's decision, Congress became concerned that the combined total of the divorced spouse's federal income taxes and state-

§ 3.07
1. See § 1001(a).
2. Id.

ordered alimony payments could in some cases exceed the payor's gross income; hence, it enacted the predecessors of current sections 71 and 215. Under section 71(a) alimony or separate maintenance payments are generally includible in the gross income of the payee spouse, and under section 215(a), such payments are generally allowed as a deduction from the gross income of the payor spouse.

[b] Definition of Alimony or Separate Maintenance Payments

Alimony or separate maintenance payments are defined in section 71(b)(1). In order to enhance administrative simplicity, section 71 distinguishes between payments that constitute (deductible and includible) alimony or separate maintenance and nontaxable, nondeductible payments by reference exclusively to objective criteria.

Payments qualify as alimony or separate maintenance if the following requirements are met: (1) payment is made in cash;[3] (2) such payment is received by, or on behalf of, a spouse under a "divorce or separation instrument;"[4] (3) the divorce or separation instrument does not designate the payment as not includible in the recipient's gross income and not deductible by the payor;[5] (4) in the case of a decree of legal separation or divorce, the parties are not members of the same household at the time of payment;[6] and (5) there is no liability to make any payments for any period after the death of the payee spouse.[7]

The requirement of section 71 that payments can qualify as alimony only if made in cash ensures that noncash property transfers between spouses or incident to divorce will always fall with the reach of section 1041, and, hence, such transfers are not deductible to the transferor, not income to the recipient, and the recipient takes the transferor's basis and holding period.[8] For purposes of section 71, cash includes checks, credit card payments and other transfers typically considered "cash."[9] Transfers of services, of the taxpayer's own debt instrument, or of a third-party debt instrument do not qualify as cash for purposes of section 71.[10]

Cash payments to third parties can qualify as alimony or separate maintenance if received "on behalf of" a spouse.[11] Not surprisingly, some questions have arisen as to exactly when cash payments made to a third party are "on behalf" of an ex-spouse. Payments made in satisfaction of the payee spouse's obligation, for example rent, taxes, or tuition due from the spouse, are "on behalf of" the recipient spouse.[12] Payments made by a spouse that maintain property *owned by the payor* are *not*

3. § 71(b)(1).

4. § 71(b)(1)(A).

5. § 71(b)(1)(B).

6. § 71(b)(1)(C).

7. § 71(b)(1)(D).

8. See § 1041(a) and (b).

9. Temp. Treas. Reg. 1.71–1T(b), Q & A–5.

10. Id.

11. Temp. Treas. Reg. 1.71–1T(b), Q & A–6.

12. Id.

treated as cash alimony payments, even if the "payee" spouse benefits from the current use of that property.

Moreover, the Service's position has been that the payment of a mortgage debt is only treated as alimony if the recipient spouse is the principal obligor on the mortgage, and, therefore, payment by the payor spouse constitutes a discharge of indebtedness.[13] Mortgage payments on property owned by the payor spouse and used by the payee thus cannot qualify as alimony.[14] Accordingly only one-half of the mortgage payment made by the payor spouse on property held in joint tenancy with right of survivorship is potentially alimony.[15]

Similarly, if the payor spouse maintains a life insurance policy on his or her life and the recipient spouse is the irrevocable beneficiary and owner of the policy, the premiums paid by the payor spouse can be considered alimony or separate maintenance payments.[16] However, premiums paid on a policy not owned by the recipient spouse or on which the recipient spouse is merely a contingent beneficiary are not deductible by the payor spouse.[17]

The second requirement for "alimony" under section 71(b)(1) is that it be paid under a "divorce or separation instrument," which is defined by section 71(b)(2) as follows: "(A) a decree of divorce or separate maintenance or a written instrument incident to such a decree, (B) a written separation agreement, or (C) a decree ... requiring a spouse to make payments for the support or maintenance of the other spouse."[18] Hence, payments not required by some written agreement or court decree will not qualify as alimony or separate maintenance payments under section 71(b).

The third requirement for payments to be treated as alimony or separate maintenance under section 71(b)(1) is that the divorce or separation instrument not designate the payments as non-alimony.[19] Any payment that technically qualifies as alimony or separate maintenance under section 71(b)(1) may be labeled as non-alimony in the divorce or separation agreement. This permits the parties to designate the portion that will be included in the recipient's income even if tax avoidance is the only motive for such designation. Congress intended to provide some flexibility for tax planning within section 71; consequently, the parties may allocate the payments based on their relative marginal tax brackets to minimize the overall federal income tax consequences.

The fourth requirement of section 71(b)(1) is that the payments must be made when the payor and payee are not members of the same

13. Temp. Treas. Reg. § 1.71–1T(b), Q & A–6; Marinello v. Commissioner, 54 T.C. 577 (1970). See also Rothschild v. Commissioner, 78 T.C. 149 (1982).

14. Temp. Treas. Reg. § 1.71–1T(b), Q & A–6; Grutman v. Commissioner, 80 T.C. 464, 472 (1983).

15. Rev. Rul. 67–429, 1967–2 CB 63.

16. Temp. Treas. Reg. 1.71–1T(b), Q & A–6.

17. Id.

18. § 71(b).

19. § 71(b)(1)(B).

household in the case of divorce or separate maintenance.[20] The purpose behind section 71(b)(1)(C) is to prevent "live-in" divorces. Obviously, Congress does not want couples who are not truly divorced (or separated) to be able to artificially shift their income to one another by utilizing section 71 to their unfair advantage.

The fifth requirement of section 71(b)(1) is that there is no liability on the part of the payor to make alimony payments after the death of the payee. The idea behind this requirement is that (deductible and includible) alimony payments should be limited to payments made for the support of the recipient spouse.[21] Any payments that are required to continue after the spouses death cannot have been required solely for the support of the spouse, and thus they cannot qualify as alimony.[22] Payments required to be made after death that are in substitution of payments made to a payee spouse disqualify lifetime payments from alimony status.[23] Payments are considered as a substitute if they begin, increase in amount, or become accelerated as a result of the death of the payee spouse.[24]

[c] Front–Loading of Alimony Payments

Section 71(f) is intended to prevent substantial property-settlement transfers made shortly after divorce or separation from being characterized as deductible alimony or separate maintenance payments. While it may accomplish this result, it does so in a somewhat roundabout, and excessively complicated fashion. Section 71(f) does not recharacterize payments that qualify as alimony under the provisions of 71(b)(1), discussed above. Even if 71(f) applies, alimony payments remain alimony in the year paid. Under 71(f), however, if the amount of alimony decreases significantly after year one or year two, some of the initial alimony payments are subject to a three-year recapture rule. The amount recaptured has no impact on the payor or recipient for either of the first two years, but it is included in the payor's gross income and is deductible by the payee in the third "post-separation year." Any payments made after the third year are not affected by 71(f).

Under section 71(f)(2) the amount recaptured in year three is the sum of the excess payments for the second and first post-separation years. The computation of the excess for the second year is set forth in section 71(f)(4). Basically, any decrease in payments from the second to the third year by more than $15,000 is treated as an "excess payment" for the second post-separation year, and it is subject to recapture.[25] In other words, so long as payments either do not decrease between years two and three, or as long as any decrease from year two to year three is $15,000 or less, there will be no "excess payment" for year two.[26] To the

20. § 71(b)(1)(C).

21. See § 71(b)(1)(D).

22. Id.

23. Temp. Treas. Reg. § 1.71–1T(b), Q & A–10.

24. Temp. Treas. Reg. § 1.71–1T(b), Q & A–13.

25. See § 71(f)(4).

26. Id.

extent the payment made in year three is more than $15,000 less than the payment made in year two, that excess is subject to recapture (in year three).[27]

The computation of the "excess payment" for the first year is set forth in section 71(f)(3). This amount depends not simply on the decrease in payments made from year one to year two, but it also depends on the difference between the payments made in year one and the average payments made in year two and year three (after accounting for the recapture of the year two payments).[28] To the extent that the decrease in payments from payments made in year one to the average payments made in years two and three exceeds $15,000, the decrease will be recaptured in year three.

To illustrate the workings of 71(f), assume that alimony payments from S1 to S2 are as follows:

Year 1—$100,000, year 2—$100,000, and year 3—$85,000. There is no section 71(f) alimony recapture, since the decrease from year 2 to year 3 does not exceed $15,000 and the decrease between year 1 and the average of years 2 and 3 ($92,500) does not exceed $15,000.

Year 1—$100,000, year 2—$60,000, year 3—$60,000. There is no excess alimony payment for year 2, because the amount of alimony did not decline by more than $15,000 between year 2 and year 3. However, the average alimony of years 2 and 3 is only $60,000, and this is a decrease of $40,000 from year one. As a result, there is an excess alimony payment of $25,000 ($100,000 year 1 payment-$60,000 year 2 payment-$15,000) for year 1. As a result, in year 3, in addition to S1 deducting and S2 including the actual alimony paid of $60,000, S1 also has alimony recapture under section 71(f)(1) (income in year 3) of $25,000, and S2 has a $25,000 deduction for alimony recapture in year 3.

Year 1—$100,000, year 2—$60,000, year 3—$0. Payments decreased between year 2 and year 3 by more than $15,000, so there is an excess alimony payment for year 2 of $45,000 ($60,000 year 2 payment-$0 year 3 payment-$15,000). When this amount is recaptured the year 3 payment becomes $45,000, so that the average payment for year 2 and year 3 becomes $52,500. The decrease from year 1 ($100,000) to the average for years 2 and 3 ($52,500) is $47,500. This amount exceeds the permissible $15,000 decrease by $32,500. There is thus an excess payment for year one of $32,500. Total excess payments equal $45,000 from year 2 and $32,500 from year 1, or $87,500. Under section 71(f)(1) this amount is treated as income to S1 in year 3 and a deduction for S2 in year 3.[29]

There are three exceptions to the application of section 71(f)(1). First, no recapture occurs merely because either spouse dies, the payee spouse remarries, or the payments cease by reason of such death or

27. Id.

28. See § 71(f)(3).

29. § 71(e)(1)(A)–(B).

remarriage.[30] Second, there is no recapture if the payments are made pursuant to a support decree.[31] If the payments are for support, there is no potential for a disguised property settlement. Third, payments are not subject to recapture if they are to be made for at least three years and are not fixed as a specific sum, but instead are a fixed percentage of the income from a business, from property, or from employment or self-employment compensation.[32] Such payments are subject to fluctuations in amount generally beyond the control of the payor, and accordingly they represent minimal opportunity for manipulation.

[d] Alimony Trusts

Section 71 does not apply to transfers in trust. Instead, if the payor spouse establishes a trust to be used to pay what would otherwise qualify as alimony (because payments are made in cash pursuant to an appropriate decree or agreement), the trust is governed by section 682.[33] Under section 682(a), the recipient beneficiary is taxed on the trust income. Moreover, the transferor may exclude the trust income from his gross income under section 682(a).

Section 682 applies only when the parties are divorced, legally separated, or separated under a written separation agreement, and it does not apply to amounts paid for child support.[34] Additionally, the transferor must be taxable on the trust income but for the application of section 682(a).[35]

[4] CHILD SUPPORT

Amounts that are fixed as child support are not taxable to the payee or deductible by the payor.[36] Under section 71(c)(2) amounts not actually fixed as child support in the decree or agreement will be deemed fixed as child support in two instances. First, amounts not specifically labeled as child support will be regarded as child support if any amount specified in the agreement or decree will be reduced upon the happening of a contingency relating to a child, including the child's attaining a specified age, marrying, or dying.[37] Second, amounts will be regarded as child support when payments are reduced at a time that can clearly be associated with a contingency of the kind specified in the preceding sentence.[38]

Assume, for example, that the divorce or separation instrument requires payments of $12,000 each year for the life of the recipient

---

30. § 71(f)(5)(A).

31. § 71(f)(5)(B).

32. § 71(f)(5)(C).

33. *Nota bene:* section 682 is not gender neutral on its face; it mandates that the "wife" include in her gross income amounts paid to her from a trust. However, § 7701(a)(17) defines husband and wife so that the genders are reversed if payments are made by the wife to the husband.

34. § 682(a).

35. The transfer could be taxable if the transferor was the beneficiary of the trust before assigning it to the transferee spouse. Moreover, the transferor could be taxable on the trust income under the grantor trust rules of §§ 671–679.

36. See § 71(c).

37. § 71(c)(2)(A).

38. § 71(c)(2)(B).

spouse. When child C, the only child of the marriage, reaches the age of majority, marries, or dies, the annual payments will be reduced to $8,000. Under these facts $4,000 is treated as child support and $8,000 is treated as alimony or separate maintenance payments.[39]

With respect to the second instance the temporary regulations provide two situations that are presumed clearly associated with a child-related contingency.[40] The first situation is where the payments are to be reduced not more than six months before or after the child is to attain the age of 18, 21, or the local age of majority.[41] The second situation applies when there are two or more children and two or more payment reductions.[42] The reductions must occur not more than one year before or after each of the children attains a certain age between 18 and 24; that age must be the same for each child, but it need not be a whole number of years.[43]

Assume the following facts:

A and B are divorced on July 1, 1985, when their children, C (born July 15, 1970) and D (born September 23, 1972), are 14 and 12, respectively. Under the divorce decree, A is to make alimony payments to B of $2,000 per month. Such payments are to be reduced to $1,500 per month on January 1, 1991 and to $1,000 per month on January 1, 1995. On January 1, 1991, the date of the first reduction in payments, C will be 20 years 5 months and 17 days old. On January 1, 1995, the date of the second reduction in payments, D will be 22 years 3 months and 9 days old. Each of the reductions in payments is to occur not more than one year before or after a different child of A attains the age of 21 years and 4 months. (Actually, the reductions are to occur not more than one year before or after C and D attain any of the ages 21 years 3 months and 9 days through 21 years 5 months and 17 days). Accordingly, the reductions will be presumed to clearly be associated with the happening of a contingency relating to C and D. Unless this presumption is rebutted, payments under the divorce decree equal to the sum of the reduction ($1,000 per month) will be treated as fixed for the support of the children of A and therefore will not qualify as alimony or separate maintenance payments.[44]

§ 3.08 SPECIFIC EXCLUSIONS RELATING TO COMPENSATION FOR SERVICES

The Code contains a number of provisions that either exclude or provide special treatment for economic benefits that would otherwise fall within the broad sweep of section 61(a)(1), which states that gross

---

39. See § 71(c)(2)(A).

40. See Temp. Treas. Reg. § 1.71–1T(c), Q & A–18.

41. Id.

42. Id.

43. Id.

44. Temp. Treas. Reg. § 1.71–1T(c), Q & A–18.

income includes "[c]ompensation for services, including fees, commissions, fringe benefits and similar items."[1] These provisions, namely sections 132 and 119, are discussed in detail hereafter.

[1]　SECTION 132: STATUTORILY EXCLUDED FRINGE BENEFITS

In addition to paying money wages or salaries, many employers frequently provide fringe benefits to the employee as compensation for services rendered. In line with the general principal that any accession to wealth in any form is taxable income, such fringe benefits are generally taxable under section 61(a)(1). As most things in tax, however, there are exceptions to the general rule.

Section 132(a) provides: "Gross income shall not include any fringe benefit which qualifies as a—

(1)　no-additional-cost service,

(2)　qualified employee discount,

(3)　working condition fringe,

(4)　de minimis fringe,

(5)　qualified transportation fringe,

(6)　qualified moving expense reimbursement,

(7)　qualified retirement planning services, or

(8)　qualified military base realignment and closure fringe."

[a]　Section 132(a)(1): No–Additional–Cost Services

For this category of excludable fringe benefits, two conditions must be met: (1) the service provided to the employee must be of the type the employer offers for sale to non-employee customers in the ordinary course of the employer's line of business in which the employee works;[2] and (2) the employer must not incur substantial additional costs in providing the service to the employee, computed without regard to any amount the employee pays for it.[3] Costs include revenues foregone because the service is furnished to an employee rather than a non-employee.[4] Generally, situations in which employers incur no substantial costs in providing services to employees are those in which the employees receive the benefit of excess capacity that would otherwise have remained unused because non-employee customers would not have purchased it. Common examples of services excludable from gross income under section 132(a)(1) include unsold airline seats, hotel rooms, and telephone service.[5]

---

§ 3.08

1.　See Treas. Reg. § 1.61–2 for items constituting compensation for services and for cross references to items treated specially.

2.　§ 132(b)(1).

3.　§ 132(b)(2)

4.　§ 132(b)(2).

5.　While employee use of unsold seats or hotel rooms may result in some extra cost to the employer because of added weight to the airplane or added services

[i] Nondiscrimination

The no-additional-cost service benefits are subject to the nondiscrimination rules set forth in section 132(j)(1); these rules prohibit discrimination in favor of highly compensated employees with respect to the availability of such benefits.

Accordingly, if Company X only allows its executive officers (and none of its rank and file employees) to utilized its no-additional-cost service benefits, these benefits are not excludable under § 132(a)(1).[6]

[ii] Reciprocal Agreements

For purposes of excluding no-additional-cost services under section 132(a)(1):

[A]ny service provided by an employer to an employee of another employer shall be treated as provided by the employer of such employee if—(1) such service is provided pursuant to a written agreement between such employers, and (2) neither of such employers incurs any substantial additional costs (including foregone revenue) in providing such service or pursuant to such agreement.[7]

Hence, assume Airline X and Airline Y have written reciprocal agreement which allows their employees to utilize each other's otherwise empty seats; so long as neither employer incurs any substantial additional costs, the services provided to the employees of Airline X and Airline Y are excludable under § 132(a)(1).[8]

[iii] Benefits for Family Members

Section 132 provides continuing tax-free treatment for no-additional-cost services for family members of employees as well as for the employees themselves.[9] Section 132(h) does so by providing that certain individuals are treated as employees for purposes of section 132(a)(1). Consequently, spouses and dependent children are treated as employees.[10] Even parents of an airline employee can receive free stand-by tickets.[11] Moreover, retired and disabled employees and surviving spouses are also treated as employees for the foregoing purposes.[12]

[b] Section 132(a)(2): Qualified Employee Discounts

The term "qualified employee discount" means any employee discount[13] with respect to qualified property or services[14] to the extent such discount does not exceed—

---

required on the part of housekeeping staff, such costs are regarded as de minimis. Significantly, when the added costs are seen as more than de minimis, however, the benefit no longer qualifies under section 132(b). The distinction between de minimis costs and costs that will subject the employee to taxation is not always apparent. For a complete discussion of de minimis fringe benefits, see § 3.08[1][d], *infra*.

6. See § 132(j)(1).

7. § 132(i).

8. See § 132(i).

9. See § 132(h).

10. § 132(h)(2).

11. § 132(h)(3).

12. § 132(h)(1).

13. "The term 'employee discount' means the amount by which—(A) the price at which the property or services are pro-

(A) in the case of property, the gross profit percentage[15] of the price at which the property is being offered by the employer to customers, or

(B) in the case of services, 20 percent of the price at which the services are being offered by the employer to customers.[16]

[i] Nondiscrimination

As is the case with the no-additional-cost service benefits described above, qualified employee discounts are also subject to the nondiscrimination rules set forth in section 132(j)(1); these rules prohibit discrimination in favor of highly compensated employees with respect to the availability of such benefits.

Accordingly, if Company Y only allows its executive officers (and none of its rank and file employees) to utilized its qualified employee discount program, these benefits are not excludable under § 132(a)(2).[17]

[ii] Reciprocal Agreements

The same reciprocal agreement rules which apply to no-additional-cost services, also apply to qualified employee discounts.[18] Thus, for purposes excluding qualified employee discounts under section 132(a)(2):

> [A]ny service provided by an employer to an employee of another employer shall be treated as provided by the employer of such employee if—(1) such service is provided pursuant to a written agreement between such employers, and (2) neither of such employers incurs any substantial additional costs (including foregone revenue) in providing such service or pursuant to such agreement.[19]

Hence, assume Store X and Store Y have written reciprocal agreement which allows their employees to utilize each other's qualified employee discounts; so long as neither employer incurs any substantial additional costs, qualified employee discounts provided to the employees of Store X and Store Y are excludable under section 132(a)(2).[20]

---

vided by the employer to an employee for use by such employee, is less than—(B) the price at which such property or services are being offered by the employer to customers." § 132(c)(3).

14. "The term 'qualified property or services' means any property (other than real property and other than personal property of a kind held for investment) or services which are offered for sale to customers in the ordinary course of the line of business of the employer in which the employee is performing services." § 132(c)(4).

15. "The term 'gross profit percentage' means the percent which—(i) the excess of the aggregate sales price of property sold by the employer to customers over the aggre-

gate cost of such property to the employer, is of (ii) the aggregate sale price of such property." § 132(c)(2)(A). "Gross profit percentage shall be determined on the basis of—(i) all property offered to customers in the ordinary course of the line of business of the employer in which the employee is performing services (or a reasonable classification of property selected by the employer), and (ii) the employer's experience during a representative period." § 132(c)(2)(B).

16. § 132(c)(1).

17. See § 132(j)(1).

18. See § 132(i).

19. § 132(i).

20. See § 132(i).

[iii]   Benefits for Family Members

Section 132 provides continuing tax-free treatment for qualified employee discounts for family members of employees as well as for the employees themselves.[21] Section 132(h) does so by providing that certain individuals are treated as employees for purposes of section 132(a)(2). Consequently, spouses and dependent children are treated as employees.[22] Moreover, retired and disabled employees and surviving spouses are also treated as employees for the foregoing purposes.[23]

[c]   Section 132(a)(3): Working Condition Fringes

A working condition fringe refers to the value of any property or services provided to an employee if the cost of the property or services would be deductible by the employee as a business or depreciation expense if the employee had to pay for such property or services.[24] An illustration of this category of excludable fringe is an employee's use of a company car or airplane for business transportation. Other examples are the employer's subscription to business periodicals for an employee, on-the-job training, and a car and driver provided to an employee for security reasons.

The exclusion of working condition fringe benefits is both eminently sensible and also worth some elaboration. Consider an attorney who works in a law firm and accepts from her employer the use of a big, nicely furnished office in a fancy building. It is true that the use of that office, as opposed to having to do research and draft memos in a shack, may be worth $15,000 per year to the attorney. However, it is also true that if the attorney herself actually paid $15,000 per year to rent the office, she would be able to deduct that amount as a cost of doing business.[25] Similarly, if the attorney was paid $15,000 cash and was told by her employer to use that amount to rent a furnished office in which to work, her $15,000 income on receipt of the cash would be offset (at least to some extent) by her $15,000 gross deduction under section 162.[26] If instead the attorney is given no cash, pays no cash, and simply is told to work in the office, she likewise ought to have no net income; that is the result of the exclusion of working condition fringe benefits.[27]

---

21.   See § 132(h).

22.   § 132(h)(2).

23.   § 132(h)(1).

24.   § 132(a)(3).

25.   Unfortunately, however, her deduction would, in fact, be substantially limited as a miscellaneous itemized deduction. Section 67(a) generally provides that miscellaneous itemized deductions such as this are only deductible to the extent they exceed 2% of the taxpayers adjusted gross income. Additionally, for alternative mini-mum tax purposes miscellaneous itemized deductions are disallowed entirely. § 56(b)(1)(A)(i). Moreover, § 68(a) generally limits itemized deductions for certain high-income taxpayers. Accordingly, due to the limitations imposed by §§ 67(a), 56(b)(1)(A)(i), and 68(a), the value of any otherwise applicable deduction may be greatly diminished.

26.   Id.

27.   § 132(a)(3).

[d] Section 132(a)(4): De Minimis Fringes

A de minimis fringe is defined in section 132(e)(1) as any property or service that would otherwise be includible in gross income but is so small that accounting for it would be unreasonable or administratively impracticable. According to the regulations, de minimis fringes may include the occasional typing of personal letters by a secretary, occasional personal use of a copying machine, occasional cocktail parties, traditional holiday gifts of property with low fair market value, occasional theater or sporting event tickets, and coffee and doughnuts.[28]

Examples of fringe benefits that are not excludable from gross income as de minimis fringes are:

> [S]eason tickets to sporting or theatrical events; the commuting use of an employer-provided automobile or other vehicle more than one day a month; membership in a private country club or athletic facility, regardless of the frequency with which the employee uses the facility; employer-provided group-term life insurance on the life of the spouse or child of an employee; and use of employer-owned or leased facilities (such as an apartment, hunting lodge, boat, etc.) for a weekend. Some amount of the value of certain of these fringe benefits may be excluded from income under other statutory provisions, such as the exclusion for working condition fringes.[29]

Under section 132(e)(2) the de minimis fringe exclusion includes an employer-operated eating facility on or near the employer's business premises that offers food to employees at less than fair market value, provided the employer is at least recovering the direct operating costs of the facility and is not discriminating in favor of officers, owners, or highly compensated employees.

[e] Section 132(a)(5): Qualified Transportation Fringes

Pursuant to section 132(a)(5), qualified parking fringes are generally excludable from gross income. A qualified transportation fringe means any of the following:

(1) Transportation in a commuter highway vehicle;[30]

(2) Transit passes;[31] and

---

28. Treas. Reg. § 1.132–6(e)(1).

29. Treas. Reg. 1.132–6(e)(2).

30. § 132(f)(1)(A).

31. § 132(f)(1)(B).

(A) The term transit pass means any pass, token, farecard, voucher, or similar item entitling a person to transportation (or transportation at a reduced price) if such transportation is—

> (i) on mass transit facilities (whether or not publicly owned), or

> (ii) provided by any person in the business of transporting persons for compensation or hire if such transportation is provided in a vehicle meeting the requirements of subparagraph (B)(i).

(B) Commuter highway vehicle.—The term "commuter highway vehicle" means any highway vehicle—

> (i) the seating capacity of which is at least 6 adults (not including the driver).

§ 132(f)(5).

(3) Qualified Parking.[32]

The monthly limitation under section 132(f)(2)(A) with respect to the aggregate amount excludable for transportation in a commuter highway vehicle and any transit pass is at least $100.[33] With respect to qualified parking, the monthly limit under section 132(f)(2)(B) is at least $175.[34]

[f] Section 132(a)(6): Qualified Moving Expense Reimbursements

Pursuant to section 132(a)(6), qualified moving expense reimbursements are generally excludable from gross income. For purposes of section 132(a)(6), the term "qualified moving expense reimbursement" means "any amount received (directly or indirectly) by an individual from an employer as a payment for (or a reimbursement of) expenses which would be deductible as moving expenses under section 217[35] if directly paid or incurred by the individual."[36]

[g] Section 132(a)(7): Qualified Retirement Planning Services

Pursuant to section 132(a)(7), qualified retirement planning services are generally excludable from gross income. For purposes of section 132(a)(7), the term "qualified retirement planning services" means "any retirement planning advice or information provided to an employee and his spouse by an employer maintaining a qualified employer plan."[37]

With respect to highly compensated employees, qualified retirement planning services are only excludable from gross income if these services are available on substantially the same terms as they are to non-highly compensated employees.[38]

[2] STATUTORILY EXCLUDED SECTION 119 MEALS AND LODGING

If an employee voluntarily took part of his or her compensation in the form of meals and lodging furnished by the employer, the value of those benefits would generally be includable in gross income.[39] On the other hand, the idea of accepting lodging from an employer as part of the

---

32. § 132(f)(1)(C).

The term "qualified parking" means parking provided to an employee on or near the business premises of the employer or on or near a location from which the employee commutes to work . . . in a commuter highway vehicle, or by carpool. Such term shall not include any parking on or near property used by the employee for residential purposes. § 132(f)(5)(C).

33. The amounts excludable as qualified transportation fringes are indexed for inflation. § 132(e)(6). For the current amount excludable under section 132(a)(5)

see the current annual "Cost-of-Living Adjustments" Revenue Procedure.

34. Id.

35. For a complete discussion of § 217, see Chapter 4, Deductions.

36. § 132(g). *Nota bene:* Qualified moving expense reimbursements do not include "any payment for (or reimbursement of) an expense actually deducted by the individual in a prior taxable year." Id.

37. § 132(m)(1).

38. See § 132(m)(2).

39. See § 61(a)(1).

job might also, in some circumstances, be seen as analogous to an attorney accepting from her employer the use of a big, nicely furnished office in a fancy building. Obviously, the use of a nice office is a working condition fringe benefit that has never been thought to be taxable, and that is now specifically excludable under section 132(a)(3). Similarly, the government and the courts long ago presumed (and ruled) that if the circumstances surrounding the activities of an employee were such that she could not do her job without living on the premises, the value of the meals and lodging would not be included in gross income of the employee.[40] The proof demanded to establish that acceptance of the lodging was actually *part* of the employee's job (and not additional compensation) was that the employee show that the lodging was furnished for the "convenience of the employer)."[41]

It is worth noting that while the analogy between meals and lodging furnished for the convenience of the employer and other working condition fringe benefits exists, it is not a perfect one. While it may be that an employer needs an employee to be on location at all hours, the employer has no real need for the employee to actually sleep. Moreover, while the employer may need the employee to be sufficiently well-fed to perform his job, the employer has no real need for the employee to actually eat. Unlike an office or an employee's other tools of her trade, section 162 generally does not permit any deduction for an employee's expenses for meals and lodging (unless away from home in pursuit of business);[42] instead, those are considered to be the epitome of personal, non-deductible expenses.[43] The mere fact that the employer may need to have the employee present does not in and of itself convert those inherently personal concerns to deductible business expenses.

Nonetheless, the courts were satisfied that if the employer needed to have the employee present at the workplace and could not meet its needs without having the employee live at the workplace and remain at the workplace even to eat, they ought not to tax the employee on the value of the meals and lodging so provided.[44] These employer requirements were incorporated into what evolved into the common law exclusion of meals and lodging provided to the employee "for the convenience of the employer."[45]

The common law exception was difficult to apply. For example, in Benaglia v. Commissioner,[46] the taxpayer was employed as manager of two hotels in Hawaii. Correspondence with the employer indicated that the taxpayer was to receive an annual salary "together with living quarters, meals, etc.," for the taxpayer and his wife. Other evidence indicated that his duties were continuous, and his presence at the hotels

---

40. See Benaglia v. Commissioner, 36 B.T.A. 838 (1937), acq., 1940–1 C.B. 1.

41. Id.

42. For a complete discussion of § 162, see Chapter 4, *Deductions*.

43. Id.

44. See Benaglia v. Commissioner, 36 B.T.A. 838 (1937), acq., 1940–1 C.B. 1.

45. See § 262.

46. 36 B.T.A. 838 (1937), acq., 1940–1 C.B. 1.

was required constantly. The majority of the Board of Tax Appeals believed that the taxpayer had established that the meals and lodging at one of the hotels were solely for the employer's convenience.

Section 119(a) excludes from gross income the value of meals or lodging which are furnished for the convenience of the employer so long as "(1) in the case of meals, the meals are furnished on the business premises of the employer, or (2) in the case of lodging, the employee is required to accept such lodging on the business premises[47] of his employer as a condition of his employment."[48]

[a] Convenience of the Employer

[i] Lodging

The "convenience of the employer" and the "condition of employment" (applicable by its terms only to lodging, but not to meals) tests are basically similar and the factual considerations substantially the same.[49] The regulations provide that the "condition of employment" test means the employee is required to accept the lodging "to enable him properly to perform the duties of his employment;"[50] they add that lodging will be regarded as so furnished if, for example, it is because the employee must be available for duty at all times or because the employee could not perform the required work unless furnished the lodging on the business premises.[51]

[ii] Meals

Ultimately, "meals furnished by an employer without charge to the employee will be regarded as furnished for the convenience of the employer if such meals are furnished for a substantial noncompensatory business reason of the employer."[52]

The following circumstances represent some common scenarios where the Service will consider meals to have been be excludable from gross income because they have been provided for a substantial noncompensatory purpose:

- Meals which are furnished to employees to have them available in case of emergency are deemed to be furnished for a substantial noncompensatory purpose.[53]

- Where employees are restricted to a short meal period, such as thirty or forty-five minutes, meals are deemed to be furnished for a substantial noncompensatory purpose so long as employees

---

47. Treas. Reg. § 1.119–1(c)(1) defines the "business premises of the employer" to mean "the place of employment of the employee."

48. § 119(a).

49. Giesinger v. Commissioner, 66 T.C. 6 (1976), acq., 1976–2 C.B. 2.

50. Treas. Reg. § 1.119-1(b).

51. Id.

52. Treas. Reg. § 1.119–1(a)(1).

53. Treas. Reg. § 1.119–1(a)(2)(ii)(a). In order to qualify for exclusion under this provision it must be demonstrated that actual emergencies either have occurred or are reasonably likely to occur.

could not reasonably be expected to eat elsewhere during such a short meal period.[54]

- Where employees are provided with meals because they could not otherwise be expected to secure proper meals within a reasonable amount of time, such meals are deemed to be provided for a substantial noncompensatory purpose.[55]

- If an employer furnishes meals to certain employees and the reason for "furnishing the meals to each of substantially all of the employees who are furnished the meals is a substantial noncompensatory business reason of the employer,[56]" the meals furnished to other employees will also be deemed to be provided for a substantial noncompensatory purpose.[57]

This is by no means intended to be an all-inclusive list. Certainly there are other circumstances which result in meals being provided to employees for noncompensatory purposes. Notwithstanding the foregoing, these other circumstances are not without limitation. For example, meals furnished to employees to: (i) promote morale or goodwill or (ii) attract perspective employees, are deemed to be provided for a compensatory purpose, and, accordingly, these meals are fully includable in gross income under section 61(a).

So what happens if an employer contracts with a third-party to operate its on-site cafeteria? Can employees still take advantage of section 119? Fortunately, this scenario was contemplated by the Service when it drafted the regulations in this area.[58] Accordingly, section 119 not only applies for those meals which are provided directly by employers, but it also applies to meals which are provided on behalf of employers.[59] Of course, in either case the meals must still be provided for the convenience of the employer and on its business premises.[60]

Notwithstanding the foregoing, section 119(b)(4) provides that if more than half of the meals furnished to employees on an employer's business premises are found to be provided for the convenience of the employer, then all meals provided to employees on that employer's business premises will be deemed to have been provided for the convenience of the employer.

[b] Business Premises

[i] Lodging

Determining whether employer-provided lodging is located on the business premises of the employer is a question of fact which turns on

---

54. Treas. Reg. § 1.119–1(a)(2)(ii)(b). The sole purpose for restricting the length of the meal period cannot be to allow employees to leave earlier in the day, otherwise this exclusion will not be applicable.

55. Treas. Reg. § 1.119–1(a)(2)(ii)(c). This provision typically applies where there are insufficient eating facilities near the employer's business premises.

56. Treas. Reg. § 1.119–1(a)(2)(ii)(e).

57. Id.

58. See Treas. Reg. § 1.119–1(e).

59. Id.

60. See § 119(a)(1).

not only the employee's duties but also the nature of the employers business.[61]

Dole v. Commissioner[62] provides a tests for whether lodging is located on an employer's business premises. In general, lodging is deemed to be located on the employer's business premises so long as the lodging in question constitutes an integral part of the property or actual business activities are carried on there. "The touchstone of the business premises test is the lodging's relationship to the business activities of the employer. That is, [(t)he property must bear an integral relationship to the business activities of the employer]."[63]

In Lindeman v. Commissioner[64] the Tax Court observed that "Congress quite obviously intended a commonsense approach" to the meaning of business premises and that the legislative history indicates that section 119 "does not embody a requirement" that lodging "be furnished in the principal structure on the employer's business premises."

In Lindeman the taxpayer was the general manager of an oceanfront hotel leased by his employer. In addition to the hotel site the taxpayer's employer leased lots across the street, which were used for employee and guest parking, and a house adjacent to these lots in which the taxpayer and his family resided. Although the lots and taxpayer's residence were across a 50–foot wide public street from the hotel, the Tax Court held that the taxpayer's residence was on the employer's "business premises" within the meaning of section 119. The court stated that "the extent or the boundaries of the business premises in each case is a factual issue" and that "consideration must be given to the employee's duties as well as the nature of the employer's business." Because the taxpayer, whose customary working hours were 8 a.m. to 5 p.m., was subject to call 24 hours a day, often returned to the hotel several times each evening, could observe the hotel from his residence to see if there were problems, and the like, the Tax Court determined that the house was "on the business premises of the employer" within the meaning of section 119.

[ii] Meals

When it comes to meals, the employer's business premises may be construed somewhat more broadly. Basically, the business premises of an employee is wherever that employee needs to be to properly perform his job. If, for example, the employee is a state trooper, the business premises may be anywhere in the state, so long as it is the place where the trooper is assigned to be on duty.

It is also worth pointing out exactly what it is that must be furnished on the employer's business premises. The regulations state

---

61. Lindeman v. Commissioner, 60 T.C. 609 (1973).

62. 43 T.C. 697, 707 (1965), aff'd *per curiam*, 351 F.2d 308 (1st Cir. 1965).

63. Vanicek v. Commissioner, 85 T.C. 731, 740 (1985), citing Benninghoff v. Commissioner, 71 T.C. 216, 221 (1978).

64. 60 T.C. 609 (1973), acq., 1973–2 C.B. 2.

that "section 119 applies only to meals and lodging furnished in kind."[65] In Commissioner v. Kowalski[66] the Supreme Court held that meal allowances for a state trooper who remained on call during a mid-shift break were not subject to exclusion because section 119 does not cover cash allowances.[67]

Nonetheless, if meals are provided on the business premises for the convenience of the employer, the fact that an employee may be required to pay a fixed fee to the employer for meals furnished will not preclude exclusion under section 119.[68] Instead, if the employer pays "cash" compensation to an employee, but the employee is required to pay a fixed amount for meals provided on the premises for the convenience of the employer, whether or not she actually consumes those meals, she may exclude from income an amount equal to that charged for the otherwise qualifying meals.[69]

[3] OTHER EXCLUSIONARY PROVISIONS

There are several other sections that specifically address employee fringe benefits, many of which are discussed at greater length elsewhere in this work.

[a] Group–Term Life Insurance

Section 79(a) excludes from gross income any premiums paid by an employer for group-term life insurance to the extent such premiums provide insurance do not exceed $50,000 in death benefits.[70]

[b] Dependent Care Assistance

Section 129 provides that an employee may exclude up to $5,000 ($2,500 for a married employee filing a separate return) paid or incurred by the employer for dependent care assistance under a qualified program. For the exclusion to apply the program must be in writing and for the exclusive benefit of employees. Further, it must be nondiscriminatory. "Dependent care assistance" is defined in section 129(e)(1) by reference to the credit under section 21 for household and dependent care necessary for gainful employment. The section 21 credit is not allowed, however, to an employee for amounts excluded under section 129.

65. Treas. Reg. § 1.119–1(e).

66. 434 U.S. 77, 98 S.Ct. 315, 54 L.Ed.2d 252 (1977).

67. The question has arisen concerning the definition of "meals." In Tougher v. Commissioner, 51 T.C. 737 (1969), aff'd per curiam, 441 F.2d 1148 (9th Cir. 1971), cert. denied, 404 U.S. 856, 92 S.Ct. 103, 30 L.Ed.2d 97 (1971), the Ninth Circuit held that "meals" meant only ready-to-eat servings of food and hence did not include groceries. In Jacob v. United States, 493 F.2d 1294 (3d Cir. 1974), however, the Third Circuit held that employer-provided groceries were not subject to inclusion merely because the intermediate step of employer preparation of the food was absent. The court in Jacob also held that nonfoodstuffs, such as napkins and soap provided to the employee, constituted an integral part of the meals and hence were excludable under § 119. The Service has chosen to follow the narrow construction of Tougher. Rev. Rul. 77–80, 1977–1 Cum. Bull. 36.

68. Treas. Reg. § 1.119–1(a)(3)(ii).

69. Id.

70. For a complete discussion of § 79(a), see § 2.11, *supra*.

[c] Cafeteria Plans

Under section 125 an employee is generally not required to include amounts in gross income merely because the employee may choose between the cash and statutory nontaxable benefits offered by the employer's plan that permits employees to select the benefits they want from an employer-provided package.[71] Of course the employee who chooses and receives cash must include it in income;[72] the employee who foregoes the cash and instead opts for tax-free benefits will not lose the exclusion just because she had (and rejected) the opportunity to choose cash.[73]

With respect to highly compensated individuals, section 125(a) does not apply to the extent the plan discriminated with respect to: "(A) highly compensated individuals as to eligibility to participate, or (B) highly compensated participants as to contributions and benefits."[74]

Moreover, with respect to key employees, section 125(a) does not apply to "any benefit attributable to a plan for which the statutory nontaxable benefits provided to key employees exceed 25 percent of the aggregate of such benefits provided for all employees under the plan."[75]

[d] Accident and Health Plan Benefits

Sections 105–106 generally exclude from gross income amounts received from an employer.[76] Thus, generally these benefits, including those received indirectly in the form of the employer's costs for them, do not constitute taxable income.

Section 106(a) excludes from gross income[77] employer contributions to accident or health plans. However, the amounts received by the employee from such accident and health plans are generally includable in gross income, subject to certain exceptions enumerated in section 105.

Section 105(b) generally provides for an exclusion from gross income for amounts received under such a plan as reimbursement for medical expenses incurred, except to the extent that a prior year's medical expense deduction resulted in a tax benefit under section 213.

Under section 105(c) amounts received under such a plan are likewise excludable from gross income if they: "(1) constitute payment for the permanent loss or loss of use of a member or function of the body, or the permanent disfigurement, of the taxpayer, his spouse, or a dependent;"[78] and (2) the payments are determined with regard to the nature of the injury and not the employee's absence from work.[79] Section

---

71. § 125(a).

72. See § 61(a)(1).

73. See § 125(a), (d)(1).

74. § 125(b)(1)(A) and (B).

75. § 125(b)(2).

76. See § 105(a); § 106(a).

77. In addition to exclusion from the employee's gross income, amounts paid to a plan subsequent to the employee's retirement or death are likewise excludable from gross income. See Rev. Rul. 82–196, 1982–2 Cum. Bull. 53. See also CCA 200206053; Rev. Rul. 2002–41, 2002–28 I.R.B. 75;

78. § 105(c)(1).

79. § 105(c)(2).

105 concerns amounts received through "accident or health insurance," and section 105(e) provides that this term encompasses "amounts received under an accident or health plan."

§ 3.09   SECTION 121: EXCLUSION OF GAIN FROM SALE OF PRINCIPAL RESIDENCE

Homeowners have long enjoyed numerous tax benefits not only by owning homes,[1] but also by selling them. In line with the benefits extended to homeowners is section 121, which allows taxpayers to exclude from income up to $500,000[2] of gain on the sale of a home.[3]

In order to qualify for the Section 121 exclusion of gain, the taxpayer must have owned the home and used it as her primary residence for at least two of the five years immediately prior to the sale.[4] If spouses file a joint return,[5] they can exclude the first $500,000 of gain on the sale[6] if either spouse has owned the home for two of the five years prior to sale,[7] and both of them have used the house as their primary residence for two of those five years.[8]

[1]   OWNERSHIP REQUIREMENTS

The ownership requirements are obviously met if the taxpayer (or her spouse) has owned the home outright for the requisite period.[9] The ownership requirements are also met if the taxpayer owns stock as a tenant-stockholder in a cooperative housing corporation and as such was entitled to occupy the particular unit sold.[10] Moreover, the ownership requirements are satisfied if the taxpayer does not own the home directly as an individual but is otherwise treated as the owner because the home is owned by a grantor trust[11] or a disregarded business entity.[12]

If one spouse dies prior to the sale, any time during which the home was owned by the deceased spouse is treated as time the home was owned by the surviving spouse,[13] so that the survivor can claim the exemption (of up to $250,000) even if their mutual residence had been the sole property of the deceased spouse prior to death (so long as either spouse or both of the spouses together had owned the property for a total of two of the five years prior to sale).[14] Similar rules apply (that is,

---

§ 3.09

1. For example, nontaxation of imputed income from use of a home, deferred taxation of appreciation of the home, deduction of mortgage interest and property taxes.

2. This is the applicable amount for qualifying couples filing a joint return; the amount is reduced to $250,000 for all other types of taxpayers. § 121(b)(2).

3. See § 121(a).

4. § 121(a).

5. § 121(b)(2).

6. § 121(b)(2)(A).

7. § 121(b)(2)(A)(i).

8. § 121(b)(2)(A)(ii).

9. See § 121(a).

10. § 121(d)(4).

11. Treas. Reg. § 1.121–1(c)(3)(i).

12. Treas. Reg. § 1.121–1(c)(3)(ii).

13. § 121(d)(2).

14. See § 121(b)(2)(A)(i) and (ii).

separate periods of ownership can be added together) if ownership of a home is transferred between spouses pursuant to a divorce.[15]

[2] USE REQUIREMENTS

In order to qualify for the 121 exclusion, the taxpayer must have used the home as her principal residence during two of the five years immediately prior to the sale.[16] If the taxpayer alternates between two properties during the year (for example, a weekend home and a workday home, or a summer home and another residence), the Service will not accept an assertion that each of the two places is her "principal" residence during the time she spends there. Instead, a taxpayer can have only a single "principal" residence. Which of two or more residences qualifies as the taxpayer's "principal" residence is determined by reference to a number of facts and circumstances, primary among them being the amount of time during the year that she uses the home.[17]

Example 1.

Taxpayer A owns 2 residences, one in New York and one in Florida. From 1999 through 2004, he lives in the New York residence for 7 months and the Florida residence for 5 months of each year. In the absence of facts and circumstances indicating otherwise, the New York residence is A's principal residence. A would be eligible for the section 121 exclusion of gain from the sale or exchange of the New York residence, but not the Florida residence.

Example 2.

Taxpayer B owns 2 residences, one in Virginia and one in Maine. During 1999 and 2000, she lives in the Virginia residence. During 2001 and 2002, she lives in the Maine residence. During 2003, she lives in the Virginia residence. B's principal residence during 1999, 2000, and 2003 is the Virginia residence. B's principal residence during 2001 and 2002 is the Maine residence. B would be eligible for the 121 exclusion of gain from the sale or exchange of either residence (but not both) during 2003.

Example 3.

In 1991 Taxpayer C buys property consisting of a house and 10 acres that she uses as her principal residence. In May 2005 C sells 8 acres of the land and realizes a gain of $110,000. C does not sell the dwelling unit before the due date for filing C's 2005 return, therefore C is not eligible to exclude the $110,000 of gain. In March 2007 C sells the house and remaining 2 acres realizing a gain of $180,000 from the sale of the house. C may exclude the $180,000 of gain. Because the sale of the 8 acres occurred within 2 years from the date of the sale of the dwelling unit, the sale of the 8 acres is treated as a sale of the taxpayer's principal residence under paragraph (b)(3) of this section. C may file an amended return for 2005 to claim an

15. See § 121(d)(3).

16. § 121(a).

17. Treas. Reg. § 1.121–1(b)(2).

exclusion for $70,000 ($250,000–$180,000 gain previously excluded) of the $110,000 gain from the sale of the 8 acres.

Example 4.

In 1998 Taxpayer D buys a house and 1 acre that he uses as his principal residence. In 1999 D buys 29 acres adjacent to his house and uses the vacant land as part of his principal residence. In 2003 D sells the house and 1 acre and the 29 acres in 2 separate transactions. D sells the house and 1 acre at a loss of $25,000. D realizes $270,000 of gain from the sale of the 29 acres. D may exclude the $245,000 gain from the 2 sales.[18]

[a] Dual Use of Property

The taxpayer who uses the home as her principal residence for at least two years and leases out the property for up to three years has clearly met the use requirements.[19] The taxpayer who uses the property for dual purposes at the same time may also meet the use requirements, but the rules are a little more complicated.[20] The taxpayer who uses the residence as her primary residences but leases out adjacent property or otherwise uses the adjacent property for business rather than residential purposes is treated as using only the portion which is not leased out for her primary residence.[21]

On the other hand, the taxpayer who lives in the residence and either leases out or otherwise uses a part of the same residence for business purposes may treat the entire residence as her principal residence during such time, except to the extent of any depreciation she has taken on the residence during such time.[22] Any gain which is the result of such depreciation does not qualify for exclusion under section 121.[23]

[b] Generous Nature of Section 121

Section 121 can be fairly generous. The taxpayer need not have been living in the home immediately prior to sale, and indeed the taxpayer may have moved out as long as three years prior to the sale, so long as she has met the ownership and residence requirements for two of the last five years.[24] In addition, there is no requirement in section 121 that any of the excluded gain have accrued during the taxpayer's use of the home as a primary residence. Finally, there is no requirement that the taxpayer have lived in the home at the same time she owned it.[25] All that is required is that she be able to meet the two separate and possibly independent tests of residence and ownership.[26]

18. Treas. Reg. § 1.121–1(b)(4), Examples 1–4.

19. See Treas. Reg. § 1.121–1(c)(4), Example 1.

20. See Treas. Reg. § 1.121–1(e).

21. Id.

22. See Treas. Reg. § 1.121–1(e) and (d).

23. Treas. Reg. § 1.121–1(e).

24. See § 121(a).

25. Treas. Reg. § 1.121–1(c).

26. Id.

Example 1.

Taxpayer A has owned and used his house as his principal residence since 1986. On January 31, 1998, A moves to another state. A rents his house to tenants from that date until April 18, 2000, when he sells it. A is eligible for the section 121 exclusion because he has owned and used the house as his principal residence for at least 2 of the 5 years preceding the sale.

Example 2.

Taxpayer B owns and uses a house as her principal residence from 1986 to the end of 1997. On January 4, 1998, B moves to another state and ceases to use the house. B's son moves into the house in March 1999 and uses the residence until it is sold on July 1, 2001. B may not exclude gain from the sale under section 121 because she did not use the property as her principal residence for at least 2 years out of the 5 years preceding the sale.

Example 3.

Taxpayer C lives in a townhouse that he rents from 1993 through 1996. On January 18, 1997, he purchases the townhouse. On February 1, 1998, C moves into his daughter's home. On May 25, 2000, while still living in his daughter's home, C sells his townhouse. The section 121 exclusion will apply to gain from the sale because C owned the townhouse for at least 2 years out of the 5 years preceding the sale (from January 19, 1997 until May 25, 2000) and he used the townhouse as his principal residence for at least 2 years during the 5–year period preceding the sale (from May 25, 1995 until February 1, 1998).

Example 4.

Taxpayer D, a college professor, purchases and moves into a house on May 1, 1997. He uses the house as his principal residence continuously until September 1, 1998, when he goes abroad for a 1–year sabbatical leave. On October 1, 1999, 1 month after returning from the leave, D sells the house. Because his leave is not considered to be a short temporary absence under paragraph (c)(2) of this section, the period of the sabbatical leave may not be included in determining whether D used the house for periods aggregating 2 years during the 5–year period ending on the date of the sale. Consequently, D is not entitled to exclude gain under section 121 because he did not use the residence for the requisite period.[27]

[c] Repeated Use of Section 121

There are some limits on the repeated use of section 121. The primary such limit is that, absent certain extenuating circumstances, a taxpayer cannot use it more than once every two years.[28] Even this limit, though, is not universally applicable. If a taxpayer who has used the section 121 exclusion within the past two years sells another residence

---

27. Treas. Reg. § 1.121–1(c)(4), Examples 1–4.

28. § 121(b)(3).

and seeks to exclude gain on that second sale, she may exclude some of the gain from that second sale under section 121(c)(2) if the second sale is "by reason of a change in place of employment, health, or other reasons provided in the regulations."[29] The amount of gain she may exclude in such cases, though, will be less than the full amount she would otherwise be allowed. Instead, her exclusion will be only a percentage of the full exclusion, and that percentage will be the lesser of the following: (1) time since the prior sale/2 years; or (2) the total period of time for which the ownership and use requirements have been met for the second home/ 2 years.[30]

To see how this limit might apply, assume that H and W owned and lived in Home 1 for two years, and then purchased and moved into Home 2 for two years, during which time they lease out Home 1. Initially, they can choose to sell either home and use the full section 121 exclusion. If they sell Home 1 and use the section 121 exclusion and wait two years, they can also obtain a full $500,000 exclusion with respect to gain recognized on the sale of Home 2. Should they sell Home 2 after, say, only 1.5 years in order to move to accommodate a change in place of employment of either spouse, they can exclude 1.5/2, or ¾ of $500,000 gain on the sale of Home 2.

Of course, it could be quite difficult for taxpayers to prove that they moved because of a change in employment or health as opposed to moving to a new place and then looking for a new job, or just feeling better, in that new place. To solve this potential problem, the regulations provide a few safe harbors.

They treat a move as "by reason of a change of employment" if during the time the taxpayer owns and uses the property as her primary residences, she changes jobs and the new job is at least 50 miles further from the residence than was the old one.[31]

Example 1.

A is unemployed and owns a townhouse that she has owned and used as her principal residence since 2003. In 2004 A obtains a job that is 54 miles from her townhouse, and she sells the townhouse. Because the distance between A's new place of employment and the townhouse is at least 50 miles, the sale is within the safe harbor of paragraph (c)(2) of this section and A is entitled to claim a reduced maximum exclusion under section 121(c)(2).

Example 2.

B is an officer in the United States Air Force stationed in Florida. B purchases a house in Florida in 2002. In May 2003 B moves out of his house to take a 3–year assignment in Germany. B sells his house in January 2004. Because B's new place of employment in Germany is at least 50 miles farther from the residence sold than is B's former place of employment in Florida, the sale is within the safe harbor of

---

29. § 121(c)(2)(B).

30. § 121(c)(1)(B).

31. Treas. Reg. 1.121–3(c).

paragraph (c)(2) of this section and B is entitled to claim a reduced maximum exclusion under section 121(c)(2).

Example 3.

C is employed by Employer R at R's Philadelphia office. C purchases a house in February 2002 that is 35 miles from R's Philadelphia office. In May 2003 C begins a temporary assignment at R's Wilmington office that is 72 miles from C's house, and moves out of the house. In June 2005 C is assigned to work in R's London office. C sells her house in August 2005 as a result of the assignment to London. The sale of the house is not within the safe harbor of paragraph (c)(2) of this section by reason of the change in place of employment from Philadelphia to Wilmington because the Wilmington office is not 50 miles farther from C's house than is the Philadelphia office. Furthermore, the sale is not within the safe harbor by reason of the change in place of employment to London because C is not using the house as her principal residence when she moves to London. However, C is entitled to claim a reduced maximum exclusion under section 121(c)(2) because, under the facts and circumstances, the primary reason for the sale is the change in C's place of employment.

Example 4.

In July 2003 D, who works as an emergency medicine physician, buys a condominium that is 5 miles from her place of employment and uses it as her principal residence. In February 2004, D obtains a job that is located 51 miles from D's condominium. D may be called in to work unscheduled hours and, when called, must be able to arrive at work quickly. Because of the demands of the new job, D sells her condominium and buys a townhouse that is 4 miles from her new place of employment. Because D's new place of employment is only 46 miles farther from the condominium than is D's former place of employment, the sale is not within the safe harbor of paragraph (c)(2) of this section. However, D is entitled to claim a reduced maximum exclusion under section 121(c)(2) because, under the facts and circumstances, the primary reason for the sale is the change in D's place of employment.[32]

Moreover, the regulations treat a move as being for health reasons if it is recommended by a physician.[33]

Example 1.

In 2003 A buys a house that she uses as her principal residence. A is injured in an accident and is unable to care for herself. A sells her house in 2004 and moves in with her daughter so that the daughter can provide the care that A requires as a result of her injury. Because, under the facts and circumstances, the primary reason for

32. Treas. Reg. § 1.121–3(c)(4), Examples 1–4.

33. Treas. Reg. § 1.121–3(d).

the sale of A's house is A's health, A is entitled to claim a reduced maximum exclusion under section 121(c)(2).

Example 2.

H's father has a chronic disease. In 2003 H and W purchase a house that they use as their principal residence. In 2004 H and W sell their house in order to move into the house of H's father so that they can provide the care he requires as a result of his disease. Because, under the facts and circumstances, the primary reason for the sale of their house is the health of H's father, H and W are entitled to claim a reduced maximum exclusion under section 121(c)(2).

Example 3.

H and W purchase a house in 2003 that they use as their principal residence. Their son suffers from a chronic illness that requires regular medical care. Later that year their son begins a new treatment that is available at a hospital 100 miles away from their residence. In 2004 H and W sell their house so that they can be closer to the hospital to facilitate their son's treatment. Because, under the facts and circumstances, the primary reason for the sale is to facilitate the treatment of their son's chronic illness, H and W are entitled to claim a reduced maximum exclusion under section 121(c)(2).

Example 4.

B, who has chronic asthma, purchases a house in Minnesota in 2003 that he uses as his principal residence. B's doctor tells B that moving to a warm, dry climate would mitigate B's asthma symptoms. In 2004 B sells his house and moves to Arizona to relieve his asthma symptoms. The sale is within the safe harbor of paragraph (d)(2) of this section and B is entitled to claim a reduced maximum exclusion under section 121(c)(2).

Example 5.

In 2003 H and W purchase a house in Michigan that they use as their principal residence. H's doctor tells H that he should get more outdoor exercise, but H is not suffering from any disease that can be treated or mitigated by outdoor exercise. In 2004 H and W sell their house and move to Florida so that H can increase his general level of exercise by playing golf year-round. Because the sale of the house is merely beneficial to H's general health, the sale of the house is not by reason of H's health. H and W are not entitled to claim a reduced maximum exclusion under section 121(c)(2).[34]

Lastly, the regulations also describe other "unforeseen circumstances" that can justify a move and merit application of the partial exclusion under section 121.[35] The regulations provide a list of events

---

34.   Treas. Reg. § 1.121–3(d)(3), Examples 1–5.

35.   Treas. Reg. § 1.121–3(e).

which are within the safe-harbor for "unforeseen circumstances;" this list includes:

(i) The involuntary conversion of the residence.

(ii) Natural or man-made disasters or acts of war or terrorism resulting in a casualty to the residence (without regard to deductibility under section 165(h)).

(iii) In the case of a qualified individual described in paragraph (f) of this section—

    (A) Death;

    (B) The cessation of employment as a result of which the qualified individual is eligible for unemployment compensation (as defined in section 85(b));

    (C) A change in employment or self-employment status that results in the taxpayer's inability to pay housing costs and reasonable basic living expenses for the taxpayer's household (including amounts for food, clothing, medical expenses, taxes, transportation, court-ordered payments, and expenses reasonably necessary to the production of income, but not for the maintenance of an affluent or luxurious standard of living);

    (D) Divorce or legal separation under a decree of divorce or separate maintenance; or

    (E) Multiple births resulting from the same pregnancy.[36]

Examples of "unforeseen circumstances" include the following:

Example 1.

In 2003 A buys a house in California. After A begins to use the house as her principal residence, an earthquake causes damage to A's house. A sells the house in 2004. The sale is within the safe harbor of paragraph (e)(2)(ii) of this section and A is entitled to claim a reduced maximum exclusion under section 121(c)(2).

Example 2.

H works as a teacher and W works as a pilot. In 2003 H and W buy a house that they use as their principal residence. Later that year W is furloughed from her job for six months. H and W are unable to pay their mortgage and reasonable basic living expenses for their household during the period W is furloughed. H and W sell their house in 2004. The sale is within the safe harbor of paragraph (e)(2)(iii)(C) of this section and H and W are entitled to claim a reduced maximum exclusion under section 121(c)(2).

Example 3.

In 2003 H and W buy a two-bedroom condominium that they use as their principal residence. In 2004 W gives birth to twins and H and W sell their condominium and buy a four-bedroom house. The sale is

---

36. Treas. Reg. 1.121–3(e)(2).

within the safe harbor of paragraph (e)(2)(iii)(E) of this section, and H and W are entitled to claim a reduced maximum exclusion under section 121(c)(2).

Example 4.

In 2003 B buys a condominium in a high-rise building and uses it as his principal residence. B's monthly condominium fee is $X. Three months after B moves into the condominium, the condominium association replaces the building's roof and heating system. Six months later, B's monthly condominium fee doubles in order to pay for the repairs. B sells the condominium in 2004 because he is unable to afford the new condominium fee along with a monthly mortgage payment. The safe harbors of paragraph (e)(2) of this section do not apply. However, under the facts and circumstances, the primary reason for the sale, the doubling of the condominium fee, is an unforeseen circumstance because B could not reasonably have anticipated that the condominium fee would double at the time he purchased and occupied the property. Consequently, the sale of the condominium is by reason of unforeseen circumstances and B is entitled to claim a reduced maximum exclusion under section 121(c)(2).

Example 5.

In 2003 C buys a house that he uses as his principal residence. The property is located on a heavily traveled road. C sells the property in 2004 because C is disturbed by the traffic. The safe harbors of paragraph (e)(2) of this section do not apply. Under the facts and circumstances, the primary reason for the sale, the traffic, is not an unforeseen circumstance because C could reasonably have anticipated the traffic at the time he purchased and occupied the house. Consequently, the sale of the house is not by reason of unforeseen circumstances and C is not entitled to claim a reduced maximum exclusion under section 121(c)(2).

Example 6.

In 2003 D and her fiance E buy a house and live in it as their principal residence. In 2004 D and E cancel their wedding plans and E moves out of the house. Because D cannot afford to make the monthly mortgage payments alone, D and E sell the house in 2004. The safe harbors of paragraph (e)(2) of this section do not apply. However, under the facts and circumstances, the primary reason for the sale, the broken engagement, is an unforeseen circumstance because D and E could not reasonably have anticipated the broken engagement at the time they purchased and occupied the house. Consequently, the sale is by reason of unforeseen circumstances and D and E are each entitled to claim a reduced maximum exclusion under section 121(c)(2).

Example 7.

In 2003 F buys a small condominium that she uses as her principal residence. In 2005 F receives a promotion and a large increase in her salary. F sells the condominium in 2004 and purchases a house because she can now afford the house. The safe harbors of paragraph (e)(2) of this section do not apply. Under the facts and circumstances, the primary reason for the sale of the house, F's salary increase, is an improvement in F's financial circumstances. Under paragraph (e)(1) of this section, an improvement in financial circumstances, even if the result of unforeseen circumstances, does not qualify for the reduced maximum exclusion by reason of unforeseen circumstances under section 121(c)(2).

Example 8.

In April 2003 G buys a house that he uses as his principal residence. G sells his house in October 2004 because the house has greatly appreciated in value, mortgage rates have substantially decreased, and G can afford a bigger house. The safe harbors of paragraph (e)(2) of this section do not apply. Under the facts and circumstances, the primary reasons for the sale of the house, the changes in G's house value and in the mortgage rates, are an improvement in G's financial circumstances. Under paragraph (e)(1) of this section, an improvement in financial circumstances, even if the result of unforeseen circumstances, does not qualify for the reduced maximum exclusion by reason of unforeseen circumstances under section 121(c)(2).

Example 9.

H works as a police officer for City X. In 2003 H buys a condominium that he uses as his principal residence. In 2004 H is assigned to City X's K–9 unit and is required to care for the police service dog at his home. Because H's condominium association does not permit H to have a dog in his condominium, in 2004 he sells the condominium and buys a house. The safe harbors of paragraph (e)(2) of this section do not apply. However, under the facts and circumstances, the primary reason for the sale, H's assignment to the K–9 unit, is an unforeseen circumstance because H could not reasonably have anticipated his assignment to the K–9 unit at the time he purchased and occupied the condominium. Consequently, the sale of the condominium is by reason of unforeseen circumstances and H is entitled to claim a reduced maximum exclusion under section 121(c)(2).

Example 10.

In 2003, J buys a small house that she uses as her principal residence. After J wins the lottery, she sells the small house in 2004 and buys a bigger, more expensive house. The safe harbors of paragraph (e)(2) of this section do not apply. Under the facts and circumstances, the primary reason for the sale of the house, winning the lottery, is an improvement in J's financial circumstances. Under paragraph (e)(1) of this section, an improvement in financial circumstances, even if the result of unforeseen circumstances, does not qualify for the reduced maximum exclusion under section 121(c)(2).[37]

§ 3.10 EXCLUSION FOR STOCK DIVIDENDS

The general rule with respect to stock dividends (that is, dividends paid in the form of additional stock to shareholders who already own stock of the issuing corporation) is that they are not taxed under section 305(a). This general rule is the direct result of the Supreme Court's holding in Eisner v. Macomber,[1] where the Court held that a stock dividend of common shares issued to shareholders in proportion to the percentage of the outstanding common stock they already owned was not taxable because there was no realization event. In other words, the Court determined that the shareholders received nothing they did not already own. Instead, their continuous ownership of the identical portion of the identical corporation was simply represented by a larger number of shares after the distribution.

It is still true that a distribution of common shares to those who already own common stock is nontaxable if, as is likely to be the case, the newly issued shares are issued in proportion to the already outstanding shares.[2] In addition, the distribution of newly-issued preferred shares to holders of common shares is also tax free so long as the distribution is proportionate and the rights of the newly-issued preferred shares are subordinate to the rights of any preferred shares already outstanding.[3]

Nonetheless, just as the holding of Eisner v. Macomber with respect to realization generally has been subjected to significant erosion, so has the specific holding with respect to the taxation of stock dividends. Under section 305(b), any stock distributions other than those described above will be taxed to the shareholders who receive them. Basically, section 305(b) makes taxable any stock distributions that result in the recipient receiving *any* rights in addition to or different from the rights she owned before the stock distribution. For example, each of the following are taxable under section 305(b): an increased proportionate interest in the corporation,[4] the receipt of *any* rights by one who previously owned only preferred shares,[5] or the receipt of shares with different rights by different shareholders.[6]

Additionally, the shareholder who receives a stock distribution will be taxed if either she or any other shareholder was given the right to receive property rather than stock.[7] One might argue that the shareholder who is given the right to receive property rather than shares is in

---

37. Treas. Reg. § 1.121–3(e)(4), Examples 1–10.

§ 3.10

1. 252 U.S. 189, 40 S.Ct. 189, 64 L.Ed. 521 (1920).

2. See § 305(b)(2).

3. See § 305(b)(5).

4. § 305(b)(2).

5. § 305(b)(4).

6. § 305(b)(3) makes taxable a distribution if some shareholders receive common shares and others receive preferred shares in the same distribution.

7. § 305(b)(1).

constructive receipt of the property offered, and should be taxed under standard realization doctrine. Nonetheless, the taxation of shareholder A, who was not given the opportunity to receive property other than a proportionate amount of stock, because shareholder B was offered but declined the opportunity to receive some other property, goes well beyond application of the standard realization doctrine. Perhaps because corporations aware of the rules of section 305 can with relative ease ensure that stock distributions will not be taxed (by making them simple and proportionate), the limitations inherent in the statute have not proven to be problematic.[8]

8. See § 305(b)(1)-(5).

Chapter 4

DEDUCTIONS

Table of Sections

§ 4.01   IN GENERAL

The first step in computing taxable income requires a determination of the taxpayer's gross income (as well as any appropriate exclusions from gross income).[1] The second step, the focus of this chapter, concerns determining the amount of allowable deductions. The amount left after all relevant deductions are taken is taxable income, the tax base; it is against this base that the applicable marginal tax rates are multiplied to arrive at an individual's tax liability.

The interpretative approach applied to the deduction provisions of the Code, unlike the broad sweep accorded the concept of gross income, is primarily one of strict statutory construction. The courts have said that deductions are allowed as a matter of "legislative grace."[2] In one sense this concept has been joined with other expressions indicating that Congress could "disallow them as it chooses."[3] In another sense "legislative grace" means that the taxpayer must show the amount claimed as a deduction is indeed allowed by the Code. In other words, the provision relied upon is construed strictly against the taxpayer.[4]

The taxpayer ordinarily is required to show a relationship between the amount claimed as a deduction and the production of taxable income. Thus, the primary focus in this chapter is on the activities of the taxpayer engaged in a trade or business or in investing.

---

§ 4.01

1. For a complete discussion of gross income, see Chapter 2, *Gross Income*; for a complete discussion of exclusions from gross income, see Chapter 3, *Exclusions from Gross Income*.

2. Interstate Transit Lines v. Commissioner, 319 U.S. 590, 593, 63 S.Ct. 1279, 1281 (1943); Deputy v. Du Pont, 308 U.S. 488, 493, 60 S.Ct. 363, 366 (1940); New Colonial Ice Co. v. Helvering, 292 U.S. 435, 440, 54 S.Ct. 788, 790 (1934); Intermet

Corp. & Subsidiaries v. Commissioner, 209 F.3d 901, 904 (6th Cir. 2000); Chrysler Corp. v. Commissioner, 436 F.3d 644, 654 (6th Cir. 2006). See also INDOPCO, Inc. v. Commissioner, 503 U.S. 79, 84 (1992).

3. Commissioner v. Sullivan, 356 U.S. 27, 78 S.Ct. 512, 2 L.Ed.2d 559 (1958).

4. See Interstate Transit Lines v. Commissioner, 319 U.S. 590, 63 S.Ct. 1279, 87 L.Ed. 1607 (1943). See also FSA 200219001; FSA 200109001.

Individuals, as distinguished from corporations, are allowed certain deductions without regard to their relationship to income.

§ 4.02   INCOME–SEEKING EXPENSES

Under section 162(a) a taxpayer engaged in carrying on a trade or business may deduct all ordinary and necessary expenses. Under section 212(1)-(2) an individual not engaged in a trade or business may deduct ordinary and necessary expenses paid or incurred "for the production or collection of income" and "for the management, conservation, or maintenance of property held for the production of income."

The presence in the Code of two sections governing income-seeking expenses requires explanation. Although the words "trade or business" in section 162(a) are broad, the Supreme Court in Higgins v. Commissioner[1] gave them a narrow construction in holding that the activities of an individual in managing his considerable securities portfolio did not constitute the "carrying on of any trade or business." Hence, the Court said that the taxpayer could not deduct for salaries of staff and rent for offices in connection with his investment activity. Congress reacted in by passing what is now section 212(1)-(2).

Sections 162(a) and 212(1)-(2) are complementary. Nevertheless, on several occasions section 162 has been amended or expanded and corresponding changes in section 212 have not been made. This is perhaps attributable to the Supreme Court's saying that section 212(1)-(2) "is comparable and *in pari materia* with"[2] section 162(a) and provides for a class of deductions "coextensive with the business deductions allowed by"[3] section 162(a) except for the requirement that the income-producing activity qualify as a trade or business.[4] Moreover, the Supreme Court has said that the committee reports make it clear that the deductions under section 212(1)-(2) are subject to the same limitations and restrictions that are applicable to those allowable under section 162(a).[5]

In Higgins v. Commissioner[6] the Supreme Court stated that the determination of whether an activity is a trade or business "requires an examination of the facts in each case."[7] The Court adhered to this position in Commissioner v. Groetzinger[8] in which it held that a full-time gambler who makes wagers solely for his own account is engaged in a "trade or business" within the meaning of section 162(a). Writing for

§ 4.02

1. 312 U.S. 212, 61 S.Ct. 475, 85 L.Ed. 783 (1941).

2. Trust of Bingham v. Commissioner, 325 U.S. 365, 373, 65 S.Ct. 1232, 1237 (1945).

3. Trust of Bingham v. Commissioner, 325 U.S. 365, 374, 65 S.Ct. 1232, 1237 (1945).

4. Trust of Bingham v. Commissioner, 325 U.S. 365, 65 S.Ct. 1232, 89 L.Ed. 1670 (1945).

5. See, e.g., United States v. Gilmore, 372 U.S. 39, 44, 83 S.Ct. 623, 627 (1963).

6. 312 U.S. 212, 61 S.Ct. 475, 85 L.Ed. 783 (1941).

7. 312 U.S. 212, 217 (1941).

8. 480 U.S. 23, 107 S.Ct. 980, 94 L.Ed.2d 25 (1987). See also Richard W. Toemo, Slot Machine Player was not a "Professional Gambler," so no "Business Loss," 17–Sep J. Multistate Tax'n 38 (2007).

the majority, Mr. Justice Blackmun said that to be engaged in a trade or business, the taxpayer must be involved in an activity "with continuity and regularity"[9] and "the taxpayer's primary purpose for engaging in the activity must be for income or profit,"[10] adding that "[a] sporadic activity, a hobby, or an amusement diversion does not qualify."[11]

With regard to the proof of expenses, the taxpayer bears the burden of proof with respect to any claimed deductions.[12]

Under section 274(d), strict substantiation is required with respect to deductions claimed for travel, entertainment, and business gifts.[13] For these expenses the Code requires that the taxpayer substantiate the amount, time, place, business purpose, and business relationship to the taxpayer of the other persons involved. The next to last sentence of section 274(d) authorizes the Service to dispense with some or all of these requirements if the expense does not exceed an amount prescribed pursuant to the regulations.[14]

A taxpayer normally will be required to establish a causal relationship between income and deductions. This means, among other things, that if a taxpayer lacks a profit motive, he will not be regarded as carrying on a trade or business or an investment activity, and his deductions will be denied.[15] For example, in Brydia v. Commissioner[16] the taxpayer was an engineer who, while employed full time, engaged in independent, freelance evangelism; he deducted from his income as an engineer the expenses incurred as an unpaid evangelist. The Tax Court denied the deductions, reasoning that in view of the taxpayer's express disaffirmance of any profit motive as an evangelist, the activity did not constitute a trade or business within the meaning of section 162.

Although a corporation may be assumed to engage in business, deductions may be denied if the corporation fails to establish that profit was the primary motive of a particular activity. For example, in Transport Manufacturing & Equipment Co. v. Commissioner[17] the corporate taxpayer, who owned freight and motor equipment, was denied deductions for the excess of maintenance and depreciation over the rents

9. 480 U.S. 23, 35, 107 S.Ct. 980, 987 (1987).

10. Id.

11. Id.

12. New Colonial Ice Co. v. Helvering, 292 U.S. 435, 440 (1934); Welch v. Helvering, 290 U.S. 111, 115, 54 S.Ct. 8, 78 L.Ed. 212 (1933).

13. See Dominic L. Daher, The Business Purpose Substantiation Requirements, 17 Tax'n of Exempts 189 (2006).

14. See, e.g., Treas. Reg. § 1.274–5(h); Rev. Proc. 83–71, 1983–2 C.B. 590.

15. See e.g., Industrial Research Products, Inc. v. Commissioner, 40 T.C. 578 (1963); Rev. Rul. 64–9, 1964–1 C.B. (Part 1) 65; Szmak v. Commissioner, T.C. Memo.

1965–301, aff'd 376 F.2d 154 (2d Cir. 1967); Brydia v. Commissioner, T.C. Memo. 1970–147, aff'd 450 F.2d 954 (3d Cir. 1971).

16. 450 F.2d 954 (3d Cir. 1971).

17. 434 F.2d 373 (8th Cir. 1970). See also International Artists, Ltd., 55 T.C. 94 (1970), in which the Tax Court limited a corporate taxpayer engaged in promoting concerts of its principal stockholder (Liberace) to 50% of claimed deductions for depreciation and operating expenses of a residence leased from the corporation by the stockholder at less than its fair rental value. Cf. Sanitary Farms Dairy, Inc., 25 T.C. 463 (1955), in which the Tax Court allowed the costs of an African safari undertaken by the taxpayer's president and his wife, hunting enthusiasts, to be deducted as advertising expenses in selling milk.

received on three residential properties it rented to family members who owned the company. The Tax Court pointed out that the ownership of the residential properties had no connection with the corporation's regular business, and there was no evidence it had ever purchased other residential property. Moreover, each residence was occupied soon after purchase by a family member, and the rent for two of the properties was substantially below fair market value.

The profit motive concept is limited in cases of expense deductions, other than those allowed independent of their relationship to income, by the requirement that the income sought must be taxable. Under section 265(a)(1) no deduction is allowed for an amount allocable to tax-exempt income.[18] In addition, section 264(a)(1) provides that no deduction is allowed for premiums paid on life insurance policies when the taxpayer is a beneficiary under the policy.[19] This is because the proceeds are excluded from gross income by section 101(a)(1).[20]

Section 267(a)(2) imposes a further limitation on an expense deduction; it defers deduction of items that accrual method taxpayers are to pay to related cash method payees until those items are includible in the gross income of the payees. Under section 267(b) related persons include certain family members, a more than 50% shareholder and the corporation, corporate members of the same controlled group, and trustees and grantors or beneficiaries. Moreover, for the purpose of determining stock ownership, section 267(c) prescribes rules of constructive ownership that are applicable to individuals, family members, corporations, partnerships, trusts, and estates.

Finally, a deduction may be denied because the purported expense represents a loan made in the course of business. For example, in Canelo v. Commissioner[21] partners in a law firm that specialized in plaintiffs' personal injury litigation made advances of costs to clients under contingent-fee contracts and claimed them as section 162(a) deductions. In

---

18. See, e.g., See Church v. Commissioner, 80 T.C. 1104 (1983); Manocchio v. Commissioner, 78 T.C. 989, 994 (1982), aff'd on other grounds, 710 F.2d 1400 (9th Cir. 1983); Rev. Rul., 1961–2 C.B. 58, Rev. Rul. 61–222, 1961; Gold v. Commissioner, 41 T.C. 419 (1963); Rev. Rul. 66–262.

19. Treas. Reg. § 1.264–1(a). See, e.g., Tunningley v. Commissioner, 22 T.C. 1108 (1954), acq., 1955–2 C.B. 3; Yarnall v. Commissioner, 9 T.C. 616 (1947), judgment aff'd, 170 F.2d 272 (3d Cir. 1948); Meyer v. United States, 175 F.2d 45 (2d Cir. 1949). See also Revenue Ruling, 1966–2 C.B. 104, Rev. Rul. 66–203, 1966 WL 15316 (1966), which holds that the deduction cannot be divided where the employer's interest is proportionate and declines depending on the employee's length of service; as long as the employer has any interest in the policy as a beneficiary, the employer cannot deduct the premiums paid.

20. Section 264(a)(1) is limited to policies covering the life of any officer or employee or of any person financially interested in any business carried on by the taxpayer.

21. 53 T.C. 217 (1969), aff'd *per curiam*, 447 F.2d 484 (9th Cir. 1971). See also Burnett v. Commissioner, 356 F.2d 755, 760 (5th Cir.), cert. denied, 385 U.S. 832, 87 S.Ct. 77, 17 L.Ed.2d 68 (1966); Herrick v. Commissioner, 63 T.C. 562, 567, 568 (1975); Silverton v. Commissioner, T.C. Memo. 1977–198, aff'd, 647 F.2d 172 (9th Cir.), cert. denied, 454 U.S. 1033, 102 S.Ct. 571, 70 L.Ed.2d 477 (1981); Watts v. Commissioner, T.C. Memo. 1968–183; Flower v. Commissioner, 61 T.C. 140, 152 (1973), aff'd, 505 F.2d 1302 (5th Cir. 1974); CCA 200730020.

denying the deductions as business expenses the court held that on the facts the payments were intended as loans to be repaid by clients only in the event of a recovery.

§ 4.03 ORDINARY AND NECESSARY REQUIREMENT

The terms of section 162(a) and section 212 require that expenses be "ordinary and necessary." Perhaps the very multiplicity of daily transactions falling under the categories of business or investment expenses guarantees that this requirement will generate considerable controversy. Moreover, the courts have not developed a bright-line test. The best that can be said is that the courts have provided benchmarks as to the meaning of "ordinary and necessary." The more important of these benchmarks concern: (1) whether the payment was customary in the particular trade or business, (2) whether the payment was voluntary or involuntary, and (3) whether the payment was proximately related to the production of income.

The classic description of what is ordinary and necessary came in 1933 from Justice Cardozo in Welch v. Helvering.[1] In that case the taxpayer, in order to strengthen his reputation and credit when he became a grain commission agent, paid some of the debts of a discharged bankrupt corporation of which he had been the secretary. The Commissioner characterized the payments as nondeductible capital expenditures made for the acquisition of goodwill and was upheld by the Tax Court, the Eighth Circuit, and the Supreme Court. Justice Cardozo reasoned that while the payments could be assumed to be "necessary," in the sense of being "appropriate and helpful,"[2] they were not "ordinary," that is, "common and accepted"[3] "in the life of the group, the community, of which"[4] the taxpayer "is a part."[5] Justice Cardozo said that persons do not "ordinarily" pay the debts of others without legal obligation. Justice Cardozo added: "The standard set up by the statute is not a rule of law; it is rather a way of life. Life in all its fullness must supply the answer to the riddle."[6]

§ 4.03

1. 290 U.S. 111, 54 S.Ct. 8, 78 L.Ed. 212 (1933).

2. 290 U.S. 111, 113 54 S.Ct. 8, 9 (1933).

3. 290 U.S. 111, 114 54 S.Ct. 8, 9 (1933).

4. Id.

5. For a discussion of the meaning of the word "ordinary," see Raymond Bertolini Trucking Co. v. Commissioner, 736 F.2d 1120 (6th Cir. 1984). In Lilly v. Commissioner, 343 U.S. 90, 72 S.Ct. 497, 96 L.Ed. 769 (1952), the Court said that "ordinary" meant of a "common or frequent occurrence" in the type of business at issue. In

Trebilcock v. Commissioner, 64 T.C. 852 (1975), aff'd, 557 F.2d 1226 (6th Cir. 1977), the taxpayer's payments to a minister for providing spiritual advice and prayer to help cope with the strain of business and to assist in solving problems of the business were held not deductible under § 162(a). Although the court agreed that the enhanced spiritual awareness experienced by the taxpayer was helpful, it nevertheless denied the deduction because of lack of proof that such payments were incurred by similar businesses.

6. 290 U.S. 111, 115 54 S.Ct. 8, 9 (1933).

Consider the search for a solution by the courts in Friedman v. Delaney[7] and Pepper v. Commissioner.[8] In Friedman an attorney had assured a client's creditors in a bankruptcy proceeding that funds would be available for a settlement. The attorney was relying on money to be derived from a loan on a life insurance policy the client owned. When the referee in bankruptcy insisted upon a deposit, the attorney discovered that his client had changed his mind about the loan. The attorney felt obligated to use $5,000 of his own funds to make the deposit. Later the settlement fell through; the client was declared bankrupt; and the attorney's petition for the return of his deposit was denied. The attorney claimed a deduction as a business expense or, in the alternative, a loss. In disallowing the deduction the First Circuit said: "It is obviously no part of a lawyer's business to take on a personal obligation to make payments which should come from his client."[9] It added that "[t]he voluntary nature of the action ... takes it outside of"[10] the provisions concerning business expenses and losses.

In Pepper the taxpayers, partners in a law firm, found lenders for a client's business. When the taxpayers discovered that the client had used fictitious invoices as security for the loans and that the business was a failure, the taxpayers felt obligated to make good on $66,000 of loans. The Tax Court allowed the deduction claimed for these payments as an ordinary and necessary business expense although the taxpayers had been under no legal obligation to repay the loans. It relied largely on the showing made by the taxpayers that the finding of financing for clients was common practice for lawyers. The Tax Court distinguished Welch v. Helvering on the ground that there the taxpayers' expenditures were made "to acquire, and not to retain or protect, the taxpayer's business"[11] and Friedman v. Delaney on the similar ground that there was no contention that the payments were made to protect or promote the taxpayers' business.

The notion of what constitutes an involuntary payment appears to have been given a broad interpretation in Gould v. Commissioner.[12] There the taxpayer was an employee and minority shareholder of one corporation and the sole shareholder of a second corporation for which bankruptcy proceedings had begun. The taxpayer paid some of the debts of the bankrupt second corporation. The court held that these payments were deductible under section 162(a) because they were necessary to protect the taxpayer's position in the first corporation. Although the taxpayer's employment was not expressly in jeopardy, the court found that the directors' outward apprehension and concern about a possible decline in credit as a result of the taxpayer's involvement with the bankrupt corporation was sufficient justification for the taxpayer to

---

7. 171 F.2d 269 (1st Cir. 1948), cert. denied, 336 U.S. 936, 69 S.Ct. 746, 93 L.Ed. 1095 (1949).

8. 36 T.C. 886 (1961), acq., 1962–1 C.B. 4. See also Field Service Advisory, 1997 WL 33314348.

9. 171 F.2d 269, 271 (1st Cir. 1948).

10. Id.

11. 36 T.C. 886, 895 (1961).

12. 64 T.C. 132 (1975). See also CCA 200402004.

believe that his employment was threatened unless he rectified the situation. If the taxpayer had been told he would lose his job if the payments were not made, there would have been no doubt as to their involuntary nature. By focusing on the taxpayer's belief about his position, the Tax Court implicitly adopted the standard that the question of voluntariness is a factual determination viewed from the perspective of the taxpayer.

The Fifth Circuit's opinion in Freedman v. Commissioner[13] provides some guidance regarding the factor of the proximity of the payment to the production of income. In Freedman, the taxpayer was engaged in two businesses, one as an employee and the other as a partner. While commuting by car from one business to the other, he was involved in an accident. He sought a business expense deduction for the cost of settling a personal injury suit brought against him. The Tax Court disallowed the deduction on the ground that such expense was too remote from either business; hence, it could not be considered ordinary and necessary. The Fifth Circuit affirmed, observing that it had been conceded that the taxpayer was not engaged in either business at the time of the accident.

The rule seems well settled that the term "ordinary and necessary" by implication limits the deduction to a reasonable amount.[14] In Audano v. United States[15] the taxpayer claimed deductions for rent paid to a family trust on medical equipment transferred to the trust by the taxpayer. The equipment cost the taxpayer $15,000, and he paid an average rental of $11,700 a year for five years. The court held that this was unreasonable, justifying disallowance of the deductions in their entirety as a matter of law.[16]

§ 4.04   PUBLIC POLICY CONCERNS

[1] HISTORICAL DEVELOPMENT

The basic concern of Congress has been to articulate a concept of net income independent of the means, legal or illegal, by which items of income and deduction are generated. Historically, for the most part the courts, have given effect to this concept despite the government's claim that under some circumstances public policy justifies the denial of a

---

13. 301 F.2d 359 (5th Cir. 1962). See also Philbin v. Commissioner, 26 T.C. 1159 (1956); Rev. Rul. 77–356, 1977–2 C.B. 317.

14. See, e.g., Treas. Reg. § 1.212–1(d); I.T. 3581, 1942–2 C.B. 88; Commissioner v. Lincoln Electric Co., 176 F.2d 815 (6th Cir. 1949), cert. denied, 338 U.S. 949, 70 S.Ct. 488, 94 L.Ed. 586 (1950); Brown Printing Co. v. Commissioner, 255 F.2d 436 (5th Cir. 1958); CCA 200411042; FSA 199938018; "Ordinary and Necessary" Business Expenses for Entertainers: What's Reasonable?, 87 J. Tax'n 63 (1997).

15. Audano v. United States (5th Cir. 1970). See also Sparks Nugget, Inc. v. Commissioner, 458 F.2d 631 (9th Cir. 1972), cert. denied, 410 U.S. 928, 93 S.Ct. 1362, 35 L.Ed.2d 589 (1973), in which the court denied a deduction for payments in excess of reasonable rent and held that the excess constituted a constructive dividend.

16. The court also justified disallowance of the deductions on the ground that the trusts established were a nullity for tax purposes.

deduction for an otherwise ordinary and necessary business expense. In Commissioner v. Sullivan,[1] for example, the taxpayer claimed deductions for rent and wages in the conduct of an illegal bookmaking establishment, the rental payments being expressly prohibited under Illinois law. The Supreme Court held that the payments were deductible. It pointed to the regulations that allowed deductions for the federal excise tax paid on wagers by bookies and felt that such a policy was broad enough to embrace such normal expenditures as rent and wages. In addition, and perhaps more significant, was the Court's rationale that disallowance would make this type of business taxable on a receipts basis, a matter better left to Congress.

The public policy limitation on the availability of a business expense deduction was expressed by the Supreme Court in two companion cases to Sullivan. In the first of these, Tank Truck Rentals, Inc. v. Commissioner,[2] the taxpayer's operations were so hindered by a Pennsylvania weight limit that it deliberately operated over-weight in the state; it incurred fines of $41,000 for over 700 willful violations and 28 innocent violations of the weight law. The taxpayer claimed an expense deduction for the amount of the fines. The Supreme Court upheld the disallowance of the fines as deductions on both the willful and innocent violations. The Court admitted that the test of the public policy limitation, "the severity and immediacy of the frustration resulting from allowance of the deduction,"[3] was flexible, but it stated that flexibility was necessary "to accommodate both the congressional intent to tax only net income, and the presumption against congressional intent to encourage violation of declared public policy."[4]

In the companion case of Hoover Motor Express Co. v. United States[5] the taxpayer, a motor carrier, was disallowed deductions for fines paid for inadvertent violations of maximum highway-weight laws. The Court reasoned that the applicable weight laws did not differentiate between innocent and willful violations and, therefore, neither type of fine was deductible.

In Commissioner v. Tellier[6] a unanimous Supreme Court recognized the validity of a deduction for legal expenses incurred in the unsuccessful defense of criminal charges. The taxpayer, an underwriter and securities dealer, was convicted, fined, and imprisoned on 36 counts for violations of the Securities Act of 1933; he claimed a deduction of $23,000 for legal

§ 4.04

1. 356 U.S. 27, 78 S.Ct. 512, 2 L.Ed.2d 559 (1958). See also Commissioner v. Tellier, 383 U.S. 687, 693 (1966); Field Service Advisory, 1998 WL 1984218; TAM 9302002.

2. 356 U.S. 30, 78 S.Ct. 507, 2 L.Ed.2d 562 (1958). See also TAM 200629030; TAM 200502041.

3. 356 U.S. 30, 35, 78 S.Ct. 507, 510 (1958).

4. Id.

5. 356 U.S. 38, 78 S.Ct. 511, 2 L.Ed.2d 568 (1958). See also Field Service Advisory, 1998 WL 1984232; Field Service Advisory, 1997 WL 33106707; Field Service Advisory, 1997 WL 33106636; Field Service Advisory, 1993 WL 1468068; John J. Pease III, Stephens v. Commissioner and the Continuing Confusion Surrounding the Public Policy Doctrine of the Internal Revenue Code, 11 J.L. & Com. 105, 122 (1991).

6. 383 U.S. 687, 693 (1966). See also CCA 200451030.

expenses incurred in his defense. In affirming the Second Circuit's allowance of the deduction, the Court said:

> No public policy is offended when a man faced with serious criminal charges employs a lawyer to help in his defense. That is not 'proscribed conduct.' It is his constitutional right. . . . In an adversary system of criminal justice, it is a basic of our public policy that a defendant in a criminal case have counsel to represent him.[7]

Some of the difficulty surrounding the public policy issue can be attributed to the need for articulating a particular policy that would be violated or frustrated if a deduction were allowed. On more than one occasion the Supreme Court has indicated that this is a basic requirement for disallowance. For example, in Lilly v. Commissioner[8] the Court allowed a deduction for kickbacks made by an optician to doctors who had prescribed glasses. It held that while customs and actions of organized professional organizations were relevant on the question of whether the payments met the ordinary and necessary requirement of section 162, such customs did not in themselves constitute "sharply defined national or state policies." The Court did suggest, however, that such customs could be translated into policy by legislation, a matter that has been accomplished by a number of states through enactment of statutes prohibiting kickbacks and similar arrangements.

Occasionally the courts have avoided the public policy issue by requiring a strict showing that the expenses claimed were ordinary and necessary. This appears to be the approach taken by the Seventh Circuit in United Draperies, Inc. v. Commissioner.[9] When the taxpayer entered the market for the manufacture and sale of draperies to mobile home manufacturers, it made kickbacks of $138,000 and gifts of $21,000 to employees of some of its customers, and over a four-year period the taxpayer claimed deductions for these amounts as commission and sales promotion expenses. The deductions were disallowed by the court on the ground that such payments were not ordinary and necessary. The Seventh Circuit stated there was nothing in the record to show that the practice of making such kickbacks or gifts was a normal incident to the drapery industry or to suppliers of mobile home manufacturers generally; it further stated that while such kickbacks do occur, it was a matter of common knowledge that "the mores of the market place of this nation is not such that 'kickbacks,' . . . are an ordinary means of securing or promoting business."[10]

Congress has established four areas that, in terms of the Senate Report, "are deemed to violate public policy" and that justify the denial of a deduction for an otherwise ordinary and necessary expense.[11] The

---

7. 383 U.S. 687, 694 (1966).

8. 343 U.S. 90, 72 S.Ct. 497, 96 L.Ed. 769 (1952). See also Richard H.W. Maloy, Public Policy–Who Should Make it in America's Oligarchy?, 1998 Det. C.L. Mich. St. U. L. Rev. 1147, 1194 (1998).

9. 340 F.2d 936 (7th Cir. 1964), cert. denied, 382 U.S. 813, 86 S.Ct. 30, 15 L.Ed.2d 61 (1965).

10. 340 F.2d 936, 938 (7th Cir. 1964).

11. S. Rep. No. 552, 91st Cong., 1st Sess. 274 (1969).

four areas for which statutory rules are now provided are: (1) fines and penalties, (2) bribes and illegal kickbacks, (3) treble damage payments under the antitrust laws, and (4) political contributions and lobbying expenses.[12] Furthermore, in circumstances for which no statutory rule is provided public policy is not to be considered "sufficiently clearly defined to justify the disallowance of deductions."[13]

[2] FINES AND PENALTIES

Section 162(f), codifies the rule of Tank Truck Rentals and Hoover Motor by denying a deduction "for any fine or similar penalty paid to a government for the violation of any law." The regulations state that a fine or similar penalty includes an amount "[p]aid as a civil penalty imposed by Federal, State, or local law."[14]

The Tax Court has observed that the method for determining whether civil penalties are "similar" penalties under section 162(f) is to distinguish those "imposed for purposes of enforcing the law and as punishment for the violation thereof"[15] from those "imposed to encourage prompt compliance with a requirement of the law, or as a remedial measure to compensate another party for expenses incurred as a result of the violation."[16]

In Mason & Dixon Lines, Inc. v. United States[17] the Sixth Circuit allowed a trucking company to deduct for "liquidated damages" paid to a state for operating overweight vehicles because the amounts were com-

12. Each of these topics is discussed in detail hereinafter.

13. S. Rep. No. 552, 91st Cong., 1st Sess. 274 (1969). Treas. Reg. § 1.162–1(a) states, in part, that a deduction for an expense that "would otherwise be allowable under section 162 shall not be denied on the grounds that allowance of such deduction would frustrate a sharply defined public policy." The deductibility of losses under § 165 is precluded if it would frustrate a sharply defined public policy. Thus, in Raymond Mazzei, 61 T.C. 497 (1974), a taxpayer who entered into a conspiracy to counterfeit United States currency could not take a loss deduction under § 165(c) when the genuine currency the taxpayer provided for use in the counterfeiting process was stolen by co-conspirators. In Rev. Rul. 81–24, 1981–1 C.B. 79, the Service concluded that no deduction is available to a taxpayer who burns down a building and fails to collect the insurance proceeds because the arson is discovered.

14. Treas. Reg. § 1.162–21(b)(1)(ii). When a civil action has been instituted for a statutory violation but is settled prior to judgment, the courts have given effect to the characterization by the parties in the negotiations and especially in the settle-

ment agreement. Thus, in Middle Atlantic Distribs., Inc. v. Commissioner, 72 T.C. 1136 (1979), a civil suit had been filed involving illegally imported property. The statute allowed both punitive and remedial recovery against the violator. The agreement between the parties characterized the settlement as liquidated damages. The payments were held compensatory in nature and therefore deductible. In Adolph Meller Co. v. United States, 220 Ct.Cl. 500, 600 F.2d 1360 (1979), which involved the same statutory violation as in Middle Atlantic, a portion of the settlement that was characterized in the agreement as being a compromise amount of the penalty allowed by the statute was held nondeductible.

15. Huff v. Commissioner, 80 T.C. 804, 821 (1983). See also Field Service Advisory, 1998 WL 1984232; Field Service Advisory, 1997 WL 33106707.

16. Huff v. Commissioner, 80 T.C. 804, 821–822 (1983).

17. 708 F.2d 1043 (6th Cir. 1983). See also FSA 200210011; Field Service Advisory, 1998 WL 1984232; Charles A. Borek, The Public Policy Doctrine and Tax Logic: The Need for Consistency in Denying Deductions Arising from Illegal Activities, 22 U. Balt. L. Rev. 45, 65 (1992).

pensatory in nature, being determined by the degree to which the vehicle exceeded the prescribed limit. This reflected the fact that damage to highways increases with added weight. Fines were also imposed, but were not claimed as deductions.

Moreover, in recognition of the Supreme Court's holding in Tellier, the regulations provide that the amount of a nondeductible fine or penalty "does not include legal fees and related expenses paid or incurred in the defense of a prosecution or civil action arising from a violation of the law imposing the fine or civil penalty."[18]

[3] BRIBES AND ILLEGAL KICKBACKS

Under section 162(c)(2)[19] no deduction is allowed for bribes, kickbacks, or other payments that subject the payor to a criminal penalty or loss of license or privilege, provided any state law involved is generally enforced.[20] The regulations provide that a law is generally enforced unless it is never enforced or enforced only as to infamous persons or flagrant violators.[21]

Additionally, the question of enforceability has been given a broad interpretation. For example, in Boucher v. Commissioner[22] the taxpayer, an insurance agent, illegally offered premium discounts to customers. Although the state took no affirmative action to detect statutory violations, the court denied deduction of the rebates upon a finding that the state agency responsible for enforcement of the statute would have instituted action against a suspected violator if a violation were brought to its attention. The court held such policy to be within the meaning of the phrase "generally enforced." The court said that to constitute a lack of enforceability the statute must be regarded as a "dead letter."

Max Sobel Wholesale Liquors v. Commissioner[23] involved a wholesaler who secretly transferred, as added consideration for sales, extra liquor to customers in violation of state law mandating minimum prices.[24] Although section 162(c)(2) clearly precluded the taxpayer from claiming the value of the extra liquor as a business expense deductible under section 162(a), the Tax Court and the Ninth Circuit held that the taxpayer could include the value of the liquor in the cost of goods sold, which decreased the taxpayer's gross income. The Ninth Circuit said: "[W]e interpret § 162(c)(2) to apply only in the netherworld of deduc-

---

18. Treas. Reg. § 1.162–21(b)(2).

19. *Nota bene:* The second sentence of § 162(c)(1) states that the burden of proof is on the Commissioner, as in a tax fraud case, to show that payment to a government official or employee is illegal.

20. See Dominic Daher and Barry Brents, Chapter 1D:27, Disallowed Deductions, LEXISNEXIS FEDTAX IN DEPTH (LexisNexis 2007).

21. Treas. Reg. § 1.162–18(b)(3).

22. 77 T.C. 214 (1981), aff'd *per curiam*, 693 F.2d 98 (9th Cir. 1982). However,

the result in Boucher may have a different outcome today under another issue. See Max Sobel Wholesale Liquors v. Commissioner, 630 F.2d 670 (9th Cir. 1980), aff'g, 69 T.C. 477 (1977), acq., 1982–2 C.B. 2.

23. 630 F.2d 670 (9th Cir. 1980), aff'g, 69 T.C. 477 (1977), acq., 1982–2 C.B. 2.

24. Max Sobel Wholesale Liquors v. Commissioner, 630 F.2d 670 (9th Cir. 1980), aff'g, 69 T.C. 477 (1977), acq., 1982–2 C.B. 2.

tions, and not to have any effect in the 'above the line' realm of cost of goods sold."[25] Thus, the Ninth Circuit reasoned that the illegal rebate was a reduction in gross receipts in the computation of gross income whereas a deduction is a reduction of gross income. It said that a tax statute should not be extended by implication beyond the clear import of its language.[26] The foregoing should not affect such cases as United Draperies,[27] in which denial of a deduction for commercial kickbacks was based upon the lack of a showing that the payments were ordinary and necessary.

Finally, section 162(c)(3) provides that kickbacks, rebates, or bribes made by physicians or other suppliers of services under Medicare and Medicaid programs are not deductible.[28]

[4] TREBLE DAMAGE PAYMENTS UNDER THE ANTITRUST LAWS

Section 162(g) provides:

If in a criminal proceeding a taxpayer is convicted of a violation of the antitrust laws, or his plea of guilty or nolo contendere to an indictment or information charging such a violation is entered or accepted in such a proceeding, no deduction shall be allowed under subsection (a) for two-thirds of any amount paid or incurred—

(1) on any judgment for damages entered against the taxpayer under section 4 of the Act entitled "An Act to supplement existing laws against unlawful restraints and monopolies, and for other purposes", approved October 15, 1914 (commonly known as the Clayton Act), on account of such violation or any related violation of the antitrust laws which occurred prior to the date of the final judgment of such conviction, or

(2) in settlement of any action brought under such section 4 on account of such violation or related violation.

Essentially, section 162(g) serves to disallow 2/3 of any deduction related to certain treble damage settlements or judgments stemming from the violation of applicable antitrust laws.

[5] POLITICAL CONTRIBUTIONS AND LOBBYING EXPENSES

Since 1918 Treasury regulations in terms similar to the current ones have denied expense deductions "for lobbying purposes, for the promotion or defeat of legislation, for political campaign purposes (including the support of or opposition to any candidate for public office) or for

25. Max Sobel Wholesale Liquors v. Commissioner, 630 F.2d 670, 672 (9th Cir. 1980).

26. In Rev. Rul. 82–149, 1982–2 C.B. 56, the Service said that price rebates that are illegal payments within the meaning of § 162(c)(2) when made by the seller directly

to the purchaser may be subtracted from gross sales to determine gross income.

27. 340 F.2d 936 (1964).

28. See Dominic Daher and Barry Brents, Chapter 1D:27, Disallowed Deductions, LEXISNEXIS FEDTAX IN DEPTH (LexisNexis 2007).

carrying on propaganda (including advertising) relating to any of the foregoing purposes."[29]

Under section 162(a) a contribution to a political cause, party, or candidate by an individual normally would not be sufficiently related to a business activity to constitute an ordinary and necessary income-seeking expense.[30] But what about a business whose very existence is threatened by a legislative proposal and where logic would compel an expenditure designed to defeat it? Must the regulations yield? Apart from the allowances provided by section 162(e), discussed below, the answer to this question is no. Here, logic gives way to history.

In Cammarano v. United States[31] the taxpayer-partners, who were wholesale beer distributors, claimed a deduction for a contribution to a fund to finance a publicity program designed to defeat a legislative proposal to turn over the retail beer business to the state. The Supreme Court denied the deduction, stating that the regulations had acquired the force of law through repeated reenactment and consistent interpretation in the lower courts. Perhaps more important, in answer to the contention that denial of the deduction violated First Amendment rights, the Court stated that the "nondiscriminatory denial of" a deduction for everyone appeared to "express a determination by Congress that since purchased publicity can influence the fate of legislation which will affect, directly or indirectly, all in the community, everyone in the community should stand on the same footing as regards its purchase so far as the Treasury of the United States is concerned."[32]

The Court's reference in Cammarano to the concern of Congress with tax equality in this area could well have been documented by reference to a number of congressional investigations into lobbying as well as to the effort made to close a loophole that had developed with the enactment of the predecessor to section 271. This provision was enacted in response to revelations that a number of rulings had been issued allowing taxpayers bad debt deductions on loans made to political parties. Thus, section 271 denies a deduction for a taxpayer (other than a bank) on loans to political parties for bad debts otherwise deductible under section 166 and for worthless securities otherwise deductible under section 165(g).[33] A political party is defined expansively in section

---

29. Treas. Reg. § 1.162–20(a)(1). Prior to 1938 the regulations addressed themselves only to corporations, thereafter to all taxpayers. An even earlier denial of deductions for lobbying expense was published in 1915. T.C. 2137, 17 Treas. Dec. Int. Rev. 48, 57–58 (1915).

30. See Shannon King, The Lobbying Deduction Disallowance: Policy Considerations, Comparisons, and Structuring Activities Under Amended Section 162(e), 15 Va. Tax Rev. 551 (1996).

31. 358 U.S. 498, 79 S.Ct. 524, 3 L.Ed.2d 462 (1959). See also Textile Mills Securities Corp. v. Commissioner, 314 U.S.

326, 62 S.Ct. 272, 86 L.Ed. 249 (1941), denying deductions for amounts paid to a publicist and two legal experts who were employed to aid in securing legislation designed to secure the return of certain property seized by the government during World War I.

32. 358 U.S. 498, 513, 79 S.Ct. 524, 533 (1959). See also Internal Revenue Manual 7.25.3.17 (2007).

33. See also Daniel L. Simmons, An Essay on Federal Income Taxation and Campaign Finance Reform, 54 Fla. L. Rev. 1, 117 (2002).

271(b) as including a national, state, or local committee of a political party and a committee, association, or organization that accepts, contributes, or makes expenditures in promotion of an individual running for elective public office.

A second loophole was plugged when it was disclosed that the major political parties had made widespread use of brochures for which advertisers were paying exorbitant rates and claiming them as business expense deductions.[34] Thus, section 276(a)(1) denies a deduction for advertising expense or for admission costs to political events if the proceeds of the affair inure to the benefit of a political party or to a committee or unit of a political party.[35]

Section 162(e),[36] allows taxpayers engaged in business a deduction for expenses, including travel, incurred in connection with appearances and communications with legislative bodies, committees, or members, provided pending or proposed legislation is of direct interest to the taxpayer, and the expense qualifies as an ordinary and necessary business expense.[37] Under section 162(e)(2) prior law is codified to deny deductions for political campaign contributions and "grassroots" promotional expenses. But the "grassroots" prohibition does not prevent deductions for goodwill advertising unrelated to the taxpayer's goods or services, such as advertisements that keep the taxpayer's name before the public in connection with encouraging contributions to the Red Cross.[38]

34. See e.g., Denise Coal Co. v. Commissioner, 29 T.C. 528 (1957), in which the court allowed a deduction for advertising at a national political convention.

35. See RJR Nabisco Inc. v. Commissioner, T.C. Memo. 1998–252.

36. See S. Rep. No. 1881, 87th Cong., 2d Sess. (1962).

37. For an explanation of § 162(e)(1)(3), see Jordan v. Commissioner, 60 T.C. 770 (1973). The taxpayer, an employee of the Georgia Highway Department, formed a lobbying organization whose aim was to improve the wages and working conditions of employees of the department. The court allowed a deduction for the taxpayer's lobbying activities, finding them to be directly related and of direct interest to his employment with the department. The court said it was of no consequence that the taxpayer was not the sole beneficiary of his lobbying activities.

38. Treas. Reg. § 1.162–20(a)(2). See Beeken, A Tax Practitioner's Primer on Grassroots Lobbying, 59 Taxes 93 (1981); Cooper, The Tax Treatment of Business Grassroots Lobbying: Defining and Obtaining the Public Policy Objectives, 68 Colum.

L. Rev. 801 (1968). In 1978 the Service issued Rev. Ruls. 78–111, 78–112, 78–113, and 78–114, 1978–1 C.B. 41–44, dealing with attempts to influence legislation and grassroots lobbying. In Rev. Rul. 78–111 expenses incurred by a corporation in printing and distributing to shareholders its president's remarks given before a state legislature regarding a pending environmental protection bill were considered a nondeductible attempt to influence legislation. The same conclusion was reached in Rev. Rul. 78–112 about advertisements in newspapers and magazines regarding proposed legislation of direct interest to a corporate taxpayer. In Rev. Rul. 78–113 a trade association urged its members to contact their employees and customers and have them communicate with elected state representatives to support the repeal of legislation. That activity was considered an attempt to influence a segment of the general public. In Rev. Rul. 78–114 a trade association contacted prospective members to urge them to write or call their Congressmen to recommend support of legislation. This was considered grassroots lobbying; however, the same communication to current members was not.

§ 4.05   PERSONAL, LIVING, AND FAMILY EXPENSES

[1]   IN GENERAL

Section 262 denies deductions for "personal, living, or family expenses." As with capital expenditures, discussed in § 4.07, an express Code prohibition is perhaps unnecessary since the concept of personal, living, or family expense is the antithesis of income-seeking expenses.

The denial of a deduction for personal, living, or family expenses ordinarily is encountered only in situations involving individuals rather than corporations. However, in Fred W. Amend Co. v. Commissioner[1] the court denied a deduction to a candy company for a retainer paid to a Christian Science practitioner who counseled the taxpayer's Chairman of the Board in order to clarify his thinking about such matters as personnel, sales, production, financing, and labor relations. In addition, the Christian Science practitioner relied upon prayer to bring enlightenment concerning the problems of the taxpayer. The Tax Court said that the spiritual services were so personal that they came within the proscription of section 262.

Because any individual who works for another person is considered as being engaged in a trade or business for purposes of the Code, some taxpayers are tempted to classify their personal, living, and family expenses as a cost of doing business. For example, in Reading v. Commissioner[2] the taxpayer, an engineering consultant, attempted to analogize his expenses to the cost of goods sold, that is, the cost of providing labor. The court, while recognizing the philosophical logic of the taxpayer's argument, held that unlike the expense of producing goods, which is a direct cost in the production of income, personal, living, and family expenses are necessary only to the maintenance of the body and the satisfaction of human needs, which are not a direct investment in the services rendered.[3]

In broad outline, the regulations classify as personal, living, and family expenses such items as premiums paid for life and homeowner insurance; expenses of maintaining a household; losses sustained on property held for personal, living, or family use; costs of commuting to (and from) work; damages paid for breach of promise to marry; and attorney's fees and general legal expenses incurred in connection with

---

§ 4.05

1. 55 T.C. 320 (1970), aff'd, 454 F.2d 399 (7th Cir. 1971). See also TAM 8140018; Joel S. Newman, On the Tax Meaning of "Ordinary;" How the Ills of Welch Could be Cured Through Christian Science, 22 Ariz. St. L.J. 231, 259 (1990).

2. 70 T.C. 730 (1978), aff'd *per curiam*, 614 F.2d 159 (8th Cir. 1980).

3. See Halperin, Business Deductions for Personal Living Expenses: A Uniform Approach to an Unsolved Problem, 122 U. Pa. L. Rev. 859 (1974), and Sutter v. Commissioner, 21 T.C. 170 (1953), acq., 1954–1 C.B. 6, in which the court stated that for the expense to be outside the scope of § 262 it must be "different from or in excess of that which would have been made for the taxpayer's personal purposes."

divorce or separation.[4] The list in the regulations is not exclusive.[5]

Section 262 involves several areas in which the concept of a personal, living, or family expense has come into conflict with the concept of income-seeking expense under sections 162(a) and 212.

[2] WORK CLOTHING

Taxpayers have been allowed deductions where their work requires special or distinctive apparel, and the clothing is not suitable for "street wear."[6] In Revenue Ruling 70–474[7] the Service said that the cost of apparel is deductible if the apparel is specifically required as a condition of employment and is not of a type adaptable to general or continued usage to the extent the apparel takes the place of regular clothing. The Service concluded that the costs of uniforms for such persons as police officers and nurses are deductible while the costs of military uniforms that replace regular clothing are not. Under the regulations, however, military reservists may deduct the costs of uniforms (except to the extent of nontaxable allowances).[8]

The courts have used a similar test. In Drill v. Commissioner,[9] for example, the taxpayer, a superintendent for a building contractor, claimed deductions for clothing on the ground that his duties resulted in inordinate wear and tear. The Tax Court denied the deductions because the taxpayer's clothing was adaptable to general street wear. In Farrior v. Commissioner[10] the taxpayer, an inspector for a port authority, was

4. Treas. Reg. § 1.262–1.

5. See, e.g., Rev. Rul. 82–168, 1982–2 C.B. 56, in which the Service held that a watch purchased by an employee of a law enforcement agency whose job required him to know the correct time of day was a nondeductible personal expense under § 262.

6. See Pevsner v. Commissioner, 628 F.2d 467 (1980); Popov v. Commissioner, 246 F.3d 1190 (9th Cir. 2001); Rev. Rul. 70–474, 1970–2 C.B. 34; Cowarde v. Commissioner, T.C. Memo. 1968–158; Farrior v. Commissioner, T.C. Memo. 1970–312, acquiescence recommended, 1971 WL 29095 (IRS AOD 1971); Rev. Rul. 70–476, 1970–2 C.B. 35; Thompson v. Commissioner, T.C. Memo. 1963–147, aff'd, 333 F.2d 845 (4th Cir. 1964); Dennert v. Commissioner, T.C. Memo. 1964–5.

7. 1970–2 C.B. 34, superseding Mim. 6463, 1950–1 C.B. 29, and I.T. 3988, 1950–1 C.B. 28. See also Rev. Rul. 70–475, 1970–2 C.B. 35, allowing a jockey deductions for riding pants, boots, and helmet; Rev. Rul. 70–476, 1970–2 C.B. 35, allowing baseball players deductions for uniforms.

8. Treas. Reg. § 1.262–1(b)(8).

9. 8 T.C. 902 (1947).

10. T.C. Memo. 1970–312. See also Pevsner v. Commissioner, 628 F.2d 467 (5th Cir. 1980), where the Fifth Circuit held that a manager of the Sakowitz Yves St. Laurent Rive Gauche Boutique in Dallas could not deduct the cost of buying and maintaining Yves St. Laurent apparel. In reversing the Tax Court, the Fifth Circuit said that "the Circuits that have addressed the issue have taken an objective, rather than subjective, approach" and that "[under] an objective test, no reference is made to the individual taxpayer's lifestyle or personal taste." The Fifth Circuit pointed out that the principal argument in support of the objective approach was "administrative necessity." In Hynes v. Commissioner, 74 T.C. 1266 (1980), the Tax Court denied the taxpayer, a television news announcer, a deduction for clothes worn only on camera. Although the taxpayer argued that he was restricted in the selection of colors and patterns to styles dissimilar from his personal taste and would not wear for personal purposes, the Tax Court concluded that the taxpayer's position was no different from other individuals whose occupation requires their work wardrobe to be limited to conservative styles and fashions. The Tax Court said that the fact the taxpayer chose not to wear the clothes as a matter of personal preference was irrelevant.

required to wear work shirts with sewed-on arm bands. His costs for the shirts and their maintenance were allowed on the ground that they were not suitable for everyday wear.

If the taxpayer is self-employed rather than an employee, the sole issue has been whether the clothing was adaptable to general street wear.[11]

[3] MEALS

As a general rule the cost of meals is not deductible.[12] In Moss v. Commissioner[13] the taxpayer was a partner in a small trial firm that met every business day for lunch to discuss current litigation problems, scheduling, assignments, and settlement of cases. The Tax Court held that the taxpayer's share of the cost of the lunches was a nondeductible personal expense under section 262. Although the court did not doubt that the partnership benefited from the luncheon meetings, it said "[t]he mere fact that this time is given over the noon hour does not convert the cost of daily meals into a business expense." The court said that the cost of nourishment is inherently personal and the fact that meals are consumed in conjunction with a business purpose does not make them deductible.

[4] PERSONAL GROOMING

The expenses of personal grooming are generally not deductible, regardless of the mandates of the job. For example, in Drake v. Commissioner[14] the taxpayer, an enlisted man in the U.S. Army, was required to have his hair cut every two weeks, which was more than his personal desires dictated. The court held that the additional amounts were not deductible because "[e]xpenses for personal grooming are inherently personal in nature"[15] and "[t]he fact that the Army may have required such grooming does not make the expenses thereafter any less personal."[16] In addition, the court observed that the requirement was to maintain a high standard of personal appearance, and it did not assist in the accomplishment of any of the taxpayer's duties of his employment.

---

11. See Mortrud v. Commissioner, 44 T.C. 208 (1965), acq., 1966–1 C.B. 3, in which the court allowed a self-employed dairy routeman deductions for the costs of a shirt, jacket, cap, and pants and their maintenance although only the first three items were stitched with the name of a dairy.

12. § 262. Notwithstanding the general non-deductibility of meals, there are certain circumstances where meals are deductible. See § 4.10, *infra*.

13. 80 T.C. 1073 (1983), aff'd, 758 F.2d 211 (7th Cir. 1985), cert. denied, 474 U.S. 979, 106 S.Ct. 382, 88 L.Ed.2d 335 (1985). See also Field Service Advisory, 1992 WL 1354947; Acupuncturist Needled for Claiming Business Meal Deduction, 62 Prac. Tax Strategies 51 (1999).

14. 52 T.C. 842 (1969), acq., 1970–1 C.B. xv. See also Rev. Rul. 78–128, 1978–1 C.B. 39.

15. 52 T.C. 842, 844 (1969).

16. Id.

[5] PHYSICAL CONDITIONING

Although the Service has taken the position that physical conditioning expenses are inherently personal,[17] in Stemkowski v. Commissioner[18] the Second Circuit was willing to allow a professional hockey player to deduct off-season expenses related to certain athletic activities. The court said that activities such as weight-lifting "to strengthen and coordinate the body may well be at the business end of the spectrum, because these activities may contribute directly to professional hockey playing ability." However, other activities, such as golf, tennis, or bowling, "may well be on the fun-and-relaxation end of the spectrum."[19]

§ 4.06 EDUCATION EXPENSES

[1] IN GENERAL

This section deals with the deduction of educational expense in certain circumstances; for a discussion of certain educational benefits which are excludable from gross income, see § 3.06.

In Welch v. Helvering[1] Mr. Justice Cardozo concluded that the taxpayer's payments to creditors of a bankrupt corporation, with which the taxpayer had been associated, in order to reestablish customer relations and solidify the taxpayer's credit and standing did not qualify as ordinary expenses. In doing so, Mr. Justice Cardozo observed that there was little difference between such payments and the price of education when a "man conceives the notion that he will be able to practice his vocation with greater ease and profit if he has an opportunity to enrich his culture."[2] Indeed, "[f]or many," reputation and learning "are the only tools with which to hew a pathway to success."[3] Nevertheless, the money spent in acquiring them "is not an ordinary expense of the operation of a business." The government treated Welch v. Helvering as standing for the proposition that education costs were personal expenses, and until 1950 it was able to maintain successfully that such costs were not deductible.

In 1950 the Fourth Circuit allowed a public school teacher to deduct the cost of attending summer school, such attendance being required under state law for her to retain her position.[4] In 1953, in a situation lacking the compulsive feature of Hill, the Second Circuit allowed an upstate New York lawyer to deduct the costs of attending the annual

---

17. See Rev. Rul. 78–128, 1978–1 C.B. 39 (law enforcement officer required as a condition of employment to keep in excellent physical condition incurred health spa expenses).

18. 690 F.2d 40 (2d Cir. 1982), aff'g in part, rev'g in part, and remanding in part, 76 T.C. 252 (1981).

19. Stemkowski was nonetheless denied a deduction for his conditioning expenses arguably related to his business because of the lack of substantiation. 82 T.C. 854 (1984).

§ 4.06

1. 290 U.S. 111, 54 S.Ct. 8, 78 L.Ed. 212 (1933).

2. 290 U.S. 111, 115, 54 S.Ct. 8, 9 (1933).

3. Id.

4. Hill v. Commissioner, 181 F.2d 906 (4th Cir. 1950). See also Jay Katz, The Deductibility of Educational Costs: Why Does Congress Allow the IRS to Take Your Education so Personally?, 17 Va. Tax Rev. 1 (1997).

New York University Tax Institute in New York City.[5] The court relied upon Hill and distinguished the dictum in Welch by saying that Mr. Justice Cardozo's "general reference to the cost of education as a personal expense was made by way of illustrating the point then under decision, and it related to that knowledge which is obtained for its own sake as an addition to ones cultural background or for possible use in some work which might be started in the future."[6] But "[t]here was no indication that an exception is not to be made where the information acquired was needed for use in a lawyer's established practice."[7] The Second Circuit added that the taxpayer's expenses were sufficiently analogous to the following items that the regulations allow as deductions: dues to professional societies, payments for journal subscriptions, and the costs of books with short useful lives.[8]

Today, regulations[9] establish objective criteria and provide an overriding test that generally allows a deduction for education expenditures that maintain or improve skills required in the taxpayer's trade or business, but these regulations deny a deduction if the educational expenditures in question are personal or are made to meet minimum requirements.[10]

[2] LEGAL EDUCATION

If the education is "part of a program of study being pursued" by the taxpayer that "will lead to qualifying him in a new trade or business," the regulations deny the deduction regardless of the relationship of the training to the taxpayer's occupation and regardless of an employer requirement.[11] This rule is illustrated in the regulations with an example of an engineer or accountant who intends to continue practicing his profession but whose employer requires him to obtain a law degree.

Those who have commenced a graduate law program shortly after receiving their first degree in law (and without having actually engaged in the practice of law) have been unable to deduct the expense of their graduate studies.[12] For example, in Wassenaar v. Commissioner[13] the taxpayer began courses in the graduate law program in taxation at New York University three months after receiving his J.D. degree from Wayne State Law School. He was not employed during the summer following graduation from Wayne State. Instead, he prepared for the bar examination. The Tax Court pointed out that "the taxpayer must be

---

5. Coughlin v. Commissioner, 203 F.2d 307 (2d Cir. 1953). Educational costs that are not deductible because they are personal cannot be capitalized and made the subject of depreciation or amortization deductions. Denman v. Commissioner, 48 T.C. 439 (1967).

6. 203 F.2d 307, 309 (2d Cir. 1953).

7. Id.

8. See Treas. Reg. § 1.162–6.

9. Treas. Reg. § 1.162–5.

10. Id.

11. Treas. Reg. § 1.162–5(b)(3).

12. See e.g., Wassenaar v. Commissioner, 72 T.C. 1195 (1979); Randick v. Commissioner, 35 T.C.M. 195 (1976); Kohen v. Commissioner, T.C. Memo 1982–625.

13. 72 T.C. 1195 (1979). See also Ralph Conley Salyer, Jr., Lawyers Going Back to School: It's All Tax Deductible, 7 Me. B.J. 40, 44 (1992).

established in the trade or business at the time he incurs an educational expense to be able to deduct such expense under section 162."[14] The Tax Court distinguished the situation in which the taxpayer was allowed an educational expense deduction because he "was already firmly established in his profession and was truly taking courses or attending a seminar for the purpose of maintaining or improving the skills of his profession."[15] The Tax Court also said that completing the requirement for admission to the bar and being formally admitted to the bar do not satisfy the "carrying on" requirement of section 162(a); it observed that "being a member in good standing of a profession is not tantamount to *carrying on* that profession."[16]

In Sharon v. Commissioner[17] the taxpayer was licensed to and had practiced law in New York City with a firm before taking a position with the Office of the Regional Counsel of the Internal Revenue Service in California. The Tax Court disallowed a deduction for the expense of a California bar review course. Although the Tax Court recognized that the taxpayer had engaged in the practice of law before taking the review course for the California bar examination, it reasoned that the expenses incurred in obtaining a license to practice law in California qualified the taxpayer to represent clients and engage in the practice of law before all California courts. Because the taxpayer could not practice law in California before passing the bar, the court held that after receiving his California license, which his employer did not require, the taxpayer qualified for a new trade or business.

[3] TEACHERS

Ever since the Fourth Circuit decided in Hill v. Commissioner,[18] that the taxpayer's summer school costs were ordinary and necessary expenses of a public school teacher, educators have experienced little difficulty in securing deductions for course work.[19] In Furner v. Commissioner,[20] for example, a junior high school teacher, who resigned her

---

14. 72 T.C. 1195, 1199 (1979).

15. 72 T.C. 1195, 1200 (1979).

16. 72 T.C. 1195, 1199 (1979).

17. 66 T.C. 515 (1976), aff'd *per curiam*, 591 F.2d 1273 (9th Cir.1978), cert. denied, 442 U.S. 941, 99 S.Ct. 2883, 61 L.Ed.2d 311 (1979).

18. 181 F.2d 906 (4th Cir. 1950).

19. For a case in which deductions were denied, see Takahashi v. Commissioner, 87 T.C. 126 (1986) (Los Angeles high school science teachers failed to demonstrate the required connection between a cultural seminar in Hawaii and their particular job skills).

20. 393 F.2d 292 (7th Cir. 1968). The Service has stated it will follow Furner when the full-time study is temporary (one year or less) and the taxpayer resumes the trade or business, but it does not endorse

the "normal incidents" rationale of the case to the extent it implies that a subjective intent to reenter the field is all that is required to satisfy the regulations. Rev. Rul. 68–591, 1968–2 C.B. 73. See also Carter v. Commissioner, 645 F.2d 784 (9th Cir. 1981), in which the taxpayers, husband and wife, left their occupations (the wife's being that of a teacher) for an indefinite time to sail around the world. The deduction for tuition in pursuit of a Masters of Education for the wife's degree paid the year the voyage began was denied. The Commissioner acknowledged that the expenses met the skills-maintenance requirement. However, because the taxpayer resigned her position as a teacher with no intent to return to her profession at any definite time, she was regarded as not engaged in a trade or business when she entered the graduate degree program.

teaching position because her school lacked a leave policy, was allowed a deduction for her full-time graduate school costs, the taxpayer having taken a new job at a different school the following year. Although the Tax Court denied the deduction because of the lack of an existing trade or business, the Sixth Circuit reasoned that a year of full-time graduate study was a normal incident of the taxpayer's trade or business, and under the circumstances her resignation was consistent with it.

The regulations state that for an employee "a change of duties does not constitute a new trade or business if the new duties involve the same general type of work as is involved in the individual's present employment."[21] The regulations also state that "all teaching and related duties shall be considered to involve the same general type of work."[22] Changes in duties that do not constitute a new trade or business include going from classroom teacher to guidance counselor or principal.[23]

The bias in favor of the teaching profession expressed in the regulations is illustrated by Laurano v. Commissioner.[24] The taxpayer, who was certified to teach in Toronto, Canada, was allowed a deduction for a course required for certification to teach in New Jersey. The taxpayer taught at a parochial school in New Jersey. The school did not require that the taxpayer take the course. While recognizing that in Sharon the California bar review course helped the taxpayer qualify for a new trade or business as a licensed California attorney even though the taxpayer was already a licensed New York attorney, in Laurano the Tax Court nonetheless found itself bound by the all-encompassing language of the regulations and allowed the deduction.

[4] SPECIALIZATION AND RELATED MATTERS

In Greenberg v. Commissioner[25] the taxpayer was a physician who had a part-time psychiatry practice and a part-time teaching position. The taxpayer enrolled in a six-year course of study designed to train psychiatrists wanting to specialize in the clinical practice of psychoanalysis. The Tax Court denied the claimed deduction for the cost of the course of study on the ground that the taxpayer's primary purpose was the acquisition of a new skill or specialty. The First Circuit agreed with this conclusion but reversed on the grounds that most professions require a bundle of skills and that if what is newly acquired is regarded as a specialty, this is irrelevant so long as the primary purpose of the training is to add to the skills used in an existing profession.

21. Treas. Reg. § 1.162–5(b)(3).

22. Id.

23. Treas. Reg. § 1.162–5(b)(3). See also Rev. Rul. 71–58, 1971–1 C.B. 55, in which the Service concluded that a teacher who had met the minimum requirements for a teaching certificate in one state may deduct the costs of courses required to qualify in another state.

24. 69 T.C. 723 (1978), acq., 1978–2 C.B. 2. See also Baist v. Commissioner, T.C. Memo. 1988–554.

25. 367 F.2d 663 (1st Cir. 1966). See also Gilmore v. Commissioner, 38 T.C. 765 (1962); Namrow v. Commissioner, 288 F.2d 648 (4th Cir. 1961), cert. denied, 368 U.S. 914, 82 S.Ct. 192, 7 L.Ed.2d 132 (1961); Treas. Reg. § 1.162–5(b)(3); Rev. Rul. 74–78, 1974–1 CB 44.

The decision of the First Circuit in Greenberg may have prompted the position implicit in the regulations that training for a specialty does not constitute a new trade or business. Relevant to this issue are the following: (1) the terms of the objective standard that deny a deduction if the study qualifies a taxpayer for a "new trade or business" without mention of new skills or specialties; (2) the liberal rule permitting teachers to change from teaching to administrative duties without being regarded as involved in a change of trade or business; and (3) the example in the regulations, apparently based on the facts of Greenberg, to the effect that a course of study taken by a psychiatrist leading to qualification as a psychoanalyst does not constitute a new trade or business.[26]

When the education qualifies the taxpayer to engage in a practice only lawfully allowed upon completion of the education, the courts have generally held that such education qualifies the taxpayer for a new trade or business regardless of whether the taxpayer previously engaged in the same general occupation. Thus, in Glenn v. Commissioner[27] a practicing public accountant was denied a deduction for a certified public accountant review course leading to the taxpayer becoming licensed as a CPA. The court found that qualification for a new trade or business requires a "commonsense approach," and an objective comparison should "be made between the types of tasks and activities which the taxpayer was qualified to perform before the acquisition of a particular title or degree, and those which he is qualified to perform afterwards."[28] The court found that the taxpayer's ability to engage in, among other things, a general tax practice that he was only qualified to do as a result of obtaining his CPA license was a significant new ability substantial enough to constitute a new trade or business.[29] The court did not find that the general practice of accounting encompassed all practices engaged in by accountants.

Although the position on specialties implicit in the regulations has reduced disagreements, it has not dispensed with the problem of defining a trade or business, and it has not eliminated the question of whether particular educational costs are sufficiently related to a taxpayer's trade or business to constitute an ordinary and necessary business expense.

---

26. Treas. Reg. § 1.162–5(b)(3)(ii), Ex. (4). Rev. Rul. 74–78, 1974–1 C.B. 44, concerned a dentist who had a general practice, but returned to dental school full time to take post-graduate studies in orthodontics. After completing the training, the taxpayer limited himself to orthodontic patients. The Service concluded that the taxpayer's expenditures "for postgraduate studies in orthodontics were not incurred in connection with qualifying him for a new trade or business but were expenditures in connection with improving his skills as a dentist," relying on Ex. (4) of § 1.162–5(b)(3)(ii).

27. 62 T.C. 270 (1974). See also Robert A. Stolworthy, Jr., No M.B.A. Left Behind: Professional Education as a Business Expense in Allemeier v. Commissioner, 59 Tax Law. 927 (2006).

28. 62 T.C. 270, 275 (1974).

29. See also Robinson v. Commissioner, 78 T.C. 550 (1982), in which the court held that a licensed practical nurse may not deduct the costs of acquiring a degree when it leads to her qualifying as a registered nurse.

In general, the Tax Court has been liberal with taxpayers engaged in business. For example, in Beatty v. Commissioner[30] an engineer, whose position at the time of the educational expenditures was research project supervisor, was allowed a deduction for obtaining a Master of Science in Administration degree, the equivalent of an MBA, for which the course of study involved an understanding of administration, management, and business organization. The court found that because the taxpayer's position as a supervisor involved the skills of administration and management the taxpayer was already engaged in a managerial position. His studies, therefore, did not qualify him for a new trade or business but, at most, a change in duties.[31]

§ 4.07 CAPITAL EXPENDITURES

[1] OVERVIEW

Section 263 is entitled "Capital Expenditures." It appears in Part IX ("Items Not Deductible") of Subchapter B ("Computation of Taxable Income") of the Internal Revenue Code. Section 261 introduces the sections in Part IX by stating that "[i]n computing taxable income no deduction shall in any case be allowed in respect of the items specified in this part."[1] The term "capital expenditures" is not defined in section 263, although section 263(a)(1) provides that no deduction shall be allowed for amounts paid for new buildings or permanent improvements or betterments made to increase the value of property.[2] While the courts have not articulated bright-line criteria, they generally have supported the statements in the regulations[3] that capital expenditures include the following: (1) the cost of acquiring or constructing buildings, machinery, furniture, fixtures, and similar property having a useful life extending substantially beyond the taxable year;[4] (2) the cost of copyrights; (3) the cost of defending or perfecting title to property; (4) the cost of architectural services; (5) commissions for purchasing securities and commissions for selling securities that reduce the amount received, except that securities dealers may treat these items as deductible expenses; (6)

---

30. T.C. Memo. 1980–196.

31. See also Robert A. Stolworthy, Jr., No M.B.A. Left Behind: Professional Education as a Business Expense in Allemeier v. Commissioner, 59 Tax Law. 927 (2006).

§ 4.07

1. See also Henry Ordower, Seeking Consistency in Relating Capital to Current Expenditures, 24 Va. Tax Rev. 263, 299 (2004).

2. Lee & Murphy, Capital Expenditures: A Result in Search of a Rationale, 1 U. Rich. L. Rev. 443 (1981); Gunn, The Requirement that a Capital Expenditure Create or Enhance an Asset, 15 B.C. Ind. & Comm. L. Rev. 443 (1974).

3. Treas. Reg. § 1.263(a)–2(a)-(h).

4. Section 263A, provides capitalization rules for inventory, self-constructed property and noninventory property produced for sale, and interest. Section 263A(a)(1) states that the "direct costs" and the "proper share of those indirect costs (including taxes)" allocable to the property "shall be capitalized." For the application of § 263A to inventory, see § 4.08 *infra*. Property produced by the taxpayer that has a long useful life or production period is subject to the interest capitalization rules of § 263A(f). See Schneider & Solomon, New Uniform Capitalization and Long–Term Contract Rules, 65 J. Tax'n 424 (1986).

voluntary shareholder contributions to capital; and (7) the cost of good-will in the purchase of the assets of a going concern.[5]

Section 162(a)(3) allows deduction of rent paid for property used in a trade or business if the taxpayer has not or is not taking title or and does not have an equity interest. Thus, the "rental" of property may result in avoiding a difficult problem of characterization. However, a sale cast in the form of a lease will not necessarily provide a means of converting a capital expenditure into a deduction for "rent" paid.

In Estate of Starr v. Commissioner[6] the taxpayer contracted for the use of a fire sprinkler system under an instrument styled and couched in the terminology of a lease. The contract provided for annual rental payments of $1,240 for five years with an optional five-year period at $32 annually. No provision was made for further renewals, but if there was none the lessor was given six months to remove the system. Under similar contracts the lessor had never reclaimed a single fire sprinkler system after installation. The Ninth Circuit held that the taxpayer had purchased the property for his "rental" payments because there was little likelihood the lessor would reclaim the custom-made installation that would have only negligible salvage value.

Often the issue of whether an item constitutes a currently deductible expense or a nondeductible capital expenditure affects only the time when a deduction is allowed. This is true when the expenditure is subject to depreciation deductions. If, however, a purchased asset, such as goodwill, is not subject to amortization for one reason or another, the issue is more critical. Moreover, an expenditure that is characterized as personal may not qualify as either a business or production of income deduction or as an asset for which the taxpayer may deduct through cost recovery or depreciation, although for an asset such as a personal residence the cost will provide the taxpayer with a basis recoverable upon sale. In still other instances what is at stake is the difference between an immediate deduction that reduces ordinary income and capitalization that will result in lower capital gain. These problems are discussed in Chapter 7, *Taxation of Property Transactions.*

[2] ELECTION TO EXPENSE OR CAPITALIZE

One of the focal points for special interest groups seeking preferential benefits is revealed by the statutory provisions that grant an election to either capitalize or expense certain items, all but one of which relate to expenditures that would otherwise have to be capitalized. The exception is provided in section 266, denying deductions for taxes and other carrying charges that the taxpayer has elected to capitalize in accordance with the regulations.[7] The regulations apply to both productive and unproductive property, but have the most relevance for unproductive

---

5. Treas. Reg. § 1.263(a)–2(a)-(h).

6. 274 F.2d 294 (9th Cir. 1959). See also FSA 200217024; Alex Raskolnikov, Contextual Analysis of Tax Ownership, 85 B.U. L. Rev. 431, 516 (2005).

7. See § 263A. See also CCA 200721015; TAM 9429001.

property.[8] For example, if a taxpayer has purchased unproductive land and does not have other taxable income, by electing to capitalize property taxes and interest on the mortgage these items can be added to the basis of the property, thereby preserving them for recovery upon sale or other disposition.[9]

On the other hand, the Code allows several items of capital expenditure to be expensed for immediate tax benefit. These include section 173 expenditures of publishers of periodicals,[10] section 174 research and experimental expenditures,[11] section 175 soil and conservation expenditures of farmers,[12] and section 180 expenditures of farmers for fertilizers and other soil conditioners.[13]

As discussed *infra*, an election to deduct rather than capitalize is also available under section 263(c) for intangible drilling and development costs of oil, gas, and geothermal wells and under sections 615–617 for exploration and development costs of mines.[14]

In addition, the Code provides a number of provisions under which capital expenditures may be amortized over limited periods (usually at least 60 months); these include, among others, expenditures for pollution control facilities under section 169, start-up expenditures under section 195, and organizational expenditures of corporations under section 248.

[3] RESEARCH AND EXPERIMENTAL EXPENDITURES

Section 174(a)(1) provides that "research or experimental expenditures" made in connection with the taxpayer's trade or business need not be capitalized and that such expenditures are currently deductible.

---

8. Treas. Reg. § 1.266–1.

9. See Rao, Section 266 Carrying Charges: Tax Planning Opportunities, 58 Taxes 787 (1980). See also Treas. Reg. § 1.162–12 pertaining to the crop method and the taking of deductions in the year gross income is realized.

10. See also Field Service Advisory, 1992 WL 1354730; Field Service Advisory, 1992 WL 1466092.

11. If not expensed such expenditures may be amortized over a period of not less than 60 months. § 174(b) (flush language).

12. The amount deductible for any taxable year under § 175 cannot exceed 25% of gross income derived from farming. § 175(b). See also Field Service Advisory, 1998 WL 1984303; TAM 9119005.

13. See also TAM 9211007; Jesse J. Richardson, Jr., Maximizing Tax Benefits to Farmers and Ranchers Implementing Conservation and Environmental Plans, 48 Okla. L. Rev. 449, 468 (1995).

14. Expenditures for oil and gas exploration and recovery, known as intangible drilling and development costs, or IDCs, are subject to special treatment under the Code. Section 263(c) gives the taxpayer the option to deduct as expenses certain amounts paid in drilling and preparing wells for oil and gas production. In Sun Co., Inc. v. Commissioner, 74 T.C. 1481 (1980), aff'd, 677 F.2d 294 (3d Cir. 1982), the taxpayer sought a deduction under the IDC option for the costs of drilling exploratory wells that were never used for production. The Commissioner argued that the IDC option should only apply to wells drilled with the intention of being used for the production of hydrocarbons. However, both the Tax Court and the Third Circuit reasoned that the congressional purpose behind the IDC option was to encourage risk taking, and the need for incentive is greatest at the initial exploratory stage. Both courts held that the intent of subsequent production is immaterial to the statutory language, and the IDC option is available for any well, regardless of its nature, if part of the process of exploration and development is capable of producing hydrocarbons upon completion.

The regulations[15] indicate that the term "research and experimental expenditures" refers to costs "in the experimental or laboratory sense," including those "incident to the development of an experimental or pilot model, a plant process, a product, a formula, an invention, or similar property" but not the costs "for the ordinary testing or inspection of materials or products for quality control or those for ... consumer surveys, advertising, or promotions." Section 174(c) provides that section 174 does not apply to the costs of acquiring or improving land or depreciable or depletable property.

In Snow v. Commissioner[16] the Supreme Court held that the costs for a special purpose incinerator that was being developed in a limited partnership, with the inventor-partner devoting about one-third of his time to the project and an outside engineering firm doing the shopwork, were deductible under section 174(a)(1), even though there had been no sales. The Court pointed out that:

> Section 174 was enacted in 1954 to dilute some of the conception of 'ordinary and necessary' business expenses under § 162(a) (then § 23(a)(1) of the Act) adumbrated by Justice Frankfurter in a concurring opinion in Deputy v. du Pont, 308 U.S. 488, 499 (1940), where he said that the section in question (old § 23(a)) 'involves holding ones self out to others as engaged in the selling of goods or services.'[17]

The Court observed that "Congress wrote into § 174(a)(1) 'in connection with,' and § 162(a) is more narrowly written than is § 174."[18]

[4] IMPROVEMENT AND ALTERATION OF PROPERTY

When property is improved or altered, resolution of the problem of distinguishing between a nondeductible capital expenditure and a deductible business or production of income expense may be aided by applying a "useful life" test. This test is expressed in the regulations that refer to capital expenditures as amounts that "substantially prolong the useful life" of property or costs for the "acquisition, construction, or erection of ... property having a useful life substantially beyond the taxable year."[19] However, the courts have disregarded this test when the taxpayer established that despite the property's useful life of more than a year, the expenditure was necessary to maintain normal operation; this principle is expressed in the regulations for mining operations as well and has been applied by the courts in such cases.[20] This principle has

15. Treas. Reg. § 1.174–2(a).

16. 416 U.S. 500, 94 S.Ct. 1876, 40 L.Ed.2d 336 (1974).

17. 416 U.S. 500, 502, 94 S.Ct. 1876, 1878 (1974).

18. See Green v. Commissioner, 83 T.C. 667 (1984), for a discussion of the phrase "in connection with his [a taxpayer's] trade or business" used in § 174; the case is analyzed in Gadarian & Dezart, The

Trade or Business Requirement Under Sec. 174 After Green, 16 Tax Advisor 348 (1985). See also FSA 200145011; Field Service Advisory, 1992 WL 1355726; TAM 9604004.

19. Treas. Regs. §§ 1.263(a)–1(b), 1.263(a)–2(a).

20. Treas. Reg. § 1.612–2; Adkins v. Commissioner, 51 T.C. 957 (1969), acq., 1970–1 C.B. xviii; Kennecott Copper Corp.

also been applied when expenditures were made to protect business property from physical harm. For example, in Midland Empire Packing Co. v. Commissioner[21] the taxpayer was permitted to expense the cost of lining its basement walls and floor with cement to prevent seepage of oil from a nearby refinery. The court stated that such repairs "merely served to keep the property in an operating condition over its probable useful life," a rationale analogous to that employed in the mining cases.

The outcome in Midland Empire Packing should be compared with that in Mt. Morris Drive–In Theatre Co. v. Commissioner.[22] There the taxpayer purchased farm land for use as a drive-in theater. The land sloped and drained toward the property of an adjoining owner, who complained that the construction of the theater increased the flow of water onto his land. After the theater was completed, the adjoining land owner filed suit for an injunction and for damages. The suit was settled by an agreement under which the taxpayer constructed a drainage system across the adjoining land. The Tax Court and the Sixth Circuit held that the cost of the drainage system was a capital expenditure.

If the taxpayer uses its own equipment and personnel to construct property for the taxpayer's own use and the useful life of the property is substantial, the direct costs are capital expenditures. The Supreme Court said in Commissioner v. Idaho Power Co.[23] that "[t]here can be little question that ... construction-related expense items, such as tools, materials, and wages paid construction workers, are to be treated as part of the cost of acquisition of a capital asset."[24] With regard to depreciation for equipment that the taxpayer owned and used in the construction of its own facilities, the Court held that section 263(a) bars deduction, explaining that "[i]t serves to prevent a taxpayer from utilizing currently a deduction properly attributable, through amortization, to later tax years when the capital asset becomes income producing."[25]

Outlays as part of a general renovation of a building normally are characterized as capital expenditures. For example, in Stoeltzing v. Commissioner[26] the taxpayer expended $22,000 in renovating a building

---

v. United States, 171 Ct.Cl. 580, 347 F.2d 275 (1965); Marsh Fork Coal Co. v. Lucas, 42 F.2d 83 (4th Cir. 1930).

21. 14 T.C. 635 (1950), acq., 1950–2 C.B. 3. Accord Oberman Mfg. Co. v. Commissioner, 47 T.C. 471 (1967), acq., 1967–2 C.B. 3, in which the cost of over $20,000 for inserting an expansion joint in the roof of leased premises and for removing and replacing the roof covering was allowed as an expense because the purpose was to prevent leakage rather than to increase the useful life or value of the property.

22. 25 T.C. 272 (1955), aff'd *per curiam*, 238 F.2d 85 (6th Cir. 1956). See also TAM 9719007.

23. 418 U.S. 1, 94 S.Ct. 2757, 41 L.Ed.2d 535 (1974). See also TAM 200521032; TAM 200512021.

24. 418 U.S. 1, 13, 94 S.Ct. 2757, 2765 (1974).

25. 418 U.S. 1, 16, 94 S.Ct. 2757, 2766 (1974). Section 263A, provides, in pertinent part, for the capitalization of the costs of "[r]eal or tangible personal property produced by the taxpayer." See § 263A(a), (b)(1).

26. 266 F.2d 374 (3d Cir. 1959). Accord Mountain Fuel Supply Co. v. United States, 449 F.2d 816 (10th Cir. 1971), cert. denied, 405 U.S. 989, 92 S.Ct. 1251, 31 L.Ed.2d 455 (1972); United States v. Wehrli, 400 F.2d 686 (10th Cir. 1968), in which the Tenth Circuit concluded that it was an error for the trial court to refuse to rule that if the jury found that the amounts were paid for a general reconditioning, the total was not

he had purchased for $11,000. The taxpayer was required to capitalize the entire amount even though the work included the costs of repairs and rubbish removal, items that standing alone would constitute deductible expenses.

As a general proposition, alterations and improvements made by lessees are subject to the principle that requires capitalization of betterments that improve the value of property. However, the betterment is to be determined with respect to the leasehold estate rather than the reversion. Thus, if a lease requires the lessee to surrender the premises in as good a condition as reasonable use permits, a question may arise concerning what is required of the lessee regarding improvements. In Hotel Kingkade v. Commissioner[27] the lease for a hotel contained such a provision. The court held that the provision did not require expenditures totaling $19,000 for the replacement of carpets, heating and plumbing fixtures, kitchen equipment, and a roof. Consequently, the taxpayer-lessee was required to capitalize the cost of these items.

On the other hand, in Journal–Tribune Publishing Co. v. Commissioner[28] the taxpayer was a lessee under a 99–year lease requiring that it maintain the leased printing plant in the condition it was in at the time the lessee took over. In allowing the taxpayer to expense the cost of replacing printing presses (but not the cost of new color equipment), the court, in effect, applied a maintenance of normal output standard. It reasoned that such an expense did not benefit or increase the value of the leasehold since the taxpayer was without the right to sell its leased rights of publication and that mere replacement of presses was to assure performance of the "obligation to continue publication and to protect the lessors' rights of reversion."

[5] ACQUISITION AND DEFENSE OF TITLE

The costs of acquiring, perfecting, or defending title to property are treated as additional capital costs of the property and may not be deducted under either section 162 or section 212. Many of the litigated cases have involved the characterization of legal and litigation expenses when some personal nature of the outlay has also been involved. For this reason legal expenses are treated separately in Chapter 11, *Tax Issues Related to Litigation Recoveries and Settlements*, at § 11.02.

As a preliminary matter to consideration of the fine line that has sometimes been drawn between title acquisition costs and deductible expenses, a distinction must be made between an expense incurred to maintain an asset and the cost of acquiring an asset. Only the former is deductible. Thus, in Stevens v. Commissioner[29] the court denied the

---

deductible even though certain of the expenditures standing alone might qualify as deductible incidental repairs

27. 180 F.2d 310 (10th Cir. 1950). See also Field Service Advisory, 1996 WL 33107174; Field Service Advisory, 1995 WL 1918295; Field Service Advisory, 1993 WL 1469609.

28. 348 F.2d 266 (8th Cir. 1965). Accord Journal–Tribune Publishing Co. v. Commissioner, 216 F.2d 138 (8th Cir. 1954).

29. 388 F.2d 298 (6th Cir. 1968), aff'g 46 T.C. 492 (1966).

maintenance expenses of a race horse that were incurred by the taxpayer because he acquired his one-half interest in the horse under an agreement to pay the full maintenance costs.

As in the case of improvements, the useful life test has been applied in drawing the line between deductible expenses and nondeductible acquisition costs. Consequently, as far back as 1935 the government announced that the costs of one-year baseball player contracts could be expensed. However, in Revenue Ruling 67–379[30] it reversed itself and held that such acquisition costs, including bonuses paid to players, must be capitalized. The Service reasoned that the club acquired an asset extending substantially beyond a year because the reserve clause, then in use, gave the club the exclusive right to a player's services so long as he was capable of playing baseball and wanted to do so.

Acquisition costs that must be capitalized include, in addition to the cost of the asset itself, expenditures that are an integral part of the acquisition. This may mean that sometimes items that are normally treated as recurring expenses must be capitalized just as the total of general renovation expenditures must be capitalized. For example, in Revenue Ruling 70–332[31] the Service concluded that premium time or overtime wages paid solely to expedite the installation of additional machinery in a steel plant must be capitalized. The Service observed that the plant was operating at capacity, that the additional equipment enabled the plant to earn substantially more than would have been earned without the accelerated installation, and that capitalization was required even though the expenditures did not add value or life to the machinery installed.

The capitalization of costs incurred in the acquisition of a proprietary interest was addressed by the Supreme Court in Commissioner v. Lincoln Savings & Loan Association.[32] The taxpayer sought a deduction for premium payments made to a reserve fund of the FSLIC. The taxpayer's contributions were found to create a proprietary interest in the fund because the insured had the right, under certain conditions, to transfer, receive a cash refund, or earn an annual credit on its pro rata share of the fund. The Court said that whether the taxpayer received a future benefit from the fund did not control the question of whether the expenditures constituted an expense. It reasoned that many deductible expenses have an effect in subsequent taxable years. In deciding that the payments were capital in nature, the Court held that the controlling factor is whether "payment serves to create or enhance ... what is

30. 1967–2 C.B. 127, revoking Rev. Rul. 54–441, 1954–2 C.B. 101, I.T. 4078, 1952–1 C.B. 39, I.T. 2932, XIV–2 C.B. 61 (1935). See also Field Service Advisory, 1994 WL 1725534; TAM 9303002; William H. Baker, Taxation and Professional Sports—A Look Inside the Huddle, 9 Marq. Sports L.J. 287 (1999).

31. 1970–1 C.B. 31. See also Rev. Rul. 70–26, 1970–1 C.B. 55, in which the Service required a real estate title company to capitalize purchased title files even though half were duplicates of the taxpayer's own files and to this extent did not add to the value of the taxpayer's assets.

32. 403 U.S. 345, 91 S.Ct. 1893, 29 L.Ed.2d 519 (1971), rev'g, 422 F.2d 90 (9th Cir. 1970), rev'g, 51 T.C. 82 (1968). See also TAM 200521032; TAM 200517030.

essentially a separate and distinct additional asset;"[33] since the premium payments gave the taxpayer a proprietary interest in the fund, the amounts were not a deductible expense.

Advertising expenses, like salary and wage costs, are normally currently deductible. The Service has not attempted to require capitalization, unless tangible property is acquired, even if the benefits of the advertising extend over more than one year.[34]

In Woodward v. Commissioner[35] the Supreme Court, as discussed in the following section, held that costs incurred in appraising the value of shares of minority shareholders, when they exercised their right to be bought out, constituted capital expenditures in the acquisition of title to shares.

The expansion of a business into new product lines or into new geographic areas has created difficulties for the courts in deciding whether the amounts expended fall under section 162 or section 263. Generally, if the costs are incurred in the acquisition of an existing trade or business or in entering into a new business different from that already engaged in by the taxpayer, the costs must be capitalized.

In Robertson v. Commissioner[36] the court held that an amount paid by a manufacturer's sales representative for customer lists and exclusive agency rights to represent a manufacturer in a state constituted a nondeductible capital expenditure. The court reasoned that the customer lists had a value in the business of greater than one year. The representation rights were an exclusive sales agency for products in a state that the taxpayer had not previously served and therefore amounted to the acquisition of a business.

In Leisure Dynamics, Inc. v. Commissioner[37] the taxpayer paid for the right to manufacture and market a line of dolls in the likeness of characters known as "Gumby" and "Gumby's Pal, Pokey" that appeared in a television cartoon series. The issue was whether the payment for the right amounted to a purchase of property, in which case it would be a nondeductible capital expenditure, or whether it was a royalty pursuant to a licensing agreement, in which case the payment would be deductible as a section 162 business expense. For an amount to qualify as a royalty, the Tax Court said that the transferor must retain substantial rights in,

33. 403 U.S. 345, 354, 91 S.Ct. 1893, 1899, 29 L.Ed.2d 519 (1971).

34. With respect to the acquisition of tangible property, see E. H. Sheldon & Co. v. Commissioner, 214 F.2d 655 (6th Cir. 1954) (catalogues); Alabama Coca–Cola Bottling Co. v. Commissioner, T.C. Memo. 1969–123 (sign, clocks, and scoreboards); Rev. Rul. 68–360, 1968–2 C.B. 197 (catalogues). See also Cleveland Elec. Illuminating Co. v. United States, 7 Cl.Ct. 220 (1985) (the cost of an advertising campaign undertaken in connection with the construction and operation of a nuclear facility was a capital expenditure).

35. 397 U.S. 572, 90 S.Ct. 1302, 25 L.Ed.2d 577 (1970). See also TAM 200502039.

36. 61 T.C. 727 (1974). See also FSA 199941008; Field Service Advisory, 1992 WL 1354730; Field Service Advisory, 1992 WL 1466092.

37. 494 F.2d 1340 (8th Cir. 1974). See also William M. Shaheen, Tax Planning for the Transfer Of Franchises, Trademarks, and Trade Names, 28 J. Corp. Tax'n 11 (2001).

or control over, property so that the interest remains vested in the transferor. The Tax Court found that the rights acquired by the taxpayer amounted to a purchase of an interest. In reversing, the Eighth Circuit found that the manufacturing and marketing rights to the dolls were interrelated with the title and actual control of the cartoon series. The rights were relatively worthless if the series was not regularly exhibited. The Eighth Circuit reasoned that retention of the film rights resulted in the transferor retaining substantial control over the marketing of the dolls. When coupled with the taxpayer's agreement to make continuing payments based on the volume of sales, the arrangement was held to be a transaction for the use of property retained by the seller; thus, the amount was merely a licensing fee and currently deductible.

[6] INVESTIGATORY EXPENDITURES

After the Supreme Court's decision in INDOPCO, Inc. v. Commissioner,[38] there is little doubt left in how investigatory expenditures must be treated for federal income tax purposes—they must be capitalized.[39]

Moreover, investigatory costs associated with the acquisition of an asset are also capital expenditures.[40] Amounts paid for investment advice are likewise capitalized if directly related to the acquisition of an asset.

[7] START–UP EXPENDITURES

Section 195 generally provides for the deduction of up to $5,000[41] of start-up expenditures; any remaining start-up expenditures are amortized over 180 months.[42]

§ 4.08 LEGAL EXPENSES

For a complete discussion of legal expenses, see § 11.02, *infra*.

§ 4.09 COMPENSATION FOR PERSONAL SERVICES

Section 162(a)(1) provides that a taxpayer may deduct the ordinary and necessary expenses in carrying on a trade or business, including "a reasonable allowance for salaries or other compensation for personal

---

38. 503 U.S. 79, 112 S.Ct. 1039, 117 L.Ed.2d 226 (1992).

39. Treas. Reg. § 1.263(a)–5(a). See also Dominic L. Daher and Robert W. Wood, INDOPCO Era of Uncertainty Comes to a Close, M & A TAX REPORT, Vol. 12, No. 12, p. 7 (CCH July 2004).

40. See, e.g., Ellis Banking Corp. v. Commissioner, 688 F.2d 1376 (11th Cir. 1982), in which the taxpayer acquired the stock of another bank and sought to deduct the costs of examination of the acquired bank's books incurred prior to making the

investment decision. The court held that even though the expenses were incurred prior to any commitment by the bank, they were nonetheless allocable to the purchase since the investment decision was affirmative.

41. This $5,000 amount is reduced (but not below zero) for every dollar in excess of $50,000 spent by the taxpayer on start-up expenditures.

42. § 195(b)(1)(A) and (B).

services actually rendered."[1] The courts have identified and applied a number of factors to determine whether compensation is reasonable and thus deductible, with no single factor being decisive of the reasonableness question. The factors include the following: (1) the education, experience, and responsibilities of the payee, (2) the amount paid in relation to profits, (3) the time compensation was fixed, (4) the relation of the payments to stockholdings, (5) the dividend history of a corporate employer, (6) the time the payee devoted to the business, and (7) the amount paid comparable persons in comparable businesses.[2] Other factors, such as family relationships[3] and whether an employment relationship existed, may bear on the threshold question of whether payment was compensation for personal services, a gift, or a dividend.[4] Thus, many if not most of the problems in this area involve closely held corporations that use the deduction for compensation for services as a means of eliminating or minimizing corporate tax liability.[5] The compensation of executives of publicly-held companies are rarely, if ever, challenged for reasonableness by the Internal Revenue Service.[6]

§ 4.09

1. Brawerman & Racine, Corporate Compensation: The Client's Compensation is More Reasonable Than he Thinks, 33 U. So. Cal. Inst. Fed. Tax'n 11 (1981); Englebrecht & Windlinger, Justifying Reasonable Compensation for Executives of Closely Held Corporations, 31 Tax Executive 321 (1978); Ford & Page, Reasonable Compensation: Continuous Controversy, J. Corp. Tax'n 307 (1979); Blanc & Victor, Unreasonable Compensation, 28 U. So. Cal. Inst. Fed. Tax'n 281 (1976).

2. See, e.g., Palmetto Pump & Irrigation Co. v. Tomlinson, 9 A.F.T.R.2d 1136 (S.D. Fla. 1962), aff'd per curiam, 313 F.2d 220 (5th Cir. 1963). The court listed nine factors in detailed instructions to the jury in what might be regarded as a typical close corporation compensation case. The jury upheld the IRS' reduction from $30,700 to $20,000 for two corporate employees. See also Elliotts, Inc. v. Commissioner, 716 F.2d 1241 (9th Cir. 1983).

3. See, e.g., Transport Mfg. & Equip. Co. v. Commissioner, 434 F.2d 373 (8th Cir. 1970), in which the Eighth Circuit upheld the Tax Court in disallowing amounts in excess of $15,000 paid to a corporate president whose father dictated policy of two family owned corporations.

4. See, e.g., Alicia Ruth, Inc. v. Commissioner, 421 F.2d 1393 (5th Cir. 1970), in which the court disallowed deductions for the full amount paid the 50% owner as "salary" for lack of proof of the extent to which his only services (steering customers into a retail store) contributed to sales. In affirming, the Court of Appeals simply stat-

ed that "no employment relationship was established." See also Kennedy v. Commissioner, 671 F.2d 167 (6th Cir. 1982), in which the Sixth Circuit overturned the Tax Court's finding of unreasonable compensation. Among several factors the Sixth Circuit cited for its finding of reasonableness was the extent of the employee's trade association, civic, and charitable activities in such organizations as the American Warehousemen's Association, the American Cancer Society, and the Rotary Club. The court said that the employee's activities increased the company's reputation and stature among its customers and in the local business community. The court held that because the employee's participation benefited the company, such activity should be considered a factor indicating the reasonableness of the compensation.

5. In Alicia Ruth, Inc. v. Commissioner, 421 F.2d 1393 (5th Cir. 1970), the taxpayer reported operating losses for four out of five years and a $1,000 gain in the fifth year that reflected claimed "salary" deductions for payments to its 50% owner ranging from $7,650 to $18,550.

6. But see § 280G that makes any excessive payment under a "golden-parachute" agreement nondeductible. A "golden-parachute" agreement calls for payment to an officer, shareholder, or highly compensated employee contingent on a change in ownership or control of a corporation or in a significant portion of a corporation's assets. See also Dominic L. Daher, Golden Parachutes of a Different Color? Square D Goes to "Excess," M & A TAX REPORT, Vol. 12, No. 5, p. 1 (CCH Dec. 2003).

The burden of proof facing the taxpayer may be even more acute when the corporate employer has paid little or no dividends. The Service warned in Revenue Ruling 79–8[7] that "the failure of a closely held corporation to pay more than an insubstantial portion of its earnings as dividends on its stock is a very significant factor to be taken into account in determining the deductibility of compensation paid by the corporation to its shareholder-employees." The ruling adds, however, that if:

> [A]fter an examination of all of the facts and circumstances (including the corporation's dividend history) compensation paid to shareholder-employees is found to be reasonable in amount and paid for services rendered, deduction for such compensation under section 162(a) will not be denied on the sole ground that the corporation has not paid more than an insubstantial portion of its earnings as dividends on its outstanding stock.[8]

Apart from the frequent need to negate possible dividend characterization, at the heart of the taxpayer's burden of proof is the need to show what was actually done by the recipient. Thus, if an owner-employee's services are unique, the full amount claimed as a compensation deduction has frequently been upheld.

For example, in Home Interiors & Gifts, Inc.[9] the Tax Court said that while the compensation received by two employees exceeded that paid to the Chief Executive Officers of many other corporations with much larger sales, more employees, and greater profits, "in view of the extraordinary services" they earned their compensation. One of the employees, Mary Crowley, formed the corporation in 1957 to engage in the direct sale of home decorations and accessories by use of the "hostess plan," whereby products were sold in homes of cooperating "hostesses." She served as president and sales manager from the outset. For the five years (1971–1975) her compensation was $570,000, $935,000, $1,083,000, $1,557,000 and $1,137,000. Another employee, Mary Crowley's son, received compensation of $457,000, $748,000, $1,081,000, $1,361,000 and $1,136,000 for the five years. He served as Executive Vice President, responsible for the design, purchase, distribution, and pricing of merchandise. Writing for the Tax Court, Judge Simpson said: "[T]he amounts of compensation paid the officers of Home Interiors were very large, but their efforts produced extraordinary results for Home Interiors and everyone connected with it. However measured, the success of Home Interiors was very impressive."[10] He observed that Mary Crowley recruited a sales organization of over 17,000, with little turnover in personnel, and motivated the organization to produce exceptional re-

7. 1979–1 C.B. 92.

8. For the "automatic dividend rule" under which an element of a disguised dividend will be presumed if a profitable corporation pays no formal dividends, see Charles McCandless Tile Service v. United States, 191 Ct.Cl. 108, 422 F.2d 1336 (1970). The rule was rejected in Elliotts, Inc. v. Commissioner, 716 F.2d 1241 (9th Cir. 1983).

9. 73 T.C. 1142 (1980). See also Field Service Advisory, 1997 WL 33313661; Andrew W. Stumpff, The Reasonable Compensation Rule, 19 Va. Tax Rev. 371, 402 (1999).

10. 73 T.C. 1142, 1157 (1980).

sults. Her son also made immense contributions to the success of Home Interiors.

On the other hand, when management functions are turned over to outsiders for which deductible expenses are allowed, there may be little to justify a deduction for substantial salaries paid the owners. In Langley Park Apartments, Sec. C, Inc. v. Commissioner[11] the taxpayer-corporation, owned by its officers, a husband and wife, turned over the management of its apartment houses to a real estate management company that charged a fee of 3% of the gross rental. The officers made withdrawals during the year that were charged to loan accounts. At the end of the year the loan accounts were charged to salary. For one of the three years involved the taxpayer claimed a deduction of $8,000 for the husband's salary and $6,300 for the wife's. Testimony of the husband indicated that as President of the company, he kept some personal records of expenditures, visited the property two or three times a month, contacted the management firm weekly, made decisions concerning painting and repairs, and signed a few corporate checks. The wife had no regular duties. The Tax Court upheld the Commissioner's allowance of a salary of $1,500 for the husband and nothing for the wife. Despite annual gross rentals of $125,000 to $136,000 for a five-year period, the court said that the corporation could hardly expect to deduct substantial salaries for officer's management services when the only important decision the President had made was to delegate almost all the actual management to the outside firm. The wife's services were regarded as de minimis.

Undoubtedly the greatest difficulty in applying the factors listed at the beginning of this section has arisen in cases involving percentages of sales, receipts, or net profits compensation arrangements. When the evidence reveals that such percentage compensation agreements have been made at arm's length, most courts have been reluctant to use hindsight in judging the reasonableness of the amount paid and have said that the analysis of what is reasonable should be made from the viewpoint of when the contract was made. Thus, in Robert Rogers, Inc. v. United States[12] an employee on a $14,000 annual salary was given a contract for $8,000 plus 1% of net profits when he took over as manager of the taxpayer. Business increased more than had been anticipated, and under the contract the taxpayer earned $177,000. It was allowed in full as a reasonable amount.

The regulations provide that the circumstances are to be viewed from the time the contract is made, and percentage arrangements will not result in disallowance even if the amount of compensation turns out to be higher than would ordinarily be paid.[13] However, this is conditioned upon the existence of a "free bargain," thereby providing the opportuni-

11. 44 T.C. 474 (1965), aff'd *per curiam*, 359 F.2d 427 (4th Cir. 1966). Cf. S & B Realty Co., 54 T.C. 863 (1970), in which the use of an outside management firm did not prevent the allowance of a $5,000 salary paid to the taxpayer's president-owner, the taxpayer having reported $7,300 of taxable income from rent.

12. 118 Ct.Cl. 126, 93 F.Supp. 1014 (1950). See also Kennedy v. Commissioner, 671 F.2d 167 (6th Cir. 1982).

13. Treas. Reg. § 1.162–7(b).

ty for a court to examine a percentage arrangement.[14] For example, in Harolds Club v. Commissioner[15] the corporate taxpayer, a Nevada gambling establishment, gave a managerial contract to the father of the taxpayer's two owners. The contract, which was made in 1941, provided for a $10,000 annual salary and 20% of the net profits, a common practice in the business. The father had taken over the management from his two sons in 1935 when the club was not doing well. As a result of the father's management, the club grew and prospered. During 1952–1956, the tax years involved, the taxpayer had annual net income ranging from $1.4 million to $2.1 million, and the amounts paid to the father-manager ranged from $350,000 to $550,000 annually.

The Tax Court applied the "free bargain" requirement of the regulations and disallowed the amounts in excess of the fixed salary plus 15% of the profits. It found that when the contract was entered into the dominance of the father over the sons was such that his will prevailed on most matters, and he had suggested the 20% contract. The Tax Court reasoned that it was therefore proper to examine the question of reasonableness from the standpoint of the time of payment. On appeal, the taxpayer did not challenge the determination of reasonableness, but argued that there was no basis for the finding of lack of a free bargain since the sons were competent adults at all times. The Ninth Circuit, however, upheld the Tax Court, determining that the regulations correctly interpreted the Code, and the record supported the finding of a lack of a free bargain.

§ 4.10 TRAVEL EXPENSES

[1] IN GENERAL

Section 162(a)(2) limits deductions for business travel expenses to those incurred "while away from home in the pursuit of a trade or business," but expressly includes amounts "expended for meals and lodging other than amounts which are lavish or extravagant under the circumstances."[1] The express reference to meals and lodging came into the statute in 1921 at the request of the Department of the Treasury in order to eliminate the problems of administering a prior regulation that limited travel expense deductions to amounts expended in excess of those "ordinarily required for such purposes when at home."[2]

---

14. Id.

15. 340 F.2d 861 (9th Cir. 1965). See also Hammond Lead Prods., Inc. v. Commissioner, 425 F.2d 31 (7th Cir. 1970), in which the court upheld the disallowance of compensation paid an owner-executive to the extent of the amount yielded by a dollar-a-ton-of-sales provision.

§ 4.10

1. Weber & Outslay, A House is Not Necessarily a Tax Home: An Examination

of the Deductibility of Away-from-Home Expenses, 65 Taxes 275 (1987). As a general rule, under § 274(n) only 50% of any expense for food and beverages is deductible.

2. T.D. 3101, amending Treas. Reg. § 45, art. 292, 3 C.B. 191 (1920). See Mim. 2698, 4 C.B. 209 (1921), for the formula used in computing the deductible excess.

The "lavish or extravagant" limitation was a product of the Revenue Act of 1962, which undertook to overhaul completely the deductions allowed for travel and entertainment. Presumably Congress did not intend to disallow the entire amount if the expenses are "lavish or extravagant" but only that portion which is unreasonable. The Revenue Act of 1962 also imposed the substantiation requirements of section 274(d) on travel expenses.[3]

If a trip involves both business and personal activities, proration may be permitted. However, proration is limited to expenses other than those for transportation. The deductibility of transportation expenses is wholly dependent upon the *primary or dominant purpose* of the trip. Thus, if the primary purpose of a trip is personal, no part of the expenses for transportation is allowed.[4]

Special allocation rules are provided in section 274(c) for foreign travel. However, if a trip outside the United States lasts for less than one week or less than 25% of the taxpayer's time is devoted to personal pursuits, allocation is not required.

[2] THE TAX HOME CONCEPT

The term "while away from home" has been a feature of the expense deduction provisions for countless decades. Therefore, it is perhaps surprising that the meaning of the word "home" remains unsettled.[5] Some of this uncertainty may be attributed to what the Supreme Court said as distinguished from what it held in the leading case of Commissioner v. Flowers.[6] There the taxpayer, a lawyer employed by a railroad, lived in a city 250 miles from his business office in Mobile, Alabama. He incurred expenses for travel, meals, and lodging when business required him to stay overnight in Mobile. In reversing the Tax Court the Fifth Circuit held that the Tax Court had erroneously construed "home" to mean place of business because Congress meant "home" as the place where the taxpayer resides.

The Supreme Court reinstated the Tax Court's judgment. The Court noted a conflict between the appellate courts and also a consistent interpretation as business home by the Tax Court and the government, but it stated that it deemed "it unnecessary here to enter into or to decide this conflict." The Court predicated its reversal of the Court of Appeals on the ground that the expenses were not incurred in pursuit of the employer's business. The Court said that the taxpayer's expenses between his residence and business office were irrelevant to the carrying on of the employer railroad's business and that deductible travel ex-

---

3. For additional rules regarding travel expenses, see § 274(c) (foreign travel), § 274(h) (conventions, seminars, and similar meetings), § 274(m) (luxury water transportation and travel as a form of education).

4. See Treas. Reg. § 1.162–2.

5. See Note, The Tax Home Doctrine: Fifty–Five Years of Confusion, 34 Maine L. Rev. 141 (1982); Note, Section 162(a)(2): Resolving the Tax Home Dispute, 2 Va. Tax Rev. 153 (1982).

6. 326 U.S. 465, 66 S.Ct. 250, 90 L.Ed. 203 (1946). See also Tsilly Dagan, Commuting, 26 Va. Tax Rev. 185, 244 (2006).

penses within the meaning of what is now section 162(a) "could arise only when the railroad's business forced the taxpayer to travel and to live temporarily at some place other than Mobile."[7] Business trips, the Court said, "are to be identified in relation to business demands and the traveler's business headquarters."[8]

Flowers clearly stands for the basic proposition that the cost of going to and from work is not deductible.[9] Further, despite the Court's avowed refusal to decide the locus of "home," the case lends support to the position of the Service that the term "home" means the traveler's business headquarters. While the Service,[10] the Tax Court,[11] and most Circuit Courts of Appeals[12] have generally adopted the principal place of business or employment interpretation of "home," the Court of Appeals for the Second Circuit said in Rosenspan v. United States[13] that the word should be given its ordinary meaning. Rosenspan involved an itinerant traveling jewelry salesman; he was employed by New York City manufacturers and spent 300 days a year on the road, returning to New York City five or six times a year to perform certain tasks in connection with his sales work. Although Rosenspan occasionally used his brother's home in Brooklyn as a personal residence, voted there, and filed tax returns from there, he did not claim Brooklyn as a tax home. Instead he contended that, in line with the Service's position, New York was his business headquarters and tax home. Therefore, he reasoned that while on the road he was "away from home."

The Second Circuit affirmed the district court's denial of the deduction. Although it ultimately predicated its decision on the fact that Rosenspan lacked a home to be away from, it used the occasion to reexamine the business headquarters concept of "home." Writing for the court, Judge Friendly reasoned that revenue could be as fully protected

7. 326 U.S. 465, 474, 66 S.Ct. 250, 254 (1946).

8. Id.

9. See, e.g., McCabe v. Commissioner, 688 F.2d 102 (2d Cir.1982), cert. denied, 459 U.S. 906, 103 S.Ct. 208, 74 L.Ed.2d 166 (1982); Kasun v. United States, 671 F.2d 1059 (7th Cir. 1982).

10. See G.C.M. 23672, 1943 C.B. 66; Rev. Rul. 75–432, 1975–2 C.B. 60.

11. See, e.g, Lee E. Daly, 72 T.C. 190 (1979), rev'd, 631 F.2d 351 (4th Cir. 1980), rev'd en banc, 662 F.2d 253 (4th Cir. 1981).

12. See, e.g., Markey v. Commissioner, 490 F.2d 1249 (6th Cir. 1974); Curtis v. Commissioner, 449 F.2d 225 (5th Cir. 1971); Chimento v. Commissioner, 438 F.2d 643 (3d Cir. 1971); Wills v. Commissioner, 411 F.2d 537 (9th Cir. 1969); England v. United States, 345 F.2d 414 (7th Cir. 1965), cert. denied, 382 U.S. 986, 86 S.Ct. 537, 15 L.Ed.2d 475 (1966); Barnhill v. Commissioner, 148 F.2d 913 (4th Cir. 1945). The First Circuit has observed, however: "The

meaning of the word 'home' in the travel expense provision is far from clear. When Congress enacted the travel expense deduction now codified as section 162(a)(2), it apparently was unsure whether, to be deductible, an expense must be incurred away from a person's residence or away from his principal place of business.... This ambiguity persists and courts, sometimes within a single circuit, have divided over the issue." Hantzis v. Commissioner, 638 F.2d 248 (1st Cir. 1981), cert. denied, 452 U.S. 962, 101 S.Ct. 3112, 69 L.Ed.2d 973 (1981).

13. 438 F.2d 905 (2d Cir. 1971), cert. denied, 404 U.S. 864, 92 S.Ct. 54, 30 L.Ed.2d 108 (1971), aff'g, 316 F.Supp. 194 (E.D. N.Y. 1970). See also John A. Lynch, Jr., Travel Expense Deductions Under I.R.C. § 162(a)(2)—What Part of "Home" Don't You Understand?, 57 Baylor L. Rev. 705 (2005); William H. Baker, Home & Away: A Tax Definition for Athletes, 2 Va. J. Sports & L. 104 (2000).

without distortion of the term "home" by applying the condition laid down in Flowers "that there must be a direct connection between the expenditure and the carrying on of the trade or business of the taxpayer or of his employer."[14] He said that most of the cases endorsing the business headquarters test, including those discussed below under the temporary-indefinite rule, could be explained on the basis that the taxpayer had no permanent residence, was not away from it, or maintained it at a locale apart from where he worked as a matter of personal choice. Therefore, the Second Circuit rejected the need of searching for a "fictional tax home," and instead it tested the claimed deductions by the "business necessity for incurring the expense away from the taxpayer's permanent residence."[15] This would not upset the basic structure of past decisions but would provide a "sounder conceptual framework for analysis while following the ordinary meaning of language."[16]

In Rosenspan the Second Circuit reasoned that the term "away from home" ("home" meaning residence) could not be read out of the statute as in effect contended by the taxpayer. The Second Circuit thought that the term reflected congressional recognition of the rational distinction between taxpayers whose travel expenses represent duplicative costs and those whose expenses do not. Moreover, the taxpayer failed to show such duplicative costs, because occasional visits to New York City, even if it qualified as a business headquarters, placed the taxpayer in no different position than the homeless traveling salesperson without even the modicum of a business headquarters.

As indicated in the Rosenspan opinion, the courts have fairly consistently denied itinerant salesmen and other taxpayers without a genuine business headquarters or permanent residence deductions for travel expenses because of the lack of duplicative costs. However, if an itinerant taxpayer can show such duplicative expenses, the cost of travel may be allowed even though the amount of the at-home expenses do not approach those incurred in business travel. For example, in Sapson v. Commissioner[17] the taxpayer, a traveling salesman, had his legal residence (a room in his sister's home for which he paid $50 a month) and his employer's place of business in the same city. The Commissioner contended that the claimed travel deductions of $6,600 and $5,500 for the two tax years should be disallowed for lack of "substantial continuing living expenses at a permanent place of residence."[18] The Tax Court disagreed. The court admitted that the amount of the payment was a relevant factor in determining whether it was for a permanent abode, but once that fact was established, the court reasoned, it would only add to the confusion of an already confused area to consider the cost of the taxpayer's permanent headquarters.

14. 438 F.2d 905, 909 (2d Cir. 1971).

15. 438 F.2d 905, 911 (2d Cir. 1971).

16. 438 F.2d 905, 912 (2d Cir. 1971).

17. 49 T.C. 636 (1968). See also See also John A. Lynch, Jr., Travel Expense Deductions Under I.R.C. § 162(a)(2)—What Part Of "Home" Don't You Understand?, 57 Baylor L. Rev. 705 (2005); William H. Baker, Home & Away: A Tax Definition for Athletes, 2 Va. J. Sports & L. 104 (2000).

18. 49 T.C. 636, 640 (1968).

The Service has issued a revenue ruling setting forth criteria to assist in the determination of whether a taxpayer maintains a home or is merely an itinerant worker.[19] The revenue ruling lists three objective factors to determine whether the residence is the taxpayer's "regular place of abode in a real and substantial sense." They are the following: (1) whether the taxpayer performs a portion of his business in the vicinity of his claimed abode and uses such abode for lodging; (2) whether the taxpayer's living expenses incurred at his claimed abode are duplicated because his business requires that he be away; and (3) whether the taxpayer (a) has not abandoned the vicinity of his historical place of lodging and claimed abode, (b) has his family (marital or lineal) residing at his claimed abode, or (c) frequently uses his claimed abode for lodging. If the taxpayer satisfies all three factors, the Service will recognize that the taxpayer has a "home" for traveling expense deduction purposes. If the taxpayer satisfies two of the three factors, the Service will closely scrutinize the facts and circumstances to determine whether the taxpayer has a "regular place of abode in a real and substantial sense." If the taxpayer cannot satisfy at least two of the three factors, he will be regarded as an itinerant.

Apart from Sapson v. Commissioner, itinerant taxpayers have generally not fared well; the same cannot be said of taxpayers with two separate businesses. In such a situation deductions have been allowed for travel to and from a secondary or minor place of business.[20]

The situation of both spouses working at some distance from one another has led the Tax Court to conclude that each spouse may have a separate tax home.[21] In Foote v. Commissioner[22] a couple had a ranch thirty miles from Austin, Texas. The wife took a job with the Austin School District that required her to maintain an Austin address. The couple resided in Austin during the week and at the ranch on weekends, while the husband made daily trips during the week to the ranch to keep it operating. Because Austin was the wife's place of employment, the court concluded that Austin was her tax home, reasoning that a taxpayer's home must be considered in the vicinity of the place of employment. The court denied a deduction for the wife's travel expenses to and from Austin and her living expenses there. The court also denied a deduction for the husband's commuting expenses to and from the ranch, which the court determined to be the husband's place of business, and his living expenses in Austin. The court dismissed the couple's argument that it was unjust to find two tax homes merely because each spouse was employed at a distance from the other; it reasoned that the couple's

19. Rev. Rul. 73–529, 1973–2 C.B. 37. See also CCA 200242038; CCA 200020055; Field Service Advisory, 1993 WL 1609130.

20. See, e.g., Downs v. Commissioner, 49 T.C. 533 (1968), acq., 1968–2 C.B. 2; Chandler v. Commissioner, 226 F.2d 467 (1st Cir. 1955); Rev. Rul. 55–604, 1955–2 C.B. 49; CCA 200020055.

21. Foote v. Commissioner, 67 T.C. 1 (1976). See also See also See also John A. Lynch, Jr., Travel Expense Deductions Under I.R.C. § 162(a)(2)—What Part Of "Home" Don't You Understand?, 57 Baylor L. Rev. 705, 784 (2005).

22. 67 T.C. 1 (1976).

decision to maintain two jobs and live together was a personal decision and not one of business necessity.

[3] SLEEP–OR–REST RULE FOR MEALS

Early in the history of the "away from home" requirement the Service took the position, in the interest of administrative convenience, that a deduction for meals would not be allowed unless the taxpayer was away from home overnight.[23] Later, the Service said it would follow a decision of the Fifth Circuit allowing a deduction to a railroad conductor who on a turnaround run rented a hotel room for some rest. Thus, the Service's interpretation became known as the sleep-or-rest rule.[24]

In United States v. Correll[25] the Supreme Court accepted the sleep-or-rest rule as a reasonable exercise of the Commissioner's administrative powers. In that case the taxpayer was a traveling salesman who left his residence early in the morning and did not return until the evening, eating only his supper at his residence. He claimed deductions for breakfast and lunch. The Supreme Court stated that Congress, as evidenced in committee reports for the 1954 Code,[26] was well aware of the long-standing sleep-or-rest rule; therefore, it came within the reenactment doctrine. The Court disagreed with the Sixth Circuit, which found the words of the statute inconsistent with a sleep or rest requirement. The Supreme Court stated that the terms of the statute were hardly self-defining, and the coupling of "meals and lodging" suggested a congressional intent to allow a deduction for meals only when a traveler would incur significantly higher living expenses when it was necessary to stop for rest. The Court also felt that the rule provided substantial fairness by placing all one-day travelers, along with commuters, on a similar footing.

In Revenue Ruling 75–170[27] the Service said that for the sleep-or-rest rule the period during which employees are not performing their regular duties:

> [N]eed not be for an entire 24–hour day or throughout the hours from dusk until dawn, but it must be of such duration or nature that the taxpayers cannot reasonably be expected to complete the round trip without being released from duty, or otherwise stopping . . ., for sufficient time to obtain substantial sleep or rest.[28]

The Service cautioned that it:

> [D]oes not consider the brief interval during which employees may stop, or be released from duty, for sufficient time to eat, but not to

---

23. See I.T. 3395, 1940–2 C.B. 64, a ruling following prior administrative practice.

24. See Williams v. Patterson, 286 F.2d 333 (5th Cir. 1961); Rev. Rul. 61–221, 1961–2 C.B. 34.

25. 389 U.S. 299, 88 S.Ct. 445, 19 L.Ed.2d 537 (1967), rev'g, 369 F.2d 87 (6th Cir. 1966). See also Tsilly Dagan, Commuting, 26 Va. Tax Rev. 185, 244 (2006).

26. S. Rep. No. 1622, 83rd Cong., 2d Sess. 9 (1954).

27. 1975–1 C.B. 60.

28. Rev. Rul. 75–170, 1975–1 C.B. 60.

obtain substantial sleep or rest, as being an adequate rest period to satisfy the requirement for deducting the cost of meals on business trips completed within one day.[29]

[4] BULKY TOOLS OR MATERIALS

In Fausner v. Commissioner[30] a commercial airline pilot who regularly traveled by driving his automobile from his residence to the airport and back again attempted to deduct the entire cost of his local transportation under section 162(a) on the theory that his automobile expenses were incurred to transport his flight bag and overnight bag, and thus they were ordinary and necessary business expenses. It was not disputed that the taxpayer would have commuted by driving his automobile regardless of whether he had transported the bags. In a *per curiam* opinion the Supreme Court held that the taxpayer was not entitled to any deduction for the cost of transporting the bags in his automobile. The Court stated:

> Congress has determined that all taxpayers shall bear the expense of commuting ... without receiving a deduction.... We cannot read § 262 of the Internal Revenue Code as excluding such expense from 'personal' expenses because by happenstance the taxpayer must carry incidentals of his occupation with him.[31]

The Court added: "Additional expenses may at times be incurred for transporting job-required tools and material to and from work. Then such allocation of costs between 'personal' and 'business' expenses may be feasible."[32]

In Revenue Ruling 75–380[33] the Service interpreted the last two sentences quoted from Fausner in the preceding paragraphs. The Service said that additional transportation costs are deductible if the taxpayer can establish they were incurred in addition to ordinary commuting expenses, and such additional costs are attributable solely to the necessity of transporting work implements to and from the job. In Revenue Ruling 75–380 the Service gave an example of a taxpayer who commuted to and from work by public transportation for $2 a day. When the taxpayer had to carry necessary work implements, he drove his automobile, which cost him $3 a day, and rented a trailer for $5 a day. The Service concluded that the allowable deduction would be the $5 a day additional expense for the trailer.

[5] TEMPORARY—INDEFINITE RULE

Suppose an employee is sent on temporary assignment to another place or maintains a residence in one area but changes the location of employment to another area. In either situation the Service, the Tax

---

29. Id.

30. 413 U.S. 838, 93 S.Ct. 2820, 37 L.Ed.2d 996 (1973). See also Field Service Advisory, 1998 WL 1984391; Field Service Advisory, 1992 WL 1466106.

31. 413 U.S. 838, 838 93 S.Ct. 2820, 2821 (1973).

32. Id.

33. 1975–2 C.B. 59. See also Field Service Advisory, 1992 WL 1466106.

Court, and other courts adhering to the business headquarters concept of home have allowed a deduction for travel expenses provided the work is temporary as distinguished from indefinite. The theory supporting this temporary-indefinite rule is that the section 162(a)(2) deduction for travel is allowed in order to equalize the tax burden between employees required to travel and those not so required, and when work is temporary a taxpayer cannot be expected to move the home, as occurs when the work is of indefinite duration.

In Peurifoy v. Commissioner[34] the Supreme Court had an opportunity to provide guidelines but did not do so. Instead the Court chose to limit its decision to the issue of whether the Court of Appeals had made a fair assessment of the record in reversing the Tax Court.

In Peurifoy three construction workers claimed deductions while employed at work locations away from their residences for eight, twelve, and twenty months. The Fourth Circuit reversed the Tax Court and denied the deductions. The Supreme Court affirmed, holding that the Fourth Circuit's decision should stand under the general rule announced in Flowers that deductions are allowable only when required by "the exigencies of business."[35] However, the Supreme Court noted that the Tax Court had "engrafted an exception which allows a deduction for expenditures of the type made in this case when the taxpayer's employment is 'temporary' as contrasted with 'indefinite' or 'indeterminate,' "[36] and neither the Commissioner nor the Fourth Circuit had challenged this exception. Therefore, the Court found the issue was of a factual nature: whether the taxpayer's employment was temporary or indefinite. It held that the determination of the Court of Appeals that the Tax Court's finding was "clearly erroneous" was made on a fair assessment of the record. The Court thereby avoided endorsing the temporary-indefinite rule, and, for the second time, found no need to define the term "home."

The temporary-indefinite rule is applicable when an existing employee is transferred to a new business locale on less than a permanent basis.[37] In Commissioner v. Stidger[38] the taxpayer was a Marine Corps flier attached to a squadron stationed at El Toro, California, where he maintained a home and family. In October, 1957 the taxpayer, along with his contingent, was assigned to duty in Japan for fifteen months. The period of assignment was subject to extension. Marine Corps orders prohibited the taxpayer's family from accompanying him on the assign-

---

34. 358 U.S. 59, 79 S.Ct. 104, 3 L.Ed.2d 30 (1958). See also CCA 200020055.

35. 358 U.S. 59, 59, 79 S.Ct. 104, 105, 3 L.Ed.2d 30 (1958).

36. Id.

37. 386 U.S. 287, 87 S.Ct. 1065, 18 L.Ed.2d 53 (1967).

38. 386 U.S. 287, 87 S.Ct. 1065, 18 L.Ed.2d 53 (1967), rev'g 355 F.2d 294 (9th Cir. 1965), rev'g 40 T.C. 896 (1963), on the ground as discussed in the text that a military taxpayer's permanent duty station constitutes the tax home whether or not it is feasible to move the family to such station. The Service has ruled that a naval officer, assigned to permanent duty aboard a ship that has regular living and eating facilities, has his tax home aboard the ship rather than at the ship's home port. Rev. Rul. 67–438, 1967–2 C.B. 82.

ment; so they remained at home during the taxpayer's entire fifteen-month tour of duty. The Marine Corps regarded the taxpayer as having been assigned to a permanent station in Japan in the sense that he was not in "travel status." Consequently, while the taxpayer received free lodging at his post in Japan, he had to pay for his own meals and claimed a $650 deduction for them for 1958. The Tax Court denied the deduction on the ground that the taxpayer's tax home was his post in Japan because his stay there was indefinite and not temporary.

The Ninth Circuit reversed, stating as a rule that if it appears unreasonable to have expected the taxpayer to move his family the expenses claimed will qualify as ordinary and necessary business expenses. There was little difficulty in applying this rule to the facts since the taxpayer had no choice but to maintain a separate residence for his family in the United States.

In reversing, the Supreme Court, for the third time in 20 years, found it unnecessary to rule on the position of the Service and most courts that home means business headquarters in "all of its myriad applications." Instead, the Court held that a military taxpayer's permanent duty station was intended by Congress to constitute his home for purposes of determining deductibility of travel expenses. The Court reasoned that the statutory system of military allowances was designed to provide complete and direct relief for the burdens of military travel and if inadequate "it is the province of Congress and the Commissioner, not the courts, to make the appropriate adjustments."[39]

If a taxpayer changes his work locations frequently because of the nature of his employment, the Service will treat the city where the taxpayer resides with his family as his tax home. In Revenue Ruling 71–247[40] the taxpayer was employed by a public utility as a member of a maintenance crew covering a 12–state area. The taxpayer maintained a family residence in that area and was sent by a regional office not in the vicinity of the residence on temporary assignments. The Service said that the residence constituted the tax home, reasoning that all the facts and circumstances must be considered in determining the location of a taxpayer's home.

In Michaels v. Commissioner[41] the taxpayer, a cost analyst for Boeing Aircraft in Seattle, was assigned to Los Angeles in June 1964 for what his employer believed would be a one-year period. The taxpayer rented out his Seattle residence and took his family and part of his furniture with him. In March 1965 the taxpayer's Los Angeles assignment was made permanent. The taxpayer received $2,000 in per diem allowances (apparently only for himself) in 1964 from his employer, which he treated as an offset against away-from-home expenses. The Commissioner contended that the taxpayer should have reported the per

---

39. 386 U.S. 287, 295 87 S.Ct. 1065, 1071 (1967).

40. 1971–1 C.B. 54. See also TAM 9641003.

41. 53 T.C. 269 (1969). See also Leach v. Commissioner, 12 T.C. 20 (1949).

diem as income and taken a smaller moving expense deduction under section 217. The Tax Court disagreed; it held that the taxpayer was in temporary status away from his Seattle home until March 1965. The Tax Court reasoned that until then he intended to return to Seattle, and the expected period of one year was long enough to justify taking his family and short enough to justify retention of his home in Seattle. The Tax Court also stated that while absence of duplicative living expenses was an important factor, it was not determinative of deductibility, and the taxpayer still had substantial duplicative expenses.

Moreover, Revenue Ruling 93–86[42] provides in pertinent part:

> [I]f employment away from home in a single location is realistically expected to last (and does in fact last) for 1 year or less, the employment is temporary in the absence of facts and circumstances indicating otherwise. If employment away from home in a single location is realistically expected to last for more than 1 year or there is no realistic expectation that the employment will last for 1 year or less, the employment is indefinite, regardless of whether it actually exceeds 1 year. If employment away from home in a single location initially is realistically expected to last for 1 year or less, but at some later date the employment is realistically expected to exceed 1 year, that employment will be treated as temporary (in the absence of facts and circumstances indicating otherwise) until the date that the taxpayer's realistic expectation changes.[43]

[6] THE COMMUTER AND LACK OF NEARBY HOUSING

Some of the more difficult applications of the "away from home" limitation have involved situations in which, because of the lack of suitable living quarters, a taxpayer is required to commute a substantial distance. Most courts, relying upon Flowers, have denied deductions for such commuting expense and have refused to make any distinction on the basis of hardship. While these courts have not failed to recognize the sometimes arbitrary nature of the rule, they have pointed out, as the Supreme Court did in Correll with respect to the sleep-or-rest rule, that nondeductibility provides a rough equality in treatment for all taxpayers.

In Coombs v. Commissioner[44] the taxpayers were employees at a remote nuclear testing facility in the Nevada desert and resided in Las Vegas. The distance the taxpayers had to commute each day varied from 65 to 200 miles in one direction. While recognizing that the nearest community from the test site was 65 miles away, the court found commuting expenses to be personal and therefore not deductible.

[7] CONVENTIONS, MEETINGS, AND SPOUSES

In carefully guarded language the regulations recognize that expenses incurred in attending a convention or a meeting may qualify as

---

42. 1993–2 C.B. 71.

43. Rev. Rul. 93–86, 1993–2 C.B. 71. See also IRS CCA 200020055; Field Service Advisory, 1995 WL 1918325.

44. 67 T.C. 426 (1976) aff'd in part, rev'd in part, remanded in part, 608 F.2d 1269 (9th Cir. 1979).

deductible business expenses, whether the taxpayer is an employee or self-employed, provided "he is benefiting or advancing the interests of his trade or business by such attendance."[45] Under this rule most business and professional conventions and meetings qualify. A deduction will also be available for the expenses of a spouse (or other family member) if that person can be shown to have made a bona fide contribution to the advancement of the other person's trade or business.[46]

Social attributes may be enough in the right situation. In United States v. Disney[47] the taxpayer, CEO of a motion picture company with markets in 58 countries, was required by his job to travel extensively and to be accompanied by his wife whose expenses were reimbursed by the company. The taxpayer's mission on the domestic and foreign trips was to promote the image of the company as a producer of family-type films and to enhance the morale of company representatives and distributors. The taxpayer established that the presence of his wife was necessary in connection with the dinners, receptions, screenings, and meetings used to carry out his mission. These special circumstances, the Ninth Circuit held, were sufficient to establish that the dominant purpose of the wife's presence was the aid she provided her husband. Hence, her expenses were deductible.

Since the Ninth Circuit's holding in Disney, Congress has enacted section 274(m)(3) which further limits business expenses incurred by spouses, dependents, or others traveling with the taxpayer. Section 274(m)(3)[48] provides:

45. Treas. Reg. § 1.162–2(d).

46. Treas. Reg. § 1.162–2(c).

47. 413 F.2d 783 (9th Cir. 1969). Cf. Sanitary Farms Dairy, Inc., 25 T.C. 463 (1955), acq., 1956–2 C.B. 8, in which the court allowed business expense deductions to a dairy for the $16,000 cost of an African safari undertaken by the corporation's president and his wife, both hunting enthusiasts. The trip was extensively and successfully exploited in various dairy product advertising campaigns during the couple's six months absence and after their return. Although the Commissioner asserted a deficiency against the President and his wife for failure to include their reimbursed costs in income, apparently no effort was made to determine the role of the wife in aiding her husband in his trade or business. In denying the deficiency, the court concluded that the evidence indicated that the trip represented hard work by the couple, undertaken for the company, and that they were not on a frolic of their own.

48. If an employer's deduction under section 162(a) for amounts paid or incurred for the travel expenses of a spouse, dependent, or other individual accompanying an employee is disallowed by section 274(m)(3), the amount, if any, of the employee's working condition fringe benefit relating to the employer-provided travel is determined without regard to the application of section 274(m)(3). To be excludible as a working condition fringe benefit, however, the amount must otherwise qualify for deduction by the employee under section 162(a). The amount will qualify for deduction and for exclusion as a working condition fringe benefit if it can be adequately shown that the spouse's, dependent's, or other accompanying individual's presence on the employee's business trip has a bona fide business purpose and if the employee substantiates the travel within the meaning of paragraph (c) of this section. If the travel does not qualify as a working condition fringe benefit, the employee must include in gross income as a fringe benefit the value of the employer's payment of travel expenses with respect to a spouse, dependent, or other individual accompanying the employee on business travel. See §§ 1.61–21(a)(4) and 1.162–2(c). If an employer treats as compensation under section 274(e)(2) the amount paid or incurred for the travel expenses of a spouse, dependent, or other individual accompanying an employee, then the expense is de-

No deduction shall be allowed under this chapter (other than section 217) for travel expenses paid or incurred with respect to a spouse, dependent, or other individual accompanying the taxpayer (or an officer or employee of the taxpayer) on business travel, unless—

(A) the spouse, dependent, or other individual is an employee of the taxpayer,

(B) the travel of the spouse, dependent, or other individual is for a bona fide business purpose, and

(C) such expenses would otherwise be deductible by the spouse, dependent, or other individual.

Additionally section 274(h) provides for further limitations with respect to conventions.[49] Section 274(h)(1) provides in pertinent part:

In the case of any individual who attends a convention, seminar, or similar meeting which is held outside the North American area, no deduction shall be allowed under section 162 for expenses allocable to such meeting unless the taxpayer establishes that the meeting is directly related to the active conduct of his trade or business and that, after taking into account in the manner provided by regulations prescribed by the Secretary—

(A) the purpose of such meeting and the activities taking place at such meeting,

(B) the purposes and activities of the sponsoring organizations or groups,

(C) the residences of the active members of the sponsoring organization and the places at which other meetings of the sponsoring organization or groups have been held or will be held, and

(D) such other relevant factors as the taxpayer may present,

it is as reasonable for the meeting to be held outside the North American area as within the North American area.

§ 4.11   MOVING EXPENSES

Section 217 provides, along with section 82, for the treatment of moving costs and employer reimbursements. Section 82 generally re-

---

ductible by the employer as compensation and no amount may be excluded from the employee's gross income as a working condition fringe benefit. See § 1.274–2(f)(2)(iii)(A).

Treas. Reg. § 1.132–5(t)(1).

49.

In the case of any individual who attends a convention, seminar, or other meeting which is held on any cruise ship, no deduction shall be allowed under section 162 for expenses allocable to such meeting, unless the taxpayer meets the requirements of paragraph (5) and establishes that the meeting is directly related to the active conduct of his trade or business and that—

(A) the cruise ship is a vessel registered in the United States; and

(B) all ports of call of such cruise ship are located in the United States or in possessions of the United States.

With respect to cruises beginning in any calendar year, not more than $2,000 of the expenses attributable to an individual attending one or more meetings may be taken into account under section 162 by reason of the preceding sentence.

quires that any amount received as reimbursement for moving expenses be included in gross income.[1]

Even so, section 217(a) provides that "moving expenses" are deductible if "paid or incurred during the taxable year in connection with the commencement of work by the taxpayer as an employee or as a self-employed individual at a new principle place of work."

In order to be eligible for deductions under section 217, the taxpayer must satisfy both a distance test and a duration of work test. With respect to distance, the taxpayer new principal place of work must be at least 50 miles further from her former residence than was her former principal place of work or, if she had no former principal place of work, at least 50 miles away from her former residence.[2] As a result, moves within the same basic geographical area will not give rise to deductions under section 217 even if they coincide with the taxpayer's new place of employment.

With respect to the duration of work, an employee must be able to show that she was employed full time (although not necessarily by the same employer) in her new location for at least 39 of the 52 weeks following the move.[3] The self-employed[4] taxpayer must not only satisfy the 39/52 week test, but also a similar, but separate, two-year test, by showing that she worked full time in the new location for at least 78 weeks during the two years directly following the move.[5]

Both the one year and two year duration tests are waived if the taxpayer suffers death, disability, or involuntary termination from employment (other than for willful misconduct) prior to the expiration of the relevant time limit.[6]

[1] WHAT MOVING EXPENSES ARE DEDUCTIBLE

Section 217 defines deductible moving expenses as including the reasonable travel expenses (including lodging, but not meals) of both the taxpayer and her household members,[7] as well as the reasonable expenses of moving household goods and personal effects of the taxpayer and her household members from the old residence to the new.[8]

If the qualifying move is to a location outside the United States, the taxpayer may also deduct the costs of storing household goods and

§ 274(h)(2).

§ 4.11

1. Although § 82 does not provide for treatment of the employer, normally the payment is deductible as an ordinary and necessary business expense under § 162.

2. § 217(c)(1).

3. § 217(c)(2)(A).

4. § 217(f).

5. § 217(c)(1)(B).

6. § 217(d)(1)(A).

7. § 217(b)(1)(B) and (2).

8. § 217(b)(1)(A).

personal effects (as well as the costs of transferring such goods to and from storage) while at the new location.[9]

[2] WHEN MOVING EXPENSES ARE DEDUCTIBLE

The taxpayer who relocates can deduct moving expenses of a potentially qualified move in the year she moves, despite the fact that she has not yet satisfied the duration tests as of the time she files her return.[10] If she later fails to satisfy the duration test(s) for reasons other than those permitted, she must include as income in the following year an amount equal to that she deducted in the year of the move.

[3] MOVING EXPENSES FOR MEMBERS OF THE ARMED FORCES

Not surprisingly, active duty members of the armed forces who move pursuant to a military order are exempted from the duration requirements.[11] In addition, to the extent that the taxpayer is either reimbursed or paid in kind for moving, she need not include any amount in income, whether the payments are for her own move or that of her spouse and dependents, and whether the spouse or dependents are moved to accompany the taxpayer or to a different location.[12]

[4] REIMBURSEMENT OF MOVING EXPENSES

Certain employer-provided reimbursements of employee moving expenses are excluded fringe benefits under section 132.[13]

§ 4.12 ENTERTAINMENT AND RELATED EXPENSES

The Code makes no express provision for the deduction of entertainment expenses and qualification must therefore depend on satisfying section 162 or section 212. Even so in order for entertainment expense to be deductible, section 274 imposes requirements that must be met in addition to those of the trade or business or the production of income provisions.

The basic section 274 limitations were enacted after Treasury and Service expressed dissatisfaction with what was regarded as abuse of the business expense deduction for entertainment and other activities in which business and pleasure were combined.

Sutter v. Commissioner[1] is illustrative of the abuses which gave rise to the enactment of section 274. The taxpayer, a physician engaged in

---

9. § 217(h)(1).

10. § 217(d)(2).

11. § 217(g)(1).

12. § 217(g)(2) and (3).

13. See § 3.08[1][f].

§ 4.12

1. 21 T.C. 170 (1953), acq., 1954–1 C.B. 6. See Rev. Rul. 63–144, 1963–2 C.B. 129, in which the Service indicated that it would limit the rule announced in Sutter to "abuse cases."

the practice of industrial medicine, claimed ordinary and necessary business expense deductions for: (1) the cost of gifts to elevator operators, parking lot attendants, hospital employees, and associates, (2) the expense of printing copies of an article, (3) the cost of a hunting trip, (4) the entertainment expenses on board a cabin cruiser and the maintenance and depreciation for the boat, and (5) the cost of lunches while attending Chamber of Commerce and other meetings. In an opinion reviewed by the entire Tax Court, it disallowed the first three items because the taxpayer failed to establish how and to what extent, if any, they contributed to his work. The fourth item was allowed under the Cohan doctrine[2] to the extent of 25% of the amount claimed. The fifth item was disallowed because there was no evidence that the cost of the lunches was greater than the cost the taxpayer would have incurred on his own account. With respect to the cost of meals, entertainment, and similar items for ones self and ones dependents the Tax Court said that "the presumptive nondeductibility of personal expenses may be overcome only by clear and detailed evidence as to each instance that the expenditure . . . was different from or in excess of that which would have been made for the taxpayer's personal purposes."

Section 274 ostensibly provides substantial limitations on the availability of a deduction for entertainment expenses that otherwise would qualify under sections 162(a) or 212.[3]

One of the principal concerns of Congress was the treatment accorded business entertainment aimed at developing goodwill. Consequently, section 274(a)(1)(A) requires that an activity "generally considered to constitute entertainment, amusement, or recreation" must be "directly related to" "the active conduct of the taxpayer's trade or business." If an expenditure is "directly preceding or following a substantial and bona fide business discussion," the requirement is that the expenditure be "associated with" "the active conduct of the taxpayer's trade or business."

Under section 274(a)(3) expenditures for social, athletic, or sporting club dues or fees are not deductible even if used for the furtherance of the taxpayer's trade or business. In that circumstance only the portion of expenses directly related to the active conduct of the trade or business is deductible.[4]

Expressly excluded by section 274(e) from the limitations are the following: (1) food and beverages furnished on the business premises primarily for employees; (2) goods, services, and facilities treated by the taxpayer with respect to the recipient as compensation for services; (3) expenses paid by a taxpayer in connection with services the taxpayer

2.   Cohan v. Commissioner, 39 F.2d 540 (2d Cir. 1930), is discussed at § 4.02 *supra.* Also discussed at § 4.02 *supra* is § 274(d), which supersedes the Cohan doctrine with respect to deductions claimed for travel, entertainment, and gifts. See Treas. Reg. § 1.274–5T.

3.   See Treas. Reg. § 1.274–1.

4.   § 274(a)(2)(C). Treas. Reg. § 1.274–2(c)(3)(iii) creates a rebuttable presumption that activity on a hunting or fishing trip or on a yacht is not considered to be principally and directly related to the active conduct of a trade or business.

performed for another person under an expense allowance or reimbursement arrangement; (4) expenses for social or similar activities primarily for lower echelon employees; (5) expenses paid by a taxpayer that are directly related to business meetings; (6) expenses directly related to and necessary for attendance at meetings of business leagues, chambers of commerce, real estate boards, and boards of trade that are tax-exempt organizations; (7) expenses for goods, services, and facilities made available by the taxpayer to the general public; (8) expenses for goods and services sold by the taxpayer to customers (in other words, the taxpayer is engaged in the entertainment business); and (9) expenses for goods, services, or facilities includible in the gross income of the recipient who is not an employee.[5]

As a general rule only 50% of the expense for food, beverages, or entertainment are allowed as a deduction.[6] Moreover, no deduction is allowed for the expense of food or beverages if lavish or extravagant.[7] Lastly, no deduction is allowed for the expense of food or beverages if the taxpayer (or an employee of the taxpayer) is not present when the food or beverages are provided.[8]

§ 4.13   BUSINESS GIFTS

The business-gift limitation made its formal appearance in the Code at the same time restrictions were imposed upon deductions for travel and entertainment. In the preceding section it was mentioned that an audit of 38,000 returns revealed that $11.5 million had been claimed as deductions for business gifts. Treasury wanted to eliminate completely their deductibility. However, Congress left the door open for small gifts. Subject to two minor exceptions, annual deductions for business gifts are limited to $25 per donee.[1] This limitation is inapplicable to: (1) fungible items not costing in excess of $4.00 each, provided they are clearly and permanently imprinted with the taxpayer's name and are distributed generally; and (2) advertising signs, display racks, or promotional material used on the business premises of the recipient.

Packaged foods and beverages are treated as business gifts rather than entertainment if transferred directly or indirectly to another person and intended for later consumption. In addition, if the taxpayer gives away tickets of admission for entertainment and does not accompany the recipient, the tickets are regarded as gifts unless the taxpayer treats them as entertainment.[2]

For purposes of section 274 "gift" means any item that is excludable from the recipient's gross income under section 102 and is not excludable under any other section. Thus, section 274(b) does not apply to scholarships excludable from gross income under section 117.

---

5. § 274(e)(1)-(9).

6. § 274(n)(1).

7. § 274(k)(1)(A).

8. § 274(k)(1)(B).

§ 4.13

1. § 274(b)(1).

2. Treas. Reg. § 1.274–2(b)(1)(iii)(b).

§ 4.14   HOME OFFICE AND RENTAL EXPENSES

[1]   IN GENERAL

Under certain circumstances, section 280A, allows taxpayers to deduct expenses attributable to the business or rental use of their homes.[1] Section 280A accomplishes this deduction in a fairly convoluted manner; section 280A(a) begins by first prohibiting any deduction "with respect to the use of a dwelling unit which is used by the taxpayer during the taxable year as a residence." Even so section 280A(b) excepts from the general prohibition of section 280A(a) deductions allowable without regard to the property's connection with the taxpayer's trade or business or income-producing activity. Thus, interest (section 163), real estate taxes (section 164), and casualty losses (section 165) on residential property are deductible under section 280A(b). Moreover, section 280A(c) excepts from the general prohibition of section 280A(a) property used for business, inventory storage, rental, or day-care services. However, section 280A(c)(5) and (e) limit the amount of deductions.

[2]   IN–HOME OFFICES

Section 280A(c) was drafted to address the confusion surrounding home office deductions. It allows a taxpayer to take home office deductions if they are allocable to that part of the residence used "exclusively" and "on a regular basis" as one of the following: (1) the taxpayer's principal place of business,[2] (2) a place of business to meet or deal with patients, clients, or customers in the normal course of a taxpayer's business, or (3) if a separate structure not attached to the residence, "in connection with" the taxpayer's business. The second sentence of section 280A(c)(1) provides that exclusive use by an employee of a home office requires that it be used "for the convenience of" the employer.

Section 280A(c) refers only to the home office used in connection with the taxpayer's trade or business; hence, a securities investor may not deduct for a place in the residence used for production of income.[3]

§ 4.14

1. Exclusive Business use Distinguishes Deductible Home Office, 74 Prac. Tax Strategies 240 (2005); Rolf Auster, Home–Office Tax Myths Discourage True Tax Savings, 64 Prac. Tax Strategies 283 (2000); Tracey Ingraham Holmes, Closing the Door on the Home Office Debate: A Case Commentary on Soliman v. Commissioner, 113 S.Ct. 701 (1993), 6 U. Fla. J.L. & Pub. Pol'y 287 (1994).

2. "[T]he term 'principal place of business' includes a place of business which is used by the taxpayer for the administrative or management activities of any trade or business of the taxpayer if there is no other fixed location of such trade or business where the taxpayer conducts substantial administrative or management activities of such trade or business." § 280A(c) (flush language).

3. Moller v. United States, 721 F.2d 810 (Fed. Cir. 1983), cert. denied, 467 U.S. 1251, 104 S.Ct. 3534, 82 L.Ed.2d 839 (1984), citing the legislative history that the deductions for use of the home must otherwise qualify under § 162 and not merely meet the less stringent income-producing-activity requirements of § 212. Accord Edwin R. Curphey, 73 T.C. 766 (1980).

[3] RESIDENTIAL RENTAL EXPENSES

Section 280A(c)(3) excepts from section 280A(a)'s general rule of nondeductibility "any item which is attributable to the rental" of a place that the taxpayer has used as a residence during the year. However, section 280A(e) limits the deduction to the total expenses multiplied by a fraction. The numerator of the fraction is the number of days during the year that the property was rented at a fair rental, and the denominator is the total number of days of use during the year. Moreover, section 280A(g) provides a rule intended as a de minimis exception. If during the year the taxpayer has used the property as a residence and has rented it for less than 15 days, no deduction is allowed under sections 162 or 212, but the income is not required to be included in the taxpayer's gross income.[4]

These rules concerning rental of residences reflect Congress' effort to provide definitive treatment of the deductibility of vacation homes. Before section 280A was enacted the allowance of deductions for a vacation home depended on whether the taxpayer's activity was profit motivated. If not, section 183, regarding an activity not engaged in for profit, applied. Section 183, provides that for such an activity deductions are limited to the gross income derived from it reduced by deductions for such items as interest and taxes. While listing factors for determining whether an activity is engaged in for profit, the regulations under section 183 state that "no one factor is determinative" and that "all the facts and circumstances with respect to the activity" must be taken into account.[5]

The Senate Finance Committee said that it was extremely difficult under the then existing law to determine when an activity was engaged in for profit with respect to vacation homes (those used both for personal purposes and for rental purposes). It commented "that frequently personal motives predominate and the rental activities are undertaken to minimize the expenses of ownership of the property rather than to make an economic profit." Indeed, "[i]n marketing vacation homes, it has become common practice to emphasize that certain tax benefits can be obtained by renting the property during part of the year, while reserving the remaining portion for personal use."[6]

---

4. See Brian Hirsch, The Extreme Home Renovation Giveaway: Constructive Justification for Tax–Free Home Improvements on ABC's Extreme Makeover: Home Edition, 73 U. Cin. L. Rev. 1665 (2005); Jennifer M. Nasner, The Unexpected Tax Consequences of "Extreme Makeover: Home Edition," 40 Gonz. L. Rev. 481 (2004 / 2005).

5. Treas. Reg. § 1.183–2(b)(1)-(9).

6. S. Rep. No. 938, 94th Cong., 2d Sess. 151 (1976). Section 183 may still apply to limit a deduction otherwise allowable under § 280A, such as a vacation home not rented for profit though not subject to personal use. H.R. Rep. No. 658, 94th Cong., 2d Sess. 165 (1976).

§ 4.15 ACTIVITIES NOT ENGAGED IN FOR PROFIT

Under section 183(a) deductions, other than those described in section 183(b), are not allowed for activities "not engaged in for profit."[1] The deductions under section 183(b) are (1) those that are allowed independent of their relationship to profit seeking and (2) those otherwise allowed in profit seeking that are in excess of the deductions in the preceding category up to the amount of the gross income from the activity. Section 183(c) provides that an activity not engaged in for profit is one that does not qualify under either section 162 or section 212.[2]

Section 183 should not be regarded as a disallowance provision. It allows deductions the taxpayer is not otherwise entitled to under section 162 or section 212 to the extent provided in section 183(b).[3] Thus, a preliminary determination must be made whether the activity falls under section 162 or section 212 before reaching the issue of deductibility under section 183.

A variety of factors have been considered in testing a taxpayer's alleged profit-seeking purpose.[4] The courts have predicated results mainly on the objective manifestations of a business operated for profit as indicative of an intent to make a profit. When a taxpayer has maintained a business-like approach to the activity with the bona fide expectation of making a profit and has kept adequate records, generally the losses have been allowed as deductions from other income. For example, in Allen v. Commissioner[5] the taxpayer operated a ski lodge that incurred substantial losses in each of the twelve years of its existence. The Tax Court held that the taxpayer had shown the necessary purpose and intent to operate for a profit because, among other things, he operated the lodge in a business-like manner, it was not an activity engaged in for personal pleasure, and the losses were economic losses representing out-of-pocket expense rather than tax losses arising from artificial deductions.

When a business-like approach is lacking, the taxpayer has had difficulty convincing a court that the venture was profit-seeking. For example, in McGowan v. Commissioner[6] the taxpayer was a retired corporate officer who exhibited films taken on three trips, including a six-month safari in Africa and the Far East. In affirming the Tax Court,

---

§ 4.15

1. See Rozzano v. Commissioner, T.C. Memo. 2007–177; Giles v. Commissioner, T.C. Memo. 2005–28.

2. See H.R. Rep. No. 658, 94th Cong., 2d Sess. 163 (1976); S. Rep. No. 938, 94th Cong., 2d Sess., pt. 1, at 151 (1976). This legislative history states: "The rules for determining whether an activity is a trade or business engaged in for the production of income are the same as those used for determining whether an activity is engaged in for profit."

3. See, e.g., Brannen v. Commissioner, 78 T.C. 471 (1982), aff'd, 722 F.2d 695 (11th Cir. 1984).

4. See Treas. Reg. § 1.183–2(b), which discusses nine factors relating to the determination of profit intention.

5. 72 T.C. 28 (1979). See also FSA 200137002; FSA 200042001; James John Jurinski, Section 183's "Hobby Loss Rules May Limit Losses," 33 Real Estate Tax'n 143 (2006).

6. 347 F.2d 728 (7th Cir. 1965). See also Adam D. Chinn, Attacking Tax Shelters: Section 183 Leaves the Farm and Goes to the Movies, 61 N.Y.U. L. Rev. 89, 123 (1986).

the Seventh Circuit concluded the taxpayer was not in the lecturing business and had not embarked on the trips with a profit motive. The Tax Court considered it significant that no copyrights were secured on the films, advertising and market surveying were meager, and there were no formal attempts to secure bookings.

When little or no possibility has existed that the income from an activity could cover the expenses, the courts have concluded that the activity was not engaged in for profit.[7] This issue arises frequently in the limited partnership context when, through the use of substantial amounts of nonrecourse debt, the limited partners are able to take depreciation or depletion deductions in excess of their investment. This was the situation in Brannen v. Commissioner[8] in which a movie-distribution limited partnership was found not to be engaged in an activity for profit. In addition to the lack of a business-like approach, the court found that because of a large nonrecourse note used to purchase the movie, the film would have to produce revenues in excess of what it could conceivably be expected to ensure that the venture would break even.[9]

Under section 183(d) if gross income exceeds deductions attributable to the activity for any three of five consecutive years (two of seven for breeding, training, showing, or racing of horses) ending with the tax year at issue, a presumption arises that the activity is engaged in for profit, and the government has the burden of showing that the activity is not engaged in for profit.[10]

§ 4.16   EXTRAORDINARY CASUALTY AND THEFT LOSSES

[1]   IN GENERAL

Under section 165(c)(3) individuals may deduct property losses (to the extent not compensated by insurance or otherwise) that arise from

---

7. See, e.g., Jasionowski v. Commissioner, 66 T.C. 312 (1976), in which the taxpayer leased a house to its former owner. The rental payments were limited to the amount of taxes and insurance on the property. Due to the additional interest expense on the mortgage, the taxpayer was bound by the terms of the lease to incur losses until its expiration, negating any possibility of a profit and thus the requisite profit intention. See also Rev. Rul. 76–287, 1976–2 Cum. Bull. 80, for a discussion of when rental of a family dwelling qualifies for deductibility of expenses under either §§ 162 or 212, or § 183.

8. 78 T.C. 471 (1982), aff'd, 722 F.2d 695 (11th Cir. 1984).

9. The courts have interpreted "profit" in § 183 to mean economic profit divorced from any artificial losses that may accrue.

See, e.g., Surloff v. Commissioner, 81 T.C. 210 (1983) (coal mining of limited partnership not engaged in for profit). See also CCA 200411042; Yoram Keinan, The Many Faces of the Economic Substance's Two–Prong Test: Time For Reconciliation?, 1 N.Y.U. J. L. & Bus. 371, 456 (2005).

10. This presumption has not been viewed lightly by the courts. In Faulconer v. Commissioner, 748 F.2d 890 (4th Cir. 1984), the taxpayer's horse breeding operation showed modest income in each of the requisite years and more significant losses in the other five. The court held that the amount of the profits was immaterial to the effect of the presumptions, and any profit in two out of seven years would shift the burden of proof.

"fire, storm, shipwreck, or other casualty, or from theft."[1]

Amounts are deductible under section 165(c)(3) if they exceed, in the aggregate, 10% of an individual's adjusted gross income, but the first $100 of each casualty is not deductible.[2] The purpose of the 10% floor is "to minimize the number of users . . . while maintaining the deduction for losses which significantly affect an individual's ability to pay taxes."[3] The need to minimize the number of individuals who can avail themselves of section 165(c)(3) arose because the deduction "creates significant problems of complexity, recordkeeping, and audit."[4] In addition to the $100 and 10% of adjusted gross income limitations, the amount deductible is the lesser of: (1) the fair market value of the property immediately before the casualty reduced by the fair market value immediately after the casualty or (2) the adjusted basis of the property.[5]

[2] CASUALTY: CRITERIA, AMOUNT, AND TIME

As a general rule a casualty loss is limited to physical damage to property. A mere decline in value of property not physically damaged is not deductible.[6] For example, in Pulvers v. Commissioner[7] a deduction was denied for the loss in value of the taxpayer's home attributable to the destruction of three nearby residences by a landslide. The court reasoned that the words "fire, storm, shipwreck" involve physical damage and that the term "other casualty" is to be read *in pari materia*. Moreover, Congress could not have intended to classify the myriad possible events giving rise to mere diminution in value as casualties. In Squirt Co. v. Commissioner[8] the taxpayer's citrus trees were damaged by a freeze with the result that its land decreased in value. Although the taxpayer was allowed a deduction for the physical damage to the trees and for the cost of returning the land to usable condition, no deduction was allowed for an alleged general decrease in value due to buyer resistance as a result of the freeze.

The courts appear in agreement on the general meaning of the term "other casualty" in that the rule of *ejusdem generis* requires a sudden event, characteristic of fires and storms, as distinguished from normal wear and tear. The event is not limited to those arising from natural

§ 4.16

1. See e.g., Francine J. Lipman, Anatomy of a Disaster Under the Internal Revenue Code, 75. 6 Fla. Tax Rev. 953 (2005).

2. See § 165(h)(1).

3. S. Rep. No. 494, 97th Cong., 2d Sess. 115 (1982).

4. Id.

5. Treas. Reg. § 1.165–7(b).

6. See Pulvers v. Commissioner, 407 F.2d 838 (9th Cir. 1969).

7. 407 F.2d 838 (9th Cir. 1969). See also Kamanski v. Commissioner, 477 F.2d 452 (9th Cir. 1973); Joel S. Newman, Of Taxes and Other Casualties, 34 Hastings L.J. 941, 968 (1983); Steven C. Thompson and Randy Serrett, Shore–Up Tax Breaks for Weather–Related Casualty Losses, 74 Prac. Tax Strategies 68, 78 (2005).

8. 51 T.C. 543 (1969), aff'd *per curiam*, 423 F.2d 710 (9th Cir. 1970); Treas. Reg. § 1.165–7. See also Tarsey v. Commissioner, 56 T.C. 553 (1971), in which the court limited a casualty loss deduction arising out of an automobile collision to the total loss less salvage value of the car and denied deductions for attorney's fees and the amount paid in settlement of a counterclaim when the taxpayer sued the other party.

causes, however, the emphasis being on result rather than cause. Hence, automobile collisions may come within the term "other casualty."[9] Moreover, the fact that the event was foreseeable will not preclude a deduction.[10] For example, in Heyn v. Commissioner[11] the Tax Court allowed a deduction for a loss caused by a landslide that had foreseeably been set in motion by excavation work.

For the most part the suddenness requirement has been interpreted broadly, a matter of no small administrative concern when the multitude of incidents giving rise to losses is considered. For this reason the Commissioner argued in White v. Commissioner[12] that the term "other casualty" should be limited to occurrences that are "cataclysmic in character." In White the taxpayer inadvertently slammed a car door on his wife's hand. The diamond in her ring was dislodged and lost in a crushed gravel drive. In allowing the deduction the court observed that this was not a situation in which a ring was lost by being misplaced or mislaid and held that the magnitude of the casualty is not controlling. It also noted that the $100 floor was enacted as the answer to the Commissioner's concern with the multitude of "minor casualties incurred by taxpayers in everyday living."[13]

In Revenue Ruling 72–592[14] the Service conceded that the accidental loss of property can qualify as a casualty, but pointed out that a casualty loss "must result from some event that is (1) identifiable, (2) damaging to property, and (3) sudden, unexpected, and unusual in nature." A "sudden" event must be "swift and precipitous and not gradual or progressive."[15] An "unexpected" event must be "ordinarily unanticipated that occurs without the intent of one who suffers the loss." An "unusual" event must be "extraordinary and nonrecurring, one that does not commonly occur during the activity in which the taxpayer was engaged when the destruction or damage occurred, and one that does not commonly occur in the ordinary course of day-to-day living of the taxpayer."

The suddenness criterion precludes damage done to property over a period of time. Consequently, losses caused by insect infestation or disease are normally not deductible.[16]

---

9. See Treas. Reg. § 1.165–7(a)(3).

10. Heyn v. Commissioner, 46 T.C. 302 (1966).

11. 46 T.C. 302 (1966). See also Brian Lester, The "Casualty" to Taxpayers From a Misapplied Application of Internal Revenue Code Section 165(c)(3): The Need for an Objective Approach, 48 S.D. L. Rev. 52, 70 (2003).

12. 48 T.C. 430 (1967), acq., 1969–1 Cum. Bull. 21.

13. 48 T.C. 430, 436 (1967).

14. 1972–2 Cum. Bull. 101. See also Rev. Rul. 87–59, 1987–28 I.R.B. 4; Chief Counsel Attorney Memorandum, 2006 WL 3885156.

15. In Ruecker v. Commissioner, T.C. Memo. 1981–257, the court held that the loss of ornamental plants and shrubs caused by a severe draught was deductible as a casualty loss. It pointed out that generally "a drought loss is sustained through the progressive and gradual deterioration of the property," but that "on the particular facts" of the case, "the withering and desiccation of the plants which took place" in three to four months was sudden.

16. In Rev. Rul. 63–232, 1963–2 Cum. Bull. 97, revoking Rev. Rul. 59–277, 1959–2 Cum. Bull. 73, the Service said that scientific studies indicate that termite damage can never be regarded as happening suddenly.

Even though physical damage to property may have been the result of gradual deterioration, this will not preclude a casualty loss deduction for damage to other property in the chain of causation of a sudden event. Thus, in Revenue Ruling 70–91[17] the Service denied a deduction for damage to a water heater that burst as a result of deterioration, but allowed a deduction for water and rust damage to household furnishings because as to them the bursting of the water heater was a sudden identifiable event.

As indicated at the outset of this section, the amount allowable as a deduction may not exceed the adjusted basis of the property. Adjusted basis is determined in accordance with section 1011. As a general rule cost is an asset's basis, adjusted in accordance with section 1016.

Suppose property is subject to a casualty loss after several years of personal use. Is the original cost of the property the basis referred to in section 165(b)? This question was presented to the Supreme Court in Helvering v. Owens.[18] In that case the taxpayers claimed a deduction for casualty losses to property used for personal purposes. The taxpayers argued that the literal terms of the predecessor of section 165(b) entitled them to use the unrecovered cost basis. The Court rejected this argument. It reasoned that because the provision allowed the deduction of losses sustained during the year, and the property was subject to wear and tear before the casualty, the deduction was limited to the actual amount of loss, the difference between the value immediately before and the value immediately after the casualty.

As a general rule a deduction for a casualty loss is available only in the year in which the loss is suffered. Under section 165(i), however, disaster losses occurring in those areas designated by the President for disaster relief are subject to special treatment. If such losses are incurred after the close of a tax year, but before the time for filing a return has expired, the taxpayer may elect to deduct the disaster losses on the tax return for the preceding year.

[3]   THEFT: CRITERIA, AMOUNT, AND TIME

For purposes of section 165(c) theft has been interpreted broadly to include any nonconsensual taking of property, including that arising by misrepresentation or fraud.[19] The courts have added a caveat that the

See Rev. Rul. 55–327, 1955–1 Cum. Bull. 25, in which the Service denied a deduction for damage to a fur coat caused by moths. It has been held that damage to wearing apparel by carpet beetles during a single winter did not constitute a casualty. Meersman v. United States, 370 F.2d 109 (6th Cir. 1966). However, in Rev. Rul. 79–174, 1979–1 Cum. Bull. 99, the Service determined that damage to ornamental trees caused by a massive beetle attack in a 5–10 day period, which was unknown in the area in which it occurred, was sufficiently sudden and unusual to constitute a casualty. See

Maher v. Commissioner, 76 T.C. 593 (1981), aff'd, 680 F.2d 91 (11th Cir. 1982) (taxpayer was denied deduction for loss of coconut palms due to vegetational disease; court held that destruction by disease occurs as a result of gradual deterioration as opposed to sudden identifiable event).

17.   1970–1 Cum. Bull. 37.

18.   305 U.S. 468, 59 S.Ct. 260, 83 L.Ed. 292 (1939).

19.   See, e.g., Gerstell v. Commissioner, 46 T.C. 161 (1966), in which a theft loss deduction was allowed because the taxpayer

appropriation must constitute a criminal act under the law of the jurisdiction in which the taking occurred.[20] However, the taking need not be adjudicated a theft in violation of the local penal code by a court of the applicable jurisdiction. All that is necessary is the opinion of the fact-finder that based on the evidence presented by the taxpayer it is reasonable to conclude a theft occurred. Because the court deciding the issue of deductibility makes its own independent determination of the existence of a criminal violation (if there had been a criminal conviction that would obviously constitute the determination), a taxpayer does not have to meet the "beyond a reasonable doubt" standard of proof necessary for a criminal conviction, only the lesser civil standard of "more probable than not." It is not even necessary that the taxpayer initiate criminal proceedings or be able to identify the alleged thief. Because the burden of proof is less stringent, evidence regarding each element of the crime that may be insufficient proof in criminal proceedings may be sufficient in tax proceedings.[21]

The mere disappearance or loss of property does not qualify as a theft.[22] Thus, in Smith v. Commissioner[23] the taxpayer's prize thoroughbred dog strayed while being exercised. The court admitted the dog would have been a tempting prize for a thief, but it denied the deduction for lack of proof of a theft.

The amount deductible for a theft loss is determined in the same manner as a deduction for a casualty loss, with the property after the theft treated as having no value.[24] However, section 165(e) prescribes that a theft loss, unlike a casualty loss, is to be treated as sustained in the year the theft is discovered rather than in the year in which it occurs. If at the time of discovery there is a reasonable possibility of recovery, a deduction must await resolution of such possibility.[25] But if remote, the possibility of recovery will not postpone the deduction.[26]

[4] REIMBURSEMENT

Regardless of the nature of the loss, under section 165(a) the amount deductible is reduced by any compensation received. Moreover, under section 165(h)(4)(E) a taxpayer is not permitted to deduct a

---

was induced to sell annuity contracts at an artificially low price due to fraudulent representations regarding their value.

20. See, e.g., Edwards v. Bromberg, 232 F.2d 107 (5th Cir. 1956). See also CCA 200406046; FSA 200305028; FSA 200242004; FSA 200217001; TAM 200625032.

21. See Jacobson v. Commissioner, 73 T.C. 610 (1979), in which the court allowed a theft loss deduction for belongings found missing from storage although the police did not follow up on the incident because the evidence was felt insufficient for criminal proceedings. See also Wilson v. Commissioner, T.C. Memo. 1982–107, in which the

failure to press charges did not by itself indicate an acquiescence in the taking.

22. See e.g., Smith v. Commissioner, 10 T.C. 701 (1948).

23. 10 T.C. 701 (1948). See also Brian Lester, The "Casualty" to Taxpayers From a Misapplied Application of Internal Revenue Code Section 165(c)(3): The Need for an Objective Approach, 48 S.D. L. Rev. 52, 70 (2003).

24. Treas. Reg. § 1.165–8(c).

25. Treas. Reg. § 1.165–1(d)(3).

26. See, e.g., Rainbow Inn, Inc. v. Commissioner, 433 F.2d 640 (3d Cir. 1970).

personal casualty loss that is covered by insurance unless the taxpayer files a timely claim.

§ 4.17 BAD DEBTS

[1] IN GENERAL

Because a bad debt is the loss of an intangible property right, it is potentially within the bailiwick of section 165; however, section 166, provides special rules for bad debt deductions, making the categories of loss and bad debt mutually exclusive. Moreover, because most bad debts of individuals (other than those owed by political parties)[1] are deductible, whereas a deduction for losses other than casualty or theft losses is generally limited for individuals to those incurred in a trade or business or a transaction entered into for profit, a critical question may arise sometimes of whether a loss is a bad debt or is a loss under section 165.[2]

For example, in Hanes v. Commissioner[3] the taxpayer was the victim of a swindle when she purchased a painting that turned out to be worthless. She gave a check for the purchase price but stopped payment on it. After spending a considerable amount in settling lawsuits over the check and learning the seller would be unable to indemnify her, she claimed a bad debt deduction. The Tax Court denied the deduction on the ground that the taxpayer had suffered a nondeductible personal loss and did not have a "debt" as the term is used in what is now section 166. The court pointed out that if there were a debt it was worthless at its inception, and such a debt would not give rise to a deduction under what is now section 166.

Probably the most common debt characterization problems occur when shareholders make advances to their corporations. In such situations the question is whether a true debt has been created or whether the advances are contributions to capital. The tax advantage frequently sought is a deduction by the corporation for interest paid on a loan as distinguished from a nondeductible dividend distribution.

Assuming that a debtor-creditor relationship has been established, section 166 permits corporations to deduct bad debts and individuals to deduct business bad debts that become wholly or partially worthless during the tax year.[4] Individuals may also deduct nonbusiness bad debts

---

§ 4.17

1. Under § 271 uncollectable loans to political parties, unless made by a bank, are not deductible.

2. See § 165(c).

3. 2 T.C. 213 (1943). See also Swenson, 43 T.C. 897 (1965); Markle v. Commissioner, 17 T.C. 1593 (1952); Bihlmaier v. Commissioner, 17 T.C. 620 (1951); Hanes v. Commissioner, 2 T.C. 213 (1943); Eckert v. Burnet, 283 U.S. 140, 51 S.Ct. 373, 75 L.Ed. 911 (1931); Dexter v. Commissioner, 99 F.2d 769 (1st Cir. 1938); Park v. Commissioner, 58 F.2d 965 (2d Cir. 1932); Crocker v. Lucas, 37 F.2d 275 (9th Cir. 1930); Estate of Moorshead v. Commissioner, T.C. Memo. 1955–215; Bernstein v. Commissioner, T.C. Memo. 1960–287; Sheldon v. Commissioner T.C. Memo. 1961–44, aff'd 299 F.2d 48 (7th Cir. 1962); Garrett v. Commissioner, 39 T.C. 316 (1962); Wilson v. Commissioner, 40 T.C. 543 (1963); Mannarino v. Commissioner, T.C. Memo. 1964–246.

4. § 166(a)(1) and (2).

when they become wholly worthless, but only as short-term capital losses.[5]

The distinction between business and nonbusiness bad debts and the special treatment accorded nonbusiness bad debts as short-term capital losses has been around for decades. The primary design of the legislation was to eliminate abuses that had arisen with prior law under which transfers to relatives frequently were held fully deductible as bad debts. Also, Congress sought to effectuate similar tax treatment for holders of debt instruments as is accorded investors in corporate stock.

[2] WORTHLESSNESS, TIME, AND AMOUNT

For purposes of section 166, the normal three-year statute of limitations is extended to seven years for filing a claim based on a bad debt deduction.[6] Nevertheless, a charge-off within the year is required, however, for a partially worthless bad debt under section 166(a)(2).

As a general proposition the question of worthlessness is basically a factual one. While collection efforts may bear on the issue of the time of worthlessness, they do not constitute an element of worthlessness.[7]

Legal action to enforce a debt is not required for a determination of worthlessness.[8] However, a taxpayer-creditor cannot unilaterally decide that a debt is worthless merely by electing not to enforce the obligation. In Southwestern Life Insurance Co. v. United States[9] the taxpayer periodically made advances against future commissions to sales agents. If an agent terminated employment before full repayment of the advances, the company's policy was to charge-off the remainder as a worthless debt without seeking repayment. The court acknowledged that legal action is not a prerequisite to a determination of worthlessness, but it held the taxpayer failed to meet its burden of proof regarding the ascertainment of worthlessness because of the lack of any effort to determine a former agent's solvency and ability to pay or any effort to request repayment.

Once a debt has been determined worthless based on all the facts and circumstances,[10] the deduction must be taken in the year of worthlessness. In Winters & Hirsch, Inc. v. United States[11] the taxpayer did not account for certain debts in the year of worthlessness because of the fraudulent activities of its key officers. The taxpayer was denied a bad debt deduction in a subsequent year for the prior unaccounted worthless

---

5. § 166(d)(1)(A) and (B).

6. See § 6511(d)(1).

7. See, e.g., Smyth v. Barneson, 181 F.2d 143 (9th Cir. 1950), in which the court rejected the government's contention that a reasonable effort to collect was required.

8. Treas. Reg. § 1.166–2(b).

9. 560 F.2d 627 (5th Cir. 1977), cert. denied, 435 U.S. 995, 98 S.Ct. 1647, 56 L.Ed.2d 84 (1978). See also Must Show Year Debt Goes Bad to Claim Bad Debt Deduction, 74 Prac. Tax Strategies 111 (2005).

10. See Treas. Reg. § 1.166–2 regarding evidence of worthlessness. A subsequent recovery does not bar a finding of worthlessness in a prior taxable year. See Estate of Mann v. United States, 731 F.2d 267 (5th Cir. 1984), in which a minimal recovery as a result of bankruptcy proceedings was included in income in the year of receipt and did not negate a conclusion of worthlessness in the year of bankruptcy.

11. 215 Ct.Cl. 518, 571 F.2d 11 (1978). See also FSA 200024004; TAM 9847004.

debts despite its inability to account for them in the proper year. The court held that a bad debt deduction must be taken in the year of worthlessness and not in some other year. To hold otherwise, the court reasoned, would allow the taxpayer to choose when to take the deduction.

[3] GUARANTORS AND INDEMNITORS

Suppose an individual, A, is considering the means by which to shore-up the financial structure of a controlled corporation, X, and desires to maximize the sharing of risks with the tax collector. In broad outline A's problem is to move from the investor category to the trade or business category so that losses can qualify as business bad debts. If A makes a contribution to X's capital and then X fails, A's loss on the stock will be treated as a capital loss, which, is limited to offsetting capital gain and up to $3,000 of ordinary income.[12] Capital loss treatment on worthless corporate stock is provided by section 165(g), which prescribes that the stock shall be treated as sold or exchanged on the last day of the tax year during which it becomes worthless.[13]

Would A fare any better if A guaranteed a bank loan made to X? Could A argue that such guarantee was a transaction entered into for profit entitling A to an unrestricted loss deduction if A was forced to pay? The Supreme Court answered in the negative in Putnam v. Commissioner,[14] involving a taxpayer-lawyer who participated in the organization of a publishing company. After the company failed it was liquidated, leaving proceeds insufficient to pay two notes given by the corporation and guaranteed by the taxpayer. The taxpayer paid the notes and claimed a deduction for their full amount, alleging that the loss was incurred in a transaction entered into for profit. The Court treated the taxpayer's deduction as a nonbusiness bad debt; it relied primarily on the basic principles of subrogation under which a guarantor simply steps into the shoes of the creditor upon payment of the debt. The Court stated that upon payment by a guarantor a new debt is not created; hence, the loss "by its very nature" was "a loss from the worthlessness of a debt."

The subrogation rationale of Putnam has been subject to criticism on two grounds: (1) the tax consequences there were dictated by the technical nicety that the taxpayer's payment of debt put him in the shoes of the creditor by subrogation, and (2) it would follow that when a taxpayer stands as an indemnitor or secures a discharge of a guarantor's liability without subrogation, debt characterization would be lacking.

---

12. See § 1211(b)(1).

13. Ordinary loss treatment is available under § 1244 for certain stock of qualifying small business corporations.

14. 352 U.S. 82, 77 S.Ct. 175, 1 L.Ed.2d 144 (1956). See also Indemnifica-

tion Payments not Deductible as Business Expense or Loss, 78 Prac. Tax Strategies 226 (2007); Paul D. Carman and David C. Blum, The Tax Aspects of Payments Made by Guarantors and Joint Obligors, 32 Real Estate Tax'n 100 (2005).

Even so, the Courts of Appeals and the Tax Court have viewed Putnam as an articulation of the congressional design of section 166(d) to provide capital loss treatment as part of a broader scheme that limits an investor who seeks capital gain to capital loss when the investment fails.

For example, in Stratmore v. United States[15] the taxpayer, a corporate officer-shareholder, guaranteed notes of his two corporations. When the corporations failed, he settled his guarantor's liability by paying part of the debts of the corporations. As an alternative to the business bad debt characterization, which the court rejected, the taxpayer contended that since under state law he was not subrogated to the rights of the corporation's creditors, there was no debt to become worthless. Therefore, the taxpayer argued, Putnam did not control and his loss was fully deductible as a loss from a transaction entered into for profit. The Third Circuit rejected this argument, and it held that Putnam controlled the characterization of the taxpayer's loss as a nonbusiness bad debt. The court stated that the "essence of Putnam"[16] was the Supreme Court's view "of the Congressional purpose behind"[17] the provision for nonbusiness bad debts "and the part it was intended to play in the statutory scheme for a common tax treatment of all losses suffered by a corporate stockholder in providing his corporation with financing."[18] Hence, the taxpayer's losses were treated as capital losses. To allow the results to turn on the right of subrogation under state law, the Third Circuit said, "would be to undermine the Putnam doctrine—taxpayers could change capital losses to ordinary losses almost at will."[19]

[4] TRADE OR BUSINESS

The demise of the subrogation rationale as a means of treating a loss from a transaction entered into for profit as fully deductible has resulted in shifting the focus in the bad debt area to whether the taxpayer has shown a sufficient relationship between the loan, guarantee, or other credit arrangement and a trade or business, including that of acting as an employee, so as to qualify as a business bad debt.[20] The basic guidelines on this issue were provided by the Supreme Court in Whipple v. Commissioner,[21] in which the primary issue was whether the taxpayer had established the existence of a business of lending or of promoting corporations.

In Whipple the taxpayer had been engaged for many years in promoting corporate and noncorporate businesses in construction, real estate, and oil. After the taxpayer acquired a soft drink bottling fran-

---

15. 420 F.2d 461 (3d Cir. 1970), cert. denied, 398 U.S. 951, 90 S.Ct. 1870, 26 L.Ed.2d 291 (1970); accord Horne v. Commissioner, 523 F.2d 1363 (9th Cir. 1975), cert. denied, 439 U.S. 892, 99 S.Ct. 249, 58 L.Ed.2d 237 (1978).

16. 420 F.2d 461, 465 (1970).

17. Id.

18. Id.

19. Id.

20. See Whipple v. Commissioner, 373 U.S. 193, 83 S.Ct. 1168, 10 L.Ed.2d 288 (1963).

21. 373 U.S. 193, 83 S.Ct. 1168, 10 L.Ed.2d 288 (1963).

chise, he formed a corporation, taking 80% of its stock, and he made loans to it of $57,000. When the loans became worthless, he claimed a business bad debt deduction. The Tax Court held that the taxpayer was entitled only to a nonbusiness bad debt deduction because he was not in the lending business and was not engaged in the business of promoting corporations engaged in bottling soft drinks.

In affirming the Tax Court the Supreme Court framed the issue in terms of whether a taxpayer who "furnishes regular services to one or many corporations"[22] is engaged in "an independent trade or business."[23] The business status of the taxpayer was rejected on the ground that the activities of the taxpayer were related to his role as an investor, since the taxpayer's return, "though substantially the product of his services,"[24] arose from the business of the corporation. The Court admonished that even if a taxpayer demonstrates he is engaged in an independent business, "care must be taken to distinguish bad debt losses arising from his own business and those actually arising from activities peculiar to an investor concerned with, and participating in, the conduct of the corporate business."[25]

If a salary taken by a corporate owner-employee is small or nominal, substantial difficulty can be expected in establishing the requisite connection between a loan and the taxpayer's business as an employee. Further, the frequency of litigation in this area led to a conflict in approach, which, as discussed below, arose out of a desire for a rule that would provide more certainty. Thus, in Niblock v. Commissioner[26] the taxpayer invested $2,500 as a 50% owner in a corporation manufacturing boats; the taxpayer was also employed at an annual salary of $7,800. From time to time he made direct loans and guaranteed bank loans to the corporation to meet its operating needs. On three previous occasions he had purchased and sold stock in small companies. When the taxpayer paid off the bank loans, he claimed they were business bad debts because they were related to his business as a corporate employee. This was so, the taxpayer contended, because he had discovered he could not work for anyone other than himself.

22. 373 U.S. 193, 202, 83 S.Ct. 1168, 1174 (1963).

23. Id.

24. Id.

25. Id. In Deely v. Commissioner, 73 T.C. 1081 (1980), acq., 1981–2 C.B. 1, the taxpayer was involved in the organization of several corporations and had sought a bad debt deduction for a worthless loan to one of the corporations. The court reasoned that in order for the taxpayer to establish that he was in the separate business of promoting corporations, he must show that the entities were organized with a view to a quick and profitable sale rather than with a view to long-range investment gains. The longer an interest is held the more the profit on the eventual disposition is attributable to the successful operation of the corporation and not to the activity of promotion. The taxpayer's acquisition of an equity interest in the corporation, as opposed to compensation for services, indicated that he was not in the business of promoting but rather assumed the role of an investor.

26. 417 F.2d 1185 (7th Cir. 1969). See also Rev. Rul. 71–561, 1971 WL 26665, 1971–2 C.B. 128; William J. Rands, The Closely Held Corporation: Its Capital Structure and the Federal Tax Laws, 90 W. Va. L. Rev. 1009, 1126 (1988).

The Tax Court and the Seventh Circuit held the losses were non-business bad debts. The Seventh Circuit found no proximate relationship between the taxpayer's job and the loans, stating that it was "quite evident that the taxpayer's dominant interest was in capital gain income."[27] However, it also stated "that the only test that will inject sufficient certainty into the interpretation of section 166"[28] is to require the taxpayer "prove that his corporate employment furnished the dominant and primary motivation for making the advances and the guarantees."[29] The court therefore rejected the significant motivation test used by the Second Circuit in Weddle v. Commissioner.[30] A dominant and primary motivation test, said the court, was justified by the Supreme Court's admonition in Whipple that "care must be taken to distinguish bad debt losses arising from his own business and those actually arising from activities peculiar to an investor concerned with, and participating in the conduct of the corporate business."[31]

The conflict between the "dominant and primary motivation test" and the "significant motivation" test was resolved by the Supreme Court in United States v. Generes.[32] In Generes the taxpayer, most of whose time was spent as president of a savings and loan association where he earned an annual salary of $19,000, had $38,000 invested in a construction company as a 50% owner and where he drew an annual salary of $12,000. In 1958 the taxpayer signed a blanket indemnity agreement with a surety on his corporation's construction contracts. In 1962 he paid $162,000 to the surety when his corporation failed. This amount he claimed as business bad debt deduction. The taxpayer repeatedly testified that he signed the indemnity agreement to protect his job and salary. The jury found that the signing of the indemnity agreement was proximately related to his job under instructions that "a debt is proximately related to a taxpayer's trade or business when its creation was significantly motivated by the taxpayer's trade or business and it is not rendered a nonbusiness debt merely because there was a nonqualifying motivation as well, even though the non-qualifying motivation was the primary one."[33]

The Fifth Circuit affirmed, stating it was impressed with the analogy drawn by the majority in Weddle between proximate cause in the law of torts and the significant motivation test. The Supreme Court, however, reversed. Writing for the court, Mr. Justice Blackmun said that the proximate relationship test of the regulations for a business bad debt was unfortunate since it tempted one to think in terms of tort law, as

27. 417 F.2d 1185, 1188 (7th Cir. 1969).

28. 417 F.2d 1185, 1187 (7th Cir. 1969).

29. 417 F.2d 1185, 1188 (7th Cir. 1969).

30. 325 F.2d 849 (2d Cir. 1963), in a concurring opinion suggesting a "primary and dominant motivation" test.

31. 417 F.2d 1185, 1188 (7th Cir. 1969), quoting Whipple v. Commissioner, 373 U.S. 193, 202, 83 S.Ct. 1168, 1174, 10 L.Ed.2d 288 (1963).

32. 405 U.S. 93, 92 S.Ct. 827, 31 L.Ed.2d 62 (1972), rev'g 427 F.2d 279 (5th Cir. 1970).

33. 405 U.S. 93, 99, 92 S.Ct. 827, 831, 31 L.Ed.2d 62 (1972).

indeed the lower court had done. But tort law "has little place in tax law where plural aspects are not usual, where an item either is or is not a deduction, or either is or is not a business bad debt, and where certainty is desirable."

In holding that a dominant motivation test served best in this area, Mr. Justice Blackmun reasoned that the Code carefully distinguishes between business and nonbusiness items and that an emphasis on significant motivation would tend to obliterate the distinction between business and nonbusiness bad debts and to undermine and circumscribe the holding in Whipple. He also reasoned that a dominant motivation standard had the attribute of workability, would strengthen the mandate of section 262, which denies deductions for personal, living, and family expenses, and was consistent with the loss provisions of section 165(c)(1) and (2).

In Generes the Court concluded that although the jury instructions were erroneous and would normally require a new trial, reasonable minds could not, on the self-serving statements in the record, ascribe a dominant motivation to the preservation of the taxpayer's salary. The Court therefore directed that judgment be entered for the government.

§ 4.18 DEPRECIATION, DEPLETION, AND AMORTIZATION

[1] IN GENERAL

Section 167(a) provides that a reasonable allowance for the exhaustion, wear and tear, and obsolescence of business or investment property is allowed as a depreciation deduction. Moreover, section 168 establishes the Accelerated Cost Recovery System for determining depreciation deductions for tangible property, and provides "the depreciation deduction provided by section 167(a) for any tangible property shall be determined" using the Accelerated Cost Recovery System described in section 168.

The depreciation deduction represents that portion of the cost or other basis of the property allocated to and written off as an expense of operation during the year. In theory, the purpose of a depreciation deduction is to distribute in a systematic and rational manner the cost of property over its useful life.

As an aid to small business, section 179 allows a taxpayer to elect to expense up to $125,000[1] of the cost of certain property[2] in the year it is placed in service.

The statutory terminology limiting depreciation deductions to gain-seeking property that is subject to "exhaustion, wear and tear"[3] pre-

---

§ 4.18

1. § 179(b)(1).

2. See § 179(d)(1).

3. § 167(a).

cludes the taking of depreciation for land; however, a depletion deduction is allowed for the extraction of oil, gas, and mineral deposits.[4]

The depreciation deduction is limited to "property used in a trade or business"[5] and "property held for the production of income"[6] that is subject to "exhaustion, wear and tear."[7] Hence, the gain-seeking requirements of section 167 are substantially similar to those imposed on expense deductions under sections 162 and 212.

Sections 167 and 168 are designed to permit the cost of property to be recovered by the taxpayer who bears the burden of the wear and tear. Normally this burden falls on the owner; however, the niceties of form and legal title do not always control.[8] For example, in Helvering v. F. & R. Lazarus & Co.[9] the taxpayer, a department store, claimed depreciation deductions on three buildings. The taxpayer had transferred the legal title of the buildings to a trustee for the benefit of land-trust certificate holders and took back a 99–year lease with an option to renew and purchase. The Commissioner argued that the statutory right to depreciation followed the legal title. The Board of Tax Appeals, however, concluded that the transaction between the taxpayer and the trustee was in reality a mortgage loan, and it therefore allowed the taxpayer the deductions for depreciation on the buildings. The Supreme Court, as had the Court of Appeals, agreed with the Board of Tax Appeals and affirmed. The Court regarded the "rent" stipulated in the leaseback as a promise to pay interest on the loan and a "depreciation fund" required by the lease as an amortization fund designed to pay off the loan in the stated period. Thus, said the Court, the Board of Tax Appeals justifiably concluded that the transaction, although in written form a transfer of ownership with a leaseback, was actually a loan secured by the property.

Lazarus was distinguished in Frank Lyon Company v. United States,[10] and it was found not to be controlling in that case. Lyon involved three parties: the taxpayer, Frank Lyon Company (Lyon); a bank, Worthen Bank & Trust Company (Worthen); and a mortgage lender, New York Life Insurance Company (New York Life). Initially, Worthen planned to construct a multistory bank and office building and to finance it by issuing debentures, but this proved unworkable because of various legal and regulatory restrictions. Worthen then sought to employ a sale-leaseback arrangement. The arrangement was approved by the regulatory authorities provided Worthen retained a repurchase option after 15 years and obtained an independent third-party buyer-lessor.

---

4. See §§ 611–613A discussed *infra* at § 4.16[4].

5. § 167(a)(1).

6. § 167(a)(2).

7. § 167(a).

8. See e.g., § 167(d) which life tenants (not the absolute owner) of property to take any allowable depreciation deductions.

9. 308 U.S. 252, 60 S.Ct. 209, 84 L.Ed. 226 (1939). See also Alex Raskolnikov, Contextual Analysis of Tax Ownership, 85 B.U. L. Rev. 431, 516 (2005); CCA 200513022.

10. 435 U.S. 561, 98 S.Ct. 1291, 55 L.Ed.2d 550 (1978). See also CCA 200513022; CCA 200620022; TAM 200604033.

Following negotiations with several prospective parties, Worthen selected Lyon as the buyer-lessor. Worthen had arranged for the financing with New York Life, and Lyon was approved as an acceptable borrower. Lyon participated actively in negotiating the terms of the sale-leaseback. Lyon was liable for the payment of the principal to New York Life, and it paid Worthen $500,000. Under the terms of the agreement Worthen would lease the land to Lyon for 76 years, sell the building, and lease it back for a primary term of 25 years and eight 5–year option terms. Lyon bought the building from Worthen as it was constructed and simultaneously leased it back to Worthen. The rent for the 25–year primary term exactly equaled the mortgage payments Lyon was required to make. Thereafter, the amount of rent decreased substantially during the option periods. The lease could not be canceled during the initial term. The options to repurchase were for the amount of the outstanding mortgage and Lyon's original $500,000 investment plus interest. The government contended the arrangement was only a financing transaction under which Worthen was the owner of the building. Hence, the government said that Worthen, not Lyon, was entitled to deductions for depreciation.

The Supreme Court held the transaction was a valid sale-leaseback. The Court found that:

> [W]here, as here, there is a genuine multiple-party transaction with economic substance, which is compelled or encouraged by business or regulatory realities, is imbued with tax-independent considerations, and is not shaped solely by tax-avoidance features that have meaningless labels attached, the Government should honor the allocation of rights and duties effectuated by the parties. Expressed another way, so long as the lessor retains significant and genuine attributes of the traditional lessor status, the form of the transaction adopted by the parties governs for tax purposes. What those attributes are in any particular case will necessarily depend upon its facts.[11]

In Hilton v. Commissioner[12] a newly constructed department store was sold to a single-purpose finance company and leased back under a long-term net lease. The Tax Court refused to recognize the sale-leaseback transaction. It concluded the transaction failed to satisfy the elements of the test the Supreme Court articulated in Frank Lyon Company.

In Rice's Toyota World, Inc. v. Commissioner[13] the taxpayer, a highly successful retail automobile dealer, entered into a sale-leaseback

11. 435 U.S. 561 562, 98 S.Ct. 1291, 1293, 55 L.Ed.2d 550 (1978).

12. 74 T.C. 305 (1980), aff'd *per curiam*, 671 F.2d 316 (9th Cir. 1982), cert. denied, 459 U.S. 907, 103 S.Ct. 211, 74 L.Ed.2d 168 (1982). See also IRS FSA 199927039; IRS FSA 199920012; Donald J. Weidner, Synthetic Leases: Structured Finance, Financial Accounting and Tax Ownership, 25 J. Corp. L. 445, 487 (2000).

13. 81 T.C. 184 (1983), aff'd in part, rev'd in part, and remanded, 752 F.2d 89 (4th Cir. 1985). See also CCA 200620022; David P. Hariton, When and how Should the Economic Substance Doctrine be Applied?, 60 Tax L. Rev. 29, 56 (2006).

arrangement with a computer equipment leasing company. Pursuant to the arrangement the taxpayer purchased a six-year-old computer for more than $1,400,000, which the Tax Court said was more than the fair market value of the computer. The purchase price was paid in the form of a 4–year promissory note for $250,000 and the balance in two nonrecourse notes payable over eight years. Simultaneously, the taxpayer leased the equipment back to the equipment company for eight years. The Tax Court concluded the taxpayer did not have a business purpose in entering into the transaction and that the transaction lacked economic substance because there was no realistic hope of profit, and there was no actual investment upon which depreciation could be predicated and which would support genuine nonrecourse indebtedness.[14]

[2] INTANGIBLES

Section 167(a) refers to "a reasonable allowance for the exhaustion, wear and tear" of property. Included within the meaning of "exhaustion" is the diminution in value due to the passage of time of intangible property having a useful life that is definitely ascertainable and is more than one year.[15] Nevertheless, intangibles are generally amortized under section 197.[16]

> Section 197 allows for the straight line method of amortization for almost all intangible assets over a fifteen year period. This rule applies to § 197 intangibles that were acquired in connection with a trade or business or in a separate transaction, but it does not apply to self-created intangible assets, such as the cost of creating a customer relationship through advertising. Those intangible assets that are included in the definition of § 197 intangibles are: goodwill, going-concern value, work force, information base assets, know-how, customer-based intangibles, supplier-based intangibles, other similar intangibles, government licenses and permits, covenants not to compete, franchises, trademarks, and tradenames. Certain other intangible assets are excluded from the definition of § 197 intangibles regardless of whether the asset was acquired as part of a trade or business, or in a separate transaction. Depending upon the asset, it may be excluded because it has been determined to be non-amortizable or to have an amortization period of less than fifteen years. These excluded assets are: interests in land, computer software, financial interests, leases of tangible property, indebtedness, professional sport franchises, transaction costs, and mortgage servicing rights. Other intangible assets are also excluded from the definition of § 197 intangibles, but only if they were acquired in a

---

14. In Mukerji v. Commissioner, 87 T.C. 926 (1986), and Estate of Thomas v. Commissioner, 84 T.C. 412 (1985), the Tax Court found that computer equipment sale-leaseback transactions satisfied the economic-substance test.

15. Section 168(a) refers to "tangible property;" hence intangible property must be depreciated under § 167 rather than § 168.

16. See Catherine L. Hammond, The Amortization of Intangible Assets: § 197 of the Internal Revenue Code Settles the Confusion, 27 Conn. L. Rev. 915 (1995).

transaction separate from the acquisition of a trade or business. These excluded assets are: any interest in a film, sound recording, or book; any right to receive tangible property under a contract, patents or copyrights; and any right under a government contract with a fixed duration of less than fifteen years.[17]

[3]　DEPRECIATION OF TANGIBLE PROPERTY

With respect to tangible property section 168 generally works in concert with 167 to mandate the utilization of the Accelerated Cost Recovery System (ACRS).[18] ACRS allows recovery of capital costs for most tangible depreciable property over prescribed periods that are generally shorter than the actual useful lives of such property. ACRS is mandatory for tangible property of a character subject to an allowance for depreciation.[19] Intangible property and tangible property placed in service prior to January 1, 1981, do not qualify for ACRS, and the depreciation deductions for such property are instead governed by section 167.

Under ACRS property is classified and recovery periods are given for each class.[20] This eliminates disputes between the Service and taxpayers about the useful life of property. Also, because salvage value is disregarded,[21] the entire cost of property may be deducted.

Under section 168, there is generally a half-year convention for both the year property is placed in service and the year of disposition.[22] Under this convention property is treated as placed in service or disposed of at the middle of year. For residential rental property and nonresidential real property there is a mid-month convention.[23] A mid-quarter convention applies to all property placed in service during the year if more than 40% of the property is placed in service during the last three months of the year.[24]

Under section 280F ACRS deductions allowed on luxury automobiles used for business are subject to the following *minimum* dollar limitations (which are indexed for inflation): $2,560 for the first recovery year, $4,100 for the second recovery year, $2,450 for the third recovery year, and $1,475 for each succeeding year in the recovery period.[25]

---

17. Catherine L. Hammond, The Amortization of Intangible Assets: § 197 of the Internal Revenue Code Settles the Confusion, 27 Conn. L. Rev. 915, 933–934 (1995) (citations omitted).

18. See § 167(b) which states: "For determination of depreciation deduction in case of property to which section 168 applies, see section 168."

19. See § 168(a); Grinalds v. Commissioner, T.C. Memo. 1993–66; C & M Amusements, Inc. v. Commissioner, T.C. Memo. 1993–527.

20. See § 168(c).

21. § 168(b)(4).

22. § 168(d)(1), (4)(A).

23. § 168(d)(2), (4)(B).

24. § 168(d)(3), (4)(C).

25. § 280F(a)(2). § 280F(d)(7)(A) provides that § 280F(a):

[S]hall be applied by increasing each dollar amount contained in such subsection by the automobile price inflation adjustment for the calendar year in which such automobile is placed in service. Any increase under the preceding sentence shall be rounded to the nearest multiple of $100 (or if the increase is a multiple of $50, such increase shall be increased to the next higher multiple of $100).

For "listed property" not having a business use exceeding 50%, the deduction allowed under section 168 is determined under the "alternative depreciation system" provided in section 168(g).[26] The straight line method of depreciation is used for the alternative depreciation system.[27] Included within the definition of listed property are automobiles and computers not used exclusively at a regular business establishment. Taxpayers must meet strict substantiation requirements with respect to the use of listed property.[28]

[4] ELECTION TO EXPENSE CERTAIN TANGIBLE PROPERTY

Section 179(a) provides that a taxpayer may elect to deduct up to $125,000 of the cost of "section 179 property" for the year it is placed in service. "Section 179 property" is defined in subsection (d)(1) as property:

(A) which is—

(i) tangible property (to which section 168 applies), or

(ii) computer software (as defined in section 197(e)(3)(B)) which is described in section 197(e)(3)(A)(i), to which section 167 applies, and which is placed in service in a taxable year beginning after 2002 and before 2011,

(B) which is section 1245 property (as defined in section 1245(a)(3)), and

(C) which is acquired by purchase for use in the active conduct of a trade or business.[29]

The $125,000 ceiling for the deduction applies to taxpayers whose total investment in section 179 property placed in service during the taxable year is $500,000 or less.[30] For other taxpayers the $125,000 ceiling is reduced by one dollar for every dollar of investment in excess of $500,000.[31] Moreover, the amount eligible for deduction is limited to the taxable income derived during the year from the active conduct by the taxpayer of the trade or business in which the property is used.[32] Married individuals filing separate returns are treated as one taxpayer for purposes of determining the amount that may be deducted and the total amount of investment in section 179 property.[33]

[5] DEPLETABLE ECONOMIC INTEREST

[a] In General

Sections 611–613A recognize the right of a taxpayer with a capital interest in a natural resource to recover the investment in a wasting asset through deductions for depletion.[34]

---

26. § 280F(b)(1).

27. § 168(g)(2)(A).

28. § 274(d)(4). See also See Dominic L. Daher, The Business Purpose Substantiation Requirements, 17 Tax'n of Exempts 189 (2006).

29. § 179(d)(1).

30. § 179(b)(1) and (2).

31. Id.

32. § 179(b)(3)(A).

33. § 179(b)(4).

34. Fenton & Davis, The Economic Interest Concept: An Illusion?, 33 Oil & Gas Tax. Q. 259 (1984).

Under the general rule of section 611(a) deduction for depletion is available with respect to "mines, oil and gas wells, other natural deposits, and timber." More often than not these natural resources are developed under arrangements in which the interests in the depletable property are divided as to ownership. Section 611(b) provides the basic framework for allocating the depletion deduction between the ownership interests as follows: (1) for a trust allocation between the income beneficiaries and the trustee is on the basis of the income allocable to each except as a trust instrument may otherwise provide;[35] (2) a life tenant is treated as the absolute owner;[36] (3) allocation between a lessor and a lessee is to be made equitably;[37] and (4) for an estate allocation between the estate and the heirs, legatees, and devisees is on the basis of the income allocable to each.[38]

[b] Economic Interest

The allocation rules of section 611(b) do not begin to provide the precision needed to determine whether the wide variety of interests owned by different taxpayers constitute depletable interests. The doctrine of economic interest, under which the right to a depletion deduction is determined, has evolved from the landmark opinion of the Supreme Court in Palmer v. Bender.[39]

The regulations state that "[a]n economic interest is possessed in every case in which the taxpayer has acquired by investment any interest in mineral in place ... and secures, by any form of legal relationship, income derived from the extraction of the mineral ... to which he must look for a return of his capital."[40] Whether a taxpayer has such an interest "in mineral in place" is normally determined by the terms of the lease or other contract. The doctrine of economic interest has engendered substantial litigation, especially in the oil and gas industry, where attempts have been made to follow the thread of an economic interest into leases, subleases, royalty payments, and a variety of income interests taken as payment or as security.

In general, the doctrine of economic interest has been given broad meaning. For example, in Commissioner v. Southwest Exploration Co.[41] an economic interest was found to be held by a landowner whose

---

35. § 611(b)(3).

36. § 611(b)(2).

37. § 611(b)(1).

38. § 611(b)(4).

39. 287 U.S. 551, 53 S.Ct. 225, 77 L.Ed. 489 (1933). See also Thomas v. Perkins, 301 U.S. 655, 57 S.Ct. 911, 81 L.Ed. 1324 (1937), in which the Court concluded that a holder of a reserved production payment "payable out of oil only" was chargeable with the production as owner of the economic interest.

40. Treas. Reg. § 1.611–1(b)(1).

41. 350 U.S. 308, 76 S.Ct. 395, 100 L.Ed. 347 (1956). See also United States v. Swank, 451 U.S. 571, 101 S.Ct. 1931, 68 L.Ed.2d 454 (1981), in which the Court held that a mineral lessee had an economic interest even though the lease was subject to cancellation by the lessor on 30-days' notice without cause.

property was adjacent to the property actually producing the mineral. The State of California had advertised for bids to develop its submerged off-shore oil lands. Under state law such land either had to be worked from filled land or slant drilled from adjacent land. As the only bidder the taxpayer was given a lease that required slant drilling (there being no available filled land) and the endorsement of the adjacent land owners to permit the drilling. To secure the endorsement of the adjacent land owners and the use of their property, the taxpayer contracted to pay them 24½% of its net profits from the extraction and sale of the off-shore deposits. Although the contract with the adjacent land owners expressly provided they did not acquire a share in the lease or oil deposit, the Supreme Court held the contract did just that, at least for the purpose of qualifying the adjacent land owners' interest as an economic interest for tax purposes. The Court reasoned that without the consent of the owners there would have been no lease, no wells, and no production, and the contribution of the use of their land in return for the rental based on the share of the net profits was an investment in oil in place sufficient to constitute an economic interest.

In Southwest Exploration the requirement that the mineral in place must constitute the source of recovery of the taxpayer's capital was obviously satisfied. This requirement, however, can constitute a serious limitation, as illustrated by Paragon Jewel Coal Co. v. Commissioner.[42] In this case the lessee of coal land entered into oral agreements with various contractors to mine the coal. The contractors were obligated to construct all necessary shafts and tunnels and to deliver the coal to the lessee for a fixed per ton amount. The court of appeals held that because the lessee had an economic interest the contractors likewise had an economic interest because they were performing the lessee's obligation to mine, and they were paid at a rate related to the market price of the coal. In reversing, the Supreme Court held that the mere right to mine, even to the extent of exhaustion of the deposit, did not amount to an economic interest. It found that an essential ingredient was lacking in that the contractors could look only to the promise of the lessee for payment rather than to the proceeds from the sale of the coal. In short, the Court found that the taxpayer had a "mere economic advantage" rather than an economic interest dependent upon an investment in the mineral as distinguished from development expenditures.

[c] Operating and Nonoperating Interests

Southwest Exploration and Paragon Jewel, however, hardly begin to portray the variety of economic interests encountered in the financing and development of natural resources. The more important of these interests and their descriptive terms may be illustrated by way of example.

42. 380 U.S. 624, 85 S.Ct. 1207, 14 L.Ed.2d 116 (1965). See also Missouri River Sand Co. v. Commissioner, 774 F.2d 334 (8th Cir. 1985) (no economic interest in sand and gravel dredged from river); Rev. Rul. 68–330, 1968–1 C.B. 291 (no economic interest in exclusive right to purchase gas at the well); Costantino v. Commissioner, 445 F.2d 405 (3d Cir. 1971) (strip miner lacked economic interest when payment based on owner's contractual obligation to pay).

Assume that A, a landowner, grants B the right to develop A's land for oil or minerals. B pays A a "bonus" or "advance royalty" before production starts, a "delay rental" to defer immediate efforts at production, and promises to pay A a one-eighth "royalty" in the production subject to a minimum royalty. Assume also that after production is underway, B is obligated to pay a "shut-in royalty" in lieu of production or a "shut-in rental" if the lease is forfeitable.

A would have economic interests with respect to the bonus or advance royalty and the one-eighth royalty, including the minimum royalty, because they are regarded as having their source in production, but because a depletion allowance follows income rather than production A would have to restore to income any depletion deductions taken if the lease expired or terminated before production. On the other hand, the delay rental and shut-in payments would not constitute depletable income since they would not have their source in the production of minerals.

B, as owner of the working interest (or operating interest), could create a "carved out overriding royalty" interest by assigning to C a fractional share of the working interest, or he could create a "retained overriding royalty" by assigning his working interest and retaining the overriding royalty. B could also carve out and sell a "production payment" out of his working interest, or he could sell his working interest and retain a production payment. (A could also create a production payment in a similar manner out of his lessor's interests.) A production payment is similar to an overriding royalty except it is limited to a fixed dollar amount, or production unit, and duration.

B could also create a "net profits" interest out of his working interest, reducing it to a nonoperating interest, under an agreement whereby his interest would be charged with stated operating costs. In a similar manner B could create a "carried interest" in himself by transferring one-half of his working interest to C in consideration of the latter's assuming the development costs with the payout to commence only after C had recovered his full costs.

B's working interest, overriding royalty, and net profits interest would qualify as economic interests. However, although production payments qualify as economic interests when created prior to 1970, as described below, section 636 now prescribes the treatment for them, and a carried interest will not qualify as an economic interest during the recoupment period.[43]

[d]　Production Payments and ABC Transactions

The working interest owner may carve out and sell a production payment (the right to a specified share of the production or a specified

---

43. See United States v. Cocke, 399 F.2d 433 (5th Cir. 1968), cert. denied, 394 U.S. 922, 89 S.Ct. 1187, 22 L.Ed.2d 455 (1969). See also Rev. Rul. 90–20, 1990–9 I.R.B. 8.

money payment), or he may sell his working interest and retain a production payment. In the latter situation, if he takes the further step of selling his production payment, the series of steps would constitute an "ABC transaction," a financing arrangement used for many years, especially in the oil and gas industry. For example, assume A, as lease owner, sells the working interest to B for cash but takes the major portion of his consideration in form of a retained production payment. A then sells his production payment to C, a bank, pledging the production payment as collateral. Under pre–1970 law the tax effect of a carved out payment was that A, through the acceleration of income received from the payment (the corresponding operating expenses would be paid by B), was able to avoid the 50% limitation imposed on the deduction for percentage depletion. For the ABC transaction similar distortions were possible with respect to B, the buyer of the working interest, and B was able to pay off what was basically a loan with pre-tax dollars because B was not charged with the production during the pay-out period.

These and other considerations, including the growing use of production payments for other natural resources and an estimated annual revenue loss ranging from $200 to $350 million, led Congress in 1969 to control this abuse. Thus, under section 636 for post-August 6, 1969 years most production payments will be characterized for tax purposes as loans by the owner of the payment to the owner of the mineral property.

The legislative history of section 636 indicates that Congress was most intrigued by the analogy of a production payment to a loan on nonmineral property secured by a mortgage. Thus, in a carve out the sale of the production payment was regarded as equivalent to the borrowing of money, and in an ABC transaction the sale of the production payment was regarded as analogous to the sale of property subject to a mortgage subsequently sold to a third person. This loan treatment, however, was not unprecedented since under pre–1970 law loan treatment resulted in the case of a carve out when the pay out of the production payment was guaranteed by the person creating it, or, in case of an ABC transaction, by B, the buyer of the working interest. The guarantee provided an additional source for payment and thereby destroyed the production payment as an economic interest.

Congress has turned proceeds of production payments into loans in the following manner. Under section 636(a), when a production payment is carved out and sold by the owner of a mineral interest, instead of depletable income in the hands of the seller and production allocable to the buyer, the money received by the seller will be treated as loan proceeds and the production when received will be allocable to the seller. In this manner the distortions created under pre–1970 law through the treatment of the sales proceeds as depletable income are avoided.

Under section 636(b) a sale of a mineral interest subject to a retained production payment will result in the production payment being treated the same as a purchase money mortgage loan rather than as an economic interest. The result is that the production used to satisfy the payment is taxable to the owner of the working interest, subject to depletion, who may deduct all his production costs. This means that in an ABC transaction, while A is not affected, B, the buyer of the working interest, unlike pre–1970 law when the income attributed to the production payment was not chargeable to him, has to include the full production in income; of course, he may offset this full inclusion in income with his full production expenses. C, the buyer of the production payment, in turn, treats the amounts received as non-taxable payments on a mortgage loan and presumably any excess as interest income.

[6] COST DEPLETION

Section 612 states that the basis upon which the deduction for depletion under section 611 is allowed is the adjusted basis provided in section 1011.[44] Cost depletion, which has been a feature of the tax laws since the Revenue Act of 1913, is computed by dividing the adjusted basis of the property by the estimated number of recoverable units and multiplying the result by the number of units sold during the year. The deduction may be taken until the total investment is recovered. Cost depletion is available with respect to "mines, oil and gas wells, other natural deposits, and timber."[45] The definitional content of "natural deposits" is prescribed for percentage depletion, discussed in the next section of this chapter, but it is not prescribed for cost depletion.

In United States v. Shurbet[46] the Fifth Circuit rejected the government's contention that the term "natural deposits" meant mineral deposits and allowed the taxpayer a deduction for cost depletion for water extracted and used in irrigation farming. While the Fifth Circuit was careful to limit its holding to the geological facts of the peculiar conditions of the Southern High Plains of Texas and New Mexico, the opinion reveals some of the fundamental concepts in the allowance of cost depletion. In this case, prior to the commencement of irrigation farming in the region, the formation from which the taxpayer and other farmers had extracted water was in a state of equilibrium in that the annual recharge from precipitation on the ground surface, the only water source of the formation, equalled the natural discharge. After irrigation pumping was started, the water storage was depleted to the extent of some 40 million acre feet over a 24–year period. These facts were held sufficient to establish the water constituted a natural deposit and to indicate that capital was being exhausted in the production of income in the taxpayer's business.

Only cost depletion may be taken for timber.[47] The depletable amount of timber property does not include any part of the cost or value of the land or depreciable equipment. On the other hand, the amount

44. See FSA 200021006; Field Service Advisory, 1994 WL 1725437.

45. Treas. Regs. §§ 1.611–2, 1.611–3. For the treatment of bonuses and advanced royalties, see Treas. Reg. § 1.612–3.

46. 347 F.2d 103 (5th Cir. 1965), acq., Rev. Rul. 65–296, 1965–2 C.B. 181, and amplified by Rev. Rul. 82–214, 1982–2 C.B. 115. See also Day v. Commissioner, 54 T.C. 1417 (1970).

47. Treas. Reg. § 1.611–1(a)(1).

qualifying for depletion is increased by costs paid or incurred in connection with preparing sites for planting.[48]

[7] PERCENTAGE DEPLETION

[a] In General

Section 613(a) provides an alternative method of computing the deduction for depletion—a method based on the percentage of gross income from the property. Under this method the annual deduction is computed on a percentage of the gross income from the property at rates prescribed in section 613(b), which range from 22% for sulphur and uranium to 5% for gravel and sand. However, the maximum deduction is limited to 50% of taxable income but not less than an amount that could be computed under the cost depletion method.[49]

Section 613(d) denies the use of percentage depletion as a general rule for oil and gas wells. Accordingly, section 613(d) results in a complete disallowance of the percentage depletion method for foreign oil and gas producers as well as major domestic companies; even so, section 613A provides limited exceptions for small independent producers and royalty owners of domestic oil and gas.

The percentage depletion deduction is generally limited to 15% under section 613A(c)(1) for independent producers and royalty owners. Percentage depletion may be taken on the income from domestic crude oil and natural gas based on the taxpayer's average daily production. However, the depletable quantity is limited to 1,000 barrels a day for oil and 6,000 cubic feet a day for natural gas.[50] Furthermore, section 613A(d)(1) disallows the deduction for percentage depletion exceeding 65% of the taxpayer's taxable income determined without regard to income attributable to domestic production activities, percentage depletion for oil and gas, and net operating loss or capital loss carrybacks. An amount so disallowed may be carried forward for subsequent tax years.[51]

Percentage depletion is not available with respect to timber, soil, sod, dirt, water, mosses, and minerals extracted from sea water.[52]

Unlike cost depletion and depreciation, percentage depletion may be taken as long as the property produces income. It operates independent of recovery of the actual investment. This deviation from one of the basic principles of taxation has given rise to the controversy over congressional policy of granting investors in natural resources what is, in effect, a subsidy through the Code mechanism once capital has been recouped.

The justification for both the subsidy feature and the computation of percentage depletion has its roots deep in the history of the depletion allowance. During the first five years of income taxation under the

---

48. Treas. Reg. § 1.611–3(a).

49. § 613(a).

50. § 613A(c)(3)(B), (4).

51. Prop. Treas. Reg. § 1.613A–4(a)(2), Ex. (2).

52. See § 613(b)(7)(A) and (B). But see § 613(e), concerning "geothermal deposits."

Sixteenth Amendment only cost depletion was available. However, in 1918, for the avowed wartime purpose of encouraging the exploration for minerals, Congress recognized the "discovery value" depletion method. Under this method the taxpayer was permitted to recover tax-free the market value of the deposit as of the date of discovery or 30 days thereafter. Discovery value depletion, which was available until 1954, did not solve the problem of estimating the number of depletable units. Percentage depletion was established for this purpose in 1924, but without any limitation on the amount of recovery.

[b] Gross Income

In general, "the gross income for the property"[53] refers to the amount extracted; amounts attributable to refining, converting, or manufacturing are excluded. For oil and gas extraction the market price in the immediate vicinity of the well controls.[54] For mineral extraction the determination of "the gross income from the property" is more complicated. The starting point is section 613(c)(1), which defines "gross income from the property" as "gross income for mining." The term "mining" is defined to include the extraction of the ores or minerals from the ground, certain "treatment processes," and in general, up to 50 miles of transportation to the place of treatment.[55]

[c] Taxable Income

As stated above, the percentage depletion deduction is limited to 50% of the taxpayer's "taxable income from the property (computed without allowance for depletion)."[56] However, in determining taxable income for the purpose of the 50% ceiling, a number of adjustments must be made in addition to the depletion deduction itself. In general, only those deductions that are attributable to depletable income will be required to be allocated to taxable income, including those capital expenditures, discussed in the next section, which may be expensed, and allocable portions of administrative expense, overhead, selling expense, depreciation, taxes, and similar items.

When a taxpayer has more than one property, deductions not directly attributable to specific properties must be allocated among all of them.[57]

Special treatment is provided in the regulations for decreasing expenses and adjusting basis when section 1245 property is sold during the tax year since gain on such property reflects previously allowed

---

53. § 613(a).

54. Treas. Reg. § 1.613–3(a).

55. § 613(c)(2). Under § 613(c)(5) certain processes are expressly excluded, and the regulations prescribe the criteria for both inclusion and exclusion. Treas. Reg. § 1.613–3(f)-(g).

56. § 613(a).

57. Treas. Reg. § 1.613–5(a). For some applications of the allocation requirements, see, e.g, Southwestern Portland Cement Co. v. United States, 435 F.2d 504 (9th Cir. 1970); Arvonia–Buckingham Slate Co. v. United States, 426 F.2d 484 (4th Cir. 1970); Occidental Petroleum Corp., 55 T.C. 115 (1970), acq., 1971–1 C.B. 2.

deductions.[58] Also, the Service has ruled that taxable income does not include the net operating loss deduction[59] or the deduction allowed for charitable contributions.[60]

[8] EXPLORATION AND DEVELOPMENT COSTS

[a] In General

Related to the depletion allowance, and greatly affecting tax liability on income from natural resources, arc the statutory rules governing exploration and development costs. Absent these statutory rules such costs would be characterized as capital expenditures that, if the acquired asset or improvement had a determinable life, would be recoverable through depreciation or depletion. However, Congress has regarded these preproduction costs of natural resources as being entitled to special treatment. This is perhaps because the costs are incurred in what are considered high-risk enterprises and perhaps because when percentage depletion is used, based as it is on income rather than on the amount of the investment, such expenditures may be wasted.

In providing for this special treatment, the Code distinguishes between oil and gas development costs and exploration and development costs for mines.

[b] Oil and Gas Intangible Drilling and Development Costs

Although no special provision is made for oil and gas exploration costs, which ordinarily must be capitalized, section 263(c) allows an election to expense rather than to capitalize intangible drilling and development costs. In general, this means that expenditures for labor, fuel, supplies, tool rental, and drilling equipment repairs, that are incurred, directly or through contract with others, in preparing for production may be deducted as ordinary business expenses if the taxpayer so elects.

The option granted under section 263(c), however, is not unlimited. First, section 263(c) does not extend to expenditures for exploration that must be capitalized. Second, only taxpayers with working interests may avail themselves of the election. Third, section 291(b)(1)(A) reduces by 30 percent the amount allowable as a deduction under section 263(c) for an "integrated oil company," defined in section 291(b)(5). The amount disallowed is capitalized to the oil or gas property and is deducted ratably over a 60–month period beginning with the month that the costs are either paid or incurred.[61] Fourth, to the extent that payment for intangibles constitutes the consideration for a working interest, such costs must be capitalized.[62] Fifth, the option is not available with respect

58. Treas. Reg. § 1.613–5(b).

59. Rev. Rul. 60–164, 1960–1 C.B. 254.

60. Rev. Rul. 60–74, 1960–1 C.B. 253.

61. § 291(b)(2).

62. Rev. Rul. 70–657, 1970–2 C.B. 70.

to tangible property that ordinarily has a salvage value and, therefore, must be capitalized.[63]

As a general rule, when intangible drilling and development costs are capitalized, they are recoverable through depreciation if they relate to the installation or construction of tangible physical property; otherwise, they are recoverable through depletion.[64] Thus, in broad outline, expensing of these items means deducting in lieu of cost depletion or depreciation; they do not serve to reduce percentage depletion, which is based on the income from the property.

[c] Mining Exploration Costs

Unlike investors in oil and gas properties who must capitalize exploration costs, under section 617(a) taxpayers engaged in the exploration of deposits located in the United States may elect to deduct the exploration costs.[65] However, the amount deducted is recaptured as ordinary income when the mine reaches the production stage.[66] If no election to deduct is made under section 617, the exploration costs are capitalized and recoverable through depreciation or depletion.

Exploration costs are current pre-development stage expenditures "for the purpose of ascertaining the existence, location, extent, or quality of any deposit."[67] The development stage is considered as commencing when the deposit is reasonably capable of commercial exploitation.[68] Exploration costs do not include otherwise deductible business expenses, amounts paid for depreciable property (except that depreciation on such property may qualify), or those incurred for nondepletiable minerals.

[d] Mining Development Costs

Once a mine reaches the development stage, that is, when commercial exploitation is reasonably possible, a taxpayer engaged in mining loses the election for exploration expenditures but gains a new one for development costs. Under section 616 he may elect to deduct such costs in the year paid or incurred or to defer them for deduction ratably as the mineral is sold. There is no recapture, and like section 263(c), which permits expensing of intangible drilling and development costs in oil and gas operations, section 616 functions as a deduction in lieu of cost depletion but not in lieu of percentage depletion.

§ 4.19 PERSONAL DEDUCTIONS
AND EXPENSES

The main focus of attention in the preceding parts of this chapter has been on deductions incurred in a trade or business or production of

63. See, e.g., Harper Oil Co. v. United States, 425 F.2d 1335 (10th Cir. 1970), in which the Tenth Circuit interpreted this rule to require the capitalization of surface casing costs even though set in cement, not removable under state law, and, therefore, nonsalvagable.

64. Treas. Reg. § 1.612–4.

65. See § 617(h) for the special rules applicable to foreign exploration. See also Field Service Advisory, 1993 WL 1470180.

66. § 617(b).

67. § 617(a)(1).

68. Treas. Reg. § 1.617–1(a).

income activity. Nevertheless, in certain instances the Code allows an individual deductions independent of the relationship of the item to a trade or business or production of income activity, including (but not limited to): (1) ordinary and necessary expenses paid or incurred in connection with the determination, collection, or refund of taxes under section 212, (2) casualty and theft losses under section 165, and (3) nonbusiness bad debts under section 166. A fourth instance concerns alimony or separate maintenance payments, deductible under section 215.

The Code also allows individuals other deductions independent of their relationship to a trade or business or production of income activity; these deductions are available for interest, taxes, charitable contributions, and extraordinary medical expenses. It is convenient to also refer to these deductions as "personal," even though corporations are also allowed to deduct interest, taxes, and charitable contributions.

In lieu of listing personal deductions on the federal income tax return, an individual may take a standard deduction, and whether an individual lists personal deductions or uses the standard deduction, he is entitled to certain personal and dependency exemptions that are taken before arriving at taxable income, the base upon which the tax rates are applied.

[1] ADJUSTED GROSS INCOME

One function of adjusted gross income is that it serves as a computational device for individuals to determine whether amounts for certain items are deductible. For example, the deduction for uncompensated medical care expenses is allowed under section 213 to the extent the amount exceeds 7.5% of adjusted gross income. Similarly, a personal casualty loss is allowed as a deduction under section 165 to the extent it exceeds 10% of adjusted gross income (and 100% per occurrence). Moreover, the deduction for charitable contributions allowed under section 170 may not exceed certain percentages of an individual's "contribution base," which is defined in terms of adjusted gross income.[1]

Section 67(a) provides that "miscellaneous itemized deductions"[2] are deductible only to the extent that in the aggregate they exceed 2% of adjusted gross income. Miscellaneous itemized deductions include (among other things) unreimbursed employee travel expenses for transportation and lodging initially deductible under section 162(a), dues to unions and professional associations, home office expenses, employment related educational expenses, work clothing, hobby expenses up to the amount of hobby income initially deductible under section 183(b)(2),

---

§ 4.19

1. § 170(b)(1)(G).

2. Section 67(b) describes "miscellaneous itemized deductions" as "itemized deductions other than" those listed in § 62(a)(1)–(21).

expenses for the production of income initially deductible under section 212(1) or (2), and tax related expenses initially deductible under section 212(3).

Adjusted gross income is gross income minus the deductions listed in section 62. It is important to note that section 62 does not authorize deductions. Those deductions enumerated in section 62 are authorized elsewhere in the Code. The items subtracted from gross income to arrive at adjusted gross income are the following:

(1) Trade and business deductions;

(2) Certain trade and business deductions of employees;

(3) Losses from sale or exchange of property;

(4) Deductions attributable to rents and royalties;

(5) Certain deductions of life tenants and income beneficiaries of property;

(6) Pension, profit-sharing, and annuity plans of self-employed individuals;

(7) Retirement savings;

(8) Penalties forfeited because of premature withdrawal of funds from time savings accounts or deposits;

(9) Alimony;

(10) Reforestation expenses;

(11) Certain required repayments of supplemental unemployment compensation benefits;

(12) Jury duty pay remitted to employer;

(13) Deduction for clean-fuel vehicles and certain refueling property;

(14) Moving expenses;

(15) Archer MSAs;

(16) Interest on education loans;

(17) Higher education expenses;

(18) Health savings accounts;

(19) Costs involving discrimination suits, etc.; and

(20) Certain attorneys fees.[3]

[2] INTEREST

[a] In General

Section 163(a) permits a deduction for interest paid or accrued by the taxpayer during the taxable year upon his indebtedness independent

---

3. § 62(a)(1)-(21) (note § 62(a)(8) has been repealed).

of the relationship of the interest obligation to the production of income.[4] Thus, the interest on the mortgage on the family home is as fully deductible as that incurred on a bank loan to provide a business enterprise with needed capital.[5]

Interest on debt secured by the taxpayer's principal residence or second residence is deductible only to the extent the amount of the debt does not exceed the purchase price of the residence plus the cost of improvements.[6] The deduction for investment interest is limited to the amount of net investment income.[7] Additionally, interest from activities subject to passive loss rules is not treated as investment interest.[8]

Since the establishment of the allowance of the interest deduction in the first revenue laws, Congress and the courts have been called upon to control both its use and abuse in a variety of situations. As a result, this area of the law bristles with refinements and exceptions.

The broad definition of interest as "compensation for the use or forbearance of money"[9] has generated problems. Probably the most frequent one has concerned shareholder advances, the issue being whether the advances are debt giving rise to corporate interest deductions or whether they are capital contributions with the alleged interest payments constituting nondeductible dividends.

Another characterization problem has involved "mortgage points," the loan processing fee paid by a mortgagor-borrower. Although the Service has ruled that fees paid by a seller to a lender in connection with the latter's assistance in securing FHA loans, performing escrow services, and issuing credit reports constitute nondeductible service fees rather than deductible interest,[10] it has held that "points" and "processing fees," regardless of their label, paid by a mortgagor-borrower constitute deductible interest,[11] and such interest is currently deductible if actually paid by a cash method taxpayer.[12] If the payment is a "prerequisite to obtaining borrowed capital," it will be considered interest even though paid prior to disbursement of the borrowed funds.[13] Howev-

---

4. McIntyre, An Inquiry into the Special Status of Interest Payments, 1981 Duke L.J. 765; Asimow, The Interest Deduction, 24 U.C.L.A. L. Rev. 749 (1977).

5. As a general rule, a deduction is not available for interest paid on the debt of another. See, e.g., Prendergast v. Commissioner, ¶ 83,419 P–H Memo TC (interest deduction denied father for payment of son's student loan). However, under § 216 interest, taxes, and depreciation deductions of a cooperative housing corporation are passed through and are available to tenant-stock-holders. This pass-through does not apply to subscription payments made during the construction period because such payments represent an equity investment. Rev. Rul. 70–92, 1970–1 C.B. 53, modified by Rev. Rul. 73–15, 1973–1 C.B. 141.

6. § 163(h)(3)(B)(i)(II) and (C)(i)(I).

7. § 163(d)(1).

8. § 63(d)(3)(B)(ii).

9. Deputy v. du Pont, 308 U.S. 488, 498, 60 S.Ct. 363, 368 (1940).

10. Rev. Rul. 68–650, 1968–2 C.B. 78; see also Rev. Rul. 67–297, 1967–2 C.B. 87, denying a deduction for a "loan originating" fee paid by a buyer.

11. Rev. Rul. 69–188, 1969–1 C.B. 54. See also Field Service Advisory, 1994 WL 1725374; Field Service Advisory, 1993 WL 1469705.

12. Rev. Rul. 69–582, 1969–2 C.B. 29. See also TAM 200624065.

13. Rev. Rul. 69–188, 1969–1 C.B. 54. See also Field Service Advisory, 1994 WL 1725374; Field Service Advisory, 1993 WL 1469705.

er, the Service has concluded that points paid to refinance a mortgage loan secured by the taxpayer's principal residence are not deductible in full for the year the points are paid, but instead they must be deducted over the period of the new mortgage loan.[14]

[b]   Tax–Exempt Securities

Under section 265(a)(2) interest paid on indebtedness incurred to purchase or carry obligations whose interest is tax exempt is not deductible. The principal target is state and local government bonds whose interest is excluded from income under section 103. The obvious purpose of section 265(a)(2) is to prevent taxpayers from obtaining a double tax advantage from borrowed funds. While section 265(a)(2) does not contain language concerning the taxpayer's purpose, the legislative history of what is now section 265(a)(2) indicates that Congress intended the critical factor to be the purpose of obtaining a double tax advantage. The courts and the Service appear to be in agreement that the proper test is whether there is a business purpose for the borrowing, and section 265(a)(2) is to be invoked only when there is a "sufficiently direct relationship" between the debt incurred and the purchase or carrying of tax-exempt securities. The Service has indicated that there must be a showing that the taxpayer borrowed the funds for the purpose of carrying tax-exempt securities before the deduction will be disallowed.[15]

The courts have rejected the argument that the holding of tax-exempt securities for sale later at a taxable gain precludes the application of what is now section 265(a)(2);[16] however, little else in this area of the law appears well-settled. Controversies involving brokerage firms seem to have been resolved as illustrated by Leslie v. Commissioner.[17] In this case a deduction was denied a brokerage firm on the amount of interest paid for borrowings from banks allocable to tax-exempt securities in the taxpayer's holdings, which amounted to some $2 million out of a total of $170 million. The Second Circuit rejected the position taken by the Tax Court that allowed the deduction because the loans were made on a day-to-day basis for all the taxpayer's business needs with no specific part of the loans directly traceable to the tax-exempt securities.

Section 265(a)(2) also poses a threat to banks in their daily operations. The Service has attempted to provide guidelines and has ruled

---

14. Rev. Rul. 87–22, 1987–14 I.R.B. 41. An acceptable method for deducting points over the period of the new mortgage loan is set forth in Rev. Proc. 87–15, 1987–14 I.R.B. 47.

15. Rev. Proc. 72–18, 1972–1 C.B. 740, modified by Rev. Proc. 87–53, 1987–41 I.R.B. 37.

16. See, e.g., Wynn v. United States, 288 F.Supp. 797 (E.D. Pa. 1968), aff'd per curiam, 411 F.2d 614 (3d Cir. 1969), cert. denied, 396 U.S. 1008, 90 S.Ct. 565, 24 L.Ed.2d 500 (1970), in which the court denied deductions for interest paid on bank loans made by a brokerage firm to support a separate account for tax-exempt securities notwithstanding findings that the purpose of the loans was to enable the taxpayer to resell at taxable gain and not to earn tax-exempt interest.

17. 413 F.2d 636 (2d Cir. 1969), cert. denied, 396 U.S. 1007, 90 S.Ct. 564, 24 L.Ed.2d 500 (1970), rev'g, 50 T.C. 11 (1968). See also CCA 200238002; Field Service Advisory, 1997 WL 33313703; Field Service Advisory, 1994 WL 1866019.

that what is now section 265(a)(2) does not apply to interest paid on bank deposits.[18]

In Revenue Procedure 70–20[19] the Service identified additional safe harbors for ordinary day-to-day banking operations. In general, under this revenue procedure interest deductions are not denied on short-term notes and similar borrowings on federal banking transactions or on repurchase agreements not involving tax-exempt securities.

Taxpayers using tax-exempt securities as collateral for loans should not be expected to be treated any differently than if they used the loan proceeds to purchase such securities. In Wisconsin Cheeseman, Inc. v. United States[20] the taxpayer invested its seasonal net receipts in tax-exempt securities, and thereafter it used the securities as collateral for working capital loans at the beginning of the next season. In denying the interest deduction the Seventh Circuit saw no reason to treat the taxpayer preferentially merely because its business was seasonal. It reasoned that when a taxpayer can reasonably foresee the need for loans to meet its recurring needs, the interest deduction should not be allowed.

On the other hand, if the need for working capital loans is unusual or unanticipated, the deduction has been allowed. In Norfolk Shipbuilding & Drydock Corp. v. United States[21] the taxpayer, a Navy contractor, made two short-term $1 million working capital loans at a time when it had $400,000 invested in tax-exempt securities. The loans were unanticipated and were required by delays in periodic payments due the taxpayer under its contracts as a result of disputes over work completions. In allowing the interest deduction the court reasoned such loans were not normal, no securities were purchased while the loans were outstanding, and the need for cash was so immediate the securities the taxpayer held could not have been sold in time to sustain normal business operations.

In Wisconsin Cheeseman the taxpayer also deducted for interest paid on a mortgage construction loan on a new plant. The government contended that the taxpayer failed to show it wanted to sell its tax-exempt bonds and could not. Hence, what is now section 265(a)(2) operated to deprive it of an interest deduction because of its tax-exempt holdings pledged as collateral. The Seventh Circuit rejected this interpretation and allowed the deduction on the mortgage loan. It reasoned that the taxpayer's testimony showed that without the bonds it would have had fewer liquid assets to meet seasonal needs, and, therefore, "business reasons dominated the mortgaging of the property."

---

18. Rev. Rul. 61–222, 1961–2 C.B. 58. See also TAM 200530027; Ronald W. Blasi, Ineffective and Inequitable: The Section 265(a) Interest Disallowance, 25 Wake Forest L. Rev. 811, 830 (1990).

19. 1970–2 C.B. 499, amplified by Rev. Proc. 80–55, 1980–2 C.B. 849, and Rev. Proc. 83–91, 1983–2 C.B. 618, modified by Rev. Proc. 83–91, 1983–52 I.R.B. 21.

20. 388 F.2d 420 (7th Cir. 1968); accord Earl Drown Corp. v. Commissioner, 86 T.C. 217 (1986).

21. 321 F.Supp. 222 (E.D. Va. 1971). See also Rev. Rul. 55–389, 1955–1 C.B. 276, in which the Service allowed a deduction for interest on working capital loans temporarily invested in tax-exempt securities.

A similar result was reached in Ball v. Commissioner[22] where the Tax Court allowed an investor to deduct for interest paid on a number of investments made at a time when he held tax exempt securities. These included the assumption of a loan to prevent the insolvency of a corporation engaged in cattle raising, an oil drilling venture, and the purchase of various properties. In allowing the taxpayer to deduct, the Tax Court relied upon Wisconsin Cheeseman and reasoned that the "loans were used to finance major, nonrecurring opportunities ... and were not foreseeable when the tax-exempt securities were purchased."

[c] Insurance Policy Loans

Life insurance policies and related investments have also provided taxpayers with opportunities to secure double tax benefits through section 101, which excludes the proceeds of life insurance from gross income, and section 163, which allows a deduction for interest. Tax avoidance practices in this area have been so widespread and of such a variety that on more than one occasion, Congress has had to enact limiting legislation.

One of the earliest limitations on the interest deduction is provided by what is now section 264(a)(2), which denies a deduction for interest on indebtedness incurred or continued to purchase or carry a single premium life insurance, endowment, or annuity policy. Under section 264(c) a policy is treated as a single premium contract if substantially all the premiums are paid within four years of the date of purchase or if an amount is deposited with the insurer to pay a substantial number of future premiums.

A second limitation in this area is 264(a)(3); under this provision a deduction is denied for interest paid on indebtedness incurred or continued to purchase or carry life insurance, endowment, or annuity contracts (other than single premium contracts covered by section 264(a)(2)) under a plan that contemplates systematic direct or indirect borrowing of part or all the increases in the cash value of such contracts. Under section 264(d) the following are excepted from the section 264(a)(3) disallowance: interest of $100 or less during the year, loans made because of unforeseen circumstances, loans made for business purposes, and when four out of the first seven annual premiums are paid with funds other than those borrowed under the plan.

The denial of an interest deduction in the case of systematic borrowings is designed to curb the use of an interest deduction as a means of increasing the amount of tax-free life insurance that may be carried. For example, insurance companies designed policies so that taxpayers would pay only the first year's premium and thereafter borrow from the insurance company or a bank against the annual increases in loan values that would equal or exceed the amount of the annual premiums. As a

---

22. 54 T.C. 1200 (1970); accord Batten   1971). See also CCA 200238002.
v. United States, 322 F.Supp. 629 (E.D. Va.

result of section 264(a)(3), taxpayers no longer have the government sharing the interest costs of such insurance programs.

[d] Miscellaneous

Section 163(e) allows a deduction for original issue discount, which is a form of interest.

Section 163(f) denies a deduction for interest on registration-required obligations not in registered form. Registration-required obligations are generally all obligations except those that have a maturity of less than one year, are issued by individuals, or are of a type not offered to the general public. Section 263A(f) requires capitalization of interest incurred for the production of property by a taxpayer if the property has a long useful life or production period. Under section 266 a taxpayer may elect to capitalize interest. Furthermore, section 263(g) requires capitalization of interest incurred to carry the offsetting positions in a straddle.

[e] Related Taxpayers

Suppose that a corporate taxpayer on the accrual method of accounting borrows money from its sole shareholder, an individual, who is on the cash method. Without more, a deduction for interest through immediate accrual is available to the corporation while inclusion in gross income of the interest to the shareholder must await actual payment, a matter that could be postponed indefinitely. To control this, section 267(a)(2) requires an accrual method taxpayer to defer deduction of interest payable to a related cash method taxpayer until the amount is includible in the latter's gross income. In general, under section 267(b) related taxpayers include family members, trusts and trust grantors, trustees and beneficiaries, owners and their controlled (more than 50%) corporations, and partners and partnerships.[23]

Section 267(a)(2) does not provide the outer limits of the nondeductibility of interest payments involving related taxpayers. The regulations state that "section 267 is not exclusive" and that "[n]o deduction for . . . interest arising in a transaction which is not bona fide will be allowed."[24]

[f] Prepaid Interest: Sham Transactions

Several decades ago schemes were devised under which a net economic advantage could be obtained through combining a prepaid interest deduction with a second tax advantage, such as a capital gain in later years. Here the Service and the courts required that the interest-generating transaction possess an economic or commercial substance apart from any designed tax saving in order to qualify the interest paid for deduction under section 163. For example, in Revenue Ruling 54–94[25] the Service concluded that the following plan lacked such substance: M

23. For additional application of § 267(a)(2) to a business expense deduction, see § 4.02, *supra*.

24. Treas. Reg. § 1.267(a)–1(c).

25. 1954–1 C.B. 53. See also TAM 9812005; Knetsch v. United States, 364 U.S. 361, 366, 81 S.Ct. 132, 135 (1960).

Insurance Company sold an "annuity bond" to the taxpayer for $100,000, the taxpayer paying $100 in cash and giving a $99,900 3% note. The bond paid 2½% interest. The plan contemplated that the ½% interest cost would be more than offset by the interest deduction and the preferential capital gain rate upon a subsequent sale of the bond.

The position of the Service was upheld in most of the cases, and in 1960 the Supreme Court provided additional support in Knetsch v. United States.[26] Knetsch indicates that realization of the second stage of the planned tax benefit is not the *sine qua non* for the disallowance of an interest deduction under the economic or commercial substance doctrine. In Knetsch the taxpayer purchased 30–year, 2½% annuity bonds from an insurance company. This purchase was made shortly before the effective date of an amendment to the Code that included the purchase of annuities within the single premium provision of section 264(a)(2). The purchase price of the bonds was $4,004,000; the taxpayer "paid" $4 million in 3½% notes and $140,000 of interest in advance. The taxpayer was permitted to borrow in advance on the $100,000 loan value of the bonds as of the end of the first year. This he did by borrowing $99,000 with a second 3½% note, paying an additional first year's interest of $3,465. If this process had been repeated for 30 years, the taxpayer would have been entitled to an annuity of a mere $43 a month based on a $1,000 equity ($8,388,000 cash or loan value less $8,387,000 of indebtedness).

Thus, there was nothing substantial for the taxpayer to gain other than the interest deduction. The taxpayer abandoned the plan after four years and surrendered the annuities to the company. In this manner he apparently abandoned a plan to convert the proceeds received into capital gains since the surrender resulted in ordinary income.[27] The taxpayer claimed deductions for his prepaid interest, and the question of how to treat the first two years of the plan came before the Supreme Court. Although the taxpayer would have suffered a net loss even with the allowance of the deductions for his prepaid interest, this did not deter the Supreme Court from disallowing the deductions under the economic or commercial substance doctrine. The Supreme Court found that the transaction was a sham because nothing of substance was realized apart from a tax deduction.

26. 364 U.S. 361, 81 S.Ct. 132, 5 L.Ed.2d 128 (1960). See also CCA 200650014; IRS CCA 200532047; TAM 200513028; Richard M. Lipton, New Tax Shelter Decisions Present Further Problems for the IRS, 102 J. Tax'n 211, 219 (2005).

27. The final chapter in the saga of Knetsch was written by the Court of Claims when he sought a deduction for his out-of-pocket costs of some $137,000 for the year he surrendered the annuity bonds to the insurance company. The court denied the deduction. It held as follows: (1) the trans-

action failed as a transaction entered into for profit under § 165(a)(2) because the only motivating factor was the tax deduction; (2) the costs did not qualify as an expense paid for the management or conservation of property under § 212 for the same lack of profit-seeking reason; (3) the government was not estopped by letter rulings granted other taxpayers (subsequently revoked); and (4) the taxpayer was not discriminated against. Knetsch v. United States, 172 Ct.Cl. 378, 348 F.2d 932 (1965), cert. denied, 383 U.S. 957, 86 S.Ct. 1221, 16 L.Ed.2d 300 (1966).

When taxpayers have been denied deductions under prepaid interest plans, some courts have reasoned that the loans were shams because they did not create genuine indebtednesses. Other courts have concluded the transactions were shams because they lacked economic substance. The Second Circuit considered both approaches—sham transactions and economic substance in Goldstein v. Commissioner.[28] In Goldstein the taxpayer won a taxable sweepstakes prize of $140,000. To reduce the taxable amount on this income, she borrowed $945,000 from two banks and prepaid some $81,000 of interest at a rate of 4%. This was followed by the purchase of $1,000,000 of 1½% Treasury notes that were pledged as collateral for the bank loans. The plan, which was devised by the taxpayer's accountant son, had a built-in economic loss of some $18,000, and the taxpayer showed an actual loss of $25,000 because of greater than anticipated losses in disposing of the Treasury notes. However, it was contemplated that the plan would effect a $47,000 reduction in tax liability because of the interest deduction.

The Tax Court, in a full court review with five dissents, denied the deduction; it concluded, on the authority of Knetsch, that the loan transactions were shams since they created no genuine indebtednesses. In affirming, the Second Circuit rejected the Tax Court's sham rationale because the lending institutions did not deal solely in such arrangements, the loans were outstanding for a substantial time, and the collateral demanded and the right of recourse of the lenders against the taxpayer provided them with genuine security. The Second Circuit denied the deduction on the ground that the loan transactions had no purpose or substance apart from the anticipated tax consequences and, hence, fell outside the intent of section 163. The Second Circuit found that the Tax Court had been correct in rejecting the taxpayer's contention that she anticipated gain on the resale of the Treasury notes because the computations made by the taxpayer's son established that an $18,000 economic loss was anticipated at the outset.

Under section 446(b), if the taxpayer's method of accounting does not clearly reflect income, the Commissioner is empowered to prescribe a method that does. Using this provision, the Service announced in Revenue Ruling 68–643[29] that a claimed prepaid interest deduction by a cash method taxpayer may not result in a clear reflection of income in the year of payment and may require allocation. The Service added that a deduction claimed for a period of up to 12 months following the year of payment will be considered on a case-by-case basis.

---

28. 364 F.2d 734 (2d Cir. 1966), cert. denied, 385 U.S. 1005, 87 S.Ct. 708, 17 L.Ed.2d 543 (1967); accord Collins v. Commissioner, 54 T.C. 1656 (1970) (prepaid interest on purchase of an apartment building by a sweepstakes winner was a sham). See also CCA 200650014; CCA 200620022; TAM 200513028; David P. Hariton, When and how Should the Economic Substance Doctrine be Applied?, 60 Tax L. Rev. 29, 56 (2006).

29. 1968–2 C.B. 76, revoking I.T. 3740, 1945 C.B. 109, followed in McMullan v. United States, 231 Ct.Cl. 378, 686 F.2d 915 (1982). Section 461(g) provides that the prepaid interest must be allocated over the life of the debt unless such interest represents points incurred in relation to the purchase or improvement of ones principle residence that also serves as security for the loan.

[3] TAXES

[a] In General

Section 164(a) permits a taxpayer to deduct the following in the year in which paid or accrued: (1) state, local, and foreign real property taxes, (2) state and local personal property taxes, (3) state, local, and foreign income taxes, (4) the environmental tax imposed on corporations that have an alternative minimum tax of at least $2 million, and (5) the generation skipping tax imposed on income distributions.[30] Other state, local, and foreign taxes paid or accrued in carrying on a trade or business or section 212 activity are also deductible. However, state, local, or foreign taxes, other than the six enumerated taxes, incurred in a trade or business or section 212 activity in connection with the acquisition or disposition of property are not deductible. Instead, such taxes must be treated on the acquisition of the property as part of the cost and on the disposition as a reduction of the amount realized. For example, a sales tax paid on the acquisition of the property for use in business is part of the cost of the property.

The basic requirement of section 164 is that the amounts paid or incurred are "taxes." The Service has observed that "[g]enerally, the word has been defined as an exaction of the state laid by some rule of apportionment according to which the persons or property taxed share the public burden and the proceeds of which go into the state's general revenue fund."[31] Labels are not determinative of whether charges are or are not taxes. Such items as turnpike tolls[32] and amounts deposited in parking meters[33] are not taxes, but "fees" paid by corporations for filing certificates of increase of capital stock are taxes.[34]

[b] State, Local, and Foreign Real Property Taxes

Deductible real property taxes are those imposed on interests in real property [35]"levied for the general public welfare by the proper taxing authorities at a like rate against all property in the territory over which such authorities have jurisdiction."[36] Such taxes are to be contrasted with those "assessed against local benefits of a kind tending to increase the value of the property assessed," which are not deductible.[37] This limitation applies to assessments for items such as street and sidewalk improvements, since the charges do not benefit the public but rather the property directly.[38] Examples of other items that the Service has ruled

---

30. Section 275 denies a deduction for certain taxes, including federal income taxes and foreign income taxes taken as a credit under § 901. Taxes may be subject to the capitalization rules of § 263A. Under § 266 a taxpayer may elect to capitalize taxes.

31. Rev. Rul. 60–366, 1960–2 C.B. 63.

32. Cox v. Commissioner, 41 T.C. 161 (1963). See also FSA 200014003; Field Service Advisory, 1995 WL 1918334.

33. Rev. Rul. 73–91, 1973–1 C.B. 71.

34. Rev. Rul. 66–184, 1966–2 C.B. 50.

35. Treas. Reg. § 1.164–3(b).

36. Treas. Reg. § 1.164–4(a).

37. § 164(c).

38. Treas. Reg. § 1.164–4(a).

are not deductible are annual fees earmarked for sanitation services imposed on all residential and commercial property in a county based on assessed value of the property,[39] sewerage service charges based upon the amount of water used,[40] and front foot benefit charges for water main and sewer improvements.[41] However, charges that may not be deducted because of section 164(c)(1) may be deducted under section 162 if they are ordinary and necessary expenses incurred in the taxpayer's business.

Section 164(d) provides for apportionment of real property taxes between the seller and the purchaser. Under section 164(d)(1) taxes for the "real property tax year" in which the property is sold are allocated to the seller and the purchaser, and the deduction allowed each is limited to the portion of taxes that corresponds to the part of the "real property tax year" during which each owned the property.[42] The term "real property tax year" "refers to the period which, under the law imposing the tax, is regarded as the period to which the tax imposed relates."[43]

The seller is deemed to have paid the portion of the year's tax that is allocable to the period ending on the day before the date of the sale, and the purchaser is deemed to have paid the balance.[44] For example, assume the real property tax year is from April 1 of one year through March 31 of the next year, and the real property tax is $365 a year. Assume also that A, who owns a parcel of real estate, sells the parcel to B on June 30, and B owns it for the balance of the real property tax year, June 30 through March 31. For purposes of section 164(a) the seller, A, is deemed to have paid 90/365 times $365, or $90, of the real property tax, while the buyer, B, is deemed to have paid 275/365 times $365, or $275, of the tax.[45]

The Code provides for the determination of the amount realized on the sale of real property and for the determination of basis of real property acquired by purchase when the taxes are apportioned under section 164(d).[46]

[c] State and Local Personal Property Taxes

To be deductible under section 164(a)(2) state and local personal property taxes must meet three requirements.[47] First, the tax must be substantially proportionate to the value of the property (ad valorem) as opposed to, for example, a motor vehicle tax based upon weight, model year, or horsepower. Second, the tax must be imposed on an annual basis regardless of whether it is collected more or less frequently. Finally, the tax must be in respect of personalty. If a tax is based partly on value and partly on other criteria, the portion of the tax based on value may be deducted while the other portion may not.

39. Rev. Rul. 77–29, 1977–1 C.B. 44. See also CCA 200630017; IRS FSA 200014003.

40. Rev. Rul. 75–346, 1975–2 C.B. 66.

41. Rev. Rul. 75–455, 1975–2 C.B. 68.

42. Treas. Reg. § 1.164–6(a).

43. Treas. Reg. § 1.164–6(c).

44. Treas. Reg. § 1.164–6(b)(1)(i).

45. Treas. Reg. § 1.164–6(b)(3), Ex. (1); §§ 1001(b) and 1012.

46. §§ 1001(b) and 1012.

47. Treas. Reg. § 1.164–3(c).

[4] EXTRAORDINARY MEDICAL CARE EXPENSES

[a] In General

Section 213 allows an individual to deduct medical care expenses paid during a taxable year and not compensated for by insurance or otherwise. The deduction is available with respect to amounts paid for the taxpayer and the taxpayer's spouse and dependents to the extent that the total exceeds 7.5% of adjusted gross income. Medical care expenses eligible for the deduction are amounts paid for the following: (1) diagnosis, treatment, or prevention of disease or malfunction of the body;[48] (2) transportation primarily for and essential to medical care;[49] (3) qualified long-term care services;[50] (4) health insurance;[51] and (5) the cost of up to $50 a night for "each individual" for lodging away from home primarily for and essential to medical care provided by a physician at a hospital or medical facility if "there is no significant element of personal pleasure, recreation, or vacation" and the lodging is not "lavish or extravagant."[52] The cost of prescription drugs and insulin is regarded as for medical care.[53]

A question may sometimes arise whether an expense is deductible under section 213 or section 162. The 7.5% floor under section 213 may be avoided if the deduction is taken as a trade or business expense. In Revenue Ruling 75–316[54] the Service said that an expense is deductible under section 162 rather than under section 213 if the item is clearly not required or used, other than incidentally, in the conduct of the taxpayer's personal activities. In Revenue Ruling 75–316 the Service concluded that payments made by a blind employee to readers for services performed in connection with the conduct of the blind employee's work were deductible under section 162. However, the Service has concluded that maintenance expenses incurred by a blind individual for his seeing-eye dog used in the conduct of his business were deductible under section 213 rather than under section 162.[55] The Service has also concluded that the expenses of a professional singer for treatments of his throat by a medical specialist were not deductible under section 162.[56]

[b] Medical Care

The statutory definition of "medical care" is a broad one, encompassing amounts paid either for treatment of a disease or for the purpose of affecting any structure of the body.[57] In Mattes v. Commissioner[58] the

48. § 213(d)(1)(A).

49. § 213(d)(1)(B).

50. § 213(d)(1)(C).

51. § 213(d)(1)(D).

52. § 213(d)(2).

53. § 213(a) and (b).

54. 1975–2 C.B. 54. See also Larry R. Garrison, Help Clients Take Advantage of Tax Breaks for the Disabled, 78 Prac. Tax Strategies 34 (2007).

55. Rev. Rul. 57–461, 1957–2 C.B. 116. See also Ron West, Diagnose Payments for Bigger Medical Expense Deductions, 62 Prac. Tax Strategies 289, 300 (1999).

56. Rev. Rul. 71–45, 1971–1 C.B. 51.

57. § 213(d)(1)(A).

58. 77 T.C. 650 (1981), acq., 1982–1 C.B. 1. The Service has ruled that expenditures for hair transplants performed by a dermatologist or plastic surgeon and for hair removal through electrolysis by a tech-

Tax Court held that the expense of a hair transplant operation for a taxpayer who suffered from premature baldness was deductible because it was "for a medical surgical procedure to correct a specific physiological condition." Similarly, the Service concluded in Revenue Ruling 76–332[59] that the cost of a face lift was deductible as a medical expense.

However, the Service has ruled that the cost of an individual's participation in a weight reduction program or a program to help cigarette smokers stop smoking are not deductible.[60] Its position is based on the language in the regulations that deductions for expenditures for medical care are confined strictly to those incurred primarily for the prevention or alleviation of physical or mental defects or illnesses and that expenditures beneficial to ones general health, such as the cost of a vacation, are not for medical care.[61] The Service regards amounts paid for treatment of alcoholism or drug addiction at therapeutic centers as medical expenses.[62]

In Greisdorf v. Commissioner[63] the Tax Court held that a special school included one established "to provide an environment where average and above-average students with special learning disabilities (usually psychological) could learn to adjust and function normally in a competitive classroom situation." It was shown that the school's staff had special training in psychology, and the programs were individualized. Hence, the Tax Court held that the tuition for the taxpayer's daughter, who suffered an emotional disturbance causing a withdrawal from reality, was deductible.

On the other hand, if the primary purpose of the private schooling is educational rather than remedial, only the costs attributable to the latter will be deductible as medical expenses. For example, in Fay v. Commissioner[64] two of the taxpayer's children who had learning disabilities were sent to a private school that employed the Montessori method and offered a regular curriculum supplemented by a special program for language development. In addition to the regular tuition a fee was charged for the language development program. Both of the taxpayer's children attended the school and were in the language development program. In 1975 the taxpayer paid some $5,100 for regular tuition and $1,800 for the language development program. The Tax Court held that the $5,100 was not deductible but that the additional $1,800 fee qualified as an amount paid for medical care.

nician constitute medical care. Rev. Rul. 82–111, 1982–1 C.B. 48.

59. 1976–2 C.B. 81.

60. Rev. Rul. 79–151, 1979–1 C.B. 116 (weight); Rev. Rul. 79–162, 1979–1 C.B. 116 (smoking). See also Deducting the Cost of Smoking Cessation Programs Under Internal Revenue Code Section 213, 81 Mich. L. Rev. 237 (1982).

61. Treas. Reg. § 1.213–1(e)(1)(ii).

62. Rev. Rul. 73–325, 1973–2 C.B. 75 (alcoholism); Rev. Rul. 72–226, 1972–1 C.B. 96 (drug addiction).

63. 54 T.C. 1684 (1970), acq., 1970–2 C.B. xix. See also Craig J. Langstraat, John M. Malloy, and Courtney Brock, Special Schooling Tuition may be a Deductible Medical Expense, 76 Prac. Tax Strategies 279 (2006).

64. 76 T.C. 408 (1981). See also James W. Colliton, The Medical Expense Deduction, 34 Wayne L. Rev. 1307, 1372 (1988).

Under the regulations the cost of a permanent improvement to property that ordinarily would not have a medical purpose is deductible if directly related to prescribed medical care but only for the portion of the cost that exceeds the increased value of the property attributable to the improvement.[65] Even so, any increase in the value of the property attributable capital improvements related to the removal of structural barriers or other accommodations (such as wheelchair ramps and shower bars) so a physically handicapped individual may live independently may be disregarded.[66]

Related operating and maintenance costs of capital improvements may also qualify as medical expenses in certain circumstances. For example, a portion of the cost of constructing an exercise pool may be deductible.[67] In Revenue Ruling 83–33[68] the taxpayer had severe osteoarthritis, a degenerative disease. To slow the effects of the disease, the taxpayer's physician prescribed a treatment of swimming several times a day. The pool, which was attached to the taxpayer's residence, was 8 feet wide by 36 feet long, varied in depth from approximately 3 to 5 feet, and had a hydrotherapy device. The Service said that the cost of the pool was incurred for the primary purpose of and was directly related to the taxpayer's medical care; hence, it was deductible to the extent the expenditure exceeded the increase in value of the taxpayer's property. The Service added that the taxpayer's costs to operate and maintain the special purpose pool were also deductible.[69]

[5] CHARITABLE CONTRIBUTION DEDUCTIONS

Under section 170 individuals and corporations, and under section 642(c) trusts and estates, are allowed deductions from gross income, subject to seemingly innumerable limitations, for contributions or gifts made to certain charitable organizations.

As indicated later in this chapter, the broad policy justifying exempt status is based on the notion that the organizations provide important public services that would otherwise have to be provided by the government. The policy underlying section 170 is related but restricted to encouraging charitable activities. Thus, the deduction under section 170 is limited to contributions or gifts made to organizations for the furtherance of their charitable purposes.

From the viewpoint of the practitioner, section 170 constitutes an integral, but complex, tool in tax planning. The complexity permeates almost all aspects of section 170.

65. Treas. Reg. § 1.213–1(e)(1)(iii).

66. Rev. Rul. 87–106, 1987–2 C.B. 67.

67. See Rev. Rul. 83–33, 1983–1 C.B. 70.

68. 1983–1 C.B. 70.

69. See Haines v. Commissioner, 71 T.C. 644 (1979).

[a] Criteria and Valuation

[i] In General

Section 170(c) defines a charitable contribution, which is allowed as a deduction under section 170(a)(1), as "a contribution or gift to or for the use of" an organization described in section 170(c)(1)-(5). When the taxpayer receives a benefit from such a payment or a transfer of property, the courts have used various tests in deciding whether the taxpayer has made "a contribution or gift." One test ascribes to the term "gift" the same meaning it has under section 102(a), which excludes gifts from gross income.[70] Under this test the taxpayer must establish that the payment or transfer proceeded from "detached and disinterested generosity."[71] Under a second test:

> [I]f the benefits received, or expected to be received, are substantial, and meaning by that, benefits are greater than those that inure to the general public from transfers for charitable purposes (which benefits are merely incidental to the transfer), then in such case . . . the transferor has received, or expects to receive, a quid pro quo sufficient to remove the transfer from the realm of deductibility under section 170.[72]

A third test allows a deduction if the amount contributed to the organization exceeds the value of the benefit received from it.[73]

In United States v. American Bar Endowment[74] the Supreme Court appears to have adopted the Service's two-part test for determining when part of a dual payment is deductible. The Supreme Court said: "First, the payment is deductible only if and to the extent it exceeds the market value of the benefit received. Second, the excess payment must be 'made with the intention of making a gift.' "[75] The Supreme Court observed that the First Circuit[76] had expressed "dissatisfaction with such subjective tests as the taxpayer's motives in making a purported charitable contribution,"[77] but noted that the Tax Court had adopted the Service's two-part test.[78] The Supreme Court said that the taxpayer "must at a minimum demonstrate that he purposely contributed money or property in excess of the value of any benefit he received in return."[79]

---

70. See DeJong v. Commissioner, 309 F.2d 373 (9th Cir. 1962). See also Field Service Advisory, 1995 WL 1770815; Field Service Advisory, 1992 WL 1355674.

71. See Commissioner v. Duberstein, 363 U.S. 278, 80 S.Ct. 1190, 4 L.Ed.2d 1218 (1960).

72. Singer Co. v. United States, 449 F.2d 413, 423 (Ct. Cl. 1971).

73. Oppewal v. Commissioner, 468 F.2d 1000 (1st Cir. 1972). See also Field Service Advisory, 1997 WL 33313757; Field Service Advisory, 1992 WL 1355666.

74. 477 U.S. 105, 106 S.Ct. 2426, 91 L.Ed.2d 89 (1986).

75. 477 U.S. 105, 117, 106 S.Ct. 2426, 2433, 91 L.Ed.2d 89 (1986), citing Rev.Rul. 67-246, 67-2 C.B. 104.

76. Oppewal v. Commissioner, 468 F.2d 1000 (1st Cir. 1972).

77. Id.

78. See Murphy v. Commissioner, 54 T.C. 249 (1970). See also Field Service Advisory, 1994 WL 1866009; Christine Roemhildt Moore, Religious Tax Exemption and the "Charitable Scrutiny" Test, 15 Regent U. L. Rev. 295, 326 (2003).

79. 477 U.S. 105, 118, 106 S.Ct. 2426, 2433-2434 (1986).

A substantial benefit to a taxpayer engaged in business may some-times work to his advantage if he can show the necessary relationship between the business and the payment to a charitable organization; in other words, if the taxpayer can show that the payment constituted an ordinary and necessary business expense deductible under section 162 this result is beneficial. Although section 162(b) precludes a charitable contribution deduction in excess of the section 170 ceiling limits on contributions, this provision functions at best as a presumption and allows a taxpayer engaged in business to show that a payment was a business expense. In Marquis v. Commissioner,[80] for example, the tax-payer operated a travel agency and made payments to certain charitable organizations. Deductions as business promotional expenses were al-lowed upon a showing that the recipient charities provided most of the taxpayer's clients. Because the taxpayer received something in return for her payments, they were considered business expenses rather than charitable contributions.

The Service has pointed out that "[a] contribution for purposes of section 170 of the Code is a voluntary transfer of money or property that is made with no expectation of procuring a financial benefit commensu-rate with the amount of the transfer."[81] Hence, tuition payments are not deductible as charitable contributions to an educational institution.[82] However, even if the actual cost of educating a student exceeds the amount of tuition charged, the payment may be a charitable contribution if it is a voluntary transfer made with no expectation of obtaining a commensurate benefit.[83]

In Revenue Ruling 86–63[84] the Service has provided guidelines concerning whether payments to athletic scholarship programs are chari-table contributions under section 170 when the payments afford the right to purchase preferred seating at a university's home football games. In its analysis of the issue in Revenue Ruling 86–63 the Service relied upon Revenue Ruling 67–246.[85] In that revenue ruling the Service set forth various examples concerning the deductibility of payments made in connection with admission to or other participation in charitable fund raising activities. The Service indicated in Revenue Ruling 67–246 that if a deduction is claimed under section 170(a) with respect to a payment for which the taxpayer receives substantial privileges or bene-

---

80. 49 T.C. 695 (1968), acq. 1971–2 Cum. Bull. 3. See also Rev. Rul. 84–110, 1984–2 Cum. Bull. 35 (§ 162 deduction per-mitted for city council member's expendi-tures for salaries, office rents, and supplies, the Service concluding that because the ex-penditures were charitable contributions under § 170 the limitation in § 162(b) did not apply).

81. Rev. Rul. 83–104, 1983–2 Cum. Bull. 46. See also Field Service Advisory, 1997 WL 33313757; Field Service Advisory, 1992 WL 1355666.

82. Id.

83. Id. In Rev. Rul. 79–99, 1979–1 Cum. Bull. 108, the Service concluded that a taxpayer whose child attended a church school that charged no tuition but solicited operating funds from parents, churches, and others was not entitled to a charitable deduction for payments that did not exceed the fair market value of the child's edu-cation.

84. 1986–1 Cum. Bull. 88. See also Field Service Advisory, 2002 WL 1315725.

85. 1967–2 Cum. Bull. 104. See also CCA 200238041; FSA 200149007.

fits, the payment is presumed not to be a charitable contribution; moreover, the burden is on the taxpayer to establish the amount paid is not the purchase price and the portion of the payment claimed as a charitable deduction represents the excess of the total amount paid over the fair market value of any substantial privileges or benefits that may be received in return.

[ii] Payment and Services

Under section 170(a)(1) a deduction for a charitable contribution is allowed only if payment is made within the taxable year. For corporate taxpayers using the accrual method, section 170(a)(2) provides a special rule: if payment is made within two and one-half months after the close of the taxable year the deduction may be taken in the year of accrual.

The actual payment requirement has been interpreted as limiting the deduction under section 170 to contributions of property, measured by the fair market value and to deny a deduction for personal services[86] rendered to a charity.

Under section 170(f)(3) (applicable to transfers other than in trust) a deduction is not available unless the taxpayer transfers his entire interest in the property, and a right of use is treated as less than an entire interest. As an exception to this rule, a gift of a remainder interest in a personal residence or a farm nevertheless qualifies for as a charitable contribution deduction.[87] Under section 170(a)(3) a gift of a future interest in personal property is not treated as complete as long as the possessory interest is held by the taxpayer or by a person or entity related to him under the rules of section 267(b) or section 707(b). For example, a gift of a painting to a qualifying charity with the taxpayer retaining possession for ten years would not qualify for a deduction until the tax year that the term expired. Further, a gift of a remainder interest, regardless of the type of property involved, will be disallowed if there is a possibility that it could be diverted from charitable use.[88]

While the value of personal services rendered to charities are not deductible, unreimbursed expenses in rendering services may be deductible as contributions "for the use of" charities.[89] Thus, such items as the cost of uniforms, transportation, meals, and lodging may be deducted as

---

86. Treas. Reg. § 1.170A–1(g). See also Rev. Rul. 53–162, 1953–2 Cum. Bull. 127 (a donation of blood is analogous to a gift of a service rather than of property); Lary v. United States, 787 F.2d 1538 (11th Cir. 1986) (a donation of blood is not deductible because it constitutes the performance of a service or the contribution of a product). Cf. Holmes v. Commissioner, 57 T.C. 430 (1971), acq., 1972–1 Cum. Bull. 2, in which the Tax Court held that a donation by the taxpayer of two films he produced qualified as a gift of property rather than of services and could be valued on the basis of what other film producers charged.

87. § 170(f)(3)(B)(i).

88. See Rev. Rul. 65–144, 1965–1 Cum. Bull. 442, in which the Service denied a deduction for a gift of a charitable remainder interest because the income could have been diverted to noncharitable uses.

89. Treas. Reg. § 1.170A–1(g). See also Rev. Rul. 84–61, 1984–1 Cum. Bull. 39, in which the Service announced it would follow Rockefeller v. Commissioner, 676 F.2d 35 (2d Cir. 1982), in allowing unreimbursed expenses under § 170(b)(1) (A), which requires that gifts be made "to" certain organizations.

well as travel expenses incurred as a delegate at charitable organization meetings.[90] No deduction will be allowed, however, if travel is undertaken for personal purposes or if it results in an economic benefit to the taxpayer.[91]

[iii]   Valuation of Property

One of the more difficult problems encountered in the administration of section 170 is the valuation of property. The Code does not prescribe criteria for valuation except insofar as it requires that a contribution will be deductible only if verified under the regulations. The regulations prescribe a standard of fair market value at the time of the contribution and define fair market value as the price at which property would change hands between a willing buyer and willing seller.[92] There is no suggestion in the regulations as to the meaning of the term "market" except that for a contribution of inventory or stock in trade the donor's usual market price controls. It seems conceded that the fair market value approach of the regulations precludes the use of a standard that would measure the deduction solely by the value to the charity, however consistent this may be with the theory underlying section 170.

Suppose the charity sells the property shortly after the contribution is made. Is the sale price conclusive as to market value at the time of the gift? In Kaplan v. Commissioner[93] the taxpayer contributed used clothing and furniture to a charity that had them appraised at $5,500 by an outside auction firm. Less than two months later they were sold at auction for $500. The Tax Court regarded the price received at the auction as the best evidence of the market value of the property at the time of the gift, and so it limited the taxpayer's deduction to $500. The Tax Court quite bluntly indicated that it believed the appraisal was a sham designed to provide the taxpayer with an inflated value for tax purposes. However, shortly after Kaplan the full Tax Court took a more liberal view in a case that involved the same charity and the same appraisal-auction process as in Kaplan.

In McGuire v. Commissioner,[94] the taxpayer's donations of high quality furniture, clothing, and art objects were made over three years.

---

90. Treas. Reg. § 1.170A–1(g). Section 170(k) denies a charitable deduction for travel expenses while away from home "unless there is no significant element of personal pleasure, recreation, or vacation in such travel."

91. See Babilonia v. Commissioner, 681 F.2d 678 (9th Cir. 1982) (cost of skating lessons and travel expenses denied because they were incurred primarily for a personal benefit and only indirectly benefited a figure skating association or an olympic committee); Seed v. Commissioner, 57 T.C. 265 (1971) (expenses in connection with a golf tour of Europe sponsored by a tax-exempt organization); Wood v. Commissioner, 57 T.C. 220 (1971), aff'd, 462 F.2d 691 (5th Cir. 1972) (travel to the Philippines as a member of a veterans organization); Rev. Rul. 71–135, 1971–1 Cum. Bull. 94 (participant in foreign study mission to which the taxpayer was not a delegate).

92. Treas. Reg. § 1.170A–1(c).

93. 43 T.C. 663 (1965). See also Field Service Advisory, 1998 WL 1984368.

94. 44 T.C. 801 (1965). See also Estate of Alexia DuPont Ortiz DeBie v. Commissioner, 56 T.C. 876 (1971), in which the Tax Court allowed a deduction for the value of tangible personal property upon the basis of the testimony of the taxpayer's experts, the Tax Court finding that a subsequent forced

The appraised value totaled some $62,000, and apart from a few items that were retained by the charity, the donations were sold at auction shortly thereafter for some $4,200. The Tax Court allowed a total of $15,200 as deductions. Three dissenting judges would have limited the deductions to the auction sales prices as contended by the Commissioner.

The Tax Court in McGuire rejected the sales price standard, finding that the best evidence of market value is not a sale consummated in a restricted market, such as the auction in McGuire where bidders were mostly retailers buying for resale. The court stated that it did not accept the appraiser's testimony, or that of an insurance broker who placed the taxpayer's insurance coverage, as to market value because both admitted their appraisals were based in large measure on replacement cost less wear and tear. The court did state, however, that some weight was to be given to the testimony that the auction prices did not reflect the true market value and to testimony indicating that the prices would have been higher had the property been held for sale over an extended period. Kaplan was distinguished on the ground that there the court did not hold that an auction price would always be determinative of market value. It is because of these valuation difficulties that the donation of vehicles are subject to special rules.[95]

A second valuation problem involves deductions claimed for the price of tickets to charitable fund-raising affairs. As indicated earlier, in Revenue Ruling 67–246[96] the Service said that payment for such tickets raises a presumption that no gift was intended; therefore, the allowance of a deduction depends upon a showing that the amount paid was in excess of the value received. If this is done, perhaps by contacting the charity to determine the value of what is being received or through comparisons with the charges for commercial events, the excess qualifies as a deduction. Revenue Ruling 67–246 says that nonuse of tickets will be regarded as irrelevant. In United States v. American Bar Endowment,[97] the Supreme Court applied the test set forth in this revenue ruling.

The Service also takes the position that a charity raffle ticket is not deductible on the ground that full consideration is received by the purchaser of a ticket who obtains a chance to win a valuable prize.[98] This position was upheld in Goldman v. Commissioner.[99] The Sixth Circuit

sale was not an adequate measure of the value at the time of the gift.

95. See Dominic L. Daher, and Joshua D. Rosenberg, Accounting for Vehicle Donations Just Made Life a Little More Complicated, 17 Tax'n of Exempts 134 (2005).

96. 1967–2 Cum. Bull. 104. The Service also indicated concern with charities misleading patrons such as by the use of the term "donation" on tickets, saying that in such instances the "event or affair will be subject to a special scrutiny and may be questioned in audit of returns."

97. 477 U.S. 105, 106 S.Ct. 2426, 91 L.Ed.2d 89 (1986).

98. See Ex. 5 of Rev. Rul. 67–246, 1967–2 Cum. Bull. 104.

99. 388 F.2d 476 (6th Cir. 1967), aff'g 46 T.C. 136 (1966). See Rev. Rul. 83–130, 1983–2 Cum. Bull. 148, for a discussion of the tax consequences of a sale of a personal residence through a raffle conducted by a charitable organization.

recognized the possible application of an excess value rule for raffle tickets, observing that "[i]t is possible to hypothesize a raffle ticket situation where the charitable nature of the gift would scarcely be debated, as where the purchase for $10.00 is one of one thousand chances and the prize a nosegay of violets." But the Sixth Circuit said that the record was deficient on this argument of the taxpayer.

Another problem concerns the valuation of a remainder interest in real property. Section 170(f)(4) requires discounting such interests 6% a year for delay in receipt. The value of the remainder must also take into account depreciation (using the straight line method) and depletion. Discounting may also be necessary for a gift-annuity. Thus, under Revenue Ruling 70–15[100] the amount paid for an annuity in excess of the value of it at the time of the purchase was allowed as a contribution deduction.

If an annuity is purchased with appreciated property, special rules are applicable, and although gain on the disposition of the property may be realized, as a general rule a charitable deduction is available for the difference between the value of the property and the present value of the annuity.[101]

[b] Qualified Recipients

The term "charitable contribution" is described in section 170(c) as a gift made "to or for the use of" one of five types of organizations. They are: (1) a state, the United States (including possessions or territories), the District of Columbia, or any subdivisions, if the gifts are made for exclusively public purposes;[102] (2) a charitable organization (corporation, trust, community chest, fund, or foundation) created or organized in the United States (or any possession) and organized and operated exclusively for charitable purposes provided no earnings inure to the benefit of any individual, no substantial part of its activities consist in carrying on propaganda or otherwise attempting to influence legislation, and the organization does not engage in any activity on behalf of a candidate for political office;[103] (3) a post or organization of war veterans organized in

100. 1970–1 Cum. Bull. 20.

101. Treas. Reg. § 1.170A–1(d).

102. See Rev. Rul. 82–169, 1982–2 Cum. Bull. 72 (voluntary contribution to federal social security trust fund is a contribution to the United States); Rev. Rul. 81–307, 1981–2 Cum. Bull. 78 (deduction allowed for contribution of reward by victim's parent to police for information leading to conviction of murderer, reward serves exclusively public purpose); Rev. Rul. 71–47, 1971–1 Cum. Bull. 92 (deduction allowed for gift to nonprofit volunteer fire company as one for the use of a qualifying political subdivision).

103. In the case of a gift by a corporation under this second category to a "trust, chest, fund, or foundation," the penultimate sentence of § 170(c)(2) provides that a deduction is allowed only if it is used within the United States; the Service has interpreted this sentence, with its lack of reference to a corporate recipient, as permitting a gift by a corporation to a domestic charitable corporation for foreign charitable use. Rev. Rul. 69–80, 1969–1 Cum. Bull. 65. See also the United States–Canada tax treaty that permits United States taxpayers with Canadian income deductions for contributions to Canadian charities if they would have qualified if organized in the United States. United States Canada Tax Treaty, Aug. 16, 1984, art. XXI, para. 5.

the United States provided no earnings inure to the benefit of any individual; (4) for an individual contributor (corporations do not qualify), a fraternal lodge provided the individual's gift is to be used exclusively for the charitable purposes enumerated in the second category; (5) a cemetery company owned and operated for its members or a corporation chartered solely for its members or a corporation chartered solely for burial purposes and not permitted by its charter to engage in any business not incidental to its purpose, both types of organizations being subject to a private individual inurement limitation.

The Service's *Cumulative List of Organizations Described in Section 170(c)* (Publication 78) identifies organizations with outstanding ruling or determination letters which means contributions to them are deductible. This list is updated periodically, but inclusion is not a condition for qualification.

As an exception to the general requirement that a deductible gift must be made to or for the use of a qualified organization, section 170(g) permits charitable contribution treatment under the second, third, or fourth categories for amounts up to $50 a month expended to maintain as a member of the taxpayer's household (other than as a dependent) high school and grade school students under certain foreign exchange programs.

Deductions have been denied when donors have earmarked contributions to qualified organizations for payment to particular individuals or when donors have paid the educational or living expenses of particular individuals studying at qualified organizations.[104]

[c] Percentage Limitations

The federal income tax has long reflected a policy that limits deduction for charitable gifts. However, Congress has been subjected to pressures in this area stemming from both abuse of the deduction and from a desire to encourage charitable giving.

Under section 170(b)(1)(A) eight categories of charitable organizations qualify for the 50% ceiling on contributions by individuals. Gifts to other section 170(c) organizations may be deducted in an amount up to 30% of a taxpayer's contribution base with the 50% ceiling rules being applied first.

These so-called public or 50% organizations (the regulations use the term "section 170(b)(1)(A) organization")[105] are designated as "public" because in most instances they have a broad base of public support. These eight categories include the following: (1) a church or association of churches; (2) an educational organization that maintains a regular faculty, curriculum, and regularly enrolled student body at a place where

---

104. See, e.g., Tripp v. Commissioner, 337 F.2d 432 (7th Cir. 1964); Rev. Rul. 79–81, 1979–1 Cum. Bull. 107. See also Domin-

ic L. Daher, The Deductibility of Restricted Gifts, 18 Tax'n of Exempts 190 (2007).

105. Treas. Reg. § 1.170A–9.

instruction is provided;[106] (3) a hospital or a hospital-connected medical research organization;[107] (4) an organization that normally receives a substantial part of its support (apart from its exempt purpose income) from a governmental unit or the general public and that is organized and operated to hold and administer property for public colleges or universities qualifying as educational organizations defined in category (2); (5) a state, the United States, any subdivision or the District of Columbia if the gift is made exclusively for public purposes; (6) a religious, charitable, scientific, or educational organization that normally receives a substantial part of its support (apart from its charitable purpose functions) from a governmental unit described in category (5) or from contributions from the general public;[108] (7) a private foundation if it qualifies as an "operating foundation," defined in section 4942(j)(3),[109] a nonoperating pass-through foundation that makes qualifying distributions within two and one-half months of the close of its tax year, or a community foundation (trust or fund) that makes similar two and one-half month distributions and that will distribute corpus within one year of the donor's (or his spouse's) death;[110] or (8) an organization described in section 509(a)(2) or (3), which generally requires that the organization receive more than one-third of its support in gifts, grants, membership fees, incidental business income from persons other than disqualified persons and less than one-third of its income from investments.[111]

106. This category includes both public and private schools but not necessarily a museum that conducts a school. Treas. Reg. § 1.170A–9(c)(1).

107. The statute also requires that contributions for research be committed to expenditure within five years of the contribution. § 170(b)(1)(A)(iii).

108. The regulations indicate that this category is intended to cover publicly supported museums, libraries, community centers, and organizations for the promotion of the arts, opera, drama, and the like as well as such organizations as the Red Cross and United Fund; in general, publicly supported means that one-third of normal support must come from the government and the general public but a lesser percentage will satisfy the requirement if other conditions are met. Treas. Reg. § 1.170A–9(e).

109. In general, operating foundation classification under § 4942(j)(3) and the regulations requires that the foundation distribute 10% or more of its income for its exempt charitable purpose and that it meets one or more of the following tests: (1) 65% or more of its assets are devoted to its exempt purpose; (2) substantially all its support is derived from five or more unrelated exempt organizations or the general

public; or (3) the endowment is no more than adequate to meet current expenses.

110. The provision for community foundations (the regulations use the term "trust" as including funds and foundations) constitutes recognition of an entity that is designed to attract gifts for public purposes from a relatively few wealthy contributors as distinguished from a broadly supported community chest or fund. A community foundation may or may not include earmarked gifts, but ultimate power over the use of the gifts must rest with the trustees. Special rules are required to insure that such entities are publicly supported. Treas. Reg. § 1.170A–9(e)(11)-(14).

111. A § 509(a)(2) charitable organization (e.g., an entity providing scholarships for needy students) is expressly excluded from private foundation characterization because of its broad based public support; a § 509(a)(3) organization is similarly excluded since it is designed to provide support for a § 509(a)(2) organization or a public charity as described in the first six categories of § 170(b)(1)(A). The regulations governing §§ 509(a)(2) and (3) are detailed and complex. See Treas. Regs. §§ 1.509(a)–3, 1.509(a)–4.

Special rules govern contributions of capital gain, ordinary income property,[112] and bargain sales to charitable organizations.[113]

[6] THE STANDARD DEDUCTION

Under section 63(b) an individual is allowed a standard deduction in lieu of itemizing deductions.[114] Section 63(d) states that itemized deductions are those other than the deductions allowable in arriving at adjusted gross income and the deduction for exemptions. For an individual who may be claimed as a dependent, such as a minor child, the standard deduction is generally limited to a reduced amount or the individual's earned income (but not in excess of the otherwise applicable standard deduction).[115] The standard deduction is unavailable for certain individuals, including all married individuals who file separate returns if either spouse itemizes deductions.[116] An additional standard deduction is allowed for a taxpayer age 65 or older or blind.[117] The standard deduction amounts are adjusted for inflation.[118]

The standard deduction was introduced in 1944 shortly after the base of the federal income tax had been expanded to include the bulk of the nation's wage earners. It was aimed at simplifying the tax computation for low-income persons and easing the administrative burden of handling the additional millions of returns that would result from the expansion of the tax base. Because the standard deduction was intended as a substitute for personal itemized deductions, the concept of adjusted gross income was to separate most gain-seeking deductions from personal ones. The adjusted gross income deductions and the personal and dependency exemptions thus remain deductible even when the standard deduction is used.

[7] EXEMPTIONS

Section 151(a) allows individuals to deduct for exemptions. The amount allowed for each exemption is indexed for inflation and changes annually.[119] Section 151(b) allows an exemption for the taxpayer and an additional exemption for the spouse of the taxpayer if they file a joint return.[120] If a joint return is not filed, a taxpayer may still claim the exemption for the spouse if the spouse has no gross income and is not the dependent of another taxpayer.

---

112. § 170(e).

113. § 1011(b). In Ebben v. Commissioner, 783 F.2d 906 (9th Cir. 1986), the court held that a transfer by gift of encumbered property to a charity is a "sale" under § 1011(b). In Estate of Pauline E. Bullard v. Commissioner, 87 T.C. 261 (1986), the court, in a reviewed opinion, held portions of Treas. Regs. §§ 1.170A–4(c) and 1.1011–2 invalid.

114. For the current amount of the standard deduction, see IRS Publication 501.

115. § 63(c)(5). For purposes of § 63(c) the amount of a scholarship or fellowship received by a dependent child that is includible in gross income constitutes earned income.

116. § 63(c)(6).

117. § 63(c)(1), (3), (f). For the current amount of any additional standard deduction, see IRS Publication 501.

118. § 63(c)(4).

119. § 151(d)(3). For the current exemption amount, see IRS Publication 501.

120. § 151(b).

A taxpayer is also allowed an exemption for each dependent, as defined under section 152, whose gross income is less than the amount of the personal exemption or who is a child of the taxpayer and either has not attained age 19 or has not attained the age of 24 and is a student.[121] A "child" is defined as an individual who is a son, stepson, daughter, or stepdaughter of the taxpayer.[122] A "student" is an individual who during five months of the year either is a fulltime student at an institution described in section 170(b)(1)(A)(ii) or in an institutional on-farm training program.[123] Certain qualifying income of a handicapped dependent is not taken into account in computing that person's gross income.[124]

121. See § 151(c) citing to the definition of "dependent" as defined in § 152. No exemption is allowed on the return of an individual who may be claimed as a dependent on another's return, for example, a child who may be claimed as a dependent by the parents. § 152(b)(1).

122. § 152(f)(1).

123. § 152(f)(2).

124. § 152(d)(4).

Chapter 5

ACCOUNTING ISSUES

Table of Sections

§ 5.01   IN GENERAL

Income tax liability is usually determined in the context of a twelve-month period referred to as a taxable year.[1] This chapter deals with the rules governing the allocation of gross income and deductions to the proper taxable year. Although the allocation may be performed in accordance with generally accepted accounting principles, there are differences between financial accounting and tax accounting. Financial accounting seeks to match revenues with the costs of producing them while tax accounting starts from the premise of a need for certainty in the collection of taxes and focuses on the ability to pay. Moreover, in the case of tax accounting, a variety of statutory, regulatory, and judicial pronouncements are necessary to counter tax avoidance. For example, if the IRS believes that a taxpayer's method of accounting does not clearly reflect income, section 446(b) authorizes the Service to change the taxpayer's method of accounting to a more appropriate one which clearly reflects income.[2]

Controversies about the proper taxable year for gross income and deductions are attributable to a variety of factors. From a taxpayer's perspective, the tax liability for the current taxable year should be minimized. Accordingly, taxpayers generally seek to recognize items of gross income in a later year while taking as many deductions as possible during the current year. Additionally, marginal tax rates may differ from one year to another. Of course, the running of the statute of limitations may preclude tax liability.[3] Moreover, changes in substantive provisions of the Code may affect inclusion in or exclusion from gross income and the availability of deductions during a particular year.[4]

§ 5.02   TAXABLE YEAR

Section 441(a) generally requires taxable income to "be computed on the basis of the taxpayer's taxable year." Typically the taxable year is a fiscal or calendar year.[1]

While a taxpayer may select either a calendar or a fiscal year,[2] a calendar year must be used if no books are kept, if the taxpayer does not have an annual accounting period, or if the taxpayer has an annual

---

§ 5.01

1. See § 441(a) and (b).

2. See Jennifer C. Root, The Commissioner's Clear Reflection of Income Power Under § 446(b) and the Abuse of Discretion Standard of Review: Where Has the Rule of Law Gone, and Can we Get it Back?, 15 Akron Tax J. 69 (2000). See also Rowell v. Commissioner, 884 F.2d 1085 (8th Cir. 1989).

3. See § 6501.

4. See e.g., The Tax Reform Act of 1986 (which provided a myriad of changes

to inclusionary and exclusionary provisions of the Code).

§ 5.02

1. See § 441(b)(1) and (2). Section 441(d) defines a calendar year as a period of twelve months ending on December 31, and § 441(e) defines a fiscal year as a period of twelve months ending on the last day of any month other than December.

2. Personal service corporations and S corporations must use the calendar year, §§ 441(i), 1378(a)-(b); partnerships must

accounting period but such period does not qualify as a fiscal year.[3] Moreover, Revenue Ruling 85–22[4] holds:

> A taxpayer who begins business operations on a date other than the first day of a calendar month and adopts an annual accounting period of exactly 12 months from the date business was begun has not satisfied the tax year requirements of section 441 of the Code. The taxpayer in this instance is required either to file an amended federal income tax return on the basis of a calendar year . . ., or to secure the approval of the Commissioner under section 442 to change its annual accounting period, if the taxpayer desires to use a fiscal year.

Unlike the commercial code requirements of civil law countries, there is no general legal requirement in the United States that merchants or others keep prescribed books of account. However, both the Internal Revenue Code and the Treasury regulations require that records be kept when necessary to reflect income properly, and in practice most enterprises maintain recording systems of varying degrees of complexity. If a taxpayer establishes a fiscal year as the annual accounting period, the books must be kept in accordance with such year.[5]

Although a taxpayer may elect either a calendar or fiscal year on the first return without permission from Treasury, section 442 generally requires consent from Treasury to change from one accounting period to another. The regulations provide that if certain conditions are satisfied certain taxpayers may change accounting periods without prior consent.[6] A change in taxable year, usually from a calendar to a fiscal year, may be allowed in certain circumstances when the taxable year sought coincides with the natural business year of the taxpayer, using the end of the peak period of the business as the close of the natural year.[7]

Under section 443 a short-period (less than twelve months) return is required when there has been a change of accounting period;[8] or when the taxpayer is in existence only part of the year.[9] For a change of

---

use (in order of priority) the taxable year of one or more of its partners who have an aggregate interest of greater than 50%, all the principal partners, or the calendar year, § 706(b)(1). An exception is made for those that establish a business purpose for having a different taxable year. Eight situations are analyzed in Rev. Rul. 87–57, 1987–28 I.R.B. 7, with regard to whether a personal service corporation, an S corporation, or a partnership established a business purpose for adopting, retaining, or changing its tax year. Rev. Proc. 87–32, 1987–28 I.R.B. 14, provides guidance for any personal service corporation, S corporation, or partnership that desires to adopt, retain, or change its tax year. Trusts, both existing and newly created, must use the calendar year according to § 645(a).

3. § 441(g)(1)-(3).

4. 1985–10 I.R.B. 5. See also C. H. Leavell & Co. v. Commissioner, 53 T.C. 426 (1969).

5. Treas. Reg. § 1.441–1(b)(5)(ii).

6. See e.g., Treas. Reg. § 1.442–1(d)(1) (which allows certain newly married individuals to change their tax year without consent). See also § 441(f) allows the use of a 52–53 week period as a fiscal year in certain circumstances.

7. Rev. Proc. 2002–39, 2002–22 I.R.B. 1046, at § 2.06(2).

8. § 443(a)(1).

9. § 443(a)(2).

accounting period taxable income is analyzed to keep the taxpayer within the proper tax bracket for the short period.[10]

§ 5.03   OVERVIEW OF ACCOUNTING METHODS

Section 446(a) requires that taxable income be computed in accordance with the accounting method regularly used by the taxpayer. Section 446(c) recognizes the cash receipts and disbursements method,[1] the accrual method,[2] any other method permitted by the Code,[3] and any combination of these methods permitted under the regulations.[4] The method of accounting used by the taxpayer concerns not only the overall method but also the treatment of any individual item.[5]

Section 451(a) requires that income items be included in the year of receipt unless the taxpayer's method of accounting requires inclusion in a different period. Section 461(a) requires a deduction or credit be taken in the proper taxable year under the method of accounting used in computing taxable income. Not surprisingly, the problems encountered under sections 451 and 461 have generally involved the two most widely used accounting methods, the cash receipts and disbursements method and the accrual method. Although a touchstone of tax (and financial) accounting is consistency, for tax purposes purity of method is the exception rather than the rule. Certain items must be reported in the period required by the Code irrespective of the method of accounting.

Section 446(b) provides that if the Commissioner believes a taxpayer's method of accounting does not clearly reflect income, taxable income may be computed under another accounting method. Furthermore, the regulations provide:

> A method of accounting which reflects the consistent application of generally accepted accounting principles in a particular trade or business in accordance with accepted conditions or practices in that trade or business will ordinarily be regarded as clearly reflecting income, provided all items of gross income and expense are treated consistently from year to year. [6]

In Thor Power Tool Co. v. Commissioner[7] the taxpayer wrote down its inventory to scrap value in accordance with generally accepted accounting principles, which created a net operating loss. The Commissioner determined that the write-down did not clearly reflect income because the inventory was still held for sale at its original price, and there was no determination made of the market value of the inventory.

---

10. See § 443(b).

§ 5.03

1. § 446(c)(1).

2. § 446(c)(2).

3. § 446(c)(3).

4. § 446(c)(4).

5. Treas. Reg. § 1.446–1(a)(1).

6. Treas. Reg. § 1.446–1(a)(2).

7. 439 U.S. 522, 99 S.Ct. 773, 58 L.Ed.2d 785 (1979). See also Total Health Center Trust v. Commissioner, T.C. Memo. 2006–226; Houchin v. Commissioner, T.C. Memo. 2006–119.

The Supreme Court held that the Commissioner did not abuse his discretion in recomputing taxable income. The Court reasoned that while the primary goal of financial accounting is to provide useful information to interested persons, the primary goal of the federal income tax system is the equitable collection of revenue. Because of these non-equivalent goals, the Court held there is no presumption that use of generally accepted accounting principles provides a clear reflection of income.[8]

As a general rule, changing from one method of accounting to another requires the consent of the Service, which will be given upon a showing of a valid business purpose.[9]

§ 5.04   CASH METHOD OF ACCOUNTING

[1]   IN GENERAL

The cash method of accounting is used by most individuals. Section 448(a), generally provides that a C corporation,[1] a partnership[2] that has a C corporation as a partner, and a tax shelter[3] may not use the cash method of accounting. Exceptions are made for farming businesses,[4] qualified personal service corporations,[5] and corporations or partnerships (other than tax shelters) with average annual gross receipts of not more than $5 million.[6]

---

8. Cf. Public Serv. Co., 78 T.C. 445 (1982), in which the court held that conformity to generally accepted accounting principles is a factor to be considered in determining whether the taxpayer's method of accounting provides a clear reflection of income.

9. § 446(e); Treas. Reg. § 1.446–1(e).

§ 5.04

1. "... [T]he term 'C corporation' means, with respect to any taxable year, a corporation which is not an S corporation for such year." § 1361(a)(2).

2. "... [T]he term 'partnership' includes a syndicate, group, pool, joint venture, or other unincorporated organization through or by means of which any business, financial operation, or venture is carried on, and which is not, within the meaning of this title, a corporation or a trust or estate." § 761(a).

3. ... [T]he term "tax shelter" means—

(A) any enterprise (other than a C corporation) if at any time interests in such enterprise have been offered for sale in any offering required to be registered with any Federal or State agency having the authority to regulate the offering of securities for sale,

(B) any syndicate (within the meaning of section 1256(e)(3)(B)), and

(C) any tax shelter (as defined in section 6662(d)(2)(C)(ii)).

§ 461(i)(3), as referenced by § 448(d)(3). Moreover, § 1256(e)(3)(B) defines syndicate as "any partnership or other entity (other than a corporation which is not an S corporation) if more than 35 percent of the losses of such entity during the taxable year are allocable to limited partners or limited entrepreneurs." And, § 6662(d)(2)(C)(ii) provides: "the term 'tax shelter' means—(I) a partnership or other entity, (II) any investment plan or arrangement, or (III) any other plan or arrangement, if a significant purpose of such partnership, entity, plan, or arrangement is the avoidance or evasion of Federal income tax."

4. § 448(b)(1).

5. § 448(b)(2). A qualified personal service corporation is one that is engaged in performing health, law, engineering, architecture, accounting, actuarial science, performing arts, or consulting services and is employee-owned. § 448(d)(2).

6. § 448(b)(3).

Under the cash method income is generally reported in the year received and deductions are generally reported in the year paid.[7] Unlike the accrual method, under which income and deductions are generally reportable when the right of receipt or the obligation to pay arises, the cash method of accounting does not attempt to correlate receipts and payments to the year of economic activity. This lack of correlation between income and deductions under the cash method has given rise to trials and tribulations with respect to whether items have been received or paid.

The word "cash" does not preclude income from being received if payment is made by means of something other than money. "Gross income includes income realized in any form, whether in money, property, or services. Income may be realized, therefore, in the form of services, meals, accommodations, stock, or other property, as well as in cash."[8]

In Revenue Ruling 80–52[9] members of a barter club received "credit units" in exchange for services performed. Once "credit units" were received by members, they could be used to purchase goods and services from other club members. Because of the use for which the "credit units" were available, they constituted receipt of income in the form of valuable rights.

Whether receipt of an instrument evidencing an obligation to pay constitutes receipt of property has been subject to varying interpretations. For example, in Cowden v. Commissioner[10] the taxpayer, as lessor, received deferred payment agreements as part of an oil, gas, and mineral lease. While recognizing that the agreements were not negotiable instruments, the Fifth Circuit reasoned that economic realities and not legal labels were determinative of what constitutes a cash equivalent. Thus, the Fifth Circuit said that "negotiability is not the test of taxability in an equivalent of cash case."[11] Rather, "a promise to pay of a solvent obligor"[12] that "is unconditional and assignable, not subject to set-offs, and is of a kind that is frequently transferred to lenders or investors at a discount not substantially greater than the generally prevailing premium for the use of the money . . . is the equivalent of cash."[13]

Ultimately, "Items of gross income and expenditures which are elements in the computation of taxable income need not be in the form of cash. It is sufficient that such items can be valued in terms of money."[14]

[2]   CONSTRUCTIVE RECEIPT

Although a taxpayer may not have actual possession of an item of income, in certain circumstances he may be deemed to control it for tax

---

7.   Treas. Regs. §§ 1.451–1(a), 1.461–1(a)(1).

8.   Treas. Reg. § 1.61–1(a).

9.   1980–1 C.B. 100. See also Rev. Rul. 79–24, 1979–1 C.B. 60; Rev. Rul. 83–163, 1983–2 C.B. 26; Barter Systems, Inc. of Wichita v. Commissioner, T.C. Memo. 1990–125.

10.   289 F.2d 20 (5th Cir. 1961). See also Monico v. Commissioner, T.C. Memo. 1998–10; FSA 200151003.

11.   289 F.2d 20, 24 (5th Cir. 1961).

12.   Id.

13.   Id.

14.   Treas. Reg. § 1.446–1(a)(3).

purposes under the theory of constructive receipt. If income is credited to a taxpayer's account, set apart for him, or otherwise made available so he may draw upon it at any time, it will be regarded as constructively received unless subject to substantial limitations or restrictions.[15]

"Thus, under the doctrine of constructive receipt, a taxpayer may not deliberately turn his back upon income and thereby select the year for which he will report it.[16]" "Nor may a taxpayer, by a private agreement, postpone receipt of income from one taxable year to another."[17]

Moreover, constructive receipt is not dependent upon subsequent physical control; command over the disposition of income is sufficient. In Geiger's Estate v. Commissioner[18] a cashier embezzled bank funds over a period of years by crediting amounts to her own account and to the accounts of other people. The taxpayer contended that the mere crediting to the accounts did not constitute constructive receipt to her because there was no taking of bank funds until a check on one of the accounts was actually presented for payment. The Eighth Circuit rejected this argument, and it held that the crediting to the accounts constituted constructive receipt because of the taxpayer's control over the funds and because of the "readily realizable economic benefit derived therefrom as a practical matter."[19] The fact that there were undrawn funds in the accounts when the embezzlement was discovered in a later year was held not to disturb the character of the funds as income or to defer the time of receipt.

Other examples of constructive receipt include the maturing of interest coupons attached to a bond, interest credited to a savings account, and receipt by an agent.[20] In Lavery v. Commissioner[21] constructive receipt was found with respect to a check when the taxpayer received the check on December 30, a Tuesday, and cashed it on January 2 of the next year. The Seventh Circuit held that the taxpayer was in constructive receipt because the check could have been cashed on the day received or the following day; this result was particularly true in light of the fact that there was no question about the validity of the check or the solvency of the drawer.

Application of the doctrine of constructive receipt with respect to a check is not dependent upon the taxpayer's ability to turn conditional

---

15. Treas. Reg. § 1.451–2(a).

16. Rev. Rul. 60–31, 1969–1 C.B. 174.

17. Rev. Rul. 60–31, 1969–1 C.B. 174, citing Lewis v. Commissioner, 30 B.T.A. 318 (1934).

18. 352 F.2d 221 (8th Cir. 1965), cert. denied, 382 U.S. 1012, 86 S.Ct. 620, 15 L.Ed.2d 527 (1966). See also Walters v. Commissioner, T.C. Memo. 1998–111.

19. 352 F.2d 221, 225 (8th Cir. 1965), citing Rutkin v. United States, 343 U.S. 130, 136–137, 72 S.Ct. 571, 575, 96 L.Ed. 833 (1952). See also United States v. Stein,

473 F.Supp.2d 597 (SD NY 2007); Han v. Commissioner, T.C. Memo. 2002–148.

20. See Treas. Reg. § 1.451–2(b).

21. 158 F.2d 859 (7th Cir. 1946). See also Rev. Rul. 68–126, 1968–1 C.B. 194, in which the Service concluded that the taxpayer was in constructive receipt of a retirement check in 1967 although it was not delivered by mail until 1968 because he could have picked it up on the last working day of 1967.

payment into actual receipt of cash. In Kahler v. Commissioner[22] the Tax Court, in an opinion reviewed by the full court, held that a taxpayer who received a check on December 31 after banking hours was in constructive receipt despite his inability to present it for payment. The court reasoned that not only do the regulations require payment for services in other than money to be measured by the value of the item received, but also under negotiable instruments law payment by check related back to the time of delivery. Accordingly, the court held that except in unusual circumstances, such as dishonor or where delivery is subject to conditions, a check is treated as payment.

On the other hand, if a check or other property "is subject to substantial limitations or restrictions," the recipient is not treated as in constructive receipt.[23] The regulations illustrate this with an example of bonus stock being credited to an employee's account, and the stock not being available until a future date.[24] For the most part, the "substantial limitations or restrictions" exception has been construed narrowly. Four situations are described in section 1.451–2(a) of the regulations in which interest, dividends, or other earnings will not be treated as subject to "substantial limitations or restrictions," including:

(1) A requirement that the deposit or account, and the earnings thereon, must be withdrawn in multiples of even amounts;

(2) The fact that the taxpayer would, by withdrawing the earnings during the taxable year, receive earnings that are not substantially less in comparison with the earnings for the corresponding period to which the taxpayer would be entitled had he left the account on deposit until a later date (for example, if an amount equal to three months' interest must be forfeited upon withdrawal or redemption before maturity of a one year or less certificate of deposit, time deposit, bonus plan, or other deposit arrangement then the earnings payable on premature withdrawal or redemption would be substantially less when compared with the earnings available at maturity);

(3) A requirement that the earnings may be withdrawn only upon a withdrawal of all or part of the deposit or account. However, the mere fact that such institutions may pay earnings on withdrawals, total or partial, made during the last three business days of any calendar month ending a regular quarterly or semiannual earnings period at the applicable rate calculated to the end of such calendar month shall not constitute constructive receipt of income by any depositor or account holder in any such institution who has not made a withdrawal during such period;

22. 18 T.C. 31 (1952). See also Bright v. United States, 926 F.2d 383, 385 (5th Cir. 1991); Millard v. Commissioner, T.C. memo. 2005–192; Walter v. United States, 148 F.3d 1027, 1029 (8th Cir.1998).

23. See Fischer v. Commissioner, 14 T.C. 792, 802 (1950); Bones v. Commissioner, 4 T.C. 415, 420 (1944); Treas. Reg. § 1.451–2(a).

24. Treas. Reg. § 1.451–2(a).

(4) A requirement that a notice of intention to withdraw must be given in advance of the withdrawal. In any case when the rate of earnings payable in respect of such a deposit or account depends on the amount of notice of intention to withdraw that is given, earnings at the maximum rate are constructively received during the taxable year regardless of how long the deposit or account was held during the year or whether, in fact, any notice of intention to withdraw is given during the year. However, if in the taxable year of withdrawal the depositor or account holder receives a lower rate of earnings because he failed to give the required notice of intention to withdraw, he shall be allowed an ordinary loss in such taxable year in an amount equal to the difference between the amount of earnings previously included in gross income and the amount of earnings actually received.[25]

In Revenue Ruling 76–3[26] the taxpayer was sent a check for severance pay by certified mail. Delivery of the check was attempted but not made on December 31 because the taxpayer was not at home. Notice was left that the check was available for pickup at the post office. The taxpayer arrived home after the post office had closed and actual delivery was made on January 2 of the following year. The Service concluded that the taxpayer was in constructive receipt. However, in Baxter v. Commissioner[27] the Ninth Circuit held that the taxpayer did not constructively receive income when a check was written on a nonbusiness day (Saturday, December 30, 1978), the taxpayer would have had to drive 40 miles to obtain the check, and the taxpayer could not have received credit for the check at a bank before January 2, 1979. The Ninth Circuit found that these fact and circumstances served as an "effective barrier" to the taxpayer's asserting control over the check, and therefore they constituted substantial restrictions.

Furthermore, proceeds received by an agent are generally treated as received by the principal.[28] Thus, an agreement between a taxpayer and his agent purporting to defer payment of proceeds received by the agent to the taxpayer will be disregarded.[29]

The Service has invoked the doctrine of constructive receipt when interest accumulates but is not actually paid.[30] In Revenue Ruling 65–

---

25. Treas. Reg. § 1.451–2(a)(1)-(4).

26. 1976–1 C.B. 114. See also United States v. Pfister, 205 F.2d 538 (8th Cir. 1953).

27. 816 F.2d 493 (9th Cir. 1987). See also Adam M. Ekonomon, Constructive Receipt of Income Baxter v. Commissioner, 5 Akron Tax J. 241 (1988).

28. Hines v. United States, 90 F.2d 957 (7th Cir. 1937); Helvering v. Schaupp, 71 F.2d 736 (8th Cir. 1934); Henritze v. Commissioner, 41 B.T.A. 505 (1940); Diescher v. Commissioner, 36 B.T.A. 732 (1937), aff'd, 110 F.2d 90 (3d Cir. 1940); Twohy v. Commissioner, 34 B.T.A. 444 (1936); United States v. Pfister, 205 F.2d 538 (8th Cir. 1953); Ebner v. Commissioner, 26 T.C. 962 (1956), acq., 1956–2 C.B. 4; Producers Gin Ass'n, A.A.L. v. Commissioner, 33 T.C. 608 (1959), acq., 1960–2 C.B. 3; Bratton v. Commissioner, 31 T.C. 891 (1959), aff'd, 283 F.2d 257 (6th Cir. 1960), acq., 1964–2 C.B. 3; Alsop v. Commissioner, 290 F.2d 726 (2d Cir. 1961); Joyce v. Commissioner, 42 T.C. 628 (1964).

29. Id.

30. See e.g., Rev. Rul. 65–199, 1965–2 C.B. 20 revoking I.T. 3513, 1941–2 C.B. 75, and Rev. Rul. 65–24, 1965–1 C.B. 31, amplified in Rev. Rul. 66–120, 1966–1 C.B. 14.

199[31] the Service ruled that any increment in value of advance or prepaid premiums on annuity or life insurance contracts that is applied to the payment of premiums or is made available for withdrawal results in income to the policy holders at that time. In Revenue Ruling 66–44[32] the same rule was applied to "growth savings certificates" issued by a bank. Each certificate had a face amount greater than its issue price and was redeemable at any time for an amount equal to the issue price plus increments that accrued regularly up to the maturity date. The Service concluded the increments were includible in gross income in each taxable year because the certificate holder had a right to redeem the certificate at any time; hence, the interest was "otherwise made available." A similar result was reached in Revenue Ruling 68–586[33] with respect to a long-term savings arrangement that permitted the depositor to withdraw only principal. The Service held that interest credited under the plan would be regarded as constructively received up to the amount of the unrestricted principal.

An escrow account for proceeds already made available to the taxpayer usually does not prevent the application of the doctrine of constructive receipt.[34] Notwithstanding the foregoing, if there is substantial uncertainty or limitations with respect to the taxpayer's ability to reduce escrowed funds to cash constructive receipt has been found not to apply to these situations, and no income is recognized by the taxpayer unless and until such time when the uncertainty or limitations in question cease to exist.[35]

[3] CONSTRUCTIVE PAYMENT

Logically, it would appear that whenever an amount is regarded as constructively received, the payor should be treated as having made a constructive payment. However, neither the courts nor the Service have generally espoused a doctrine of constructive payment. For example, in Vander Poel, Francis & Co., Inc. v. Commissioner[36] the Tax Court denied a cash method corporate taxpayer an expense deduction for the year that

31. 1965–2 C.B. 20, revoking I.T. 3513, 1941–2 C.B. 75, and Rev. Rul. 65–24, 1965–1 C.B. 31, amplified in Rev. Rul. 66–120, 1966–1 C.B. 14.

32. 1966–1 C.B. 94, revoking Rev. Rul. 57–452, 1957–2 C.B. 302 (which permitted deferral of interest income to the time of redemption). See also Charlene Davis Luke, Beating the "Wrap:" The Agency Effort to Control Wraparound Insurance Tax Shelters, 25 VA Tax Rev. 129, 199 (2005).

33. 1968–2 C.B. 195.

34. See, e.g., Williams v. United States, 219 F.2d 523 (5th Cir. 1955), in which the escrow account was a limitation imposed by the taxpayer; Kuehner v. Commissioner, 214 F.2d 437 (1st Cir. 1954), in which the taxpayer was entitled to interest from the funds in escrow. See also Holden v. Com-

missioner, 6 B.T.A. 605 (1927); Vaughn v. Commissioner, 81 T.C. 893 (1983); Hamilton Nat. Bank of Chattanooga v. Commissioner, 29 B.T.A. 63 (1933); Bailey v. Commissioner, 18 B.T.A. 105 (1929).

35. Ware v. Commissioner, 906 F.2d 62 (2d Cir. 1990); Johnston v. Commissioner, 14 T.C. 560 (1950); Reed v. Commissioner, 723 F.2d 138 (1st Cir. 1983). See also Bedell v. Commissioner, 30 F.2d 622, (2d Cir. 1929); Commissioner v. Tyler, 72 F.2d 950 (3d Cir. 1934); Olson v. Commissioner, 67 F.2d 726 (7th Cir. 1933); Depew v. Commissioner, 27 B.T.A. 515 (1933); Murray v. Commissioner, 28 B.T.A. 624 (1933).

36. 8 T.C. 407 (1947), citing J H Martinus & Sons v. Commissioner, 116 F.2d 732 (9th Cir. 1940).

compensation for services was credited to employees' accounts under circumstances in which the recipients were admittedly in constructive receipt. The Tax Court said that "the weight of authority . . . is against the doctrine that 'constructive payment' is a necessary corollary of 'constructive receipt.' "[37] In Revenue Ruling 76–135[38] a cash basis taxpayer issued a negotiable promissory note to a lawyer for services rendered that the lawyer discounted at a bank. While the fair market value of the note was includible in the lawyer's income in the year of receipt, the issuance of the note was not regarded as payment in cash or its equivalent, and the taxpayer was only allowed a deduction as cash payments were made on the note in the following years.

[4] PAYMENT WITH BORROWED MONEY AND RELATED MATTERS

When payment is made with borrowed money, the deduction is not postponed until the year in which the loan is repaid.[39] If the taxpayer uses a credit card, payment occurs when the charge is made.[40] The charge is viewed as the equivalent of payment with borrowed money since the charge creates an obligation. Moreover, payment made by the taxpayer's agent is considered as made by the taxpayer.[41] Of course, regardless of the fact that a payment has been made, a deduction will not be permitted if the payment does not satisfy the statutory provision of the Code which authorizes the deduction in question.[42]

[5] PREPAID INTEREST

Section 461(g) requires that a cash method taxpayer capitalize and deduct prepaid interest over the period of a loan. Notwithstanding the

37. Vander Poel, Francis & Co., Inc. v. Commissioner, 8 T.C. 407, 411 (1947). See also Citizens Federal Sav. and Loan Ass'n of Covington v. Commissioner 30 T.C. 285 (1958), acq., 1958–2 C.B. 3; Hancock County Federal Sav. and Loan Ass'n of Chester v. Commissioner, 32 T.C. 869 (1959), acq., 1959–2 C.B. 3.

38. 1976–1 C.B. 114. See also Pinellas Ice & Cold Storage Co. v. Commissioner, 287 U.S. 462, 53 S.Ct. 257, 77 L.Ed. 428 (1933); Estate of Silverman v. Commissioner, 98 T.C. 54 (1992); Griffith v. Commissioner, 73 T.C. 933 (1980); FSA 200151003.

39. Crain v. Commissioner, 75 F.2d 962, 964 (8th Cir. 1935); Battelstein v. Commissioner, 631 F.2d 1182, 1184 (5th Cir. 1980), cert. denied, 451 U.S. 938, 101 S.Ct. 2018, 68 L.Ed.2d 325 (1981); Granan v. Commissioner, 55 T.C. 753, 755 (1971); Blumeyer v. Commissioner, T.C. Memo. 1992–647.

40. See Rev. Rul. 78–38, 1978–1 C.B. 67; Rev. Rul. 78–39, 1978–1 C.B. 73; Granan v. Commissioner, 55 T.C. 753, 755 (1971); McAdams v. Commissioner, 15 T.C.

231, 235 (1950), affd. 198 F.2d 54 (5th Cir.1952).

41. In Rev. Rul. 80–335, 1980–2 C.B. 170, a cash method taxpayer's use of a "pay-by-phone" account with a financial institution constituted payment by the taxpayer when the financial institution, acting as the taxpayer's agent, made payment. See also Griffin v. Commissioner, 49 T.C. 253 (1967).

42. In Hradesky v. Commissioner, 65 T.C. 87 (1975), aff'd per curiam, 540 F.2d 821 (5th Cir. 1976), a cash method taxpayer made payments to a mortgage company's escrow account for real estate taxes on the property. The mortgage company did not make payment out of the escrow account for certain taxes until the following year. The Tax Court held that § 164 only allows a deduction when payment is made to a taxing authority and not to an intermediary. Accordingly, the taxpayer could not deduct the payments to the escrow account until the amounts were paid to the taxing authority. See also Arnold v. Commissioner, T.C. Memo. 2007–168.

foregoing, points on a home mortgage may be deductible when paid so long as each of the foregoing are satisfied:[43]

(1) The Uniform Settlement Statement ... must clearly designate the amounts as points payable in connection with the loan, for example as "loan origination fees ...," "loan discount," "discount points," or "points."[44]

(2) "The amounts must be computed as a percentage of the stated principal amount of the indebtedness incurred by the taxpayer."[45]

(3) "The amounts paid must conform to an established business practice of charging points for loans for the acquisition of principal residences in the area in which the residence is located, and the amount of points paid must not exceed the amount generally charged in that area."[46]

(4) "The amounts must be paid in connection with the acquisition of the taxpayer's principal residence, and the loan must be secured by that residence."[47]

(5) "The amounts must be paid directly by the taxpayer. An amount is so paid if the taxpayer provides, from funds that have not been borrowed for this purpose as part of the overall transaction, an amount at least equal to the amount required to be applied as points at the closing."[48]

Ultimately, points paid which do not meet the aforementioned criteria are not currently deductible. Moreover, point may not be currently deducted if any of the following criteria exist:

(1) The points are paid with respect to "principal in excess of the aggregate amount that may be treated as acquisition indebtedness under section 163(h)(3)(B)(ii) of the Code."[49]

(2) The points are paid "for loans the proceeds of which are to be used for the improvement, as opposed to the acquisition, of a principal residence."[50]

(3) The points are "paid for loans to purchase or improve a residence that is not the taxpayer's principal residence, such as a second home, vacation property, investment property, or trade or business property."[51]

---

43. Rev. Proc. 94–27, 1994–1 C.B. 613.

44. Rev. Proc. 94–27, 1994–1 C.B. 613 at § 3.01.

45. Rev. Proc. 94–27, 1994–1 C.B. 613 at § 3.02.

46. Rev. Proc. 94–27, 1994–1 C.B. 613 at § 3.03.

47. Rev. Proc. 94–27, 1994–1 C.B. 613 at § 3.04.

48. Rev. Proc. 94–27, 1994–1 C.B. 613 at § 3.05.

49. Rev. Proc. 94–27, 1994–1 C.B. 613 at § 4.01.

50. Rev. Proc. 94–27, 1994–1 C.B. 613 at § 4.02.

51. Rev. Proc. 94–27, 1994–1 C.B. 613 at § 4.03.

(4) The points are "paid on a refinancing loan, home equity loan, or line of credit, even though the indebtedness is secured by a principal residence."[52]

[6] PREPAID RENT AND INSURANCE

Section 1.461–1(a)(1) of the regulations states, in part, "[i]f an expenditure results in the creation of an asset having a useful life which extends substantially beyond the close of the taxable year, such an expenditure may not be deductible, or may be deductible only in part, for the taxable year in which made." In Zaninovich v. Commissioner[53] a cash method taxpayer was contractually required to make one-year rental payments in advance (payable December 20) for a period running from December 1 to November 30 of the following year. The Tax Court only allowed a deduction in the year of payment for one-twelfth of the amount paid, holding that a deduction is allowed only for the portion attributable to the year of payment. In reversing, the Ninth Circuit reasoned that the "substantially beyond" language "implements § 263 which disallows a deduction for capital expenditures." Since the rental payment did not result in the taxpayer receiving a benefit beyond a one-year period, the court held that the payment was fully deductible in the year when made.

Pursuant to section 446(b) the taxpayer's method of accounting must clearly reflect income. Thus, if a cash method taxpayer consistently deducts a prepaid expenditure either fully or on a pro rata basis, and the practice does not result in a material distortion of income, the practice may be allowed in order to clearly reflect income.[54] For example, in Commissioner v. Boylston Market Association[55] the cash method taxpayer was allowed to deduct each year insurance premiums applicable to the year regardless of when the premiums were actually paid. The taxpayer managed real estate owned by it and purchased fire and other insurance policies covering periods of three years or more. The First Circuit reasoned that to permit a full deduction in the year the premiums were paid would distort the taxpayer's income and that in the interest of consistency the prepaid expense should be treated as a capital expenditure amortized over the three or more years for which the insurance protection was paid. On the other hand, in Waldheim Realty & Investment Co. v. Commissioner[56] the taxpayer consistently deducted the entire amount of insurance premiums when paid, even though the coverage extended into subsequent years. The Eighth Circuit held that

---

52. Rev. Proc. 94–27, 1994–1 C.B. 613 at § 4.04.

53. 69 T.C. 605 (1978), rev'd, 616 F.2d 429 (9th Cir. 1980). See also Kauai Terminal, Ltd. v. Commissioner, 36 B.T.A. 893 (1937); Hillsboro Nat. Bank v. Commissioner, 460 U.S. 370, 103 S.Ct. 1134, 75 L.Ed.2d 130 (1983); U.S. Freightways Corp. v. Commissioner, 270 F.3d 1137 (7th Cir. 2001), rev'g 113 T.C. 329 (1999).

54. See e.g., Commissioner v. Boylston Market Ass'n, 131 F.2d 966 (1st Cir. 1942).

55. 131 F.2d 966 (1st Cir. 1942). See also TAM 200514020; TAM 9218004; Rev. Rul. 70–413, 1970–2 CB 103; GCM 23587, 1943–1 CB 213 .

56. 245 F.2d 823 (8th Cir. 1957). See also Calvin H. Johnson, The Illegitimate "Earned" Requirement in Tax and Nontax Accounting, 50 Tax L. Rev. 373, 414 (1995).

the practice was not improper. The court's reasoning was based upon the theory that, in the long run, no material distortion of income would result since no deductions would be allowed the taxpayer in later years to which the insurance coverage was applicable.[57]

[7] CLAIM OF RIGHT DOCTRINE

As a broad principle applicable to both cash and accrual method taxpayers, payment received under a claim of right is includible in income even though there is a possibility that all or part of the amount may have to be returned at some point in the future.

In North American Oil Consolidated v. Burnet[58] the taxpayer operated government oil properties. In an ejectment action brought by the government, a receiver was appointed in 1916 who impounded the receipts for that year. In 1917 the action was dismissed by the trial court, and the receiver turned over the net profits for 1916 to the taxpayer. The government appealed but lost in the Court of Appeals in 1920 and dismissed its appeal to the Supreme Court in 1922. In a subsequent tax proceeding the Supreme Court held that the taxpayer had to include the 1916 net profits turned over by the receiver in its gross income for 1917. The actual receipt in 1917 under a claim of right was held to be the controlling factor regardless of the accounting method employed and regardless of the possibility that the taxpayer might have had to repay the amount had the government prevailed on appeal. In the latter event, the Court stated, the taxpayer would have been entitled to a deduction in the year it made the repayment.

An exception to the application of the claim of right doctrine exists when in the year of receipt the taxpayer recognizes the obligation to repay the amount received and makes provision for repayment.[59] However, this exception will not be applied simply because the taxpayer has filed an action to rescind a sale of property since such a suit imposes no restriction on the taxpayer's use of the proceeds.[60]

---

57. See also Treas. Reg. § 1.461–1(a)(3) (i), which says, in part, that "in a going business there are certain overlapping deductions. If these overlapping items do not materially distort income, they may be included in the years in which the taxpayer consistently takes them into account."

58. 286 U.S. 417, 52 S.Ct. 613, 76 L.Ed. 1197 (1932). See Boyce v. United States, 186 Ct.Cl. 420, 405 F.2d 526 (1968); Board v. Commissioner, 51 F.2d 73 (6th Cir. 1931), cert. denied 284 U.S. 658, 52 S.Ct. 35, 76 L.Ed. 557; Commissioner v. Gaddy, 344 F.2d 460 (5th Cir. 1965), aff'g on this issue 38 T.C. 943 (1962), acq (1969) 1969–2 CB xxiv; Hope v. Commissioner, 471 F.2d 738 (3d Cir. 1973), aff'g 55 T.C. 1020 (1971); Latimer v. Commissioner 55 T.C,

515 (1970). See also Dominic L. Daher and Joshua D. Rosenberg, Tax Aspects of Incentive Compensation Disgorgement: Good Motives Raise Serious Questions About Deductibility, 166 DTR J–1, 2005 (August 29, 2005).

59. See, e.g., United States v. Merrill, 211 F.2d 297 (9th Cir. 1954); Bates Motors Transp. Lines v. Commissioner, 200 F.2d 20 (7th Cir. 1952); FSA 200124008; Bishop v. Commissioner, 25 T.C. 969 (1956).

60. Hope v. Commissioner, 55 T.C. 1020 (1971), aff'd, 471 F.2d 739 (3d Cir. 1973), cert. denied, 414 U.S. 824, 94 S.Ct. 126, 38 L.Ed.2d 57 (1973). See also Hightower v. Commissioner, T.C. Memo. 2005–274.

Although the possibility of return or even a restriction on the use of the receipt has not prevented inclusion in gross income, more difficulty has been experienced with situations in which there has been uncertainty as to the purpose of the receipt. For example, in Gilken Corporation v. Commissioner[61] the taxpayer leased property in 1940 for ten years at a monthly rental of $1,600, taking a deposit of $3,200 that could be used as security for repairs, applied to the last two months' rent, or applied to the purchase price if the tenant exercised an option to purchase. In 1941 the lease was amended and an additional $5,000 deposit was made on the same terms. The Tax Court held the deposits constituted rental income in the years received because the lease indicated they were to serve primarily as advance rental payments.

A similar result was reached in Astor Holding Co. v. Commissioner.[62] In this case the taxpayer gave a ten-year lease to a tenant in 1936 at an annual rental of $21,500. The lease provided for an advance payment of $17,500 as "part payment of the tenth year's rent" and for three additional payments in January and February of 1946 for the balance. The Fifth Circuit had no difficulty in concluding the parties intended the $17,500 as rent since the taxpayer was in no way restricted as to its use or required to account for interest on it, which would have been evidence of the parties' intention to treat the amount as a security deposit.

An analogous issue has arisen in cases involving deposits by lessees that may be applied either to rent or to the purchase price under an option to purchase. While most courts have adopted an approach that attempts to characterize the transaction as a sale or lease, depending on the circumstances, some courts have adopted an approach of holding the matter in abeyance pending the ultimate outcome. In Commissioner v. Dill Co.[63] the taxpayer received a deposit that either was to serve as consideration for an extension of a licensing contract or was to be applied to the purchase price of a licensed trademark if an option to purchase was exercised. If the option lapsed, the amount would have been treated as ordinary income; if the option was exercised, as capital gain. The Third Circuit held that the uncertainty about the use of the deposit prevented inclusion in income in the year of receipt.

§ 5.05   ACCRUAL METHOD OF ACCOUNTING

[1]   IN GENERAL

The accrual method of accounting provides better matching between income and deductions. Generally, under the accrual method, actual receipt and payment of funds is irrelevant. The accrual method of accounting is used by most significant commercial enterprises, and it

---

61.   10 T.C. 445 (1948).

62.   135 F.2d 47 (5th Cir. 1943); accord Van Wagoner v. United States, 368 F.2d 95 (5th Cir. 1966).

63.   294 F.2d 291 (3d Cir. 1961).

must be used in computing taxable income when the production, purchase, or sale of merchandise is an income-producing factor.[1]

Section 451(a) requires that "[t]he amount of any item of gross income shall be included" in the year of receipt unless "under the method of accounting used in computing taxable income, such amount is to be properly accounted for as of a different period." Section 461(a) provides that a deduction "shall be taken for the taxable year" that is proper "under the method of accounting used in computing taxable income." These provisions are broad and provide the courts with latitude for the exercise of discretion in dealing with accrual method taxpayers. Accordingly, litigation involving accrual method taxpayers has been fairly substantial. The issues center on the following areas: (1) those concerning the circumstances in which accrual must be made, (2) those relating to advance receipts under a claim of right, (3) those concerning the treatment of prepaid and estimated expenses and liabilities, and (4) those situations in which accrual method taxpayers are placed on the cash method.

[2] REQUIREMENTS FOR ACCRUAL

The regulations provide that accrual of an item is required when all events have occurred that fix the right to receive income or that determine the fact of the liability and the amount can be determined with reasonable accuracy.[2] General guidelines as to when a right to receive income becomes fixed are given in Revenue Ruling 79–292,[3] which provides that all events occur when the required performance takes place, payment is due, or payment is made.

Section 461(h) provides that certain liabilities will not be treated as incurred under the all events test unless economic performance has occurred. In general, economic performance occurs when services or property are provided or used.[4]

In Lucas v. North Texas Lumber Co.[5] the taxpayer gave to Southern Pine Company a ten-day option on December 27, 1916, to purchase its

§ 5.05

1. Treas. Regs. §§ 1.446–1(a)(4)(i), 1.471–1. See Wilkinson–Beane, Inc. v. Commissioner, 420 F.2d 352 (1st Cir. 1970), in which the court upheld an IRS determination that the taxpayer's cash method did not clearly reflect income and required the use of the accrual method because the taxpayer, an undertaker, realized income from an inventory of caskets.

2. See Treas. Regs. §§ 1.451–1(a), 1.461–1(a)(2).

3. 1979–2 C.B. 287, clarified by Rev. Rul. 89–122, 1989–2 C.B. 200. See also Rev. Rul. 79–195, 1979–1 C.B. 177; Commissioner v. Hansen, 360 U.S. 446, 79 S.Ct. 1270, 3 L.Ed.2d 1360 (1959).

4. § 461(h)(2)(A)(i)-(iii). Special rules provide for worker's compensation and tort

liability (economic performance occurs as payments are made) and for certain recurring items. *Nota bene:* § 461(h) does not apply to § 463, relating to vacation pay, and any other provision that specifically allows a deduction for a reserve for estimated expenses.

5. 281 U.S. 11, 50 S.Ct. 184, 74 L.Ed. 668 (1930). See also Major Realty Corp. v. Commissioner, 749 F.2d 1483, 1486–87 (11th Cir. 1985); Claiborne v. United States, 648 F.2d 448, 451 (6th Cir. 1981); Bradford v. United States, 444 F.2d 1133 (Ct. Cl. 1971); Wiseman v. Scruggs, 281 F.2d 900, 902 (10th Cir. 1960); Rich Lumber Co. v. United States, 237 F.2d 424, 427 (1st Cir. 1956); Commissioner v. New Jersey Title Ins. Co., 79 F.2d 492 (3d Cir. 1935); Merrill v. Commissioner, 40 T.C. 66, 76(1963); Rev. Rul. 73–369, 1973–2 C.B.

timber lands for a specified price. On December 30, 1916, Southern Pine notified the taxpayer that it would exercise the option. In the notice Southern Pine declared itself ready to close the transaction and pay the purchase price "as soon as the papers were prepared." On January 5, 1917, the papers were delivered, the purchase price paid, and the transaction closed. The taxpayer was not allowed to accrue the gain on the sale for 1916. The Court said:

> Respondent did not prepare the papers necessary to effect the transfer or make tender of title or possession or demand the purchase price in 1916. The title and right of possession remained in it until the transaction was closed. Consequently, unconditional liability of vendee for the purchase price was not created in that year.[6]

In Flamingo Resort, Inc. v. United States[7] a casino extended credit to its customers for gambling. Gambling debts were not enforceable under state law and could not be recovered in court. Nonetheless, the Ninth Circuit reasoned that legal enforceability may be indicative, but it is not controlling in determining when the right to receive income becomes fixed. Based upon findings that approximately 96% of the casino's receivables were paid, and that the existence of legal enforceability would not increase the recovery rate to any significant extent, the court held the taxpayer had to accrue the debts as they were incurred.[8]

In Commissioner v. Hansen[9] the taxpayers were two retail automobile dealers and a house trailer dealer who discounted installment obligations received from customers to finance companies. The finance companies credited a small percentage of the amounts due the taxpayers to reserve accounts to secure their guarantees. The reserve accounts were to be repaid to the taxpayers or applied to any liability the taxpayers had incurred. The Supreme Court held that the amounts credited to the reserve accounts on the books of the finance companies must be reported as income accrued during the tax years they were so credited. The taxpayers argued their lack of a currently enforceable right to recover the amounts in the reserve accounts prevented accrual, but the Supreme Court held that the acquisition of a fixed right to receive the reserve amounts and not present receipt was determinative of accrual. The taxpayers also claimed they did not have a fixed right to receive the reserve amounts because of the possibility of offset. The

155; Alex Raskolnikov, Contextual Analysis of Tax Ownership, 85 B.U. L. Rev. 431, 516 (2005).

6.   281 U.S. 11, 13 (1930).

7.   664 F.2d 1387 (9th Cir. 1982), cert. denied, 459 U.S. 1036, 103 S.Ct. 446, 74 L.Ed.2d 602 (1982); cf. Desert Palace, Inc. v. Commissioner, 72 T.C. 1033 (1979), rev'd and remanded, 698 F.2d 1229 (9th Cir. 1982), cert. denied, 464 U.S. 816, 104 S.Ct. 73, 78 L.Ed.2d 86 (1983). See also Joseph Kelly, Caught in the Intersection Between

Public Policy and Practicality: A Survey of the Legal Treatment of Gambling–Related Obligations in the United States, 5 Chap. L. Rev. 87, 158 (2002).

8.   Accord Rev. Rul. 83–106, 1983–2 C.B. 77.

9.   360 U.S. 446, 79 S.Ct. 1270, 3 L.Ed.2d 1360 (1959). See also CCA 200048001; FSA 200049003; TAM 200310003; TAM 200110002; Hitachi Sales Corp. v. Commissioner, T.C. Memo. 1992–504.

Court responded that the reserve amounts were received by the taxpayers whether paid in cash or applied to the payment of their obligations. Thus, the taxpayers were held to have a fixed right to receive the reserve amounts and were required to accrue income when the amounts were credited to the reserve accounts by the finance companies.

In United States v. Hughes Properties, Inc.[10] the Supreme Court held that an accrual method taxpayer who owned a casino in Nevada could deduct amounts guaranteed for payment on progressive slot machines but not yet won. In addition to paying fixed amounts when certain symbol combinations appear, these machines have a progressive jackpot that is won only when a different specified combination appears. The amount increases as money is gambled on the machine. The amount of the jackpot at any given time is registered on a payoff indicator on the face of the machine. A Nevada Gaming Commission regulation, which is strictly enforced, prohibited reducing the jackpot, and by statute the Commission was authorized to impose severe administrative sanctions upon a casino that wrongfully refused to pay a winning customer the jackpot.

The Supreme Court rejected the government's argument in Hughes Properties that the taxpayer's liability for the progressive jackpots did not satisfy the all events test prescribed in the regulations because until the jackpots were won no person could assert a claim. The Supreme Court said that the effect of the Nevada Gaming Commission's regulation is to fix the taxpayer's liability; therefore, it is not contingent. Moreover, the identity of a winner is unnecessary because "[t]he obligation is there, and whether it turns out that the winner is one patron or another makes no conceivable difference as to basic liability."[11]

If a taxpayer or its debtor is contesting a liability, the obligation is not regarded as fixed until there is a final settlement or judgment. In Dixie Pine Products Co. v. Commissioner[12] the taxpayer accrued a deduction for a state tax on gasoline for 1937 when it was contesting the validity of the tax. The tax was never paid and the taxpayer made a compensating inclusion in income in 1938 when it was ultimately determined that the tax was invalid. The Supreme Court denied the deduction in 1937, holding that all events determinative of liability had not occurred because the liability was contingent and was being contested by the taxpayer. The Court has not deviated from this position even if the taxpayer makes full payment but still contests the liability.[13]

However, under section 461(f) the transfer of money or other property to provide for the satisfaction of the asserted liability permits

10. 476 U.S. 593, 106 S.Ct. 2092, 90 L.Ed.2d 569 (1986). See also CCA 200726023; CCA 200521026; TAM 200619022; TAM 200440023; United States v. General Dynamics Corp., 481 U.S. 239, 243, 107 S.Ct. 1732, 95 L.Ed.2d 226 (1987); Globe Products Corp. v. Commissioner, 72 T.C. 609, 621–622 (1979), acq., 1980–2 C.B. 1.

11. 476 U.S. at 602, 106 S.Ct. at 2097.

12. 320 U.S. 516, 64 S.Ct. 364, 88 L.Ed. 270 (1944). See also CCA 200236007.

13. United States v. Consolidated Edison Co., 366 U.S. 380, 81 S.Ct. 1326, 6 L.Ed.2d 356 (1961).

the taxpayer to take the deduction in the taxable year of the transfer. If the payment and deduction are in excess of the ultimate liability, the excess must be reported as income in the year of final determination; if the payment and deduction are less than the taxpayer's ultimate liability, an additional amount is allowed as a deduction.[14] Section 461(f) applies to contested liabilities and governs in cases of actions for recovery on commercial accounts when goods have been prepaid as well as in cases of claims for refunds or resistance to asserted tax liability, provided payment has been made.[15] The amount of the contested liability need not be paid to the opposing party, but it can be placed in an escrow account by the taxpayer as long as the funds are "beyond his control."[16]

As indicated earlier, accrual of an item is required when all events have occurred that fix the right to receive income or that determine the fact of the liability and the amount can be determined with reasonable accuracy.[17] Whether the amount can be determined with reasonable accuracy is largely a factual question. In Continental Tie & Lumber Co. v. United States[18] the taxpayer, a railroad, was entitled to a statutory award to compensate it for operating losses during a period when it was under federal control during World War I. The Supreme Court held that the taxpayer's right to the award was fixed by legislation enacted in

14. See Treas. Reg. § 1.461–2(a)(3).

15. Treas. Reg. § 1.461–2. Section 461(f)(4) requires that the deduction would have been allowed for the year of the transfer or an earlier year but for the contest and that the economic performance test of § 461(h) is satisfied. Section 461(h)(2)(C) indicates that if the liability arises under a workers compensation act or out of a tort, economic performance occurs as the payments are made.

16. Treas. Reg. § 1.461–2(c)(1). See, e.g., Specialized Servs., Inc. v. Commissioner, 77 T.C. 490 (1981), in which a sufficient transfer to an escrow account was not made within the meaning of § 461(f) because the taxpayer could withdraw funds on its own volition and maintained authority over the disposition of funds to claimants for settlement. See also Poirier & McLane Corp. v. Commissioner, 547 F.2d 161 (2d Cir. 1976), rev'g 63 T.C. 570 (1975), cert. denied, 431 U.S. 967, 97 S.Ct. 2925, 53 L.Ed.2d 1063 (1977), in which the taxpayer who unilaterally transferred funds in trust to cover future contested liabilities, relinquishing all authority and control over the funds, was denied accrual. The Second Circuit held that, to be deductible, payment in trust must be equivalent to direct payment, requiring that the claimant agree and be made a party to the trust agreement rather than the trust being created unilaterally. In Chem Aero, Inc. v. United States, 694 F.2d 196 (9th Cir. 1982), the taxpayer, in appeal-

ing a judgment, was required by state law to post a bond equal to one-and-one-half times the amount of the award. The Ninth Circuit held that the transaction resembled a typical escrow agreement because the bond was collateralized with sufficient cash to satisfy the judgment and the bonding company's functions were similar to that of a trustee or escrowee. The Ninth Circuit allowed a deduction for the purchase of the bond, reasoning that the statutory purpose of § 461(f) is satisfied whenever the taxpayer irrevocably parts with money in settlement of a contested liability. It also held that the claimant's assent to the bonding agreement could be implied to satisfy the "among the parties" language in the regulations.

17. See Treas. Regs. §§ 1.451–1(a), 1.461–1(a)(2).

18. 286 U.S. 290, 52 S.Ct. 529, 76 L.Ed. 1111 (1932). See also Gillis v. United States, 402 F.2d 501 (5th Cir. 1968), in which the Fifth Circuit allowed accrual for losses on damage claims under a contract providing for arbitration pursuant to which the taxpayer could estimate the losses to within one-half of one percent. But see AB-KCO Indus., Inc. v. Commissioner, 56 T.C. 1083 (1971), aff'd, 482 F.2d 150 (3d Cir. 1973), in which the Tax Court denied accrual for royalties payable in excess of fixed minimum amounts, the minimum amounts never being reached during the tax year involved.

1920, and the amount of the award, made in 1923, was capable of determination from the taxpayer's books with reasonable accuracy in 1920 despite the requirement that the amounts of certain elements in the computation were based on subjective determinations.

As another prerequisite to accrual, collection or payment of the amount must be reasonably certain. In Georgia School–Book Depository, Inc. v. Commissioner[19] the taxpayer, a book broker, had a contract with the State of Georgia under which it was to receive commissions for its services in purchasing school books for the state. Under the contract both the publishers and the taxpayer were paid from a textbook account that was funded by a tax on beer. During the years involved the account was exhausted, the state regarding its liability as a charge on the subsequent year's account. The Tax Court acknowledged that "[w]here there is a contingency that may preclude ultimate payment, whether it be that the right itself is in litigation or that the debtor is insolvent, the right need not be accrued when it arises."[20] However, "[t]o allow the exception there must be a definite showing that an unresolved and allegedly intervening local right makes receipt contingent or that the insolvency of [the] debtor makes it improbable."[21] In requiring accrual the Tax Court reasoned there was no serious doubt about the ultimate collection of the commissions.

Two provisions of section 461 concern the accrual of state and local taxes.[22] Section 461(c) allows taxpayers to accrue ratably real property taxes that relate to a definite period of time. According to the Tax Court in Epoch Food Service, Inc.,[23] the legislative history of section 461(d) suggests that Congress intended to deny accrual method taxpayers the right to accrue and deduct taxes for two years in one tax year when they only paid the tax for the one year. The taxpayer in Epoch Food Service was a California corporation. The California corporate franchise tax was incurred in a tax year based on the previous year's business activities. However, the law was amended so that dissolving corporations would pay the franchise tax based on activities in the year of termination plus the prior year. The Tax Court held that although the amendment accelerated the taxpayer's corporate franchise tax liability, section 461(d)(1) limited the taxpayer's right to accrue the franchise tax using the new calculation, and it allowed the deduction only for taxes that related to the prior year's activities.[24]

19. 1 T.C. 463 (1943). See also TAM 9143083.

20. 1 T.C. at 468. But see Spring City Foundry Co. v. Commissioner, 292 U.S. 182, 54 S.Ct. 644, 78 L.Ed. 1200 (1934), in which the Supreme Court required accrual of goods sold on open account even though it was probable that the account would turn out to be partially worthless. But cf. § 448(d)(5) (a service provider is not required to accrue amounts that on the basis of experience will not be collected if no interest is charged and no penalty for late payment is imposed).

21. 1 T.C. at 469.

22. See § 461(c) and (d).

23. 72 T.C. 1051 (1979). See also FSA 200122008.

24. See also Rev. Rul. 74–244, 1974–1 C.B. 118, and Rev. Rul. 76–474, 1976–2 C.B. 135. In both revenue rulings the taxpayer was a lessee who agreed to pay the real estate taxes that the lessor was liable for;

[3] ADVANCE RECEIPTS

The Supreme Court has decided several cases involving advance receipts. In Automobile Club of Michigan v. Commissioner,[25] decided in 1957, the taxpayer deferred prepaid dues to monthly periods; it claimed a right to do so on the ground that deferral clearly reflected income under the accrual method. The Supreme Court, however, upheld the Commissioner's determination that the claim of right doctrine did not permit deferral. The Court found that the allocation of the dues to monthly periods was "purely artificial" and was without relation to the services the taxpayer would be called upon to provide.

Four years later the Supreme Court reviewed a similar question in American Automobile Association v. United States.[26] The taxpayer in this case received dues attributable in part to the following year. The taxpayer deferred both the income attributable to the following year and certain operating expenses, although the taxpayer did not and could not know its costs for rendering such services for its members as towing and routing, which were to be performed only upon demand. Again the Court denied the right to defer the advance receipts, holding that the taxpayer's system was artificial because it had deferred income to a period in which the costs of services, for which the income was paid, could not be determined.

In Schlude v. Commissioner[27] the accrual method taxpayers formed a partnership to operate a ballroom dancing studio. Lessons were offered under contracts that provided for advance payments. The taxpayers reported as gross income only that portion of the advance payments that corresponded with the number of hours taught during the year. The balance was reserved for accrual in future years. The Court said that "the considerations expressed" in American Automobile Association "are apposite here." Moreover, it pointed out that in American Automobile Association the retroactive repeal of section 452 "was regarded as reinstating long-standing administrative and lower court rulings that accounting systems deferring prepaid income could be rejected by the

---

the lessor became liable for the real estate taxes on January 1, but the taxes were not due until June 1 of the following year when the bills were sent. In Rev. Rul. 74–244 the lessee was not required under the terms of the lease to pay the tax until the lessor was obligated to do so on June 1 of the following year. Under the terms of the lease his liability did not arise until that date. Thus, the liability did not become fixed, and the taxpayer was not allowed to accrue and deduct the taxes, until June 1. However, in Rev. Rul. 76–474 the taxpayer-lessee's liability for the real estate taxes, in accordance with the terms of the lease, became fixed when the taxes accrued on January 1. The taxpayer was allowed a deduction in the year the taxes accrued, even though he was not obligated to pay the tax until June 1 of the following year.

25. 353 U.S. 180, 77 S.Ct. 707, 1 L.Ed.2d 746 (1957). See also W. Eugene Seago, Do Advance Trade Discounts Represent a Liability or Income?, 105 J. Tax'n 144, 144 (2006).

26. 367 U.S. 687, 81 S.Ct. 1727, 6 L.Ed.2d 1109 (1961). See also Cinergy Corp. v. United States, 55 Fed.Cl. 489, 504 (2003); Tampa Bay Devil Rays, Ltd. v. Commissioner, T.C. Memo. 2002–248; FSA 200203004; TAM 200619023.

27. 372 U.S. 128, 83 S.Ct. 601, 9 L.Ed.2d 633 (1963); accord Angelus Funeral Home v. Commissioner, 407 F.2d 210 (9th Cir. 1969), cert. denied, 396 U.S. 824, 90 S.Ct. 65, 24 L.Ed.2d 74 (1969).

Commissioner." In Schlude the Court concluded it was proper for the Commissioner in the exercise of his discretion under section 446(b) to reject the taxpayer's accounting system as not clearly reflecting income and to include advance payments in income when received.

In Commissioner v. Indianapolis Power & Light Co.[28] the Court considered whether deposits received by a power company were properly taxable as gross income or instead nontaxable as capital being held to secure performance. The Court decided the deposits were analogous to loans because they would ultimately have to be repaid upon the customers' cessation of service; accordingly, the deposits were determined to be nontaxable.

RCA Corp. v. United States,[29] makes clear that to defer prepaid income the certainty of performance must be unconditional and not based on predictions. In RCA the taxpayer rendered repair services for customers on demand and deferred the income received on prepaid service contracts "based on reasonably accurate forecasts of monthly variations in the demand for service." The Second Circuit held the forecasts were not determinative of revenue because of the uncertainty of the extent of services that would actually be demanded by the customers.[30]

In Farrara v. Commissioner[31] the taxpayer, a retail merchant, formed "suit clubs" under which customer-members made weekly advance payments for a fixed period. Each week a drawing resulted in a member winning a suit; those members who did not win a suit received certificates that entitled them to merchandise equal to the amount of their payments. The Tax Court held that American Automobile Association and Schlude precluded deferral of the advance payments. The Tax Court acknowledged that refundable deposits on merchandise would not be included in income under American Automobile Association and Schlude, but it found that in this case the taxpayer had unrestricted use of the payments.

The Tax Court in Farrara did not face the issue of the distortion that results from inclusion in closing inventory of goods for which advance payments have been received, if the payments may not be deferred. Suppose, for example, that a corporation receives an advance payment of $100,000 for goods to be manufactured and delivered in a

---

28. 493 U.S. 203, 110 S.Ct. 589, 107 L.Ed.2d 591 (1990). See also Vivian R. King, Commissioner of Internal Revenue v. Indianapolis Power & Light Co.: Federal Income Tax Treatment of Customer Deposits by an Accrual–Basis Electric Company, 16 T. Marshall L. Rev. 355 (1991).

29. 664 F.2d 881 (2d Cir. 1981), cert. denied, 457 U.S. 1133, 102 S.Ct. 2958, 73 L.Ed.2d 1349 (1982). See also Johnson v. Commissioner, 108 T.C. 448 (1997).

30. See also Morgan Guar. Trust Co. v. United States, 218 Ct.Cl. 57, 585 F.2d 988

(1978), in which the taxpayer was allowed a deferral for prepaid interest over the life of the loan because of the certainty of the periods to which the interest was attributable.

31. 44 T.C. 189 (1965), distinguishing Consolidated–Hammer Dry Plate & Film Co. v. Commissioner, 317 F.2d 829 (7th Cir. 1963) and Veenstra & DeHaan Coal Co., 11 T.C. 964 (1948), on the ground that the amounts in those cases were refundable deposits.

future year and spends $90,000 for raw materials and labor on the order. If at the close of its tax year the $90,000 of goods are included in closing inventory, the cost of goods sold (opening inventory plus purchases less closing inventory) is reduced in a corresponding amount and gross income (receipts less cost of goods sold) is increased. Does it follow that if the advance payment is subject to inclusion in income, the taxpayer is being taxed on capital, and, consequently, the claim of right doctrine is inapplicable and deferral allowed?

This problem was presented to the full Tax Court in Hagen Advertising Displays, Inc.[32] and again the court found that the claim of right doctrine controlled. In this case the taxpayer was engaged in the manufacturing of advertising signs. Some of its larger customers placed prepaid blanket orders for signs for delivery in the future. The taxpayer recorded these prepaid amounts in an "advance from customers" liability account. When a prepaid sign was shipped, the taxpayer recorded a sale and removed the appropriate amount from the "advance" account. In many instances the taxpayer had begun, and in some instances had completed, the signs that were prepaid. However, it did not maintain separate inventory records pertaining to the prepaid signs; and its closing inventory, 80% of which related to signs on order, simply included material costs and direct and overhead costs of all finished signs and goods in process. The taxpayer contended that deferral of the prepaid amounts was proper because an accrual method taxpayer engaged in selling property, as distinguished from services, does not realize gross income until its cost of goods sold can be determined and subtracted from gross receipts, and that income is not realized until a sale is completed and the right to payment becomes unqualified by the passing of title or possession. The Tax Court rejected these arguments, and it held the advance receipts must be included in income when received under the claim of right doctrine. The Tax Court reasoned the taxpayer "would in effect place its regular business on a 'transactional' basis insofar as advance payments are concerned instead of on the annual basis required in tax accounting."[33] The court also noted that no attempt was made to record the precise cost or amount of gain realized from the sale of any particular sign.

The litigation in this area reveals the reluctance of accrual method taxpayers to accept the applicability of the claim of right doctrine when it arguably runs counter to generally accepted accounting practice for prepaid income. The resultant pressure on the courts has been matched by similar pressure on Congress. In 1954 Congress added section 452, which would have permitted accrual method taxpayers a general right to defer prepaid income; however, in 1955 the section was repealed retroactively because of the potential revenue loss that would have occurred. In 1957 Congress added section 455, which allows publishers to elect to defer subscription income,[34] and in 1960 added section 456, which

---

32. 47 T.C. 139 (1966), aff'd, 407 F.2d 1105 (6th Cir. 1969).

33. 47 T.C. at 146.

34. See also § 458 which allows an accrual method publisher or distributor to exclude from gross income amounts re-

permits prepaid dues received by accrual method membership organizations to be deferred up to 36 months. While the latter statutory provision would reverse the automobile club cases on their facts, it does not disturb the principle of those cases.

Accrual method taxpayers have received some relief at the administrative level in the form of a revenue procedure and an amendment to the section 451 regulations, both allowing deferral of prepaid income in limited circumstances. Under Revenue Procedure 2004–34[35] certain types of income (including, but not limited to, income from services and the sale of goods) may be deferred, at the taxpayer's election, to the second year after receipt. However, subject to certain exceptions, deferral is limited to the second year after receipt. Expressly excluded from Revenue Procedure 2004–34 are amounts received under guaranty and warranty contracts, as prepaid rent, prepaid interest, and payment with respect to financial instruments.

The regulations under section 451 permit a taxpayer using the accrual method of accounting for purchases and sales of goods to report advance receipts for the payment of goods in the year of receipt or to defer reporting in accordance with accounting practice, such as on shipment.[36] However, deferral is restricted for the sale of identifiable inventory if the taxpayer receives "substantial advance payments" equal to or in excess of the estimated total inventory cost of the goods and has similar goods on hand or readily available through supply channels to satisfy the contract in the year of receipt. In that situation all untaxed amounts received by the end of the second year following the year of substantial advance payments must be included in income in the second year. Moreover, in the second year adjustment for the cost of inventory on hand attributable to unfilled contracts (or, if none, an estimate of the needs to fill the contracts) must be made. Since no further deferral is permitted, any subsequent payments must be included in the year of receipt, and appropriate adjustment made where estimates are used to prevent inventory from being taken into account a second time.

[4] PREPAID AND ESTIMATED EXPENSES

Section 1.461–1(a)(2) of the regulations states that under the accrual method of accounting "any expenditure which results in the creation of an asset having a useful life which extends substantially beyond the close of the taxable year may not be deductible, or may be deductible only in part, for the taxable year in which incurred." Consequently, an accrual method taxpayer may be precluded from taking an immediate deduction for a prepaid expense. Moreover, accrual method taxpayers have not

---

ceived from sales of magazines, paperbacks, or records when the taxpayer is under a legal obligation to make an adjustment if such items are not sold and are returned within a specified period during the following taxable year.

35. 2004–1 C.B. 991. See also TAM 200725029; Dennis J. Gaffney, Richard O.

Davis, Richard P. Weber, and Maureen H. Smith–Gaffney, Advance Payments: Rev. Proc. 2004–34 Expands Rev. Proc. 71–21 and Provides Needed Clarity, 101 J. Tax'n 84 (2004).

36. Treas. Reg. § 1.451–5.

been able to convince the Supreme Court that estimated expenses may be deducted through the use of reserve accounts. Thus, most taxpayers must use the specific charge-off method in accounting for losses on bad debts. The specific charge-off method allows a deduction at the time and in the amount that a particular debt is wholly or partially worthless.

In United States v. General Dynamics Corp.[37] the Supreme Court held that the taxpayer, a self-insurer of employee medical care plans beginning in October 1972, could not deduct for reserve accounts that reflected services rendered to employees or their dependents during the final quarter of 1972 and for which the taxpayer had not made payment as of the end of the year. The Court held that all the events necessary to fix liability had not occurred during 1972 because the taxpayer was liable only if a person covered by a plan filled out and submitted a benefit claim form. The Court stated that the taxpayer had not demonstrated that the estimates "represented claims for which its liability was firmly established." Because "all events necessary to establish liability were not shown to have occurred," the Court held that deduction for 1972 was not permitted.

The Court noted that although the taxpayer may have been able to make a reasonable estimate of its liability based on actuarial data, "that alone does not justify a deduction." The Court said that "[a] reserve based on the proposition that a particular set of events is likely to occur in the future may be an appropriate conservative accounting measure, but does not warrant a tax deduction."[38]

In General Dynamics Corp. the Supreme Court referred to Brown v. Helvering.[39] In Brown the taxpayer, a general insurance agent, received overriding commissions on policies written by other agents for periods of three years and more. However, the taxpayer was required to return commissions on canceled policies. On the basis of five years of experience the rate of cancellation was some 22%. To reflect this the taxpayer changed his method of accounting for tax purposes from taking deductions when he actually returned the commissions to making entries to a "return commission" reserve account. The Supreme Court rejected the use of the reserve account because "the events necessary to create the liability" did "not occur during the taxable year."

Under section 461(h)(1) as a general rule for determining whether liabilities are incurred during a taxable year the all events test is not

37. 481 U.S. 239, 107 S.Ct. 1732, 95 L.Ed.2d 226 (1987). See also CCA 200521026; CCA 200521026; Rev. Rul. 2007–3, 2007–4 I.R.B. 350; Rev. Rul. 2003–3, 2003–2 I.R.B. 252; TAM 200619022; Michael Dubetz, United States v. General Dynamics: The Deduction of Estimated Liabilities by Accrual Method Taxpayers: The All Events Test and Economic Performance, 49 Ohio St. L.J. 1439 (1989); Larissa L. Renshaw, Federal Taxation–Timing of Deduc-

tions–Deduction by Accrual Basis Taxpayer of its Liability for Medical Services Received by Employees for Which Claims Have not Been Filed Disallowed. United States v. General Dynamics Corp., 481 U.S. 239, 107 S.Ct. 1732, 95 L.Ed.2d 226 (1987), 19 Rutgers L.J. 1133 (1988).

38. 481 U.S. at 247, 107 S.Ct. at 1737.

39. 291 U.S. 193, 54 S.Ct. 356, 78 L.Ed. 725 (1934).

satisfied until there has been economic performance.[40] Economic performance occurs as services or property are provided to the taxpayer or as property is used by the taxpayer. An exception is made for certain recurring items.

In order to qualify for the recurring items exception:[41]

(1) The all-events test must be fulfilled with respect to the item at issue during the taxable year in question;

(2) Economic performance for the liability in question occurs no later than 8½ months after the close of the taxable year;

(3) The item is "recurring in nature and the taxpayer consistently treats items of such kind as incurred in the taxable year in which the requirements"[42] of the all-events test are met; and

(4) Either the item is immaterial, or "the accrual of such item in the taxable year in which the requirements of . . . [the all-events test] are met results in a more proper match against income than accruing such item in the taxable year in which economic performance occurs."[43]

[5] ACCRUAL METHOD TAXPAYERS MADE TO ACCOUNT ON THE CASH METHOD

In some instances the Code allows a deduction only when an item is actually paid. As a general rule such provisions override the use of the accrual method of accounting, and the deduction may not be taken upon the creation of an obligation. For example, an accrual method individual must account for tax purposes on a cash method with respect to charitable contributions, medical expenses, and alimony payments.[44]

On the income side, dividends declared are not reportable by an accrual method taxpayer until actual or constructive receipt. In Commissioner v. American Light & Traction Co.[45] dividends were declared in December 1936 to stockholders of record as of a date during that month, but they were not payable until 1937. The Seventh Circuit considered as possible candidates for reporting the dates of declaration, record, payment, and receipt. The Seventh Circuit concluded that in the interest of uniformity in characterizing the dividend as income or capital in the hands of both cash and accrual method taxpayers, as well as for the purpose of alleviating administrative difficulties in auditing, the year of receipt would be the most desirable.[46]

---

40. See Jensen, The Deduction of Future Liabilities by Accrual–Basis Taxpayers: Premature Accruals, The All Events Test, and Economic Performance, 37 U. Fla. L. Rev. 443 (1985).

41. § 461(h)(3)(A).

42. § 461(h)(3)(A)(iii).

43. § 461(h)(3)(A)(iv)(II).

44. See §§ 170(a)(1), 213(a), 215(a).

45. 156 F.2d 398 (7th Cir. 1946).

46. See also Treas. Reg. § 1.301–1(b) (distribution made by corporation to shareholders is included in gross income when cash or other property is unqualifiedly made subject to their demands); Tar Products Corporation v. Commissioner, 130 F.2d 866 (3d Cir. 1942); American Light & Traction Co. v. Commissioner, 3 T.C. 1048 (1944), aff'd, 156 F.2d 398 (7th Cir. 1946); Koppers Co. v. Commissioner, 3 T.C. 62 (1944), aff'd, 151 F.2d 267 (3d Cir. 1945).

In response to a variety of schemes previously perpetrated by related parties, Congress concluded that related parties should be required to use the same accounting method for transactions between themselves to prevent the allowance of a deduction without the corresponding inclusion in gross income.[47] Hence, under section 267(a)(2) an accrual method payor is placed on the cash method with respect to the deduction of an amount owed to a related cash method payee. In other words, the deduction by an accrual method payor is not allowed until the cash method payee includes the item in gross income.[48]

§ 5.06 LONG–TERM CONTRACT METHODS

As an alternative to the cash method or the accrual method, taxpayers engaged in building, installing, constructing, or manufacturing under contracts not completed during the taxable year the contracts are entered into must report income under the percentage of completion method.[1] Except for certain construction contracts,[2] the percentage of completion method is the exclusive method under which long-term contracts may be reported.[3]

Section 460(e) allows the completed contract method if the contract is for the building, construction, or improvement of real property, is expected to be completed within two years, and is performed by a taxpayer whose average annual gross receipts do not exceed $10 million for the preceding three taxable years. No reporting of gain or loss is made under the completed contract method until the contract is finally completed and accepted.[4] In the year of completion the contract price is included in gross income and all costs properly allocable to the contract are deducted.[5]

Under the percentage of completion method the amount included in gross income during the taxable year is the portion of the gross contract price corresponding to the percentage of the entire contract completed during the year.[6] The percentage of completion of a contract can be determined by comparing either the costs incurred with the estimated total contract costs or the work performed with the estimated total work to be performed.[7] Under the percentage of completion method all costs incurred during the taxable year with respect to a contract must be deducted.[8]

§ 5.07 INSTALLMENT SALES TREATMENT

The treatment of gain from installment sales under section 453 represents an exception to the general rules of inclusion in gross income

---

47. Staff of Joint Comm. on Tax'n, 98th Cong., 2d Sess., General Explanation of the Revenue Provisions of the Deficit Reduction Act of 1984, at 542 (Joint Comm. Print 1984).

48. § 267(2).

§ 5.06

1. § 460(a).

2. See § 460(e).

3. See § 460(a).

4. Treas. Reg. § 1.451–3(b)(2).

5. Treas. Reg. § 1.451–3(d)(1).

6. § 460(b)(1)(A) and (B).

7. Treas. Reg. § 1.460–4(b)(1).

8. Treas. Reg. § 1.460–4(b)(2)(i).

applicable to cash and accrual method taxpayers.[1] Were it not for section 453, a taxpayer would usually be taxed on the entire gain in the year the property is disposed of, even though the payments are spread over more than one year.[2] Under section 453 gain is recognized on a proportionate basis as payments are received unless the taxpayer elects out of the installment method. This method of reporting only applies to gain from the disposition of property; a loss is reported in full in the year of the disposition.[3]

An installment sale concerns any disposition of property if at least one payment is to be received in a taxable year subsequent to the taxable year of disposition.[4] The income from payments received on an installment sale is reported in the proportion that the total gross profit realized or to be realized bears to the total contract price.[5]

Section 453 may be illustrated by the following example of a sale of land. Assume that the taxpayer's basis for the land is $6,000 and that the land is sold for $13,000, the buyer taking it subject to a $5,000 mortgage, making a $2,000 down payment, and agreeing to pay the balance at the rate of $2,000 a year for three years. The taxpayer's gross profit is $7,000 ($13,000 amount realized minus $6,000 basis); the total contract price is $8,000 ($13,000 selling price less the $5,000 mortgage). Thus, the gross profit ratio is 7,000/8,000, or 87.5%.[6] In the year of sale the taxpayer would report 87.5% of the $2,000 down payment, or $1,750, and in each of the following three years he would report 87.5% of the

§ 5.07

1. In Commissioner v. South Texas Lumber Co., 333 U.S. 496, 68 S.Ct. 695, 92 L.Ed. 831 (1948), the Court stated:

The installment basis of reporting was enacted, as shown by its history, to relieve taxpayers who adopted it from having to pay an income tax in the year of sale based on the full amount of anticipated profits when in fact they had received in cash only a small portion of the sales price. Another reason was the difficult and time-consuming effort of appraising the uncertain market value of installment obligations.

2. See Treas. Reg. § 15a.453–1(d).

3. See § 165(a); Treas. Reg. § 1.165–1(d)(1).

4. § 453(b)(1). Section 453(b)(2) makes an exception for dispositions by dealers of personal property or dispositions of personal property included in inventory. Section 453A provides rules similar to § 453 for dispositions by dealers in personal property.

5. § 453(b). See Treas. Reg. § 15a. 453–1(b)(2) for the definitions of "gross profit" and "contract price." The includibility of sales tax in the contract price is determined by whether the tax is imposed on the seller or the buyer. According to Rev. Rul. 79–196, 1979–1 C.B. 181, when the sales tax is imposed on a retailer, it is included in the contract price because the price paid is only for the goods, even though the price includes the sales tax. However, according to Rev. Rul. 83–4, 1983–1 C.B. 102, when the sales tax is imposed on the consumer, it is excluded from the contract price because the tax paid by the consumer is not for the goods themselves. Gain under the installment method refers only to the sale of the property and not to any interest accrued to the seller as a result of the deferral of payments; the interest must be accounted for under the taxpayer's usual method of accounting. Rev. Rul. 75–171, 1975–1 C.B. 140. Gain on an installment sale does not include amounts otherwise excluded by specific Code sections. In Rev. Rul. 80–249, 1980–2 C.B. 166, the amount of gain excluded by § 121 on the sale of a principal residence was not considered as gross profit for § 453 installment reporting purposes.

6. See Treas. Reg. § 15a.453–1(b).

annual $2,000 payment. In this manner the taxpayer accounts for the total $7,000 gain over four years.

For a complete discussion of installment sales, see § 8.05, *Receipt of Periodic Payments: Installment Sales.*

§ 5.08 ACCOUNTING FOR INVENTORIES

[1] IN GENERAL

If the production, purchase, or sale of merchandise is an income-producing factor, an inventory is necessary.[1] Normally, this requires determining the cost of goods, which is subtracted from gross receipts or gross sales to arrive at gross income. The role of inventories in the process of computing gross income can be expressed as follows: Gross Income = Gross Receipts – Cost of Goods Sold, where Cost of Goods Sold = Opening Inventory + Purchases – Closing Inventory.

Sound accounting requires that accounting procedures and inventory methods be tailored to the business enterprise. Congressional recognition of the need for flexibility in this area is evidenced by the substantial discretionary authority delegated to the Commissioner under section 471. The Commissioner is authorized to determine whether the use of inventories is necessary to clearly reflect income, and, if so, to prescribe rules for handling them in accordance with the best accounting practices in the trade or business.[2] Under this broad authority the Service has promulgated regulations concerning (among other things) when the use of inventories is required, what they should include, and the methods of valuation.[3]

When inventories are required, the taxpayer must, as a general rule, use the accrual method of accounting to properly reflect income.[4]

Inventory includes goods held for sale,[5] goods in process, and raw materials. The definition of inventory excludes such items as cash, accounts receivable, machinery used in manufacturing, and mortgages purchased by a lending institution.[6] Certain businesses, including real estate dealers, may not use inventories because of the impracticality of valuing the property held for sale each year.[7]

---

§ 5.08

1. Treas. Reg. §§ 1.446–1(a)(4)(i), 1.471–1.

2. § 471(a).

3. See Treas. Regs. §§ 1.471–1 through 1.471–11.

4. Treas. Reg. § 1.446–1(c)(2)(i).

5. See, e.g., Thompson Electric, Inc. v. Commissioner, T.C. Memo. 1995–292; J.P. Sheahan and Assoc. v. Commissioner, T.C. Memo. 1992–239.

6. See e.g., Rev. Rul. 65–95, 1965–1 C.B. 208. See also Treas. Reg. 1.471–1.

7. Atlantic Coast Realty Co. v. Commissioner, 11 B.T.A. 416 (1928); Rev. Rul. 86–149, 1986–2 C.B. 147; Rev. Rul. 69–536, 1969–2 C.B. 109; Homes by Ayres v. Commissioner, 795 F.2d 832 (9th Cir. 1986); W.C. & A.N. Miller Development Co. v. Commissioner, 81 T.C. 619 (1983). See also Jerry S. Williford and C. Todd Sinnett, Tax Planning for the Developer: Allocating Costs Among Land and Improvements, 103 J. Tax'n 335, 348 (2005).

[2] VALUATION

From the formula above for determining gross income, it follows that the smaller the closing inventory the larger the cost of goods sold and the less gross income. Hence, the lower the closing inventory, the lower the tax liability. Consequently, many of the controversies involving inventories have concerned the valuation of closing inventories, even though a lower closing inventory means a correspondingly lower opening inventory for the determination of the following year's gross income.

Section 471 provides that inventory practices must conform to the best accounting practices in the industry and they must clearly reflect income. The regulations recognize the two most commonly used methods: cost and the lower of cost or market.[8]

The regulations also provide for the following: valuation at market for security dealers,[9] the right of miners and manufacturers producing two or more products from a single process or processes to allocate between such products on the basis of selling values,[10] and, as discussed below, special rules for retail merchants, farmers, and livestock raisers.

Section 263A deals, in part, with inventory costs. Section 263A(a) provides that "direct costs"[11] and the "proper share"[12] of "indirect costs (including taxes)"[13] of "property which is inventory in the hands of the taxpayer, shall be included in inventory costs."[14] The legislative history[15] states that the rules implementing this provision should be "patterned after the rules applicable to extended period long-term contracts, set forth in the final regulations issued under section 451."

Hence, taxpayers "will be required to capitalize not only direct costs but also an allocable portion of most indirect costs that benefit the assets produced or acquired for resale, including general and administrative and overhead costs and other costs described in section 1.451–3 of the regulations."[16] However, it was recognized that "modifications of the rules set forth in the long-term contract regulations may be necessary or appropriate in order to adopt such rules to production not involving a contract."[17]

Section 263A(a) applies to all persons who produce or acquire property for resale, but an exception is made for personal property held for resale by retailers and wholesalers whose average annual gross receipts do not exceed $10 million.[18]

8. Treas. Reg. § 1.471–2(c).

9. Treas. Reg. § 1.471–5. The use of market value permits the taking of unrealized gain and loss into account annually.

10. Treas. Reg. § 1.471–7.

11. § 263A(a)(2)(A).

12. § 263A(a)(2)(B).

13. Id.

14. § 263A(a)(1)(A).

15. S. Rep. No. 313, 99th Cong., 2d Sess. 141–42 (1986).

16. Id.

17. Id.

18. § 263A(b)(1) and (2). Moreover, § 263A(i)(2) directs the Secretary to provide for a simplified method for applying the rules in the case of taxpayers acquiring property for resale.

When the taxpayer elects the lower of cost or market, each item is valued at both cost and market, and the lower of the two is used as the inventory value.[19] Market is the current bid price or, if there is no open or active market, the best evidence of that price.[20] When a taxpayer wishes to use a market value that is lower than replacement cost, he has the burden of proving a bona fide selling price by actual offerings, sales, or contract cancellations.[21]

[3] IDENTIFICATION: FIFO AND LIFO

The option of valuing inventories at the lower of cost or market recognizes the conventional accounting practice of keeping inventory balance sheet figures current during periods of price decline. However, identification of items is impossible in inventorying fungible goods. For this reason it is presumed that the inventory for tax purposes consists of the goods most recently purchased. In other words, goods first-in are presumed first-out (FIFO). This is the general rule, although actual valuation of identifiable goods is a permissible alternative.

The effect of a price change on FIFO with the option of the lower of cost or market may be summarized as follows: On the upswing of an economic cycle, gross income is increased. On the downswing of an economic cycle, a price decline below cost at the end of the inventory period will result in an inventory loss.

Although in the long run the distortions resulting from the use of FIFO tend to even out, substantial dissatisfaction developed in the late 1930s from reporting what were allegedly "paper profits" on cyclical upswings under the FIFO presumption. Taxpayers in the leather and nonferrous metal industries were able to induce Congress to permit an elective variant, now section 472, predicated upon their customary base stock method of inventory valuation under which inventory is identified on the basis of a presumption that the latest items produced or purchased are sold first, in other words, last-in first-out (LIFO).[22]

In using LIFO the taxpayer must value its inventory at cost. On the upswing of an economic cycle, this results in the LIFO taxpayer having an increased cost of goods sold and a corresponding decrease in gross income. This effect is the result of the presumption that the most recently purchased, higher priced goods are sold first. On the downswing of the cycle, because the taxpayer must maintain inventory at cost and

---

19. Treas. Reg. § 1.471–4.

20. Treas. Reg. § 1.471–4(a)(1).

21. Treas. Reg. § 1.471–2(c). In Thor Power Tool Co. v. Commissioner, 439 U.S. 522, 99 S.Ct. 773, 58 L.Ed.2d 785 (1979), the taxpayer wrote down, in accordance with generally accepted accounting principles, what it regarded as excess inventory to its own estimate of net realizable value. Despite the write-down the taxpayer continued to hold the goods for sale at original prices. The Court held the Commissioner did not abuse his discretion in determining that the write-down failed to reflect the taxpayer's income clearly since it was plainly inconsistent with the regulations. See also CCA 200728001; TAM 200545043; Celia Whitaker, How to Build a Bridge: Eliminating the Book–Tax Accounting Gap, 59 Tax Law. 981, 988 (2006).

22. See Treas. Reg. § 1.472–3(a); Rev. Proc. 74–2, 1974–1 C.B. 412, regarding the election to adopt LIFO.

cannot mark down as is the case with FIFO, inventory losses are excluded. In theory, over a full cycle and everything else being equal, the impact of taxes in the aggregate would be the same whether the taxpayer was on FIFO or LIFO. However, the bird-in-hand approach to tax benefits has induced a substantial number of taxpayers during periods of general price increases to convert to the LIFO method of identifying opening and closing inventories.

When LIFO was first made available to all taxpayers in 1939, the Service took the position that the identification of specific items in an inventory was a prerequisite for its use. This would preclude using LIFO in retailing where inventories are valued by the retail price method, which is discussed below. Present regulations no longer restrict the use of LIFO, and indexes compiled currently by the United States Department of Labor, Bureau of Labor Statistics, are used by retailers in applying LIFO.[23]

[4] RETAIL MERCHANTS

The regulations permit retail merchants to use the retail method in valuing inventories;[24] this method consists of reducing the retail selling price of goods on hand by a percentage representing selling expenses and profit to arrive at cost.[25] In general, the method must be used on a department by department basis,[26] and if the taxpayer deals in goods carrying different percentages of gross profit, a separate computation for each class of goods must be made.[27] The retail method can be adapted to the lower of cost or market valuation method or to the LIFO identification system.[28]

§ 5.09   CHANGING ACCOUNTING METHODS

Section 446(e) provides that a taxpayer must secure the consent of the Commissioner before changing a method of accounting. This consent must be obtained regardless of whether the taxpayer in question is using a permissible method of accounting.[1] Moreover, section 481(a)[2] provides

---

23. Treas. Reg. § 1.472–8(e).

24. Treas. Reg. § 1.471–8(a).

25. Treas. Reg. § 1.471–8(a)(1) and (2).

26. Treas. Reg. § 1.471–8(c).

27. Id.

28. See Hutzler Bros. Co. v. Commissioner, 8 T.C. 14 (1947).

§ 5.09

1. See § 1.446–1(e)(2)(i). For procedures on how to change a method of accounting, see Rev. Proc. 97–27, 1997–2 I.R.B. 11 (as modified and amplified by Rev. Proc. 2002–19, 2002–1 C.B. 696, modified and clarified by Rev. Proc. 2002–54, 2002–2 C.B. 432) and Rev. Proc. 2002–9, 2002–1 C.B. 327, (as modified and clarified

by Announcement 2002–17, 2002–1 C.B. 561, modified and amplified by Rev. Proc. 2002–19, 2002–1 C.B. 696, and amplified, clarified, and modified by Rev. Proc. 2002–54, 2002–2 C.B. 432). See also Treas. Reg. § 1.446–1(e)(3)(ii).

2. Section 481(a) was designed to require adjustments whether the change in accounting method was from a proper or improper method and whether the change was initiated by the taxpayer or by the Service. Thus, as a general rule under section 481(a), if a taxpayer computes his income in the "year of the change" under a method of accounting different from that used in the preceding year, adjustments attributable "solely by reason of the change" must be taken into account "in order to

that in computing taxable income for the year of change, there shall be taken into account adjustments necessary to prevent amounts from being duplicated or omitted.[3]

The purpose of section 446(e) is to provide the Commissioner with the authority to monitor changes in methods of accounting to ensure that no duplication or omission of items of income or expense result. Furthermore, section 446(e) allows the Commissioner to impose on the taxpayer the terms and conditions under which any change of accounting may take place.

In order to change accounting methods, taxpayers generally must file IRS Form 3115, "Application for Change in Accounting Method."[4] "Taxpayers are encouraged to file the Form 3115 as early as possible during the year of the change to provide the IRS adequate time to process the application prior to the original due date of the taxpayer's return."[5] Even so, extensions for filing Form 3115 will be granted in "unusual and compelling circumstances."[6]

A change in method of accounting includes a change "in the overall plan of accounting for gross income or deductions" or "in the treatment of any material item."[7] Changes in the overall plan include a change: (1) from the cash method to an accrual method, (2) a change involving the method or basis of valuing inventories, (3) certain changes in computing depreciation or amortization, and (4) a change involving the adoption, use, or discontinuance of a specialized method of computing taxable income.[8] However, a change in accounting method does not include correction of mathematical errors or errors in computing tax liability, such as errors in computing the net operating loss.[9]

§ 5.10   RESTORATIONS

Although receipt under a claim of right must be included in income even though there is a possibility the item may have to be restored, what

prevent amounts from being duplicated or omitted." However, to prevent bunching of taxable income in one year, under section 481(b) proration may be made through election of one of two methods. First, when the adjustments increase taxable income of the year of change more than $3,000, and the old method of accounting had been used for the two preceding years, then the taxpayer is subject to the increase in tax in the year of change to the extent of the increase that would have been payable had the adjustments been included ratably in the year of change and the two preceding years. In the alternative, the taxpayer may, using the new method, reconstruct income for all prior years that the old method was employed and allocate the adjustments accordingly.

   3.   *Nota bene:* For purposes of § 481(a), adjustments can in certain circumstances include amounts properly attributable to tax years which are otherwise closed by the statute of limitations. Graff Chevrolet Co. v. Campbell, 343 F.2d at 571–572; Rankin v.

Commissioner, 138 F.3d 1286, 1288 (9th Cir. 1998); Superior Coach of Florida v. Commissioner, 80 T.C. 895, 912 (1983); Weiss v. Commissioner, 395 F.2d 500 (10th Cir. 1968); Spang Industries, Inc. v. United States, 6 Cl. Ct. 38, 46 (1984), rev'd on other grounds 791 F.2d 906 (Fed. Cir. 1986).

   4.   Treas. Reg. § 1.446–1(e)(3)(i).

   5.   TD 8719, 62 Fed. Reg. 26,740 (May 15, 1997). The idea behind this rule is that the Service needs to have sufficient time to process the taxpayer's request for a change in accounting methods prior to processing the taxpayer's return for the year in question. Rev. Proc. 97–27, 1997–1 CB 680, § 5.01(1)(b).

   6.   Temp. Reg. § 301.9100–3T(c)(2); Rev. Proc. 97–27, 1997–1 CB 680, § 5.01(2).

   7.   Treas. Reg. § 1.446–1(e)(2)(ii)(a).

   8.   Id.

   9.   Treas. Reg. § 1.446–1(e)(2)(ii)(b).

treatment is to be given the restoration in a subsequent year?[1] Is the old year to be reopened, or are the two tax years separate time components limiting the taxpayer to qualifying the restoration under some deduction provision of the Code? United States v. Lewis[2] addresses these issues.

The taxpayer in Lewis received a $22,000 bonus in 1944 that he reported as income. In 1946 he was required to restore some $11,000 as a result of litigation pertaining to the computation of the bonus. The government contended that the taxpayer should have taken a loss deduction in 1946; the taxpayer sought to reopen the 1944 year. The Supreme Court denied his right to do so on the ground that nothing under the claim of right doctrine permitted an exception because the taxpayer was mistaken about the validity of the claim or because it resulted in an advantage or disadvantage to the taxpayer.

Under section 1341, which was enacted largely in response to Lewis, if the amount of the restoration exceeds $3,000, a taxpayer may compute the tax in the year of restoration by either of two methods. The taxpayer may, take a loss or expense deduction or may take a credit in the amount of tax attributable to the inclusion of the amount in the earlier year. While this latter alternative does not reopen the year of receipt, it does provide a transactional approach.

Unfortunately, section 1341 will not necessarily make taxpayers whole under all circumstances. The primary reason for this result is the Code's utilization of an annual system of accounting.[3] For it is under this annual accounting system that the amount of a taxpayer's income and tax liability for a given year must be quantifiable at each year's end. "It is the essence of any system of taxation that it should produce revenue ascertainable, and payable to the government, at regular intervals."[4] For example, in the case of executives who are forced to repay ill-gotten bonuses under the Sarbanes Oxley Act,[5] the executives included their bonuses in the year received, and they will deduct their repayments in the years those repayments are made.[6]

§ 5.10

1. Dubroff, The Claim of Right Doctrine, 40 Tax L. Rev. 729 (1985); Wootton, The Claim of Right Doctrine and Section 1341, 34 Tax Lawyer 297 (1981).

2. 340 U.S. 590, 71 S.Ct. 522, 95 L.Ed. 560 (1951). See also CCA 200327053; FSA 200129001; FSA 200124008; FSA 200102009; Rev. Rul. 2004–17, 2004–1 C.B. 516; TAM 200050005; Dominic L. Daher and Joshua D. Rosenberg, Tax Aspects of Incentive Compensation Disgorgement: Good Motives Raise Serious Questions About Deductibility, BNA Daily Tax Report, Aug. 29, 2005 (166 DTR J–1); reprinted by publisher in Corporate Accountability, Vol. 3, No. 36 (September 2005).

3. See Burnet v. Sanford and Brooks Company, 282 U.S. 359, 365–366 (1931).

4. Burnet v. Sanford and Brooks Company, 282 U.S. 359, 365 (1931).

5. In fact, as a result of Section 304 the Sarbanes–Oxley Act of 2002, CEOs and CFOs are now personally liable for the repayment of any incentive compensation or short-swing stock sale profits when their companies are forced to restate earnings due to accounting irregularities.

6. North American Oil Consolidated v. Burnett, 286 U.S. 417, 424 (1932).

Because of the annual system of accounting, even if the net amount deducted upon repayment is exactly equal to the net amount of income included on receipt of the bonuses, the value of the tax benefit received in the year of repayment may not necessarily offset the increased taxes paid in the year of receipt.[7] How can this happen? Tax rates may have decreased or the taxpayer may be in a lower marginal tax bracket at the time of repayment.[8] For that matter, other limitations may apply, such as those found in sections 67, 68, and 56. "But as the doctrine was originally formulated, these discrepancies were accepted as an unavoidable consequence of the annual accounting system."[9] Accordingly, Congress added section 1341 to the Code in an attempt to rectify the inequities which Congress felt existed in this area of the law.[10]

Where a taxpayer would otherwise not be made whole by the deduction of an amount originally included in income under the claim of right doctrine, as articulated by North American Oil Consolidated, and subsequently paid back and deducted, section 1341(a)(5) now permits taxpayers to reduce their taxes for the current tax year by the amount their taxes were previously increased in the year of receipt. The idea here is to attempt to make the taxpayer whole; i.e., the idea behind section 1341 is to attempt to make claim of right situations followed by deductible repayments tax neutral.[11] If for any reason section 1341(a)(5) fails to achieve a more favorable result than a current deduction, section 1341(a)(4) applies the North American Oil Consolidated incarnation of the claim of right doctrine, allowing a deduction in the year repayment is made.

Section 1341 has three disparate requirements:

(1) The item at issue must have been previously included in gross income by the taxpayer in an earlier year because it appeared the taxpayer had an unrestricted right to it;[12]

(2) A deduction is allowable for the current (or future) taxable years because it turned out after the close of the prior taxable year that the taxpayer did not in fact have an unrestricted right to the item;[13] and

(3) The item at issue must exceed $3,000.[14]

If each of the foregoing requirements are satisfied, then the taxpayer is allowed relief under either section 1341(a)(4) or section 1341(a)(5), whichever provides the greater tax benefit.

---

7. See Healy v. Commissioner, 345 U.S. 278, 284–285, 73 S.Ct. 671, 97 L.Ed. 1007 (1953).

8. Id.

9. United States v. Skelly Oil, 394 U.S. 678, 680 (1969).

10. Id., citing H.R. Rep. No. 1337, 83d Cong., 2d Sess., 86–87 (1954); S. Rep. No. 1622, 83d Cong., 2d Sess., 118–119 (1954), U.S. Code Cong. & Admin. News, p. 4629.

11. See Cinergy Corp. v. United States, 55 Fed.Cl. 489 (2003); Dominion Resources,

Inc. v. United States, 219 F.3d 359, 363 (4th Cir. 2000).

12. § 1341(a)(1). See Bailey v. Commissioner, 756 F.2d 44, 47 (6th Cir. 1985).

13. § 1341(a)(2). See United States v. Skelly Oil, 394 U.S. 678, 683 (1969); Bailey v. Commissioner, 756 F.2d at 46; Griffiths v. United States, 54 Fed.Cl. 198, 201–02 (2002).

14. § 1341(a)(3).

In the case of executives repaying incentive compensation under section 304 of Sarbanes–Oxley, it is a near certainty they will have no problem meeting the first prong of section 1341(a); i.e., it is extraordinarily probable they previously included these bonuses in gross income in an earlier year. Assuming the executives' employer issued the executives accurate IRS Forms W–2, these bonus amounts would have been delineated on them, and the executives would have accordingly reported them on their individual IRS Forms 1040 in the year of receipt. When the executives received these payments some years ago they had no way of knowing they would be paid back in a later year; hence, it appeared the executives had an unrestricted right to these bonuses.[15]

The second prong of section 1341(a) may prove to be more troubling to the executives in this example. Section 1341(a)(2) has been interpreted by some courts as having within it two separate and distinct prongs: (i) a deduction is available because of the repayment of the previously included income; and (ii) "it turned out ... that the taxpayer did not in fact have an unrestricted right to the item. In other words, repayments that are deductible because they arise out of the taxpayer's trade or business and are *motivated* by trade or business concerns may nonetheless fail to qualify for section 1341 treatment because, regardless of the taxpayer's *beliefs* about the need for repayment, it was never *established* that the taxpayer did not have an unrestricted right to the funds. These cases suggest that in order to qualify for treatment under section 1341, the taxpayer must be compelled to make the repayment, either by suit, threat of suit, or under pain of imprisonment."[16]

The last prong of section 1341(a)'s qualifying provisions does not appear to be a problem for the executives in this example. Section 1341(a)(3) requires that the amount at issue must exceed $3,000.

Section 1341 essentially recasts the bonus payments as if they never happened; i.e., the whole idea behind section 1341 is to put the taxpayer in the same tax position he would have been in if the payment had never been received.[17] This result is achieved by allowing the executives to choose between the greater of the recomputed tax benefit during the original year of receipt or a deduction in the year of repayment. As Justice Stewart once said about section 1341, "the taxpayer always wins and the Government always loses."[18]

The real beauty of section 1341 is that it avoids the taint of being characterized as a miscellaneous itemized deduction; accordingly, as discussed above, the limits of sections 67 and 68 are avoided and the limitations of section 56(b)(1)(A)(i) do not apply. Hence, section 1341

---

15. See § 1341(a)(1).

16. See Rev. Rul. 62–14, 1962–1 C.B. 1, revoked by Rev. Rul. 78–16, 1978–1 C.B. 31, on other grounds; Pike v. Commissioner, 44 T.C. 787 (1965), acq. 1968–2 C.B. 2; Kappel v. United States, 437 F.2d 1222 (3d Cir. 1971), cert. denied 404 U.S. 830, 92 S.Ct. 71, 30 L.Ed.2d 59 (1971) (each holding that § 1341 only applies to *involuntary* repayments).

17. See Cinergy Corp. v. United States, 55 Fed.Cl. 489 (2003); Dominion Resources, Inc. v. United States, 219 F.3d 359, 363 (4th Cir., 2000).

18. United States v. Skelly Oil, 394 U.S. 678, 682 (1969).

actually has the ability to make the executives in this example whole. After all, in a perfect world, the receipt and subsequent repayment of incentive compensation should be a tax-neutral event.

§ 5.11   THE TAX BENEFIT RULE

The tax benefit rule[1] is a limitation upon the general principle that recovery of property that was once the subject of a deduction must be treated as income when recovered.[2] The Court of Claims once said that the "rule permits exclusion of the recovered item from income so long as its initial use as a deduction did not provide a tax saving."[3]

Section 111(a) expresses the tax benefit rule by providing that recovery of a deducted item is not included in gross income if the item did not reduce income subject to tax. Section 111 assumes that a taxpayer first recovers the portion (if any) of the amount deducted in the prior year that did not reduce taxable income. "The assumption that the first dollars recovered are not those which produced a tax benefit may, in certain cases, be erroneous and produce a windfall to the taxpayer."[4]

Section 111 provides that the recovered amount may be excluded only to the extent it did not reduce income subject to tax. Also, when an amount is recovered that relates to a credit, other than the foreign tax credit claimed in a prior year, the tax is increased by the amount of the credit attributable to the recovered amount but only to the extent the credit reduced the tax.

Must an allowance be made under the tax benefit rule for any difference in tax rates in effect in the two years?   No. Alice Phelan Sullivan Corp. v. United States[5] held that rate differences in the year of deduction and the year of recovery must be ignored.[6]

§ 5.12   CORRECTION OF ERRORS IN CLOSED YEARS

[1]   IN GENERAL

When the statute of limitations runs on a taxpayer's return, errors pertaining to the inclusion or exclusion of income and to deductions may

---

§ 5.11

1. Del Cotto & Joyce, Double Benefits and Transactional Consistency Under the Tax Benefit Rule, 39 Tax L. Rev. 473 (1984); Bittker & Kanner, The Tax Benefit Rule, 26 U.C.L.A. L. Rev. 265 (1978); Matthew J. Barrett, Determining an Individual's Federal Income Tax Liability When the Tax Benefit Rule Applies: A Fifty–Year Checkup Brings a New Prescription for Calculating Gross, Adjusted Gross, and Taxable Incomes, 1994 B.Y.U. L. Rev. 1 (1994); Steven J. Willis, The Tax Benefit Rule: A Different View and a Unified Theory of Error Correction, 42 Fla. L. Rev. 575 (1990).

2. Rothensies v. Electric Storage Battery Co., 329 U.S. 296, 67 S.Ct. 271, 91 L.Ed. 296 (1946); Estate of Block v. Commissioner, 39 B.T.A. 338 (1939), aff'd sub nom. Union Trust Co. v. Commissioner, 111 F.2d 60 (7th Cir. 1940), cert. denied, 311 U.S. 658, 61 S.Ct. 12, 85 L.Ed. 421 (1940).

3. Alice Phelan Sullivan Corp. v. United States, 180 Ct.Cl. 659, 381 F.2d 399, 401 (1967).

4. H.R. Rep. No. 432, Part II, 98th Cong., 2d Sess. 1368–69 (1984).

5. 180 Ct.Cl. 659, 381 F.2d 399 (1967).

6. See also American Mut. Life Ins. Co. v. United States, 267 F.3d 1344 (Fed. Cir. 2001).

not be corrected as a general rule.[1] The underlying policy is that a statute of limitations is an indispensable element of the income tax system. In other words, there must be a point of finality in the interest of fairness as well as practical administration. However, notions of fairness cannot be articulated with precision.

Suppose a taxpayer treats an income item as constructively received and includes it in gross income. After the statute of limitations on the return has run, it is determined that the taxpayer is properly taxable on the item for an open year. Should the taxpayer be required to pay tax twice on the same item? Conversely, should the taxpayer be entitled to a double deduction if he erroneously claimed such an item as income for a closed year? In these situations the courts have occasionally been willing to depart from the strictness of the limitations generally imposed by the Code, especially when judicial doctrines are available.

The common law doctrines that have been used include equitable estoppel and recoupment. From an early date, however, it became apparent that these doctrines showed little promise of being applied with the degree of certainty desired. Hence, in 1938 provisions for mitigating the effect of the statute of limitations were enacted. The provisions are now contained in sections 1311–1314. Nevertheless, they were not intended as an exclusive remedy for the correction of errors in closed years since they are limited to prescribed transactions, and the legislative history indicates that the provisions were intended to supplement, and not to supplant, estoppel and recoupment.[2]

These approaches for correcting errors in closed years do not apply unless a transaction in an open year is related to a transaction in a closed year. Mere plain error on a closed return is not sufficient.

The courts have by no means been consistent in their use of terms in this area, especially in the use of "estoppel." While "estoppel" connotes a misrepresentation of fact, when misrepresentation has been lacking, relief has sometimes been granted in the name of "equitable estoppel," "quasi-estoppel," or "duty of consistency." Regardless of the particular label used, the doctrine is designed to prevent a party from taking advantage of an error barred by the statute of limitations. The line between these expressions of estoppel and the twin doctrines of collateral estoppel and res judicata is reasonably clear. The latter two procedural devices are designed to limit repeated litigation between the same parties on the same issue; they do not normally concern the correction of errors in statute-barred returns.

§ 5.12

1. See § 6501(a) (which generally provides for a three year statute of limitations).

2. S. Rep. No. 1567, 75th Cong., 3d Sess. 48–52 (1938). See also dictum in Be-

nenson v. United States, 385 F.2d 26 (2d Cir. 1967), to the effect that in the interest of certainty recoupment would not be available if the situation falls within the scope of the statutory mitigation provisions.

[2] EQUITABLE ESTOPPEL

Broadly, equitable estoppel is based upon conduct amounting to misrepresentation of facts unknown to the other party and relied upon by that party. As a general rule, it cannot be invoked by the taxpayer against the government.[3] Although some courts, in limited situations where the Commissioner has taken affirmative action against the wrong taxpayer or asserted a tax for the wrong year,[4] have estopped the government from collecting a second tax, ordinarily the required conduct by government personnel is not present in tax controversies.

On the other hand, courts are divided on the government's right to invoke estoppel against the taxpayer. Some courts have applied the doctrine restrictively, requiring a showing of the usual elements. A few, including the Fifth Circuit, have apparently ignored the basic elements and have gone so far as to require only a showing of inconsistency on the part of the taxpayer.

In Wichita Coca Cola Bottling Co. v. United States[5] the taxpayer had treated amounts received from customers for containers as deposits and had excluded them from income for a closed year. In a subsequent year it asserted that the amounts constituted proceeds of a sale that should have been reported as income in the closed year. The Fifth Circuit disagreed. It held that neither a misrepresentation nor all the elements of a technical estoppel need be established, and the taxpayer's duty to disclose and handle its accounts so they would fairly subject its income to tax required consistency in tax accounting.

[3] RECOUPMENT

The equitable doctrine of recoupment permits "a taxpayer to recoup an erroneously paid tax, the refund of which is time-barred, against a timely and correctly asserted deficiency by the government" and permits "the government to recoup a correctly assessed tax, which ordinarily could not be collected because of a statute of limitations bar, against a timely refund of a tax erroneously collected."[6] As expressed by the Court in Bull v. United States,[7] the doctrine of recoupment "is in the nature of a defense arising out of some feature of the transaction upon which the

---

3. See, e.g., Automobile Club of Michigan v. Commissioner, 353 U.S. 180, 77 S.Ct. 707, 1 L.Ed.2d 746 (1957), in which the Court held that the doctrine of equitable estoppel was not a bar to a retroactive revocation of a private letter ruling. In Estate of Vitt v. United States, 706 F.2d 871 (8th Cir. 1983), the court observed that "at least traditionally, conduct amounting to a representation or concealment of a material fact is an element which must be demonstrated before the doctrine of equitable estoppel will be applied."

4. See, e.g., Vestal v. Commissioner, 152 F.2d 132 (D.C. Cir. 1945). See also Camilla E. Watson, Equitable Recoupment:

Revisiting an old and Inconsistent Remedy, 65 Fordham L. Rev. 691 (1996).

5. 152 F.2d 6 (5th Cir. 1945), cert. denied, 327 U.S. 806, 66 S.Ct. 964, 90 L.Ed. 1031 (1946). See also Steve R. Johnson, The Taxpayer's Duty of Consistency, 46 Tax L. Rev. 537, 581 (1991).

6. O'Brien v. United States, 766 F.2d 1038, 1049 (7th Cir. 1985). See also Gerald A. Kafka, Equitable Recoupment After Dalm: Sustained, but Clarified and Narrowed, 72 J. Tax'n 340, 344 (1990).

7. 295 U.S. 247, 55 S.Ct. 695, 79 L.Ed. 1421 (1935).

plaintiff's action is grounded.'"[8] Hence, recoupment has been applied in tax cases when the bar of the statute of limitations has resulted in inequitable consequences to either taxpayers or the government.[9]

Application of the doctrine of equitable recoupment is limited to circumstances in which "a single transaction constitute[s] the taxable event claimed upon and the one considered in recoupment."[10] Thus, it is predicated upon the offsetting amount from the year barred by the statute of limitations resulting from the same transaction that gave rise to the refund or deficiency in the open year.[11]

[4] STATUTORY MITIGATION

As previously indicated, the enactment of what are now sections 1311–1314 was attributable primarily to uncertain and confusing case law concerning estoppel and recoupment, and in some measure to an alleged one-sided application of estoppel against taxpayers.

In broad outline, the underlying theory of the statutory solution (which is the converse of the effect of estoppel that freezes the error of the earlier year) is that the item is to be properly handled in the later year, but the statute of limitations and other procedural bars should be lowered for the limited purpose of requiring a proper adjustment of the earlier year. For example, if the taxpayer had erroneously taken a deduction in a closed year, he would be allowed a deduction in the later proper year, but he must recompute the tax for the year of error and pay any deficiency with interest. In this respect the provisions function in a manner similar to the adjustments that must be made under section 481 for a change in accounting method.

Fundamental to the applicability of sections 1311–1314 is an error in the handling of an item or transaction. These provisions do not apply to items or transactions that are merely similar in nature;[12] nor are they available to a taxpayer merely because tax planning has gone astray.[13]

In broad outline sections 1311–1314 are applicable only if: (1) the government or the taxpayer, subject to two exceptions, successfully maintains an "inconsistent" position (2) in a "determination" (3) in any one of seven prescribed "circumstances" of adjustment.

---

8. 295 U.S. 247, 262, 55 S.Ct. 695, 700.

9. See, e.g., Stone v. White, 301 U.S. 532, 57 S.Ct. 851, 81 L.Ed. 1265 (1937); CCA 200727015. See also Richard J. Wood, Supreme Court Jurisprudence of Tax Fairness, 36 Seton Hall L. Rev. 421, 479 (2006).

10. Rothensies v. Elec. Storage Battery Co., 329 U.S. 296, 299, 67 S.Ct. 271, 91 L.Ed. 296 (1946). See also Suzette M. Malveaux, Statutes of Limitations: A Policy Analysis in the Context of Reparations Litigation, 74 Geo. Wash. L. Rev. 68, 122 (2005).

11. See, e.g., Estate of Vitt v. United States, 706 F.2d 871 (8th Cir. 1983). See also Camilla E. Watson, Equitable Recoup-

ment: Revisiting an old and Inconsistent Remedy, 65 Fordham L. Rev. 691, 788 (1996).

12. See, e.g., Rev. Rul. 70–7, 1970–1 C.B. 175, in which the Service held that §§ 1311–1314 did not apply to a real estate developer who was entitled to allocate his correct cost basis to remaining lots of a tract even though he had erroneously recovered his total basis through prior sales in statute-barred years.

13. See, e.g., Knowles Electronics, Inc. v. United States, 365 F.2d 43 (7th Cir. 1966).

The requirement of an inconsistent position is illustrated by G–B, Inc. v. United States.[14] The taxpayer first successfully maintained, in a refund action for taxes paid for 1960, that an incorporation of a mortgage company was either a tax-free transaction or took place in 1959. Following this refund action the Commissioner asserted a deficiency for 1959 upon the same theory. The taxpayer paid the deficiency and brought a second refund action, pleading the statute of limitations. The court held for the taxpayer on the ground that because the taxpayer had maintained at all times that the transaction was not a taxable event, an inconsistent position had not been adopted; therefore, sections 1311–1314 were not available to the government.

An inconsistent position also requires more than an acquiescence in the position of the other party. Thus, in Heineman v. United States[15] the taxpayer was denied the right to open closed years where the Commissioner had first treated corporate distributions to the taxpayer as ordinary income; in a deficiency paid by the taxpayer without dispute and subsequently allowed the taxpayer's refund claim for an open year based on a theory that the distributions were liquidating dividends as held in another case. The court reasoned that the Commissioner's second position, the allowance of the claim, was merely the adoption of the taxpayer's position and did not constitute an inconsistent position on the part of the Commissioner.

Ultimately, the taxpayer or the government must also show the error made falls within one of the seven "circumstances" of adjustment. These circumstances are detailed in section 1312 and concern determinations that:

(1) Require an inclusion in gross income of an item erroneously included in the income of the taxpayer or a related taxpayer[16] in another tax year;[17]

(2) Allow a deduction or credit erroneously allowed the taxpayer or a related taxpayer for another tax year;[18]

(3) Require the exclusion from gross income of an item included in a return but that was erroneously excluded by the taxpayer or a related person in another tax year, or require the exclusion from gross income of an item not included in a return filed by a taxpayer but that is includible in the gross income of the

---

14. 302 F.Supp. 851 (D. Colo. 1969), aff'd per curiam, 422 F.2d 1035 (10th Cir. 1970). See also Edward G. Lavery, New and Renewed Proposals to Revise the Mitigation Provisions of the Code, 46 Tax Law. 785, 799 (1993).

15. 183 Ct.Cl. 17, 391 F.2d 648 (1968). See also John D. Rice, When and How Will the Courts Apply the Mitigation Provisions?, 69 J. Tax'n 106 (1988).

16. For purposes of § 1312, "related taxpayer" includes the following: (1) husband and wife; (2) grantor and fiduciary; (3)

grantor and beneficiary; (4) fiduciary and beneficiary, legatee, or heir; (5) decedent and decedent's estate; (6) partner; and (7) member of an affiliated group of corporations (defined in section 1504). § 1313(c). The "related taxpayer" concept does not apply to determinations of basis since § 1312(7) provides its own criteria in this respect.

17. § 1312(1).

18. § 1312(2).

taxpayer or a related person in a tax year that was open when the claim resulting in the determination[19] was first made (in the latter situation inconsistency in position is not required);[20]

(4) Disallow a deduction or credit that should have been allowed to the taxpayer or a related taxpayer but was not;[21]

(5) Allow or disallow an item of trust or estate income or deduction in a manner inconsistent with its treatment in the hands of the beneficiary or fiduciary;[22]

(6) Allow or disallow a deduction or credit of a corporation in a manner inconsistent with the way it has been treated in the income of an affiliated corporation;[23] and

(7) Determine the basis of property, and, for any purpose on which basis depends, errors were made in prior transactions with respect to the inclusion or exclusion of income, the determination or recognition of gain or loss, deductions, or charges to capital account.[24]

Most often the closed year of error will be a year proceeding the correct year. Cory v. Commissioner[25] illustrates that this is not always the case. The court in Cory interpreted the finality requirement of a determination with some liberality, the case demonstrating the manner in which a closed year may be kept open for the purpose of the section 1311 adjustments. The taxpayers reported some $42,000 of royalty income as capital gain in their return for 1944. Later, they filed a claim for refund, contending that $30,000 of such amount was reportable in 1945 although the taxpayers did not report it for 1945. The Commission-

---

19. For purposes of § 1312, a "determination" includes a final decision by a court, a closing agreement made under § 7121, a final disposition by the Service on a claim for refund, and a written agreement for purposes of §§ 1311–1314 between the Service and a taxpayer. Once a determination has been made, § 1314(b) provides the taxpayer or the Service one year to proceed by way of claim for refund or deficiency. The adjustments cannot be made in a "determination" because finality of the determination is a prerequisite to the adjustment. Wiener Mach. Co. v. Commissioner, 16 T.C. 48 (1951). A taxpayer must therefore proceed by way of a claim for refund. Benenson v. United States, 385 F.2d 26 (2d Cir. 1967). However, a compromise settlement under § 7122 cannot be reopened by these provisions. In making the adjustment § 1314(a) limits it to the increase or decrease in the tax "which results solely from the correct treatment of the item which was the subject of the error." However, it is sometimes best for the taxpayer or government to let the error remain buried beneath the statute of limitations. This is because the amount of the adjustment in the closed

year can exceed, and sometimes has, the amount claimed in an open year in a deficiency by the government or under a claim for refund by the taxpayer.

20. § 1312(3).

21. § 1312(4).

22. § 1312(5).

23. § 1312(6).

24. § 1312(7). See also O'Brien v. United States, 766 F.2d 1038 (7th Cir. 1985); Chertkof v. United States, 676 F.2d 984 (4th Cir. 1982); Gary L. Maydew, Mitigation Offers Escape from Expired Limitations Period, 65 Prac. Tax Strategies 153, 156 (2000); John A. Lynch, Jr., Income Tax Statute of Limitations: Sixty Years of Mitigation–Enough, Already!!, 51 S.C. L. Rev. 62, 152 (1999).

25. 261 F.2d 702 (2d Cir. 1958), aff'g, 29 T.C. 903 (1958), cert. denied, 359 U.S. 966, 79 S.Ct. 877, 3 L.Ed.2d 834 (1959). See also Gary L. Maydew, Mitigation Offers Escape from Expired Limitations Period, 65 Prac. Tax Strategies 153, 156 (2000); Steve R. Johnson, The Taxpayer's Duty of Consistency, 46 Tax L. Rev. 537, 581 (1991).

er rejected the claim and contended the $42,000 received in 1944 was ordinary income and issued a deficiency. In 1955 the Tax Court upheld the taxpayer with respect to the proper year issue, and the Commissioner was upheld on the ordinary income issue. However, only the taxpayer appealed, the Commissioner failing to file a timely cross appeal. In 1956 the Second Circuit affirmed the Tax Court, and the Supreme Court denied certiorari. The Commissioner then issued a deficiency for the failure to include the $30,000 in income in 1945. The taxpayers contended they had not maintained an inconsistent position, and since the Commissioner had not cross-appealed he was barred under section 1314(b), more than a year having lapsed since the Tax Court's determination became final.

The Tax Court's decision for the Commissioner was upheld by the Second Circuit. It held that the position of the taxpayers brought them squarely within the "circumstance" of adjustment of section 1312(3)(A). Moreover the court found the "determination" of the Tax Court in the deficiency suit for the year 1944 required the exclusion of an item of gross income from a return filed by the taxpayers for that year which was erroneously excluded from another tax year, the 1945 year that was then closed. In short, the court held that the position the taxpayers successfully maintained in the "determination" (the income was received in 1945) was inconsistent with the position they took in the return for 1944 (the income was received in 1944).

As to the finality of the determination, the Second Circuit admitted that technically the determination became final when the time for appeal had expired. However, it held that the assessment was timely on the ground that to break down a Tax Court decision for a single year into separate issues—the time and the character of the income—for decisional and assessment purposes would add unnecessarily to the complexities in administering sections 1311–1314. Hence, it would treat the statute as running from the final adjudication on the monetary issue. In this manner the Commissioner would not be forced to make an unnecessary assessment of a deficiency for 1945 during pendency of an appeal that might upset the Tax Court's finding.[26]

§ 5.13   NET OPERATING LOSSES

Section 172 functions in large measure as an averaging device for net operating losses from business operations, although, as described below, the computation of operating loss is not strictly limited to business operations. Section 172 generally permits a taxpayer who conducts a business to average net operating losses over the two years

---

26. A third issue, also decided for the Commissioner, involved the computation of the amount to be taken into account in making the adjustment in the closed year. Under the statute then in force only one-half of long-term capital gains was taken into gross income. The Second Circuit held that the full amount of the royalties received, not one-half, must be accounted for in computing the adjustments.

prior to the year of the loss[1] and the twenty years after the year of the loss.[2]

The carryback or carryforward of operating losses prevents the income tax from functioning as a tax on capital in years of loss when expenditures devoted to the production of income would be otherwise wasted; it has also been justified on the ground that it reduces the incidence of risk-taking in investing, thereby causing the income tax to function with more neutrality in the context of investment decisions.

Under section 172(c) the net operating loss for any tax year is gross income less the allowable deductions subject to the modifications prescribed by section 172(d). The most important modifications are as follows: (1) net operating losses from other years are not allowed as deductions;[3] (2) capital gains and losses of non-corporate taxpayers;[4] (3) no deduction is allowed for personal exemptions under section 151;[5] (4) nontrade or nonbusiness deductions of taxpayers other than corporations are allowed only to the extent of income not derived from a trade or business;[6] (5) deductions for dividends received by corporations are computed without regard to the limitations imposed by section 246(b).[7]

When a loss is carried back or forward, additional adjustments are required in each year in which it is used.[8] Thus, the loss is first deducted from the taxable income of the applicable year. If any loss remains, it must be reduced by net capital losses, the long-term capital gain deduction, and personal exemptions before being carried to the next applicable year.[9] This means that taxable income for the years to which a loss is carried will have to be recomputed.[10] When there are carryovers from different years, they are added together, and the total becomes the net operating loss deduction.[11]

The most significant limit on the use of section 172 is that for the most part, it is only losses incurred in operating a business that can be used. Any deductions or losses incurred by a taxpayer with respect either to investments (including recognized net capital losses) or consumption-related activities (other than casualty losses allowed deductible after the limitations imposed by section 165(h)) cannot either create or increase a net operating loss.[12] Although, as explained below, income from such activities will decrease or eliminate an otherwise apparent NOL from business.[13]

In the corporate area, much has been made of corporations attempting to take advantage of losses that generated NOLs for other corporations by acquiring those loss corporations, and there are, as a result,

§ 5.13

1. § 172(b)(1)(A)(i).
2. § 172(b)(1)(A)(ii).
3. § 172(d)(1).
4. § 172(d)(2).
5. § 172(d)(3).
6. § 172(d)(4).

7. § 172(d)(5).
8. See § 172(e).
9. See Treas. Reg. § 1.172–5.
10. § 172(b)(2)(A) and (B).
11. Treas. Reg. § 1.172–1(b)(3).
12. § 172(d).
13. Id.

significant statutory limitations on the continued existence of corporate NOLs after corporate takeovers.[14] While individuals have not generally engaged in similar attempts, the regulations make it clear that the NOL can be deducted only by the same taxpayer who incurred it.[15] Any other result might enable taxpayers with substantial NOLs to marry high income taxpayers, who could then use their new spouse's old NOLs to avoid paying taxes. While individuals may still choose to marry for money, and even for tax advantages, this is one such advantage that does not come along with marriage.[16]

14. See § 382 which generally limits the use of another taxpayer's NOLs.

15. Treas. Reg. § 1.170–7.

16. See Calvin v. United States, 354 F.2d 202 (10th Cir. 1965) (pre-marriage NOL could be used only against income attributable to spouse who sustained the loss). See also FSA 200118003; Rev. Rul. 80–6, 1980–1 C.B. 296.

Chapter 6

ASSIGNMENT OF INCOME

Table of Sections

---

§ 6.01 IN GENERAL

This chapter concerns a deceptively simple question; who is the proper taxpayer? The inquiry into who must report income and who may take a deduction is frequently encountered in a variety of areas of tax law. It arises when a taxpayer attempts to transfer or shift income or a deduction to another taxpayer, often a family member. Since the result is usually a reduction of the collective tax liability, such transfers have been subjected to close scrutiny by the Service in an attempt to curb abuses. The tax law in this area is detailed and complex.

Because our federal income tax system has a progressive rate structure,[1] it encourages the use of transfers to reduce ones tax liability.

§ 6.01

1. In a progressive rate tax system is one where the taxpayer pays a higher rate of tax as the tax base increases.

In 1913, in adopting the income tax with respect to individuals rather than family units, Congress opened the door to the assignment of income issue; accordingly, this allows family members to potentially take advantage of the progressive rate structure by transferring income to lower-bracket taxpayers and deductions to higher-bracket taxpayers.

The true value of a successful assignment of income is depicted in the following table.

Tax Rate of Individual Providing Services	Tax Rate of Recipient Payee	Approximate Percentage of Tax Liability Saved from Assignment of Income
35%	10%	71.5%
33%	10%	70%
28%	10%	64.3%
25%	10%	60%

The early cases addressing the proper taxpayer issue involved income transfers between spouses. For example, in Lucas v. Earl[2] the husband entered into an agreement with his wife under which he assigned her one-half of his salary. The Supreme Court refused to recognize the transfer for federal income tax purposes by refusing to permit "the fruits [to be] attributed to a different tree from that on which they grew."[3] The fruit-and-tree metaphor serves as a shorthand expression of the principle that the economic realities underlying a transaction must control its outcome or result for federal income tax purposes.

An introduction to the complexities underlying the proper taxpayer issue is provided by a companion case to Lucas. In Poe v. Seaborn[4] a husband and wife were residents of the State of Washington, a community property state. Filing separate income tax returns, each spouse reported one-half the income produced by the community property, consisting of interest, dividends, and profits on sales as well as the earnings from the husband's personal services. The Supreme Court held that the reporting was proper and in so doing implicitly approved state-created community property interests to assign income. The Court rejected the government's argument that the husband's extensive management powers over the community property granted by state law and the interest in national uniformity of federal tax law justified attributing all the income to the husband. The management argument was rejected on the ground that the community needed an agent and the husband's powers in this respect did not interfere with the wife's vested interest.

---

2. 281 U.S. 111, 50 S.Ct. 241, 74 L.Ed. 731 (1930). For further discussion of the case, see § 6.03 *supra*.

3. In this famous metaphor the tree represents the person or property generat-

ing the income and the fruit the income itself.

4. 282 U.S. 101, 51 S.Ct. 58, 75 L.Ed. 239 (1930).

The differences among the states, the Court said, could not be interpreted as creating a lack of uniformity in a constitutional sense.

In 1948, after a number of traditional common law states had switched from separate ownership to community ownership, Congress provided for the joint return of spouses to place a married couple in a common law state on an equal basis with a married couple in a community property state. This legislation, now section 6013, which allows a husband and wife to make a joint return, has reduced the number of tax controversies involving arrangements between spouses. Additionally, the joint return is reflected in section 1 of the Code in the form of a separate table of rates applicable to spouses filing joint returns.

§ 6.02 ASSIGNMENT OF INCOME FROM PROPERTY

Who must report the income generated by income-producing property? A fundamental principle of tax law is that the income from property is taxable to the owner of the property.[1] The principle permits a taxpayer to shift income from property only if the income-producing property is also transferred.[2] However, if the taxpayer does not transfer the property but merely transfers the right to receive the income, the assignment of income doctrine applies, and the transferor remains taxable.[3]

What constitutes a transfer of income-producing property rather than a transfer of income from property? As a basic proposition, the donor must part with ownership of the property. The seminal case supporting this proposition is Helvering v. Horst.[4] In Horst the taxpayer-father was the holder of coupon bonds. He attempted to shift income by detaching the coupons before their due dates and giving them to his son (in a lower marginal tax bracket), who in the same year collected the income. The Supreme Court held that "[t]he power to dispose of income is the equivalent of ownership of it. The exercise of that power to procure the payment of income to another is the enjoyment, and hence the realization, of the income by him who exercises it."[5] In Horst the

§ 6.02

1. Helvering v. Horst, 311 U.S. 112, 61 S.Ct. 144, 85 L.Ed. 75 (1940).

2. Id.

3. Id.

4. 311 U.S. 112, 61 S.Ct. 144, 85 L.Ed. 75 (1940).

5. 311 U.S. 112, 118, 61 S.Ct. 144, 147–148 (1940). The exact meaning of the quote is uncertain, although the tax liability to the father-transferor is clear. Did realization occur when the coupons were transferred or when collected at maturity? The fact pattern precludes a determination because transfer and collection occurred during the same tax year. Later cases interpreting the quote have said that realization to the transferor occurs when the transferee receives the income. See Jones v. United States, 395 F.2d 938 (6th Cir. 1968), in which accrued interest at the time of a gift of endowment policies was held taxable to the taxpayer-donor when the interest was received by the donee on the rationale that relinquishment of the tree does not prevent taxation of the fruit that has already ripened upon it; the Court observed that the language in Horst referring to the exercise of a "power to dispose of income" as constituting realization was capable of being taken to mean realization at the time of payment to an assignee. See also Austin v. Commissioner, 161 F.2d 666 (6th Cir. 1947), cert. denied, 332 U.S. 767, 68 S.Ct. 75, 92 L.Ed. 352 (1947); Anthony's Estate

taxpayer merely transferred income (the coupons) and retained the property (the bond); hence, the income remained taxable to him.

[1] DIFFERENTIATING BETWEEN PROPERTY AND INCOME TRANSFERS

A difficulty with the entire notion of assignment of income from property is that it relies on the distinction between "property," on the one hand, and "income" from property, on the other. This distinction, while apparent on the surface, fades under scrutiny. The problem basically arises from the fact that our tax system is theoretically aimed at *individuals* rather than at particular assets. The notion that underlies the federal income tax system is that each person should be taxed on her income; each person's annual income, in turn, is a product of that person's receipts during the year. Without putting too fine a point on it, if T is made richer by some receipt during the year, normally T has income.

The Court in Horst,[6] though, focused not on individuals, but on "property" that exists independent of any person. The Court's basic premise was not that *people have* income, but that *property generates* income, which must then ultimately be taxed to individuals. To see the difference in these approaches, assume that T owns a 10 year bond with a face amount and value of $100,000 that pays $10,000 per year interest at a time when all applicable interest rates are 10%. T transfers to her son S the right to receive the interest payment due in three years. According to Horst, T retains the bond, which is the "property," so T, and not S, will be taxed on the $10,000 of interest income when that amount is paid to S at the end of year three.

If instead one looked not at the "property" but at the *taxpayers* involved, it would be clear that in year one T transferred to her son the right to receive $10,000 at the end of three years. Assuming a 10% interest rate, the present value of the right S receives at the time S receives it is $7,510. In other words, T has made a present transfer of "something" worth $7,510. If it is assumed that this gift is not taxable for federal income tax purposes,[7] S would have received a nontaxable gift of $7,510 in year one. When S holds the "something" for three years, at which time it has grown in value to $10,000, and then sells it in for $10,000, T has made a profit of $2,490 on his "something."

By the same token, T starts out owning something with a value of $100,000 (the entire bond and the right to all future interest). After T transfers the right to the year three interest to S, T owns something worth $92,490 (the right to collect all but one of the interest payments and the right to receive $100,000 at the end of 10 years). Horst rests on the predicate that the something that S receives is not "property," nor is

v. Commissioner, 155 F.2d 980 (10th Cir. 1946).

6. Helvering v. Horst, 311 U.S. 112, 61 S.Ct. 144, 85 L.Ed. 75 (1940).

7. This assumption only holds true if the gift is ultimately determined to be a gift of "property" rather than a gift of "income from property." § 102(a) and (b)(1).

the something that T retains "property." Instead, the only "property" to be found is apparently T's right to collect $100,000 at the end of ten years. Everything else is merely inchoate "income."

The property-income distinction made in Horst has found its way not only into other areas of case law, but also into the Code. Section 102(b)(2) provides that the taxpayer who receives, as either a gift or inheritance, income from property must include such amounts in income. As a result, if Parent owns income-generating property worth $200,000 and leaves ½ of the property to each child, neither child will be taxed on the inheritance, but both children will be taxed on any income generated by the inherited property.[8] If rather than divide the property into halves, Parent divides it temporally, for example by putting it in a trust that gives Child 1 a 12 year income interest worth $100,000 and giving Child 2 a remainder interest also worth $100,000, Child 1, whose interest is "income" will be taxed on everything she receives from the trust, and Child 2 will be taxed on nothing she gets from the trust.[9] The Code simply does not provide for allocation of basis between the two interests, but it instead allocates all basis to the interest treated as "property."

The Service and courts have remained attached to the property-income distinction in large part because they understand that if T holds onto her bond that pays $10,000 per year interest, T ought to be taxed on the entire $10,000 received each year. The Service and the courts were concerned that if T's transfer to S of the right to receive year three's interest payment were treated as a gift of property with a value of $7,510 (and S ought to be taxed on income of only $2,490 when he collects the $10,000 in year three), then T would argue that when T retains the entire bond and collects $10,000 in year three T, like S, ought to be taxed on only $2,490. The only choices the Services and the judiciary saw were to either overtax S by taxing him on an amount in excess of his real "income" or under-taxing T on her income when T holds onto the bond and all its accompanying rights to payment.

Examples of the difficulty in distinguishing between property and income transfers and application of the above concepts are provided by Blair v. Commissioner[10] and Harrison v. Schaffner.[11]

In Blair the father, a life beneficiary of a trust, assigned to his children a portion of the trust income for the rest of his life. The Supreme Court observed that local law established the interests in the

---

8. See § 102(b)(2).

9. See § 102(a) and (b).

10. 300 U.S. 5, 57 S.Ct. 330, 81 L.Ed. 465 (1937). See also United States v. Newell, 239 F.3d 917 (7th Cir. 2001); Steingold v. Commissioner, T.C. Memo. 2000–225; Chambers v. Commissioner, T.C. Memo. 2000–218; FSA 200146025; William G. Ross, When Did The "Switch In Time" Actually Occur?: Re–Discovering The Su-

preme Court's "Forgotten" Decisions of 1936–1937, 37 Ariz. St. L.J. 1153, 1220 (2005).

11. 312 U.S. 579, 61 S.Ct. 759, 85 L.Ed. 1055 (1941). See also Rauenhorst v. Commissioner 119 T.C. 157 (2002); CCA 200246003; Martin J. McMahon, Jr., Random Thoughts on Applying Judicial Doctrines to Interpret The Internal Revenue Code, 54 SMU L. Rev. 195, 208 (2001).

trust. A lower state court had held that the father's interest was assignable and the children were the beneficial owners of the assigned interests. The Supreme Court held that the father had made a complete transfer of income-producing property. Consequently, the children were taxable on the trust income.

In Schaffner the mother, a life beneficiary of a trust, assigned part of the trust income for one year. The Supreme Court ignored the assignment and said:

> [T]he gift by a beneficiary ... of some part of the income derived from the trust property for the period of a ... year involves no ... substantial disposition of the trust property as to camouflage the reality that he is enjoying the benefit of the income from the trust of which he continues to be the beneficiary.... Even though the gift of income be in form accomplished by the temporary disposition of the donor's property which produces the income, the donor retaining every other substantial interest in it, we have not allowed the form to obscure the reality.[12]

The Court noted that " '[d]rawing the line' is a recurrent difficulty in those fields of the law where differences in degree produce ultimate differences in kind."[13]

Accordingly, an assignor may be subject to the assignment of income doctrine by retaining control over the property's capacity to produce income. This nuance of retained control concerns an assignor's ability to determine the amount of income the property will generate for the assignee. In Commissioner v. Sunnen[14] the taxpayer transferred licensing contracts to his wife for patents he held. The taxpayer contended that since the contracts were property, the assignment of income doctrine was inapplicable. The Supreme Court rejected this contention as inconclusive and said that "[t]he crucial question remains whether the assignor retains sufficient power and control over the assigned property or over receipt of the income to make it reasonable to treat him as the recipient of the income for tax purposes." The Court then reviewed the circumstances of the assignment. The assigned contracts were with a corporation, 89% of which the taxpayer owned. The corporation was not required to pay a minimum amount of royalties, and the contracts were cancellable by either party upon giving appropriate notice. The contracts were not exclusive license agreements. Consequently, the taxpayer could have licensed another manufacturer and effectively regulated the income flow to his wife. Accordingly the Court concluded that the taxpayer retained control of the income-producing property.

Even though property is transferred and the assignor relinquishes control of it, the assignment of income doctrine can nevertheless be applicable. If property is transferred with income attached, the assignor is taxed on the income. Similarly, if the transfer of appreciated property

12. 312 U.S. at 582–583, 61 S.Ct. at 761–762.

13. 312 U.S. at 583, 61 S.Ct. at 762.

14. 333 U.S. 591, 68 S.Ct. 715, 92 L.Ed. 898 (1948).

occurs after the transferor completes the earning process or an event makes certain the receipt of income, the income or gain is taxed to the transferor. The assignment of income doctrine also applies when earned income is not separated from the income-producing property but is transferred along with it. An example is interest earned while a bond or certificate of deposit is owned by the transferor; such interest is taxable to the transferor in the year the transferee receives the interest.[15]

The identity of the proper taxpayer becomes most difficult when the subject of the transfer is property that has appreciated in value. This is because a fundamental principle of tax law is that the transferor of appreciated property does not include in gross income the unrealized appreciation of the property at the time of transfer. The gain is shifted to the donee through adoption of the transferor's basis pursuant to section 1015(a).

[2] GIFTS OF INVENTORY

In two rulings the government said that gifts of inventory (wheat and feeder cattle) to a charitable organization and to a child constituted assignments of income.[16] These rulings relied primarily upon the previously quoted language of Horst.

In Campbell v. Prothro[17] the Fifth Circuit rejected the blanket application of Horst to gifts of appreciated property. Prothro, a cash basis farmer, made a gift of calves to a charitable organization, who sold them one month later. The government relied upon the position taken in the two rulings and contended that Horst justified the treatment of the gift as an assignment of income. The Fifth Circuit disagreed; it held that Horst did not disturb the principle that unrealized appreciation does not constitute income. The livestock, unlike the bonds in Horst, was not income in the hands of the transferor because the value could only be realized upon sale; whereas the bonds were transferred with interest due.

A year after Prothro the government withdrew its earlier rulings and said that a gift of inventory does not constitute a realization event.[18] However, in the case of a gift to an exempt organization a double tax benefit occurs due to the deduction for the cost of the inventory and the

15. See Jones v. United States, 395 F.2d 938 (6th Cir. 1968), in which accrued interest at the time of a gift of endowment policies was held taxable to the taxpayer-donor when the interest was received by the donee on the rationale that relinquishment of the tree does not prevent taxation of the fruit that has already ripened upon it; the court observed that the language in Horst referring to the exercise of a "power to dispose of income" as constituting realization was capable of being taken to mean realization at the time of payment to an assignee. See also Austin v. Commissioner, 161 F.2d 666 (6th Cir. 1947), cert. denied, 332 U.S. 767, 68 S.Ct. 75, 92 L.Ed. 352 (1947); Anthony's Estate v. Commissioner, 155 F.2d 980 (10th Cir. 1946).

16. I.T. 3910, 1948–1 C.B. 15; I.T. 3932, 1948–2 C.B. 7.

17. 209 F.2d 331 (5th Cir. 1954); accord Visintainer v. Commissioner, 187 F.2d 519 (10th Cir. 1951), cert. denied, 342 U.S. 858, 72 S.Ct. 85, 96 L.Ed. 646 (1951).

18. Rev. Rul. 55–138, 1955–1 C.B. 223; Rev. Rul. 55–531, 1955–2 C.B. 520; see also Treas. Reg. § 1.170–1(c).

deduction for the charitable contribution.[19] In order to eliminate the double deduction an adjustment to inventory, to the expense deduction, or to the charitable contribution deduction must be made.[20]

[3] ANTICIPATORY ASSIGNMENTS OF INCOME

In Doyle v. Commissioner[21] the taxpayer purchased a claim that would entitle him to judgment proceeds if a pending suit against the government was successful. After the government's request for *certiorari* had been denied, but before payment of the judgment, the taxpayer assigned a portion of the claim to his wife and children. The court held that the proceeds were taxable to the donor. The court reasoned that the assignees simply had to wait for the fruit to fall without any effort on their part as owners of the income-producing property, and the assignment was made when "it was just about to snow in their hats."[22]

Another application of these principles is found in the case of Susie Salvatore v. Commissioner[23] in which taxpayer contracted to sell her service station to Texaco. After she negotiated the sale, but prior to the actual transfer of title, she gave one-half of the service station to her children, who then joined her in concluding the sale. The court held that because the taxpayer had negotiated the sale prior to transferring partial title to her children, she was properly taxable on the entire gain recognized on the sale. The court treated the transactions as if the taxpayer made the sale and then transferred a part of the sale proceeds, rather than a transfer of title followed by a sale.

While the above cases relate to re-characterization by the Service and/or the courts of a purported gift-sale as a sale-gift, there are also numerous instances of the taxpayer treating transactions as a gift followed by current income from the asset (rather than gain on a sale) and the IRS re-characterizing them, for tax purposes, as the production of income on the property followed by the gift; hence, the original owner of the property is taxed on the current income.

Even if no one disputes the fact that a taxpayer transfers property, and even if all agree that the transfer occurred prior to the realization or recognition of any income on or from the property, the assignment of income doctrine can apply if property is transferred with income "attached." The idea behind this aspect of the assignment of income doctrine is that if the transfer of property occurs after the transferor completes the earning process, or after an event makes certain the receipt of income, the gain or income is taxed to the transferor. While this idea is similar to the concept of taxing the transferor on income by re-characterizing gift/income as income/gift, it is not premised on the application of any kind of substance versus form analysis. Instead, even if it is clear that the gift occurs before the income is realized and

---

19. See Treas. Reg. § 1.17–1(c).

20. Id.

21. 147 F.2d 769 (4th Cir. 1945).

22. 147 F.2d at 772–773. See also Moorefield v. Commissioner, T.C. Memo. 1996–98.

23. 29 T.C.M. 89 (1970), aff'd 434 F.2d 600 (2d Cir. 1970).

recognized, the transferor will nonetheless be taxed on income which was fully earned and fixed prior to the transfer.

A similar result was reached in Townsend v. Commissioner[24] where the taxpayers, after an installment sale of corporate shares, made gifts to their children of the sale proceeds. The proceeds were payable in securities of the buyer corporation. The parties had stipulated that gain was not fully realized at the time of the sale, but, instead, it was reportable as the proceeds were received. The Tax Court held that the postponement of the year of taxation did not prevent allocation of the gain to the assignors because it was their activity that had created the profit.

Other cases have reached similar results without reliance on the assignment of income doctrine. Instead, the realized gain has been attributed to the assignor on the ground that the assignee was merely a conduit for the passage of title. For example, in Malkan v. Commissioner,[25] the taxpayer concluded an agreement to sell unregistered shares of stock to underwriters on June 10. On July 21 he signed a declaration of trust naming himself trustee and ostensibly made a gift of a portion of the shares to the trust for family members, the certificate representing the taxpayer's shares then in escrow. On July 29 the sale to the underwriters was closed. The court held that the taxpayer had to include the gain on all the shares in his gross income, including those transferred to the trust. Pointing out that at no time prior to concluding the details of the sale did the taxpayer act in his capacity as trustee, the court reasoned that the transaction as a whole indicated that the taxpayer, rather than the trust, made the sale.

It does not follow, however, that every tax motivated series of steps in a sale will result in attributing the gain to the donor. The line here has sometimes been finely drawn and in numerous instances, which are hardly distinguishable from Doyle, Townsend, or Malkan, the assign-

24. 37 T.C. 830 (1962); accord Seyburn v. Commissioner, 51 T.C. 578 (1969), in which a partner was taxed on rental income despite an assignment of his partnership interest while the partnership was in the process of liquidation. See also Nick Marsico, Chopping Down The Fruit Tree: Caruth Corp. v. United States Applies Assignment of Income Doctrine to Gift of Stock Between Declaration and Record Dates, 40 Depaul L. Rev. 845, 902 (1991).

25. 54 T.C. 1305 (1970). See also Salvatore v. Commissioner, 434 F.2d 600 (2d Cir. 1970), in which the assignor was taxable for all gain on the sale of a gas station despite a transfer of a partial interest to the taxpayer's children after conclusion of the negotiations but prior to execution of the deed; both courts relied upon Commissioner v. Court Holding Co., 324 U.S. 331, 65 S.Ct. 707, 89 L.Ed. 981 (1945). In Court Holding, the taxpayer-corporation concluded negotiations with a buyer of an apartment building. However, when the parties met to reduce an oral agreement to writing, the buyer was told that the sale could not be consummated because of the large corporate tax that the seller would have to pay. The next day the taxpayer declared a liquidating distribution of all its assets and the sale was concluded by the shareholders. The Supreme Court, reversing the Court of Appeals for the Fifth Circuit, upheld the Tax Court's findings that the corporate taxpayer had not abandoned the sale and that the liquidation and transfer of legal title by the shareholders were mere formalities; hence, the tax on the gain was properly imposed on the corporation.

ment of income doctrine or the title conduit principle has been rejected so long as gain has not fully matured prior to the gift.[26]

A sale of anticipated income from property, as distinguished from a gratuitous transfer of income, may prevent the application of the assignment of income doctrine. Initially, the Tax Court disallowed the scheme, which is an attempt to accelerate future income into the current tax year.[27] The Tax Court held that the transaction was in economic substance a loan rather than a sale. The assignment of income doctrine was then applied to the transfer and the assignor remained taxable on the income.

In Estate of Stranahan v. Commissioner[28] the assignor needed to increase his current income to fully absorb a large interest deduction. He sold to his son future undeclared dividends on stock. The price was determined by discounting the expected future dividends at the prevailing market interest rate. The assignor-father reported the income in the year of the sale. The Tax Court held the transaction was in substance a loan. The Sixth Circuit, however, regarded the transfer as a bona fide sale of the dividends due to the risk incurred by the son, who could only look to the corporation for repayment from the declaration and payment of dividends. Given the sale, the Sixth Circuit held the anticipatory assignment of income doctrine did not apply since the transfer was for value. The Sixth Circuit did not clearly articulate the risk that made the transaction in substance a sale. Arguably, in Stranahan the risk was similar to that in the earlier Tax Court cases.[29] In any event, a taxpayer contemplating such a transaction should observe all appropriate formalities. Nevertheless, the cases do not provide much additional guidance as to what factors need be present or absent to establish the requisite risk that qualifies a transaction as a bona fide sale.[30]

§ 6.03 ASSIGNMENT OF INCOME FROM PERSONAL SERVICES

A fundamental principle of taxation is that income from personal

26. See e.g., S.C. Johnson & Sons, Inc. v. Commissioner, 63 T.C. 778 (1975). See also Rauenhorst v. Commissioner, 119 T.C. 157 (2002); FSA 200149007.

27. Martin v. Commissioner, 56 T.C. 1255 (1971), in which rental income was charged to partners in the year collected despite an attempt to accelerate the income to a prior year by a sale of future rents, the sale being treated as a loan. See also FSA 199927039.

28. 472 F.2d 867 (6th Cir. 1973). See also Hart Schaffner & Marx and Subsidiaries v. Commissioner, T.C. Memo. 1982–348; CCA 200519048; FSA 200001001; FSA 199930004; TAM 200512020; David S. Miller, Taxpayers' Ability to Avoid Tax Owner-

ship: Current Law and Future Prospects, 51 Tax Law. 279, 349 (1998); Brant J. Hellwig, The Supreme Court's Casual Use of the Assignment of Income Doctrine, 2006 U. Ill. L. Rev. 751, 797 (2006).

29. Note, Sale of Future Income Successful in Accelerating Income into Taxable Year to Fully Utilize a Personal Deduction, 20 Wayne L. Rev. 933 (1974).

30. A common assignment of income for value transaction is the sale of inventory. Criteria for determining whether a loan or sale has occurred have been identified. See Mapco Inc. v. United States, 214 Ct.Cl. 389, 556 F.2d 1107 (1977); Hart Schaffner & Marx v. Commissioner, T.C. Memo. 1982–348.

services is attributable to the individual who performs the services.[1] In Lucas v. Earl,[2] the leading case on this proposition, the taxpayer-lawyer entered into a contract with his wife under which all acquisitions of both parties were to be owned equally, including future income from personal services. In Earl, Justice Holmes explained that:

> There is no doubt that the statute could tax salaries to those who earned them and provide that the tax could not be escaped by anticipatory arrangements and contracts however skillfully devised to prevent the salary when paid from vesting even for a second in the man who earned it. That seems to us the import of the statute before us and we think that no distinction can be taken according to the motives leading to the arrangement by which the fruits are attributed to a different tree from that on which they grew.[3]

Essentially the Supreme Court held that all of the taxpayer's salary and fees were attributable to Earl for tax purposes. Although the contract was made in 1901, prior to the enactment of the federal income tax, the Court nevertheless held that the general import of the gross income provision, now section 61(a), was to charge income to the person who rendered the services, and nontax motives could not control the attribution of the fruits to a different tree than the one on which they grew.

An assignment of the right to receive income already earned met with a similar result in Helvering v. Eubank,[4] a companion case to Horst.[5] In Eubank the taxpayer, an insurance agent, assigned to his wife renewal commissions on insurance policies he had written. The assignments were made in 1924 and 1928 and the tax deficiencies were assessed against the taxpayer in 1933 when the commissions were paid to the taxpayer's wife. In holding the taxpayer liable as assessed, the Court relied on Horst without elaboration.

[1] ULTIMATE DIRECTION AND CONTROL OVER THE EARNING OF INCOME

In some cases, courts have been using a more refined test to tax the person who has ultimate direction and control over the earning of

§ 6.03

1. Lucas v. Earl, 281 U.S. 111, 50 S.Ct. 241, 74 L.Ed. 731 (1930). See also CCA 200608038; Rev. Rul. 2006–19, 2006–15 I.R.B. 749; Greene v. United States, 13 F.3d 577 (2d Cir. 1994); Sargent v. Commissioner, 929 F.2d 1252 (8th Cir. 1991); Saenger v. Commissioner, 69 F.2d 631 (5th Cir. 1934); Wofford v. Commissioner, 5 T.C. 1152 (1945); Guaranty Trust Co. v. United States, 139 F.2d 69 (9th Cir. 1943).

2. 281 U.S. 111, 50 S.Ct. 241, 74 L.Ed. 731 (1930).

3. 281 U.S. at 115, 50 S.Ct. at 242.

4. 311 U.S. 122, 61 S.Ct. 149, 85 L.Ed. 81 (1940). See also United States v. Magin-

nis, 356 F.3d 1179 (9th Cir. 2004); Doll v. Commissioner, T.C. Memo. 2005–269; CCA 200246003; Rev. Rul. 2006–19, 2006–15 I.R.B. 749.

5. Horst is discussed above at § 6.02. In Horst the Supreme Court was unclear on the issue of when realization occurred to the transferor. In Eubank the Supreme Court avoided the realization issue by stating that the parties had briefed and argued the case on the assumption that the transfer consisted of assignments of the right to collect the commissions "when they became payable."

income. For example, in Vnuk v. Commissioner[6] a taxpayer attempted to shift income to a trust by transferring to the trust the right to the income from his services as a physician. The court decided that the taxpayer (and not the trust) was taxable on the income because of the trust's lack of supervisory powers over the performance of services and because the taxpayer had no legal duty to earn money or perform services for the trust.

The Service and the courts have been reluctant to push Earl and Eubank beyond the narrow compensation-for-personal-services area. The transfer of property created by personal efforts has escaped application of the assignment of income doctrine. However, a blurry line separates the transfer of earned income from the transfer of income-producing property that the transferor has created.

[2] ASSIGNMENTS OF COPYRIGHTS, PATENTS, ROYALTIES, AND CHOSES IN ACTION

An assignment of a copyright generally is treated as the transfer of income-producing property. In Revenue Ruling 54–599[7] the Service indicated that a copyrighted work is divisible into separate properties as to the medium of exploitation, such as television or the stage, and that a gift of the exclusive right to exploit a copyrighted work in a specific medium transfers a property right so that the income therefrom is taxable to the donee.

Although the courts have divided on the question of the allocation of proceeds from assigned royalties and similar items, taxpayers have won most of the cases, including those where donors have first contracted for royalty payments and then made outright gifts of the royalty contracts. For example, in Heim v. Fitzpatrick[8] the taxpayer was an inventor of a new type of rod end and spherical bearing. After the taxpayer applied for a patent and for a further patent on his original invention, he made a formal assignment of this invention and of the patents that might be issued for it and for improvements to a corporation. The taxpayer owned one percent of the stock of the corporation and his wife and children the balance. The nontransferable agreement gave the taxpayer specified

---

6. 621 F.2d 1318 (8th Cir. 1980). See also United States v. Schmidt, 935 F.2d 1440, 1448 (4th Cir. 1991); Minnesota Lawyers Mut. Ins. Co. & Subsidiaries v. Commissioner, 285 F.3d 1086, 1092 (8th Cir. 2002).

7. 1954–2 C.B. 52. See also Rev. Rul. 71–33, 1971–1 C.B 30, in which the Service held that a taxpayer who made an outright and irrevocable gift to a foundation of a manuscript containing his memoirs and who gratuitously assisted in preparing the manuscript for publication did not realize income from the foundation's use or disposition.

8. 262 F.2d 887 (2d Cir. 1959). The lack of agreement on the application of the assignment of income doctrine to royalty contracts is illustrated by two cases involving P. G. Wodehouse, the British writer, who assigned an undivided one-half interest in two of his manuscripts and their copyrights to his wife followed by a sale by the taxpayer and his wife of their interests to publishers. In the Second Circuit the assignment of one of the manuscripts was recognized, Wodehouse v. Commissioner, 177 F.2d 881 (2d Cir. 1949), and in the Fourth Circuit the assignment of the other manuscript was not, the taxpayer-donor being held taxable on all the proceeds, Wodehouse v. Commissioner, 178 F.2d 987 (4th Cir. 1949).

royalties on certain types of bearings, rights to royalties on new types of bearings, and a right to cancel if monthly royalty payments fell below stated amounts. Prior to receipt of royalties the taxpayer assigned 25%-interests in his agreement with the corporation to his wife and each of two children. Thereafter, all four participated in setting the amount of the royalties as new bearings were put into production by the corporation. In reversing the district court the Second Circuit held that the assignments were gifts of income-producing property and fell outside the purview of Horst and Eubank. The district court had held that the taxpayer was left with only an income interest under the royalty agreement. The Second Circuit noted the taxpayer's retained power to bargain for future royalties, and it held that the agreement, including the retained rights, was substantial enough to constitute income-producing property.

The result in Heim should be compared with Strauss v. Commissioner[9] where the Second Circuit found that an assigned royalty interest consisted of nothing more than assigned income. The taxpayer performed personal services in connection with the financing of the Kodachrome process, and in return he received a share of the royalties the inventors obtained under a licensing agreement. The royalties were assigned to a trustee who collected and distributed the proceeds. The taxpayer gave his interest in the royalties to his wife and so advised the trustee, who paid her the taxpayer's share. The Second Circuit held the transfer ineffective for tax purposes; it found that the taxpayer's interest was never greater than a contract right to share in the proceeds rather than an interest in "the process itself or any right to control disposition of that process." The court found nothing to distinguish this gift from the one in Eubank; it therefore concluded that the taxpayer had made an assignment for compensation due in the future for personal services rendered in the past.

When the taxpayer's personal efforts have contributed to enhancing the value of property prior to its transfer, the created property exception to the assignment of income doctrine has been held inapplicable. In Wilkinson v. United States[10] the taxpayer, a lawyer, paid $12,000 for a percentage interest in a contingent-fee contract owned by a non-lawyer who represented an Indian tribe in its claim against the government. The taxpayer worked on the case as the lead attorney until twelve years after the purchase, when a $32 million judgment was entered. The next

9. 168 F.2d 441 (2d Cir. 1948), cert. denied, 335 U.S. 858, 69 S.Ct. 132, 93 L.Ed. 405 (1948). See also FSA 200149019; Siegel v. United States, 464 F.2d 891 (9th Cir. 1972), cert. dismissed, 410 U.S. 918, 93 S.Ct. 978, 35 L.Ed.2d 581 (1973); Heim v. Fitzpatrick, 262 F.2d 887 (2d Cir. 1959); Nick Marsico, Chopping Down the Fruit Tree: Caruth Corp. v. United States Applies Assignment of Income Doctrine to Gift of Stock Between Declaration and Record Dates, 40 DePaul L. Rev. 845, 902 (1991);

Paul B. Stephan III, Federal Income Taxation and Human Capital, 70 Va. L. Rev. 1357, 1427 (1984).

10. 157 Ct.Cl. 847, 304 F.2d 469 (1962). See also Rev. Rul. 55–2, 1955–1 C.B. 211, in which the Service concluded that unpaid accounts receivable representing compensation for personal services transferred by a cash method taxpayer were taxable to the donor upon collection by the donee.

year the taxpayer made gifts of his purchased fee contract to two charitable organizations. That same year legal fees were awarded, some $191,000 of which was paid to the charities, representing the amount attributable to the taxpayer's purchased interest. In a suit for refund the taxpayer claimed a charitable deduction. The government asserted a counterclaim alleging that the difference between the taxpayer's cost of $12,000 and the $191,000 paid to charities was ordinary income to the taxpayer. The taxpayer contended that he had made a nontaxable gift of property. The majority of the Court of Claims (there were three separate opinions dissenting in part) upheld the position of the government that the taxpayer realized gain and that it was ordinary income. The majority recognized the general rule that a gift of appreciated property does not constitute realization and that, broadly, a contract is property, but it felt that the contract was not property either for the purpose of the charitable deduction or for the purpose of qualifying as a capital asset under section 1221. The court reasoned that the gain was attributable to the taxpayer's own personal efforts exerted between the purchase of the claim and its realization, and, hence, it was properly taxable as ordinary income.

[3] IMPACT OF ORDINARY INCOME PRODUCING PROPERTY

Application of the assignment of income doctrine is less certain when the post-gift activity of the donor consists of personal services that have contributed to the production of ordinary income from the donated property. For example, in Henson v. Commissioner[11] the taxpayer, a sole proprietor, made a gift of the entire enterprise to his wife who lacked any business experience. The wife retained her husband as manager at a salary of $300 a month, the same amount he had drawn prior to the transfer. The wife did not maintain an office at the place of business and normally was not consulted about its operations. Nevertheless, the Fifth Circuit held the income from the business was attributable to its owner, the wife. It noted that every owner of a business has the right to have it managed by another even though that person is married to the owner. However, later cases have held that if personal services produce the income, rather than contributing to the income-generating capacity of the donated property, the assignment of income doctrine applies to attribute income to the donor from his post gift personal services.[12]

---

11. 174 F.2d 846 (5th Cir. 1949); accord Alexander v. Commissioner, 194 F.2d 921 (5th Cir. 1952) (gift of cattle and land to daughter followed by continued management by donor); Visintainer v. Commissioner, 187 F.2d 519 (10th Cir. 1951), cert. denied, 342 U.S. 858, 72 S.Ct. 85, 96 L.Ed. 646 (1951).

12. Hogle v. Commissioner, 132 F.2d 66 (10th Cir. 1942). In Hogle security trading profits were held taxable to the donor although the trading account was owned by a trust for his children. The profits realized were not merely income accruing from the corpus of the trust or from capital gains realized from disposition of corpus but included profits earned through trading involving the exercise of personal skill and judgment of the donor and were in substance his personal earnings. He could trade for the benefit of the trust as he saw fit.

[4] INELIGIBILITY OF THE DONOR TO RECEIVE THE AS-SIGNED INCOME

The assignment of income doctrine has not been applied when the personal efforts of the donor occur after the gift if the donor was ineligible to receive the income. In Teschner v. Commissioner[13] the taxpayer entered an essay contest that required entrants over the age of 17 years and 1 month to designate a person under that age as winner in the event the essay won. The taxpayer designated his seven-year-old daughter who was awarded a $1,500 annuity as a prize. A majority of a sharply divided Tax Court held that the prize was income to the daughter. The court reasoned that the Commissioner's reliance on the language of Horst ("the power to dispose of income is the equivalent of ownership") was misplaced because the power of disposition assumes possession or a right to possession and in this case the taxpayer did not have the right to possession under the contest rules. Hence, the court concluded that it could not be said that the taxpayer had a power to dispose of income, and the power to appoint or designate the recipient alone did not give rise to taxable income in the hands of the taxpayer. This latter point was regarded by the minority of seven judges as resting on "attenuated subtleties" that the Supreme Court had repeatedly rejected.

[5] IMPACT OF EXTERNALLY–IMPOSED RESTRICTIONS ON THE ASSIGNED INCOME

An example of an externally-imposed restriction is provided in Commissioner v. First Security Bank of Utah.[14] A federal banking law prohibited the taxpayer-bank from receiving the proceeds of credit life insurance sales. The court held the assignment of income doctrine inapplicable to a transfer of the proceeds to another corporation and the income taxable to the assignee-recipient.

On the other hand, if a taxpayer has any opportunity to bargain for and agree to an anticipatory arrangement, the assignment of income doctrine applies.[15] The opportunity to bargain need not be a complete and unrestricted power to designate the manner and form in which income is to be received.[16] Any possibility of negotiated results will

13. 38 T.C. 1003 (1962). See also Zaal v. Commissioner, T.C. Memo. 1998–222; Zorc v. Commissioner, T.C. Memo. 1990–620.

14. 405 U.S. 394, 92 S.Ct. 1085, 31 L.Ed.2d 318 (1972). See also Texaco, Inc. v. Commissioner, 98 F.3d 825, 828 (5th Cir. 1996).

15. See Armantrout v. Commissioner, 67 T.C. 996 (1977), aff'd per curiam, 570 F.2d 210 (7th Cir. 1978), in which the employer had established a plan to provide the children of the employees with funds for their college education. The Tax Court said that the employees "in effect consented to having a portion of their earnings paid to third parties."

16. See United States v. Basye, 410 U.S. 441, 93 S.Ct. 1080, 35 L.Ed.2d 412 (1973), in which physician-taxpayers, members of a limited partnership, could elect to be beneficiaries of a retirement trust established by the limited partnership. The Court ignored the fact that the taxpayers could not elect to receive additional compensation or other benefits in lieu of the retirement plan and the fact that strict plan rules limited vesting and payment.

typically be considered sufficient to enable invocation of assignment of income principles.

[6]   WHAT IS INCOME AND HOW IS IT EARNED?

Two other related questions remain which, while not unique to questions of assignment of income, nonetheless impact this area of the law substantially. These questions are: (1) What is "income?" and (2) What does it mean to "earn" income?

As noted in Chapter 1, the federal income tax system tax system bases the notion of income on realization and receipt. To put this in the context of assignment of income, if T works for X and earns the right to receive a payment of $100, T will be taxed on that payment even if she directs that it be made directly to a different person (D).[17] If T's motivation for directing the payment to D is something other than the detached disinterested generosity necessary to support gift treatment to D, T will be taxed under the principles of Old Colony Trust[18] (T has received a benefit equal to the amount transferred to D). If T's motivation for directing the transfer to D is donative, T will be taxed under the assignment of income doctrine. Either way, T is taxed on $100 of income that she in turn directs to D.

If T performs services *directly* for D in a non-donative setting, then T will be compensated by D and will in turn be taxed on that compensation. Whether the compensation takes the form of cash, property, release of some pre-existing obligation, or any other type of benefit does not change the taxability of that compensation.

On the other hand, if T performs services directly for D in a donative setting, there is no "income" to tax anyone on because the only benefit T has received is her ability to benefit D by making the gift of services, and federal income tax law is clear that making a gift is not a realization event.[19] As a result, by performing services directly for D as a gift, T can avoid any "income" to anyone for federal income tax purposes.

Unfortunately, the distinction between what is and what is not a gift of services is not always clear. Consider, for example, the following. T typically is paid $400 per hour for her services as an attorney. T knows that if she performs 10 hours worth of services for X and directs X to pay D, T will be taxed on D's receipt of the $4,000. Instead, in order to avoid tax, T decides to simply make a gift of 10 hours worth of services directly to D. D, who has no personal need for those services, instead contacts X. D and X agree that D will provide X with 10 hours of legal services (to be

---

17.   See Lucas v. Earl, 281 U.S. 111, 50 S.Ct. 241, 74 L.Ed. 731 (1930). See also CCA 200608038; Rev. Rul. 2006–19, 2006–15 I.R.B. 749; Greene v. United States, 13 F.3d 577 (2d Cir. 1994); Sargent v. Commissioner, 929 F.2d 1252 (8th Cir. 1991); Saenger v. Commissioner, 69 F.2d 631 (5th Cir. 1934); Wofford v. Commissioner, 5 T.C.

1152 (1945); Guaranty Trust Co. v. United States, 139 F.2d 69 (9th Cir. 1943).

18.   Commissioner v. Glenshaw Glass Co., 348 U.S. 426, 75 S.Ct. 473, 99 L.Ed. 483 (1955). For a detailed discussion of Old Colony Trust, see § 2.02[1][a].

19.   See § 102(a).

performed by T) in exchange for X's payment to D of $4,000. T contends that: (1) She has made a gift of her services to D, (2) D has made a $4,000 profit on those services, and (3) D, and not T, is taxed on that profit.

[7] SUBSTANCE VERSUS FORM

The issue in cases such as this is whether or not the Service believes that the form of the transaction reflects the real substance.[20] If the Service believes that the "substance" of the transactions is T's performance of services for X and an attempted assignment of the income to D, T will be taxed. On the other hand, if the Service believes that the "substance" of the transaction is T's performance of services for D, and D's separate arrangement with X, only D (and not T) will be taxed.

As is always the case in questions of substance versus form, the answer is never completely clear. Since the form of the transaction is under the taxpayer's control, the Service feels no obligation to respect that form when it is self-serving. On the other hand, to the extent that the form of the transaction does affect legal rights and obligations and is adopted in order to accomplish non-tax goals, the Service will normally honor the taxpayer's choice to participate in whatever transactions he desires. Because the law is uncertain, it is worth reviewing a few specific decisions to get a general understanding of the approach taken by the Service and the courts.

[8] ANTICIPATORY ASSIGNMENTS OF INCOME TO CHARITY AND THE DOCTRINE OF WAIVER

A taxpayer who waives compensation to avoid tax liability on earned income may avoid application of the assignment of income doctrine.[21] In Commissioner v. Giannini[22] the taxpayer, President and Director of the predecessor of Bank of America, contracted to receive five percent of the profits of the corporation as compensation. For the first half of 1927 the amount was $445,704.20. Prior to receipt of the share for the second half of 1927, the taxpayer absolutely and unconditionally advised the corporation "he would not accept any further compensation" for the year. He suggested "that the corporation do something worthwhile with the money."[23] The Ninth Circuit held that "we cannot say as a matter of law that the money was beneficially received by the taxpayer."[24]

The doctrine of waiver is not without limitation. In Revenue Ruling 66–167[25] the taxpayer-executor made no claim for statutory commissions after entering upon performance of his duties as executor. The Service said that the "crucial test" of whether income is realized despite a

20. For a complete discussion of the substance vs. form doctrine, see § 14.06[1][b].

21. Commissioner v. Giannini, 129 F.2d 638 (9th Cir. 1942).

22. 129 F.2d 638 (9th Cir. 1942). See also Emery v. Commissioner, 156 F.2d 728,

731 (1st Cir. 1946); Hedrick v. Commissioner, 154 F.2d 90, 91 (2d Cir. 1946).

23. 129 F.2d at 639.

24. 129 F.2d at 641.

25. 1966–1 C.B. 20.

waiver was whether "the timing, purpose, and effect of waiver make it serve any other important objective."[26] In holding that the taxpayer had effected a valid waiver, the Service focused on the early and continually manifested intent by the taxpayer to serve gratuitously.

[9] IMPACT OF AGENCY RELATIONSHIPS ON ASSIGNMENT OF INCOME

A common arrangement that may shift income arises from the creation of an agency relationship. For example, a salesperson-agent need not include in his gross income the amount of sales made for the employer-principal. The question that sometimes arises concerns what constitutes an agency relationship. For example, in Revenue Ruling 74–581[27] the Service said fees earned by an attorney who was a law school faculty member from the court appointed representation of clients in a clinical program resulted in no gross income to the attorney. Prior to participation in the clinical program each attorney agreed to remit all fees to the school. The rationale for the position taken was the existence of an agency relationship; however, the operative facts creating the agency are not discernable. The revenue ruling concludes "that amounts that would otherwise be deemed income are not, in certain unique factual situations, subject to the broad rule of inclusion provided by section 61(a)." Hence, while an agency relationship will avoid the assignment of income doctrine, the factors necessary for creation are uncertain.[28]

Another area in which the assignment of income doctrine has been invoked in connection with personal efforts pertains to services rendered for charitable organizations. The regulations and revenue rulings reveal concern with taxpayer attempts to avoid the limitations on charitable deductions imposed by section 170 while recognizing a need to pursue a

---

26. Rev. Rul. 66–167, 1966–1 C.B. 20. See also Rev. Rul. 74–613, 1974–2 C.B. 153.

27. 1974–2 Cum. Bull. 25.

28. To determine the existence of an agency relationship in the context of a member of a religious order under a vow of poverty who seeks to direct income to the order that has been earned by performing services for a third person, the Service has said that the "relationship is established when it appears, based on all the facts and circumstances, that the payer of the income is looking directly to the order, rather than to the individual member, for the performance of services." Rev. Rul. 79–132, 1979–1 Cum. Bull. 62. In Schuster v. Commissioner, 84 T.C. 764 (1985), aff'd, 800 F.2d 672 (7th Cir. 1986), the issue was whether the petitioner's wages were paid to her in her individual capacity or as agent of her religious order. The eleven-member majority of the Tax Court looked for some indication of an agreement between the principal (the order) and the third party and required

that the service performer (the petitioner) be an employee of the principal who had the right to direct or control the employee in a meaningful sense. The seven-member minority would have found an agency relationship based on the existence of an established agreement between the principal and the agent rather than the principal and the third party. In Fogarty v. United States, 780 F.2d 1005 (Fed. Cir. 1986), the court said that it preferred "a flexible approach that will take account of diverse factual circumstances" to the Tax Court's " 'triangle theory' which requires a contractual arrangement between the third party employer and the order, as in Schuster." The Seventh Circuit agrees with the Fogarty court's conclusion that the agency determination requires a flexible test that allows consideration of all relevant factors. Schuster v. Commissioner, 800 F.2d 672 (7th Cir. 1986), aff'g 84 T.C. 764 (1985).

flexible policy in applying the assignment of income doctrine. The regulations[29] provide that services rendered gratuitously and directly to a charity followed by a third party's payment to the charity for these services do not constitute income, but services rendered directly to a person who then makes payment to a charity subjects the person rendering the services to tax on the payment. This rule was explained in Revenue Ruling 53–71[30] as applying typically in situations where a radio sponsor or motion picture company engages the services of an artist and by agreement with the artist turns over the payment for the services to a charity designated by the artist.[31] The revenue ruling also draws a distinction between taxable payments made to a charity by such a sponsor for services by an artist who is under contract with respect to the charity and nontaxable payments made to an employer (charity or non-charity) pursuant to an arrangement that is not participated in by the artist whereby the latter performs services as an incident to his normal duties and obligations.

§ 6.04 ASSIGNMENTS OF INCOME TO CHILDREN AND THE KIDDIE TAX

Prior to the enactment of the Kiddie Tax, it was common practice for wealthy families to assign income producing assets to children to take advantage of the federal income tax system's progressive nature (and the children's lower marginal tax rates). Of course, the Service was not particularly pleased with these purported assignments of income; accordingly, Congress enacted the Kiddie Tax, which is now found in section 1(g).

Under section 1(g) certain unearned (investment) income of children under the age of 18[1] (or who are still dependents[2]) is taxed as if it were the income of the children's parents.[3]

Unearned income is nothing more that income which is not earned income.[4] Hence, unearned income generally consists of (but is not limited

---

29. Treas. Reg. § 1.61–2(c).

30. 1953–1 C.B. 18. Compare with Rev. Rul. 68–503, 1968–2 C.B. 44, in which the Service concluded that a gratuitous appearance by the taxpayer, a professional entertainer, on a program planned, organized, promoted, and scheduled by a political fund raising organization was not an assignment of income; hence, no amount was includible in the taxpayer's gross income.

31. See also Rev. Rul. 71–33.

§ 6.04

1. § 1(g)(2)(A)(i).

2. § 1(g)(2)(A)(ii).

3. § 1(g)(1)(A) and (B).

4.

The term "earned income" means wages, salaries, or professional fees, and other amounts received as compensation for personal services actually rendered, but does not include that part of the compensation derived by the taxpayer for personal services rendered by him to a corporation which represents a distribution of earnings or profits rather than a reasonable allowance as compensation for the personal services actually rendered.

§ 911(d)(2) (as referenced by § 1(g)(4)(A)(i) and Treas. Reg. § 1.1(i)–1T, Q & A–6).

to) investment income, such as interest, dividends, rents, royalties, annuities, and income received as a trust beneficiary.[5]

The kiddie tax is generally applicable the "net unearned income" of children under the age of 18 (or who are still dependents) so long as the child has at least one living parent,[6] and her net unearned income exceeds a threshold amount which is indexed for inflation.[7]

Ultimately, the kiddie tax is computed on IRS Form 8615; this form generally aggregates the net unearned income of all the parent's children and taxes it at the parents rate.

Despite the application of the kiddie tax to unearned certain children's unearned income; any earned income of children will generally be taxed at their own marginal tax rate.[8] Section 73(a) provides, "Amounts received in respect of the services of a child shall be included in his gross income and not in the gross income of the parent, even though such amounts are not received by the child." Additionally, any expenditures by the parent or the child which are attributable to the child's earned income are treated as paid or incurred by the child.[9]

§ 6.05   SECTION 7872 INTEREST–FREE AND BELOW–MARKET LOANS AND ASSIGNMENT OF INCOME

For a detailed discussion of the assignment of income doctrine and section 7872 interest-free and below-market loans, see § 2.02[1][d].

5. Temp Reg § 1.1(i)–1T, Q & A–9; Temp Reg § 1.1(i)–1T, Q & A–16.

6. § 1(g)(2)(B).

7. § 63(c)(5)(A) (as referenced by § 1(g)(4)(A)(ii)(I)).

8. § 73(a).

9. § 73(b).

Chapter 7

TAXATION OF PROPERTY TRANSACTIONS

Table of Sections

§ 7.01   INTRODUCTION

Gain from the disposition of property has long been recognized as gross income.[1] More specifically, "Gain[2] realized on the sale or exchange of property[3] is included in gross income, unless excluded[4] by law."[5]

§ 7.02   STATUTORY STRUCTURE

Section 61(a)(3) provides that gross income includes "[g]ains derived from dealings in property."

Regarding losses, section 165(a) provides that a deduction is allowed for "any loss sustained during the taxable year and not compensated for by insurance or otherwise." The regulations provide that "a loss shall be

§ 7.01

1. Merchants' Loan & Trust Co. v. Smietanka, 255 U.S. 509, 41 S.Ct. 386, 65 L.Ed. 751 (1921). See also Walsh v. Brewster, 255 U.S. 536, 41 S.Ct. 392, 65 L.Ed. 762 (1921); Goodrich v. Edwards, 255 U.S. 527, 41 S.Ct. 390, 65 L.Ed. 758 (1921); Eldorado Coal & Mining Co. v. Mager, 255 U.S. 522, 41 S.Ct. 390, 65 L.Ed. 757 (1921).

2. "Generally, the gain is the excess of the amount realized over the unrecovered cost or other basis for the property sold or exchanged. The specific rules for computing the amount of gain or loss are contained in section 1001 and the regulations thereunder." Treas. Reg. § 1.61–6(a).

3. "For this purpose property includes tangible items, such as a building, and intangible items, such as goodwill." Treas. Reg. § 1.61–6(a).

4. Certain realized gains or losses on the sale or exchange of property are not "recognized," that is, are not included in or deducted from gross income at the time the transaction occurs. Gain or loss from such sales or exchanges is generally recognized at some later time. Examples of such sales or exchanges are the following:

(1) Certain formations, reorganizations, and liquidations of corporations, see sections 331, 333, 337, 351, 354, 355, and 361;

(2) Certain formations and distributions of partnerships, see sections 721 and 731;

(3) Exchange of certain property held for productive use or investment for property of like kind, see section 1031;

(4) A corporation's exchange of its stock for property, see section 1032;

(5) Certain involuntary conversions of property if replaced, see section 1033;

(6) Sale or exchange of residence if replaced, see section 1034;

(7) Certain exchanges of insurance policies and annuity contracts, see section 1035; and

(8) Certain exchanges of stock for stock in the same corporation, see section 1036.

Treas. Reg. § 1.61–6(b).

5. Treas. Reg. § 1.61–6(a). See also § 61(a)(3).

treated as sustained during the taxable year in which the loss occurs as evidenced by closed and completed transactions and as fixed by identifiable events occurring in such taxable year."[1]

The amount of gain or loss "from the sale or other disposition of property" is computed under section 1001(a). Gain is determined by subtracting from the "amount realized" the "adjusted basis" of the property.[2] Loss is the excess of the "adjusted basis" over the "amount realized."[3] The terms "amount realized" and "adjusted basis" are defined in sections 1001(b) and 1011, respectively. The "amount realized" is the amount of money plus the fair market value of any other property received.[4] The "adjusted basis" is, as a general rule, the basis of the property determined in accordance with section 1012 and adjusted in accordance with section 1016.

Section 1012 prescribes the general rule for determining basis—it is the cost of the property. Two important exceptions to this general rule are contained in sections 1014 and 1015.[5] Under section 1014(a), the basis of property acquired from a decedent is the property's fair market value at the date of death or at an alternate valuation date. Section 1015(a) provides that the basis of property acquired by gift is the donor's basis, but if the adjusted basis at the time the gift is made is greater than the fair market value of the property, then section 1015(a) uses the latter to compute the donee's loss. Once the basis of the property has been determined, section 1016 outlines the general rules regarding adjustments that must be made to the basis. For example, basis is adjusted upward, or increased, for capital expenditures,[6] and it is adjusted downward, or decreased, for depreciation.[7]

As a general rule, gains and losses are recognized pursuant to section 1001(c). The word "recognized" is not defined in the Code, but the regulations indicate that it means "included in or deducted from gross income at the time the transaction occurs."[8] However, the concept of recognition should not be confused with realization.

Certain types of transactions result in realized, but unrecognized, gains or losses, referred to as "tax-free" or "nontaxable" exchanges. The underlying assumption of nonrecognition "is that the new property is substantially a continuation of the old investment still unliquidated."[9] The provisions concerning common nontaxable transactions are set forth

§ 7.02

1. Treas. Reg. § 1.165–1(d)(1).

2. § 1001(a).

3. Id.

4. § 1001(b).

5. These exceptions are described in detail hereinafter at § 7.03[2][f] and [g].

6. § 1016(a)(1). See also Jeffrey H. Roberts, Allocation of Costs of Common Improvement to Bases of Benefited Properties Disallowed Under Section 1016(a) (1): Nor-

west v. Commissioner, 52 Tax Law. 425 (1999).

7. § 1016(a)(2). See also Robyn L. Dahlin and Mike R. Gardner, Recent Guidance on Accounting Method Changes Provides Clarity in Computing Depreciation, 31 Real Estate Tax'n 187 (2004).

8. See Treas. Reg. § 1.61–6(b).

9. Treas. Reg. § 1.1002–1(c).

in the Code starting with section 1031 and are discussed hereafter in Chapter 9, *Nonrecognition Provisions.*

The concept of nonrecognition of a loss should not be confused with the disallowance of a loss. For example, if an individual sustains a loss on the sale of a personal residence, such a loss is not deductible because it does not satisfy the limitations listed in section 165(c). Hence, while the loss is realized, it is not recognized or deductible, because section 165(c) disallows the deduction of losses for individuals which are not "incurred in a trade or business," "incurred in any transaction entered into for profit," or does not arise from a casualty or theft.[10]

§ 7.03 DISPOSITION OF PROPERTY

[1] IN GENERAL

Normally, a disposition of property, which is a prerequisite to the determination of gain or loss, is a readily identifiable event. However, when the question arises whether there was in fact a disposition, the resolution has frequently turned on the facts and circumstances surrounding the finality of the disposition. For example, leased property normally will be regarded as retained by the lessor even if the lessee is given a purchase option on the property. It is well settled, however, that mere retention of title alone, as with a conditional sales contract, will not preclude a transaction as being treated as an "other disposition" under section 1001.[1] If, as is usual, title is retained for security purposes only, a disposition normally results. Additional factors other than the passage of title that will be taken into account include the taking of possession, the definiteness and nature of the terms of the contract, the amount of the price paid, and the intent of the parties.[2]

---

10. For a complete discussion of the deductibility of losses, see Dominic L. Daher and Joshua D. Rosenberg, Chapter 1D:11, Deductibility of Losses, LEXISNEXIS FEDTAX IN DEPTH (LexisNexis January 2007).

§ 7.03

1. In sale or exchange cases courts have considered: (1) Whether legal title to the property has passed, Merrill v. Commissioner, 40 T.C. 66, 74, affirmed per curiam 336 F.2d 771 (9th Cir. 1964); (2) whether the transferee has obtained possession of the property, Clodfelter v. Commissioner, 48 T.C. 694, 701 (1967), affd. 426 F.2d 1391 (9th Cir. 1970); (3) whether the sale price of the property is definitely fixed, Clodfelter v. Commissioner, *supra*; (4) whether there has been a significant amount of the agreed price paid, Hay v. Commissioner, 25 B.T.A.

96, 101 (1932); (5) the intention of the parties, Merrill v. Commissioner, *supra* at 75; (6) descriptive terms utilized in the agreements such as 'buyer' or 'seller,' Clodfelter v. Commissioner, *supra*; and (7) whether an effective date has been agreed upon fixing a specific time for recognition of the rights and obligations of the parties, Clodfelter v. Commissioner, *supra*.

Maher v. Commissioner, 55 T.C. 441, 451–452 (1970).

2. See e.g., Commissioner v. Segall, 114 F.2d 706, 709 (6th Cir. 1940), cert. denied, 313 U.S. 562, 61 S.Ct. 838, 85 L.Ed. 1522 (1941); Grodt & McKay Realty, Inc. v. Commissioner, 77 T.C. 1221, 1237–38 (1981); Gilmartin v. Commissioner, 47 T.C.M. (CCH) 1532, 1542–44 (1984).

[2] ADJUSTED BASIS

[a] Overview

Given a qualifying "sale or other disposition" of property, the determination of the amount of gain or loss is then dependent upon two factors: the "adjusted basis" of the property and the "amount realized."[3]

The term "adjusted basis" rather than simply "basis" is used in the Code because the taxpayer's initial basis, whether determined by reference to cost or something else, will often have to be adjusted.[4] The taxpayer who purchases a building for $1,000,000 and then spends another $2,000,000 on improvements should not to be taxed on gain upon the sale of the improved building unless she nets some amount in excess of her $3,000,000 investment, and the proper tax result is accomplished by allowing her to adjust her basis by increasing it by the $2,000,000 she spent on improvements.

On the other side of the equation, consider the taxpayer who purchases an asset for $1,000,000 and deducts that entire $1,000,000 as depreciation over the first six years she holds the asset. She has fully accounted for her entire investment. If she later sells the asset for $1,000,000 and is permitted to exclude from income her $1,000,000 initial investment, she will have spent $1,000,000, gotten back $1,000,000, so that she is economically even, but her taxes would show only deductions of $1,000,000 and no income. Requiring basis to be adjusted downwards to reflect depreciation[5] ensures this does not happen.

[b] Required Adjustments to Basis

Often, after property is acquired, certain adjustments (increases or decreases to the dollar amount of the original basis) must be made.[6] After these adjustments, the property then has an "adjusted basis."

A common and recurring adjustment is required by section 1016(a)(2), under which a downward adjustment must be made for depreciation "allowed" or "allowable" as a deduction in computing taxable income.[7] Because the deduction for depreciation is basically a cost allocation technique, a reduction must be made in the dollar amount of the basis of the property.

The requirement that a reduction in basis must be made for depreciation that is "allowable" recognizes that the property is subject to wear and tear.[8] Thus, a reduction in basis must be made whether or not the

---

3. See § 1001(a).

4. Section 1011 provides that the adjusted basis is generally cost the basis determined under § 1012 and adjusted by the rules of § 1016.

5. § 1016.

6. See § 1016.

7. Section 1016(a) simply provides that "[p]roper adjustment" shall be made for a

list of 27 transactions but does not prescribe the nature of the adjustment; this is done in the regulations under § 1016. Section 1016(b) brings within the purview of § 1016(a) adjustments prescribed in other sections of the Code.

8. See Virginia Hotel Corporation of Lynchburg v. Helvering, 319 U.S. 523, 63 S.Ct. 1260, 87 L.Ed. 1561 (1943).

taxpayer has actually taken a deduction for depreciation.[9] This some-times focuses attention on the determination of the correct amount of unadjusted basis. For example, in Commissioner v. Superior Yarn Mills, Inc.[10] the taxpayer purchased a business in 1929, allocating some $244,000 of the $500,000 purchase price to depreciable property. The $244,000 figure was used as the basis for depreciation deductions until 1944. In 1945 the taxpayer contended that the $500,000 purchase price should be reallocated. The Tax Court allowed the taxpayer to allocate an additional $73,000 to the depreciable property, but it did not require the taxpayer to reduce the basis by the allowable depreciation resulting from the $73,000 increase. The Fourth Circuit reversed, holding that the statute required that allowable depreciation must be computed in accordance with the original basis of $317,000 ($244,000 plus $73,000), even though this basis was not actually determined until 1945.

Section 1016(a)(1) provides for correlative upward adjustments to property for expenditures chargeable to a capital account. For example, an expenditure for an addition to a manufacturing facility is capitalized, thereby increasing the basis of the property. However, a taxpayer cannot take a deduction from gross income and also make an upward adjustment to basis. For example, if the Code permits the taxpayer to elect either to expense or to capitalize an amount, basis may be increased only if the taxpayer does not take the deduction.[11]

Section 1016(a) provides for a host of other adjustments; section 1016(b) brings within the purview of section 1016(a) property that was acquired with a substituted basis as under section 1015, which states that as a general rule a donee takes the basis of the donor.

[c] Allocation

Many adjustments to basis require simply a decrease or increase in basis. Even so, some adjustments to basis require an allocation rather than a simple increase or decrease; for example, section 307 provides that the receipt of a nontaxable stock dividend under section 305

---

9. § 1016(a)(2); Treas. Reg. § 1.1016–3(b)(2); Treas. Reg. § 1.1016–3(d)(2); United States v. Ludey, 274 U.S. 295, 47 S.Ct. 608, 71 L.Ed. 1054 (1927); Fidelity–Philadelphia Trust Co. v. Commissioner, 47 F.2d 36 (3d Cir. 1931), aff'g. 18 B.T.A. 43 (1929); Hinckley v. Commissioner, 410 F.2d 937, 940 (8th Cir. 1969), aff'g. T.C. Memo. 1967–180. In Virginian Hotel Corp. v. Helvering, 319 U.S. 523, 525–526, 63 S.Ct. 1260 (1943), the Supreme Court stated:

That provision [for depreciation] makes plain that the depreciation basis is reduced by the amount "allowable" each year whether or not it is claimed. Moreover the basis must be reduced by that amount even though no tax benefit results from the use of depreciation as a deduction. Wear and tear do not wait on net income. Nor can depreciation be accumulated and held for use in that year in which it will bring the taxpayer the most tax benefit. Congress has elected to make the year the unit of taxation. Thus the amount "allowable" must be taken each year. [Citations omitted.]

10. 228 F.2d 736 (4th Cir. 1955). See also Virginia Hotel Corporation of Lynchburg v. Helvering, 319 U.S. 523, 63 S.Ct. 1260, 87 L.Ed. 1561 (1943).

11. See e.g. § 179 (which allows taxpayers to elect to currently deduct certain depreciable business assets). Absent an election under § 179, taxpayers must capitalize costs associated with depreciable business assets.

requires the shareholder to spread the basis of his original shares over both that stock and the dividend in proportion to their relative values.

Moreover, the regulations indicate that if a part of a larger property is sold, the cost or other basis of the whole must be apportioned equitably to the part sold. Hence, gain or loss on the part sold will not be deferred until all of the property has been disposed.[12]

When property is fungible, such as shares of stock, ratable apportionment is possible. However, in some situations ratable apportionment may be impracticable or inequitable, necessitating the consideration of additional factors. Thus, in Beaver Dam Coal Co. v. United States[13] the Sixth Circuit rejected the use of per-acre apportionment where the taxpayer acquired land, a portion of which was to be used for the strip mining of coal. Instead, the court held that a greater percentage of the basis of the property should be allocated to that portion beneath which the coal lay.

A similar rule applies when a taxpayer acquires a number of different assets for a lump sum, as with the purchase of a going business. As indicated in Commissioner v. Superior Yarn Mills, Inc.,[14] the purchase price must be allocated to the different assets acquired in accordance with their relative values at the time acquired. However, if an item in the group of assets purchased cannot be fairly valued, allocation will not be forced, and gain or loss will be deferred. For example, in Piper v. Commissioner[15] the taxpayer had acquired, as part of a tax-free reorganization, stock and warrants to purchase stock from a corporation in exchange for stock with a basis of $118,000 that he owned in a predecessor corporation. When the taxpayer sold the warrants three years later for $28,500 ($.50 each), the question arose as to how much of the $118,000 basis should be allocated to the new stock and how much to the warrants. The warrants were limited to a four-year period and had been quoted at prices ranging from $.75 to $3.50. The taxpayer had assigned a basis of $37,000 to them, but the Commissioner contended that they had a zero basis because they lacked market or actual value. The Tax Court held that since there was no ascertainable market value, there was no practical method whereby an allocation could be made. Consequently,

---

12. Treas. Reg. § 1.61–6(a). The Service has ruled that compensation awarded as severance damages to 100 acres of a 600 acre tract, after the taking of 26 acres in condemnation, must be allocated to the basis of the 100 acres, Rev. Rul. 68–37, 1968–1 C.B. 359, and that the consideration received for an easement affecting only a specified 20–acre portion of a 600 acre tract must be allocated to the 20 acres, Rev. Rul. 68–291, 1968–1 C.B. 351.

13. 370 F.2d 414 (6th Cir. 1966). See also see also Rev. Rul. 86–24, 1986–1 C.B. 80; Leigh Mckee, Income Tax Consequences of Dispositions of Development Rights in Property, 97 J. Tax'n 347 (2002).

14. 228 F.2d 736 (4th Cir. 1955). See also Davock v. Commissioner, 20 T.C. 1075 (1953); Fairfield Plaza Inc. v. Commissioner, 39 T.C. 706 (1963); Hazeltine Corp. v. Commissioner, 32 B.T.A. 4 (1935), nonacq, rev'd89 F.2d 513 (3d Cir. 1937).

15. 5 T.C. 1104 (1945), acq., 1946–1 C.B. 4. See also Tricou v. Commissioner, 25 B.T.A 713 (1932), acq., aff'd on other issue 68 F.2d 280 (9th Cir. 1933), cert. denied 292 U.S. 655, 54 S.Ct. 865, 78 L.Ed. 1503 (1934); Domestic Management Bureau v. Commissioner, 38 B.T.A 640 (1938), acq.; Green v. Commissioner, 33 B.T.A. 824 (1935), nonacq, petition dismissed 84 F.2d 1004 (9th Cir. 1936).

the taxpayer was entitled to recover his entire original basis before gain or loss was recognized.

[d] Identification

Related to the problem of allocation of basis is the determination of the basis of fungible property that has been acquired at different times for different amounts. If fungible property is acquired as inventory at different times by a dealer, the inventory valuation method will provide the means for determining the basis of the property that has been sold and of the property on hand.

Section 1013 provides that if property should have been included in the last inventory, its basis shall be the last inventory value. Unless the dealer has adopted LIFO (last-in, first-out), this will normally result in identification on a first-in, first-out (FIFO) basis.

FIFO is also dictated in the regulations where the identification of shares of stock is impossible.[16] In Kluger Associates, Inc. v. Commissioner[17] the Second Circuit endorsed the use of FIFO in the absence of adequate identification by the taxpayer; the Tax Court arrived at a similar conclusion in Joseph Gann, Inc. v. Commissioner[18] despite the taxpayer's argument that the average cost method more clearly reflected income.

On the other hand, neither first-in, first-out nor average cost may be satisfactory to a taxpayer accustomed to picking and choosing among the securities he desires to sell. The regulations recognize that adequate identification of securities may justify a different calculation, with accurate record keeping being the key.[19]

[e] Acquisition by Purchase: Section 1012

Section 1012 provides that, as a general rule, the basis of property is its cost. Although this section makes no reference to the method of acquisition, it covers the most usual one, a purchase;[20] it also applies to situations in which the property received is the measure of income. For example, property received as compensation for services is included in gross income at its fair market value; this value is also the taxpayer's "cost" basis.[21] Furthermore, the basis of property includes not just the purchaser's equity, but it also includes liabilities assumed or encumbering the property.[22] However, liabilities are not included in the cost basis if they are contingent or indefinite in amount.[23]

---

16. Treas. Reg. § 1.1012–1(c).

17. 617 F.2d 323 (2d Cir. 1980). See also Treas. Reg. § 1.1012–1(c)(1).

18. T.C. Memo. 1982–104. See also Treas. Reg. § 1.1012–1(c)(1).

19. Treas. Regs. §§ 1.1012–1(c)(2), (3), (4) and 1.1012–1(e). Treas. Reg. § 1.1012–1(e) permits purchasers of certain mutual fund shares to elect an average-cost basis.

20. Greenbaum, The Basis of Property Shall Be the Cost of Such Property: How Is Cost Defined?, 3 Tax L. Rev. 351 (1948).

21. See Treas. Reg. § 1.61–2(d).

22. Crane v. Commissioner, 331 U.S. 1, 67 S.Ct. 1047, 91 L.Ed. 1301 (1947).

23. See, e.g., Albany Car Wheel Co. v. Commissioner, 40 T.C. 831 (1963), aff'd per curiam, 333 F.2d 653 (2d Cir. 1964).

Difficulty with determining the cost basis may occur when property is received in a taxable exchange. For example, in Philadelphia Park Amusement Co. v. United States[24] the taxpayer operated a street railway. In 1934, the taxpayer transferred an old bridge it owned to the city in exchange for an extension of the taxpayer's franchise for a fixed term of years. The adjusted basis of the bridge was some $229,000 at the time of the exchange. In 1944, an issue arose as to the basis of the franchise for the purpose of computing the deduction for amortization. The Court of Claims noted that, as a general rule, the basis of property received in a taxable exchange is its fair market value rather than the value of the property given up. However, the court held that when a transaction is at arm's length and the value of the property received cannot be determined with reasonable certainty, the value of the property given up may be used as a measure of the value of the property received, which value will then be the acquired property's basis.

As a general rule, costs incurred in acquiring property, including amounts paid for options, constitute part of the cost basis.[25] Also, as discussed below (although under section 1014 property acquired from a decedent takes a basis measured by its market value at death) if a recipient acquires property from a decedent charged with an obligation, such as the payment of a legacy, then section 1012 applies rather than section 1014. As a result, the taxpayer will acquire a cost basis to the extent of any payments made;[26] in other words, to this extent the taxpayer is treated as having purchased the property rather than acquiring it by inheritance, bequest, or devise.

[f] Tax Cost Basis

Not all property is acquired by purchase. There are, though, numerous properties that may be acquired by neither purchase nor donative transfer, but nevertheless, these transactions are at arm's length. Perhaps the most obvious of these is property transferred in connection with the performance of services.

Assume that T performs services for B, and in return, B transfers to T a car worth $17,000. T will have income equal to the fair market value of the property received, or $17,000.[27] Clearly, if T immediately turns around and sells the car for $17,000, she should not be taxed on any additional income, since she will simply have $17,000 cash, and she has just paid tax on that amount. To approach the issue from another

---

24. 130 Ct.Cl. 166, 126 F.Supp. 184 (1954). See also FSA 200218022; FSA 200005005; TAM 200604033; TAM 200346007; TAM 200147032; Joseph M. Dodge, Debunking the Basis Myth Under the Income Tax, 81 Ind. L.J. 539 (2006).

25. See Treas. Reg. § 1.263(a)–2.

26. See, e.g., Vaira v. Commissioner, 444 F.2d 770 (3d Cir. 1971), reversing and remanding on another issue, 52 T.C. 986 (1969), while upholding the Tax Court's

findings of a cost basis limited to legacy payments and refusing to permit the taxpayer to include capital expenditures and support costs to a life tenant on a farm devised to the taxpayer's brother because they were not made in discharge of the obligation imposed on the taxpayer by his father's will.

27. See § 83. For a more complete discussion of § 83, see § 13.03[2].

perspective, T's basis in the car ought to be $17,000, the amount she included in income upon receipt of the property. That way, if she sells the car for $17,000 she will pay no further tax; if she sells it for $20,000 she will pay tax on $3,000 of gain, giving her total taxable income of $20,000 (the amount of cash she now has); and if she sells the car for $14,000 she will have a $3,000 realized loss, giving her net income of $14,000 (again, equal to the amount of cash she nets from the transactions).

Some might argue that section 1012 provides T with the appropriate basis, because her basis is "cost," and the car has cost her $17,000 of services. Unfortunately, even if that argument were to carry the day in this particular case, it might not apply to give T the proper basis if the car were simply a bonus, or if T won the car worth $17,000 on a game show, and she was required to include that $17,000 value in gross income.

Fortunately, though, the tax law provides another route to give T the proper basis in this and similar situations. The concept of "tax cost" or "tax paid" makes it clear that if a taxpayer receives property and includes that property in income on receipt, her basis in that property is the same as if she had received (and been taxed on) cash and used that cash to purchase the property. In other words, T's basis in the above hypothetical would be the same as if T received cash of $17,000 and used that cash to purchase the car. Note, by the way, that despite the reference to a "tax cost" basis, the taxpayer's basis is unrelated to the actual tax paid, but it is instead determined by the amount the taxpayer included in income upon receipt of the property.

Often situations arise where an employee (or stockholder) in an arm's length relationship receives some property not entirely in exchange for services or entirely for free, but instead the employee (or stockholder) receives property at a discount. And, the discount represents either compensation or some other normally taxable transfer. These slight variations of the situation described above do not change the tax law's ability to come up with the proper basis.

For example, if a corporation allows its shareholders to buy corporate property for less than the fair market value of the property, then the excess of the fair market value of the property over its adjusted basis in the hands of the corporation will be considered to be a dividend to the shareholder.[28] The basis of the property in the hands of the shareholder will be its fair market value.[29] This is the result of the shareholder taking a cost basis to the extent of the amount she pays for the property and a "tax cost" basis to the extent that she receives property that is taxable receipt.

This same general "cost" plus "tax cost" approach is applied to the case of employees getting a bargain purchase of property from an

28. Treas. Reg. § 1.301–1(j).   **29.** Treas. Reg. § 1.301–1(h).

employer.[30] In the case of an employee, this bargain element is taxed as wages.[31]

[g] Acquisition by Gift: Section 1015

Section 1015(a) prescribes two rules pertaining to the basis of property in the hands of a donee. The first rule provides that, to compute gain, the donee must take the basis of the donor, a substituted basis.[32] This statutory requirement, which, upon disposition by the donee, subjects to taxation the appreciation in value during the period the property was owned by both the donor and the donee, was upheld as constitutional by the Supreme Court in Taft v. Bowers.[33] The Court said there is nothing in the Constitution that limits taxation to the appreciation in value during the time the property was owned by the donee, and, furthermore, Congress had not acted unreasonably or arbitrarily in requiring the donee to take the donor's basis in order to prevent tax avoidance.

Section 1015 was first enacted in 1920 and was amended in 1958, when Congress added section 1015(d)(1)-(5) under which basis is increased for the gift tax paid. In 1976 Congress amended 1015(d) to distinguish between gifts made: (1) before September 2, 1958, (2) on or after September 2, 1958, but before 1977, and (3) after December 31, 1976.

The basis of property acquired by gift before September 2, 1958, and that has not been disposed of before such date is increased by the amount of gift tax paid. However, the increase in basis represented by the gift tax paid cannot bring the donee's basis above the property's fair market value measured as of the date of the gift.

Gifts made between September 2, 1958, and 1977 continue to receive the treatment provided in the 1958 amendment: basis is increased by the amount of the gift tax paid but not to exceed the property's fair market value at the date of the gift.

Under section 1015(d)(6) post–1976 gifts receive an increase in basis by an amount that bears the same ratio to the gift tax as the net appreciation in the value of the property when given bears to the total value of the property, with the net appreciation in value and the property's total value being measured as of the date of the gift. However, that increase cannot exceed the gift tax actually paid. This treatment demonstrates Congress' rationale that the gift tax is a cost of the property, but only to the extent of the tax allocable to appreciation while the property was in the hands of the donor.

The second rule of section 1015(a) applies when the donee realizes a loss upon disposition of the property. Here the basis in the hands of the

30. See § 61(a)(1); Treas. Reg § 1.61–2(d)(2); Commissioner v. LoBue, 351 U.S. 243, 76 S.Ct. 800, 100 L.Ed. 1142 (1956); Akers v. Commissioner, T.C. Memo. 1992–476 (1992).

31. Id.

32. See § 1015(a).

33. 278 U.S. 470, 49 S.Ct. 199, 73 L.Ed. 460 (1929). See also James B. Lewis, Exploring Section 1015 and Related Topics, 43 Tax Law. 241, 294 (1990).

donee is either the donor's basis, adjusted as required under section 1016, or the fair market value at the time of the gift, whichever is lower. This mechanism prevents the donor from making a gift of an unrealized loss.

The combined application of the two rules in section 1015(a) can result in a situation where neither gain nor loss is realized by a donee upon disposition of the property. For example, assume a gift of property with an adjusted basis of $100,000 is made at a time when its fair market value is $90,000. If the donee later sells the property for $95,000, neither gain or loss would be realized. This is so because the basis used to compute the gain is $100,000, while the basis used to compute a loss is $90,000.[34]

What constitutes a gift under section 1015? In Farid–Es–Sultaneh v. Commissioner[35] the Second Circuit found "that a transfer which should be classed as a gift under the gift tax law is not necessarily to be treated as a gift income-tax-wise." In this case the taxpayer received shares of common stock of S. S. Kresge Company from its founder, the taxpayer's fiancé. The shares had an adjusted basis in Sebastian S. Kresge's hands of $.16 a share. The taxpayer acquired the shares under an antenuptial agreement whereby the taxpayer released all her marital and support rights. If the release constituted good consideration, the taxpayer acquired the stock at a cost basis of $10.67 a share.

The Second Circuit held that for federal income tax purposes the taxpayer had acquired the shares by purchase rather than by gift. The Second Circuit reasoned that the legislative history of section 1015 indicated it was limited to closing a preexisting loophole under which a donee was permitted to use the value at the time of the gift as the basis on the subsequent disposition, and there was nothing in the legislative history of the problem of consideration in the estate and gift taxes indicating the concept employed therein should be applied in construing the income tax.

While it is clear the concept of donative intent is central to the meaning of a gift in section 1015, sometimes it may be a critical and a close question whether the requisite donative intent has been established. For example, suppose a shareholder in a family corporation contributes a portion of his shares to the corporation. Has the shareholder made a contribution to corporate capital, retaining his full basis, and simply increasing the economic interests of the other shareholders? Or has the shareholder made a gift to the other shareholders, reducing his own basis, and increasing the tax bases of the donees' interests?

In Estate of Julie B. Hitchon v. Commissioner[36] a family corporation was owned 99% by the father of the family and less than 1% by his three

34. Treas. Reg. § 1.1015–1(a)(2).

35. 160 F.2d 812 (2d Cir. 1947). See also See also James B. Lewis, Exploring

Section 1015 and Related Topics, 43 Tax Law. 241, 294 (1990).

36. 45 T.C. 96 (1965), acq., 1966–1 C.B. 2; see also Rev. Rul. 74–329, 1974–2

sons, who each owned one share. In 1935, at a time when the corporation had a deficit, the father, as revealed by the corporate minutes, made a "donation" of some 1500 shares to the corporation, retaining one share, which then represented one-fourth of the corporate capital. Resolutions were passed authorizing the directors "to sell or otherwise dispose of" the stock as they might deem advisable. The stock was thereafter carried on the books as "donated surplus," and each of the four shareholders was on record as owning one share, with each share representing $100 of capital stock. The corporation was liquidated in 1960, and two taxpayer sons reported capital gains on the liquidation as permitted under section 331; they claimed a basis of $37,800, all but $100 of which they contended accrued to them by virtue of the donation made by their father in 1935. The Commissioner argued that the transfer to the corporation in 1935 was not a gift to the taxpayers because it was not intended as such, but it was instead a capital contribution that resulted in an increase in basis of the share retained by the transferor, with no effect on the basis of each son's interest.

The Tax Court, with four judges dissenting, decided in favor of the taxpayers. The court reasoned that a gift was made to the sons because the net effect was to reduce the donor's interest as well as to increase proportionately the interests of his sons, "and not upon the theory that a transfer of property to a corporation is tantamount to a transfer to the stockholders merely because there may be an increase in the value of their existing interests." The court found nothing inconsistent with an intent to make a gift from the terms in the minutes or from the manner in which the shares were treated on the balance sheet; it pointed out that the shares were not carried as assets nor did they otherwise improve the financial statement of the corporation.

Suppose a transfer is part gift and part sale. How is the basis determined? The regulations provide that the transferee's basis is the greater of the amount paid or the transferor's basis.[37] If, for example, property with an adjusted basis of $30,000 and a value of $90,000 is sold for $60,000, the transferee acquires a basis of $60,000. If the sale price had been $30,000 and the adjusted basis $60,000, the transferee would again have a $60,000 basis.[38] As under the general rule, for purposes of determining loss the transferee's unadjusted basis may not exceed the fair market value of the property as of the date of the gift.[39]

[i] Loss Property

Section 1015, attempts to ensure that someone, at some time, will pay federal income tax on the appreciation in the property;[40] accordingly,

C.B. 269 (effect of property bequest to decedent's wholly owned corporation on basis of stock acquired from decedent).

37. Treas. Reg. § 1.1015–4(a).

38. Treas. Reg. § 1.1015–4(b); see also Fincke v. Commissioner, 39 B.T.A. 510 (1939). For correlative treatment of the transferor, see Treas. Reg. § 1.1001–1(e).

For bargain sales of appreciated property to charitable organizations, see § 1011(b).

39. Treas. Reg. § 1.1015–4(a).

40. But see § 1014 (which generally provides for a stepped-up basis to FMV upon death).

the donee may well end up paying tax on appreciation that occurred while the property belonged to the donor. The converse, though, is not the case. If property has *declined* in value in the hands of the donor prior to the gift, it is likely that the loss resulting from that decline in value will never be deducted by anyone.

Section 1015 provides that if the donor's adjusted basis in the gifted property "is greater than the fair market value of the property at the time of the gift, then for purposes of determining loss the (donee's) basis shall be such fair market value."[41] The general rule of section 1015 allows a wealthy donor to transfer the tax liability of a built-in gain to a poor donee who will pay less tax on the same gain; nevertheless, this provision prevents the poor donor from transferring her high basis (and a built-in loss) to a wealthy donee who could otherwise get more tax savings by deducting the same built-in loss.

To see how this works, assume that L bought stock for $20,000 and gifted the stock to H when its fair market value was $1,000. For purposes of determining H's *loss* on any subsequent sale, her basis is the value of the property at the time of the gift rather than whatever L's basis was.[42] As a result, if H subsequently sells the stock for $1,000, she has no loss on that sale, because her amount realized of $1,000 equals her basis of $1,000. If H later sells the stock for $300 instead of its $1,000 value at the time of the gift, her basis for determining loss is still $1,000, the value of the property at the time of the gift, and she has a realized loss of $700. The result of all of this is that the donee will be permitted to deduct as a loss on sale any decline in value the property suffers while held by the donee, but any loss due to a decline in value in the hands of the donor prior to making the gift basically disappears.

Hence, if the donee receives property with a fair market value less than the donor's basis at the time of the gift, then for purposes of calculating further loss in the donee's hands, the donee shall use that fair market value as his basis.[43]

It is important to note that this special rule that gives the donee a basis equal to fair market value at the time of the gift applies only "for the purpose of determining *loss*" by the donee on a subsequent sale.[44] To return to our example, then, assume that L bought stock for $20,000 and gifted the stock to H when its fair market value was $1,000. Assume further that H holds onto the property for long enough for the property to increase in value to $30,000, and thereafter H sells the property for $30,000. While H's basis for determining *loss* is only $1,000, H does not have a loss on this sale, because her amount realized exceeds her basis of $1,000, and unless the seller's amount realized is less than her basis in the property sold, there can be no loss.

Since the special rule for loss does not apply to H in this situation, her basis is governed by the default general rule of section 1015—the

---

41. § 1015(a).   **43.** § 1015(a).

42. Id.   **44.** Id.

donee's basis is the same as that of the donor. Because the donor's cost basis for the property was $20,000, and her amount realized is $30,000, she has a $10,000 taxable gain on the sale.

Finally, suppose L owns property in which she has a basis of $20,000, she gives the property to H when it is worth $1,000, and H subsequently sells the property for $15,000 (or any other amount that is not less than the $1,000 value at the time of the gift and not more than the donor's $20,000 cost basis). Since the property was worth less than the donor's basis at the time of the gift, H's basis for determining loss is only the value at the time of the gift, or $1,000. Clearly, since H's amount realized is not less than $1,000, H has no loss on the sale under section 1015.

On the other hand, generally for purposes *other* than determining H's loss on a subsequent sale, H's basis is determined by the more general rule of section 1015, which states that H's basis in the gifted property is the same as the donor's basis immediately prior to the transfer.[45] In this case, the only purpose for which H's basis is relevant, aside from determining whether and to what extent she may have a *loss* on the sale is for the purpose of determining whether and to what extent she has a gain on the sale. H's basis for determining gain is the same as L's basis was, or $20,000 (L's original cost). H's gain would be the excess of her amount realized ($15,000) over her adjusted basis ($20,000 so long as the question being asked is not about H's loss on a sale). Since $15,000 does not exceed $20,000, H has no gain on the sale of the gifted property.

The net results here are that if (and only if) the donee receives as a gift property whose fair market value at the time of the gift is less than the donor's basis, then (1) the donee will realize no loss on a subsequent sale unless, and only to the extent that, the property further declines in value in her hands after the gift, but (2) the donee will recognize no gain on a subsequent sale of the property unless she sells it for an amount in excess of the donor's cost basis.[46]

[ii] Part Sale Part Gift

Instead of making an outright gift, a transferor may confer a benefit by selling property to a transferee at a price substantially below the property's fair market value.

Where a transfer of property is in part a sale and in part a gift, the unadjusted basis[47] of the property in the hands of the transferee is the sum of—

45. Notwithstanding the forgoing, H's basis for depreciation purposes may well differ.

46. § 1015(a); Treas. Reg. § 1.1015–1(a).

47. "For determining loss, the unadjusted basis of the property in the hands of

the transferee shall not be greater than the fair market value of the property at the time of such transfer. For determination of gain or loss of the transferor, see Treas. Reg. § 1.1001–1(e) and § 1.1011–2. For special rule where there has been a charitable contribution of less than a taxpayer's entire interest in property, see § 170(e)(2) and

(1) Whichever of the following is the greater:

   (i) The amount paid by the transferee for the property, or

   (ii) The transferor's adjusted basis for the property at the time of the transfer, and

(2) The amount of increase, if any, in basis authorized by section 1015(d) for gift tax paid (see section 1.1015–5).[48]

Some examples from the regulations illustrate the effect of the foregoing:

> Example 1. If A transfers property to his son for $30,000, and such property at the time of the transfer has an adjusted basis of $30,000 in A's hands (and a fair market value of $60,000), the unadjusted basis of the property in the hands of the son is $30,000.

> Example 2. If A transfers property to his son for $60,000, and such property at the time of transfer has an adjusted basis of $30,000 in A's hands (and a fair market value of $90,000), the unadjusted basis of such property in the hands of the son is $60,000

> Example 3. If A transfers property to his son for $30,000, and such property at the time of transfer has an adjusted basis in A's hands of $60,000 (and a fair market value of $90,000), the unadjusted basis of such property in the hands of the son is $60,000.

> Example 4. If A transfers property to his son for $30,000 and such property at the time of transfer has an adjusted basis of $90,000 in A's hands (and a fair market value of $60,000), the unadjusted basis of the property in the hands of the son is $90,000. However, since the adjusted basis of the property in A's hands at the time of the transfer was greater than the fair market value at that time, for the purpose of determining any loss on a later sale or other disposition of the property by the son its unadjusted basis in his hands is $60,000.[49]

[h]   Acquisitions From Decedents: Section 1014

As a general rule, under section 1014(a) property acquired from a decedent receives a stepped-up basis to fair market value as of the date of the decedent's death. Consequently, any appreciation in value during the time the property was held by the decedent escapes federal income taxation completely.[50] Conversely, any decrease in value is not deductible.[51]

Alternatively, a decedent's executor may, under section 2032 of the Code, elect to use a valuation date six months after death or at the time of any prior disposition by the estate, if the election decreases the value of the gross estate for federal estate tax purposes and the amount of any

---

Treas. Reg. § 1.170A–4(c)." Treas. Reg. § 1.1015–4(a) (flush language).

48. Treas. Reg. § 1.1015–4.

49. Treas. Reg. § 1.1015–4(b).

50. See Joseph M. Dodge, Debunking the Basis Myth Under the Income Tax, 81 Ind. L.J. 539, 600 (2006).

51. Id.

applicable federal estate tax. If such an election is made under section 2032, it governs the date of valuation for the purpose of section 1014(a).[52]

The section 1014(a) rules also applies to inter vivos transfers otherwise subject to the basis rules for gifts that are included in the decedent's gross estate for federal estate tax purposes; even so, this assumes the donee has not disposed of the property before the decedent's death.

In broad terms section 1014(a) simply provides that the basis of property acquired "from a decedent or to whom the property passed from a decedent" is its value at death or its alternate after death value if the proper election is made. Section 1014(b) provides a list of ten categories that "[f]or purposes of subsection (a) [section 1014(a)], the . . . property shall be considered to have been acquired from or to has passed from the decedent." As discussed below, this language has been interpreted to mean that "property must meet the definition of at least one of the . . . categories of subsection (b) [section 1014(b)]" to qualify under section 1014 (a) as property passing from a decedent.[53]

The first category of section 1014(b), which covers property "acquired by bequest, devise, or inheritance, or by the decedent's estate from the decedent," and the sixth category, which covers a surviving spouse's one-half share of community property if at least one-half of the whole community property was included in the decedent's estate for estate tax purposes,[54] have been strictly interpreted. In Collins v. United States[55] the taxpayer widow received monthly payments of $1,000 from her deceased husband's employer under contracts requiring such payments for five years. The right to receive these payments constituted community property under California law, and one-half the value of the contracts was included in the decedent's gross estate for federal estate tax purposes. The taxpayer claimed a stepped-up basis for the payments, on alternative grounds, under section 1014(a), (b)(1), and (b)(6). The court rejected all three grounds. Section 1014(a) was rejected because, as stated above, that provision requires the taxpayer bring the transfer within one of the section 1014(b) categories. Section 1014(b)(1) was held not to apply, the court observing the taxpayer's counsel conceded in oral argument that the taxpayer's rights were in all probability not part of the probate estate.

With respect to section 1014(b)(6) the district court in Collins admitted there was literal compliance with the statute, but it held that more was required. The court pointed out that section 1014(b)(6) was

---

52. § 1014(a)(2).

53. Collins v. United States, 318 F.Supp. 382 (C.D. Cal. 1970), aff'd per curiam, 448 F.2d 787 (9th Cir. 1971).

54. Two of the categories of § 1014(b) no longer have operative effect; two others pertain to inter vivos transfers in trust; one to the exercise of a general power of appointment by the decedent; another to stock or securities in foreign personal holding companies; the ninth to certain inter

vivos transfers includible in the decedent's gross estate for estate tax purposes; and the tenth to property includible in the decedent's gross estate under § 2044.

55. 318 F.Supp. 382 (C.D. Cal. 1970), aff'd per curiam, 448 F.2d 787 (9th Cir. 1971). The court also held that § 1014 did not apply because the payments were items of income in respect of a decedent under § 691.

designed, as part of a broader program, to equalize the effect of section 1014 in common law and community property states. Thus, prior to 1948, a surviving spouse's one-half interest in community property did not acquire a new basis at death because it vested in interest prior to death, while in a common law state a bequest or devise of one-half of a decedent's property to a surviving spouse did acquire a new basis at death. Section 1014(b)(6) was designed to provide equal treatment. It followed, said the district court, that for the taxpayer to acquire a stepped-up basis for the contract rights, it must be shown that such rights would acquire a stepped-up basis in a common law state. The court then held that such payments clearly would not fall within any of the other categories of section 1014(b). Accordingly, the taxpayer was not entitled to a stepped-up basis under section 1014(b)(6).

A limitation on section 1014(a) is provided by section 1014(c). Section 1014(a) does not apply to property passing from a decedent that constitutes a right to receive an item of "income in respect of a decedent" under section 691.[56]

Moreover, section 1014(e) denies a step-up in basis for appreciated property acquired by the decedent as a gift within one year of death if the property passes from the donee decedent to the original donor or the donor's spouse. The basis of such property in the hands of the original donor or his spouse is its basis to the donee immediately before death rather than its fair market value on the date of death. Section 1014(e) is aimed at thwarting attempts to effect a tax-free step-up of basis of appreciated property by the gift of it to a person who is expected to die shortly (and who is willing to accommodate the donor by having the property pass back to the donor or the donor's spouse).

[i] Acquisitions in Other Nontaxable Transactions

Subject to the exception of section 1014(a), property acquired in a transaction in which gain or loss is not recognized generally takes a substituted basis as distinguished from a cost basis that is acquired in a taxable transaction or purchase. A transaction in which gain or loss is not recognized normally involves an exchange of properties. The substitution of basis is effected by the taxpayer's retention of the basis he had in the property disposed of, which he then uses as his basis for the property acquired in the nontaxable exchange. The effects on basis are described in this volume in the discussion of the various transactions in which gain or loss is not recognized.[57]

[j] Acquisitions of Property in Exchange for Other Property

Purchases made for property rather than for cash are subject to the principals of section 1012.[58] The buyer's basis is her cost.[59] Whether the

---

56. § 1014(c).

57. See e.g., Chapter 9, *Nonrecognition Provisions.*

58. Treas. Reg. § 1.1012–1(a).

59. Id.

cost takes the form of cash or property or a combination of the foregoing is irrelevant.[60] One problem that may arise in cases where property is exchanged for other property that is not likely to arise in cash purchase situations is that it may be that the actual values of the properties exchanged may be difficult to determine. Assuming that the exchange is made at arm's length, it is reasonable to assume that the properties exchanged are of equal value, so that if either property is readily subject to valuation, each person's cost basis (and amount realized) can be easily ascertained.[61]

Indeed, there is support for courts to make the assumption that properties exchanged in an arm's length transaction are of equal value even if even if the court itself believes that might not be the case. In Farid-Es-Sultaneh v. Commissioner,[62] SS Kresge transferred property to Farid "in consideration for her promise to marry him coupled with her promise to relinquish all rights in and to his property which she would otherwise acquire by the marriage."[63] Furthermore, "Her inchoate interest in the property of her affianced husband greatly exceeded the value of the stock transferred to her."[64] Despite this statement, however, the court held that the transfer "was a fair consideration under ordinary legal concepts of that term for the transfers of the stock. She performed the contract under the terms of which the stock was transferred to her and held the shares as a purchaser for a fair consideration."[65] The court thus found her basis in the shares was equal to the fair market of those shares at the time they were transferred to her.[66]

If neither property involved in a taxable exchange is easily subject to valuation, though, problems may arise. In such cases, it is likely that the biggest opportunity for the taxpayers to maximize their tax benefits (by minimizing their tax liability) lies not in manipulating the values of the exchanged assets in order to obtain a high basis, but in manipulating the values in order to report a low amount realized for the property each exchanges. This will minimize taxable gain or maximize a deductible loss on the exchange itself. Regardless of taxpayers' motivations, the IRS can require adequate proof of proper valuation in these cases.

Philadelphia Park Amusement Co. v. United States,[67] was a case where inaccurate prior reporting, a somewhat unclear relationship between the parties, a transaction that may or may not have been an actual exchange but was treated as one by the court, and the passage of time after the initial, basis-determining exchange, gave rise to both an

60. Id.

61. Philadelphia Park Amusement Co. v. United States, 130 Ct.Cl. 166, 126 F.Supp. 184 (1954). See also FSA 200218022; FSA 200005005; TAM 200604033; TAM 200346007; TAM 200147032; Joseph M. Dodge, Debunking the Basis Myth Under the Income Tax, 81 Ind. L.J. 539 (2006).

62. 160 F.2d 812 (2d Cir. 1947).

63. 160 F.2d 812, 815 (2d Cir. 1947).

64. Id.

65. Id.

66. Farid-Es–Sultaneh v. Commissioner 160 F.2d 812, 815 (2d Cir. 1947).

67. 130 Ct.Cl. 166, 126 F.Supp. 184 (1954).

appropriate analysis of the law, but a strange outcome in the case at hand.

In the case, the taxpayer had engaged in what the court believed should have been a taxable exchange in a year not subject to review (because of the expiration of the statute of limitations). In that earlier year the taxpayer had not reported the transfer as an exchange. Rather than reporting a taxable "exchange," the taxpayer had treated the transaction as an abandonment of worthless property. As a result, the taxpayer did not report any realized gain or loss from the "exchange;" instead, it simply deducted as a loss its entire basis in the asset it transferred.

The court was asked to determine the taxpayer's basis in the property *acquired* in that prior "exchange," while at the same time (because of the statute of limitations) disregarding what the tax consequences of the exchange itself should have been. In another significant deviation from the norm, it appeared to the court that in the earlier "exchange," the fair market value of the property the taxpayer transferred was substantially less than the fair market value of the property received.

As a result of this setting, the court found itself having to determine whether the taxpayer's basis in the acquired property was the fair market value of the property *given* in the exchange, even though that amount was substantially lower than the value of the property received. Alternatively, the court also examined whether the taxpayer's cost basis ought to be determined by reference to the value of the property *received* in the exchange, even though that amount was substantially in excess of what the court believed the taxpayer had actually paid. Ultimately, the court determined that in the specific case before it, the proper way to determine the taxpayer's basis in the acquired property was by reference not to the value of the property *transferred*, but to the value of the property *received* by the taxpayer.

Although perhaps not apparent from the court's opinion because of the unique factual setting of the case, the court was simply, and accurately, applying a version of a "tax cost" basis theory. To understand the court's holding in Philadelphia Park, assume that T owns property with a basis and apparent "value" of $10,000; assume further that T transfers that property to X in a taxable exchange for property worth $50,000. Under section 1001, T will be taxed on the $40,000 gain on the exchange (the excess of her amount realized of $50,000 over her adjusted basis of $10,000). Unless her cost basis in the acquired property is $50,000, she will be overtaxed on the subsequent sale of the property. If a court determined the property T exchanged was worth only $10,000 so her basis in the new property was only $10,000, then when T sold the new property for its $50,000 value, she would be taxed a second time on the single $40,000 profit she had earned.

The more interesting issue in Philadelphia Park is: how could the taxpayer have transferred property worth only $10,000 in exchange for property worth $50,000, especially in light of the fact that the fair market value of any property is equal to what a willing buyer would pay a willing seller in an arm's length transaction. The response (but not an actual answer) to that question is that the initial taxable transaction was not entirely a single arm's length exchange.

The taxpayer was said to have transferred a drawbridge it owned to the city of Philadelphia in exchange for the city's agreement to extend for 10 years a license the city had granted to the taxpayer many years earlier. While it is true the taxpayer did transfer to the city its draw-bridge (the asset worth $10,000), however, it was not at all clear that the contract extension (the $50,000 value) was granted by the city entirely in *exchange* for that bridge. Instead, the license extension might well have been granted even absent the existence of the bridge, since the possibility of a 10 year extension had been written into the original license agreement.

In other words, if the bridge was worth only $10,000 and the transaction was at arm's length, then whatever the taxpayer got in exchange for the bridge must have been $10,000. Any additional value it received as a result of the license extension was likely not received in exchange for the bridge, but in exchange for some value the city itself put on the license extension. On the other hand, if the license extension was worth $50,000, and it was issued entirely in exchange for the bridge by a city that saw no other benefit in the license extension (other than acquiring the bridge), then the bridge must have been worth $50,000 to the city.

[3]　AMOUNT REALIZED

[a]　Overview

Once the adjusted basis of property has been ascertained, the taxpayer must then determine the "amount realized" to compute gain or loss.[68] Section 1001(b) describes the amount realized in terms of "money" and "property" received. Additionally, services received are generally regarded as falling within section 1001(b), and they may be valued in accordance with the principles of Philadelphia Park Amusement Co. v. United States.[69] Hence, any services received in this manner are assumed to be equal in value to the property disposed of in the transaction at issue.[70]

As a corollary to the rule that treats expenses incurred in acquiring property as part of the cost of acquisition, expenses incurred in selling

---

68. See also Alvin D. Lurie, How Tax Shelters Evolved: The Road From Crane Has Been Paved With Bad Contentions, 100 J. Tax'n 274 (2004); Erik M. Jensen, The Unanswered Question In Tufts: What was the Purchaser's Basis?, 10 Va. Tax Rev. 455 (1991).

69. 130 Ct.Cl. 166, 126 F.Supp. 184 (1954).

70. See Riley v. Commissioner, 37 T.C. 932 (1962), aff'd, 328 F.2d 428 (5th Cir. 1964).

certain types of property are treated as a reduction of the amount realized.[71]

[b]　Inability to Value the Amount Realized

The regulations indicate that the fair market value of property is used to determine the amount realized, and "only in rare and extraordinary cases will property be considered to have no fair market value."[72] What happens when property cannot be currently valued? The Supreme Court considered this question in Burnet v. Logan,[73] where the taxpayer sold stock in a company for cash and a promise by the buyer to pay the stockholders $.60 a ton for iron ore obtained by the buyer from a mine. The taxpayer did not report any portion of the payments made by the buyer during 1918, 1919, and 1920. The government contended the promise had a fair market value when it was made, and the transaction was closed in 1916, the year of the sale. The Supreme Court, however, agreed with the Court of Appeals and held it was impossible to determine with certainty the fair market value of the promise to pay $.60 a ton. Therefore, the taxpayer was entitled to the return of her capital, represented by the basis of her shares, before she could be charged with income. The Supreme Court remarked: "When the profit, if any, is actually realized, the taxpayer will be required to respond."[74] It added that because the promise "had no ascertainable fair market value ... [t]he transaction was not a closed one."[75]

In Commissioner v. Kann's Estate[76] the Logan principle was applied to a sale of property where the consideration received was in the form of a noncommercial annuity. In Kann's Estate, the taxpayer sold securities to her children in return for their unsecured promise to pay her life annuities.[77] The Third Circuit said it found no reason to deviate from the

---

71. See Treas. Reg. § 1.263(a)–2(e). Commissions paid in purchasing securities are offset against the selling price, except for dealers in securities who may deduct the commissions as an ordinary and necessary business expense.

72. Treas. Reg. § 1.1001–1(a).

73. 283 U.S. 404, 51 S.Ct. 550, 75 L.Ed. 1143 (1931).

The open transaction doctrine is a 'rule of fairness designed to ascertain with reasonable accuracy the amount of gain or loss realized upon an exchange, and, if appropriate, defer recognition thereof until the correct amounts can be accurately determined.' Dennis v. Commissioner, 473 F.2d 274, 285 (5th Cir.1973). The open transaction treatment applies only in "rare and extraordinary circumstances." McShain v. Commissioner, 71 T.C. 998, 1004 (1979); Parrish v. Commissioner, T.C. Memo. 1997–474 (1997), aff'd, 168 F.2d 1019 (Em.App. 1948). The open transaction doctrine is only applicable, however, when it is not possi-

ble to determine the value of either of the assets exchanged. Davis v. Commissioner, 210 F.3d 1346, 1348 (11th Cir. 2000). In an arm's length transaction, where only one of the assets has an unascertainable value, it is presumed equal to the property for which it was exchanged. United States v. Davis, 370 U.S. 65, 82 S.Ct. 65, 8 L.Ed.2d 335, 1962–2 C.B. 15 (1962). See also, Philadelphia Park Amusement Co. v. United States, 126 F.Supp. 184, 189, 130 Ct.Cl. 166 (1954) (the value of two properties exchanged in an arm's length transaction are presumed to be equal.)

TAM 200604033

74. 283 U.S. 404, 413, 51 S.Ct. 550, 75 L.Ed. 1143 (1931).

75. Id.

76. 174 F.2d 357 (3d Cir. 1949).

77. In Estate of Lloyd G. Bell v. Commissioner, 60 T.C. 469 (1973), the Tax Court declined to apply the cost recovery

established rule that such obligations of "individuals, whether rich or poor," do not have "such standing as to" possess value "by way of ordinary business." The Third Circuit said this rule was salutary because of the uncertainty of both the annuitant's life span and the obligor's ability to pay.

In Inaja Land Co. v. Commissioner[78] the taxpayer owned acreage that had a cost basis of $61,000. The taxpayer recovered $50,000 from the City of Los Angeles as damages to property resulting from a diversion of river water and for an easement to continue such diversion. The Commissioner argued that the damages represented, at least in part, compensation for loss of income, and absent a showing of allocation between taxable and nontaxable items, the whole amount should be reported as income. The Tax Court disagreed, concluding that the whole amount was paid for damages to the land, and for the easement; it found apportionment to the impacted portion of the land to be impracticable. Accordingly, under Logan, since the amount received was less than the taxpayer's basis, it was a return of capital to be applied in reduction of the basis of the property.

The Installment Sales Revision Act of 1980 provides "new rules . . . to reduce substantially the justification for treating transactions as 'open' and permitting the use of the cost-recovery method sanctioned by Burnet v. Logan. . . ."[79] Through the Act the Senate Finance Committee intended "that the cost-recovery method not be available in the case of sales for a fixed price . . . and that its use be limited to those rare and extraordinary cases involving sales for a contingent price where the fair market value of the purchaser's obligation cannot reasonably be ascertained."[80]

In Warren Jones Co. v. Commissioner[81] a cash method taxpayer sold an apartment building for $153,000, receiving a cash down-payment of $20,000 and the buyer's promise in a real estate contract to pay the $133,000 balance, plus interest, over 15 years. The Tax Court held that the real estate contract did not constitute "property (other than money)" under section 1001(b). The Tax Court reasoned that while the contract was salable, it was not the equivalent of cash because the taxpayer could not receive for it an amount anything near its face value. In reversing the Tax Court, the Ninth Circuit said that if the fair market value of an obligation received in a sale can be ascertained, that value must be included in the amount realized under section 1001(b). The Ninth Circuit then observed that the installment method under section 453 is "Congress' [sic] method of providing relief from the rigors of

rule of Burnet v. Logan when property was exchanged for a secured promise to pay a private annuity.

78. 9 T.C. 727 (1947), acq., 1948–1 C.B. 2. See also Stephen B. Cohen, Apportioning Basis: Partial Sales, Bargain Sales and the Realization Principle, 34 San Diego L. Rev. 1693 (1997).

79. S. Rep. No. 1000, 96th Cong., 2d Sess. 24 (1980).

80. See Goldberg, Open Transaction Treatment for Deferred Payment Sales After the Installment Sales Act of 1980, 34 Tax. Lawyer 605 (1981).

81. 524 F.2d 788 (9th Cir. 1975), rev'g and remanding, 60 T.C. 663 (1973).

section 1001(b)," suggesting that the taxpayer could have chosen the installment basis to avoid the alleged hardship of realizing the "equivalent of cash."

The Installment Sales Revision Act of 1980 has greatly reduced the controversies concerning the meaning of the words "property (other than money)" in section 1001(b) when a cash method taxpayer receives a deferred payment obligation in a sale.[82] Furthermore, the Act facilitates the installment reporting of gains from deferred payment sales. If a taxpayer elects not to report using the installment method, the temporary regulations for section 453 state that:

> Receipt of an installment obligation shall be treated as a receipt of property, in an amount equal to the fair market value of the installment obligation, whether or not such obligation is the equivalent of cash. An installment obligation is considered to be property and is subject to valuation ... without regard to whether the obligation is embodied in a note, an executory contract, or any other instrument, or is an oral promise enforceable under local law.[83]

[c] Indebtedness

In Crane v. Commissioner[84] the taxpayer inherited property that was subject to a mortgage debt of $255,000 and unpaid interest of $7,000. The taxpayer used the total of $262,000, which was also the appraised value of the property at the testator's death, as the basis for taking depreciation over a period of years. However, when the taxpayer sold the property subject to the mortgage, she claimed that all that had been sold was her "equity," for which she received $2,500 net cash proceeds. The taxpayer contended that this $2,500 constituted the entirety of the amount realized on the sale.

The Supreme Court held that the term "property," in what is now section 1014 (which prescribes that property at death takes a basis equal to its fair market value), meant the value of the property apart from the mortgage. Thus, $262,000 was found to be the proper basis for the computation of depreciation. Further, the Court held that the term "property" had the same meaning in what is now section 1001(b).[85]

---

82. The Senate Finance Committee report says that payments regarded as being received do not include the purchaser's obligation of future payment unless it is a bond or other evidence of indebtedness either payable on demand or issued by a corporation or government and that is readily tradable. S. Rep. No. 1000, 96th Cong., 2d Sess. 7 (1980).

83. Treas. Reg. § 15a.453–1(d)(2)(i).

84. 331 U.S. 1, 67 S.Ct. 1047, 91 L.Ed. 1301 (1947). See also Alvin D. Lurie, How Tax Shelters Evolved: The Road From Crane has been Paved with bad Contentions, 100 J. Tax'n 274 (2004).

85. Relying in part on Crane, the Supreme Court held in Diedrich v. Commissioner, 457 U.S. 191, 102 S.Ct. 2414, 72 L.Ed.2d 777 (1982), that a donor who makes a gift on the condition that the donee pay the gift tax realizes income to the extent that the gift tax paid by the donee exceeds the donor's adjusted basis. The Court observed that in Crane it held that the amount of the mortgage was included in the amount realized because "it was the 'reality,' not the form, of the transaction that governed." In Diedrich the Supreme Court observed that the donee's discharge of the gift tax liability, statutorily imposed on the donor, was analogous to a discharge

Therefore, the amount of the mortgage on the property was to be included in the "amount realized."

The Crane rationale was followed by the First Circuit in Parker v. Delaney.[86] There the taxpayer, during 1933, 1934, and 1936, took deeds for apartment houses from banks and gave back mortgages and notes totaling some $273,000. During the years the taxpayer owned the apartments, the taxpayer paid $14,000 on the mortgages and deducted $45,000 for depreciation. In 1945 the taxpayer reconveyed in consideration of the banks' discharges of the mortgages, then totaling $259,000. The First Circuit held that the taxpayer realized a gain of $31,000, computed as the difference between his adjusted basis of $228,000 ($273,000 less a $45,000 adjustment for depreciation allowed) and the amount realized of $259,000, equal to the amount of the liability discharged when the taxpayer reconveyed to the bank.[87]

In Crane the Supreme Court held that a taxpayer who sold property encumbered by a nonrecourse mortgage that was less than the property's fair market value had to include the unpaid balance of the mortgage in the computation of the amount the taxpayer realized on the sale. In Commissioner v. Tufts[88] the Supreme Court concluded that the same rule applies, even if the unpaid amount of the nonrecourse mortgage exceeds the value of the property. The Supreme Court said in Tufts that the fair market value of the property is irrelevant to the calculation of the amount realized.[89] The Court observed that:

> From the mortgagor's point of view, when his obligation is assumed by a third party who purchases the encumbered property, it is as if the mortgagor first had been paid with cash borrowed by the third party from the mortgagee on a nonrecourse basis, and then had used the cash to satisfy his obligation to the mortgagee.[90]

of indebtedness, which had to be included in the donor's amount realized.

86. 186 F.2d 455 (1st Cir. 1950), cert. denied, 341 U.S. 926, 71 S.Ct. 797, 95 L.Ed. 1357 (1951). See also Diane M. Anderson, Federal Income Tax Treatment of Nonrecourse Debt, 82 Colum. L. Rev. 1498, 1530 (1982).

87. In a concurring opinion Chief Judge Magruder observed that a similar result could be reached, without putting a strain on the statutory terms, by ignoring the inclusion of the mortgages on both ends and starting with a zero basis, adding $14,000 for the amount paid on the mortgage (the real investment), then deducting $45,000 for depreciation taken, yielding a minus $31,000 as adjusted basis. Under the statutory formula this would yield a $31,000 gain.

88. 461 U.S. 300, 103 S.Ct. 1826, 75 L.Ed.2d 863 (1983). See also Richard B.

Dagen, Federal Income Tax–Amount Realized–Tufts v. Commissioner, 31 Emory L.J. 242 (1982); Patricia A. Cain, From Crane to Tufts: In Search of a Rationale for the Taxation of Nonrecourse Mortgagors, 11 Hofstra L. Rev. 1 (1982); Alvin D. Lurie, Crane's Ghost Not Laid to Rest: Still a Work in Progress, According to Owen, 27 J. Real Est. Tax'n 257 (2000).

89. Treas. Reg. § 1.1001–2(b) states that the fair market value of property that secures a liability is not relevant for determining the amount realized. The regulation was promulgated in 1980 while Tufts was pending in the court of appeals and formalized the Commissioner's prior interpretation.

90. Commissioner. v. Tufts, 461 U.S. 300, 312, 103 S.Ct. 1826, 1834, 75 L.Ed.2d 863 (1983).

If a taxpayer purchases for cash and later borrows on the property, giving a mortgage as security, the amount of the mortgage would be included only in the amount realized in event of a reconveyance, as in Parker v. Delaney; it would not increase the cost basis. Note that when property is purchased subject to a mortgage, as in Parker v. Delaney, the taxpayer may acquire a basis for depreciation and consequent deductions from ordinary income with little or no actual investment. However, a portion of the depreciation may be recaptured, that is, characterized as ordinary income, upon the disposition of the property; moreover there are limits on the use of depreciation deductions where little or no actual investment is present.[91]

[d]   Special Situations Which Impact the Amount Realized

[i]   Seller as Creditor—Seller Financing

If the seller finances the sale by extending credit to the purchaser, the seller's amount realized will still include all the cash and the value of services and property received for the property. The amount realized for the property will *not* include any amounts that represent interest, however, since the interest is paid for the use of money and not for the acquisition of the property. The seller will be taxed on the interest,[92] of course, but it must be tracked separately from gain or loss on the sale. This is because the character and timing of interest income (and the interest deduction for the purchaser) may differ from those of the taxpayer's gain or loss on the sale.

Because the timing and character of interest may differ from those of amounts actually paid for the property, and because characterization of amounts as interest or as principal can affect the purchaser's basis in the property in significant ways, purchasers and sellers have had incentives to (mis)characterize amounts as one or the other in the face of what appears to be a different economic reality. In response to these efforts, Congress has enacted several provisions that characterize certain amounts as interest rather than as principal.

It is also important to note that when the seller of property will receive some or all of her payments at some time after the taxable year in which the sale occurs, it is not just the seller's amount realized that warrants attention (because of potential stated or imputed interest). It is quite possible that the timing of the seller's gain will be subject to the special rules that govern "installment sales."[93]

[ii]   Seller as Debtor—Recourse Debt

In addition to paying cash for property, the buyer may also, as part of the purchase price, assume a liability for which the seller had

---

91. For a complete discussion of the limits of depreciation deductions where there is little or no actual investment, see Chapter 14, *Tax Shelters and Tax Avoidance.*

92. See § 61(a)(4).

93. The installment sale rules are discussed in detail in § 8.05.

previously been personally liable. If she does so, the value to the seller of that debt assumption is part of her amount realized for the property. Just as a person's assumption or payment of T's personal obligation in exchange for the performance of services by T is typically income to T in an amount equal to the obligation paid or assumed on T's behalf,[94] the assumption or payment of T's obligation in exchange for the transfer of property by T is part of T's amount realized.

If the liability assumed by the purchaser was the personal liability of the seller, whether the property exchanged was pledged to secure that liability does not impact the outcome. Either way, the purchaser's assumption of the seller's personal liability is part of the seller's amount realized.[95]

In the vast majority of cases, the amount included in the seller's amount realized is equal to the amount of debt assumed; because that is both the benefit to the seller and the cost to the buyer. Other times, the amount realized is not quite so clear. If the assumed liability is contingent on the happening of events that may or may not occur at some point in the future, the actual benefit of the liability assumption may be far from clear. Indeed, if the contingency giving rise to the liability is very remote, the amount of the liability assumed may in some cases be completely disregarded.[96]

[iii] Seller as Debtor—Nonrecourse Debt

As discussed in connection with determination of the taxpayer's basis in property, her amount realized on the disposition of property includes not only any recourse debt that is assumed as part of the exchange, but it also includes any nonrecourse debt attached to the transferred property. As the Court explained in Crane, a taxpayer who holds property subject to a nonrecourse liability less than the fair market value of the property "must and will treat the conditions of the mortgage exactly as if they were his personal obligations" because failure to fulfill those loan obligations will result in loss of the property and any equity she has in the property. As a result, "If [the taxpayer] transfers subject to the mortgage, the benefit to him is as real and substantial as if the mortgage were discharged, or as if a personal debt in an equal amount had been assumed by another."[97]

Crane is one of the most famous cases in the history of federal income taxation, and footnote 37 in Crane is perhaps the most famous footnote in the history of federal income tax jurisprudence. Prior to that footnote, the Court had just explained that nonrecourse debt should be

---

94. Old Colony Trust v. Commissioner, 279 U.S. 716, 49 S.Ct. 499, 73 L.Ed. 918 (1929).

95. United States v. Hendler, 303 U.S. 564, 58 S.Ct. 655, 82 L.Ed. 1018 (1938), reh'g denied 304 U.S. 588, 58 S.Ct. 940, 82 L.Ed. 1548 (1938). See also William J. Rohrbach, Jr., The Disposition of Properties Se-

cured by Recourse and Nonrecourse Debt, 41 Baylor L. Rev. 231, 265 (1989).

96. Rev. Rul. 55–675, 1955–2 CB 567. See also FSA 200217021.

97. Crane v. Commissioner, 331 U.S. 1, 14, 67 S.Ct. 1047, 1055, 91 L.Ed. 1301 (1947).

treated the same as a recourse liability because the owner of the property would necessarily treat the nonrecourse liability as a personal liability, since she must do so to retain her interest in the property. If she failed to honor the nonrecourse liability, she would lose the property and all of her equity on foreclosure. In footnote 37, the Court went on to explain that:

> [I]f the value of the property is less than the amount of the mortgage, a mortgagor who is not personally liable cannot realize a benefit equal to the mortgage. Consequently, a different problem might be encountered where a mortgagor abandoned the property or transferred it subject to the mortgage without receiving boot.[98]

What the Crane Court saw as a relatively insignificant issue eventually grew into an issue of monumental importance. At the time Crane was decided, it must have appeared that in only the rarest of cases would a nonrecourse liability to which a property was subject exceed its value. In the days when Crane was decided, lenders, not anxious to lose money, generally did not lend amounts on a nonrecourse basis in excess of the security. Just as Crane pointed out that the presence of equity would guarantee that the borrower would treat the loan as her own, lenders wanting to ensure that the borrower would honor the nonrecourse debt sought to ensure that the borrower was left with equity sufficient to motivate her.

As discussed in § 14.03 herein the holding in Crane gave rise to the era of tax shelters. As a result, what seemed only marginally relevant at that time became a highly significant issue. Ultimately, purchasers would buy heavily leveraged (depreciable) property at high prices using nonrecourse debt. When prices came down, it often turned out that the nonrecourse debt exceeded the value of the property it secured. Taxpayers argued in these cases the nonrecourse debt was not one they would treat as their own, so when they transferred the property subject to that debt that, the debt relief was not part of their amount realized. The IRS thought differently.

To see how these cases often developed, assume that T purchased a building for $15,000,000 by paying $1,000,000 down and taking the property subject to a nonrecourse debt of $14,000,000. The loan requires T to pay interest at 10% annually, and it requires principal to be paid in a lump sum at the end of 15 years. Under Crane and its progeny, T's basis in the building would include both her cash outlay and the nonrecourse debt, since they are both part of T's cost of acquiring the property, and T is presumed to treat the debt as her own in order to protect her $1,000,000 equity.

Assume that T then holds and manages the property for several years, during which she pays all interest due on the loan, and takes the depreciation deductions to which she is entitled. At the end of 8 years, she has taken depreciation deductions totaling $8,000,000, and her basis

98. Id.

in the property has been reduced, as a result of those depreciation deductions,[99] to $7,000,000. Assume that at that time the property declines in value to $5,000,000. When the property is under threat of foreclosure, T agrees to transfer the property to P, and P agrees to take the property subject to the nonrecourse debt for no cash down.

This was the basic fact pattern (simplified by substituting individuals for a partnership and inserting nice round numbers, neither of which changes either the analysis or the outcome) that arose in Commissioner v. Tufts.[100] Consistent with the implications of footnote 37 in Crane, T argued that given the facts of this case, the general principle of Crane ought not to apply.

As the Crane Court had explained, a taxpayer-owner of property will usually treat a nonrecourse debt to which the property is subject as her own personal liability in order to protect her equity in the property. In this case, however, T had no equity in the property to protect. Property worth $5,000,000 was pledged to secure a liability of $14,000,000. No taxpayer in her right mind would treat that $14,000,000 nonrecourse liability as a personal obligation. To do so would be to voluntarily pay $14,000,000 for property admittedly worth only $5,000,000. Instead, any reasonable person would simply ignore the liability, allow the creditor to foreclose, and be rid of the property.

T argued that if relief of the debt were any benefit at all, the amount of benefit she received upon disposition of the property and release from the constraints of the nonrecourse debt could not exceed the $5,000,000 value of the property securing it.

Not surprisingly, the IRS took issue with this argument. As the Service pointed out, T had included the $14,000,000 in her cost basis for the property, and T had deducted $8,000,000 of that basis as depreciation. If the Court adopted T's position, the net result would be that T would have paid a total of $1,000,000 (the down payment); T would have already deducted $8,000,000; and T would be entitled to an additional loss of $2,000,000 on the sale (because her basis was $7,000,000 and she was arguing that her amount realized was only $5,000,000). T would have received total tax deductions of $9,000,000 based on a total outlay of $1,000,000. If T's marginal tax rate is 40%, the $9,000,000 of deductions would have saved her taxes of $3,600,000, or almost four times her total expenditures.

The Court agreed with the Service, explaining that as a matter of tax law, as a matter of economics, and as a matter of logic, the full amount of the nonrecourse debt was required to be included in T's amount realized, regardless of the value of the underlying property. More specifically, the Court explained that:

---

99. See § 1016.

100. 461 U.S. 300, 103 S.Ct. 1826, 75 L.Ed.2d 863 (1983), reh'g denied 463 U.S. 1215, 103 S.Ct. 3555, 77 L.Ed.2d 1401

(1983). See also Daniel J. Glassman, "It's Not a Lie if You Believe it:" Tax Shelters and the Economic Substance Doctrine, 58 Fla. L. Rev. 665, 711 (2006).

When encumbered property is sold or otherwise disposed of and the purchaser assumes the mortgage, the associated extinguishment of the mortgagor's obligation to repay is accounted for in the computation of the amount realized. Because no difference between recourse and nonrecourse obligations is recognized in calculating basis, Crane teaches that the Commissioner may ignore the nonrecourse nature of the obligation in determining the amount realized upon disposition of the encumbered property. He thus may include in the amount realized the amount of the nonrecourse mortgage assumed by the purchaser.[101]

The rationale for this treatment is that the original inclusion of the amount of the mortgage in basis rested on the assumption that the mortgagor incurred an obligation to repay. Moreover, this treatment balances out the fact that the mortgagor originally received the proceeds of the nonrecourse loan tax-free on the same assumption. Unless the outstanding amount of the mortgage is deemed to be realized, the mortgagor effectively will have received untaxed income at the time the loan was extended, and it will have received an unwarranted increase in the basis of his property. Hence:

> [T]he mortgagor received the loan proceeds tax-free and included them in his basis on the understanding that he had an obligation to repay the full amount. When the obligation is canceled [because the mortgagor no longer owns the property], the mortgagor is relieved of his responsibility to repay the sum he originally received and thus realizes value to that extent within the meaning of § 1001(b). From the mortgagor's point of view, when his obligation is assumed by a third party who purchases the encumbered property, it is as if the mortgagor first had been paid with cash borrowed by the third party from the mortgagee on a nonrecourse basis, and then had used the cash to satisfy his obligation to the mortgagee.[102]

[iv]   Non–Cash Sales and Exchanges

The taxpayer's amount realized for any property includes, in addition to any cash and debt relief received in exchange for the property, the value of any property and/or services received in exchange for the property.[103] The difficulty in determining the taxpayer's amount realized when that amount consists of something other than cash and debt relief lies in determining the value of the property or services received. Assuming the exchange is made at arm's length, it is reasonable to assume the properties exchanged are of equal value, so that if either property is readily subject to valuation, each person's amount realized can be easily arrived at by reference to the property that is subject to

---

101. Commissioner v. Tufts, 461 U.S. 300, 308–309, 103 S.Ct. 1826, 1832, 75 L.Ed.2d 863 (1983) (citations omitted).

102. Commissioner v. Tufts, 461 U.S. 300, 312, 103 S.Ct. 1826, 1834, 75 L.Ed.2d 863 (1983) (citations omitted).

103. See International Freighting Corp. v. Commissioner, 135 F.2d 310 (2d Cir. 1943); Treas. Reg. § 1.83–5(b); Riley v. Commissioner, 328 F.2d 428 (5th Cir. 1964); Rev. Rul. 69–181, 1969–1 C.B. 196.

valuation.[104] This rule of Philadelphia Park Amusement Co. v. United States[105] was cited favorably by the Supreme Court in United States v. Davis,[106] in connection with determining the purchaser's basis in a transaction such as the one described heretofore. In that case, Davis, pursuant to a divorce settlement,[107] transferred stock worth approximately $70,000 to his wife in satisfaction of her inchoate property rights against him. The Court set forth its analysis clearly and succinctly:

> The 'amount realized' is ... defined as 'the sum of any money received plus the fair market value of the property (other than money) received. In the instant case the 'property received' was the release of the wife's inchoate marital rights. The Court of Claims, following the Court of Appeals for the Sixth Circuit, found that there was no way to compute the fair market value of these marital rights and that it was thus impossible to determine the taxable gain realized by the taxpayer. We believe this conclusion was erroneous.

> It must be assumed, we think, that the parties acted at arms-length and that they judged the marital rights to be equal in value to the property for which they were exchanged. There was no evidence to the contrary here. Absent a readily ascertainable value it is accepted practice where property is exchanged to hold ... that the values 'of the two properties exchanged in an arms-length transaction are either equal in fact or are presumed to be equal.'[108]

The same principle holds true if property is transferred in satisfaction of other kinds of obligations, or if transferred as compensation.[109] In either case, and in any taxable arm's length exchange, the transferor's amount realized is presumed to be the value of the property transferred.

If neither property involved in a taxable exchange is easily subject to valuation, though, problems may arise. Taxpayers may seek to avoid tax liability by understating the value of both of the properties exchanged, thereby enabling both parties to under-report their amount realized and their gain by the same amount. In such cases, the IRS can require the taxpayers to provide adequate proof of proper valuation.

[v] Part Sale Part Gift Transactions

So far, it has been assumed that any exchange is either an arm's length taxable sale or exchange, or a nontaxable, donative transfer; the difference between the two types of transfers is not always clear. In some

---

104. Philadelphia Park Amusement Co. v. United States, 130 Ct.Cl. 166, 126 F.Supp. 184 (1954).

105. 130 Ct.Cl. 166, 126 F.Supp. 184 (1954).

106. 370 U.S. 65, 82 S.Ct. 1190, 8 L.Ed.2d 335 (1962).

107. *Nota bene:* Today, this transaction would now be governed by § 1041, which provides that no gain or loss is recognized on transfers between spouses or incident to divorce. For a complete discussion of § 1041, see § 3.07.

108. United States v. Davis, 370 U.S. 65, 72–73, 82 S.Ct. 1190, 8 L.Ed.2d 335 (1962) (citations omitted).

109. See International Freighting Corp. v. Commissioner, 135 F.2d 310 (2d Cir. 1943).

cases, a taxpayer may transfer property partly as a gift, but also partly for consideration.

An example of such a case is Diedrich v. Commissioner.[110] In that case, taxpayers, Victor and Frances Diedrich, transferred to their children stock worth approximately $300,000. The taxpayers had been informed they would incur gift tax of about $70,000 on that transfer; however, while they were happy to part with the stock, they had no desire to part with any cash or other property. As a result, the Diedrichs transferred the stock to their children on the condition that the children pay the resulting gift taxes for which the parents would be liable.

The Diedrichs contended they had made a net gift equal to the excess of the value of the stock (about $300,000) over the amount of their personal liability that the children agreed to pay (that is, the amount of gift tax due to the federal government on account of the gift). Ultimately the gift tax due from the Diedrichs and paid by the children was about $60,000. This amount was less than the $70,000 that would have otherwise been due on a gift of $300,000 because the amount of the gift was not the full $300,000 value of the stock, but, instead it was only the net of the value of the stock less the amount of the liability the children assumed. As a result, according to the Diedrichs, they had merely made a net gift to their children of $240,000 ($300,000 worth of stock less the $60,000 gift tax debt assumed).

Since the making of a gift is not a realization event, the Diedrichs claimed that any gift tax liability paid by their children were not taxable; i.e., the Diedrichs' claimed there were no income tax consequences because the transfer was not a realization event. The IRS did not agree with this conclusion.

The Service noted that the Diedrichs had transferred to their children stock with a basis of approximately $50,000, and that while they characterized the transfer as a gift, it was clear that under the principles of Crane[111] and Old Colony,[112] the children's payment of their parents' $60,000 gift tax liability was an economic benefit to the parents and thus an "amount realized" to the parents. Since the parents transferred property with a basis of $50,000 and had an amount realized of $60,000, they had a taxable gain regardless of how they might seek to characterize the transaction.

The Court, agreed with the Service, and it concluded that the transfer should be "treated as if the donor sells the property to the donee for less than the fair market value. The 'sale' price is the amount necessary to discharge the gift tax indebtedness; the balance of the value of the transferred property is treated as a gift." [113]

110. 457 U.S. 191, 102 S.Ct. 2414, 72 L.Ed.2d 777 (1982). See also Stephen B. Cohen, Apportioning Basis: Partial Sales, Bargain Sales and the Realization Principle, 34 San Diego L. Rev. 1693, 1717 (1997).

111. Crane v. Commissioner, 331 U.S. 1, 67 S.Ct. 1047, 91 L.Ed. 1301 (1947).

112. Old Colony Trust Co. v. Commissioner, 279 U.S. 716, 49 S.Ct. 499, 73 L.Ed. 918 (1929).

113. Diedrich v. Commissioner, 457 U.S. 191, 198–199, 102 S.Ct. 2414, 2419, 72 L.Ed.2d 777 (1982).

After determining that the transfer of property in exchange for the children's agreement to pay the Diedrichs' personal tax liability was a realization event, and that the Diedrichs' amount realized was equal to the amount of the liability assumed ($60,000), the Court next determined: "the gain thus derived by the donor is the amount of the gift tax liability less the donor's adjusted basis in the entire property. Accordingly, income is realized to the extent that the gift tax exceeds the donor's adjusted basis in the property."[114]

The Court's determination of the transferor's basis, and ultimate gain realized, was in accord with Treasury regulation section 1.1001–1(e), which makes it clear that gain is realized to the transferee only if, and to the extent that, the transferor's amount realized (here, the gift tax paid) exceeds her basis in the entire property transferred. It appears, though, that this result may actually shortchange the IRS.

If the Diedrichs had sold stock in order to pay the gift tax themselves and then had given the balance of the stock to their children, they would have ended up selling approximately 1/5 of their stock ($60,000 of $300,000). The Diedrichs basis in the stock sold would have been 1/5 of their total basis in their stock; that would be $10,000 (1/5 of $50,000). The Deidrichs' gain would be $50,000 ($60,000–$10,000), rather than only the $10,000 of gain they were ultimately taxed on by the Service.

Similarly, if the Court had treated the transfer to the children as a sale by the parents of 1/5 of the stock (worth $60,000, with a basis of $10,000) in exchange for the children's payment of the Diedrich's $60,000 gift tax obligation, and a gift of 80% of the stock (worth $240,000 with a basis of $40,000), the gain realized would increase from $10,000 to $50,000.

By allowing the transferors to use their entire basis to offset their amount realized, rather than only a portion of that basis, the Service provides a clear benefit to the transferor in a net-gift transaction. As a matter of tax planning, making a conditional gift can provide significantly improved results over selling the stock and paying the tax.

The regulations provide that the purchaser/donee in a part gift, part sale transaction takes a basis in the transferred property equal to the greater of either the transferor's basis or the donee's cost.[115]

The result for both the transferor and the transferee in these transactions is that the entire transaction is treated either entirely as a sale or entirely as a gift. If the amount paid (or the liability assumed) by the donee exceeds the donor's basis in the property transferred, then the donor is treated as if she has *sold* the entire property for an amount equal to the amount paid. Accordingly, the donor pays tax only on the excess of her amount realized over her basis in the entire property. In that case, the donee is treated as if she has *purchased* the entire

114. Diedrich v. Commissioner, 457 U.S. 191, 199, 102 S.Ct. 2414, 2419, 72 L.Ed.2d 777 (1982).

115. Treas. Reg. § 1.1015–4.

property for an amount equal to the amount paid, because that is the amount of her "cost" basis in the entire property.

On the other hand, if the donor's amount realized is less than her basis in the entire property, she realizes no gain, so that she is treated exactly the same as the donor in any pure gift situation (no gain or loss realized). Similarly, if the donor's amount realized (the donee's cost) is less than the donor's basis, then the regulations provide that the donee takes a basis equal to that of the donor, which means that from the donee's perspective as well, the transaction is treated the same as any other gift (with a carryover basis).[116]

Thus, while these transactions are often referred to as "part-gift, part-sale," for income tax purposes they are always treated either as *exclusively* a sale (if the amount paid exceeds the donor's basis) or *exclusively* as a gift (if the amount paid is less than the donor's basis).[117]

§ 7.04 REALIZATION AND INCOME FROM PROPERTY

[1] OVERVIEW

Many people earn income by working, and some may simply inherit money, but a great deal of income is the result of returns on invested capital. One of the major problems running throughout the field of federal income taxation is the problem of when to treat investment returns as taxable income; when to not tax them at all; and when to treat them as a mere return of invested capital. This sounds like a simple problem, but it is actually an extraordinarily complex set of issues.

Questions of when to tax income from property arise primarily because of the realization requirement. If each taxpayer was simply taxed annually on their combined consumption during the year plus (or minus) the change in their net worth between the beginning and end of the year, none of these timing issues would arise. Whether investment returns took the form of appreciation, interest, rents, insurance payments, capital gains or anything else would be of no consequence. All that would matter would be the difference between the taxpayer's net worth at the beginning of the year and the end of the year. This is not to suggest that such a system would be simple. Issues of valuation, administrability, and fairness would arise constantly. It is only to suggest that, unlike in our current federal income tax system, the issues would not be ones of timing.

Because our federal income tax system is based on the realization principle, however, timing issues arise constantly. The realization principle means, basically, that a person is not taxed until and unless she gets something she did not have before. The realization principal is applicable

116. Treas. Reg. § 1.1015–4(a).   **117.** Id.

to income for services and other sources as well as income from capital, but it plays an incredibly important role in the taxation of income from capital. Accordingly, it is discussed at length here.

The most significant single aspect of the realization requirement is that the person who holds property that appreciates pays no tax on that appreciation until there is some realization event. This simple rule has tremendous economic implications as well as tremendous implications for the structure of the federal income tax.

Consider the following example: Taxpayer T pays $100,000 for land in January. By the end of the year, the land is worth $1,100,000. Clearly T is richer. In economic terms he has $1,000,000 of income from this investment, because his net worth has increased by that amount. Under our federal income tax system, though, T will pay no tax until or unless there is some "realization event"—basically, until or unless he gets something different from the original land. If he leases out the land, he will have taxable income equal to the rents collected, but if he simply continues to hold the land for investment, he will have no taxable income at all, regardless of how valuable the land becomes. Instead, T will pay tax on his gain only when he sells or exchanges the land. Indeed, if T never sells the land but instead holds until he dies and leaves it to his heirs, that $1,000,000 gain will *never* be taxed![1]

To see the enormous potential benefits of deferral of taxation until realization, assume that T holds the land for 40 years prior to selling. For simplicity, assume: (1) that the land does not further appreciate during the remaining 39 years, (2) the interest rate remains at 10% during the entire time, and (3) T's tax rate remains at 40% the entire time.[2]

When T sells the land at the end of 40 years, he will be taxed on his $1,000,000 gain, and will be required to pay tax of $400,000. If T were taxed on his economic income (the increase in value of his land) at the end of year one (when his net worth increased) as opposed to year 40 (when there is a realization event), he would still owe the same tax of $400,000. The only difference between the two systems (realization versus taxation of economic income as it accrues) is in the timing of taxation.

Because of the time value of money, timing is important. Again, to keep things simple, assume that T's only other asset is $400,000 in cash. If T were taxed in year one on his $1,000,000 of economic income, he would have nothing left (other than the land). If, instead, T can put off paying the tax for 40 years and keep his $400,000 invested at 10%, then by the time he sells the land and is required to pay the $400,000 in tax, his original $400,000 would have turned into more than $18 million!

§ 7.04

1. See § 1014.

2. None of these assumptions are necessary to establish the value of deferral; they are adopted as a matter of convenience.

Another way to view the economic benefit of deferral is to note that if T is allowed to defer taxation until realization (that is, in 40 years), he could fund that future tax liability by setting aside a mere $8,830 in year one, which would grow to $400,000 at the end of 40 years. The rest of his $400,000 (which he need not pay in current taxes because of the realization requirement) remains his to use as he sees fit.[3]

From the government's perspective, perhaps the most significant aspect of deferral is potential revenue that goes either uncollected or delayed (potentially for decades). Of course, the realization requirement has behavioral impacts, in addition to economic ones. One of these behavioral impacts is to encourage taxpayers to invest in assets that generate income primarily from appreciation (and the increase in value of which remains untaxed until sale). Another is to discourage taxpayers who hold appreciated assets from selling them, since that sale will generate current tax liability that could otherwise be deferred (or avoided altogether at death under section 1014).

While the realization requirement generally works in favor of taxpayers wishing to defer tax on appreciation, it can also work to the disadvantage of taxpayers. Most obviously disadvantaged is the taxpayer who invests in assets that decline in value and who is not permitted to deduct her loss until she sells them.

Additionally, application of the realization requirement may also result in imposition of taxation on the person who has a "realization event," even in the absence of any income in any meaningful sense of the word. To see how this can happen, consider the consequences if T purchases shares of stock for $100,000. Assume that at some time after T's purchase, the stock pays a $5,000 dividend, and after payment of the dividend the stock is worth $95,000. In other words, T has received cash, but his net worth is unchanged from the time of his investment. In all likelihood, T will be taxed on that amount (although at a reduced rate of 15%).[4] Indeed, T will likely be taxed on the dividend even if his original $100,000 investment is worth substantially *less* than it was at the time he purchased it. It is the realization event, rather than an increase in net worth, that triggers taxation.

This all may seem simple, but it also means that one investor who holds onto his original investment which pays no dividends may actually

---

3. Does the "simplifying" assumption that the land retains its $1,100,000 value for 40 years after appreciating by $1,000,000 in year one in fact somehow exaggerates the results? It does not. Consider that if the land continued to increase in value by 10% each year beginning in year two, then T would have additional income (from an economic perspective) each year. That income, as the initial appreciation, would go untaxed until sale, resulting in more deferred taxation and more savings for T. If T's land instead generated *current* taxable income after year one, perhaps be-

cause T leased out the more valuable land for an annual rent of $110,000 (10% of its $1,100,000 value), that also would not change the implications of deferral of taxation on the initial appreciation. T might then be taxed at the 40% rate on his $110,000 current income each year, but he would nonetheless still continue to avoid tax on the appreciation until sale.

4. See §§ 316, 301 (This result assumes sufficient current or accumulated earnings and profits.)

make millions in appreciation and defer paying tax. Alternatively, another who receives dividends on a losing investment may pay significant taxes currently despite his loss.

Why is realization so important? One argument is simply one of convenience—it would be an administrative nightmare for every taxpayer to attempt to annually appraise their assets.

Of course, from a wherewithal to pay perspective, absent a realization event, it is unlikely most taxpayers would have the funds available to pay any amount of tax due. Some tax experts respond to this assertion by pointing out the fact that most people with substantial appreciated investments also have substantial liquid assets that could be used to pay tax. These same tax experts also explain that if taxpayers holding appreciated assets do not have cash on hand to pay the tax, then at least if the assets are publicly traded securities it is easy enough to sell some of the securities to pay the tax. If the appreciation is in an illiquid asset such as real estate, the taxpayer can usually borrow against the property to pay the tax.

Some suggest that taxation awaits realization because when our federal income tax system was first constructed by Congress and the courts, they simply were not alert to either the economic realities or the potential stakes. Others suggest that the realization requirement is constitutionally mandated.

[2]   IS THERE A REALIZATION EVENT?

Put simply, if the taxpayer gets something, anything, different from what she had before, there is a realization event.

In the vast majority of cases, determining whether there has been a realization event is fairly straightforward. It matters not whether the taxpayer's receipt takes the form of money, property, services, the temporary use of money or property, the cancellation of the taxpayer's debt, the making of a payment on the taxpayer's behalf, or any other benefit to the taxpayer. So long as the taxpayer receives *something, anything,* she did not already have, there is a realization event. Of course, in the tax law, one can never simply leave anything put quite so simply.

In general, income must be realized before it is taxed. While this is a fundamental concept of federal income taxation, neither Congress nor the courts have developed or marked the boundaries of the realization requirement. The amorphous state of the law in this area may be attributed, at least in part, to the statutory rules concerning the computation of gain or loss upon the sale or other disposition of property. These rules virtually eliminate the need to consider the contours of the realization requirement. Moreover, Congress has not attempted to tax the mere appreciation in value of property held by the taxpayer.

In Helvering v. Horst[5] the Supreme Court said that the "realiza-

5.   311 U.S. 112, 61 S.Ct. 144, 85 L.Ed. 75 (1940).

tion" requirement is based upon "administrative convenience."[6] Even so, this is not to say that the realization requirement lacks an operative meaning as a limitation on the income concept in federal tax law. It has relevance in a myriad of areas. For example, it has emerged in transactions involving the disposition of property when the amount received was incapable of being valued or determined. In such a circumstance taxation was postponed until final disposition[7] unless apportionment was possible, such as on the sale of parcels of subdivided land.[8] Further, the realization requirement has provided Congress with a policy rationale for tax legislation. Thus, under section 305 of the Code the receipt of a stock dividend is not regarded as income but simply a division of the prior investment represented by the corporate stock.

Also related to the realization requirement is the imputed income that arises when, for example, individuals prepare their own income tax returns or occupy their own residences rent free. Congress has not attempted to tax imputed income from the use of taxpayers' efforts or the use of their own property. Moreover, the Service, mainly for reasons of equity and administrative convenience, has not argued that such benefits constitute income within the broad meaning of section 61(a).

Conversely, if the taxpayer has derived economic benefit from a transaction in a commercial context, the courts have held that there is realization. In Dean v. Commissioner[9] the taxpayer and his wife were the sole shareholders in an investment company. Upon the insistence of a bank, a creditor of the corporation, the family residence was transferred to the corporation. The court upheld the Commissioner's treatment of the rental value of the house as additional income to the taxpayer after the transfer, presumably as a dividend or as compensation for services. No attempt was made to treat the rental value of the house as income prior to the transfer.

Taxing imputed income from a taxpayer's use of her own property is not unheard of in tax systems of other countries. Moreover, some economists have suggested the availability of such income as a means of expanding the base of the U.S. income tax. Nevertheless there is no requirement to include such imputed income in gross income for federal income tax purposes. The failure to include such income is probably a self-imposed limitation of the government, perhaps based upon political or administrative, rather than upon legal[10] or economic, considerations.

---

6. See Deborah H. Schenk, A Positive Account of the Realization Rule, 57 Tax L. Rev. 355 (2004).

7. See, e.g., Burnet v. Logan, 283 U.S. 404, 51 S.Ct. 550, 75 L.Ed. 1143 (1931).

8. See Inaja Land Co. v. Commissioner, 9 T.C. 727 (1947), acq., 1948–1 C.B. 2.

9. 187 F.2d 1019 (3d Cir. 1951).

10. In dictum, the Supreme Court observed that rental income imputed from the use of real property would not withstand attack on constitutional grounds because it did not constitute income within the meaning of the sixteenth amendment. Helvering v. Independent Life Ins. Co., 292 U.S. 371, 54 S.Ct. 758, 78 L.Ed. 1311 (1934). See also the comment in Morris v. Commissioner, 9 B.T.A. 1273 (1928), that farm products consumed by a farmer and his family were comparable to the rental value of a private residence and neither were intended to be regarded as income by Congress.

[3] CONTINUING IMPORTANCE OF THE REALIZATION RE-QUIREMENT

There are a few provisions in the Code, such as the original issue discount rules[11] and the mark to market rules,[12] that provide for taxation even absent a "realization event," but such provisions are rare. None of these provisions have been successfully challenged at any level, and most people now believe that the realization requirement, although continuing to be a very important aspect of the tax system, is a matter of common law and codification, and it is not constitutionally mandated.

[4] TAXATION AND BASIS

It is worth noting that the issues surrounding most realization cases, are basically issues of timing rather than amounts of income.[13] If T receives something (additional shares of stock, a building, or anything else) and is taxed at the time of receipt, T will have a basis in that asset equal to the amount included in income on receipt.[14]

As a result, assume that T receives property worth $100,000 and that the receipt is a "realization event" resulting in T being required to include that $100,000 in income. T will also take a basis in that asset of $100,000. If the asset maintains its value and T later sells it for $100,000, T's amount realized and basis will both be $100,000, and T will recognize no gain or loss at the time of the sale or exchange.[15]

On the other hand, if T receives property worth $100,000 in a transaction that is not considered a realization event, T will pay no tax on receipt, and T's basis in the property received will be zero.[16] As a result, if T later sells the property for $100,000, she will have a taxable gain of $100,000 at that time.

[5] TAXATION OF PROPERTY TRANSFERS DURING MAR-RIAGE OR PURSUANT TO DIVORCE

Issues surrounding the taxation of property during marriage or pursuant to divorce are discussed in detail in § 3.07.

11. See § 1272 et. seq. For a discussion of the original issue discount rules, see § 8.02[4].

12. See § 1256. For a discussion of the mark to mark rules, see Stanley I. Langbein, Fed. Inc. Tax'n Banks & Financial Inst. ¶ 7.05, STRADDLES AND SECTION 1256 CONTRACTS (WG & L 2007).

13. This is true unless the taxpayer dies prior to selling the property in question and her heirs take a "stepped-up" basis under § 1014, eliminating permanently the taxation on any appreciation. For a discussion of § 1014, see § 7.03[2][g].

14. See discussion of tax cost basis at § 7.04[1][a][iii].

15. See § 1001(a).

16. See e.g., § 1019. Under § 307, the shareholders basis in shares received as part of a tax-free stock distribution will not be zero, because some basis will be allocated away from other shares and onto the newly received shares. Nonetheless, the shareholder's total aggregate basis in all her stock will remain the same.

[6]   GIFTS AND BEQUESTS

[a]   In General

Gifts and bequests are not generally taxable to the *recipient* for federal income tax purposes.[17] Some have suggested that gifts nonetheless ought to be treated as realization events, and thus taxable transactions, to the *transferor*. The argument is that if T purchases property for $50,000, the property becomes worth $90,000, and T transfers it to her child, T has realized from the transfer a $90,000 benefit, consisting of her use of the property to enrich her child by that $90,000. It is well established, though, that gifts and bequests are not realizing events and therefore do not give rise to income to the transferor. Indeed, it appears that the very definition, for tax purposes, of a gift precludes the possibility that giving the gift can be a realization event. As discussed at § 3.02[2], a transfer is not a gift for tax purposes unless made out of "detached and disinterested generosity." If a transfer is made as compensation for, or in exchange for, any past, present or future benefit to the donor, if it is not a gift. As a result, if the transfer is a gift, the conclusion that the transferor receives, or realizes, nothing is inevitable.

[b]   Part Gift Part Sale

The Supreme Court has held that where a donor gives a gift on the condition that the donee pay the gift tax (or any other obligation or potential obligation of the donor), a realizing event—namely a sale—may have occurred.[18] Basically, if the transferor's amount realized exceeds her basis in the property transferred, the transaction is treated as a sale or exchange. If, however, the donor's amount realized is less than her basis in the property transferred, the transaction is treated as entirely a nonrealization event.

The Tax Court has also ruled that a charitable contribution of property encumbered by non-recourse indebtedness may also be a sale that can give rise to a taxable gain.[19]

[c]   Other Non-Gift "Transfers" and "Receipts"

[i]   Pledging Property as Security for Loans

As explained in Chapter 2, a taxpayer who borrows money has no taxable income as a result of that borrowing because while the loan provides her with cash, she simultaneously incurs an obligation to return that cash and appropriate interest (payment for the temporary use of the money). As a result, she has no accession to wealth, and her net worth

---

17. § 102(a).

18. See Diedrich v. Commissioner, 457 U.S. 191, 102 S.Ct. 2414, 72 L.Ed.2d 777 (1982), discussed heretofore at § 7.03[3][d][v]. See also Stephen B. Cohen, Apportioning Basis: Partial Sales, Bargain Sales and the Realization Principle, 34 San Diego L. Rev. 1693, 1717 (1997).

19. Guest v. Commissioner, 77 T.C. 9 (1981). See also R. Robert Woodburn, Jr., Handling Charitable Gifts of Debt–Encumbered Property, 21 Est. Plan. 287, 295 (1994).

remains the same. The fact that a taxpayer pledges property as security for a loan has no impact on whether the loan itself represents income.

Despite the fact that merely borrowing money, and simultaneously incurring an obligation to repay the same amount does not result in income, a somewhat different issue may be raised when the loan is nonrecourse. If a loan is "nonrecourse," the borrower has no personal liability to repay the entire loan. Instead, if the borrower defaults on the payment of either principal or interest due on the loan, the lender's only legal option is to foreclose on the property pledged to secure the loan.

The tax effect of this limitation was at issue in Woodsam Associates, Inc. v. Commissioner;[20] in that case, the taxpayer held property with a cost basis of approximately $300,000. The property was worth substantially in excess of that amount. However, at some point the taxpayer took out a $400,000 nonrecourse loan, pledging the property as the only security for the debt. As soon as these events occurred, the taxpayer, who had paid $300,000 for the property, was in receipt of $400,000; she had no personal liability to repay that $400,000. While the lender might foreclose on the property if the taxpayer failed to make payments on the loan, even such a foreclosure would leave the taxpayer with a profit of $100,000 on the property. Given that the taxpayer had a guaranteed profit and that she had the cash in hand, the court was asked to determine whether she had a realized gain at such time.

The court held that the taxpayer's nonrecourse borrowing even of an amount in excess of her basis in the pledged property did not result in taxable gain. Since that time, the law has appeared well-established and has not been challenged, but it is nonetheless worth noting exactly how the court arrived at its conclusion. The Woodsam court stated that the taxpayer:

> [N]ever 'disposed' of the property to create a taxable event which [section 1001] makes a condition precedent to the taxation of gain. 'Disposition' ... is the 'getting rid, or making over, of anything; relinquishment' ..... Nothing of that nature was done here by the mere execution of the second consolidated mortgage; [the taxpayer] was the owner of this property in the same sense after the execution of this mortgage that she was before ..... Realization of gain was, therefore, postponed for taxation until there was a final disposition of the property at the time of the foreclosure sale.[21]

The court's reasoning is interesting primarily because it appears to be backwards. Rather than determining whether the taxpayer's acquisition of cash subject only to a nonrecourse debt was a realization event that might generate taxable income, the court determined first that the

---

20. 198 F.2d 357 (2d Cir. 1952). See also Patricia A. Cain, From Crane to Tufts: In Search of a Rationale for the Taxation of Nonrecourse Mortgagors, 11 Hofstra L. Rev. 1, 61 (1982); Deborah L. Paul, Another Uneasy Compromise: The Treatment of Hedging in a Realization Income Tax, 3 Fla. Tax Rev. 1, 50 (1996).

21. Woodsam Associates, Inc. v. Commissioner, 198 F.2d 357, 359 (2d Cir. 1952).

taxpayer had not disposed of her property and from that concluded her receipt of the cash could not have been a taxable realization event.

While a realization event is a prerequisite to taxation, a complete disposition of property has never been thought to be a prerequisite to realization. True, section 1001 talks only about gain from the sale or other disposition of property, but if there was a realization event, some or all of the taxpayer's amount realized might be taxable under any of several different sections of the Code, including section 61, which defines gross income. Certainly the landlord who holds property and receives rent has not disposed of her property, but while that ensures section 1001 does not apply, it does not permit her to exclude from gross income the rents she receives.[22]

In fact, it is likely that the Woodsam court reasoned backwards because it actually reached its conclusion backwards, starting with its desired end result and finding its way back to its justification. The reason for this lies in the rather unusual factual underpinnings of the case. While one would assume that it is the IRS that would be the party arguing there had been a "realization event," in fact it was the taxpayer who was making that argument. This was not because the taxpayer was patriotic and wanted to pay her fair share of tax, but the sought-after realization event occasioned by the nonrecourse borrowing (had the court found that there was one) would have occurred several years prior to the case.

While the taxpayer had not reported any of the loan proceeds as income at the time she took out the nonrecourse loans in excess of her basis in the property, she knew that by the time the case arose, the statute of limitations on the year in which the borrowing had occurred had already run. She was arguing that she should have been taxed several years ago, but that she had improperly failed to pay the tax due at that time, and the IRS had improperly failed to ask her to pay in time. In reality, the taxpayer was arguing that she should have been taxed in that earlier year because that result would give her a higher basis in the later year, when she disposed of the property. That higher basis would in turn result in substantially less tax due in the year for which the statute of limitations was still open.

Because the court likely did not fully appreciate the taxpayer's stance, and because the IRS was arguing against the finding of a realization event, the court ruled that no realization was occasioned by the nonrecourse borrowing. The Woodsam holding has been and continues to be universally accepted as an accurate description of the current law.

[ii] Employer/Employee Transfers

Section 102(c) makes it clear that transfers from an employer to an employee are not gifts, but are taxable income to the employee. For the

---

22. See § 61(a)(5).

same reasons, International Freighting Corporation v. Commissioner[23] makes it clear that when the employer transfers property to an employee, that transfer is a realization event for the employer. Whether the transfer is part of a wage package or is a bonus not required to be paid pursuant to contract, the transfer by the employer is in exchange for services rendered or to be rendered, and the value of those services is the "amount" realized by the employer.[24]

[iii] Abandonment

Abandonment of property, although not a sale or exchange, is a realization event.[25] Since the amount realized on abandonment is generally zero, the treatment of abandonment as a realization event typically inures to the benefit of the taxpayer, who may be allowed a deduction equal to her basis in the abandoned property. As a result, there may be disputes between the taxpayer and the IRS with respect to whether an abandonment has actually transpired. Once that potential factual dispute is resolved, however, there is no dispute that an abandonment is a realization event.[26]

[iv] Transfer of Property Subject to Debt

As discussed above at § 7.03[3][c], the surrender of property subject to mortgage indebtedness in exchange for extinguishment of the indebtedness is a realization event, with the mortgage indebtedness constituting the amount realized, whether the indebtedness was with personal liability.[27]

[7] INCOME VERSUS RETURN OF CAPITAL

While a realization event presents a proper *time* to tax income, it does not answer the questions of whether the taxpayer actually *has* any income to tax, and if so, *how much* of that income ought to be taxed at the time of each realization event. Instead, the realization requirement essentially poses two distinct, but related, questions that must be answered before one can know the tax consequences of any investment: (1)

23. 135 F.2d 310 (2d Cir. 1943).

24. Dealing with determination of the amount realized, since the employer/employee relationship is one at arm's length, the best determinant of the value of services received or to be received by the employer for the bonus paid is the value of the property transferred at the time of the transfer.

25. Treas. Reg. § 1.165–2(b). See also Gerald V. Thomas II, The Art Of Abandoning Securities and Taking an Ordinary Loss, 104 JTAX 22 (2006); Joseph A. Rieser, Jr., Leo N. Hitt, and Jeffrey G. Aromatorio, Obtaining an Abandonment or Worthlessness Deduction for a Partnership Interest, 15 JPTAX 42 (1998).

26. See A.E. Staley Mfg. Co. and Subsidiaries v. Commissioner, 119 F.3d 482

(7th Cir. 1997); Standley v. Commissioner, 99 T.C. 259 (1992), aff'd, 24 F.3d 249 (9th Cir. 1994); Echols v. Commissioner, 950 F.2d 209 (5th Cir. 1991); CRST, Inc. v. Commissioner, 909 F.2d 1146 (8th Cir. 1990); Capital Blue Cross v. Commissioner, 431 F.3d 117 (3d Cir. 2005); Middleton v. Commissioner, 693 F.2d 124 (11th Cir. 1982); El Paso Co. v. United States, 694 F.2d 703 (Fed. Cir. 1982); Duffy v. United States, 231 Ct.Cl. 679, 690 F.2d 889 (1982).

27. Parker v. Delaney, 186 F.2d 455 (1st Cir.1950), cert. denied 341 U.S. 926, 71 S.Ct. 797, 95 L.Ed. 1357 (1951). See also Diane M. Anderson, Federal Income Tax Treatment of Nonrecourse Debt, 82 Colum. L. Rev. 1498, 1530 (1982).

is there a realization event; and (2) if so, what part of what the taxpayer realizes should be treated as gain, as opposed to return of capital. In addition, and as mentioned in the introduction of this chapter, these two fundamental questions are later supplemented by other issues and concerns that have led Congress and the IRS to allow certain gains to go untaxed regardless of a realization event, and to tax some gains at reduced rates.[28]

When there is a realization event, on what amount is the taxpayer to be taxed? The answer to this question corresponds inversely to the answer of a related question. What part should be treated as a return of the taxpayer's original invested capital?

As demonstrated in Chapter 2, if the realization event does not involve the disposition of property, but is the receipt of money, property, or services in exchange for the performance of services (or as treasure trove or some other enrichment due to anything other than the disposition of property), then the entire amount received is generally gross income. This is because whether the receipt is by chance (e.g., treasure trove) or in exchange for services, the entire amount received represents taxable income.[29]

Where the realization event involves the receipt of money or other things of value in exchange for property, however, the results change. The taxpayer ultimately should be (and is) taxed only on that portion of her amount realized that represents "profit," and not on that part that represents a mere return of her own invested capital.[30]

As discussed in the introduction to this chapter, the basic rule is set forth in section 1001, which provides, in part, that the "gain from the sale or other disposition of property shall be the excess of the amount realized therefrom over the adjusted basis ... and the loss shall be the excess of the adjusted basis ... over the amount realized."[31]

Assume that taxpayer T purchases some land for $200,000 cash on January 1, year one, simply holds it for one year (without either making or receiving any payments of any kind with respect to the land), and then sells her entire interest for $200,000 on January 1, year two. Upon the sale in year two, T's amount realized is $200,000. Since this equals her cost basis for the property, she has an "amount realized," but no "gain" realized, and thus no income.[32] Instead, this realization event is simply a "return of capital." T is merely getting back her own invested capital. T has no profit, no income, and no tax liability.

---

28. For a complete discussion of capital gains, see Chapter 10, *Capital Gains and Losses*.

29. Some have argued that, theoretically, not all amounts received for services ought to be included in income because the taxpayer should have a "basis" in her "human capital," so that some of her receipts for services represent a return of capital rather than profit. This argument has never progressed beyond the theory stage. See

Louis Kaplow, Human Capital Under an Ideal Income Tax, 80 VA. L. Rev. 1477, 1497 (1994). See also Louis Kaplow, Response: The Income Tax Versus the Consumption Tax and the Tax Treatment of Human Capital, 51 Tax L. Rev. 35 (1995).

30. § 1001(a).

31. § 1001(a).

32. See § 1001(a).

Obviously, if T sells her entire interest in the land in year two for $222,000 rather than $200,000, $200,000 of her $220,000 amount realized represents a recovery of her original investment (return of capital) and is not taxable, while the remaining $20,000 represents taxable gain, or profit.[33]

On these facts, T's sale of the property in year two does not appear to be her only realization event. In year one she receives land worth $200,000 in exchange for $200,000 cash. Some (including the Supreme Court) have in fact suggested that a cash purchase is *not* a "realization event."[34]

The term "return of capital" does not actually appear in the Code, but it is nonetheless an important concept. As the example demonstrates, an amount is a return of capital if it represents a mere return to the taxpayer of her investment. Because a return of capital merely gives back to the taxpayer what she has invested, it does not represent any kind of profit or gain, and it is not taxed. Perhaps the most easily understood example is the taxpayer who deposits $100 in a bank account and later withdraws that $100. Unlike any interest she may receive, her withdrawal of her invested capital (the $100) is not taxable. Similarly, if the taxpayer invests $100 in a bank account and withdraws $85 of that amount, the $85 is a return of her capital, and she has remaining an investment of $15.

It is important to understand that since a return of capital means the taxpayer is getting back some or all of her investment, after she has received that (non-taxed) return of capital, the amount she has invested (and her basis in the investment) has been reduced by the amount of capital "returned." Thus, if T puts $100 in the bank and subsequently withdraws $85, that $85 represents a return of capital and is not taxed; but thereafter T has only $15 invested in her account. Again, although the return of capital is not taxed, it *does* reduce her basis in the account by the amount returned and not taxed, so that afterwards, T's basis in her bank account is only $15.

While the Code does not explicitly define "return of capital," it does frequently employ the concept. Several sections explain that amounts received by the taxpayer (as a result of investments) that are not taxed on receipt are to be applied against and reduce the taxpayer's adjusted basis in the investment from which the non-taxed payment comes.[35]

If the taxpayer pays money and *deducts* the amount paid, she has fully accounted for her invested capital by that deduction. The deduction

---

33. Id.

34. "When one buys property for cash, it might have been argued that in theory he too 'realizes' a gain upon the cash if the property received has a value greater than the cash; but that would have involved the premises that there had been an increase in the value of the cash, 'realized' by purchase, and that would have done great violence to our notions about money. Hence the doctrine that a cash purchase is always 'unrealized' gain." Elverson Corporation v. Helvering 122 F.2d 295, 297–298 (2d Cir. 1941). See also Palmer v. Commissioner, 302 U.S. 63, 68–69, 58 S.Ct. 67, 82 L.Ed. 50 (1937); Hunt v. Commissioner, 90 T.C. 1289, 1304–05 (1988); FSA 200013006.

35. §§ 301, 705(a)(2).

is premised on the assumption that the taxpayer has *parted* with the capital, and for tax purposes that capital is no longer treated as hers (if it were, she would not be permitted the deduction). As a result, if the taxpayer deducts an amount paid and later somehow gets back that amount, the receipt is not treated as a return of capital.

Chapter 8, *Timing Issues Surrounding Capital*, deals with situations where additional timing questions arise because either the taxpayer receives more than a single payment with respect to an asset, or because the asset is not completely disposed of in a single transaction.

§ 7.05 LUMP SUM PURCHASES

Where a taxpayer buys several different properties for a single lump-sum amount, the purchase price must be allocated in order to ascertain the basis of each individual asset.[1] This situation arises frequently upon the sale of an ongoing business, where the buyer and seller may agree on an overall price for the business as a whole, rather than for each particular asset.

If the buyer and seller were left unchecked in these kinds of cases, they would likely have very different views (for tax purposes) of how much of the overall purchase price was paid for each asset. The seller would likely report that most of the purchase price was received in exchange for those assets whose sale would generate the least tax liability for her (that is, capital assets). The buyer, on the other hand, would likely claim that the majority of her cost (and, as a result, the highest basis) went to the assets for which a high basis would provide *her* with the maximum tax benefits (depreciable property and/or inventory). The Service feared getting "whipsawed" and ultimately losing on both counts.

The Service responded to its initial fears of the taxpayers' taking inconsistent positions by simply requiring consistency—it allowed the buyer and seller to allocate amounts paid among the different assets and respected that allocation so long as the buyer and seller adopted consistent allocations. Ultimately, though, the IRS and Congress realized that requiring consistency was not enough. It was still possible for the buyer and seller to allocate disproportionate amounts of the sales price to assets for which a high amount realized for the seller combined with an inflated basis for the buyer worked well for both taxpayers but ultimately shortchanged the government.

Under current law, independent (and specifically detailed) appraisals are required on the sale of a going business.[2] In addition, in all cases that involve the simultaneous sale of several assets, the Service may reallocate the purchase price to prevent substantial tax avoidance.[3]

§ 7.05

1. Treas. Reg. § 1.61–6(a). § 1060.

2. See § 1060.

3. Rev. Rul. 77–168, 1977–1 C.B. 248; Rev. Rul. 77–413, 1977–2 C.B. 298.

[1] GOODWILL

The basis of goodwill is established either by showing that the goodwill was purchased as part of an ongoing business,[4] or by establishing that certain non-deductible expenditures were made to attempt to improve the prospects of the business.[5]

[2] STOCK, SECURITIES, AND MUTUAL FUND SHARES

Stock and securities are acquired or transferred in a variety of unique transactions that occasion the use of special rules for ascertaining basis. Substituted and carryover basis techniques are used in the corporate organization, reorganization and division areas.[6] A substituted basis is used in wash sale transactions.[7] A cost plus taxable income approach is used for stock transferred as compensation for services.[8]

Where a taxpayer has bought identical shares of stock at different times for different prices, a problem is presented where he sells some (but not all) of his holdings. The size of his gain or loss and its character of being held long-term or short-term may well depend on which of his identical shares he is deemed to have sold. The regulations provide that unless the taxpayer can in fact identify the particular shares sold, he will be deemed to have sold the shares he purchased earliest in time.[9] The regulations set forth steps the taxpayer can take to ensure that he can identify the particular shares he is selling, whether he holds the certificates himself or whether they are held by his broker.[10] Unless such steps are taken to identify the shares sold, the Service's "first-in first-out" rule will apply.

Similar problems are presented where the taxpayer has purchased shares of an open-end mutual fund at different times for different prices. A redemption or sale of some but not all of his holdings leads to questions of which shares were redeemed or sold. Here again there are two basic possibilities. If the taxpayer can in fact identify the actual mutual fund shares disposed of, then actual cost will be used as basis. If the shares, as will often be the case, have been left by the taxpayer in the custody of a transfer agent, then the taxpayer may elect to use an average cost approach to ascertain basis.[11]

[3] PURCHASE PRICE ADJUSTMENTS

Purchase prices for assets may in some cases be reduced through negotiations; should that happen, the cost basis of the property is reduced to the new lower price. Close questions can arise as to whether the whole transaction should be regarded as a reduction in purchase

4. Grace Brothers, Inc. v. Commissioner, 173 F.2d 170 (9th Cir.1949).

5. Cf. Cooperative Publishing Co. v. Commissioner, 115 F.2d 1017 (9th Cir. 1940) (dicta); cf. also Welch v. Helvering, 290 U.S. 111, 54 S.Ct. 8, 78 L.Ed. 212 (1933).

6. See §§ 358, 361.

7. § 1091.

8. § 83.

9. Reg. § 1.1012–1(c)(1).

10. Reg. § 1.1012–1(c)(2) and (3).

11. See Treas. Reg. § 1.1012–1(e).

price or rather a discharge of indebtedness of the buyer, resulting in immediate income.[12]

12. § 108 contains an exception to the taxation of cancellation of indebtedness income if it is the result of a reduction of the purchase price made by the seller to the buyer.

Chapter 8

TIMING ISSUES SURROUNDING CAPITAL

Table of Sections

---

§ 8.01 INTRODUCTION

One set of problems in taxation arises from the fact that numerous different investments involve more than a simple purchase followed only by a simple sale of the entire investment asset. The taxpayer may dispose of an asset over time rather than in a single realization event, either because she transfers less than the entire asset at once or, more frequently, because the asset wears out over time and its disposition is the result of its being used up rather than being transferred. Other times the taxpayer may dispose of the asset at one time, but she may receive some sort of payments or return with respect to the asset either prior to or after (or both) its complete disposition. In all of these cases, determining the extent to which the different amounts realized represent profit can be challenging.

It is clear that over the entire term of any investment, the taxpayer will have gross income to the extent of any gain,[1] but determining *which* parts of *which amounts realized* should be taxed as income and which parts should be treated as a nontaxable return of capital can be surprisingly complex.

The federal income tax system has devised numerous different ways to reach the proper tax result in these cases. Sometimes when a taxpayer receives more than a single payment with respect to an asset, she is allowed to exclude as nontaxable return of capital her earliest receipts; i.e., she may treat as nontaxable all amounts received until the total amounts received exceed her entire capital investment in the asset. Of course, thereafter she will be taxed in full on any additional amounts realized.[2]

Other times the taxpayer will be required to *include* in income her earliest receipts, and she will be allowed to exclude only her latest receipts.[3] Hence, the taxpayer may have to pay tax on all amounts received until her final and complete termination of interest in the asset; of course, at that time she will be able to recover her basis tax-free.[4] Still other times, the taxpayer will be permitted or required to exclude a part of each payment received.[5]

§ 8.01

1. See § 61(a)(3); § 1001(c).

2. For example, when a taxpayer sells stock he is generally entitled to recover his basis prior to pay tax on any gain. See § 1001(a).

3. For example, when a taxpayer receives a dividend, it is generally taxable. See § 61(a)(7).

4. See § 1001(a).

5. See e.g., § 72 (dealing with annuities); § 453 (dealing with installment sales).

Even these three possibilities, though, do not exhaust the variations available. When the taxpayer is permitted to exclude a portion of amounts received over time, sometimes she may be permitted to exclude a pro rata *percentage* of each payment;[6] other times she is allowed to exclude the same *dollar* amount of each payment;[7] still other times she is permitted to exclude higher dollar amounts (or percentages) up front with the amount excluded decreasing over time; and still other times she can exclude only smaller amounts up front, with the amounts permitted to be excluded *increasing* over time.

To further complicate things, sometimes the tax law requires, even with respect to payments received for property, that instead of being able to exclude some receipts as a return of capital and being taxed only on amounts received in excess of her investment, the taxpayer must include in income *all* amounts received at *any* time. When that is the case, the tax law typically *separately* allows the taxpayer to deduct (at some point) the entire amount she invested, so that the net result is to tax her only on her *gain realized*; i.e., (the excess of all amounts received during the course of the investment over the entire amount she invested).[8] Examples of this approach are the taxation of income from investments in business supplies or section 179 properties, investments in nondepreciable rental property that later becomes worthless, and investments in depreciable property.

Deductions of invested amounts, just as the exclusion of some amounts received, as return of capital, can take many forms and can occur over many different times. In some cases (business supplies and 179 property), the taxpayer is permitted to deduct her entire investment when made (up front). Other times she is permitted to deduct the amount invested only at the end, when her entire interest in the investment is terminated (for example, with nondepreciable income property that becomes worthless). Still other times she is allowed to deduct her investment over some or all of the time period during which she holds the property (for example, as depreciation).

In the event that deduction is allowed over time, there may be several different possible ways to determine exactly what percentage of the amount invested can be deducted in any year. The taxpayer may be permitted to deduct a ratable amount of her investment each year; the deductions may start larger and decrease as time goes on; or the deductions may increase over time.

§ 8.02 TIMING AND CHARACTERIZATION OF INTEREST

Perhaps the most common form of return on capital is interest. The basic tax treatment of interest as income to the recipient and as a

---

6. See e.g. § 453.

7. For example this happens in the case of an installment sale with open-ended payments. See § 453.

8. See generally § 1001(a).

potential deduction to the payor is fairly straightforward.[1] Interest is typically included in income.[2] Interest paid is generally deductible if it is incurred in a trade or business; for investment;[3] or with respect to qualified home mortgage indebtedness.[4] The timing of interest, however, is significantly more interesting and complex.

The need for concerted attention to the timing of interest income and deductions evolved from taxpayers who learned to use the tax system's earlier lack of attention to such timing to accomplish results that were nothing short of amazing. Until the enactment of section 7872, taxpayers who sought to avoid assignment of income[5] principals with respect to property needed only to make interest-free cash loans rather than temporary transfers of any other kinds of interests in property.[6] But the manipulation of the timing of interest deductions and income makes mere assignment of income tactics pale by comparison.

Games with interest have been played both by lenders seeking to defer interest income and by borrowers seeking to accelerate interest deductions. To get a sense of the stakes involved in these shenanigans, assume for simplicity that current long and short-term interest rates are 10%, and interest is compounded annually. Further assume that all of the following transactions between B (borrower) and L (lender) are at arm's length, so that L will charge a market rate of interest. If B borrows $100,000 on January 1, year one, with interest and principal from L payable in full at the end of the year, then at the end of one year B will owe $100,000 principal plus $10,000 interest. Regardless of the term of the loan, so long as B pays 10% interest annually, the amount due at maturity will remain $100,000, and each year's interest will remain $10,000.

Obviously, if interest is not paid in full each year, the results change dramatically. If, for example, B is required to pay interest and principal only at the end of several years, then in year one interest will accrue at the rate of 10% on the loan amount of $100,000. At the end of year one, B's obligation, although not yet due and payable, will be $110,000. During year two, interest will accrue at the 10% rate on that year's initial balance of $110,000, so that the interest accrued during year two will be 10% of $110,000, or $11,000. At the end of year two and the beginning of year three, the debt owed by B to L will be the $110,000 owed at the beginning of year two plus the $11,000 interest accrued during year two, for a total of $121,000. During year three interest will accrue on $121,000 at 10%, so that during the year, interest accrued will equal $12,100 (10% of $121,000). The same pattern continues for as long as the debt and accrued interest remain unpaid and the interest contin-

§ 8.02

1. See § 61(a)(4); § 163(a).

2. § 61(a)(4). But see § 103(a) (which generally excludes from gross income interest on state and local bonds).

3. § 163(a), (h)(1), (h)(2)(A) and (B).

4. § 163(a), (h)(1), (h)(2)(D).

5. For a complete discussion of assignment of income, see Chapter 6, *Assignment of Income*.

6. For a complete discussion of § 7872, see § 6.05.

ues to accrue. The table below shows the beginning balance, interest accrued, and ending balance for each successive year for which the interest and principal remain unpaid.

Year	Balance Owing at Beginning of Year	Interest that Accrues During Year (at 10%)	Amount due at end of Year
1	$100,000	$10,000	$110,000
2	$110,000	$11,000	$121,000
3	$121,000	$12,100	$133,100
4	$133,100	$13,310	$146,410
5	$146,410	$14,641	$161,051
6	$161,051	$16,105	$176,156
7	$176,156	$17,616	$193,782
8	$193,782	$19,378	$214,060
9	$214,060	$21,406	$235,466
10	$235,466	$23,547	$259,013
11	$259,013	$25,901	$284,914
12	$284,914	$28,491	$313,405
13	$313,405	$31,341	$344,746
14	$344,746	$34,475	$379,221
15	$379,221	$37,922	$417,143

Because the balance owed at the beginning of each year is higher than the year before, the amount of interest that accrues each year increases even though the interest rate remains constant at 10%. If a taxpayer kept going in the same manner for 30 years (because no payments are due or made until the end of year 30), the total amount due at that time would be about $1,740,000. Of that, $100,000 would be the original borrowed principal and the remaining $1,640,000 would be the interest that had accumulated and compounded over 30 years.

The borrower who borrows the $100,000 in year one and agrees to pay a total of $1,740,000 at the end of year 30 is simply entering into a transaction in which he borrows money at market rates, but left to its own devices, the borrower might choose one of several different ways to characterize the terms of this transaction.

[1] FRONTLOADING

B might first attempt to "frontload" the interest deduction; i.e., to structure the transaction as one in which the interest accrues towards the beginning of the transaction. Continuing with the above example, an extreme version of frontloading might be for the borrower to frame the terms of the transaction as one in which it becomes unconditionally liable for all $1,640,000 of the interest (as well as the $100,000 principal) as soon as it borrows the money. Since B knows it will not have to actually make any payments until 30 years have passed, and since B knows that at the end of 30 years it will have to pay $1,740,000 regardless of whether the interest is frontloaded, the fact that B's liability may be "fixed" at the beginning of year one is likely irrelevant for economic purposes. For *tax* purposes, though, B might choose to adopt the accrual method of taxation,[7] under which liabilities are deductible in the year when the liability is fixed, and the amount can be determined with reasonable accuracy.

By frontloading its interest deduction, B would be deducting immediately amounts it would not be required to pay for many years. Indeed, if this worked as intended, B will be entitled to an interest deduction (subject to the limitations of section 163) of $1,640,000 in year one! If B's marginal tax rate is 40%, that deduction would result in a tax savings of $656,000. If B could in turn invest that $656,000 at 10% for 30 years, B would have $11,414,400 in 30 years. B could pay L the measly $1,174,000 it owed and retain the rest. If B invested its year one tax savings at only 6%, it would still have almost $4 million at the end of thirty years, and could easily pay back L and be left with a substantial profit. Unfortunately for B, as discussed below, the frontloading of interest no longer works because of the original issue discount rules contained in section 1272 *et seq.*

[2] PRO–RATING

It did not take long for the Service to take the position that B in our example above could not frontload its interest deduction in anything close to the manner suggested heretofore. In 1969, Congress instead required most taxpayers to account for accrued interest on a pro rata basis. Under this provision, if a borrower accrued interest over several years that was not actually payable until some future time, the taxpayer/borrower could deduct each year only a pro rata portion of the total interest. As a result, since B in our example would be accruing interest over 30 years, it would be allowed to deduct only 1/30 of the total accrued interest each year.

While the requirement that taxpayer/borrowers pro rate interest deductions over the course of a loan was somewhat better from the government's perspective than allowing frontloading of interest deductions, it failed to solve the problems at which it was directed. To see why, note that in our example, if B is allowed to pro rate its interest deduction over 30 years, B will be entitled to deduct 1/30 of $1,640,000 ($54,667) each year for 30 years. This still results in B being granted a deduction of $54,667 in year one for doing nothing other than borrowing $100,000, when in fact the real interest accrued in that year is only $10,000!

[3] THE LENDER'S SHARE

In the situations described above, where B deducts significant amounts of interest long before they are either due or accrued, the lender, of course, must include interest in income, but inclusion of interest income by the lender almost never balanced out the revenue loss caused by the borrower's early deductions. In many of these situations,

---

7. For a complete discussion of the ac-   *Accounting Issues.*
crual method of taxation, see Chapter 5,

the lender was a tax-exempt organization (such as a large pension plan), and in the other situations, the lender typically accounted for income under the cash receipts method of accounting rather than the accrual method of accounting, so that while the borrower took deductions beginning in year one, the lender incurred no tax liability at all until year 30.[8]

[4]   THE ORIGINAL ISSUE DISCOUNT RULES

In 1982, Congress finally enacted the rules that still govern the taxation of interest today. The basic notion underlying the original issue discount (OID) rules can be set forth much more simply than the technicalities of the rules would suggest.[9] Basically, if L lends money to B, then interest will be *taxed as it accrues economically*. If all interest is paid annually, the payer deducts it, and the recipient includes it in income annually. If some or all interest is not paid annually as it accrues but instead is deferred and to be paid later, the OID rules put both the borrower and the lender on the accrual method with respect to that deferred interest for tax purposes. The OID rules require that the parties determine the interest rate actually being charged by comparing the amount loaned with the amount and times of the payments to be made.[10] Once that rate is determined, the parties treat interest as accruing at that rate. Any interest not paid when it accrues is nonetheless *taxed* to the lender and deductible (subject to the limits of section 163) to the borrower.

[a]   Mischaracterizing Interest

Interest is ordinary income (as opposed to capital gains) for the recipient and provides an ordinary deduction to the payer. The seller of property that might otherwise qualify for the reduced tax rates applicable to long-term capital gains often had an incentive to characterize transactions as ones which produced more long-term capital gain and less interest. To see how taxpayers attempted to convert interest income to capital gains, assume that T lends D $100,000, and in return, D promises to pay T $259,013 at the end of 10 years. Rather than hold the note for the 10 years and pay tax on the $159,013 interest earned, T might sell the note after nine years for $235,466. T would then claim that her gain of $135,466 on the sale of the note was long-term capital gain; after all, it was gain from the sale or exchange of investment property. By ensuring that interest is taxed as it accrues, the OID rules prevent T from claiming long-term capital gain treatment on the sale, because all of the interest that accrued during the first nine years would have already been taxed.[11] As the gain is taxed to T, T's basis in the note

---

8. For a complete discussion of the cash receipts method and accrual methods of accounting, see Chapter 5, *Accounting Issues*.

9. The OID rules are set forth in § 1272 *et seq.*

10. For these purposes, the OID rules assume that interest compounds semi-annually (not annually as the above example suggests).

11. See § 1274(a)(1).

is increased by the amount taxed; hence, T is not taxed again on amounts already included in her income.[12]

[b] OID: A Few Specifics

The general principals embodied in the OID rules are much easier to understand than the specific rules. Perhaps the best place to begin is with a general understanding of "original issue discount," or "OID." Simply put, OID means any interest other than interest that is set at a fixed rate, stated, and required to be paid at least annually.[13]

The Code uses the term "OID" rather than "unstated interest" mostly as a result of historical context. When Congress first addressed the general problem of unstated interest, it was in the context of corporate bonds. To see how the problem developed in this context, assume that X Corp. decides to issue bonds for $100,000 payable in ten years at an interest rate of 8% to be paid annually, but at the time the bonds come on the market, the going interest rate is 10%. When X Corp "originally issues" these bonds, it will not receive the full face amount of $100,000, because the bonds pay below market interest. In order to sell these bonds, it will have to do so at a "discount." Thus was born the term "original issue discount."[14] The OID rules as they now work treat as OID the excess of all amounts the lender will receive (other than interest that is set at a fixed rate, stated, and required to be paid at least annually) over the amount loaned.[15] In other words, all imputed interest is "OID."

Once one knows (1) the amount loaned; (2) the amount to be received; (3) when that amount is to be received; and (4) how often interest is presumed to be compounded (for example, annually in the chart above), one can determine the interest rate that would be applied to the amount loaned to generate the payments received. That is the rate at which OID is deemed to accrue.[16]

Section 1272(a)(3) sets out the principal that for purposes of the OID rules, interest is deemed to be compounded semi-annually rather than annually. As a result, once one knows the amount loaned, the amount to be repaid and when it is to be repaid, one can determine the interest rate to be applied.

Section 1272(a)(1) puts the lender on the accrual method of accounting with respect to OID by stating that the holder of any debt instrument must include in income the "sum of the daily portions of the original issue discount for each day during the taxable year on which such holder held such debt instrument." This means simply that if a

---

12. § 1272(a)(4).

13. See § 1273(a)(1) and (2).

14. Similar rules apply to "market discount," which is unstated interest inherent in a bond because the bond was sold at a discount at a time later than its original issue date. See § 1276.

15. § 1273(a). The Code uses the term "issue price" to refer to the amount loaned and "stated redemption price at maturity" as the total amount to be received excluding interest that is stated, fixed, and payable at least annually.

16. See § 1272(a)(1).

taxpayer holds the debt instrument for less than the full year, she will be taxed on the amount of OID that accrued during the time she held it, and the transferee will be taxed on the OID that accrues thereafter during her holding period. The borrower is put on the same accrual method of accounting with respect to accrued OID by section 163(e).

There are some exceptions to the application of the OID rules to the lending of money, but the exceptions are rare. Common examples include tax-exempt bonds,[17] US Savings Bonds,[18] and any loans between individuals of less than $10,000.[19]

§ 8.03   PAYMENTS OTHER THAN INTEREST

To put all of this in a context other than interest, consider some of the many ways the tax system might treat the taxpayer in the following example. Assume that Taxpayer who is in the 40% tax bracket purchases a single premium life annuity that she can sell at any time for its current fair market value. She pays $200,000 for the annuity. Current short and longer term taxable interest rates are 10%. The terms of the annuity are that she will receive annual payments of $23,500 per year for 20 years, which also represents a 10% annual rate of return on her investment.[1] The total amount she will receive under this arrangement is 20 times $23,500, or $470,000. She puts in $200,000, and over twenty years, she makes a net profit of $270,000.

It is obvious that this transaction will generate a profit of $270,000. Assume a tax rate of 40%, and there will be tax liability of 40% of her $270,000 profit, or $108,000.

When (at the beginning, at the end, or over a period of years) and how (by inclusion of all receipts and deduction of her investment, or by exclusion of only some of her receipts) this $270,000 is included in gross income will not impact the overall amount of tax she must pay. The gross income resulting from this transaction is $270,000, and that amount, in this hypothetical, will always be taxed at a 40% rate.

Nonetheless, w*hen* that $108,000 tax is paid has considerable economic implications for the taxpayer. The more quickly T can get deductions to reduce her tax liability, and/or the longer she can put off including amounts in gross income (which will increase her tax liability), the longer she can hold onto her money (instead of paying it to the IRS). The longer she can hold onto that money, the longer she can leave it invested and earning interest in her own account, and the greater her investment return will be as a result of this transaction.

---

17.   § 1272(a)(2)(A).

18.   § 1272(a)(2)(B).

19.   § 1272(a)(2)(E).

§ 8.03

1. In other words, the yield on her investment will be the same as if her invested funds grow at 10% per year, and each year her account balance is reduced by the $23,500 that is distributed to her.

[1] ALTERNATIVE THEORIES OF TAXATION

To return to the hypothetical, consider the various possibilities for accounting for the taxpayer's gains. A single payment of $200,000 goes out in year one. Payments of $23,500 are coming in every year for 20 years. At the end of that time, the transaction will be complete. Some of the possible ways to determine when T ought to be taxed on her $270,000 of income are:

1) *Accrual Taxation* (ignoring the realization requirement and applying the equivalent of the OID rules): Include in income each year the net amount by which the value of the taxpayer's total investment increases during the year. That increase in value is equal to the difference between (1) the fair market value of her investment as of the first day of that year, and (2) the total of (a) all amounts received during the year, plus (b) the value of her remaining rights to payments as of the last day of the same year.

2) Allow the deduction of the entire cost immediately upon entering into the deal and include all payments received in gross income: *Immediate Deduction or "Expensing."*[2]

3) Include in income only a portion of each receipt, so that at the end of 20 years, the taxpayer has included in income a total of $270,000 and has excluded from income $200,000.

4) Exclude from income (as a nontaxable return of invested capital) the first $200,000 received, and then include in income all subsequent receipts: *Open Treatment*.

Before evaluating these possible ways to treat the transaction, it is important to note that methods 3 and 4 involve determining whether some or all of a specific receipt should be included in income, with method 3 excluding a portion of each receipt and method 4 excluding 100% of some receipts and no portion of others. Both of these results can be achieved by either taxing some (or all) of a receipt and treating the rest as a nontaxable return of capital. In other words, assume the goal is to tax the same net portion of each receipt. Since T must include in income $270,000 of her total receipts of $470,000, she would have to pay tax on a net of 270,000/470,000 of each receipt, and she should not be taxed on the other 200,000/470,000 of each receipt. Obviously, the federal income tax system might reach this result by providing that T must include in income 270/470 of each payment she receives (270/470 x $23,500 = $13,500) and can exclude the remaining 200/470 of each payment (200/470 x $23,500 = $10,000) as a nontaxable return of a part of T's initial invested capital. The tax system can also reach the same net result by requiring T to include in income 100% of each payment received ($23,500) and providing separately for T's invested capital by allowing her a deduction for the amount invested. In this case, since T

---

2. The term "expensing" is used to indicate that the cost of the transaction is treated as an "expense;" i.e., it is to say it is immediately deductible. This is contrast-ed with a "capital expenditure" which is not immediately deductible (it is "capital-ized"). Instead, a deduction of a capital expense is spread out over time.

will receive equal payments for 20 years, she would be allowed to deduct 1/20 ($10,000) of her total investment each year. T's net income each year would thus be her gross income of $23,500 minus her deduction of $10,000.

[a] Accrual Taxation

Note that the results of the first method and the second method *require* separate treatment of T's investment (by way of deduction) and T's income (by way of including all receipts in income) and cannot be achieved by simply excluding from income some or all of a receipt. Under the second method, immediate deduction or expensing, T's *deduction* in year one ($200,000) will exceed the amount she receives ($23,500), so that even excluding from income her entire receipt in year one would not replicate the result of allowing her to deduct her entire investment at the time it is made. The first method, the accrual method, may not be able to be replicated by excluding some, all, or none of a receipt because T's *income* may exceed her receipt in any year. For example, if T received no payment until year two, she would nonetheless have *income* in year one, and even taxing all of her receipts would not properly measure her year one income.

Ultimately, the first method would include in income each year the amount by which the value of the taxpayer's total investment increases during the year. Economists would undoubtedly proffer that this is the sole accurate measure of the taxpayer's income each year. This is because the annuity generates no direct consumption; hence it is income to the extent that it increases her net worth during the year. In turn, the taxpayer's net worth includes the cash she receives during the year (and any income she earns by investing that cash, which will be separately accounted for) plus or minus the change in value of her continuing rights under the contract.

At the start of year one, when she makes the $200,000 investment, the taxpayer's rights are simply the right to receive $23,500 per year for 20 years. At a pre-tax interest rate of 10%, the right to these payments has a present value of $200,000.[3] At the end of year one, she has the right to receive $23,500 per year for the next 19 years. Assuming that the pre-tax interest rate stays at 10%, the value of the right to receive payments for 19 additional years has a present value of $196,500.[4] The total value of the taxpayer's property at the end of the year is thus $196,500 (value of future contract rights) plus $23,500 (cash on hand), for a total of $220,000. Her taxable income for the year under the accrual method is the excess of her year-end value of $220,000 over the

---

3. The present value of a future payment is the amount of money one would have to set aside now in order to have the amount of the future payment at the time it must be made. Thus, assuming an interest rate of 10%, the present value of a payment of $100 to be made at the end of one year is approximately $91, since one would have to deposit $91 in an account bearing 10% interest for one year in order to have $100 at the end of the year.

4. The present value of a stream of annual payments is determined by adding up the present values of each of the payments.

beginning value of $200,000, or $20,000. Basically, her $200,000 investment earned 10% interest for the year ($20,000), and she is taxed on that amount for the year.

At the beginning of year two, T has the right to 19 more annual payments, with a present value of $196,500. At the end of year two, she has the right to only 18 more annual payments. Assuming that the interest rates stay at 10%, the year-end present value of her rights to these payments is $192,650. In addition, T has another $23,500 cash on hand (the payment she receives during year two), leaving her with a total value from this investment (at the end of the year) of $216,150 ($23,500 cash plus the $192,650). Her income for the year is the excess of that year-end total value of $216,250 over the beginning value of $196,500, or $19,650. This makes sense, since it represents a 10% annual rate of return on the $196,500 she had invested throughout the year.

At the beginning of year three, T has the right to 18 more annual payments, with a present value of $192,650. At the end of year three, she has the right to receive only 17 more payments. Assuming that interest rates stay at 10%, the present value of her rights to these future payments is $188,415. The total value of her investment at year-end is the $188,415 year-end present value of her future receipts plus the $23,500 cash on hand from the year three payment, or $211,915. Her income for the year is the excess of that year-end value (of the cash received plus her right to future payments) over the beginning value of $192,650, or $19,265. Again, this represents a 10% return on the $192,650 that she had invested throughout the year. By the beginning of year 20, T will have only the right to receive a single $23,500 payment at the end of the year. That right will be worth only about $21,361 (the present value of the right to receive $23,500 in one year, assuming the interest rate is 10%). The year-end value will be $23,500 (the amount she will receive), so that her income for that year will be only $1,639.

So long as the interest rate remains constant, the taxpayer's income each year will be predictable. Throughout year one, she has $200,000 invested at 10%, and she earns $20,000. Throughout year two the amount she continues to have invested is $196,500, and her income (a return of 10% on that investment) is only $19,650. Each year she *receives* $23,500, which is more than the 10% return she actually earns on her continuing investment. Basically, each year she is taking from the investment all of that year's income plus some of her capital; hence each year the amount she has invested is reduced (until, after 20 years, it is reduced to 0). As the amount she has invested decreases each year, so does the income generated by the 10% return that her invested funds are earning. Accordingly, each year less of what she receives is income, and more represents a mere return of her own funds.

All of this assumes that the interest rate stays stable at 10%. It is not really likely, however, that the interest rate will remain constant. The interest rate may go up in some years and down in others, but it is not likely to remain exactly 10% at the end of each year. It is true that the taxpayer's investment will yield to her a return of 10% regardless of whether the market interest rate goes up or down, and the total income she will have over 20 years will be $270,000 regardless of the interest rate that others may be earning at any time during that 20 years. But the amount of the taxpayer's real economic income during any single year nonetheless varies each year as the market interest rate available on other investments changes.

When the interest rate changes, the value of the taxpayer's future payments will change along with it. As the interest rate increases, the present value of the taxpayer's future payments of $23,500 will decrease. As the present value of those future payments decreases, the taxpayer's actual income will also decrease, because that income is simply $23,500 plus or minus the change in the present value of the remaining future payments. Correspondingly, as the interest rate decreases, the present value of the taxpayer's future payments of $23,500 will increase. And, as the present value of those future payments increases, the taxpayer's current income will increase.

In the real world with fluctuating interest rates and corresponding fluctuations in value and in income, it is impossible to know the taxpayer's real income without being able to value the future payments at the end of each year. The federal income tax system almost never requires such real-time annual valuation to determine income, however. Instead, although our federal income tax system attempts to measure income annually, that measurement is tied to certain transactions (realization) rather than to annual valuation. As a result, at different times and in different circumstances, different transaction-based methods of attempting to measure annual income are appropriate.

All of the other methods of accounting for the taxpayer's income each year are forms of transaction-based ways to account for the taxpayer's income throughout the 20 years which do not require any annual valuation of her investment. Instead, each method simply represents one possible way to take into account the facts that: (1) the taxpayer invested $200,000 and (2) she will receive $23,500 per year for 20 years. Again, each method ultimately results in $270,000 of income and, assuming a 40% marginal tax rate, tax of $108,000. The difference among the methods is only with respect to *when* they require the taxpayer to include income or take deductions. The more closely the timing of income corresponds to the accrual method described above, the more accurate the measurement of the taxpayer's income and the less are the distortions in investment choice caused by the federal income tax system.

[b] Immediate Deduction or "Expensing"

Alternatively, allowing the deduction of the entire cost immediately upon entering into the deal and including all payments received in gross income when received results in *immediate deduction or "expensing."* Under this method, the taxpayer would be allowed to deduct her entire

$200,000 investment in the year she acquires the policy. Having then deducted her full cost, she would thereafter pay tax on the full amount she receives each of the next 20 years.

In the first year, then, the taxpayer has a deduction of $200,000, which will save her $80,000 in taxes (40% of $200,000), and she has income of $23,500, which will cost her $9,400 in tax (40% of $23,500). This leaves the taxpayer with a net tax *savings* of $70,600. In every subsequent year, she will owe tax of $9,400. Because under this method the taxpayer gets a tax refund in year one, she has more to invest early on in the investment period. Because she can earn a return (presumably 10%) on that investment, she will be significantly better off after-taxes than she would be under the accrual taxation method. As a result, allowing immediate deduction of the amount invested provides significant tax benefits (over and above any non-tax gains) to the taxpayer-investor.

One might note the extent of this benefit by seeing that T could invest her $70,600 year-one tax savings in a separate annuity, the proceeds of which she could use to pay about 90% of all of the tax due in subsequent years. Indeed, consider the present value results if T could get her $80,000 tax refund at the *beginning* of year one (when she makes the payment) and pay tax on her $23,500 receipt only at the *end* of year one (when she actually receives the payment). In that case, as of the beginning of year one, T would have $80,000 cash (her tax refund) in addition to the annuity. Assuming the same 10% interest rate, T could invest that $80,000 in an annuity that would pay $9,400 per year each year for the next 20 years, beginning at the end of year one.[5] T could then use those annuity payments to pay the $9,400 tax due on the $23,500 received each year. In other words, T could use her year one tax *savings* to finance 100% of her taxes due in years 2–20. In still other words, T could keep all of the $23,500 cash received each year (because her taxes due could be paid by her $9,400 payments on her second annuity). That means that in present value terms, the result is identical to simply not taxing T at all on her income from the annuity![6]

---

5. $200,000 will yield $23,500 per year for 20 years. The ratio of $200,000/$23,500 is the same as the ratio of $80,000/$9,400; they both equal 8.51, meaning T must invest $8.51 in year one for each $1 20 year annual return.

6. One might imagine another alternative, which would require T to include all receipts in income and take the $200,000 deduction at the end of the 20 years when the annuity terminates.

Like the expensing alternative, this new alternative would allow T to deduct her entire $200,000 investment in the annuity. The difference between the expensing alternative and this new alternative, though, is that in the new alternative T's $200,000 deduction would be allowed at the *termination* of the investment rather than at the beginning. If T is taxed on each of the $23,500 payments as they come in each year and allowed a $200,000 deduction only at the end of 20 years, then she will have taxable income of $23,500 (and tax due of 40% of that amount, or $9,400 per year) for 20 years, plus a taxable loss of $176,500 in year 20. By deferring the $200,000 deduction for 20 years, the present value of that deduction decreases from $200,000 to only $29,600. The result of this treatment would be to overtax the taxpayer substantially in years 1–19, and then to under-tax her by a substantial amount in year 20. By accelerating the tax liability, this results in substantially increasing the present-value (or, from

[c] Partial Inclusion

As an initial matter, it is important to keep in mind that the results of this alternative may be achieved either by requiring the taxpayer to include in income her entire receipt each year ($23,500) and allowing her to deduct each year some portion of her invested capital, or by simply requiring her to include in gross income each year only a portion of her receipt for the year. It is also important to keep in mind that at different places in the Code, the net percentage of each payment received that is included in income may vary. While alternative three will always require that over the 20 years, T will include net income of $270,000 and will exclude from net income $200,000, the amount of income T must report *each year* may vary. The method may be applied by using a pro-rata apportionment, so that T will include in income the same net percentage of her receipt (and the same dollar amount, since the amount received each year will remain constant) each year.[7] The method can also be applied to make it so that T includes in income either a higher amount in early years and a lower amount in later years (similar to accrual taxation),[8] or it can be applied so that T includes a lower amount in income in earlier years and a higher amount in later years.[9] As noted, each of these variations is used at various places in the Code.

Assume the same net percentage (and amount) of each payment received will be included in T's income. Each year for 20 years, T would include in income a net of $13,500, so that over the 20 years T would be taxed on $270,000.

This treatment is somewhat similar to the accrual treatment described above, in that it treats some of each payment as income and some as return of capital. But, it is important to note what can be very significant differences between the pro-rata recovery of basis in this method and the accrual treatment described *supra*. Rather than requiring the taxpayer to report an equal amount of income each year for 20 years, as this method would, the accrual method described above requires the taxpayer to include in income greater amounts in earlier years (for example, $20,000 instead of $13,500 in year one, $19,265 instead of

the taxpayer's perspective, the present cost) of the tax payments, and it therefore significantly decreases the after-tax value of the investment.

To put the difference between the expensing alternative and this new alternative in different terms, each method requires the taxpayer to include in income $23,500 per year (generating an annual tax liability of $9,400), and each method also allows the taxpayer to deduct $200,000 (for a net tax savings of $80,000). The only difference is that the expensing method allows the $200,000 deduction and $80,000 tax savings in year one, while new alternative method allows that deduction and savings only in year 20. If the taxpayer using

the expensing method takes the $80,000 year one savings and invests it until year 20, by that time she will have not just the $80,000 that the new alternative method nets her in year 20, but, instead, she will have $488,000 (if invested at a presumed pre-tax return of 10%). Obviously, the difference between the net result in the expensing methods and the new alternative method is quite significant.

7. See e.g., § 453 (which deals with installment sales and is discussed, *infra*).

8. See e.g., § 1272 *et seq.* (which deal with the OID rules, discussed *supra*).

9. See e.g., § 168 (which deals with accelerated depreciation and is discussed in Chapter 4, *Deductions*).

$13,500 in year two, $18,841 instead of $13,500 in year three, etc.) and smaller amounts in the later years (for example, $1,169 instead of $13,500 in year 20).

As a result, when compared to the accrual method, pro-rata recovery of basis allows T to defer tax on $6,500 in year one, on another $5,765 in year two, etc. T will not be required to pay these amounts until later years; at that time T will be required to include in income $13,500 each year instead of the smaller amounts that would be generated by accrual taxation in those later years. To the extent that T's tax liability is deferred, T can retain and invest her money (presumably at 10%) until she is required to pay the deferred tax in the later years; this leaves her with a reduced tax burden in present value terms and a higher after-tax return on her investment. If the amounts at stake are relatively small, and the payments are made over a relatively short period, the tax savings to the taxpayer generated by pro-rating deductions rather than using accrual taxation may be minimal. If the amounts invested are very large and/or the payments will be made over a long time, the tax savings will increase accordingly.

[d] Open Treatment

The final alternative includes amounts received in income only when the total amount received exceeds the taxpayer's entire investment (*open treatment*).[10] What this means is that as the $23,500 comes in each year, it is treated as a return of the taxpayer's initial investment until the $200,000 is exhausted. After the $200,000 initial cost has been excluded, the entire investment has been accounted for, and all future payments are taxable in full.

Although not quite as favorable as the expensing method described above, which provides the taxpayer with a tax refund in year one, this treatment is nonetheless quite favorable to the taxpayer. Rather than paying more tax earlier on and less tax later, as accrual taxation would require, and rather paying tax on $13,500 each year, as pro-rata return of capital would require, this allows her to defer any and all tax payments for almost eight years. T can therefore keep and invest her money, defer tax liability, and happily know that this investment provides clear tax benefits in addition to the 10% return on her investment.[11]

---

10. "Open treatment," especially for property sold for payments to be received in the future, has historically been a part of the tax law, although it is not widely used today. See Burnet v. Logan, 283 U.S. 404, 51 S.Ct. 550, 75 L.Ed. 1143 (1931).

11. Some have argued for still a different method of taxation, which would deem the present value of each payment at the beginning of the arrangement to be its cost. Deduct that cost from each payment as it arrives. Assume that the taxpayer paid

$200,000 for the annuity. The annuity consists of 20 payments. The taxpayer has paid a part of her $200,000 for each of those payments. Because of the time value of money, the payments to be received in years 1 through 20 each have a different present value. Therefore, it is necessary to ascertain the present value of each payment of $23,500. (Their total present value will add up to $200,000—since that is what T paid for the policy and that is what the payments are presently worth in total). Obviously, the earlier the payment will be

[2] RECONCILING THE ALTERNATIVE THEORIES OF TAXATION

Each of the above methods of measuring income (as well as variations of each and combinations of two or more) is used at various points throughout the Internal Revenue Code. Some of these methods require the taxpayer to include higher net amounts in income (and thus pay more taxes) early on;[12] some methods allow the taxpayer to include *lower* net amounts in income early on (and thus to defer more taxes);[13] others require proportionate inclusion of net income throughout the life of the investment;[14] and some situations call for combinations of different methods.[15] While each situation will be discussed when it arises, it is important to any basic understanding of federal income taxation to understand the different ways to account for invested capital, as well as the notion of the time value of money and how often and in how many different disguises these issues can arise. At this point, it is enough to keep in mind that the more that the earlier payments are treated as a return of capital rather than income, and the more that income is deferred, the better the result for the typical taxpayer.

§ 8.04   RECEIPT OF PERIODIC PAYMENTS: ANNUITIES

Given the various possibilities discussed above, one might wonder how annuities are actually taxed. The answers are given in section 72. The basic rule is that the taxpayer who invests in an annuity is taxed on a portion of each payment received and excludes a portion of each payment as a return of capital. To determine the percentage of each payment that the taxpayer can exclude, section 72 requires the taxpayer

received, the higher its present value. For example, the first payment, to be received at the end of year one, has a present value of $21,361.50; accordingly, this is the amount one would need to deposit at the beginning of the year in order to have exactly $23,500 at year-end. On the other hand, the final payment of $23,500, to be received at the end of 20 years, would have a present value (and thus a present cost) of only $3,478, since that amount, earning 10% interest, would yield $23,500 at the end of 20 years.

Because this method results in less income (and less tax) in the early years, it would, of course, be helpful to the taxpayer. While this method would accurately measure the amount of each *annual payment* received that represents the appreciation (or income component) in that particular payment, it mismeasures the taxpayer's actual income each year because it does not include the amount by which all of the taxpayer's future payments increase in val-

ue each year. In other words, it may be the case that at the end of year one, when the taxpayer receives her first payment of $23,500, she initially paid $21,365 for the right to that payment, so that only a small part of that payment is income. However, it is also true that the taxpayer has the right to 19 additional payments, and each of those has increased in value by 10% during the year (because each payment is one year closer to being received). To fail to tax the annual increase in value of each of those payments would be to mismeasure her income and to provide significant tax benefits.

12. An example is the treatment of a loan which requires annual payments to the taxpayer-lender by the borrower.

13. An example is the use of accelerated depreciation with respect to equipment.

14. An example is annuity payments.

15. See e.g., § 453 (dealing with annual interest payments related to installment sales).

to determine the total amount paid for the annuity and the total amount to be received under the annuity.[1] The percentage of each individual payment received that is treated as a return of capital is the same as the percentage of the *total* amount to be received that is represented by the taxpayer's cost.[2] For example, if the taxpayer pays $85,000 for the right to receive $10,000 per year for 20 years (a 10% rate of return), the total cost for the annuity is $85,000; the total amount to be received is $200,000. Hence 85/200 of every payment received will be treated as return of capital, and 115/200 of every payment received will be taxable income.

In terms of the above presentation of alternative methods of taxation, the treatment of annuities is governed by the pro-rata application of the third alternative; i.e., the same portion of each payment received is excluded from income, and the remainder is taxed. As discussed above, this treatment is ultimately beneficial (when compared to accrual taxation) to the taxpayer-investor. Although the investor's real economic income is more in the earlier years and less in the later years, the tax consequences are spread evenly over all the years during which she receives payments, resulting in deferral of taxation to some extent.

[1] TAX BENEFITS PROVIDED BY SECTION 72

The potential tax benefits provided by section 72 become much *more* obvious if the taxpayer who purchases an annuity does not begin receiving payments until some point in the future. For example, assume that instead of paying $85,000 for an annuity that will pay $10,000 per year beginning at the end of year one, T purchases an annuity that will pay $10,000 per year for 20 years *beginning 10 years from the date of purchase.* Assume the same 10% interest rate; accordingly, T will pay about $32,725 (the present value) for this annuity. At the end of nine years, just when the payments are about to start, the annuity will be worth $85,000 (the value of the right to receive 20 annual payments of $10,000, beginning in year ten, when the interest rate is 10%). In reality, T has more than doubled her money in those 10 years, but because section 72 defers taxation until receipt of payment and then spreads T's income ratably over the entire annuity period, she will pay no tax at all until she receives her first payment (at the end of 10 years). Even then she will be able to exclude 32,725/200,000 of each $10,000 payment she receives. In this case it is not the mere fact that T includes an identical amount in income each year rather than a higher amount in early years that provides the primary benefit to T. Instead, it is the fact that under section 72 T is not taxed at all on any income until she receives her payments (a basic application of the realization requirement), despite the fact that her investment is increasing in value each year.

§ 8.04   2. Id.

1. § 72(b)(1).

[2]   TAX ISSUES RELATED TO PAYMENTS FOR LIFE

While the basic tax treatment of annuities (if not the economic implications of that treatment) is, straightforward, numerous aspects of actual annuities require adjustment to the basic rule. To begin with often annuities are not issued for a fixed period, so that the total amount to be received under the annuity contract is not determinable at the date of purchase. Instead, many annuities involve the taxpayer who makes a premium payment, often one lump amount, to an insurance company (or other party) in exchange for which the insurance company agrees to make periodic payments to the taxpayer commencing on a particular date for the rest of the taxpayer's life. This, of course, is a method for the taxpayer to guarantee himself an income for the rest of his life.

Where the taxpayer will receive payments for life, section 72 requires initially that the taxpayer determine her life expectancy under tables issued by Treasury.[3] The taxpayer uses her published life expectancy to determine the number of payments she is expected to receives, and from that she calculates the total amount she expects to receive under the annuity. Once that determination is made, the taxpayer simply applies the formula above to determine the percentage of payment received that is treated as a nontaxable return of capital.[4] If the taxpayer then dies when expected to do so (pursuant to the published tables), the result is no different from the way an annuity for a fixed period is treated.

Of course, annuities for life are not always quite that easy. Essentially, annuities for life are the inverse of life insurance. Hence, if the taxpayer annuitant dies prior to reaching his estimated life expectancy, he experiences a mortality loss on his annuity, which is deductible under section 72(b)(3). Correspondingly, if the taxpayer dies at an age beyond his life expectancy, he reaps a mortality *gain* on his annuity. The annuitant who lives beyond his life expectancy and reaps more than expected is taxed in full on that gain. Once the annuitant has excluded an amount equal to his investment (which he will have done by the time he reaches his life expectancy) he has recovered the cost of his annuity, and he can no longer exclude any portion of any additional payments he receives.

Taxpayers who invest in annuities for life cannot be assured that they will actually receive anything at all for their investment, and it is common for such annuitants to insist on a refund feature. Such a refund feature typically takes the form of a promise by the annuity provider that should the annuitant die prior to receiving payments equal at least to her total cost, she will be refunded the difference between that total cost and all amounts paid prior to death. The presence of a refund feature does not alter the method by which the taxpayer calculates the amount of each payment which is taxable income, but it does alter the numbers used in that calculation. Simply put, if the taxpayer pays some

---

3. See Treas. Reg. § 1.72–9.   **4.** See § 72(b)(1).

amount for a refund feature, that amount is not a part of the taxpayer's cost for the periodic payments; hence the taxpayer's cost for the annuity does not include any amount paid for the refund feature. The value, and presumed cost, of the refund feature is determined by reference to tables published by Treasury.[5]

§ 8.05   RECEIPT OF PERIODIC PAYMENTS: INSTALLMENT SALES

[1]   THE BASICS

Section 453 governs the treatment of periodic payments received in exchange for property. Absent section 453, a taxpayer who sells property would generally be taxed on any realized gain (or would potentially deduct any realized loss) in the year of sale, regardless of whether she receives any actual cash payments in that year.[1] Concerned that taxpayer's might be required to pay tax before receiving any money and might be unable to do so, Congress enacted section 453; this section allows most taxpayers to defer reporting income from a sale of property until payments are actually received. Losses are not governed by section 453, so a loss is reported in full in the year of the disposition.[2]

Section 453 defines an installment sale as any disposition of property if at least one payment is to be received in a taxable year subsequent to the taxable year of disposition.[3] As section 72 does with annuities, section 453 directs that gain be recognized on a pro-rata basis as payments are received (unless the taxpayer elects[4] out of the installment method), but the specifics of the statute are somewhat reversed. While section 72 directs the taxpayer to determine what part of her total payments represent a *return of capital* and to then *exclude* that proportion of each payment received, section 453 directs the taxpayer to determine what percentage of her entire amount realized (referred to as the "total contract price"[5]) represents *profit* (referred to as "gross profit"),[6] and to then *include* as gain recognized that same portion of each principal payment received.[7]

The application of section 453 may be illustrated by the following example. Assume that T has land with a basis of $60,000 and that the land is sold for $130,000 on January 1, year one. Rather than paying cash, P promises to make 10 annual principal payments of $13,000 each beginning on December 31, year one. T's gross profit is $70,000 ($130,000 amount realized minus $60,000 basis); the total contract price is $130,000. Thus, the gross profit ratio is 70,000/130,000, or about 54%. In

---

5.   See Treas. Reg. § 1.72–9.

§ 8.05

1.   See § 1001(c).

2.   See § 453(a); § 1001(c).

3.   § 453(b)(1).

4.   See § 453(d).

5.   Treas. Reg. § 15a.453–1(b)(2)(iii).

6.   Treas. Reg. § 15a.453–1(b)(2)(v).

7.   § 453(a), (b)(1), (c). Some portion of each payment may also represent interest rather than principal. That part is taxed separately as interest.

the year of sale T receives $13,000 and reports as gain 54% of the $13,000 payment, or $7,000. In each of the following nine years she would report 54% of the annual $13,000 payment. In this manner the taxpayer accounts for the total $70,000 gain over 10 years. If payments instead were $30,000 in year one and $20,000 per year in years 2–6, T would report as taxable gain 54% of $30,000 ($17,200) in year one and 54% of $20,000 ($10,800) in each subsequent year.

[2] PRINCIPAL AND INTEREST

It is essential to understand that section 453 applies only to amounts the seller will receive *in exchange for property*, and it does not apply to interest payments.[8] To see the implications of this distinction, note that immediately upon sale in the above example (as of January 1, year one), P receives the property and owes T $130,000, the price of the property. Assuming that this is an arm's length transaction, T will demand, and P will have to pay, interest on the $130,000 debt. If the interest rate is 10%, then the parties may agree that P will pay annual interest of 10% on the outstanding balance each year, or they may instead provide that any interest accrued and not paid will be compounded until it is eventually paid. The difference between principal payments, taxable under section 453, and interest taxable under section 483, is that the principal payments are made by P to T in exchange for the *property*. On the other hand, the interest payments are made in exchange for T's extension of credit to P (the extension of credit exists because P acquires possession of the property at the time of sale but does not pay the full price at that time).

Another way to see the difference between gain governed by section 453 and interest is to note that any gain that is taxed (at any time) under section 453 represents gain that accrued while T, the seller, held the property. The installment sale represents the event that triggers realization of the gain and locks in the pre-sale gain, and section 453 ultimately governs only the timing of that gain by determining which part of each principal payment represent gain and what parts of each principal payment represent (nontaxable) return of capital. Interest, though, represents profit T makes *after* the installment sale is made, by continuing to extend credit to the purchaser. Thus, while section 453 operates in a manner similar to that of section 72, which governs annuities, section 453 applies only to gain accrued *prior* to the time T and P enter into a transaction together. On the other hand, section 72 applies only to income (essentially interest) earned after T and P enter into the transaction.

[3] BENEFITS OF INSTALLMENT SALE TREATMENT

Section 453 defers taxation of gain that has already accrued and been realized. Section 72, dealing with annuities, defers taxation of income earned only *after* the taxpayer enters into the transaction. This

---

8. See Treas. Reg. § 15a.453–1(b)(1), (b)(2)(ii).

necessarily means that the deferral offered by section 453 is even more significant than the deferral offered by section 72. Under section 453, T pays no tax on income accrued *and realized* until she receives principal payments. This is true even if the debt instrument she receives is well secured, and her accession to wealth is undeniable. The longer she puts off receiving payments, the longer she puts off taxation on her already realized gain.

[4] DEBT RELIEF

If the seller's amount realized includes not only cash (received in the year of sale or to be received in the future) but also debt relief, the regulations assure that, in line with Congress's intent to defer taxation until the taxpayer has cash in hand, debt relief is not treated as a payment received.[9] As a result, in our example, assume that T held the property with a basis of $60,000 and a value of $130,000, subject to a debt of $50,000, and the purchaser took the property subject to the $50,000 debt and promised to pay $20,000 per year for four years. T's total amount realized would be $130,000 ($50,000 debt relief plus four payments of $20,000 each). Since her basis is $60,000, her total profit is $70,000. Since the $50,000 debt relief is not treated as a "payment," T's total payments will only equal the $80,000 cash she will receive. As her profit is $70,000, and her total payments will be $80,000, 70,000/80,000 of each $20,000 payment received will be taxable as gain. And, T will report profit of $17,500 (7/8 x $20,000) each year for four years. Again, T will be taxed on her total profit of $70,000, but only as she receives cash payments.[10]

If the taxpayer sells property subject to debt that exceeds her basis in the property, then it is impossible for the taxpayer to defer reporting gain until she receives cash, because her total gain recognized will necessarily exceed the total cash she will receive. To see how this is the case, assume that T holds the same property (basis $60,000, value $130,000) subject to a debt of $75,000. Any purchaser who takes the property subject to the $75,000 debt will acquire property with a net equity of $55,000 ($130,000 value minus the $75,000 liability). As a result, the purchaser would pay no more than $55,000 cash for the property. Assume that this $55,000 will be paid at the rate of $11,000 per year beginning in year two. Since T's total gain is still $70,000 (the excess of her amount realized of $130,000 [$75,000 debt relief plus

---

9. Treas. Reg. § 15a.453–1(b)(3)(i). Not surprisingly, the regulations provide that if the debt was incurred as part of the sale transaction or somehow appears to be the result of the taxpayer's attempt to defer taxation by borrowing money and having the purchaser take the property subject to the debt instead of simply receiving cash (now or later), the debt relief indeed will be treated as payment received. Id.

10. This procedure not only establishes the timing for the reporting of a taxpayer's gain, but it also establishes the basis in the installment notes that the taxpayer holds. The rule is that the taxpayer's basis in his installment notes is the face amount of the note less the amount which would be reportable as income were the note satisfied in full. Treas. Reg. § 1.453–9(b)(2). Thus, should the taxpayer sell the note before it is satisfied, he can calculate his gain (or loss) since the installment method has established his basis in each note. See Treas. Reg. § 1.453–9(b)(1) and (2).

$55,000 cash] over her basis of $60,000), even if every penny of her cash payments were taxed, she would be taxed on only $55,000 of her $70,000 gain. In order to avoid this result, the regulations provide that to the extent that debt relief exceeds the seller's basis, that debt relief is treated as a payment received.[11] As a result, in the example, if T's basis is $60,000 and she is relieved of $75,000 of debt in the year of sale, she is treated as having received a payment of $15,000 (the excess of $75,000 debt relief over her basis of $60,000) in the year of sale, and her total payments will be $70,000 ($15,000 excess debt relief plus the $55,000 cash she will receive). Since her total profit is $70,000 and her total payments will be $70,000, the $15,000 excess debt relief will be taxed in full, as will every other dollar of payment she receives.[12]

The regulations also provide rules for contingent payment sales.[13] These are sales or other dispositions of property in which the aggregate selling price cannot be determined at the close of the taxable year in which the sale or other disposition occurs.[14] In a contingent payment sale, if a maximum selling price can be ascertained, the selling price is calculated in a manner such that all contingencies are resolved to maximize the price and accelerate the payment or payments to the earliest possible date or dates.[15] If the maximum amount is subsequently reduced, the gross profit ratio is recomputed with respect to payments received in or after the year in which the event requiring reduction occurs.[16] If the stated maximum selling price cannot be determined but the maximum period over which payments are to be received is fixed, the taxpayer's basis in the property is allocated in equal annual amounts over the payment period, and the excess of payments received for a taxable year over the basis allocated to that year is recognized as income.[17] If there is neither a maximum selling price nor a fixed period of payment, the basis of the property is allocated in equal annual amounts over a 15-year period.[18]

[5] EXCEPTIONS

[a] Inventory and Property Held Primarily for Sale to Customers

Section 453 does not apply to every transaction that would seem to qualify as an installment sale under section 453(b)(1). Sometimes installment treatment is unavailable to the seller, and at other times the seller

---

11. Treas. Reg. § 15a.453–1(b)(3)(i).

12. Clever taxpayers who held property subject to debt in excess of basis and who sought to avoid current recognition of gain attempted to avoid the taxation due to excess debt relief by having the purchasers not take the property subject to the debt. Instead, these taxpayers arranged to leave the seller liable on the underlying debt secured by the property and to have the purchaser make extra payments to the seller sufficient to enable the seller to make payments on that debt. These "wraparound

mortgages" are now treated as debt relief to the seller. Treas. Reg. § 15a.453–1(b)(3)(ii).

13. See Treas. Reg. § 15a.453–1(c).

14. Treas. Reg. § 15a.453–1(c)(1).

15. Treas. Reg. § 15a.453–1(c)(2)(i)(A).

16. Id.

17. Id.

18. Treas. Reg. § 15a.453–1(c)(4).

may decide to forgo it despite its availability.[19] Perhaps the most significant restriction on the application of section 453 is that it does not apply to the sale of inventory[20] or of property held for sale to customers in the ordinary course of business.[21]

[b] Losses

Section 453 does not apply to losses, which are recognized at the time of the sale or exchange regardless of when payments are to be received.[22]

[c] Election Out of Installment Sale Treatment

A taxpayer may elect out of the installment method and report the transaction under his usual method of accounting.[23] With respect to a taxpayer who has elected not to report on the installment method, receipt of an obligation is considered the receipt of property without regard to whether it is embodied in a note, an executory contract, or any other instrument, or is an oral promise enforceable under local law.[24] Thus, the fair market value of the installment obligation constitutes the amount realized in the year of sale by a cash basis taxpayer while the amount realized by an accrual basis taxpayer is the total amount payable under the installment obligation (exclusive of interest or original issue discount).[25]

In some cases, the payments to be received by the seller may be contingent, and not subject to easy valuation. For example, if T sells her closely held corporation for 50% of the corporation's net profits during each of the next ten years, her amount realized, and the amount of the resulting gain, depend entirely on the corporation's future success, and it may be impossible to accurately predict what the corporation's future holds in store. If the taxpayer elects out of section 453 treatment and can establish that it is impossible to even approximate the amount or value of her right to future contingent payments, so that it is impossible to reasonably estimate whether or not she will realize any gain, and if so, how much, she may be able to defer reporting any gain despite opting out of section 453. Under "open transaction" treatment, approved by the Supreme Court in Burnett v. Logan,[26] the seller who is to receive contingent payments whose amounts cannot be reasonably estimated may defer reporting any gain at all until or unless she receives total payments that exceed her basis in the property sold (at which point it first becomes apparent that she will in fact realize some gain). Once she

---

19. See § 453(d) (which allows a taxpayer to elect out of installment sale treatment).

20. § 453(b)(2)(B).

21. § 453(b)(2)(A).

22. See § 453(a); § 1001(c). See also Martin v. Commissioner, 61 F.2d 942 (2d Cir. 1932).

23. § 453(d).

24. Treas. Reg. § 15a.453–1(d)(2)(i).

25. Cf. Burnet v. Logan, 283 U.S. 404, 51 S.Ct. 550, 75 L.Ed. 1143 (1931).

26. 283 U.S. 404, 51 S.Ct. 550, 75 L.Ed. 1143 (1931).

has received payments equal to her basis in the property sold, all subsequent payments received represent gain and are taxable in full.

Perhaps the most important aspect of open transaction treatment is that it is *very rarely* permitted. Especially since section 453 itself provides ways to account for contingent payments,[27] the Service does not believe that open treatment should ever be available. Courts are likely to accede to the Service's perspective on this issues unless the taxpayer can make a very strong showing not simply that payments to be received are contingent, but also that they are impossible to value or estimate. Since the taxpayer who sells property for contingent payments must have made some estimate of their value prior to deciding to sell, making the required showing will be difficult if not impossible.

[6]   LIMITATIONS ON BENEFITS OF INSTALLMENT SALES

Although section 453 was intended to assist taxpayers who did not have access to cash, it allows taxpayers to intentionally structure most sales as installment sales in order to defer taxes, even if the seller is willing to pay cash. Not surprisingly, almost as soon as section 453 was enacted, taxpayers attempted to figure out how to get the benefits of deferral permitted by installment treatment without actually having to defer the receipt of cash or its equivalent. Rather than making an attempt to determine whether cash might have been available in a particular situation, the Code restricts some of the deferral benefits of section 453 in order to prevent abuse. The most significant of these restrictions are discussed herein.

[a]   Receipts Treated as "Payment"

[i]   Receipt of Readily Tradable Securities

One way taxpayers envisioned that they might receive what was equivalent to payment from their perspective but what appeared to be an "installment obligation" as defined in section 453(b) was to sell their property in exchange for an "evidence of indebtedness." But, taxpayers also wanted to ensure ready access to cash by making the "note" a readily tradable security, such as an investment grade corporate bond. Obviously, the taxpayer who receives such a readily tradable bond may at any time turn that instrument into cash; hence there is no need to allow her to defer paying her tax liability. As a result, section 453(f)(4)(B) provides that receipt of a readily tradable debt instrument is treated as receipt of payment, notwithstanding that such instrument would otherwise qualify as an installment obligation under section 453(b).

[ii]   Demand Notes

The seller who receives a debt instrument payable on demand obviously can receive payment whenever she wants it; hence there is no

---

27. See Treas. Reg. § 15a.453–1(c). *Nota bene:* § 453 was not in existence when   Burnett v. Logan was decided.

need to help her defer her tax liability. As a result, receipt of notes payable on demand are also treated as receipt of payments.[28] What this means is that installment treatment is available only to the seller who is willing to specify payment dates *prior* to receipt of the note.

[b]   Pledges of Installment Obligations

Perhaps the simplest way for taxpayers to defer taxation while receiving actual cash was to sell property on the installment method, and then to pledge the installment obligation as security for a loan. Under Woodsam Associates, Inc. v. Commissioner,[29] pledging property to secure indebtedness is not generally treated as a disposition of the property; hence the taxpayer who pledges her installment obligation might hope to cash in on that obligation while still deferring tax. This potential is eliminated by section 453A(d), which provides that a taxpayer who pledges an installment obligation shall be treated as receiving cash equal to the lesser of the amount of indebtedness secured by the installment obligation or the total principal payments to be made under the note.

[c]   Related Party Sales

Another technique designed to allow receipt of cash without current taxation was to use related parties to hold the cash. To see how this might work, assume that T wants to sell property with a basis of $100,000 and a value of $600,000. Rather than selling the property for cash, T sells the property to her son S on the installment method, with principal payments due only in the future. Immediately after this sale, T has no tax due because of section 453, and T's son S owns the property with a cost basis of $600,000.[30] If T then sells the property for $600,000 cash, the family has cashed out of the property, and neither T nor S owes one penny of tax (T because she can defer taxation until she receives payments from S, and S because his amount realized of $600,000 was not in excess of his cost basis in the property).

Congress decided to address this practice by treating payments received by S (or any other related party[31] to whom T makes the initial sale) as though they were also received by T, resulting in T's recognition of gain upon S's receipt of payments.[32] In order to ensure that T is not taxed again when actually paid by S, no payments made by S to T are taxed until the amounts S pays T exceed the amount T has already been treated as having received.[33] Only if and to the extent that T receives amounts from S in excess of the payments she has been treated as having already received will she be treated as receiving any payments from S.

Significantly, however, section 453(e) does not apply if: (1) the property sold is not marketable securities and the related party purchas-

---

28. § 453(f)(4)(A)

29. 198 F.2d 357 (2d Cir. 1952).

30. See Crane v. Commissioner, 331 U.S. 1, 67 S.Ct. 1047, 91 L.Ed. 1301 (1947).

31. See § 453(f)(1).

32. § 453(e)(1).

33. See § 453(e)(1) and (3).

er holds the property subject to market risk[34] for at least two years before selling it to an unrelated party,[35] or (2) if the taxpayer can establish that neither the sale to the related party nor the subsequent sale by the related party was motivated by tax avoidance.[36]

[d] Depreciation Recapture

Installment sale treatment is not permitted with respect to any gain that represents depreciation recapture under section 1245 or section 1250.[37] Instead, any recapture income must be recognized by the seller in the year of sale, even though installment treatment may be available with respect to other gain realized by the seller on the sale.[38]

To see the impact of the exclusion of recapture from installment sale treatment, assume: S sells to P property in which S has a basis of $300,000; the property is worth $1,000,000; and S will receive principal payments of $200,000 per year for 5 years (with adequate interest stated and paid annually). Assume further that S initially purchased the property for $500,000 and the difference between his initial basis of $500,000 and his current adjusted basis of $200,000 is the result of $300,000 of depreciation deductions he has taken; hence the property is subject to recapture under section 1245 of $300,000.[39] If S sold this property for cash (rather than on the installment method), he would have an amount realized of $1,000,000, an adjusted basis of $200,000, and a total gain of $800,000. Of that amount, the $300,000 that represents section 1245 recapture would be taxed as ordinary income.

Since installment sale treatment is unavailable with respect to the $300,000 section 1245 recapture, S must recognize his $300,000 of recapture gain in the year of sale. Installment sale treatment is available with respect to the remaining $500,000 of gain, however. Since S can report gain of $500,000 under the installment method, that method provides that his profit percentage is determined by dividing his total profit reportable under the installment method ($500,000, because the remaining $300,000 of profit is section 1245 recapture and not eligible for installment treatment) by the total principal payments he will receive ($1,000,000). Thus, $500,000/$1,000,000 (½) of each principal payment S receives will be taxable as gain.

The net result for S is that in year one he reports section 1245 recapture income of $300,000 immediately upon the sale. When he receives a principal payment of $200,000 at the end of the year, ½ of that payment represents gain taxable under the installment method, and the remaining ½ of that payment represents a nontaxable recovery of basis ($200,000/$500,000) and a nontaxable receipt of a portion of the recap-

---

34. § 453(e)(2)(B).

35. § 453(e)(2)(A).

36. § 453(e)(7).

37. § 453(i)(1) and (2).

38. Id.

39. The basic notion underlying § 1245 is that when S sells depreciable personal property, any part of her gain that represents depreciation previously taken is § 1245 recapture and will be taxed as ordinary income on sale.

ture on which he has already been taxed ($300,000/$500,000). In year two (and 3, 4 and 5 as well), when he receives another principal payment of $200,000, he is again taxed on ½ of that amount as gain under the installment sales rules and treats the remainder as nontaxable.

[e] Interest on Deferred Taxes

One way to allow taxpayers to defer paying tax until they receive cash but to not enable them to take undue advantage of this deferral would be to (1) make tax on the seller's gain due and owing at the time of the sale (rather than only when the seller receives payments), but (2) extend *credit* to the seller until she receives her actual payments. The result would be that the seller could defer *paying* her taxes until she receives cash, but because her liability was due and *owing* from the time of the sale, she would owe interest on that deferred tax each year until she actually paid it.

Section 453A approximates this result in certain cases. Basically, section 453A requires sellers to pay interest each year (at the rate imposed on any tax underpayment)[40] on their "deferred tax liability,"[41] and that deferred tax liability is essentially the amount of tax they would have owed on the sale if it had been taxed in full in the year of sale.

What makes section 453 remain attractive, though, is the limited application of section 453A. Interest on a deferred tax liability is due only if the sales price of the property sold exceeds $150,000.[42] In addition, even if the sales price exceeds $150,000, section 453A applies to require interest payments only if, and to the extent, that the seller holds (at the end of the year) installment obligations with total face amounts in excess of $5,000,000.[43] If the seller's total installment obligations (whenever received) do not exceed $5,000,000, no interest is due.[44] If the total does exceed $5,000,000, interest is due only on the excess portion of those obligations (over $5,000,000).[45]

[7] BASIS AND DISPOSITION OF INSTALLMENT NOTES

[a] Disposition

For the most part, the taxpayer who disposes of an installment obligation is taxed just as the taxpayer who disposes of any other property; i.e., her gain realized and recognized is equal to the difference between her amount realized and her adjusted basis in the note.[46] Since her gain is ultimately from the sale of the property that she transferred when she received the note, the character of her gain (that is, capital or ordinary) on the sale of the note is determined by reference to the

---

40. § 453A(c)(2)(B).

41. § 453A(c)(3).

42. § 453(b)(1).

43. § 453(b)(2)(A) and (B).

44. Id.

45. In other words, if T holds notes totaling $7,000,000, interest would be due only on 2/7 of that total, because only 2/7 of the total is in excess of $5,000,000. § 453A(c)(4).

46. § 453B(a).

character of gain she would have had on the sale or exchange of the asset she transferred to receive the note.[47]

Interestingly, section 453B also provides that the taxpayer who disposes of an installment obligation other than by sale or exchange also recognizes gain on that disposition, in an amount equal to the excess of the note's fair market value over its adjusted basis.[48] While this suggests that the taxpayer who gives a note as a gift or transfers it in some other transfer that is typically tax-free might be in for an unpleasant surprise, it turns out that under the regulations, transfers that are typically untaxed, such as gifts, like-kind exchanges, tax-free incorporations etc. are excluded from this provision.[49] Hence, dispositions of installment obligations are by and large treated the same as dispositions of other property.

[b] Adjusted Basis

Section 453B(b) provides that the basis of an installment obligation is "the excess of the face value of the obligation over the amount that would be returnable as income were the obligation satisfied in full." At the time of sale, this simply means that the seller's basis in the obligation is the same as her basis was in the property sold. In other words, if T sells property with a basis of $20,000 for 6 annual principal payments of $20,000, her basis in the note is $20,000, the same as her basis was in the property. The more complicated wording of the statute represents an attempt to describe how the seller's basis in the note changes as she receives payments. To see how this works, note that T will be taxed on 5/6 of each payment she receives (T's amount realized and total payments will be the six $20,000 principal payments [a total of $120,000]; her basis was $20,000; and her total profit is $100,000. As a result, her profit percentage is $100,000/$120,000, or 5/6). When she receives her first payment of $20,000, she will be taxed on 5/6 x $20,000, or $16,667. When that happens, her basis in the note will be increased by that same $16,667 to prevent double taxation. After that payment, T's adjusted basis in the note will be $20,000 + $16,667, or $36,667. Section 453B(b) reaches the same result by beginning with the note's face amount of $120,000, subtracting from that the gain not yet taxed ($100,000 total gain minus $16,667 already taxed, for a total of $83,333) and ending with the same basis of $36,667 ($120,000 minus $83,000).

[c] Accounting for Interest and Principal in Installment Sales

As explained above, section 453 applies only to payments made in exchange for the property being sold.[50] The fact that one or more payments will be made after the year in which the sale is made means that in addition to paying for the property, the purchaser will also pay some amount of interest for the interim use of money. As suggested

47. § 453B(a) (flush language).

48. § 453B(a)(2).

49. Treas. Reg. § 1.453–9(b)(1).

50. See § 453(a).

heretofore, both the seller and the purchaser of property might well be tempted to mischaracterize some or all of that interest as payments for the property. The seller might prefer to report long-term capital gains rather than ordinary interest income, and the buyer might wish to characterize as much as possible as payments for property in order to maximize her basis and potential depreciation or section 179 deductions. Each of the foregoing can provide deductions prior to any interest, which can be deducted only as it accrues under the OID rules.[51]

Indeed, without some way to impute interest in installment sales, taxpayers would have used installment sales to manipulate both the character and timing of income. To see how this might have happened, assume that L sells to B a long-term capital asset with a basis and value of $100,000. Rather than get paid $100,000 at the time of the sale, however, L agrees to allow B to defer making any payments for ten years. Assuming an arm's length transaction and a 10% interest rate, the amount due from B at the end of ten years will be approximately $259,000, which represents $100,000 principal plus interest at 10% compounded annually for 10 years.

If B and L arranged a transaction according to whose terms payment of $259,000 was due at the end of ten years, and that payment was treated as including no interest but was treated as representing only payment due for the property, B could assert that the entire $159,000 profit was long-term capital gain rather than ordinary income, and it is properly taxable only when payments are actually received in year ten rather than accruing over the entire ten years, as the OID rules would require. In addition, if the property sold were depreciable, L would be happy to go along with this characterization because she could assert that she paid $259,000 for depreciable property (much of which she might well be able to deduct in year one under section 179) rather than only $100,000 for the depreciable property and the remainder in interest which she could deduct only over time.

Under the OID rules, unstated interest would be taxed to L and deductible by B as it accrues each year ($10,000 in year one, $11,000 in year two, $12,100 in year three, etc.). The Code now generally requires the parties to a sale which involves deferred payments to characterize an appropriate amount of such payments as interest and to include and deduct that interest as it accrues.[52] The mechanism by which that recharacterization takes place, and the rules that govern the timing of interest income and deductions in installment sales, are somewhat flexible. The general rule, to which there are numerous exceptions, appears in section 1274. As an initial matter, section 1274 characterizes as interest any amounts to be paid to the seller by the purchaser to the extent they exceed the "imputed principal amount."[53] This imputed

---

51. The OID rules are contained in § 1272 *et seq.*

52. There are several exceptions to this general rule. See § 1274(c)(3).

53. See § 1274(a)(2).

principal amount is determined by calculating the *present value*, as of the time of the sale or exchange, of all payments to be made by the purchaser to the seller, using as the interest rate the applicable federal rate.[54]

The idea of section 1274 is that the present value (using the AFR[55] as the discount rate) of all present and future payments made and to be made by the purchaser to the seller represent the value of the *property* sold at the time of the sale. Since the fair market value of any property is the *value* (as opposed to a stated *"price,"* which may actually include unstated interest in addition to principal) as determined by the purchaser and seller in an arm's length agreement, the present value of the payments to be made is the best available estimate of the value of the property at the time of sale. Because the present value of all payments to be made by the purchaser is by definition the value of what the purchaser is *paying* for the property, it must also be the value that the seller is *receiving* for the property.

Once one knows (or presumes, as required by section 1274) the value, and *actual* (as opposed to "stated") sales price of the property, it is a fairly non-controversial next step to presume that any amounts paid by the purchaser in *excess* of the value of the property represent amounts paid for the extension of credit by the seller to the purchaser rather than for the property itself. Thus, the excess of the *total payments* (in absolute dollar terms rather than present value terms) called for in the agreement over the value of the property itself (the present value of all payments) payments must represent payment for the extension of credit rather than payment for the property, and as such it is treated as interest.

If the stated (in the agreement between the parties) interest equals or exceeds the interest as determined under section 1274, no other amounts will be characterized as interest.[56] If no interest is stated or if the stated interest is less than the interest determined by applying section 1274, then interest will be imputed.[57] The total amount of interest imputed will equal the excess of the amount determined under section 1274 over the interest stated in the agreement between the parties.

The determination of the amount of interest in the transaction is only the beginning of the determination of how the transaction will be taxed. Initially, even prior to accounting for the imputed interest, it is important to note that the seller's amount realized for the property and the purchaser's cost (and cost basis) for the property are equal to the principal, or present value, of the payments to be made. Thus, the first step after determining the amount of principal and interest under section 1274 is to determine the seller's amount realized, profit, and

---

54. § 1274(b). The interest rate to be used is capped at 9% in cases where the principal amount of the debt instrument does not exceed $2,800,000. § 1274A(a).

55. See § 1274(d) for determination of the AFR or applicable federal rate.

56. See § 1274(a)(1).

57. See § 1274(a)(2).

profit percentage, so that installment sale treatment can be applied to the correct sales price.

Once the sales price and the proper treatment of principal payments under section 453 has been determined, the next step is to determine how and when the interest is taxed. In smaller transactions, which, because of their size, create less opportunity for abuse and are less likely to involve sophisticated taxpayers and tax attorneys, interest may be accounted for under the cash method; this means that the seller will include in income and the purchaser will deduct interest only as it is paid. Such cash method accounting is permitted only if: (1) the principal amount (present value) of the obligation does not exceed $2,000,000, (2) both parties *elect* to use the cash method, and (3) the seller is neither an accrual method taxpayer nor a dealer in the type of goods sold.

In all cases in which either the principal amount exceeds $2,000,000, or the seller is either a dealer in the goods sold or an accrual method taxpayer, or in which the purchaser and seller do not both affirmatively elect to account for interest under the cash method, interest must be accounted for as accrued, regardless of when it is paid.

Unfortunately, even knowing the amount of principal and interest and knowing that interest is accounted for when paid may not provide complete guidance as to how the sale is taxed. Since interest in these cases is often imputed and not stated, the agreement between the parties typically provides no basis for determining which part of which payments made represent interest and which parts represent principal. Of course, if interest is taxed only when paid, it is essential to know how much of each payment is actually interest. In addition, in order to apply section 453 to each principal payment (but not to any interest payment), it is necessary to first know what part of each payment made is principal as opposed to interest. In these cases, it is presumed that any payment made represents interest to the extent interest has accrued (and not been already paid) up to the time the payment is made. Any payment made is treated as a principal payment (treated under the installment sales rules of section 453) to the extent the payment exceeds any interest accrued up to and including the date of payment.

[d] Examples

[i] Cash Method, Single Payment Example

To see how the imputed interest rules work in conjunction with installment sales, assume that S owns land with a basis of $100,000. At a time when the applicable federal rate is 8%, S sells the land to P for a single payment of $1,000,000 to be made at the end of 10 years. The present value of the payments, using the 8% applicable federal rate, is $463,000. That is also presumed by section 1274 to be the fair market value of the property sold. If the taxpayers can and do elect to have interest taxed under the cash method, then no interest is taxed until the payment is made at the end of year 10. At that time, when P pays S $1,000,000, $463,000 of that amount is principal (S's amount realized, and P's cost basis). S would owe tax on her gain of $363,000 (amount realized of $463,000 minus S's adjusted basis in the property sold of $100,000). In addition, in year 10 when the payment is made, S has interest income of $537,000 (the excess of total payments made over the present value of those payments as of the date of sale) in year 10 when she receives the payment, and P has an interest deduction (subject to the restrictions of section 163) of $537,000 in year 10 when she makes the payment.

[ii]   Cash Method, Annual Payments Example

The transaction can get a little more complicated if the parties properly elect to account for interest using the cash method and some payments are made annually. Consider, for example, the result if S sells property in which she has a basis of $100,000 in exchange for P's promise to pay $200,000 per year for five years beginning at the end of year one, and none of that amount is specified as interest. One would first have to determine the total present value of the five payments at the appropriate AFR discount rate (that present value, assuming an interest rate of 8%, is $798,000). The present value is then presumed to be the value of the property, which is both the amount P pays for the property and S's amount realized for the property (as opposed to interest).

Since the principal amount to be paid in this transaction is $798,000, S will recognize a total gain of $698,000 (the excess of her amount realized of $798,000 over her basis of $100,000). Under the installment sale rules, then, since S will recognize a total gain of $698,000 and S will receive total principal (as opposed to interest) payments of $798,000, 698/798 of each dollar of principal S receives will be taxed as gain, and the remaining 100/798 of each dollar of principal received will represent return of capital.

When P pays $200,000 at the end of each year, that payment represents a payment of both accrued interest and principal. While it is clear how the interest will be taxed (income and deduction when paid) and it is clear how the principal will be taxed to S (698/798 gain, 100/798 return of capital), it is necessary first to determine how much of that $200,000 payment made at the end of year one is principal and how much is interest. Since the payment is treated as interest to the extent that there is accrued but unpaid interest at the end of year one, it is in turn necessary to determine the amount of accrued interest as of the end of year one. To determine the interest that accrues during any year, one must simply determine the amount of the debt outstanding as of the beginning of the year (in this case, the $798,000 principal amount of the note) and apply to that amount the appropriate interest rate (in this case, the given AFR of 8%). The interest that accrues during year one is thus 8% of $798,000, or $63,840.

Of the $200,000 payment made at the end of year one, $63,840 is deemed to be interest, deductible (subject to the restrictions of section

163) to P and taxable to S when paid. The rest of the payment is principal. The principal payment made at the end of year one is thus $136,160. Of that amount, 698/798 ($119,097) is taxed as gain recognized to S at the end of year one, and the remainder is treated as a return of capital.

The next step in the process is to determine the balance of the note (the "adjusted issue price") as of the beginning of year two. Recall that the original principal of the note was $798,000, and that interest accrued at the rate of 8% during year one. As a result, immediately prior to P's year one payment, the total balance of the note was the $798,000 original issue price, increased by the $63,840 interest that accrued during the year, for a total balance of $861,840. Since P paid $200,000 of that balance ($63,840 interest and $136,160 principal) at the end of year one, the balance as of the beginning of year two is $661,840 ($861,840–$200,000).

When P pays $200,000 at the end of year two, that payment is deemed to be interest to the extent that interest has accrued on the principal and not yet been paid. Since the balance of the note (adjusted issue price) as of the beginning of year two was $661,840, interest accrued during year two equal to 8% of $661,840, for total interest of $52,947 (deductible to P and income to S when paid) and principal of $147,053. Of that principal amount, 698/798 is taxed as gain recognized to S at the end of year one (698/798 x $147,053 = $128,625), and the remainder is treated as a return of capital.

[iii] Accrual Method, Single Payment Example

To see how the imputed interest rules work when either the parties are ineligible for the cash method treatment of interest or do not elect cash method treatment, let us return to the original example. At a time when the applicable federal rate is 8%, S sells land to P for a single payment of $1,000,000 to be made at the end of 10 years. As in the original example, the present value of the payments, using the 8% applicable federal rate, is $463,000. That is also presumed by section 1274 to be the fair market value of the property sold. Because the taxpayers either cannot or do not elect to use the cash method with respect to interest, the accrual method will apply. As a result, even though no payments are made until year 10, interest is deductible to P and includable for S as it accrues (at the appropriate AFR). In year one, P will deduct and S will include interest of $37,040 (8% of $463,000).

As of the end of year one, the balance on the debt (the adjusted issue price) will be the original principal of $463,000 plus the $37,040 interest that accrued in year one, for a total of $500,040. In year two, interest will accrue at the rate of 8% on that balance, so that during year two P will deduct and S will include interest of $40,000. Interest will accrue on the increasingly higher balance until year ten, when payment is made. When P pays S $1,000,000 at the end of year 10, $463,000 of that amount will represent principal, and the rest will represent interest which has already been taxed as it accrued. The $463,000 principal will be taxed under the installment sales rules. Under those rules, since S's basis was $100,000 and her amount realized was $463,000, she has a gain of $363,000. As a result, 363/463 of every dollar of principal she receives is taxable gain. S is taxed on her gain of $363,000 when she receives the payment in full in year ten.

[iv]   Accrual Method, Annual Payments Example

To complete all possible variations of this example, assume that S sells property in which she has a basis of $100,000 in exchange for P's promise to pay $200,000 per year for five years beginning at the end of year one, and none of that amount is specified as interest. Again, one would first have to determine the total present value of the five payments at the appropriate AFR discount rate (that present value, assuming an interest rate of 8%, is $798,000). The present value is then presumed to be the value of the property, which is both the amount P pays for the property and S's amount realized for the property (as opposed to interest).

When P pays $200,000 at the end of each year, that payment represents a payment of both accrued interest and principal. At the end of year one, the total interest that has accrued is 8% of the initial principal of $798,000, or $63,840. When P makes a payment of $200,000, $63,840 of that amount is interest, which is taxed to S and deductible by P on the accrual method. The remaining $136,160 is a payment of principal. Of that amount, 698/798 ($119,097) is taxed as gain recognized to S at the end of year one, and the remainder is treated as a return of capital.

Again, the next step in the process is to determine the balance of the note (the "adjusted issue price") as of the beginning of year two. Recall that the original principal of the note was $798,000, and that interest accrued at the rate of 8% during year one. As a result, immediately prior to P's year one payment, the total balance of the note was the $798,000 original issue price, increased by the $63,840 interest that accrued during the year, for a total balance of $861,840. Since P paid $200,000 of that balance ($63,840 interest and $136,160 principal) at the end of year one, the balance as of the beginning of year two is $661,840 ($861,840 – $200,000).

When P pays $200,000 at the end of year two, that payment is deemed to be interest to the extent that interest has accrued on the principal (and been taxed to S and deducted by P using the accrual method) and not yet been paid. Since the balance of the note (adjusted issue price) as of the beginning of year two was $661,840, interest accrued during year two equal to 8% of $661,840, for total interest of $52,947 (deductible to P and income to S when paid) and principal of $147,053. Of that principal amount, 698/798 is taxed as gain recognized to S at the end of year one (698/798 x $147,053 = $128,625), and the remainder is treated as a return of capital.

Chapter 9

NONRECOGNITION PROVISIONS

Table of Sections

§ 9.01 OVERVIEW OF NONRECOGNITION TRANSACTIONS

Taxpayers are generally not taxed on the increase in value of property they own until they sell or exchange that property.[1] When a sale or exchange does occur, section 1001(c) provides that "except as otherwise provided ... the entire amount of gain or loss ... on the sale or exchange of property shall be recognized." As used in the Code, "recognized" means nothing other than "taken into consideration for tax purposes." Thus, when taxpayers sell or exchange property, that transaction may result in the imposition of substantial tax on gains which may have been accumulating for years. Congress has decided that there are a few occasions when taxpayers ought to be permitted to sell or exchange property without the imposition of taxation (or, at times, without the benefit of receiving a current tax deduction). These occasions are typically governed by the Code's "nonrecognition" provisions.

When a sale or exchange is *not* recognized under the Code, the intended result is that the Code should come as close as possible to simply ignoring the transaction for tax purposes. Nonrecognition treatment is *not* intended to exempt gain (or loss) from tax, but, instead, it is intended only to defer that gain (or loss)—to leave the inherent gain or loss intact to be taxed on a later taxable sale or exchange. Nor is nonrecognition treatment intended to change the character of any gain or loss (or any other applicable tax attributes). Instead, nonrecognition provisions come as close as possible to simply *ignoring* the unrecognized sale or exchange and pretending it never happened. To the extent possible,[2] tax attributes such as the taxpayer's basis, holding period, depreciation and recapture that attached to the property sold or exchanged by the taxpayer in the nonrecognition exchange will attach themselves to the asset received in the exchange. This enables the taxpayer and the Service to simply pretend that the unrecognized exchange never happened.

Congress has enacted relatively few nonrecognition provisions, and those that it has enacted apply only to situations that Congress has determined are particularly inappropriate occasions to impose the federal income tax. The most important examples not covered in this chapter are the formation of corporations, partnerships or LLCs.[3] If Congress had not exempted the mere formation of business entities from tax, people would never form such entities, or at least might never transfer

---

§ 9.01

1. See § 1001(a).

2. As explained below, sometimes it is not possible to simply ignore a transaction, because the type of asset the taxpayer owns

changes from depreciable to nondepreciable, etc.

3. See § 351 and § 721.

to such entities any appreciated property. The other significant nonrecognition provisions are covered below.

§ 9.02 SECTION 1031: LIKE–KIND EXCHANGES

To return to basics, a taxpayer realizes (and generally recognizes) gain whenever she receives *anything* different from what she had before.[1] The receipt of something different does not itself make the taxpayer any wealthier than she was immediately prior to the receipt; unless the taxpayer is a gifted bargainer, the gain realized on the sale or exchange simply represents appreciation in value that has occurred but not yet been taxed over the entire time the taxpayer has held the asset. Nonetheless, it provides an appropriate occasion for taxation in part because the exchange suggests the taxpayer has voluntarily transformed her asset. Whether she has received cash, other property, or services, she has transformed her property into *something* different from what it was previously.

Section 1031 generally provides for nonrecognition when the taxpayer, although engaging in something that is an "exchange" and therefore results in the realization of gain under section 1001, does not sufficiently transformation her relationship with the asset to justify the imposition of tax. Hence, section 1031 grants nonrecognition of gain or loss when a taxpayer exchanges certain property for certain other property of a "like kind."

The two major requirements for section 1031 are that (1) the property traded and the property received must both qualify under section 1031, and (2) the taxpayer must in fact *"exchange"* one qualified property for another.[2] These are both discussed below.

[1] PROPERTY POTENTIALLY SUBJECT TO SECTION 1031

[a] Property Held for Productive Use in a Trade or Business or for Investment

In order for section 1031 to apply, the taxpayer must exchange property held for productive use in a trade or business (e.g., equipment or real property used in a business) or property held for investment for other property which she will also hold for productive use in a trade or business or for investment.[3] So long as the other requirements of section 1031 are met, a taxpayer can trade property used in one business for property to be used in a different business, and the taxpayer can trade property held for investment for other property to be held for productive use in a trade or business, or vice versa.[4] This assumes both the property traded and the property used each are held for one of the permissible

§ 9.02

1. See § 1001(a).

2. See § 1031(a)(1).

3. § 1001(a)(1).

4. See Treas. Reg. § 1.1031(a)–1(a)(1).

uses.[5] If either the property traded or the property received is held by the taxpayer either for personal use or as inventory or property held primarily for sale or exchange in a business,[6] section 1031 treatment is unavailable.

[b]   Exceptions

For the most part, section 1031 is available only for the taxpayer who trades and receives a direct ownership interest in *tangible* property. There are exceptions to this requirement, though, so rather than put this requirement directly into the statute, section 1031(a)(2) instead provides that the section shall *not* apply if either the property traded or the property received is stocks, bonds, notes,[7] other securities or evidence of indebtedness or interest,[8] interests in a partnership,[9] certificates of trust or beneficial interests,[10] or choses in action.[11] As a result, intangible assets may qualify for 1031 treatment so long as they meet the other requirements and are not among the specifically excluded types of intangibles in section 1031(a)(2)(A)–(F). The regulations give at least two examples of intangibles that can qualify, if the other requirements are met, including: (1) a leasehold interest in real property that has at least 30 years of occupancy remaining[12] and (2) assets such as patents or copyrights.[13]

[c]   The Meaning of "Like–Kind"

The most significant restriction on property imposed by section 1031 is that the property received must be "like-kind" to the property traded.[14] The regulations state that "like-kind" refers to the "nature and character" of the property, rather than to the quality of the property.[15]

[d]   Application of Section 1031 to Real Property

Section 1031 has long been popular among real estate investors. The reason for this is simple—the regulations very generously treat all real property as like-kind to all other real property.[16] In other words, undeveloped rural land is like-kind to densely-used urban office buildings, and a lease on any real property with 30 years or more to run is like-kind to any other real property.[17] As a result, any real property held for investment or for productive use in a trade or business can be exchanged for any other real property to be so held under section 1031. So long as they

---

5.   Id.

6.   § 1031(a)(2)(A).

7.   § 1031(a)(2)(B).

8.   § 1031(a)(2)(C).

9.   § 1031(a)(2)(D).

10.   § 1031(a)(2)(E).

11.   § 1031(a)(2)(F).

12.   Treas. Reg. § 1.1031(a)–1(c).

13.   Treas. Reg. § 1.1031(a)–2(c). The regulations make it clear, though, that not

all patents are like kind to other patents, and copyrights are not necessarily like-kind to all other copyrights.

14.   See § 1031(a)(1).

15.   Treas. Reg. § 1.1031(a)–1(b).

16.   Commissioner v. Crichton, 122 F.2d 181 (5th Cir. 1941); Treas. Reg. § 1.1031(a)–1(b). See also Peabody Natural Resources Co. v. Commissioner, 126 T.C. 261 (2006); TAM 200424001; TAM 200035005.

17.   Treas. Reg. § 1.1031(a)–1(b).

are content to remain in real estate, investors can diversify and change their investments drastically and routinely and remain untaxed on any realized gains.[18]

On a few occasions, the breadth of the definition of like-kind with respect to real property has come back to haunt taxpayers who thought they had engaged in transactions that generated deductible losses. To see how this has transpired, assume that T owns real property with a basis of $10,000,000 and a value of $5,000,000, and T wants to be able to deduct the $5,000,000 loss in the property without actually fully disposing of the right to the underlying property. T might sell the property for $5,000,000 and simultaneously take back a 99 year lease on the property. In some similar instances, T believed she was entitled to deduct the $5,000,000 loss on the property and to subsequently deduct the annual rental payments. T learned only later that the Service viewed the transaction as an exchange of real property for another interest in real property (a lease for more than 30 years),[19] so that the exchange was governed by section 1031 and the result was nonrecognition of the desired loss.[20]

[e] Depreciable Tangible Property

The regulations refer to two tables prepared by the government that contain virtually every type of tangible depreciable property and classify it for purposes initially unrelated to section 1031.[21] Rev. Proc. 87–56[22] classified all types of depreciable tangible property frequently used in business into "general asset classes" so that taxpayers could use the tables provided in order to determine the proper classification of property for depreciation purposes. Regulation section 1.1031(a)–2(b)(1) provides that, for purposes of section 1031, any assets within the same "general asset class" under Rev. Proc. 87–56 will be treated as like kind for purposes of section 1031. In case assets do not appear in Rev. Proc. 87–56, the section 1031 regulations look instead to tables maintained by OMB, and the section 1031 regulations treat as like-kind any assets classified as within the same "product class" in those tables.[23]

[f] Intangibles

The definition of what intangibles are like-kind to other intangibles continues to be somewhat less clear than the definition of like-kind for other types of property. Whether intangibles are like-kind depends on both the character of the rights involved (e.g., patent, copyright, or

18. See § 1031(a)(1); Treas. Reg. § 1.1031(a)–1(b).

19. See Treas. Reg. § 1.1031(a)–1(b).

20. Of course, in some cases the Service might apply substance versus form and view the entire transaction as some sort of financing rather than as an exchange of properties.

21. See Treas. Reg. § 1.1031(a)–2(a) and (b)(1).

22. 87–2 C.B. 674.

23. See the North American Industry Classification System (NAICS), set forth in Executive Office of the President, Office of Management and Budget, North American Industry Classification System, United States, 2002 (NAICS Manual).

goodwill) and the character of the underlying property.[24] In other words, no patent is like-kind to a copyright or to goodwill, but that does not mean that a patent is necessarily like-kind to another patent.[25] The regulations give as an example of like-kind properties two copyrights on novels, but they exclude from like-kind status a copyright on a novel and a copyright on a song.[26] The regulations do make clear, however, that any goodwill or going concern value is not like-kind to any other goodwill or going concern value, simply because the business involved are always different.[27]

[2] EXCHANGES

In order to qualify for nonrecognition under section 1031, the taxpayer must *exchange* property for other qualified property.[28] The taxpayer who sells property for cash or exchanges property for nonqualified property can never qualify for nonrecognition of gain under section 1031; this rule is applicable even if she immediately uses the cash received to purchase property that would have qualified had the property been received in a direct exchange.[29]

Unfortunately for the taxpayer, the converse of the above principal is not equally true. A taxpayer who seeks to replace property held for investment or for use in a business may note that the property she seeks to trade away has a basis in excess of its value. If so, rather than simply engage it in a like-kind exchange to procure replacement property, she may sell the original property for cash and immediately use the cash to purchase the replacement property. This avoids the application of section 1031 and entitles the taxpayer to a loss deduction on the sale of the original property. Such a sale followed by a purchase of similar property will certainly result in the nonapplication of section 1031 to any gain realized, and it will usually allow the taxpayer to recognize any loss inherent in the exchanged property. However, if the taxpayer engages in the sale and repurchase of like-kind property with the same seller-purchaser, the Service may potentially restructure the transaction as a single exchange that is governed by section 1031, thereby disallowing, for now, the desired loss deduction.[30]

[a] Three–Party Exchanges

Often, a taxpayer who owns investment real estate, and who wants to exchange it for like-kind property, may find a property on the market that suits her needs. But, it is indeed rare that the owner of that other property will be interested in receiving the taxpayer's exact piece of property. Most of the time, the owner of the other property will want cash for her property, rather than the taxpayer's property. The taxpayer

---

24. See Treas. Reg. § 1.1031(a)–2(c)(1).

25. Id.

26. Treas. Reg. § 1.1031(a)–2(c)(3) Examples 1 and 2.

27. Treas. Reg. § 1.1031(a)–2(c)(2).

28. § 1031(a)(1).

29. See § 1031(a)(1).

30. See Rev. Rul. 61–119, 1961–1 C.B. 395; Redwing Carriers, Inc. v. Tomlinson, 399 F.2d 652 (5th Cir. 1968).

will likely be able to find someone interested in her property and willing to pay cash for it, but, again, the taxpayer who receives cash and then uses the cash to purchase like-kind property will not be entitled to nonrecognition treatment under section 1031 no matter what her intentions and regardless of how short a time she holds the cash.[31]

In order to facilitate taxpayers who seek nonrecognition in situations like that above, third parties often act as intermediaries. Typically in these cases, the taxpayer (T), the would-be purchaser of the taxpayer's property (P), and the would-be seller of the replacement property (S) will all transfer their assets (T's property that P wants to acquire, S's property that T wants to acquire, and the cash that P will pay for T's property (and that S ultimately will acquire)) to the chosen third party ("E" for Escrow agent). In turn, E will then transfer to T the property that T wants, so that T has only entered into an exchange with E, in which T has traded her property for the property she wants. Accordingly, T gets nonrecognition under section 1031. E will also transfer T's property to P, who will end up with that property in exchange for the cash he pays, and E will transfer the cash from P to S, who will receive it in exchange for the property ultimately transferred to T.

In the above exchange, all parties ultimately get exactly what they wanted, in exchange for what they are willing to transfer. The tax consequences to S, who sells for cash, and to P, who makes a cash purchase, are not impacted by the structure of this transaction. The sole purpose of the arrangement is to ensure that T can receive nonrecognition on the "exchange" with E of her property for the property formerly owned by S.

There are two potential tax issues that may be raised by such exchanges. First, it is likely that all of the parties involved in the above three-party exchanges will demand guarantees from E, to ensure that he does not damage or dispose of the properties prior to distribution to the parties. Such guarantees, accompanied by security arrangements, will not negatively affect T's nonrecognition *unless* the IRS determines that such arrangements result in T's "constructive receipt" of cash or property other than like-kind property.[32]

In turn, the Service will find that T is in constructive receipt of property other than the proper replacement property if T has the right to receive, pledge, borrow or otherwise obtain the benefits of that property (including cash or its equivalent) other than as a result of the third-party's default of its obligation to transfer to T the property T has agreed to receive.[33] In other words, any type of security or guarantee to T will not interfere with nonrecognition treatment under section 1031 *unless* T has a right to access the security or guarantee even absent a default by the third party.[34] If T can access money or other property in such cases, T has a current right to receive the cash or other property

31. See § 1031(a).

32. See Treas. Reg. § 1.1031(k)–1(a).

33. Id.

34. Id.

pledged instead of waiting for the like-kind property, and that current right to take the cash or other property is treated as the constructive receipt by T of that property and will result in current taxation.[35]

The other limit on the use of three-party exchanges to qualify for section 1031 treatment is that such exchanges must be time limited.[36] If T transfers her property to the third party in anticipation of making a like-kind exchange, section 1031 requires that: (1) T must identify proper replacement properties within 45 days of her transfer[37] and (2) the entire exchange must be completed within 180 days of T's initial transfer of her property to the third party.[38]

[b] Operative Provisions

Section 1031(a) provides that "no gain or loss shall be recognized" on qualifying exchanges; even so, several other provisions work in concert with section 1031 to ensure that whatever gain goes unrecognized as a result of section 1031 does not go untaxed in perpetuity. That is to say that any amount which qualifies for nonrecognition treatment under section 1031 merely defers any built-in gain or loss on the transaction until such time as the taxpayer sells or exchanges the replacement property in a taxable transaction.

[c] Basis

If a transaction qualifies for section 1031, the realized gain on the transaction is not recognized, except to the extent that the party receives boot in excess of any boot paid.[39] It is important to understand, though, that in this as in other nonrecognition transactions, the unrecognized gain is not permanently exempted from tax. Rather, the basis rules ensure that any realized and unrecognized gain (or loss) will be accounted for upon subsequent disposition of the newly-acquired property. This is achieved by substituting the basis of the old property for that of the new property.[40]

To see how section 1031 defers any unrecognized gain or loss, suppose that T transfers to X an office building with a fair market value of $200,000 and an adjusted basis of $120,000, for an apartment building owned by X with a fair market value of $200,000. On the transaction T realizes a gain of $80,000 (the excess of the value of what T has received [$200,000] over T's basis in the property exchanged [$120,000],[41] but section 1031 provides that none of this gain is recognized.[42] To ensure that T's $80,000 of realized gain is deferred and does not disappear

---

35. Id.

36. See Treas. Reg. § 1.1031(k)–1(b).

37. § 1031(a)(3)(A). Note: The taxpayer may identify a single replacement property, up to three alternative properties, or any number of properties so long as the value of such properties does not exceed twice the value of the property she is exchanging. Treas. Reg. § 1.1031(k)–1(c).

38. § 1031(a)(3)(B)(i) and (ii).

39. See § 1031(a)(1) and (b).

40. § 1031(d).

41. See § 1001(a).

42. § 1031(a).

permanently, section 1031(d) provides that T's basis in the apartment building she has just received is the same as her basis was in the office building she has just exchanged [$120,000].

Hence, T's unrecognized gain on the office building is preserved in the apartment building. If and when T sells the apartment building for $200,000, she will recognize the $80,000 gain that was realized, but not previously recognized. If T later sells the newly acquired apartment building for either more or less than $200,000, of course, her gain or loss on that sale may vary. Regardless of how much T eventually sells the apartment building for, though, her gain on any subsequent sale of the apartment building will always be $80,000 more than it would be if her basis were her $200,000 cost for that building. Thus for example if T sells the office building three years later for $340,000, her gain will be [$340,000 – $120,000] or $220,000. If her basis had been the fair market value of the apartment building (or her $200,000 cost), then her gain on a sale for $340,000 would be $140,000. Thus T will still recognize the extra $80,000 of gain that she did not recognize on the earlier transaction. Alternatively, any subsequent loss on sale of the apartment building will always be $80,000 less than it would be if he basis were $200,000.

Ultimately, the purpose of the basis rule in 1031(d) is to ensure that the taxpayer who avoids recognition on her current exchange of property will *at some point in the future* recognize that deferred gain.

[d] Holding Period

If both the property exchanged and the property acquired in a section 1031 transaction are either capital assets or section 1231 assets, not only the basis of the property, but also the length of time the taxpayer has held the property are important.[43] Generally, capital assets or section 1231 property held for more than a year will result in long-term capital gain (or 1231 gain) rather than short-term gain (or ordinary income) upon their disposition.[44] In line with the general idea of pretending the section 1031 exchange simply never happened, section 1223(1) provides that in any exchange, if the taxpayer takes the same basis in the new property as she had in the old property (for example, because of section 1031(d)), the taxpayer will also be deemed to have held the *new* property for as long as she held the property transferred.

[e] Depreciation

In most cases not involving real property, if the taxpayer exchanges depreciable property for other depreciable property in an exchange governed by section 1031, the newly-acquired property will have the same recovery period and depreciation method as that applied for the property transferred.[45] This result is because the properties exchanged are likely to have been considered "like-kind" under the regulations

---

43. See § 1031(d) and § 1223(1).

44. See § 1(h).

45. Treas. Reg. § 1.168(i)–6(c).

precisely because they were included in the same general asset class.[46] In such cases, the regulations provide that the newly-acquired asset simply take the place of the transferred asset in terms of depreciation.[47] It will be depreciated as if it actually were the same asset transferred.[48] As a result, if T trades five-year recovery property for other like-kind property and the traded property has only two years remaining depreciation, the newly-acquired property will be depreciated over the remaining two years just as the exchanged property would have been had it not been exchanged.[49]

Most property subject to section 1031 exchanges has of course been real property. Because residential real property held as an investment and business real estate are, though like-kind under section 1031, subject to different depreciation schedules, the regulations do not necessarily allow the taxpayer to treat newly-acquired (in a section 1031 exchange) real estate to step into the shoes of the real property traded away.[50] If both properties are subject to the same depreciation schedules, or if the property received would normally be depreciated more rapidly than the property traded away (that is, if the taxpayer trades nonresidential real property for residential real estate held for investment or for productive use in a trade or business), the regulations provide that the newly-acquired property will be treated the same as the exchanged property was being treated (that is, the new property simply steps into the shoes of the other property for purposes of depreciation).[51] On the other hand, if the newly-acquired property is subject to slower depreciation (business property acquired in exchange for residential rental property), the new property must be depreciated over the slower schedule applicable to such property.[52]

[f] Depreciation Recapture

Just as the replacement property accedes to the traded property's basis, holding period, and depreciation schedule, the new property received in a like-kind exchange also takes on any depreciation recapture previously in place on the traded property.[53] Section 1245 generally provides that if property has been subjected to depreciation by the taxpayer, any gain on the subsequent sale of that property will be treated as recapture up to the difference between the property's "recomputed basis" (generally, the amount the taxpayer originally paid to acquire the property) and the property's adjusted (for depreciation taken) basis. Since replacement property received in a section 1031 exchange already has the same basis as the property traded, section 1245 incorporates the recapture from the old property into the new one by providing that the "recomputed basis" of the new property is the basis

46. See Treas. Reg. § 1.1031(a)–2(b)(1).

47. Treas. Reg. § 1.168(i)–6(c).

48. Id.

49. See Treas. Reg. § 1.168(i)–6(c).

50. See Treas. Reg. § 1.168(i)–6(c)(1)-(5).

51. Id.

52. Id.

53. See § 1245(a)(1) and (2).

of that property increased not only by depreciation taken on the new property but also by depreciation taken on the exchanged property.[54] As a result, on a sale of the new property, the entire difference between the adjusted basis of the new property and the original cost of the old property will be recaptured.[55] Once again, the new property simply assumes the tax characteristics previously inherent in the exchanged like-kind property.

[3] BOOT

When two parties wish to exchange property (or when a taxpayer engages in a three-party exchange designed to ensure nonrecognition under section 1031), it is unlikely that their two properties will have exactly the same value. The person whose property is worth less will be asked to either pay cash or to transfer some other property to make up the difference (generally referred to as "boot").

Although section 1031(a)(1) provides nonrecognition only where property is exchanged "solely for property of a like kind," the transfer of cash or other boot in addition to the like kind property is contemplated by section 1031(b) and (c), and the receipt of boot does not remove the entire transaction from 1031 treatment. It does, however, require recognition of any realized gain (but not loss) to the extent of any boot received.[56]

To see how section 1031 works when boot is received, assume that T transfers to X an office building with a fair market value of $200,000 and an adjusted basis of $120,000 in exchange for an apartment building owned by X with a fair market value of $200,000 and in which X has a basis of $70,000. On the transaction T *realizes* a gain of $80,000 (the excess of the value of what T has received [$200,000] over T's basis in the property exchanged [$120,000], but section 1031 provides that none of this gain is *recognized*).

Suppose instead that T exchanges his office building with a fair market value of $200,000 and a basis of $120,000 for an apartment building worth $180,000, and $20,000 of cash. T will still have a realized gain of $80,000, and section 1031 will still apply, but it will be 1031(b) rather than 1031(a) that governs the tax treatment for T. As a result, T will *recognize* that realized gain to the extent of the cash, or $20,000. Section 1031 will nonetheless prevent T from recognizing the remaining $60,000 of his realized gain.

In some cases, the cash boot received may exceed the realized gain. To see how this can occur, suppose that T exchanges his apartment building (basis of $120,000, fair market value $200,000) for an office building worth $110,000, and $90,000 of cash. Again, T *realizes* a gain of $80,000 (the excess of the total cash and value of the property received over T's basis in the property transferred). Pursuant to section 1031(b),

54. § 1245(a)(2)(A).   **56.** § 1031(b).

55. See § 1245(a)(1).

T recognizes that realized gain to the extent of the $90,000 cash received. Importantly, although T receives cash boot of $90,000, his gain recognized is only *$80,000*. This is because T's gain *recognized* will *never* exceed his gain *realized*.

To avoid confusion, it is worth noting that even if T sold his property (basis $120,000, value $200,000) for $200,000 cash, his recognized gain would be the same $80,000 as it is when T trades for like-kind property plus $90,000 cash. Whenever the boot received in a like-kind exchange (or any other nonrecognition exchange) equals or exceeds the taxpayer's realized gain, *all* that realized gain (and no more) will be recognized. In fact, in these situations, while some may assert that section 1031 applies, T actually has no unrecognized gain. Because he recognizes his entire gain realized, he is taxed in full, and the exchange is more appropriately treated as one governed by the general recognition rule of section 1001(c) rather than by the more complicated rules of section 1031.

[a] Basis Where Boot Is Involved

If T transfers property in a 1031 exchange and receives not only like kind property but also boot, the process for determining T's basis in the new property changes, although typically the end result will be the same as it is when no boot is received.[57] T's basis in the new property will be the same as her basis was in the property transferred.[58] As explained, to the extent that T receives boot, any gain realized will be recognized. To the extent that gain is recognized currently, it would be inappropriate to build into the new property received *all* of T's gain realized on the property transferred. Only the gain that was realized but *not recognized* ought to be built into the new property.

To return to our example, if T transfers property with a basis of $120,000 and a value of $200,000 in exchange for like-kind property worth $180,000 and $20,000 cash, T realizes a gain of $80,000, and T must *recognize* that gain to the extent of the cash received—$20,000. Since T must pay tax *currently* on $20,000 of his $80,000 realized gain, it would be inappropriate to require him to pay tax on the full $80,000 when he sells the new building. In order to ensure that T will not be taxed again on gain recognized currently, section 1031(d) provides that T's basis in the property he receives shall be "increased in the amount of gain ... recognized on such exchange." In other words, to the extent T recognizes gain now, he increases his basis to avoid recognizing that gain a second time when he sells the new property.

In the example above, T receives a building worth $180,000 and $20,000 cash boot. His basis *in all of this* (the new building and the $20,000 cash) is his old basis (exchange basis) of $120,000, increased by his $20,000 of gain recognized on the exchange. Thus, his total basis in the *new building and cash boot* is $140,000. While the tax law does not

---

57. See § 1031(d).   **58.** Id.

refer to cash as having a "basis," section 1031(d) does require that T's basis in the "property" (everything other than money) received must be reduced by the amount of *cash* T receives. This requirement effectively allocates to each dollar of cash received a basis of one dollar.

Thus, in our example, T's total basis in *everything* he receives (the building and the cash) is $140,000, and T's basis in the "property" received (everything T receives except the cash) is $140,000 minus $20,000 (the cash received). T begins with a basis in his *old* building of $120,000, and his basis in the *new* building is $120,000, *increased* by the $20,000 gain T recognizes on the exchange, and *decreased* by the $20,000 basis allocated to the cash boot.

The result of all of these adjustments is that T's basis in the new building is exactly the same as his basis was in the old building— $120,000. Significantly, despite the complex workings of section 1031(d), this will always be the case whenever there is realized but unrecognized gain under section 1031. In other words, *whenever section 1031 results in any realized gain going unrecognized, T's basis in the new like-kind property will always be identical to T's basis in the like-kind property he exchanged.* If T gets boot, he will recognize gain. If T recognizes gain, T's basis in whatever he receives will be adjusted *upwards*. If the boot is cash, then section 1031(d) provides that T's basis in the "property" received is reduced by the cash received. And, if the boot is other than cash (that is, "property" that is not like-kind to the property exchanged), section 1031 provides that boot will be "allocated" a basis equal to its fair market value (which is also the amount of boot received, the amount of gain recognized, and the amount by which T's basis has been increased), so that the amount of basis allocated to the boot (and away from the like kind property) will necessarily equal the amount of basis step-up caused by the gain recognition.

Note that if T received a cash boot of $30,000 rather than $20,000, he would recognize gain of $30,000, his basis in *everything* he received would be increased by $30,000, and that basis would also be *decreased* by the same $30,000 cash received. If T received a noncash boot of $30,000 rather than $20,000, he would again recognize gain of $30,000, his basis in the property (including the like-kind property and the noncash boot) he received would again be increased by $30,000, and $30,000 of that basis would be *allocated* to the boot, again leaving the like-kind property with the same basis that the old like-kind property had in T's hands. The more the boot, the more gain, the more the gain, the higher T's *total* basis, but that increase in basis will in turn either be offset by a corresponding *decrease* in basis (if the boot is cash), or the extra basis will be *allocated* in full to the boot if the boot is property other than cash.

Boot always takes a basis equal to its fair market, under section 1031(d), and like-kind property always takes a basis equal to the like-kind property exchanged (if the transaction resulted in the nonrecognition of any realized gain for T).

Again, the purpose of the section 1031(d) basis rules is to ensure that any gain or loss realized but not recognized in the current exchange because of section 1031(a)(1) is built into the new like-kind property received by T. To the extent that T receives *boot* in addition to the like-kind property, it is because the like-kind property he receives must be worth *less* than the property he transferred (in the example, the new like kind property is worth only $180,000 rather than $200,000, which is why T also receives $20,000 boot). Because T's *basis* in the new property remains the same as his basis was in the old property, while the *value* of the new property is *reduced* (thus the need for boot to make up the difference), T will recognize less gain on sale of the new property (in the example, the new property is worth $180,000 and has a basis of $120,000) than he would have recognized on a sale of the old property. This is because T has already recognized some gain on the section 1031 exchange.

As a result, T recognizes gain on a 1031 exchange only if and to the extent he receives boot. T's receipt of boot means that the like-kind property T receives must be worth *less* than the property T transfers (or there would be no boot paid). The more gain T recognizes on the initial section 1031 exchange (because of boot), the less gain T ought to recognize when he sells the new property. Because the new property has the same basis as the old, but it is worth less (because of and in an amount equal to the boot), T will recognize less gain on a sale of the new property.

The idea of section 1031, and of nonrecognition provisions generally, is that any realized but unrecognized gain or loss is built into the property that is permitted to be received without the recognition of gain (the like-kind property, in section 1031 exchanges). To the extent the taxpayer receives either cash or nonlike-kind property, any realized gain *is* recognized currently.[59] Since the receipt of boot provides no "nonrecognition" of any currently realized gain or loss, it is only appropriate that there should be no gain or loss "built in" to the boot on its receipt. This result is accomplished by providing that boot always takes a basis equal to its fair market value at the time it is received.[60]

[b] Transactions Where All Realized Gain Is Recognized

As discussed above, a taxpayer may transfer property for other property of a like kind in a transaction to which 1031 would appear to apply, but in which the transferor nonetheless is required to *recognize* any realized gain.[61] This is the case whenever (and only if) the transferor receives an amount of boot that equals or exceeds his realized gain.[62] Because such a transaction results does not result in nonrecognition, it is arguably outside the scope of section 1031, and the transferor's basis in the new property is a cost basis.[63] Assuming an arm's length transaction,

59. § 1031(b).

60. See § 1031(d).

61. See § 1031(a) and (b).

62. Id.

63. See § 1012.

the cost basis is simply the value of the acquired property at the time of the exchange.[64] Fortunately, the basis rules of section 1031 provide the same result, although they follow a more circuitous route.[65]

To see how this can play out, assume that T transfers property with a basis of $120,000 and a value of $200,000 for like-kind property worth $110,000 and cash of $90,000. If the transaction is treated under section 1031, T realizes a gain of $80,000 and recognizes that gain in full because he receives boot of more than $80,000.[66] In turn, T's basis in everything he receives is $120,000 (his old basis) increased by the $80,000 recognized gain.[67] Of this $200,000 total, $90,000 is allocated to the $90,000 cash received, leaving T with a basis in the new property of $110,000 (and properly building into the new property no gain or loss, because T's entire gain on the old property has already been recognized).[68]

If one treated this exchange in which there is no unrecognized gain as simply outside the parameters of section 1031, the result would be that T would simply recognize his $80,000 gain and would take a cost basis of $110,000 in the new property.[69] Thus there is no difference in result between applying section 1031 or ignoring it in the situation where there is no unrecognized gain.

[c] Losses

Taxpayers who transfer property in a like-kind exchange with a built-in loss are also subject to the nonrecognition rules of section 1031.[70] If a taxpayer makes an exchange of loss property, the receipt of boot will not alter the fact that she will not be permitted to recognize any realized loss.[71] As with gains, though, the basis rules ensure that any loss not recognized on the section 1031 exchange will be built into the like-kind property the taxpayer receives on the exchange.[72]

To see how the basis rules work to build-in any unrecognized loss, assume that T exchanges property with a basis of $320,000 and a value of $200,000 for like-kind property worth $180,000 and $20,000 cash. Although T realizes a loss of $120,000, section 1031(c) makes it clear that T will *recognize* no loss, and the section 1031(d) basis rules ensure that T's basis in the new property will reflect his unrecognized loss. T's basis in everything he receives will be the same $320,000 basis he had in the old property, *not* increased by any amount, because T recognizes no gain.[73] Of that $320,000, $20,000 will be allocated to the cash received, leaving T with a basis in the new building of $300,000. Because the new building (value $180,000 is worth $20,000 less than the old one) and has

---

64. § 1012.

65. § 1031(d).

66. See § 1031(a) and (b).

67. See § 1031(d).

68. Id.

69. See § 1001(a) and (c); § 1012.

70. See § 1031(a)(1).

71. See § 1031(c).

72. See § 1031(d).

73. Id.

a basis ($300,000 that is $20,000 less than the old one), T's unrecognized loss of $120,000 is built into the new building.

Gain Recognized Under Section 1031:[74]

(1) Gain Realized: Amount Realized – Adjusted Basis

(2) Boot Received: cash plus property that is not like-kind

(3) Gain Recognized = lesser of (1) or (2)

Basis:[75]

(1) Basis of Boot received = fair market value of boot when received

(2) Basis of like-kind property = Basis of old like-kind property + gain recognized – cash received – other boot received

(3) Another way of determining basis of like-kind property: Same as basis of like-kind property exchanged, so long as T has any gain realized that is not recognized.

(4) Still another way of determining basis of like-kind property: Fair market value of the new property – any realized and unrecognized gain + any realized and unrecognized loss.

[d] Debt Relief as Boot

Under Crane v. Commissioner,[76] when a taxpayer disposes of property subject to nonrecourse debt, the amount of debt relief is treated as part of the transferor's amount realized. The same holds true if the transferor transfers property and part of the consideration received is the transferee's assumption of the nonrecourse debt secured by the property. Since most section 1031 exchanges over the years have involved real property and most real property is either subject to nonrecourse debt or secured recourse debt of the owner, it should not be surprising that assumption of debt and relief from debt often play a part in like-kind exchanges.

Neither Congress nor the Treasury believed it appropriate to essentially remove nonrecognition from like-kind exchanges when both properties were subject to similar amounts of debt, and each transferor basically takes on debt similar in amount to the debt of which she was relieved.[77] As a result, the regulations treat relief from debt as boot only to the extent that the taxpayer has a *net* relief from debt pursuant to the exchange.[78] Thus, if T transfers property for other like-kind property in a 1031 exchange, and T takes on debt (either recourse or nonrecourse or both) equal to or greater than the debt from which T is relieved on the

---

74. See § 1031(a) and (b).

75. See § 1031(d).

76. 331 U.S. 1, 67 S.Ct. 1047, 91 L.Ed. 1301 (1947) (holding that a taxpayer who sold property encumbered by a nonrecourse mortgage that was less than the property's fair market value had to include the unpaid balance of the mortgage in the computation

of the amount the taxpayer realized on the sale).

77. See e.g., Treas. Reg. § 1.1031(d)–2.

78. Treas. Reg. § 1.1031(d)–2. In making the determination of whether the taxpayer has a net relief from debt, both nonrecourse and recourse liabilities are taken into account.

exchange, T will not be treated as receiving boot.[79] Of course, if T takes on debt equal to or greater than the amount of debt from which she is relieved, T will be treated as paying boot.[80] To the extent T has a net relief from liabilities, that amount will be treated as cash boot received by T.[81]

[e] Section 1031 as Applied to the Boot Payor

[i] Basis

All of the above examples have involved a taxpayer who transfers property for like-kind property and also receives boot. It is, of course, possible and often true that a party who qualifies for section 1031 treatment *pays* boot rather than receives it. While the same section 1031 rules apply to the party who pays boot, it is important to pay separate attention to the boot payor because in such a case section 1031 may not be the only operative Code section.

As with other aspects of section 1031, this problem is most easily explained by way of example. Assume that X is the other party to T's exchange, and that X transfers to T, in exchange for T's building (basis for T, $120,000, value $200,000) a building with a value of $180,000, in which X has a basis of $70,000, and cash of $20,000. X *receives* no boot and recognizes no gain on this exchange. Her basis, however, is not simply the $70,000 basis she had in the property she transferred, but, instead, it is that $70,000 exchange basis *increased* by the $20,000 X paid. The appropriateness of this result may be understood by noting that the property X has acquired is worth $20,000 more than the property she exchanged, and it now has a basis that is $20,000 higher than that of the exchanged property, so that the unrecognized gain of $110,000 remains built into the new property.

The result for X may be explained most easily by noting that in fact while T has engaged in only a single exchange governed by section 1031(c) (that is, a section 1031 exchange that includes the receipt of boot), X can best be described as having engaged in *two simultaneous but separate exchanges*. In one exchange X trades a building with a basis of $70,000 and a value of $180,000 to T for an interest in T's building worth $180,000. This transaction is a pure section 1031 exchange in which X recognizes no gain, and pursuant to which X takes an exchange basis of $70,000 in $180,000 worth of T's building. In a separate (albeit simultaneous) exchange, X pays T $20,000 cash for $20,000 worth of T's building. X takes a $20,000 cost basis in that part of the building. When combined, these two exchanges give X ownership of all of T's building with a combined basis of $70,000 (exchange basis) plus $20,000 (cost basis).

---

79. See Treas. Reg. § 1.1031(d)–2.   **81.** Id.
80. Id.

[ii]   Gain Recognition on Payment of Boot

To take the above example a step further, assume that rather than transferring a building and cash, X transfers to T a building (basis $70,000), value $180,000) and non-cash boot (a car, basis $5,000, value $20,000). Looking at X as engaging in two simultaneous but separable transactions would mean that: (1) X has acquired $180,000 worth of T's building in a like-kind exchange, from which X takes a basis of $70,000 in that part of the building and (2) X has acquired $20,000 worth of T's old building in exchange for a car in which she has a basis of $20,000. Because the second part of the exchange is separate from section 1031, X must recognize any gain or loss *on the car* under the general principals of section 1001. By exchanging a car with a basis of $5,000 for $20,000 worth of T's building, X recognizes $15,000 of gain on the sale or exchange of the car. Her basis in the $20,000 worth of T's building that she acquires in exchange for the car is $20,000, giving her a total basis of $90,000 in that building.

§ 9.03   SECTION 1033: INVOLUNTARY CONVERSIONS

[1]   IN GENERAL

Generally, the destruction or loss of property by casualty, theft, or condemnation and the resulting receipt of insurance or award proceeds is a taxable transaction, and any gain or loss realized is recognized.[1] Section 1033 does not change this general rule, but it does restrict its application in situations where the taxpayer realizes a gain and reinvests the insurance or other proceeds in property that is "similar or related in service or use" to the property destroyed.[2]

The justification for section 1033 lies in the fact that without it (or some similar provision) the taxpayer whose property is damaged and who seeks only to put herself back in the position she was in prior to the casualty would likely be unable to do so. By way of example, assume that T owns an apartment building with a basis of $250,000 and a value of $4,000,000 and the building is destroyed by fire. Further assume that T has insured the building to its full $4,000,000 value, and T seeks only to use the $4,000,000 insurance proceeds to restore the building to how it was immediately prior to the fire. If 1033 did not exist, T would be unable to do so. The receipt of insurance proceeds of $4,000,000 would result in a realized and recognized gain of $3,750,000.[3] If T's marginal tax rate is 40%, she would incur tax liability of $1,500,000, and she would be left with only $2,250,000, only 60% of what she would need to restore the building to its original condition.

Section 1033 was enacted specifically to assist T and others in her position. Section 1033 provides that if a taxpayer's property is compul-

---

§ 9.03

1.   See § 1001(c).

2.   See § 1033(a).

3.   § 1001(c).

sorily or involuntarily converted (into cash or other property), the taxpayer can *elect* to defer (by way of nonrecognition) any gain realized to the extent that she ends up with property that is "similar or related in service or use" to the converted property.[4]

Eligibility to elect[5] the application of section 1033 requires that: (1) property be compulsorily or involuntarily converted "as a result of its destruction in whole or in part, theft, seizure, or requisition or condemnation or threat or imminence thereof;"[6] (2) replacement occurs within two years of the close of the tax year of the conversion;[7] and (3) the replacement consist of property that is "similar or related in service or use."[8]

[2] SPECIFIC REQUIREMENTS

As indicated, section 1033(a) requires that the taxpayer's property be converted by destruction, theft, seizure, requisition, condemnation, or by the threat or imminence of condemnation.[9] Typically, the "conversion" of one property into another is by way of the taxpayer receiving cash proceeds as either insurance, damages or as compensation for condemnation, and then reinvesting those proceeds in the replacement property. The taxpayer is given two years from the realization of gain (that is, from the receipt of damages or insurance proceeds) to complete the acquisition of the replacement property.[10] Even so, if the amount reinvested in replacement property is less than the amount realized, realized gain is recognized to the extent of the deficiency.[11]

On occasion, involuntary conversion treatment may be permitted for what might at first appear to be a "voluntary" sale. For example, in Masser v. Commissioner,[12] the taxpayer operated an interstate trucking business on two parcels of property located across a street from one another. On one parcel stood the taxpayer's freight terminal, while on the other parcel there was a truck parking and storage area that was involuntarily converted as a result of the threat or imminence of condemnation. Unable to secure adjacent property for parking and storage, the taxpayer sold the terminal property and reinvested the proceeds of both properties in new terminal and parking facilities in the same general area. The Tax Court held that the sale of the terminal property qualified as an involuntary conversion because both properties had been

---

4. See § 1033(a).

5. An election is considered to be made simply by the taxpayers failure to include the otherwise recognized gain on her return.

6. § 1033(a).

7. § 1033(a)(2)(B).

8. § 1033(a)(1).

9. Section 1033(c)-(e) states that the following are treated as involuntary conversions: property within an irrigation project sold to conform to the acreage limitations of federal reclamation laws, livestock destroyed by or on account of disease or sold or exchanged because of disease; and certain livestock sold or exchanged on account of drought.

10. See § 1033(a)(2)(B).

11. See § 1033(a)(1) and (2).

12. 30 T.C. 741 (1958). See also Willamette Industries, Inc. v. Commissioner, 118 T.C. 126 (2002); FSA 200035002; TAM 200722013; TAM 200627024.

used as an economic unit and continuation of the business on the terminal property was impractical.

On the other hand, if the taxpayer has a choice between retaining property and disposing of it and the circumstances are not beyond his control, section 1033(a) is inapplicable. For example, in C. G. Willis, Inc. v. Commissioner[13] the taxpayer, an inter-coastal water carrier, suffered some $140,000 of damage to a motor cargo vessel that ran aground. After securing repair bids and collecting $100,000 of insurance proceeds, it sold the vessel as is for $100,000 and reinvested the insurance and sales proceeds in a barge. At the time of the damage the taxpayer had a second cargo vessel laid up, apparently for lack of business. The Tax Court held that the vessel that ran aground was not involuntarily converted. The sale, the court concluded, was not dictated by the partial destruction but by the taxpayer's belief that the money would better serve its other business interests.

[3] SIMILAR OR RELATED IN SERVICE OR USE

Probably the greatest difficulty under section 1033 has been with the meaning of the phrase "similar or related in service or use," which is the standard that must be met by the replacement property.[14] It is clear that the standard for 1033 is narrower than the "like-kind" standard of section 1031 (for example, unimproved real property may not be similar in use or service to improved real property, although it is of like kind), but it is not always clear precisely what standard is applicable under section 1033.

When the taxpayer is an investor-lessor of the converted property, the Service compares the extent and type of the taxpayer-lessor's management activity, the amount and kind of services rendered by the taxpayer-lessor to the tenants, and the nature of the business risks connected with the properties to determine if the replacement property is similar or related in service or use to the original property.[15] As a result, the taxpayer-lessor might replace a gas station with a bowling alley and still qualify for nonrecognition so long as the taxpayer's activities, services provided to the lessee, and business risks were similar for the two properties.[16]

For owner-users of property, however, the Service applies a much different test.[17] Basically, the taxpayer must use the replacement proper-

---

13. 41 T.C. 468 (1964), aff'd *per curiam*, 342 F.2d 996 (3d Cir. 1965). See also Lakewood Associates v. Commissioner, 109 T.C. 450 (1997); Kurata v. Commissioner, T.C. Memo. 1997–252; Rev. Rul. 89–2, 1989–2 I.R.B. 4; TAM 200625032; TAM 200408027.

14. Section 1033(a)(2)(A) allows the acquisition of control of a corporation that owns such property to be sufficient to give the taxpayer nonrecognition of gain. Section 1033(a)(2)(E)(i) states that "control"

means ownership of stock possessing at least 80% of the voting power of all classes and 80% of the total number of shares in all other classes.

15. Loco Realty Co. v. Commissioner, 306 F.2d 207 (8th Cir. 1962).. See also Rev. Rul. 64–237, 1964–2 C.B. 319.

16. Id.

17. Id.

ty for the same purposes she used the original property.[18] If an office building that was used in a trade or business burns down and T replaces it with a factory building, section 1033 does *not* apply because a factory is not "similar or related in service or use" to an office building.[19] Similarly, if T owns and operates a bowling alley that is condemned, and T uses the proceeds to purchase a pool hall, section 1033 will not apply because a pool hall is not "similar or related in service or use" to a bowling alley.[20]

Regardless of the properties, if the taxpayer replaces a property she had held as an owner-user with a different property which she holds as a lessor, or vice versa, the replacement property will not qualify for nonrecognition under section 1031.[21]

Section 1033(g) provides for application of section 1031's "like-kind" test in limited situations under section 1033.[22] In the case of an involuntary conversion of real property held for productive use in a trade or business or for investment through condemnation, a replacement by like-kind property is to be regarded as property similar or related in service or use.[23]

The replacement property can be acquired directly by purchase of the property itself, or indirectly by purchasing the stock of a corporation which owns such property (if such stock purchase represents the acquisition of at least 80% of the stock of the corporation).[24]

[4] GAIN RECOGNIZED AND BASIS

Not surprisingly, any proceeds not reinvested in qualifying replacement property are treated as boot.[25] Section 1033 provides that any realized gain is recognized to the extent that the taxpayer does not reinvest the proceeds in qualified replacement property.[26]

The rules for the determination of the basis of the acquired property are similar to those under section 1031 and other nonrecognition provisions, in that any unrecognized gain in the original property is built into the replacement property.[27] Accordingly, section 1033(b) provides that the basis of the acquired property is the same as the basis of the converted property, decreased by any money received and not expended for the new property, and increased by the amount of any gain recognized. This ensures that section 1033 provides deferral of gain recognition rather than elimination of it.

18. Maloof v. Commissioner, 65 T.C. 263 (1976). See also Sim–Air, USA, Ltd. v. Commissioner, 98 T.C. 187 (1992); FSA 200035002; TAM 200722013.

19. Id.

20. Id.

21. Id.

22. See § 1033(g)(1); Treas. Reg. § 1.1033(g)–1(a).

23. Id.

24. See § 1033(a)(2)(A) and (E).

25. See § 1033(a)(1) and (2).

26. Id.

27. See § 1033(b).

[5] APPLICATION OF SECTION 1033 IN COORDINATION WITH SECTION 121

Section 121, generally allows taxpayers to exclude from income up to $500,000[28] of gain on the sale or exchange of the taxpayer's primary residence once every two years[29] so long as the taxpayer has lived there for two out of the last five years.[30] So what happens if there is an exchange to which both section 1033 and section 121 are potentially applicable?[31] If this is the case, the taxpayer can elect to avoid treatment under section 121.[32]

Why would any rational taxpayer want to elect to avoid treatment under section 121? The answer is simple—the taxpayer may not want to waste section 121 treatment on a small gain and thereafter have to pay tax on a large gain. This is perhaps best illustrated by way of example. T (who is married and files a joint return) purchases Primary Residence in the current year for $100,000. After living in this home for two years, T moves out and purchases New Primary Residence for $2,000,000. After living in New Primary Residence for two years, the values of the two homes are $110,000 ($110,000 – $100,000 = built-in gain of $10,000) for Primary Residence and $2,500,000 ($2,500,000 – $2,000,000 = built-in gain of $500,000) for New Primary Residence. Unfortunately for T, both New Primary Residence and Primary Residence are involuntarily converted. Of course, section 121 can only be potentially applicable to either the involuntary conversion of Primary Residence ($10,000 built-in gain) or New Primary Residence ($500,000 built-in gain).[33] Naturally, T will choose to forego section 121 treatment for the involuntary conversion of Primary Residence,[34] and, instead, T will apply section 121 to the involuntary conversion of New Primary Residence. Of course, section 1033 can still apply to the involuntary conversion of Primary Residence.

§ 9.04   OTHER NONRECOGNITION PROVISIONS

[1] SECTION 1032: EXCHANGES OF STOCK FOR PROPERTY

Section 1032 generally provides that a corporation recognizes no gain or loss upon the exchange of its own corporate stock for money or property.[1]

---

28. For qualifying married couples filing a joint return.

29. See § 121(b)(3).

30. For a complete discussion of § 121, see Chapter 3, *Exclusions from Gross Income*.

31. See § 121(d)(5)(A)-(C).

32. § 121(f).

33. See § 121(b)(3).

34. See § 121(f).

§ 9.04

1. It is important to note that § 1032 is applicable regardless of the application (or in-application) of § 351 (which generally provides that no gain or loss is recognized by transferors to a corporation who are in control of it immediately after the exchange). Hence, even if for whatever reason a transaction may be taxable to the transferors; it is still nontaxable to the issuing corporation.

Additionally, as noted by section 1032(b), section 362(a) provides for a substituted basis in whatever property is contributed in exchange for the corporation's stock. Hence, any built-in gain or loss inherent in the contributed property at the time of the exchange will be taxed in the future upon the disposition of the property in a taxable transaction.[2]

[2] SECTION 1035: CERTAIN EXCHANGES OF INSURANCE POLICIES

Section 1035 generally provides that no gain or loss shall be recognized upon the exchange of various insurance contracts. Interestingly, the section 1031 rules relating to transfers involving boot, as well as the section 1031 basis rules, are applicable to section 1035 exchanges;[3] hence, any built-in gain or loss inherent in the exchanged property at the time of the exchange will be taxed in the future upon the disposition of the property in a taxable transaction. [4]

The following types of exchanges qualify for nonrecognition under section 1035:

(1) The exchange of one life insurance contract[5] for another life insurance contract;[6]

(2) The exchange of a life insurance contract for an endowment[7] or annuity contract;[8]

(3) The exchange of a life insurance contract for a qualified-long-term care contract;[9]

(4) The exchange of an endowment contract for another endowment contract (or annuity contract or qualified-long-term care contract) "which provides for regular payments beginning at a date not later than the date payments would have begun under the contract exchanged;"[10]

---

2. See § 1032(b); § 362(a). See also § 1001(a); § 1001(c).

3. Treas. Reg. § 1.1035–1(c).

4. Treas. Reg. § 1.1035–1(c); § 1031(d). See also § 1001(a); § 1001(c).

5. The term "life insurance contract" for purposes of § 1035 is defined as: "A contract of life insurance is a contract to which paragraph (1) applies but which is not ordinarily payable in full during the life of the insured. For purposes of the preceding sentence, a contract shall not fail to be treated as a life insurance contract solely because a qualified long-term care insurance contract is a part of or a rider on such contract." § 1035(b)(3).

6. § 1035(a)(1).

7. The term "endowment contract" for purposes of § 1035 is defined as: "A con-

tract of endowment insurance is a contract with an insurance company which depends in part on the life expectancy of the insured, but which may be payable in full in a single payment during his life." § 1035(b)(1).

8. Id. The term "annuity contract" for purposes of § 1035 is defined as: "An annuity contract is a contract to which paragraph (1) [referring to the definition of 'endowment contract] applies but which may be payable during the life of the annuitant only in installments. For purposes of the preceding sentence, a contract shall not fail to be treated as an annuity contract solely because a qualified long-term care insurance contract is a part of or a rider on such contract.' " § 1035(b).

9. Id.

10. § 1035(a)(2).

(5) The exchange of "an annuity contract for an annuity contract or for a qualified long-term care insurance contract;"[11] or

(6) The exchange of "a qualified long-term care insurance contract for a qualified long-term care insurance contract."[12]

[3] SECTION 1036: EXCHANGE OF STOCK FOR STOCK OF SAME CORPORATION

Section 1036 generally provides, "No gain or loss shall be recognized if common stock in a corporation is exchanged solely for common stock in the same corporation, or if preferred stock in a corporation is exchanged solely for preferred stock in the same corporation."[13]

The section 1031 rules relating to transfers involving boot, as well as the section 1031 basis rules, are applicable to section 1036 exchanges;[14] hence, any built-in gain or loss inherent in the exchanged property at the time of the exchange will be taxed in the future upon any disposition of the property in a taxable transaction. [15]

[4] SECTION 1038: REACQUISITION OF REAL PROPERTY

Section 1038 provides a nonrecognition rule governing the repossession of real property previously sold on the installment method.[16] Prior to the enactment of section 1038 the repossession of real property resulted in recognition of gain or loss to the seller, depending on the fair market value of the property at the time of the repossession.[17] Congress believed that apart from any payments actually received prior to the repossession the seller was no better off than before the original sale.[18] Hence, instead of treating the repossession as a second sale of the property to its original owner, Congress believed that it was more desirable "to consider instead that the first sale has been nullified."[19]

Section 1038 requires a sale of real property that gives rise to an indebtedness to the seller secured by the real property sold and a reacquisition by the seller in partial or full satisfaction of the indebtedness.[20] If these conditions are met, then as a general rule no gain or loss on the repossession is recognized, and the seller cannot claim a bad debt deduction.[21] In addition, if the seller has taken a bad debt deduction prior to the repossession, under section 1038(d) the amount so deducted is treated as a recovery on repossession. Gain on section 1038 repossession is recognized to the extent of the cash or other property received prior to the repossession less any previously-reported gain.[22] However,

11. § 1035(a)(3).

12. § 1035(a)(4).

13. Section 1036 is applicable to exchanges between shareholders as well as exchanges between shareholders and the corporation. Treas. Reg. § 1.1036–1(a).

14. § 1036(c)(1) and (2).

15. § 1036(c)(1) and (2); § 1031(d). See also § 1001(a); § 1001(c).

16. Treas. Reg. § 1.1038–1(a)(1).

17. See S. Rep. No. 1361, 88th Cong., 2d Sess. 5 (1964).

18. Id.

19. S. Rep. No. 1361, 88th Cong., 2d Sess. 5 (1964).

20. § 1038(a)(1) and (2).

21. § 1038(a) (flush language).

22. § 1038(b)(1).

under section 1038(b)(2) recognized gain cannot exceed the gain on the original sale less gain reported and repossession costs.

If property is sold subject to a first mortgage and the seller takes a second mortgage, payments by the buyer on the first mortgage inure to the benefit of the seller; such payments are treated as amounts received by the seller in computing any repossession gain.[23]

A special rule is provided for the repossession of a principal residence.[24] Under section 1038(e), if gain was excluded under section 121, repossession gain is not recognized if the residence is resold within a year of the repossession.[25] In such event, the resale is treated as part of the original sale.[26]

Section 1038 makes no provision for the characterization of repossession gain. Arguably, if the theory of nullification of the original sale, as stated in the Senate Report,[27] is carried to its logical conclusion, all gain would be ordinary gain for lack of a sale or exchange or even a disposition of property. However, the regulations provide that if the original sale was reported on the installment method, the character of the gain on the repossession is determined by the character of the gain on the original sale.[28]

Under section 1038(c) the basis of repossessed property is the adjusted basis of the underlying debt, as of the date of the repossession, increased by any recognized gain and repossession costs.[29] This means gain on the seller will be subject to tax upon resale to the extent of any increase in market value. If the indebtedness to the seller is not discharged as a result of the repossession, such indebtedness acquires a zero basis.[30]

Under section 1038(g) the estate or beneficiary of a deceased seller recognizes no gain or loss on the reacquisition of real property.[31]

[5] SECTION 1041: TRANSFERS BETWEEN SPOUSES OR INCIDENT TO DIVORCE

Section 1041(a) provides for nonrecognition of gain or loss on the transfer of property between spouses or between former spouses if incident to divorce.[32] Under section 1041(c) a transfer between former spouses is treated as incident to divorce if it occurs within one year after,

---

23. Treas. Reg. § 1.1038–1(b). If after the sale the purchaser borrows money and uses the property as security for the loan, payments made in satisfaction of the indebtedness are not considered as amounts received by the seller in computing repossession gain. Id.

24. See § 1038(e).

25. § 1038(e)(1) and (2).

26. § 1038(e) (flush language).

27. See S. Rep. No. 1361, 88th Cong., 2d Sess. 5 (1964).

28. Treas. Reg. § 1.1038–1(d).

29. See § 1038(c)(1) and (2).

30. § 1038(c) (flush language).

31. In this case the basis is the same as if the property had been acquired by the original seller plus an amount equal to the deduction under § 691(c) that would have been allowable. § 1038(g)(2).

32. For a more complete discussion of § 1041, see Chapter 12, *Tax Aspects of Separation and Divorce*.

or is related to, the cessation of the marriage.[33] Section 1041(b)(2) provides that the transferee's basis in the property received is equal to the transferor's adjusted basis before the transfer.

The enactment of section 1041 was aimed at overturning United States v. Davis.[34] In that case the Supreme Court held that a transfer of appreciated property to a former spouse pursuant to a property settlement agreement executed prior to divorce was a taxable event, resulting in recognition of gain to the transferor. The Court noted that under administrative practice the release of marital rights in exchange for property was not considered a taxable event to the recipient.

Congress enacted section 1041 for several reasons;[35] it believed that to tax transfers between spouses is inappropriate since a husband and wife may be regarded as a single economic unit.[36] Furthermore, the rules governing transfers of property between spouses or former spouses incident to divorce had resulted in controversy and litigation.[37] Finally, in divorce situations the government was often whipsawed by the transferor's neglecting to report gain on a transfer while the recipient, upon the subsequent sale of the property, was entitled to compute gain by reference to a basis equal to the fair market value of the property at the time it had been received.[38]

It is important to note that section 1041 is not limited to transfers of property incident to divorce.[39] It applies to any transfer of property between spouses, regardless of whether the transfer is a gift or is a sale or exchange between spouses acting at arm's length.[40] Moreover, even if the transfer is a bona fide sale, the transferee does not acquire a basis in the transferred property equal to the transferee's cost.[41]

[6] SECTION 1044: ROLLOVER OF PUBLICLY TRADED SECURITIES GAIN INTO SPECIALIZED SMALL BUSINESS INVESTMENT COMPANIES

Section 1044 generally provides taxpayers[42] with an opportunity to *elect* to defer certain gains upon the sale of publicly traded securities.[43] If section 1044 is elected, the gain from the sale of any publicly traded securities is only recognized:

> [T]o the extent that the amount realized on such sale exceeds: (1) the cost of any common stock or partnership interest in a specialized

---

33. § 1041(c)(1) and (2).

34. 370 U.S. 65, 82 S.Ct. 1190, 8 L.Ed.2d 335 (1962).

35. See H.R. Rep. No. 432, 98th Cong., 2d Sess. 1491–92 (1984).

36. Id.

37. Id.

38. id.

39. See § 1041(a).

40. Id.

41. See § 1041(b)(2) (providing that the basis of the transferred property in the hands of the transferee is the adjusted basis of the property in the hands of the transferor).

42. Estates, trusts, partnerships, and S corporations are ineligible to elect § 1044. § 1044(c)(4).

43. *Nota bene:* Section 1044 treatment is unavailable to any stock sale (for example stock sales within certain types of retirement accounts) which would result in ordinary income treatment absent § 1044.

small business investment company[44] purchased by the taxpayer during the 60–day period beginning on the date of such sale, reduced by (2) any portion of such cost previously taken into account under this section.[45]

Given the generous nature of section 1044, certain annual limits are applicable. For individuals, the applicable annual limit is lesser of (A) $50,000, or (B) $500,000, reduced by the amount of gain excluded under § 1044(a) during all prior tax years.[46]

In the case of a C corporation,[47] the applicable annual limit is: (A) $250,000, or (B) $1,000,000, reduced by the amount of gain excluded under § 1044(a) for all prior tax years.[48]

[7] SECTION 1045: ROLLOVER OF GAIN FROM ONE QUALIFIED SMALL BUSINESS STOCK TO ANOTHER

Section 1045(a) generally provides that a taxpayer may generally postpone recognition of gain realized upon the sale of qualified small business stock[49] held for more than six months so long as the taxpayer acquires other qualifies small business stock within 60 days.

Of course, any amount which is not appropriately reinvested in timely manner to satisfy the requirements of section 1045(a) will trigger recognition of any realized gain to the extent of the deficiency.[50]

Ultimately, section 1045, through its basis adjustment rules, preserves any built-in gain inherent in the exchanged stock at the time of the exchange so it can be appropriately taxed in the future upon any disposition of the property in a taxable transaction.[51]

---

44. "The term "specialized small business investment company" means any partnership or corporation which is licensed by the Small Business Administration under section 301(d) of the Small Business Investment Act of 1958 (as in effect on May 13, 1993)." § 1044(c)(3).

45. § 1044(a)(1) and (2).

46. § 1044(b)(1)(A) and (B).

47. All corporations within a controlled group of corporations (within the meaning of § 52(a)) are treated as a single taxpayer for purposes of § 1044. § 1044(b)(4)(A). And, any gain excluded by any predecessor of a C Corporation is treated as having been excluded by it for purposes of § 1044. § 1044(b)(4)(A).

48. § 1044(b)(2)(A) and (B).

49. Qualified small business stock is generally stock which was acquired by the taxpayer upon its issuance by a domestic corporation with assets which do not exceed $50M either before or after the issuance of the small business stock at issue. See § 1045(b)(1) (referring to the definition of "qualified small business stock" contained in § 1202(c).)

50. See § 1045(a).

51. See § 1045(b)(3).

Chapter 10

CAPITAL GAINS AND LOSSES

Table of Sections

§ 10.01   IN GENERAL

Capital gains and losses are generally required to be accounted for separated from other types of gains and losses. The primary reason for this is because the Internal Revenue Code provides for favorable tax treatment for long-term capital gains;[1] a secondary reason for this is because the Internal Revenue Code limits individuals' capital losses to the amount of their capital gains plus $3,000[2] each year.[3]

§ 10.02   STATUTORY STRUCTURE

Capital gains and losses are dealt with in Subchapter P of the Internal Revenue Code. Under section 1(h), "net capital gains" are generally taxed at a maximum rate of 15%. Section 1222(a)(11) defines "net capital gain" in terms of "net long-term capital gain" over "net short-term capital loss." "Long-term capital gain" is defined in section 1222(a)(3) as a "gain from the sale or exchange of a capital asset held for more than 1 year." Hence, the three requirements for preferential long-term capital gain treatment are: "sale or exchange,"[1] "capital asset,"[2] and "held for more than 1 year."[3] The first requirement specifies two modes of disposition, but the Code defines neither "sale" nor "exchange." The term "capital asset" is defined by exception (rather than directly); section 1221(a) defines a "capital asset" as "property held by the taxpayer," which is not any of the following:

(1) Inventory or property held primarily for sale to customers;[4]

---

§ 10.01

1. See § 1(h).

2. This $3,000 annual limit is changed to $1,500 per year for those taxpayers who are married and filing separate returns. § 1211(b)(1).

3. § 1211(b)(1) and (2).

§ 10.02

1. Raytheon Production Corp. v. Commissioner, 144 F.2d 110 (1st Cir. 1944), cert. denied, 323 U.S. 779, 65 S.Ct. 192, 89 L.Ed. 622 (1944). See also § 1001(a).

2. § 1221.

3. § 1222(3).

4. § 1221(a)(1).

(2) Depreciable property (including real estate) used in a trade or business;[5]

(3) Certain copyrights, literary works, musical compositions, artistic works, letters or memorandum or similar property held by the creator, (in the case of a letter, memorandum, or similar property the "taxpayer for whom such property was prepared or produced"[6]), or held by any taxpayer "in whose hands the basis of such property is determined, for purposes of determining gain from a sale or exchange, in whole or part by reference to the basis of such property in the hands of a taxpayer; . . ."[7]

(4) Accounts or notes receivable acquired in the ordinary course of business;[8]

(5) Certain publications of the United States Government;[9]

(6) Certain "commodities derivative financial instrument held by a commodities derivatives dealer;"[10]

(7) Hedging transactions;[11] or

(8) Business supplies.[12]

Section 1211(a) provides that capital losses of corporations are allowed against capital gains but not against ordinary income. Section 1211(b) provides that capital losses of individuals are allowed against capital gains and up to $3,000 of ordinary income in any one year.

Section 1212 provides for carrybacks and carryovers of "net capital loss." Section 1222(10) defines "net capital loss" as "the excess of the losses from sales or exchanges of capital assets over the sum allowed under section 1211." Corporations may carry back net capital losses for three years[13] (beginning with the earliest year) if the carryback does not create or increase section 172 net operating losses. After such carryback, net capital losses of corporations may be carried forward for five years.[14] Individuals may carry forward net capital losses without limitation.[15]

§ 10.03 SALE OR EXCHANGE REQUIREMENT

The term "sale or exchange" came into the tax law with the Revenue Act of 1921 when Congress first accorded preferential treatment to capital gains. It is not clear whether Congress intended the words "sale or exchange" to impose a specific limitation under what is now section 1001(a), providing for the computation of gain or loss upon a "sale or other disposition of property." The problem arises not from the

---

5. § 1221(a)(2). *Nota bene:* depreciable property (including real estate) used in a trade or business is a § 1231 asset; § 1231 is described in detail *infra*.

6. § 1221(a)(3).

7. § 1221(a)(3)(A)-(C).

8. § 1221(a)(4).

9. § 1221(a)(5).

10. § 1221(a)(6).

11. § 1221(a)(7).

12. § 1221(a)(8).

13. § 1212(a)(1)(A).

14. § 1212(a)(1)(B).

15. § 1212(b)(1).

differences between section 1001(a) and section 1222 but primarily from the use of "sale or exchange" in section 1001(c), which requires recognition of gain or loss as a general rule. Ambiguity exists because a section 1001(c) "sale or exchange" is not regarded as a limitation on the mode of disposition if gain or loss does not otherwise go unrecognized under a specific statutory provision. This is not true, however, of the "sale or exchange" requirement of section 1222. In this context the term serves as a definite limitation on qualifying property for capital treatment, and subsequent legislation suggests that Congress indeed regards the term as having such a limiting function.

Congress has not attempted a definition of "sale or exchange;"[1] rather, it has dealt with the problem by providing for sale or exchange treatment on an ad hoc basis for certain assets. For example, section 165(g) provides that if a security that is a capital asset becomes worthless during the year, it is regarded as sold or exchanged on the last day of the year.[2]

Perhaps some indication of the reasons why Congress has not attempted to formulate a comprehensive definition of "sale or exchange" can be found in the difficulty the courts have had with the term. Furthermore, although the courts treat the "sale or exchange" requirement as a distinct problem, the opinions have often blended the analyses of "sale or exchange" and "capital asset." It is for this reason that many of the sale or exchange problems are considered in conjunction with the treatment of capital assets in the latter part of this chapter.

§ 10.04 SATISFACTION OF CLAIMS, FORECLOSURES, ABANDONMENTS, AND RELEASES

When property is transferred in satisfaction of a claim, the transfer by the obligor is regarded as an exchange.[1] Thus, in Kenan v. Commissioner[2] a testamentary trust was required to pay a beneficiary of the trust $5,000,000 on the beneficiary's fortieth birthday. In satisfaction of the obligation, the trust transferred to the beneficiary securities that had appreciated in value. The Second Circuit regarded the transaction as an exchange of the securities for the beneficiary's claim on the assets of the trust and rejected the Commissioner's argument that the income was ordinary in character rather than capital gain.

§ 10.03

1. But see Raytheon Production Corp. v. Commissioner, 144 F.2d 110 (1st Cir. 1944), cert. denied, 323 U.S. 779, 65 S.Ct. 192, 89 L.Ed. 622 (1944).

2. § 165(g).

§ 10.04

1. Kenan v. Commissioner, 114 F.2d 217 (2d Cir. 1940). See also Amlie v. Com-

missioner, T.C. Memo. 2006–76; CCA 200644020.

2. 114 F.2d 217 (2d Cir. 1940). See also Amlie v. Commissioner, T.C. Memo. 2006–76; CCA 200644020.

When mortgaged property is disposed of through a foreclosure sale, the transaction is treated as a sale.[3] In Helvering v. Hammel[4] the taxpayer and other members of a syndicate had purchased land on an installment contract. When a default on the payments occurred, the seller brought an action to foreclose which resulted in a judicial sale. The taxpayer contended that his loss was an ordinary loss because it was suffered in an involuntary sale and that the nature of the sale brought it outside the intendment of the Revenue Act of 1934. The taxpayer argued that the 1934 Act was designed simply to prevent tax avoidance by not permitting a taxpayer to take ordinary losses at any time during the first two years a capital asset was held, the pre–1934 law having defined a capital asset as property held more than two years. In rejecting the taxpayer's argument, the Supreme Court in Hammel held that the 1934 Act was not limited to voluntary sales. The Court found nothing in the Act's history to indicate that such was the intent of Congress. This interpretation, said the Court, was supported by the 1934 Act's introduction of limitations on capital losses, which provided expressly for sale or exchange treatment for stock redemptions, bond retirements, short sales, and lapses of options.

A voluntary reconveyance to the mortgagee in satisfaction of the debt has also been treated as a sale or exchange.[5] This is so even if the debt is nonrecourse and the value of the property is less than the remaining debt.[6] The courts have reasoned that a voluntary conveyance should have the same effect as an involuntary (or voluntary) foreclosure sale, as when the Fifth Circuit in Yarbro v. Commissioner[7] held that the abandonment of property subject to a nonrecourse debt constituted a sale or exchange. The court suggested that the practical effect of a foreclosure, conveyance, and abandonment were the same and noted that in many cases abandonment had been followed by foreclosure.

---

3. Helvering v. Hammel, 311 U.S. 504, 61 S.Ct. 368, 85 L.Ed. 303 (1941). See also Helvering v. Nebraska Bridge Supply & Lumber Co., 312 U.S. 666, 61 S.Ct. 827, 85 L.Ed. 1111 (1941); Commissioner v. Peterman, 118 F.2d 973 (9th Cir. 1941); Abelson v. Commissioner, 44 B.T.A. 98 (1941) (nonacq.); Rev. Rul. 70–63, 1970–1 C.B. 36; Aizawa v. Commissioner, 99 T.C. 197 (1992), affd. 29 F.3d 630 (9th Cir.1994); Ryan v. Commissioner, T.C. Memo. 1988–12, affd. sub nom. Lamm v. Commissioner, 873 F.2d 194 (8th Cir.1989); Great Plains Gasification Associates v. Commissioner, T.C. Memo. 2006–276.

4. 311 U.S. 504, 61 S.Ct. 368, 85 L.Ed. 303 (1941). See also Amlie v. Commissioner, T.C. Memo. 2006–76; CCA 200644020; Helvering v. Nebraska Bridge Supply & Lumber Co., 312 U.S. 666, 61 S.Ct. 827, 85 L.Ed. 1111 (1941); Commissioner v. Peterman, 118 F.2d 973 (9th Cir. 1941); Abelson v. Commissioner, 44 B.T.A. 98 (1941) (nonacq.); Rev. Rul. 70–63, 1970–1 C.B. 36; Aizawa v. Commissioner, 99 T.C. 197 (1992), affd. 29 F.3d 630 (9th Cir.1994); Ryan v. Commissioner, T.C. Memo. 1988–12, affd. sub nom. Lamm v. Commissioner, 873 F.2d 194 (8th Cir.1989); Great Plains Gasification Associates v. Commissioner, T.C. Memo. 2006–276.

5. See, e.g., Stamler v. Commissioner, 145 F.2d 37 (3d Cir. 1944).

6. See Eugene L. Freeland, 74 T.C. 970 (1980); Rev. Rul. 78–164, 1978–1 C.B. 264; Rev. Rul. 76–111, 1976–1 C.B. 214. See also 2925 Briarpark, Ltd. v. Commissioner, 163 F.3d 313 (5th Cir. 1999); Cox v. Commissioner, 68 F.3d 128 (5th Cir. 1995).

7. 737 F.2d 479 (5th Cir. 1984), cert. denied, 469 U.S. 1189, 105 S.Ct. 959, 83 L.Ed.2d 965 (1985). See also Matz v. Commissioner, T.C. Memo. 1998–334; Sands v. Commissioner, T.C. Memo. 1997–146; TAM 200049009.

As a general rule, a transaction in which a creditor receives amounts from his debtor in satisfaction of his claim is not a "sale or exchange."[8] In Hudson v. Commissioner[9] the taxpayer purchased a judgment debt from a judgment creditor for approximately $10,000. Later, the taxpayer collected some $20,000 from the judgment debtor in a settlement. The Tax Court, in an opinion reviewed by the entire court, held that the gain was ordinary gain for lack of a sale or exchange. The Tax Court reasoned that in ordinary commercial parlance such a transaction would not be regarded as a sale and that it was not a transfer of property since the debt simply vanished.

The principle of the creditor-release rule, the lack of something surviving the transaction, has been the subject of searching reexamination by the courts. Many courts have expressed considerable dissatisfaction with the formal niceties of the distinction between a sale to a third person and a release of an obligor in which nothing survives the transaction. For example, in Commissioner v. Ferrer[10] the Second Circuit retreated from its prior position that with a release there is no sale or exchange.[11] In Ferrer the taxpayer released an exclusive right to produce a play, along with certain other rights in copyrighted material, to the owner-author. The Second Circuit found "no sensible business basis for drawing a line between a release of" the taxpayer's rights to the author and a sale of them to another person. Hence, the capital gain issue, discussed below, was decided on the basis of the nature of the rights owned by the taxpayer, and the sale or exchange issue was skipped entirely.

The retreat of the Second Circuit was more than matched by the Fifth Circuit in Bisbee–Baldwin Corp. v. Tomlinson.[12] In that case the taxpayer was a mortgage banker that earned its income under servicing contracts with institutional investors, who had taken the mortgages by assignment from the taxpayer. The servicing contracts were not assignable, but they were subject to termination by the institutional investor. When the contracts were terminated, the taxpayer received a termination fee from the investor, who then was reimbursed by the new servicing company. The termination fees amounted to some $200,000 in the tax year, and the taxpayer contended that they constituted proceeds of a sale of the servicing contracts. The Fifth Circuit agreed, reasoning that "[i]n substance the transaction was a two-party transfer." Since it was found that there would have been no termination or cancellation of

---

8. Hudson v. Commissioner, 20 T.C. 734 (1953), aff'd sub nom., Ogilvie v. Commissioner, 216 F.2d 748 (6th Cir. 1954). See also Nahey v. Commissioner, 111 T.C. 256, 262 (1998); Breen v. Commissioner, T.C. Memo. 1962–230; No Sale, No Exchange– No Capital Gains Treatment, 62 Prac. Tax Strategies 54 (1999).

9. 20 T.C. 734 (1953), aff'd sub nom., Ogilvie v. Commissioner, 216 F.2d 748 (6th Cir. 1954). See also Nahey v. Commissioner, 111 T.C. 256, 262 (1998); Breen v. Commissioner, T.C. Memo. 1962–230; No Sale, No

Exchange–No Capital Gains Treatment, 62 Prac. Tax Strategies 54 (1999).

10. 304 F.2d 125 (2d Cir. 1962).

11. See, e.g., Commissioner v. Pittston Co. 252 F.2d 344 (2d Cir. 1958), cert. denied, 357 U.S. 919, 78 S.Ct. 1360, 2 L.Ed.2d 1364 (1958).

12. 320 F.2d 929 (5th Cir. 1963). See also FSA 200238045; TAM 200427023; TAM 200427025.

the taxpayer's contracts unless the new servicing agent had agreed to reimburse the investor for the termination fees, the payor was simply a conduit for the fee.

§ 10.05   RELATED TRANSACTIONS: THE ARROWSMITH DOCTRINE

Suppose an admitted sale or exchange is followed in a subsequent year by a restoration or a recovery. Is the nature of the restoration or recovery, as a product of a sale or exchange, determined in accordance with the strict tax year concept? Or does the transaction in the prior year characterize the transaction in the subsequent year? In general, the answer is that the prior related transaction provides the means for characterizing both recoveries and restorations.

In Merchants National Bank v. Commissioner[1] a year after the taxpayer bank had charged-off and deducted certain notes as worthless, it sold them to a third party for $18,000. The Fifth Circuit held that the recovery was ordinary income rather than capital gain on the ground that the notes were no longer capital assets once the taxpayer had recovered its investment through its prior deduction. Thus, to permit the taxpayer to treat its gain as capital when it had received a full deduction from ordinary income would give an advantage not contemplated by the tax law.

The same principle was applied by the Supreme Court in Arrowsmith v. Commissioner[2] with respect to a restoration. In that case the taxpayer shareholders caused a liquidation of their corporation and reported gain upon the liquidation as capital gain. In a later year the taxpayers were forced to pay, as distributees in liquidation, a judgment rendered against the corporation. The taxpayers claimed an ordinary loss for the payment. However, the Supreme Court held that the payment was a capital loss because the liability was imposed upon them as transferees in the liquidating distribution, a transaction that had produced a capital gain.

When the value of property received in a sale or other disposition is incapable of valuation, the transaction may be kept open until the proceeds are realized in a form in which they can be valued. In such a situation the proceeds take character as capital gain or ordinary income from the original disposition.[3] However, if the property received is

§ 10.05

1. 199 F.2d 657 (5th Cir. 1952). See also Rev. Rul. 80–56, 1980–9 I.R.B. 14; Cohen v. Commissioner, T.C. Memo. 2003–303; Feinberg v. Commissioner, T.C. Memo. 2003–304.

2. 344 U.S. 6, 73 S.Ct. 71, 97 L.Ed. 6 (1952). See also Rees Blow Pipe Mfg. Co. v. Commissioner, 41 T.C. 598 (1964), nonacq., 1966–2 C.B. 8, aff'd *per curiam*, 342 F.2d 990 (9th Cir. 1965); Kimbell v. United States, 490 F.2d 203 (5th Cir. 1974), cert. denied, 419 U.S. 833, 95 S.Ct. 58, 42 L.Ed.2d 59 (1974); Rosenberg v. Commissioner, T.C. Memo. 2000–108; Seagate Technology, Inc. v. Commissioner, T.C. Memo. 2000–388; CCA 200238041; TAM 200427023.

3. See, e.g., Dorsey v. Commissioner, 49 T.C. 606 (1968); Commissioner v. Carter, 170 F.2d 911 (2d Cir. 1948).

capable of valuation, the transaction is regarded as closed for tax purposes, and any proceeds received in later years in excess of the amount closed out are treated as ordinary income.[4] While this latter treatment is consistent with the annual accounting concept, no satisfactory theory has been developed for distinguishing between it and the Arrowsmith doctrine.

In a restoration, such as in Arrowsmith where the taxpayers were limited to a capital loss in the year of restoration, the benefits of section 1341 are available. Thus, the taxpayer could use the capital loss in the year of restoration or could elect to reduce his tax in the year of restoration to the extent of the tax attributable to the inclusion in income in the prior year.

The election accorded the taxpayer under section 1341 in an Arrowsmith restoration provides for a computation that permits the use of the lesser of "such deduction" in the year of restoration under section 1341(a)(4), or a tax computed without the deduction but less the decrease in tax that would result solely from the exclusion of the restored item in the year of inclusion under section 1341(a)(5).

In United States v. Skelly Oil Co.[5] the taxpayer claimed the right to use section 1341(a)(4) for the full amount restored to its customers, without taking into account the percentage depletion taken upon corresponding amounts of gross income in prior years. The Supreme Court held that Congress could not have intended such a result despite the taxpayer's literal compliance with section 1341(a)(4) and the annual accounting concept. The Court held that Arrowsmith was on point and justified its application with this explanation: "The rationale for the Arrowsmith rule is easy to see; if money was taxed at a special lower rate when received, the taxpayer would be accorded an unfair tax windfall if repayments were generally deductible from receipts taxable at the higher rate applicable to ordinary income."[6]

§ 10.06 HOLDING PERIOD

[1] IN GENERAL

A long-term capital gain or a long-term capital loss is defined in section 1222 as a gain or loss "from the sale or exchange of a capital

---

4. See, e.g., Waring v. Commissioner, 412 F.2d 800 (3d Cir. 1969); Slater v. Commissioner, 356 F.2d 668 (10th Cir. 1966).

5. 394 U.S. 678, 89 S.Ct. 1379, 22 L.Ed.2d 642 (1969). See also Cities Service Oil Co. v. United States, 199 Ct.Cl. 89, 462 F.2d 1134 (1972), cert. denied, 409 U.S. 1063, 93 S.Ct. 558, 34 L.Ed.2d 517 (1972); Dominion Resources, Inc. v. United States, 219 F.3d 359 (4th Cir. 2000); Cinergy Corp. v. United States, 55 Fed.Cl. 489 (2003); CCA 200431014; CCA 200423027; Richard

DeLossa, Eureka! California Strikes Gold with the Claim of Right Doctrine in Ackerman v. Franchise Tax Board, 38 Loy. L.A. L. Rev. 2275, 2296 (2005); Charlie Boer, The Right Intention but the Wrong Result: the Misapplication of Section 1341 in Cooper v. United States, 59 Tax Law. 1109, 1121 (2006).

6. 394 U.S. at 685, 89 S.Ct. at 1383 (1969).

asset held for more than 1 year."[1] In general, the courts have equated "held" with "acquired," and, in turn, the latter with ownership. Moreover, ownership has been held to embrace equitable ownership. Hence, the holding period of property in the hands of a beneficiary of a trust begins with the trust's purchase of the property.[2] Also, the holding period rule functions mechanically, unfettered by tax avoidance motives. As a result, the holding requirement is within the control of the taxpayer, and the difficulties in this area, which pertain to the beginning and end of the holding period, normally involve factual inquiries as to when the parties to a transaction intended legal or beneficial ownership to pass.

In Dyke v. Commissioner[3] the taxpayer and others entered into an escrow agreement to sell their shares in a freight carrier, conditioned upon approval of the Interstate Commerce Commission (ICC). The agreement provided that ten days after the "closing date" (the last day of the month during which the buyer notified the sellers of ICC approval) the parties would consummate the sale. The agreement also required the sellers to satisfy certain conditions. The buyer notified the sellers of ICC approval on July 31, 1941, making the delivery date August 10. However, the sellers requested and were granted an extension to September 10, at which time all the conditions of the escrow were satisfied. The Tax Court rejected the Commissioner's contention that the holding period terminated on July 31, or on any other date prior to the September 10 closing date; the Tax Court said that it was not until then that all the conditions of the escrow agreement had been complied with as intended by the parties.

Actual delivery or physical possession, however, is not necessarily a requirement for the commencement or the termination of the holding period. For example, buy and sell orders executed through brokers on stock exchanges normally are concluded on a contract or trade date prior to a settlement date when delivery is effected or payment made. In such cases the holding period commences and ends on the trade date.[4]

In Revenue Ruling 66–7[5] the Service ruled that the day of acquisition is excluded and the day of disposition is included in computing the holding period.

For newly constructed property the holding period is allocated according to completion dates. For example, in Paul v. Commissioner[6] a

§ 10.06

1. § 1222(3) and (4).

2. Helvering v. Gambrill, 313 U.S. 11, 61 S.Ct. 795, 85 L.Ed. 1155 (1941).

3. 6 T.C. 1134 (1946), acq., 1946–2 C.B. 2. See also Texon Oil & Land Co. v. United States, 115 F.2d 647 (5th Cir. 1940); Big Lake Oil Co. v. Commissioner, 95 F.2d 573 (3d Cir. 1938); Carpenter v. Commissioner, 34 T.C. 408, 409, 414 (1960); Alex Raskolni-

kov, Contextual Analysis of Tax Ownership, 85 B.U. L. Rev. 431, 516 (2005).

4. Rev. Rul. 70–598, 1970–2 C.B. 168, superseding I.T. 3705, 1945–1 C.B. 174, and holding that intervening holidays do not affect the application of the stated rule.

5. 1966–1 C.B. 88. See also Rev. Rul. 70–598, 1970–2 C.B. 168; Rev. Rul. 66–6, 1966–1 C.B. 160.

6. 206 F.2d 763 (3d Cir. 1953). See also Petroleum Exploration v. Commissioner,

newly constructed building was sold shortly after completion. The Third Circuit held that the part of the building completed more than six months prior to the sale satisfied the then applicable six-month holding period requirement and was entitled to capital gain treatment on a cost expended basis.

When a taxpayer cannot identify property sold out of a larger holding of similar property, such as shares of stock, the regulations prescribe a first-in, first-out rule similar to that employed for determining basis.[7]

[2]   SUBSTITUTED BASIS AND TACKED HOLDING PERIODS

Section 1223 prescribes a number of rules governing the holding period of capital assets, most of which pertain to the acquisition of property in tax-free transactions under which the taxpayer acquires a substituted basis. Generally, the taxpayer acquires the holding period of the transferor and tacks it to the time for which the taxpayer has held the property.[8] For example, securities acquired in corporate formations, reorganizations, and divisions, and property acquired in a like-kind exchange under section 1031 are subject to tacking of holding periods.[9]

Tacking of holding periods is permitted only if the property disposed of is also a capital asset or entitled to capital-asset treatment under section 1231.[10] For example, if a proprietor transfers his inventory to a corporation in a tax-free exchange for the corporation's stock under section 351, he cannot tack the holding period of the inventory to the holding period of the stock.

Under section 1223(9), if property acquired from a decedent under section 1014 is sold within one year, it is deemed to have been held more than one year.[11] Here the effect is to transmute short-term gain or loss into long-term gain or loss.

§ 10.07   SECTION 1231 NETTING PROCESS

[1]   IN GENERAL

Section 1221(a)(2) excludes from the definition of "capital asset" depreciable property used in a trade or business and real property used in a trade or business; notwithstanding the foregoing, gains or losses realized on the sale or exchange of such property are subject to special treatment under section 1231. Section 1231 gains and losses are netted against one another.[1] If the result is a net gain, all component gains and losses are treated as involving capital assets.[2] If the result is a net loss,

---

193 F.2d 59 (4th Cir. 1951); TAM 9214009; TAM 9147004.

7. Treas. Reg. § 1.1223–1(i), which refers to the regulations under § 1012.

8. § 1223(1) and (2).

9. § 1223(1)(A) and (B); § 1223(2).

10. § 1223(1).

11. § 1223(9)(A) and (B).

§ 10.07

1. See Treas. Reg. § 1.1231–1(a).

2. Id.

all component gains and losses are treated as not involving capital assets.[3] The netting process requires a consideration of three elements: the holding period of the property, the mode of disposition, and the type of property to which section 1231 applies.[4]

The holding period of the property must be more than one year.[5] However, cattle and horses owned for draft, breeding, dairy, or sporting purposes must be held for 24 months or more, while other livestock owned for similar purposes must be held for 12 months or more.[6]

With respect to the mode of disposition, section 1231 embraces only sales or exchanges (or dispositions so treated) and involuntary conversions.[7] The latter includes an exercise of the power of requisition or condemnation (or threat or imminence thereof) and deprivation by casualty or theft.[8]

Subject to the preliminary netting rule described below, section 1231 applies to recognized gains and losses from the sale or exchange or involuntary conversion[9] of property used in the taxpayer's trade or business as defined in section 1231(b) and from the involuntary conversion of a capital asset held for more than one year (but only if such asset is held in connection with a trade or business or a transaction entered into for profit).[10]

The preliminary netting rule requires that gains and losses from casualty and theft (but not condemnation) of business assets held for more than one year be offset against each other.[11] If losses exceed gains, such gains and losses are excluded from the full section 1231 netting process.[12] Conversely, if gains exceed losses, all such gains and losses go into the full section 1231 netting process.[13]

Under the section 1231 netting process net gains from casualty and theft are added to gains and losses from the disposition of business assets held for more than one year.[14] This amount is then added to condemnation gains or losses.[15] The result of these three elements will be a net section 1231 gain or loss.[16]

The preceding rules may be illustrated with a simple example consisting of the following items, each of which was concluded during the

3. Id.

4. Id.

5. § 1231(b)(1).

6. § 1231(b)(3).

7. See Treas. Reg. § 1.1231–1(c)(1).

8. See Treas. Reg. § 1.1231–1(e)(1).

9. By bringing involuntary conversions into the § 1231 netting process Congress has in effect eliminated the sale or exchange requirement normally required for capital treatment. For example, the recovery of insurance proceeds after the taxpayer's plant was destroyed by fire was held

not to constitute a sale or exchange. Helvering v. William Flaccus Oak Leather Co., 313 U.S. 247, 61 S.Ct. 878, 85 L.Ed. 1310 (1941).

10. See Treas. Reg. § 1.1231–1(a).

11. Id.

12. § 1231(a)(4)(C). See also Treas. Reg. § 1.1231–1(a).

13. See Treas. Reg. § 1.1231–1(a).

14. Id.

15. Id.

16. Id.

same taxable year. Assume that each item satisfies the one-year holding requirement.[17]

		Gain	Loss
(1)	Gain on condemnation of residential rental property to which section 1033 does not apply	$10,000	
(2)	Loss on sale of machinery used in a trade or business		($11,000)
(3)	Gain on theft of insured property	$4,000	
(4)	Loss from accident involving auto used in business		($1,000)
(5)	Loss from storm damage to personal boat used by taxpayer		($2,000)
		$14,000	$14,000

The preliminary netting of items (3) and (4) yields a net gain of $3,000.[18] Consequently, both items go into the full section 1231 netting process. The full netting process would thus include the $3,000 net gain from the preliminary netting, the loss from the disposition of business property of $11,000 in item (2), and the condemnation gain of $10,000 in item (1). Note that item (5) is ignored for the section 1231 calculations because it is *not* a loss from an asset used in the taxpayer's trade or business or other profit-seeking activity. The full section 1231 netting process results in a net section 1231 gain of $2,000. Since total section 1231 gains exceed total section 1231 losses each loss is characterized as a long-term capital loss and each gain as a long-term capital gain.[19]

An alternative illustration is to reverse the amounts in items (3) and (4) so that the gain on the theft of insured property is $1,000, and the loss on the business automobile is $4,000. Under these circumstances the preliminary netting of items (3) and (4) would yield a negative $3,000. Since losses exceed gains the net loss would be deductible without regard to section 1231. This would leave items (1) and (2) subject to the netting process, and because the amount of the loss (item (2)) exceeds the gain (item (1)), the items would constitute ordinary loss and ordinary gain, respectively.

Two points are worth mentioning regarding the treatment of involuntary conversions under section 1231. First, casualty losses are more likely to occur than are casualty gains. Therefore, as a practical matter the effect of the preliminary netting is to remove casualty losses from the netting process, leaving them deductible in full from ordinary income. Second, for involuntary conversions, recognized gain is defined to

17. For additional examples of the application of these rules, see Treas. Reg. § 1.1231–1(g).

18. § 1231(a)(4)(C).

19. § 1231(a)(1).

include conversion of property used in the trade or business without regard to the one-year holding period.[20] Therefore, all involuntary conversions of business property are included under section 1231 without regard to the holding period of such property.

Section 1231(c) provides for a "lookback" rule which prevents taxpayers from planning dispositions so that all losses are grouped in one year and all gains in another year. Of course, absent section 1231(c), the result would be that losses would be treated as ordinary, offsetting gross income dollar for dollar, while gains would be given long-term capital treatment. To preclude such use of section 1231 the lookback rule of section 1231(c) forces the taxpayer to treat net section 1231 gain as ordinary income to the extent of section 1231 net losses for any of the preceding five years.[21]

By way of illustration suppose that in 2012 the full section 1231 netting process resulted in a net section 1231 capital loss of $500. Assume further that in 2014 a net section 1231 loss of $1,000 occurred. Finally, assume that it is 2015, and there is a net section 1231 gain of $2,000 as indicated in the preceding example. The $2,000 net section 1231 gain must be recaptured to the extent of the unrecaptured section 1231 net losses. As a result, only $500 of the $2,000 gain would be long-term capital gain, and $1,500 is recaptured by section 1231(c). If a net section 1231 loss of $1,000 occurred, that amount would become another unrecaptured section 1231 net loss to be recaptured by future gains, if any.

[2] PROPERTY USED IN A TRADE OR BUSINESS: SECTION 1231(b)

Section 1231(b) specifies four categories of assets that qualify as property used in a trade or business for the section 1231 netting process,[22] the first being a general category and the other three special categories[23] applicable only to specific enterprises. The categories are as follows: (1) depreciable property and real property used in a trade or business other than inventory,[24] property held primarily for sale to customers,[25] copyright, literary, and other property as described in section 1221(a)(3),[26] and certain United States Government publications;[27] (2) timber, coal, and iron ore to the extent qualifying under section 631;[28] (3) livestock held for draft, breeding, dairy, or sporting purposes as described in section 1231(b)(3);[29] and (4) unharvested crops disposed of with the land as described in section 1231(b)(4).[30]

---

20. § 1231(a)(3)(A)(ii).

21. The legislative history for § 1231(c) indicates that the unrecaptured losses are recaptured in the chronological order in which they arose. H.R. Rep. No. 861, 98th Cong., 2d Sess. 1034 (1984).

22. § 1231(b)(1)-(4).

23. § 1231(b)(2)-(4).

24. § 1231(b)(1)(A).

25. § 1231(b)(1)(B).

26. § 1231(b)(1)(C).

27. § 1231(b)(1)(D).

28. § 1231(b)(2).

29. § 1231(b)(3).

30. Section 268 disallows deductions attributable to production of an unharvested crop that is considered "property used in

With respect to the first category, inventory and property held primarily for sale to customers (and literary property as defined in section 1221(a)(3) as well as certain United States Government publications defined in section 1221(a)(5)) are expressly excluded under section 1231(b) from qualifying as section 1231 assets. Since such property is also expressly excluded from the definition of a capital asset in section 1221, along with "stock in trade," gain or loss upon the disposition of such assets will always be ordinary gain or loss.

It is not clear whether Congress intended to establish three distinct categories of so-called inventory assets (stock in trade, inventory, and property held primarily for sale to customers) or simply has used language regarded as necessary to ensure that general sales income will be excluded from capital gain or loss treatment. The language of section 1221(a)(1) taken in conjunction with section 1231(b) seems to indicate that three separate types of property were intended. Section 1221(a)(1) employs the disjunctive "or" between each of the terms, and, perhaps more persuasive, the exclusion of section 1231(b) uses two paragraphs that separate inventory from property held primarily for sale to customers, although no mention is made of stock in trade.[31]

The last three categories of section 1231 assets were later additions to the statutory framework; they are primarily the products of successful efforts of special interest groups to secure the benefits of section 1231.

§ 10.08 PROPERTY USED IN BUSINESS OR HELD PRIMARILY FOR SALE TO CUSTOMERS

Although the list of property used in business in the preceding section covers a wide range, the main impact of section 1231 is with respect to depreciable property used in a trade or business. Most of the following discussion concerning section 1231 relates to such property and is independent of the netting process contained in that section. Therefore, when section 1231 is considered in connection with the definition of a capital asset in section 1221, the tax effects of these two Code provisions with respect to the transactions most frequently encountered are as follows:

(1) Inventory, stock in trade, and property held for sale to customers: *Ordinary gain and ordinary loss.*

(2) Depreciable property and real property used in a trade or business: *Capital gain and ordinary loss.*

(3) All other property: *Capital gain and capital loss.*[1]

---

the trade or business" under § 1231. The disallowed deductions are adjustments to basis. § 1016(a)(11).

31. See Gilbert v. Commissioner, 56 F.2d 361 (1st Cir. 1932), in which the court construed a predecessor of § 1221(a)(1) as containing three distinct categories.

§ 10.08

1. This summary ignores the noncapital asset classification provided for literary

This basic statutory structure is only a starting point for the determination of whether a particular asset is a capital asset, used in the trade or business, or held primarily for sale. The caselaw in this area is extensive and varied; it is considered, along with other special statutory provisions, later this chapter. Here, the focus is limited to several preliminary issues that are essential to an understanding of these competing concepts.

Suppose taxpayer A sells machines not currently in productive use in a trade or business. If A realizes a gain, it normally makes little difference whether such assets are characterized as capital assets under the general rule of section 1221 or as property used in a trade or business excluded from capital asset characterization by section 1221(a)(2) but entitled to capital gain treatment under section 1231. However, if A had other transactions subject to the netting process of section 1231, or a loss on the sale of the machines, then the question of whether the machines were used in a trade or business might be critical.[2] If the machines were used in a trade or business, then the loss would qualify as an ordinary loss under both section 1221(a)(2) and section 1231 (if the netting yielded a loss); if the property were not so used, it would be characterized as a capital loss.

In general, the courts have construed "used" requirement of the statute very broadly. For example, in Carter–Colton Cigar Co. v. Commissioner[3] the taxpayer purchased a vacant lot in 1926 for the purpose of building a warehouse. It had plans and specifications prepared but construction was postponed and then fully abandoned in 1935 due to the Great Depression. The lot was offered for sale, but because no buyers were found the property was rented for billboard space for nominal amounts from 1937 to 1943. It was finally sold in 1943 at a loss of some $3,000, with the taxpayer contending that the loss was ordinary under what is now section 1221(a)(2) on the grounds that the property was used in the taxpayer's business. The Tax Court agreed, reasoning that while maximum use had not been made of the lot, its purchase for the purpose of building a warehouse on the lot together with the steps taken to consummate that purpose was a sufficient business use. The Tax Court noted that the similar requirement in what is now section 167(a)(1), which limits a depreciation deduction to property used in a business, had been interpreted to mean property "devoted to the trade or business," and, hence, it includes property whether or not in actual use during the taxable year.[4]

property, certain publications of the United States Government, accounts and notes receivable, and capital gain and ordinary loss treatment provided for other § 1231 assets that are subject to the netting process.

2. See Reg. § 1.1231–1(a).

3. 9 T.C. 219 (1947). See also Rev. Rul. 58–133, 1958–1 C.B. 277; Azar Nut Co. v. Commissioner, 931 F.2d 314, 317 (5th Cir. 1991); TAM 9214009.

4. Cf. Kittredge v. Commissioner, 88 F.2d 632 (2d Cir. 1937); P. Dougherty Co. v. Commissioner, 159 F.2d 269 (4th Cir. 1946), cert. denied, 331 U.S. 838, 67 S.Ct. 1515, 91 L.Ed. 1850 (1947) (idle property was depreciable, requiring basis adjustments).

In Carter–Colton the Tax Court regarded the small scale rental activity as not "particularly pertinent." This raises the question of how much activity is necessary before rental activities become a trade or business. Generally, trade or business characterization, as distinct from investment characterization, will be found with respect to such rental property as apartment or office buildings, regardless of the degree of activity of the taxpayer.[5] Taxpayers have been treated as engaged in a trade or business even when renting only a single family residence.[6] However, exceptions should be noted. For example, in Grier v. United States[7] the taxpayer, a securities adviser and salesman, inherited a one-family house that had been leased to a tenant by the taxpayer's mother. The taxpayer simply continued to accept the rent and pay repair bills as they were presented to him by the tenant. The court observed that the cases had not been consistent but said that the line had been drawn on the basis of the activity of the taxpayer in connection with the renting. The court found that under the facts the taxpayer had treated the property with the passivity of an investor. Consequently, the court concluded that the taxpayer was not engaged in a trade or business.

Suppose that a taxpayer develops or purchases property with the thought of renting or selling it, depending on what appears most advantageous as events develop. Is such property "held by the taxpayer primarily for sale to customers in the ordinary course of his trade or business" so that gain or loss will fall under section 1221(a)(1) as ordinary gain or loss? The issue may arise in various types of business activities, and the meaning to be attributed to the term "primarily" may provide the answer to close questions involving the characterization of assets under sections 1221 and 1231.

Prior to 1966 the lower courts had not agreed on the definition of "primarily." Many, if not most courts, regarded the question simply as an aspect of the overall problem of characterization, which in turn depends upon a variety of factors. However, from this all-factors approach the Tax Court and at least two Courts of Appeals concluded that the term "primarily" meant "essential" or "substantial," rather than "principal" or "chief."[8]

The conflict was resolved by the Supreme Court in Malat v. Riddell.[9] In a brief *per curiam* opinion the Court vacated and remanded the case

---

5. Fackler v. Commissioner, 133 F.2d 509 (6th Cir. 1943). See also Larry J. Brant, The Evolution of the Phrase "Trade or Business" Flint v. Stone Tracy Company to Commissioner v. Groetzinger—An Analysis With Respect to the Full–Time Gambler and the Investor, 23 Gonz. L. Rev. 513, 571 (1988).

6. See, e.g., Leland Hazard, 7 T.C. 372 (1946). In Curphey v. Commissioner, 73 T.C. 766 (1980), the Tax Court said: "This Court held repeatedly ... that the rental of even a single piece of real property for production of income constitutes a trade or business" and cited five cases.

7. 120 F.Supp. 395 (D.Conn. 1954), aff'd per curiam, 218 F.2d 603 (2d Cir. 1955). See also Murtaugh v. Commissioner, T.C. Memo. 1997–319.

8. Rollingwood Corp. v. Commissioner, 190 F.2d 263 (9th Cir. 1951); Contra Municipal Bond Corp. v. Commissioner, 341 F.2d 683 (8th Cir. 1965); Gotfredson v. United States, 303 F.2d 464 (6th Cir. 1962); United States v. Bennett, 186 F.2d 407 (5th Cir. 1951).

9. 383 U.S. 569, 86 S.Ct. 1030, 16 L.Ed.2d 102 (1966), reversing and remanding 347 F.2d 23 (9th Cir. 1965). On remand, the district court simply concluded, without

on the ground that "the courts below applied an incorrect legal standard." The Supreme Court recognized that departure from a literal construction may, at times, be indicated to effect the legislative purpose of a statute, which in this case was to differentiate between gain and loss from everyday business operations and the realization of appreciation in value of property over a substantial period of time. However, in this instance the Court said that a literal reading of the statute, that "primarily" means of first importance or principally, was consistent with the legislative purpose.

In International Shoe Machine Corporation v. United States[10] the First Circuit considered the meaning of "primarily" in the context of section 1231.[11] The taxpayer's leasing of its shoe machinery was its main source of income prior to 1964. Beginning in 1964, when the investment tax credit made it more attractive for shoe manufacturers to buy equipment rather than lease it, the taxpayer began to sell a larger proportion of its machinery. The Commissioner argued that the machinery was "property held by the taxpayer primarily for sale to customers in the ordinary course of his trade or business" and that the taxpayer had ordinary income rather than capital gain.

The First Circuit reasoned that an interpretation of "primarily" as defined by the Supreme Court in Malat did not require a comparison of the relative value of lease income and sale income to determine which was of first importance. Rather, the First Circuit said that "a more meaningful distinction could be made between on-going income generated in the ordinary course of business and income from the termination and sale of the venture." Thus, the court rejected a mechanical application of Malat[12] and classified the sales as ordinary because sales of the machinery were accepted and predictable and, therefore, were in the ordinary course of business.

giving its rationale, that the property had not been held primarily for sale to customers. Malat v. Riddell, 275 F.Supp. 358, 18 A.F.T.R.2d 5015 (S.D.Cal. 1966). See also Biedenharn Realty Co. v. United States, 526 F.2d 409, 422–423 (5th Cir. 1976); David Taylor Enterprises, Inc. v. Commissioner, T.C. Memo. 2005–127; Phelan v. Commissioner, T.C. Memo. 2004–206; Medlin v. Commissioner, T.C. Memo. 2003–224.

10.   491 F.2d 157 (1st Cir. 1974), cert. denied, 419 U.S. 834, 95 S.Ct. 59, 42 L.Ed.2d 60 (1974). See also Hollywood Baseball Association v. Commissioner, 423 F.2d 494 (9th Cir. 1970); Continental Can Co. v. United States, 422 F.2d 405 (Ct.Cl. 1970); Recordak Corp. v. United States, 325 F.2d 460 (Ct.Cl. 1963); Honeywell Inc. v. Commissioner, 87 T.C. 624 (1986); TAM 200203001; Joseph B. Cartee, A Historical Essay and Economic Assay of the Capital

Asset Definition: The Taxpayer and Courts Are Still Mindfully Guessing While Congress Doesn't Seem to (Have a) Mind, 34 Wm. & Mary L. Rev. 885, 931 (1993).

11.   Note that the same phrase, "property held by the taxpayer primarily for sale to customers in the ordinary course of his trade or business," appears in §§ 1221(a)(1) and 1231(b)(1)(B) and has been given the same construction. See, e.g., Hollywood Baseball Ass'n v. Commissioner, 423 F.2d 494 (9th Cir. 1970), cert. denied, 400 U.S. 848, 91 S.Ct. 35, 27 L.Ed.2d 85 (1970).

12.   See also Bynum v. Commissioner, 46 T.C. 295 (1966). Judge Tannenwald, joined by three of his colleagues, said "primarily" does not imply a "quantitative measurement of more than 50 percent;" the required purpose would be served so long as it was first among equal considerations.

§ 10.09   GAIN ON DEPRECIABLE PROPERTY UNDER SECTION 1239

Under section 1239 gain on the sale or exchange of property that is depreciable in the hands of the transferee produces ordinary income for the transferor if the transaction is either between a person and a "controlled entity" or between the taxpayer (or the taxpayer's spouse) and any trust of which the taxpayer is a beneficiary.[1] A "controlled entity" includes a corporation or partnership in which the taxpayer owns, directly or indirectly, "more than 50 percent of the value of the outstanding stock" or "more than 50 percent of the capital interest or profits interest."[2]

§ 10.10   RECAPTURE OF DEPRECIATION: SECTIONS 1245 AND 1250

Two additional limitations on capital gain benefits inherent in depreciable property are imposed by section 1245, which typically applies to depreciable personal property,[1] and by section 1250, which typically applies to depreciable real property.[2] Subject to certain limitations, section 1245 and section 1250 are generally applicable when gain is realized upon the disposition of depreciable property. Essentially, section 1245 provides for reporting gain as ordinary income to the extent of the depreciation taken with respect to depreciable personal property.[3] Moreover, section 1250 provides for the reporting gain as ordinary income to the extent of any additional (any depreciation taken in excess of straight-line depreciation).[4]

The broad scope of sections 1245 and 1250 is found primarily in their applicability not only to sales and exchanges, but also to other dispositions, some of which do not ordinarily constitute taxable events. Specifically, the rules apply to any disposition not expressly excepted in sections 1245 and 1250. Sections 1245(d) and 1250(h) provide that the sections "shall apply notwithstanding any other provision of this subtitle." Among the transactions expressly excepted are: (1) gifts, (2) transfers at death, like-kind exchanges and involuntary conversions, and (4) certain tax-free transactions, but if gain is partially recognized because boot is received, such gain is subject to recapture.[5] Because sections 1245 and 1250 do not apply to losses, gains and losses on the sale of similar properties do not offset each other.[6]

The technique used under section 1245 is designed to separate the amount of the depreciation recapture from any additional gain that

---

§ 10.09

1. § 1239(a).

2. § 1239(c)(1)(A)-(C).

§ 10.10

1. See § 1245(a)(3).

2. See § 1250(c).

3. See § 1245(a)(1).

4. See § 1250(a)(1).

5. §§ 1245(b); 1250(d).

6. See Treas. Reg. § 1.1245–1(d); Treas. Reg. § 1.1250–1(a)(5)(i).

ordinarily will continue to be treated as capital gain under section 1231.[7] Generally, this is accomplished by the concept of recomputed basis, which is equal to the adjusted basis plus depreciation or amortization deductions.[8] On sale of the property the excess of the amount realized over the recomputed basis is capital gain, while the remainder of the gain, represented by the difference between the recomputed basis and the adjusted basis, is characterized as ordinary income.[9]

Assume, for example, the early 2013 sale of a machine for $20,000 that had an adjusted basis of $15,000, on which the depreciation deduction for 2012 was $3,000. Recomputed basis would be $18,000, and the computation of ordinary gain and capital gain would be as follows:

Amount Realized	$20,000	
Less: Adjusted Basis	($15,000)	
Gain	$5,000	
Recomputed Basis		$18,000
Less: Adjusted Basis		($15,000)
Ordinary Income		$3,000
Capital Gain		$2,000

If the amount realized or the value of the property received, as the case may be, is lower than the recomputed basis, the former is used as the measure of the recapture gain.[10] In this manner recapture gain is limited to the gain actually realized.

With respect to section 1231 property, any section 1245 or section 1250 recapture gain is determined first, and only the balance, if any, is subject to the section 1231 netting process.[11] Also, section 453(i) requires that the recapture amount computed under section 1245 or section 1250 be recognized in the year of disposition. Hence, with respect to any installment sale under section 453, gain is recaptured in the year of sale even though no principal is received.

Section 1250, is much milder in effect, clearly reflecting no small amount of political pressure. In general, section 1250 only applies to real property that is or has been subject to an additional allowance for depreciation above and beyond straight-line depreciation.[12] Accordingly, since depreciable real property placed into service after 1986 must be depreciated using straight-line depreciation, § 1250 is rarely applicable today.[13]

7.   See § 1245(a)(1).
8.   § 1245(a)(2)(A).
9.   § 1245(a)(1)(A) and (B).
10.   § 1245(a)(1).

11.   Treas. Reg. § 1.1245–6(a).
12.   See § 1250(a)(1)(A).
13.   See § 168(b)(3).

§ 10.11 SPECIFIC TYPES OF CAPITAL ASSETS

[1] IN GENERAL

Assume A is engaged in the real estate business and his usual activities consist of buying and selling real property, renting real property, and acting as a broker. Assume in 2006 he owns the following: (1) 20 vacant homes in a subdivision that he advertises for sale; (2) 30 homes acquired in a devise from his father that he rents out; (3) vacant land on the edge of a city, held for speculation; (4) a lakeside summer cottage that he built himself; (5) a ten-year leasehold estate in the property occupied by his business; (6) a life estate in a trust the corpus of which consists of an apartment building, with the taxpayer being entitled to periodic payments of net income from the trust; and (7) 20 surplus government Jeeps stored in a warehouse.

In any attempt A may make to minimize his tax liability by claiming capital gain treatment on the sale or other disposition of the foregoing properties, he has the benefit of the general rule under section 1221 that all property is a capital asset. Understandably, Congress has removed certain categories of property from the definition of a capital asset, and it has expressly granted capital asset treatment upon fulfillment of certain conditions, such as when the netting process of section 1231 yields a net gain. Unfortunately, the statutory structure frequently provides merely an outline for the solution of a particular characterization problem.

The characterization benchmarks similarly provide no precise guide for accurate prediction. Consider, for example, what Congress asked the courts to do under the general rule of section 1221: to provide definitional content for "property," a term that has few equals in the broadness of its meaning.

What is "property" for purposes of section 1221? Assume that A realizes gain upon the sale of vacant land held for speculation. Has A sold property that is a capital asset? Or would A's more frequent sales of inventory or stock in trade taint the transaction and result in a denial of capital gain treatment? It is clear that lack of identity as section 1221(a)(1) assets (stock in trade, inventory, and property held for sale to customers) will not of itself result in capital asset characterization. For example, in Corn Products Refining Company v. Commissioner[1] the Supreme Court admitted that the futures contracts sold did not fall within the stock in trade or inventory exception, yet it found that these sales generated ordinary gain and loss because of their close relationship to the taxpayer's normal manufacturing activities.

Furthermore, even when there has not been competition between the general rule and the inventory exception of section 1221, the courts have at times been reluctant to characterize a protectable interest as property within the meaning of sections 1221 and 1231. For example, in Commissioner v. Gillette Motor Transport, Inc.[2] the taxpayer, a motor

---

§ 10.11
1. See § 10.08 *supra.*

2. 364 U.S. 130, 80 S.Ct. 1497, 4 L.Ed.2d 1617 (1960). See also United States

carrier, received compensation from the government for the temporary requisition of its operating properties during World War II, for which the taxpayer claimed capital gain treatment under what is now section 1231. The Supreme Court held that the proceeds were ordinary income, reasoning that although the taxpayer's right to use its transportation facilities was a protectable property right it was not a capital asset within the meaning of sections 1221 and 1231. Therefore, though the facilities themselves were property, which if taken would have qualified as capital assets, the taking was only that of the use to which the facilities were to be put. This use, the Court said, was not anything in which the taxpayer had an investment apart from the physical assets. Thus, it was held that the right to the use of the facilities was not a capital asset but simply an incident of the underlying physical property and that the compensation was in the nature of rent.

Protectable interests not regarded as property for the purpose of section 1221 are numerous. Some interests that have been subject to judicial analysis have involved personal interests. For example, in Miller v. Commissioner[3] a widow's interest in the public fame of her deceased husband was denied capital asset characterization. In Miller the taxpayer was the widow of Glenn Miller, a world-famous band leader. The taxpayer granted to a motion picture company the exclusive right to produce movies based on the life of her deceased husband, receiving over $400,000 as her share of the income from a movie. The Second Circuit held that the proceeds were ordinary income since the taxpayer failed to establish that a decedent's successor has a property right to the public image of a deceased entertainer, reasoning that not everything that will command a payment may be regarded as property.

Even if a protectable interest qualifies as property, the taxpayer may have the burden of establishing that what was once an investment asset remained as such at the time of sale. Suppose that in the preceding example A decided to dispose of the vacant land, the rental properties, and the surplus Jeeps. In that situation, two competing factors or criteria regarding characterization might present themselves. First, the intensity and frequency of A's sales activity might result in a finding that all the property was converted to or was held as inventory, stock in trade, or for sale to customers. On the other hand, if A sold all the rental houses in one transaction shortly after acquiring them by devise, a court might conclude that A was simply liquidating an investment in business assets, and any gain was entitled to capital treatment. In some situations, if the values of the properties are attributable to economic forces

v. Maginnis, 356 F.3d 1179, 1182 (9th Cir. 2004); Watkins v. Commissioner, 447 F.3d 1269, 1271 (10th Cir. 2006); CCA 200211042; FSA 200238045; TAM 200722013; TAM 200627024.

3. 299 F.2d 706 (2d Cir. 1962), cert. denied, 370 U.S. 923, 82 S.Ct. 1564, 8 L.Ed.2d 503 (1962). See also Runyon v. United States, 281 F.2d 590 (5th Cir. 1960), in which the right of privacy was treated in a similar manner; Rev. Rul. 65–261, 1965–2 C.B. 281, in which the Service concluded that the sale of an individual's name, signature, or portrait to be used in connection with the advertising and selling of merchandise does not constitute a sale of property.

over a long holding period, then the liquidation of an investment
criterion might outweigh substantial sales activity. Perhaps contributing
to this last result has been the need that the courts may have felt to
ignore allocation and choose between treating all gain as either ordinary
or capital.[4]

If the taxpayer can show that he did not replace the property sold,
this may add weight to the argument that he was liquidating his
investment. However, if sales activity was contemplated at the time the
property was acquired, the Service is unlikely to be impressed by such an
argument even if the enterprise was of the single venture type. For
example, if A should contend that, in order to liquidate the assets of his
single venture in surplus government property, he had to advertise and
otherwise actively promote the sale of the Jeeps, it is unlikely that his
argument for capital treatment would prevail on this ground.

In Hollis v. United States[5] the taxpayer, a museum curator, resigned
his position and organized a syndicate to purchase art objects in Japan
for resale in the United States. The members agreed that the syndicate
was to be a "one venture proposition," and the partnership (joint
venture) agreement referred to the enterprise as an "investment" in a
"limited number of oriental art objects." The taxpayer took a 50%
capital interest and was to receive a 10% commission on gross sales. The
taxpayer purchased some 157 art objects in Japan for the syndicate, and
thereafter he engaged in selling them through personal contacts in the
United States. When it became apparent that the venture was going to
be successful, a second permanent syndicate was organized, and the
taxpayer continued his purchasing and selling for both enterprises,
keeping separate accounts and inventory. The taxpayer admitted that
the second syndicate was disposing of inventory, but contended that with
respect to the first syndicate there was capital gain. The court disagreed,
finding no reason to differentiate between the two enterprises merely
because the first syndicate was a one venture proposition, denominated
an "investment," or because it did not contemplate replenishing its
inventory.

A third major factor relates to the personal efforts embedded in
property that is created, produced, or developed by the taxpayer. Suppose A were to sell his summer cottage and his real estate business,
receiving for the business a substantial sum for goodwill. Although the
Code prescribes the tax treatment in the analogous situations of literary
and invented property, the courts have been less than consistent in
handling the personal effort element in uncodified areas. A, however,
would not be challenged in claiming capital gain on the sale of either the
cottage or the goodwill, although the values may be attributable, in part
at least, to his personal efforts. Only if A engaged in such transactions
on a fairly regular basis would his personal efforts be recognized as

4. But see § 1237 under which allocation between ordinary income and capital
gain is provided when land is subdivided
and sold.

5. 121 F.Supp. 191 (N.D. Ohio 1954).

generating ordinary income. Otherwise, A could rely upon the characterization of these properties as capital assets.[6]

Suppose A accepted a lump sum from a tenant in discharge of the latter's obligation to pay rent under the terms of a lease on one of the rental houses. Such collapsed or anticipated income does not escape ordinary income treatment. However, the treatment of collapsed income has not always been carried to such a logical conclusion. For example, as a general rule the concept of the property interest possessed by a life tenant is given precedence over ordinary income characterization. Thus, if A were to sell his life estate in the trust, the proceeds received would not be regarded as the collapsed receipt of ordinary income even though the periodic receipts from the trust would be treated as such. Similarly, if A were to accept a lump sum from his landlord for the release of his rights under his ten-year lease to occupy his business premises, the proceeds would be regarded as from the sale or exchange of a capital asset (the leasehold estate).

Somewhat related to the anticipated or collapsed ordinary income criterion, and frequently compounding the problem of asset characterization is the assignment of income doctrine, a matter discussed in Chapter 6. The principle involved may be stated as follows: as a basic tenet of tax liability, income is attributable to the person rendering the services or owning the property from which such income is derived.[7] For example, if A were to make a gift of rental contracts to his son, as owner of the income-producing property A would be charged with the rental income as it was received by his son.[8]

The relationship of the assignment of income doctrine to the problem of characterizing assets as capital assets is illustrated by Rhodes' Estate v. Commissioner.[9] In this case the taxpayer, a shareholder entitled to a cash dividend of $12,000, "sold" his dividend shortly before the payment date. In a brief *per curiam* opinion, the Sixth Circuit upheld the finding of the Tax Court that the amount received from the buyer constituted ordinary income rather than capital gain, as contended by the taxpayer. Although the court provided no rationale, it did invite comparison to three Supreme Court cases that are included in any listing of landmark decisions on the assignment of income doctrine.[10]

6. For a discussion of goodwill see § 10.10 *infra*.

7. Lucas v. Earl, 281 U.S. 111, 50 S.Ct. 241, 74 L.Ed. 731 (1930) (which deals with assignment of income from services); Helvering v. Horst, 311 U.S. 112, 61 S.Ct. 144, 85 L.Ed. 75 (1940) (which deals with assignment of income from property).

8. See Helvering v. Horst, 311 U.S. 112, 61 S.Ct. 144, 85 L.Ed. 75 (1940).

9. 131 F.2d 50 (6th Cir. 1942). See also United States v. Dresser Industries, Inc., 324 F.2d 56 (5th Cir. 1963); Commissioner v. Ferrer, 304 F.2d 125 (2d Cir. 1962); Foy v. Commissioner, 84 T.C. 50 (1985); Estate of Shea v. Commissioner, 57 T.C. 15 (1971), acq., 1973–2 C.B. 3; Guggenheim v. Commissioner, 46 T.C. 559 (1966), acq., 1967–2 C.B. 2.

10. Harrison v. Schaffner, 312 U.S. 579, 61 S.Ct. 759, 85 L.Ed. 1055 (1941); Helvering v. Horst, 311 U.S. 112, 61 S.Ct. 144, 85 L.Ed. 75 (1940); Helvering v. Eubank, 311 U.S. 122, 61 S.Ct. 149, 85 L.Ed. 81 (1940).

In summary, the following are the major criteria that the courts have used in determining whether property is entitled to capital asset characterization: (1) the frequency and intensity of sales efforts; (2) the purpose of the acquisition as an income-producing investment that is being liquidated in the most practical manner; (3) the nature of the proceeds as reflecting personal efforts; (4) the nature of the proceeds as a substitute for recurring ordinary income receipts (anticipated or collapsed); and (5) the nature of the proceeds as either the fruits of income-producing property or the services of another (the assignment of income doctrine).

Other factors, as previously indicated, have been considered. These include the meaning to be ascribed to such statutory terms as "primarily" and "used in a trade or business," the meaning of the statutory terms restricting or expanding the characterization of particular properties, and factors bearing on such overall questions as whether the transaction was a sale or a license yielding ordinary rental or royalty income. Two additional factors are the unarticulated premises of an elusive congressional policy that has accorded preferential capital treatment to assets reflecting gain accumulated over a long period and an announced judicial policy of requiring a strict interpretation of the revenue laws implementing preferential tax treatment. Fortunately, as the following discussion reveals, only a few fact patterns have required that all of these factors be weighed in any particular case.

[2] SECURITIES

[a] In General

The principal beneficiary of preferential capital gain treatment has been the securities investor because the bulk of capital gains have been attributable to securities transactions. The investor is relatively easy to identify because of the infrequency with which he buys and sells and because of his long-term holdings. But what about the person who trades securities daily on his own account? Here the answer is found in the language of section 1221(a)(1), which defines one category of noncapital assets in terms of stock in trade, inventory, or property held "primarily for sale to customers in the ordinary course of his [the taxpayer's] trade or business." To deal with securities traders, Congress added the words "to customers" in 1934, a time of declining securities' prices; its purpose was to remove traders from the purview of what is now section 1221(a)(1) so that they would not have capital losses, with their limited deductibility. Hence, only if a security holder qualifies as a dealer in securities may losses be fully deductible as ordinary losses.

The design of the 1934 legislation, as well as the efforts of traders to qualify as dealers to obtain the advantages of ordinary loss deductions, are illustrated by Van Suetendael v. Commissioner,[11] in which the

---

11. 152 F.2d 654 (2d Cir. 1945). See also King v. Commissioner, 89 T.C. 445, 457–58 (1987); Mirro–Dynamics Corp. v. United States, 247 F.Supp. 214, 217 (S.D.

taxpayer was engaged in buying and selling securities. The taxpayer's income for the three tax years in question, 1936–1938, however, was primarily derived from interest on bonds that he bought, which constituted 90% of his purchases, and from bank deposits. The taxpayer claimed dealer status and asserted that his sales were of noncapital assets. On his return he deducted the total cost of his purchases from his total receipts.

In support of his claimed dealer status Van Suetendael attempted to show that he was recognized in the security trade as a dealer through listings in financial publications and through registration with the Securities and Exchange Commission and the State of New York. The Commissioner, on the other hand, noted that most of the losses Van Suetendael claimed as ordinary were on securities held for more than five years in two of the tax years, and for more than 18 months in the third. Moreover the Commissioner asserted that the losses resulted from the taxpayer's practice of selecting for sale securities that had declined in value, a practice that Van Suetendael had engaged in since 1929.

The Tax Court concluded that Van Suetendael had not overcome the presumption that the securities sold were capital assets; accordingly, it stated that the issue was not whether he was a trader or a dealer but whether the securities sold were property held for sale to customers. This, the Tax Court said, was a factual inquiry, reasoning that a dealer normally buys at wholesale for resale to persons other than his seller; while in this case the taxpayer bought mostly in small quantities and resold through the same brokers. Furthermore, many of the purchases and sales were one-day transactions, with the taxpayer never taking delivery. In short, Van Suetendael was a trader on his own account without stock in trade, inventory, or customers. Thus, the securities fell within the general rule that defines a capital asset simply as "property." However, trader classification has been denied to taxpayers dealing in real property, and is presumably otherwise unavailable. The implication is that capital asset characterization depends primarily on the mode of disposition, in other words, on whether the disposition is made through an exchange.

The assets of a securities investor and trader are thus capital assets. The inventory items, of course, of a security dealer are noncapital assets under section 1221(a)(1). But is it possible for a dealer also be an investor or a trader? The answer is found in section 1236. Under the terms of section 1236 a security dealer may treat gain, and must treat loss, as capital gain or loss on the sale or exchange of corporate securities if the securities are clearly identified in his records before the close of

Cal. 1965) (securities bought and sold solely for taxpayer's account may not be considered business inventory), aff'd, 374 F.2d 14, 16 (9th Cir.), cert. denied, 389 U.S. 896, 88 S.Ct. 215, 19 L.Ed.2d 214 (1967); Martin v. Commissioner, 147 F.3d 147, 152 (2d Cir. 1998), affg. T.C. Memo.1997–24; United States v. Wood, 943 F.2d 1048, 1051 (9th Cir.1991); Swartz v. Commissioner, 876 F.2d 657, 659 (8th Cir.1989), affg. per curiam T.C. Memo. 1987–582; United States v. Diamond, 788 F.2d 1025, 1029 (4th Cir. 1986).

the date acquired as securities held for investment and if after acquisition they are not held for sale to customers.[12] However, once so set apart, a dealer has no effective way of returning such classified investments to his inventory as may be desired if their market value drops so that their disposition could generate ordinary loss.[13]

Identification in a security dealer's records in compliance with section 1236 does not guarantee capital asset characterization. If the dealer actually holds such securities as inventory after acquisition, capital treatment will be denied. In general, the test employed by the courts as to whether a security dealer is a trader or a dealer has been whether he functions as a merchant in buying and selling securities. This has sometimes been a close question of fact. For example, in two cases that arose from the same syndicate all the members of a partnership participated with an outsider in the purchase and resale of stock. The partnership identified the purchase in its records as required by section 1236. In Nielsen v. United States[14] the Sixth Circuit upheld the finding with respect to one partner that after the acquisition the stock was held for sale to customers. In Bradford v. United States[15] the Court of Claims found that a second partner sold capital assets. The Court of Claims reasoned that the syndicate "performed no merchandising functions" and that "it was not acting as a middleman in bringing together buyer and seller, nor did it perform the usual services of retailer or wholesaler of goods."

On the other hand, failure to identify securities in compliance with section 1236 does not guarantee inventory characterization if it works to a dealer's advantage. Thus, an incorporated securities dealer may sometimes be tempted to keep stock of controlled companies in inventory to secure the advantage of the dividend-received deduction under section 243. For example, in Stephens, Inc. v. United States[16] the taxpayer was an incorporated investment firm. Following a standard practice, it acquired the shares of stock of five companies knowing, in some instances, that it could not recover its purchase price on resale without causing the companies to pay substantial dividends. Hence, it had the companies pay substantial dividends and took the dividend-received deduction that was available under section 243. It then increased its cost of goods sold by writing down the depressed value of the stock caused by the dividends, as it was permitted to do under section 471, using the lower of cost or market value for its closing inventory.

---

12. § 1236(a) and (b).

13. Id.

14. 333 F.2d 615 (6th Cir. 1964).

15. 195 Ct.Cl. 500, 444 F.2d 1133 (1971). See also International Paper Co. v. United States, 33 Fed.Cl. 384, 394 (1995); Bielfeldt v. Commissioner, 231 F.3d 1035, 1037 (7th Cir. 2000); Alex Raskolnikov,

Contextual Analysis of Tax Ownership, 85 B.U. L. Rev. 431, 516 (2005).

16. 464 F.2d 53 (8th Cir. 1972), aff'g, 321 F.Supp. 1159 (E.D.Ark. 1970), cert. denied, 409 U.S. 1118, 93 S.Ct. 911, 34 L.Ed.2d 702 (1973). See also Pacific Securities v. Commissioner, T.C. Memo. 1992–90; Laureys v. Commissioner, 92 T.C. 101, 136 (1989); FSA 200016002.

The Commissioner in Stephens, Inc. attacked the double tax benefit on several grounds, one of which was that the taxpayer was not a dealer with respect to the securities of the five companies. The Eighth Circuit agreed, reasoning that it was well established that investor status attached to anyone, including a dealer, "who acquires securities with the primary intent to profit from their income yield."[17] Furthermore, the taxpayer "was engaging in the merchandising of business"[18] that was "not within the traditional meaning of 'dealing' in securities."[19] It therefore followed that the taxpayer could not inventory the securities of the five companies.

Congress has made a considerable effort to treat investment losses in a similar manner regardless of the form the investment may take or the manner in which the loss is realized. Thus, section 165(g) prescribes special sale or exchange treatment for certain security losses. Under this provision a corporate or government security issued with interest coupons or in registered form that becomes worthless during the taxable year and is a capital asset is treated as a loss from the sale or exchange of a capital asset on the last day of the taxable year.[20]

Under section 166(d) nonbusiness bad debts in the hands of an individual are declared short-term capital losses; this section is not applicable if section 165(g) is applicable under which a loss is either a long-term or a short-term capital loss, depending on the holding period. Section 166(d) always yields a short-term capital loss regardless of the holding period.

Thus, as a general rule, both individuals and corporations have to treat losses on stocks, bonds, debentures, and other securities held more than one year as long-term capital losses. There are, however, exceptions. For example, under section 165(g)(3) a loss is allowed as an ordinary loss to a parent corporation on securities of an 80% or more owned operating subsidiary[21] in which more than 90% of the gross receipts of the subsidiary are not investment-type income.[22] Another exception is provided in section 1244, discussed at the end of this section.

In addition to special provisions pertaining to capital losses, security investors are subject to special treatment with respect to wash sales, discount obligations, short sales and options. These matters are discussed hereafter.

[b]   Bonds and Other Evidences of Indebtedness

The problems in this area have been two-fold. First, when a bond or other evidence of indebtedness is finally paid off at redemption by the debtor, is the transaction a sale or exchange so as to afford capital gain treatment to the holder of the bond or note? Under a vanishing-asset treatment the extinguishment of an obligation by payment is denied

---

17. 464 F.2d at 57.

18. 464 F.2d at 58,

19. Id.

20. § 165(g)(1).

21. § 165(g)(3)(A).

22. § 165(g)(3)(B).

capital gain characterization. Generally, the Code provides sale or exchange treatment for payment of certain debts at maturity. Second, is ordinary interest income characterized as capital gain? This question is dealt with in sections 1271–1288 and section 483.

Under section 1272 the holder of any debt instrument includes in income the daily portions of original issue discount[23] for the period the instrument is held. The original issue discount provisions are best explained by way of example.[24] Suppose a $1,000 zero-coupon bond (one for which there are no periodic interest payments) with a ten-year maturity is purchased for $386. This is an effective yield of 10%. The $614 difference between maturity and issue is original issue discount. The difference is in reality interest, and it is therefore not characterized as capital gain. Prior to the enactment of section 1272 the $614 would have been included in the holder's income ratably ($61.40 a year for 10 years), and the discount would then be added to basis each year to avoid double taxation upon sale or redemption. However, section 1272 mandates the utilization of the economic accrual method to reflect more clearly the underlying transaction. Invested at 10%, $386 would yield $39 in year one; 10% of $386 plus the $39 of year one interest would yield $42 in year two. Under the section 1272 regime interest for year three through year ten ranges from $46 to $91, but the total amount is still $614.[25]

The market discount provisions in section 1276 work in a manner similar to the original issue discount provisions in section 1272. Market discount occurs when the purchase price of a debt instrument acquired from someone other than the issuer is less than the amount to be paid at maturity.[26] However, the taxpayer may elect between ratable or economic accrual.[27] Another important difference between original issue discount and market discount is that market discount is included in income only upon a sale or other disposition, or upon retirement of the debt.[28]

Section 483 imputes interest on a transaction if none is otherwise provided, or if it is not provided for at an adequate rate.[29] Section 483 applies to contracts for the sale or exchange of property.[30] Of course, a sale for inadequate interest would produce an inflated sales price, causing the conversion of ordinary income into long-term capital gain.[31]

[c] Options to Buy or Sell Property: Section 1234

Section 1234 regulates the character of gain or loss attributable to

---

23. "Original issue discount" is defined in § 1273(a)(1) as the "stated redemption price at maturity" over the "issue price." The terms "stated redemption price at maturity" and "issue price" are defined in §§ 1273(a)(2) and 1273(b).

24. The amounts in this example are rounded off to whole dollars.

25. Under § 163(e) the issuer is allowed to deduct for original issue discount.

26. § 1276(b)(1).

27. § 1276(b)(2).

28. Compare § 1276(a)(1) (dealing with market discount) to § 1272(a)(1) (dealing with original issue discount).

29. § 483(a).

30. § 483(a)(1).

31. Because § 483 was designed to prevent this particular problem, it does not apply to original issue discount obligations. See § 1276(d)(1).

the sale, exchange, or nonexercise of an option to buy or sell property.[32] Broadly speaking, such gain or loss would be characterized by the property that is the subject matter of the option.[33] Thus, if the option relates to a capital asset or property that would be a capital asset if acquired, gain or loss upon the sale or exchange of the option, or loss upon the failure to exercise it, would be capital gain or loss.[34] A failure by the optionee to exercise an option is treated as a sale or exchange on the date of expiration of the option.[35]

Section 1234(a)(3) expressly excludes the following from the purview of the favorable capital treatment granted under section 1234(a): (1) options that constitute stock in trade, inventory, or property held primarily for sale to customers under section 1221(a)(1);[36] (2) gain attributable to the sale or exchange of an option that is treated as other than gain from the sale or exchange of a capital asset;[37] and (3) a loss attributable to a failure to exercise an option to sell (a "put") under section 1233(c).[38]

Under section 1234(b) gain or loss from a closing transaction with respect to, or gain on the lapse of, an option in stock, securities, or commodities is treated as short-term capital gain or loss. Section 1234(b) does not apply to options granted in the taxpayer's trade or business, which would generate ordinary gain or loss.[39] A closing transaction is the termination of the grantor's obligation other than through lapse or exercise of the option, such as the repurchase of the option or the purchase of an identical option and designating it a closing transaction.[40]

If the taxpayer wrote a straddle (a combination of a put and a call), the premium must be allocated based on the relative fair market value of each option;[41] it may also be allocated 55% to the call option and 45% to

---

32. Treas. Reg. § 1.1234–1(a)(1). Section 1234 it is not limited to transactions involving securities. However, it has its greatest application to writers of security options and to investors in such options. A wide variety of the two basic types of security options, puts and calls, are used. The put, an option in which the writer agrees to buy stock (to have it "put to" him), and the call, an option in which the writer agrees to sell (to have it "called away" from him), are often written in combination and sometimes are subject to special conditions. For example, a "down-and-out" call provides for automatic expiration if the stock's price drops a fixed percentage below the "striking price." This is the specified purchase price to the investor and is usually the market price at the time the option is written.

33. Treas. Reg. § 1.1234–1(a)(1).

34. Id.

35. Treas. Reg. § 1.1234–1(b).

36. § 1234(a)(3)(A).

37. § 1234(a)(3)(B). The intent with respect to § 1234(a)(3)(B) was to ensure the inapplicability of § 1234 to options that produce ordinary income, such as certain restricted employee stock options.

38. § 1234(a)(3)(C). The property to which the option relates must be acquired on the same day the option is written. § 1233(c). Loss is not recognized, but the cost of the option is added to the basis of the property that is acquired at the same time as the option. Treas. Reg. § 1.1234–1(c).

39. § 1234(b)(3).

40. § 1234(b)(2)(A); Treas. Reg. § 1.1234–3(b)(1).

41. Rev. Rul. 78–182, 1978–1 C.B. 265. This ruling deals extensively with the tax consequences to the holders and writers of options. See also Rev. Rul. 84–121, 1984–2 C.B. 168, in which the Service deals with the exercise of an option to buy real property.

the put option.[42]

[d] Other Special Rules

Similar to the treatment afforded options is the treatment under section 1234A. Gain or loss attributable to the cancellation, lapse, or other termination of a right or obligation with respect to personal property of which is (or would be) a capital asset in the hands of the taxpayer if acquired is treated as gain or loss from the sale of a capital asset.[43]

Section 1234A also governs section 1256 contracts that are capital assets in the hands of the taxpayer.[44] Section 1256 contracts include regulated futures contracts, foreign currency contracts, nonequity options, and dealer equity options.[45] Such contracts must be treated as if sold on the last day of the taxable year.[46] Gain or loss is treated as 40% short-term capital and 60% long-term capital, regardless of the actual holding period or character of the contracts.[47]

If offsetting positions make up a straddle, such as the taxpayer holding a put and a call on the same property, the special straddle rules of section 1092 apply. The section 1092 straddle rules prevent a taxpayer from shifting ordinary income and short-term capital gain into long-term capital gain. A straddle is defined in section 1092 as an offsetting position with respect to personal property of a type that is actively traded.[48] Generally, loss is deferred upon the disposition of one offsetting position of an unidentified (unreported) straddle to the extent of the unrecognized gain in the other offsetting position.[49] Notwithstanding the general rule of section 1092(a)(1), losses on identified straddles are deferred until disposition of the last offsetting position.[50]

[e] Small Business Corporation Stock: Section 1244

Losses incurred on securities held more than one year usually must be treated as long-term capital losses. However, sections 1242–1244 generally provide for ordinary loss treatment with respect to certain corporate securities. Section 1244, which has the widest application, is limited in its application to individuals, including members of a partnership, who are original owners of stock in a "small business corporation,"[51] and ordinary loss treatment cannot exceed $50,000[52] a year

---

42. See Rev. Rul. 78–182, 1978–1 C.B. 265 citing Rev. Proc. 65–29, 1965–2 C.B. 1023.

43. § 1234A(1).

44. See § 1234A(2).

45. See § 1256(g).

46. See § 165(g).

47. § 1256(a)(3)(A) and (B).

48. § 1092(c).

49. § 1092(a)(1). For example, a loss on the sale of a put will be deferred if there

is unrecognized gain on the call held by the same taxpayer on the same property.

50. § 1092(a)(2).

51.

[A] corporation shall be treated as a small business corporation if the aggregate amount of money and other property received by the corporation for stock, as a contribution to capital, and as paid-in surplus, does not exceed $1,000,000. The determination under the preceding sentence shall be made as of the time of the issuance of the stock in question but

($100,000[53] on a joint return of a husband and wife). Additionally, the stock must have been issued for money or property other than stock or securities.[54] The regulations state that "[s]tock issued for services rendered or to be rendered to, or for the benefit of, the issuing corporation does not qualify as section 1244 stock."[55]

In order for section 1244 treatment to apply, the issuing corporation must be a corporation formed in the United States that, for five years (or for the period of the corporation's existence if less than five years) prior to the loss, derived more than 50% of its income from other than investment income or capital gains,[56] and, its equity capital at the time of the issuance of the stock must not exceed $1,000,000, including contributions to capital and paid-in surplus.[57]

[3] REAL ESTATE

[a] In General

With respect to capital gains transactions, real estate probably ranks second to securities in terms of frequency of transactions and total dollars involved. However, from the standpoint of caselaw complexity and frequency of interpretative problems, real estate ranks first. This is particularly true with respect to the identification of a real estate dealer's property as investment assets, property used in business, or inventory or property held primarily for sale.[58]

Unlike the owner of securities, the owner of real estate has not had the benefit of trader classification, nor has a real estate dealer been assured of capital gain treatment through a statutory method of recording his land holdings as held for investment. Consequently, litigation has been frequent, and substantially similar fact patterns have yielded wildly different results with respect to the weight to be given the factors considered controlling.

The Fifth Circuit in United States v. Winthrop[59] identified the following factors to determine whether property was held primarily for sale in the ordinary course of business:

> (1) the nature and purpose of the acquisition of the property and the duration of the ownership; (2) the extent and nature of the taxpayer's efforts to sell the property; (3) the number, extent, continuity, and substantiality of the sales; (4) the extent of subdividing, developing, and advertising to increase sales; (5) the use of a business office for the sale of the property; (6) the character and

shall include amounts received for such stock and for all stock theretofore issued.

§ 1244(c)(3).

52. See § 1244(b)(1).

53. See § 1244(b)(2).

54. See § 1244(c)(1)(B).

55. Treas. Reg. § 1.1244(c)–1(d)(1).

56. § 1244(c)(1)(C).

57. See § 1244(c)(3)(A).

58. Forney, Appellate Review of Dealer Status in Realty Sales under § 1221, 45 U. Pitt. L. Rev. 847 (1984); Friedlander, "To Customers:" The Forgotten Element in the Characterization of Gains on Sales of Real Property, 39 Tax L. Rev. 31 (1983).

59. 417 F.2d 905 (5th Cir. 1969).

degree of supervision or control exercised by the taxpayer over any representative selling the property; and (7) the time and effort the taxpayer habitually devoted to the sales.[60]

[b] Sales Activity

One of the principal factors considered in determining whether gain is attributable to inventory or property held for sale is the extent of the taxpayer's sales activity.[61] However, Municipal Bond Corporation v. Commissioner[62] illustrates the difficulties of making the determination. The court was faced with the problem of examining the circumstances surrounding thirty-two sales of real property spread over a five-year period that had been concluded by a corporate taxpayer in the real estate business. Most of the properties had been acquired through the purchase of tax certificates. Twenty-three of the sales were found to have produced ordinary income. These sales included nine parcels of improved property in poor neighborhoods that were in a bad state of repair and that were subject to few improvements, with low rental income being regarded as incidental to the taxpayer's principal purpose of holding the property for sale.

Ordinary income resulted from the sale of an unimproved lot that had been held because it was believed the value would increase. Also yielding ordinary income were five sales to related corporations and the sales of four parcels in an industrial park to a railroad because of the taxpayer's substantial sales efforts. On the other hand, the taxpayer was able to establish that property in nine transactions was not held primarily for sale to customers and that the property produced capital gains. The transactions included properties leased for substantial rent, lots sold to an automobile dealer who had solicited the sale, property sold to a school district and to a public utility that had the power of eminent domain, property sold to a church and to a neighbor who had made a determined effort to purchase, and service station property that was sold pursuant to the terms of a high yield lease containing an option to buy.

The role of subdividing and promotional activity in the characterization of property as that held primarily for sale to customers is well illustrated in Bynum v. Commissioner.[63] The unanimous decision of the full Tax Court was rendered after the Supreme Court held that "primarily" meant "principally" or "of first importance."

In Bynum, the taxpayer was engaged in the nursery business. To raise funds to pay off a mortgage, the taxpayer subdivided a portion of a

60. 417 F.2d at 909–910.

61. See e.g., Municipal Bond Corporation v. Commissioner, 341 F.2d 683 (8th Cir. 1965).

62. 341 F.2d 683 (8th Cir. 1965). On a second appeal by the taxpayer, three of the five sales of lots to the railroad were found to yield capital gain on the ground that they were made under an option contained in a lease, the option having been insisted upon by the lessee-buyer; in other respects the decision of the Tax Court was affirmed. 382 F.2d 184 (8th Cir. 1967).

63. 46 T.C. 295 (1966). See also Nadeau v. Commissioner, T.C. Memo. 1996–427; Thomas O. Wells and Franklin H. Caplan, Achieving Capital Gains Treatment on Predevelopment Real Property Appreciation, 80–APR Fla. B.J. 36, 39 (2006).

farm used in the taxpayer's nursery business. The taxpayer personally supervised and sold 38 improved lots in the initial subdivision and advertised that a total of 233 lots would eventually be offered for sale. The taxpayer invested some $650 to improve each lot. The proceeds from the first 26 sales exceeded the amount needed to pay off the mortgage. The Tax Court concluded that while the taxpayer remained in the nursery and landscaping business during the period of subdividing, he had entered a second business of selling the subdivided lots, and the lots were then held "primarily and principally for sale to customers"[64] so that "this purpose was of first importance to"[65] the taxpayer. The court also noted that the value of the raw land had appreciated only $35 an acre since its acquisition, but the gain on the 13 acres sold during the tax years at issue amounted to $4,000 an acre. Such gain, the court said, was generated by the taxpayer's own activities.[66]

In Adam v. Commissioner[67] the taxpayer had capital gain on the purchase and sale of unimproved waterfront lots. The Tax Court reasoned that the lack of solicitation or improvement, as well as the limited amount of time devoted to the property, precluded a finding that the sales were made in the course of the taxpayer's trade or business.

However, at least in the Fifth Circuit it appears that frequency and substantiality of sales has predominated over lack of advertising, solicitation, or improvement. In an en banc decision in Biedenharn Realty Co. v. United States[68] frequency and substantiality of sales was regarded as the most important factor. Lack of advertising was not considered important because of a favorable market, and activities of a broker in selling the property were attributed to Biedenharn. This was also the case in Suburban Realty Co. v. United States,[69] in which the court broke down the inquiry into three questions: (1) Was the taxpayer engaged in a trade or business and, if so, what business? (2) Was the taxpayer holding the property primarily for sale in that business? (3) Were the sales contemplated by the taxpayer "ordinary" in the course of that business? The Fifth Circuit held that the frequency and substantiality of sales was

---

64. 46 T.C. at 300.

65. 46 T.C. at 298.

66. See also Hansche v. Commissioner, 457 F.2d 429 (7th Cir. 1972), in which the court, in finding that gain realized on lots subdivided out of a farm was ordinary gain, observed that the notes had appreciated some 30 times in value as against a 10 times general increase in value in land in the locality.

67. 60 T.C. 996 (1973). See also Pacific Securities v. Commissioner, T.C. Memo. 1992–90.

68. 526 F.2d 409 (5th Cir. 1976), cert. denied, 429 U.S. 819, 97 S.Ct. 64, 50 L.Ed.2d 79 (1976). See also David Taylor Enterprises, Inc. v. Commissioner, T.C. Memo. 2005–127; Medlin v. Commissioner, T.C. Memo. 2003–224.

69. 615 F.2d 171 (5th Cir. 1980), cert. denied 449 U.S. 920, 101 S.Ct. 318, 66 L.Ed.2d 147 (1980). See also Major Realty Corp. & Subs. v. Commissioner, 749 F.2d 1483 (11th Cir. 1985), affg. in part and revg. in part T.C. Memo. 1981–361; Byram v. United States, 705 F.2d 1418 (5th Cir. 1983); Parkside, Inc. v. Commissioner, 571 F.2d 1092, 1096 (9th Cir. 1977), revg. T.C. Memo. 1975–14; Biedenharn Realty Co. v. United States, 526 F.2d 409 (5th Cir. 1976); United States v. Winthrop, 417 F.2d 905 (5th Cir. 1969); Estate of Freeland v. Commissioner, 393 F.2d 573 (9th Cir. 1968), affg. T.C. Memo. 1966–283; Los Angeles Extension Co. v. United States, 315 F.2d 1 (9th Cir. 1963).

pivotal in answering all three of the questions. The absence of advertising was not conclusive in determining whether a trade or business existed, and the taxpayer was held to be in the business of selling unimproved real property. The scope of review in both Biedenharn and Suburban Realty Co. may, however, have been thrown into doubt by Bynum, noted above.

[c] Use of Agents and Corporations

When extensive selling activity is dictated by business exigencies, taxpayers have sometimes reverted to the use of agents and controlled corporations in an effort to turn the gain on such sales into capital gain. The results here, as elsewhere, have varied.

In Voss v. United States[70] the taxpayer, a dentist, purchased farm land in 1929 and 1930 near the city limits of Racine, Wisconsin. After several unsuccessful attempts to sell it, in 1954 the taxpayer was persuaded by a broker to let the latter develop and subdivide the property for a 5% broker's fee and a 5% development fee. The taxpayer refrained from actively participating in the subdividing and selling, except for signing deeds of conveyance. The district court rendered judgment for the government on the grounds that the property had been held for sale, a finding based on a special jury verdict. The Court of Appeals reversed; it rejected the government's contention that the right to control the agent was sufficient to impute the selling activities of the broker to the taxpayer. Accordingly, the court held that the question turned on the degree of control actually exercised over the agent and stressed the fact that the taxpayer had held the property for 25 years.

The taxpayer's use of a corporation in subdividing and selling has not always met with success. In Browne v. United States[71] three taxpayers, sole shareholders of a corporation engaged in building and selling prefabricated houses, purchased an undeveloped tract of land. The taxpayers took title to the property in the same ratio as their stockholdings. After the taxpayers had improved the property with utility facilities and streets, they caused the corporation to build a model home for display. When sales were assured, they sold the land to the corporation in one transaction for a price five times their cost and three times their basis; the corporation thereafter continuing with the development. The taxpayers had engaged in similar transactions in the past. The Court of Claims concluded that the property had been held primarily for sale to customers, and the substantial personal development activity, coupled with the sale to a controlled corporation that continued the development and the earlier transactions, justified a finding that the property fell outside the capital gain provisions.

70. 329 F.2d 164 (7th Cir. 1964); accord Smith v. Dunn, 224 F.2d 353 (5th Cir. 1955). See also Riddell v. Scales, 406 F.2d 210 (9th Cir. 1969), But see Pointer v. Commissioner, 419 F.2d 213 (9th Cir. 1969); Hansche v. Commissioner, 457 F.2d 429 (7th Cir. 1972), in which the use of an agent did not prevent treatment of gain as ordinary gain, with the court distinguishing its own decision in Voss.

71. 174 Ct.Cl. 523, 356 F.2d 546 (1966); accord Tibbals v. United States, 176 Ct.Cl. 196, 362 F.2d 266 (1966).

[d] Length of Holding Period

When property has been held a substantial number of years, the courts have often stressed the original congressional purpose that preferential capital gain treatment was to alleviate the burden of taxing gain arising over a long period.[72] However, most courts appear to regard the length of the holding period as only one factor to be considered.

On the other hand, in Scheuber v. Commissioner[73] the Seventh Circuit, relying on Malat,[74] appeared to raise this factor to a position of dominance. The taxpayer, a real estate dealer, purchased two vacant tracts of land with the intent of holding them for long-term appreciation and sale. One tract was held for nine years and the other for fourteen years. Before the sale of the latter the taxpayer informed his wife that he expected it to provide an annuity for her in her old age. The Commissioner argued that Malat was distinguishable because it dealt with the question of primary purpose when there is more than one while in Scheuber the only purpose was a sale. This, the Seventh Circuit said, was "a very strained interpretation of Malat and a misapplication of its principles." The court concluded that because the properties were purchased for appreciation over a long period and to provide an annuity for the taxpayer's wife, the properties were not intended to be "disposed of to customers in the ordinary course of trade," thereby entitling the taxpayer to capital treatment.

[e] Change in Purpose

Once a taxpayer has engaged in the disposition of real estate from inventory, he can anticipate difficulty in convincing a court that he has terminated the real estate business and subsequent sales are of investment property.[75] For example, in Mauldin v. Commissioner[76] the taxpayer, a contractor, purchased cattle land in 1920 near Clovis, New Mexico. Depression conditions prevented the taxpayer from going into the cattle business as he had intended, and he could not sell the land. In 1924 he platted the property for residential lots. Sales were minimal until 1939 when the property, then within the city limits, was assessed $25,000 for paving. Through active selling in 1939 and 1940 the taxpayer sold enough lots to pay off the assessment. From 1940 to 1949 the taxpayer devoted his time to a lumber business and made no active effort to sell lots. However, the city had grown, and by the end of 1945 all but 20 of an original 160 acres had been sold. During 1944 and 1945, the two tax years in question, the taxpayer entered into three and fifteen transactions respectively. The Tenth Circuit upheld a Tax Court finding that the taxpayer was engaged in holding the lots for sale at all times. Although the Tenth Circuit recognized that a taxpayer may discontinue a business and sell its remnants, it held that the record indicated this

---

72. See, e.g., Voss v. United States, *supra.*

73. 371 F.2d 996 (7th Cir. 1967).

74. See § 10.08 *supra.*

75. See e.g., Mauldin v. Commissioner, 195 F.2d 714 (10th Cir. 1952).

76. 195 F.2d 714 (10th Cir. 1952), aff'g 16 T.C. 698 (1951). See also Olstein v. Commissioner, T.C. Memo. 1999–290.

had not been done. The Tenth Circuit further noted that the business volume depended primarily on the prevailing economic conditions resulting from wartime activities.

On the other hand, even if property is acquired with the intent to sell to customers, a subsequent event may permit its disposition as a capital asset. In Commissioner v. Tri–S Corp.[77] the Tenth Circuit upheld capital treatment for gain realized on a forced sale to the state under threat of condemnation of a 20–acre portion of a residential development the taxpayer had intended to develop as a shopping center and sell in the future. The Tenth Circuit reasoned that the taxpayer "never at any time held such 20–acre tract for sale in its raw state to customers in the ordinary course of its trade or business." However, other courts have abandoned any per se rule that condemnation threats convert ordinary income property into capital gain.[78]

[4] LIFE ESTATES, LEASEHOLDS, AND REMAINDERS

Section 1234A(1) provides in pertinent part:

Gain or loss attributable to the cancellation, lapse, expiration, or other termination of a right or obligation (other than a securities futures contract, as defined in section 1234B) with respect to property which is (or on acquisition would be) a capital asset in the hands of the taxpayer ... shall be treated as gain or loss from the sale of a capital asset.

Accordingly, under section 1234A(1) as it exists today essentially overrules the Supreme Court's famous decision in Hort v. Commissioner,[79] which held that that early termination payments received by a lessor constituted ordinary income instead of capital gain. The Court found that the early termination payment was a replacement for lost rent, and hence it represented ordinary income rather than capital gain.

Hence, under section 1234A(1) any gain or loss attributable to the "cancellation, lapse, expiration, or other termination of a right or obligation" involving life estates, leaseholds, and remainder interests is treated as a capital gain or loss.[80]

Notwithstanding the foregoing, section 1001(e) eliminates some of the benefits from dealings in life estates. Under section 1001(e) a seller of a life or term interest (including an interest in a trust) acquired by

77. 400 F.2d 862 (10th Cir. 1968); accord Ridgewood Land Co., Inc. v. Commissioner, 477 F.2d 135 (5th Cir. 1973). See also Maddux Constr. Co., 54 T.C. 1278 (1970), in which the court characterized gain realized on a tract of undeveloped land by a taxpayer engaged only in residential development as capital gain, the taxpayer having abandoned plans for development when it was discovered that the land would have greater potential as commercial property.

78. See e.g., Daugherty v. Commissioner, 78 T.C. 623 (1982); Juleo, Inc. v. Commissioner, 483 F.2d 47 (3d Cir. 1973), cert. denied, 414 U.S. 1103, 94 S.Ct. 737, 38 L.Ed.2d 559 (1973); Case v. United States, 633 F.2d 1240 (6th Cir. 1980).

79. 313 U.S. 28, 61 S.Ct. 757, 85 L.Ed. 1168 (1941).

80. See Edward J. Roche, Jr., Lease Cancellation Payments are Capital Gain? Yes! The TRA '97 Change to 1234A Overturned Hort, 102 J. Tax'n 364 (June 2005).

gift or inheritance or incident to divorce, must treat the basis as zero unless the sale effects a transfer of the entire interest in the property, such as when the owners of the life interest and the remainder interest join in the transfer.

Moreover, under section 1241 amounts received by a lessee for the cancellation of a lease or by a distributor of goods for the cancellation of a distributor's agreement (if the distributor has a substantial capital investment in the distributorship) are considered as amounts received in exchange for such lease or agreement.

[5]   CONTRACTS

[a]   In General

As noted above, section 1234A(1) provides in pertinent part:

Gain or loss attributable to the cancellation, lapse, expiration, or other termination of a right or obligation (other than a securities futures contract, as defined in section 1234B) with respect to property which is (or on acquisition would be) a capital asset in the hands of the taxpayer . . . shall be treated as gain or loss from the sale of a capital asset.

Therefore, under section 1234A(1) any gain or loss attributable to the "cancellation, lapse, expiration, or other termination of a right or obligation" involving contracts which are with respect to property "which is (or on acquisition would be) is treated as a capital gain or loss."

[b]   Employment Contracts

In general, courts have rejected taxpayer efforts to have employment contracts treated as capital assets for tax purposes. Some courts have reasoned that the transaction was not a sale or exchange; others found that the contracts do not constitute property for purposes of the definition of a capital asset in section 1221.

In McFall v. Commissioner[81] the taxpayers entered into five-year employment contracts with a corporate employer. The contracts called for a weekly salary and a percentage of profits. When these contracts still had two and one-half years to run, the taxpayers "sold" them to a second corporation, which apparently was securing an interest in the employer corporation, for $175,000 and releases from their employer. The Board held that the $175,000 constituted ordinary income because the taxpayers could not "sell" such contracts calling for personal services in the future. The Board added that since the purpose of what is now section 1221 would not be served by treating such contracts as property, there was no necessity to resort to the Commissioner's substituted ordinary income argument.

---

81.   34 B.T.A. 108 (1936). See also Jeremy L. Hirsh, The Wages of Not Working: FICA Liability for Severance Payments in Associated Electric Cooperative, Inc. v. United States, 54 Tax Law. 811, 821 (2001).

A somewhat similar rationale was employed by the Court of Claims in Wilkinson v. United States,[82] involving the gift of a contract rather than its sale. In 1938 the taxpayer, a lawyer, purchased for some $12,000 a percentage interest in a contingent fee contract of a non-lawyer who was representing an Indian tribe in their claim against the government. The taxpayer worked on the case as principal attorney until 1950 when a $32 million judgment was recovered for the tribe. In 1951, before legal fees were awarded, the taxpayer made gifts of his purchased contingent fee contract to two charitable organizations. In the same year the court awarded $2.8 million in legal fees, of which the taxpayer was entitled to some $1 million; in addition, approximately $191,000, representing the amount attributable to the taxpayer's purchased interest, was paid to the two charities. In a tax suit for refund for the year 1951, for which the taxpayer claimed a charitable deduction, the government asserted a counterclaim on the ground that the difference between the taxpayer's cost of $12,000 and the $191,000 paid the charities was ordinary income to the taxpayer. The taxpayer contended he had made a nontaxable gift of property.

In Wilkinson the Court of Claims sustained the government's position. Three judges filed separate, partially dissenting opinions. The majority opinion recognized the general rule expressed in the regulations that a gift of appreciated property to a charity is not taxed and that for most purposes a contract is property, but the majority felt that the contingent fee contract was not property either for the purpose of the charitable deduction or for the purpose of qualifying as a capital asset under what is now section 1221. The Court of Claims reasoned that the gain was attributable to the taxpayer's own personal efforts exerted between the purchase of the claim and its realization and, hence, was ordinary income. As such, it was not property under the predecessor of section 1221.

On the other hand, merely because an individual with an employment contract relinquishes his rights for a settlement with his employer does not automatically mean the proceeds are ordinary income. There has been no hard and fast rule applied to all cases, and there is no substitute for an independent analysis of the nature of the underlying right relinquished. For example, in Turzillo v. Commissioner[83] the taxpayer, a corporate officer, was given a 15–year employment contract at a stated salary and 5% of the net profits in excess of $100,000 when he purchased 50% of the employer's Class B stock for $10,000. Other contracts made at the same time included one under which the corporation acquired a right of first refusal to redeem all the Class A stock that was exercisable to two-fifths of the directors elected by the Class B stock and a contract under which the corporation could redeem the Class B stock held by the taxpayer and another employee upon death or termi-

82. 157 Ct.Cl. 847, 304 F.2d 469 (1962). See also Ronald H. Jensen, Scheer v. Commissioner: Continuing Confusion over the Assignment of Income Doctrine and Personal Service Income, 1 Fla. Tax Rev. 623, 680 (1993).

83. 346 F.2d 884 (6th Cir. 1965). See also TAM 200427025; TAM 200049009.

nation of employment. On termination of employment the right of the corporation to redeem could be exercised only if the termination was for cause. A year later the taxpayer was discharged and, as a result, brought an action against the corporation for his alleged wrongful discharge. He claimed $1 million in damages for interfering with his possibility of becoming a 50% owner of the corporation through redemption of the Class A stock and demanded an accounting for 5% of the profits. Two years later, in a settlement under which all parties made blanket releases of past and future claims, the taxpayer received $11,000 for his Class B stock and $95,000 for all claims to continued employment.

The Tax Court in Turzillo held that the $95,000 was ordinary income as payment for the loss of future salary because the taxpayer's Class B stock could have been redeemed under the terms of the contract. In reversing and remanding, the Sixth Circuit rejected this analysis of the Class B stock redemption provision; it noted that the taxpayer's ownership of the Class B stock would have continued if his employment were terminated without cause or if he left with cause. The other contingencies standing between the taxpayer and the 50% ownership through redemption of the Class A stock the Sixth Circuit regarded as merely going to the value of the taxpayer's rights rather than their nature. Accordingly, the Sixth Circuit found that the contract rights acquired under the contracts constituted property and capital assets; it regarded any claim for future services as having little or no value because the taxpayer was under a duty to mitigate damages. The taxpayer achieved this through the successful development of another business after his discharge.

[6]   FRANCHISES, TRADEMARKS, AND TRADE NAMES

[a]   In General

The franchise system of marketing goods and services has generated complex capital gain definitional problems. The difficulties in applying the basic tax principles arise largely out of the unique business relationship existing between the grantor and grantee of a franchise and, in particular, the continuing control maintained by the grantor over the grantee's activities.

In broad outline the grant of a franchise to promote a product or service normally consists of a license to use a trademark or trade name (or a secret process or other technology) in a particular geographic territory for a royalty based upon use or receipts. The arrangement often consists of a grant by the trademark or trade name owner to a grantee with stated territorial bounds and subfranchises granted within the territory by the initial grantee. Tax problems may arise at both levels of this process as well as upon subsequent transfers by a subgrantee.

[b]   Section 1253

Section 1253, which provides rules for both the transferor and transferee, focuses on two main features of transfers of franchises, trademarks, and trade names: the nature of the retained rights and the contingency of the payments.[84] Under section 1253(a) a transfer or renewal of a franchise, trademark, or trade name is not treated as a sale or exchange of a capital asset if the transferor retains "any significant power, right, or continuing interest," and under section 1253(c) any amount received that is contingent upon productivity, use, or disposition is treated as gain from the disposition of a noncapital asset.

Section 1253(b)(2) specifies six nonexclusive categories of significant rights; the retention of any one results in the proceeds being treated as ordinary income. They are: (1) a right to disapprove any assignment,[85] (2) a right to terminate at will,[86] (3) a right to prescribe standards of quality,[87] (4) a right to limit the transferee to the use of the transferor's goods or services,[88] (5) a right to require the transferee to purchase substantially all supplies and equipment from the transferor,[89] and (6) a right to payments based on productivity, use, or disposition if such payments are a substantial element under the agreement.[90]

Section 1253(d) prescribes that ordinary income payments are deductible by the transferee as a business expense, that lump sum payments may be amortized over a ten-year or shorter use period, and that contingent installment payments may be deducted as they are made. If the transaction is a sale yielding capital gain, presumably nonproduction or use payments may be amortized only if the rights acquired have a fixed limited life.[91]

[7]　FARMING AND LIVESTOCK RAISING

[a]　In General

Taxpayers engaged in farming and livestock raising have been confronted with the same basic asset characterization problems under sections 1221 and 1231 as other taxpayers. However, Congress has provided those in farming and ranching with additional routes into section 1231(a) with respect to certain property. These routes are alternatives and do not preclude qualification under the more general provisions of sections 1221 and 1231. Under section 1231(b)(3) property qualifying for section 1231 treatment includes cattle and horses (regardless of age) held for draft, breeding, dairy, or sporting purposes if held for 24 months or more and other livestock[92] (regardless of age) held for similar purposes if held for 12 months or more. Under section 1231(b)(4) unharvested crops qualify for section 1231 treatment if sold with the land that was held for more than one year.

---

84. See § 1253(a) and (b)(2)(A)-(F).

85. § 1253(b)(2)(A).

86. § 1253(b)(2)(B).

87. § 1253(b)(2)(C).

88. § 1253(b)(2)(D).

89. § 1253(b)(2)(E).

90. § 1253(b)(2)(F).

91. Treas. Reg. § 1.1251–1(c).

92. Treas. Reg. § 1.1231–2(a) gives the term "livestock" a broad meaning; it includes cattle, hogs, horses, mules, donkeys, sheep, goats, fur-bearing animals, and other mammals but does not include poultry, other birds, fish, frogs, or reptiles.

Section 1231(b)(3) solves the characterization problem for breeding, dairy, sporting, and draft animals in favor of section 1231 treatment, even when a dual purpose of business-use and sale exists. Section 1231(b)(3) does not completely close the door, however, on the question of whether particular property consists of section 1221(a)(1) assets, namely, stock in trade, inventory, or property held for sale. Thus, the main inquiry in the controversies in this area normally has shifted from whether such property was held for sale to whether the property was held for draft, breeding, or dairy purposes.

For example, it has been held that gain from the sale of breeder fox and mink pelts qualifies for capital treatment under section 1231.[93] The courts have reasoned that pelting only makes the animals marketable, and it does not change the purpose for which they were held.

For horse breeders, syndication allows recognition of capital gain while substantial control over, or ownership of, the income-producing property is retained. In Guggenheim v. Commissioner[94] the taxpayer was the owner of a breeding stallion and former race horse, Turn–To. Turn–To sired an increasing number of successful race horses. In January 1958, when Turn–To had from eight to ten years of productive life remaining, the taxpayer sold five lifetime breeding rights to five different individuals for $22,500 each. Late in the same year, after one of Turn–To's sired colts had won an important race, the taxpayer syndicated Turn–To. This consisted of dividing ownership of Turn–To into 35 shares. The taxpayer sold 15 shares to 15 individuals for $40,000 each and retained 20 shares, 5 of which represented the coverage rights under the earlier lifetime agreements. The taxpayer retained full management rights over Turn–To. The principal reason for the acquisition of a share was that the syndication agreement gave each share owner access to Turn–To for breeding one mare a year without payment of the stud fee. The agreement also provided that each shareholder was liable for his share of Turn–To's upkeep, was to share in breeding fees earned outside the syndicate, and, subject to a right of first refusal with respect to the syndicate members, could sell his annual right or his entire interest. However, the evidence indicated that Turn–To would be restricted to breeding only 40 mares a season, 35 to cover the shares outstanding and the balance to defray upkeep costs. The taxpayer contended that the gain from the sale of the 15 shares in Turn–To was capital gain because the horse was held for breeding purposes, as the Commissioner stipulated. The Commissioner took the position that the gain was ordinary income on the grounds that the taxpayer was in the business of selling breeding rights and that what the taxpayer received was collapsed ordinary income for future stud fees.

The Tax Court agreed with the taxpayer and held that the gain was capital gain from the sale of a three-seventh's (15 shares) property

93. Herbert A. Nieman & Co. v. Commissioner, 33 T.C. 451 (1959), acq., 1965–1 C.B. 4; United States v. Cook, 270 F.2d 725 (8th Cir. 1959); Edwards v. Commissioner, 32 T.C. 751 (1959).

94. 46 T.C. 559 (1966).

interest in livestock held for breeding purposes under section 1231(b)(3). Although the proceeds from the five lifetime agreements were not at issue, the Tax Court stated it would assume, without deciding, that such gain was ordinary income in order to present the Commissioner's position in its strongest light. The Tax Court admitted that from an economic point of view there was no significant difference between what the syndicate members received and what the owners of the lifetime agreements received; both primarily had only the right to breed mares. However, the Tax Court held that retention of control did not require a finding that the shares sold yielded ordinary income and more important, that the sale of shares effected a significant change in risk bearing. Thus, the share owners, unlike the owners of the lifetime agreement, shared in the expenses and profits, were subject to state ad valorem taxes on livestock, had a right of first refusal to other shares, and could participate in the election of a successor manager. The Tax Court rejected the Commissioner's argument based on the nature of the shares in the owner's hands as ordinary assets. It held that the character of the assets in the hands of the shareholders had no bearing on the characterization of what was sold by the taxpayer.

[b] Farm Losses and Sales: Section 1252

Section 1252 provides for mild recapture, as ordinary income upon the disposition of farm land, for deductions taken for soil and water conservation expenses and for land clearing costs. The mildness is found in a diminishing percentage of recapture after five years of holding. Thus, a sale during the sixth, seventh, eighth and ninth years results in 80%, 60%, 40%, and 20%, respectively, of the amount of the recapture being treated as ordinary income, and after ten years of holding none at all.[95]

[8] NATURAL RESOURCE DEVELOPMENT

[a] In General

The capital gain and loss problems that have confronted taxpayers engaged in natural resource development have been compounded not only by the special legislative treatment of certain transactions but also by intricate financing practices, especially in the oil and gas extraction industry.[96] As a result, this area of the tax law is highly specialized and effective tax planning requires a thorough knowledge of the industry.

[b] Oil and Gas and Hard Minerals

When a land owner grants a mineral lease, retaining a royalty interest, the lessee acquires a working interest that generally qualifies as property used in business under section 1231 unless it is held for sale to

---

95. See § 1252(a)(3).

96. Siegel & Ballou, The "Primarily for Sale" Provisions of Sections 1221 and 1231 of the Internal Revenue Code as Related to Timber Transactions, 39 Ark. L. Rev. 73 (1985).

customers; this means that gain on the sale of such an interest normally constitutes a capital gain.[97]

However, in the development of natural resources, and especially in the oil and gas industry, the means for financing the development of such property has frequently been effected through the assignment or retention of production payments, a contract right usually calling for a fixed dollar amount payable out of production. This has meant that because both the lessor and the owner of the working interest had economic interests in the oil and gas, amounts received for the assignment of such a payment, carved out of the economic interest, yielded ordinary income. Thus, the Service ruled that except when payment is pledged for development, if an assigned production payment carved out of an economic interest extended for less than the life of the economic interest, the amount received for the carved-out payment is ordinary income because it is a substitute for anticipated ordinary income.[98] The Supreme Court sustained this position in Commissioner v. P. G. Lake, Inc.,[99] in which it held that the proceeds from such carved-out interests constituted ordinary income both as to the owner of a royalty interest and to the owner of a working interest.

[c] Coal and Iron Ore

The rules governing production payments and other interests discussed above are equally applicable to hard minerals. However, for coal and iron ore, capital gain treatment has often provided a greater tax advantage than lease arrangements subject to percentage depletion. Hence, the owners of coal and iron ore have convinced Congress of the need for special treatment on the grounds that they do not benefit from the general appreciation in property values under long-term leases yielding ordinary royalty income. Consequently, under section 1231(b)(2), as detailed in section 631(c), the disposal of coal and iron ore deposits, in which the owner has retained an economic interest, is treated as a sale as of the date the mineral is mined, and it is accorded section 1231 treatment.

The taxpayer's gain or loss is measured by the difference between the amount received and the cost-depletable adjusted basis, which is computed on a per ton unit basis, for the product sold. Gain is capital gain and loss is ordinary loss. The benefits of section 631(c) are available only to the owner of an economic interest in coal or iron ore;[100] mine

---

97. In Rev. Rul. 68–226, 1968–1 Cum. Bull. 362, the Service concluded that a sale of a lessee's entire interest, or a portion thereof, in oil and gas constitutes a sale of property for purposes of §§ 1221 and 1231, independent of characterization as real property or personal property under state law.

98. I.T. 4003, 1950–1 C.B. 10.

99. 356 U.S. 260, 78 S.Ct. 691, 2 L.Ed.2d 743 (1958). See also Prebola v.

Commissioner, 482 F.3d 610, 611 (2d Cir. 2007); Lattera v. Commissioner, 437 F.3d 399, 403 (3d Cir. 2006); Watkins v. Commissioner, 447 F.3d 1269, 1272 (10th Cir. 2006); CCA 200519048; CCA 200513022.

100. For a discussion of the requirement under § 631(c) that the owner must retain an economic interest, see Deskins v. Commissioner, 87 T.C. 305 (1986).

operators are excluded.[101]

[d] Timber

Similar benefits are available to owners of timber lands who retain an economic interest (for example, payment on a percentage basis out of sales proceeds) under timber cutting contracts. Such transactions had been held to constitute leases yielding ordinary royalty income rather than sales until the timber special interest was able to convince Congress of the need for relief. This was granted by classifying in section 1231(b)(2) timber to which section 631 applies as "property used in the trade or business." As detailed in section 631(b), receipt under a cutting contract is treated as from a sale at the time of cutting. The benefit of the provision also extends to a sublessor or to the holder of a cutting contract provided, as required for a lessor, an economic interest is retained or exists. Section 1231 gain or loss is computed by determining the difference between the cost depletion basis of the timber (allocating original cost to timber units sold or cut) and the amount received.

However, failure to qualify under section 631(b), such as by the lack of a retained economic interest, does not mean that capital treatment may not be available under the more general rules of sections 1221 and 1231. Hence, in Revenue Ruling 62–81[102] the Service held that to the extent annual payments received by a lessor under a 60–year cutting lease constituted proceeds from timber in existence at the time of the lease, the lease would be treated as a sale of such timber, and the lessor was entitled to capital treatment, provided the other requirements of section 1221 or section 1231 were satisfied.[103]

The Fifth Circuit invoked Revenue Ruling 62–81 in Dyal v. United States,[104] a case that also illustrates the nature of the economic interest requirement. In this case the taxpayer gave three 99–year leases of timber lands to a paper company for the purpose of conducting tree farming operations and producing crops of pulpwood and timber. Each contract gave the lessee complete and exclusive use of the land, including the right to remove the trees and other products, but each contract prohibited cutting during the first seven years except for specified purposes. During this period, timber could be cut for sawmill lumber, buildings, construction, fuel, and for scientific thinning. The lessee agreed to pay an annual amount equal to 5% of the fixed value of the fee; in addition, timber cut pursuant to the seven year exception was to be paid for on a per-unit basis.

---

101. Section 631(c) applies only to "the disposal of" coal or iron ore; thus, the provision does not apply to payments received for the use of surface rights. Martin v. United States, 409 F.2d 13 (6th Cir. 1969).

102. 1962–1 C.B. 153; accord Rev. Rul. 62–82, 1962–1, C.B. 155.

103. However, § 483 may apply to the transaction. See Rev. Rul. 78–267, 1978–2 C.B. 171.

104. 342 F.2d 248 (5th Cir. 1965), aff'g in part and rev'g and remanding in part 13 A.F.T.R.2d 446 (S.D.Ga. 1963); contra Union Bag–Camp Paper Corp. v. United States, 163 Ct.Cl. 525, 325 F.2d 730 (1963).

In Dyal the Fifth Circuit sustained the district court in its finding that, with respect to the fixed annual payments, the lessor did not retain an economic interest because these payments, whether in cash or in kind, were not contingent upon the severance of the timber and were not payable solely out of the proceeds of the natural resource itself. On this basis the Fifth Circuit noted that the parties apparently agreed that capital gain treatment was available under sections 631(b) and 1231 with respect to the payments made for specified timber that was measured and computed on a per-unit cut basis. In this timber the taxpayer had retained an economic interest. However, the case was remanded for a determination of the extent to which the annual payments were attributable to the fair market value of the timber standing at the time of the agreement. To such extent the lease constituted an absolute sale. Thus, if such timber was held as an investment or was used in the taxpayer's business, the taxpayer would be entitled to capital gain treatment despite the failure to retain an economic interest. The Fifth Circuit did not regard the seven-year noncutting requirement as relevant; it held that the critical question was the existence of the timber at the time of the lease, not the time of its removal.

If section 631(b) does not apply, the issue in an outright sale of timber by a landowner normally involves the question of whether the timber was held for sale to customers, yielding ordinary income, or was used in business, yielding capital gain under section 1231, or was simply a section 1221 capital asset.[105]

As a final concession, timber land owners and timber contract owners engaged in the lumbering business have induced Congress to grant them capital gain treatment on the growth value of their timber. This concession was granted to encourage the reforestation of timber lands. Thus, section 1231 treatment is available to timber land owners and timber contract owners on the cutting of their own standing timber whether the timber is used by the taxpayer or marketed as inventory. In general, section 631(a), which prescribes the statutory details, is designed to separate the gain due to natural growth of the timber, which is treated as capital gain, from any additional increase in value due to marketing, which is treated as ordinary income. The separation is accomplished by treating the cutting as a sale and the market value of the timber at the time of cutting as the amount realized. Any resulting gain is subject to tax as capital gain regardless of whether the timber is later sold; if it is sold, the market value used for determining the capital gain on the cutting serves as a basis for computing any additional ordinary gain or loss.

---

105. See, e.g., Huxford v. United States, 441 F.2d 1371 (5th Cir. 1971), in which the court held that timber was sold in the ordinary course of business, the taxpayer having abandoned a naval stores business; Kirby Lumber Corp. v. Phinney, 412 F.2d 598 (5th Cir. 1969), in which the court held that sales of hardwood tie timber by a manufacturer of softwood lumber yielded capital gain rather than ordinary inventory gain.

Section 631(a) treatment must be elected on the taxpayer's return and is mutually exclusive of capital gain treatment under section 631(b).[106] Also, for cutting contracts the capital gains benefits are limited to contracts in which the taxpayer has a proprietary interest in the timber at the time of the cutting.[107]

[e] Soil and Sand

A landowner whose property did not contain a mineral subject to a relatively high depletion rate may have found it more desirable to sell the mineral or soil in place rather than to give a lease with a retained economic interest.[108] In some instances careful planning of the transaction has produced the desired classification as a sale or exchange of a capital asset or of property used in a business. For example, in Dann v. Commissioner[109] the taxpayer, a dairy farmer, entered into an agreement with a contractor under which the taxpayer was to receive a specific price per-cubic-yard of all the soil removed by the contractor from a certain portion of the taxpayer's land, the portion being described by metes and bounds. The Tax Court held that the transaction was a sale of soil in place, yielding capital gain, rather than a lease with a retained royalty; it reasoned that the parties had employed sale terminology in the contract. Moreover, the purpose of the transaction was to provide the contractor with the soil he needed for a construction job rather than to exploit a mineral with the taxpayer participating on the basis of a retained economic interest.

On the other hand, taxpayers have lost most sand and gravel cases.[110] This has been the result despite a propensity on the part of the district courts to find for the taxpayer, with the appellate courts, in reviewing the lower courts's interpretation of the contract between the parties, not being bound by the clearly erroneous standard.[111] The

---

106. Ray v. Commissioner, 32 T.C. 1244 (1959), aff'd per curiam, 283 F.2d 337 (5th Cir. 1960). But see Varn, Inc. v. United States, 192 Ct.Cl. 272, 425 F.2d 1231 (1970), in which the court held that the taxpayer was entitled to § 631(b) treatment, a § 631(a) election not being required because the taxpayer had not sold his timber under a fee arrangement as contended by the government.

107. See, e.g., Weyerhaeuser Co. v. United States, 402 F.2d 620 (9th Cir. 1968), in which the court held that § 631(a) did not apply to logs received under a pooling arrangement between two timberland owners that were in excess of the amount removed from the taxpayer's own land, the taxpayer taking title only after delivery

108. As a general rule, sand, gravel, and certain clays are limited to a 5% depletion rate while soil, dirt, and water are not depletable. §§ 611, 613.

109. 30 T.C. 499 (1958).

110. See, e.g., the following all of which constituted reversals of district court findings for the taxpayer: Dingman v. United States, 429 F.2d 70 (8th Cir. 1970); Rutledge v. United States, 428 F.2d 347 (5th Cir. 1970); Oliver v. United States, 408 F.2d 769 (4th Cir. 1969); Belknap v. United States, 406 F.2d 737 (6th Cir. 1969); United States v. Peeler, 377 F.2d 531 (5th Cir. 1967), cert. denied, 389 U.S. 977, 88 S.Ct. 465, 19 L.Ed.2d 472 (1967); United States v. Green, 377 F.2d 550 (5th Cir. 1967), cert. denied, 389 U.S. 978, 88 S.Ct. 482, 19 L.Ed.2d 473 (1967). See also the following that affirmed lower court findings for the government: Alkire v. Riddell, 397 F.2d 779 (9th Cir. 1968); Hair v. Commissioner, 396 F.2d 6 (9th Cir. 1968); Schreiber v. United States, 382 F.2d 553 (7th Cir. 1967); Wood v. United States, 377 F.2d 300 (5th Cir. 1967), cert. denied, 389 U.S. 977, 88 S.Ct. 465, 19 L.Ed.2d 472 (1967).

111. See, e.g., Dingman v. United States, 429 F.2d 70 (8th Cir. 1970).

difficulty for some taxpayers may have stemmed from the use of a standard mineral lease designed to leave the lessor with an economic interest. Other government victories include situations in which payment was conditioned upon acceptance of a prescribed quality of the extracted product determined by an outside agency, a contract clause limiting the amount to be taken to a quantity desired, or a contract whose terms called for payment only upon actual removal. A finding of a sale of minerals in place is highly unlikely despite the care taken with contract formalities and the use of such terms as "sale," "vendor," and "vendee," or an expressed capital gain objective.[112]

[9]   PATENTS AND RELATED TECHNOLOGY

[a]   In General

Patents and related technology have generated significant capital gain characterization problems.[113] One reason for some of the difficulties in this area is that Congress has provided both a general statutory route and a specific statutory route to capital gains for individual patent inventors and their investor-backers, while leaving other taxpayers and technology to be tested under the general rules of sections 1221 and 1231. As discussed below, both routes to capital gain are dependent upon a transfer under which the transferor assigns "all substantial rights" to the property. With either route the assignment of income doctrine may be applicable.[114]

[b]   Inventors and Their Investor–Backers: Section 1235

Pursuant to a congressional purpose to provide an incentive to individual inventors in the interest of the general welfare of the nation, section 1235 mandates capital gain treatment when there is a transfer of "all substantial rights" to a patent by a "patent holder."[115] Given a qualifying transfer, section 1235 takes care of all three capital gain requirements: the transfer is regarded as: (1) a sale or exchange, (2) of a capital asset, (3) held more than one year.[116] Under section 1235(b) a "patent holder" includes an individual whose efforts created the property and any other individual (an investor-banker) who acquired an

---

112. See, e.g., Ellis v. Commissioner, 56 T.C. 1079 (1971), in which the court denied capital gain treatment for removal of dirt despite the taxpayer's testimony that he sought "legal advice about the proper method of obtaining capital gain treatment."

113. Heyde, Transfers of Technology: The Appropriateness of Capital Gain Treatment, 64 Taxes 3 (1986); DiBernardo, The Taxation of High Technology, 61 Taxes 813 (1983); Olson, Federal Income Taxation of Patent and Know–How Transfers, 28 St. Louis U.L.J. 537 (1984).

114. The transfer of patents and other technology between related entities may

also raise problems involving the exercise of the Service's power to reallocate income and deductions under § 482.

115. Under Treas. Reg. § 1.1235–1(c)(2) due to the lack of a transfer the benefits of § 1235 are not available to employees who are required to release patent rights to their employers. See William Tiffin Downs, 49 T.C. 533 (1968). However, § 1235 does apply to a transfer of an "undivided interest" in a patent, meaning a transfer of a fractional share rather than of an interest based on time or use.

116. § 1235(a).

interest for a money's worth consideration paid to the creator prior to reducing to practice the invention covered by the patent. However, an employer or a person related to the creator under section 267(a) or section 707(b) may not qualify as a "patent holder."

The regulations interpret the term "patent" broadly. The term includes a patent granted by the United States or any foreign country that grants rights similar to those under a United States patent.[117] The regulations provide that the patent or patent application need not be in existence, presumably at the time of the transfer, if the terms of section 1235 are otherwise met.[118]

Additionally, section 1235 ensures capital treatment regardless of whether or not payments are made periodically or are contingent on the productivity, use, or disposition (for example, relicensing) of the property transferred.[119]

In Poole v. Commissioner[120] the taxpayer argued that even if his transfer to a related corporation prevented qualification under section 1235, he was still entitled to capital gain treatment under the general provisions of the Code as provided in the regulations.[121] The Tax Court rejected this argument on the ground that the legislative history was to the contrary,[122] and that such a holding would constitute a nullification of section 1235(d). The Tax Court concluded that when a transfer is to a related person (as defined in section 1235(d)) or when the payments are contingent upon productivity, use, or disposition or are payable periodically, section 1235 is the only provision under which the holder may qualify for capital gain treatment.

Relying on the regulations, the Service in Revenue Ruling 69–482,[123] which reviewed Poole, concluded that a patent holder who transferred a patent to a one-third owned corporation that made contingent payments

117. Treas. Reg. § 1.1235–2(a).

118. Id.

119. § 1235(a)(1) and (2).

120. 46 T.C. 392 (1966). See also Cascade Designs, Inc. v. Commissioner, T.C. Memo. 2000–58; Edward J. Jennings, The Taxation and Reporting of Distributions Derived from Licensing Intellectual Property, 15 Tax'n of Exempts 207, 210 (2004).

121. Treas. Reg. § 1.1235–1(b) states that if § 1235 does not apply it:

[S]hall be disregarded in determining whether or not such transfer is the sale or exchange of a capital asset. For example, a transfer by a person other than a holder or a transfer by a holder to a related person is not governed by section 1235. The tax consequences of such transfers shall be determined under other provisions of the internal revenue laws.

122. Section 1235 was drafted in the Senate, but the Senate Report, which has proved to be so crucial in this conflict, is equivocal. Thus, while it states that "if the mode of payment is as described" in § 1235 (a), a sale "must qualify under the section for" a holder "to obtain capital gain treatment," it also observes that "your committee has no intention of affecting the operation of existing law in those areas without its scope. For example, the tax consequences of the sale of patents ... by individuals who fail to qualify as 'holders,' or by corporations, is to be governed by ... existing law." S. Rep. No. 1622, 83rd Cong., 2d Sess. 438, 441 (1954).

123. 1969–2 C.B. 164. See also Cascade Designs, Inc. v. Commissioner, T.C. Memo. 2000–58; Edward J. Jennings, The Taxation and Reporting of Distributions Derived from Licensing Intellectual Property, 15 Tax'n of Exempts 207, 210 (2004).

as set forth in section 1235 qualified for capital gain treatment under section 1221.

[c] All Substantial Rights

The sale or exchange qualification under both section 1235 and the general provisions of the Code is troublesome when the taxpayer makes a transfer other than pursuant to an out-and-out sale or exclusive license and retains rights for himself. For section 1235 treatment to be applicable the transfer must consists of "all substantial rights to a patent, or an undivided interest therein which includes a part of all such rights."[124]

The regulations under section 1235 are more stringent than some of the cases and exclude from qualification a transfer that: (1) is limited geographically within the country of issuance,[125] (2) is limited in duration to a period of less than the remaining life of the patent,[126] (3) grants rights in fields of use within trades or industries that are less than all the rights covered by the patent,[127] or (4) grants less than all the claims or inventions covered by the patent.[128] Retention of the right to prohibit a sublicense or a sale also may be treated as a retention of substantial rights.[129]

[d] Assignment of Income Doctrine

Presumably an inventor who has sold his patent under section 1235 or under the general capital gain provisions could commute his periodic payments into a lump-sum capital gain by a sale of his contract rights to the payments. Conversely, if the original transfer fell outside section 1235 and the general capital gain provisions, an inventor would realize ordinary gain upon a disposition of his right to periodic payments. However, the purchaser in both situations may well be treated as an investor in any further sale of the flow of income.

With respect to assignment of rights to receive royalties, if the assigned rights result from compensation for personal services the assignor (not the assignee) is taxed upon the receipt of future royalty payments.[130] Even so, the Tax Court has found that an assignment of profits (rather than compensation for personal services) from license exploitation was properly taxable to the assignee.[131]

[10] SALE OF A BUSINESS: GOODWILL v. COVENANT NOT TO COMPETE

If on the disposition of a business, assets are sold, one problem that

124. § 1235(a).

125. Treas. Reg. § 1.1235–2(b)(1)(i).

126. Treas. Reg. § 1.1235–2(b)(1)(ii).

127. Treas. Reg. § 1.1235–2(b)(1)(iii).

128. Treas. Reg. § 1.1235–2(b)(1)(iv).

129. Treas. Reg. § 1.1235–2(b)(3)(i) and (ii).

130. See Strauss v. Commissioner, 168 F.2d 441 (2d Cir. 1948).

131. Cohen v. Commissioner, 15 T.C. 261 (1950); Chamberlin v. Commissioner, 32 T.C. 1098 (1959), aff'd 286 F.2d 850 (7th Cir. 1960); Scott v. Commissioner, 26 T.C. 869 (1956); Wood v. Commissioner, 274 F.2d 268 (5th Cir. 1960). See also McCullough v. Commissioner, 326 F.2d 199 (9th Cir. 1964).

arises is characterizing each item. In Williams v. McGowan[132] the taxpayer, a sole proprietor, sold his hardware business. The Second Circuit held that the predecessor of section 1221 required that the sale of a sole proprietorship must be fragmented into the underlying assets.[133]

The rule of Williams v. McGowan is well settled.[134] Essentially, Williams rejects treating the sale of a whole business as a single asset; it applies broadly to sales by corporations, partnerships, and, as in Williams, to sales by a sole proprietor. However, unlike the interest of a sole proprietor, a shareholder and a partner are regarded as owning a separate capital interest. Such interests normally qualify as capital assets except that a special fragmentation rule is applicable on the sale of a partner's interest when the partnership holds certain property that is productive of ordinary income.[135]

A premium paid by the buyer for the assets of a going concern may have the effect of establishing that some amount was paid for goodwill.[136] This is the result unless the facts and circumstances indicate that the premium was allocated to a covenant not to compete or to some other ordinary income producing intangible.[137]

Suppose that the business is, in essence, simply the embodiment of the personal efforts of the seller, such as a professional service enterprise. Is such a seller also entitled to regard his developed clientele as "property" within the meaning of section 1221?

The Service has acknowledged that both the sale of a professional business and the sale of goodwill to new partners may qualify for capital gain treatment rather than consisting of "merely an anticipatory assignment of future earnings of the practice."[138] Of course, the Service has nevertheless regarded the issue as a factual one, and it has scrutinized

132. 152 F.2d 570 (2d Cir. 1945).

133. Auster, Allocation of Lump–Sum Purchase Price upon the Transfer of Business Assets After–Tax Reform, 65 Taxes 545 (1987).

134. See Watson v. Commissioner, 345 U.S. 544, 73 S.Ct. 848, 97 L.Ed. 1232 (1953) (where the Supreme Court adopts the rule of Williams v. McGowan).

135. See § 751.

136. Section 1060 requires that for an "applicable asset acquisition," both the buyer and the seller must allocate the purchase price in the same manner as amounts are allocated to assets under § 338(b)(5). An "applicable asset acquisition" is a transfer of assets constituting a business in which the transferee's basis is determined wholly by reference to the purchase price. Temp. Treas. Reg. § 1.338(b)–2T mandates a residual method of allocation. Under this method the value of goodwill is the excess of the purchase price over the aggregate fair market values of the tangible and the identifiable intangible assets other than goodwill. Temp. Treas. Reg. § 1.338(b)–2T provides that the purchase price of the assets is first reduced by cash and items similar to cash and is then allocated sequentially to two defined classes of identifiable tangible and intangible assets; any excess is allocated to "assets in the nature of goodwill and going concern value." After the reduction for cash items, no amount may be allocated to any asset in the next two classes in excess of its fair market value.

137. See Treas. Reg. § 1.160–1(b)(2)(iii).

138. Rev. Rul. 70–45, 1970–1 C.B. 17, modifying Rev. Rul. 64–235, 1964–2 C.B 18; Rev. Rul. 60–301, 1960–2 C.B. 15; Rev. Rul. 57–480, 1957–2 C.B. 47; United States v. Stafford, 727 F.2d 1043, 1052 (11th Cir. 1984). See also Morton Harris, Selling or Disposing of Professional Practices, C472 ALI–ABA 37, 58 (1990).

transactions to determine that there was in fact goodwill (and that the consideration allocated to goodwill actually represented payment for it).

Suppose that during the negotiations for the purchase of a going business the buyer indicates that he expects the seller to take part of the consideration for a covenant not to compete, and the seller indicates his willingness to do so. Consequently, the final agreement clearly allocates a fixed dollar amount in consideration of the seller's agreeing not to compete with the buyer in the same type of business for several years in a certain geographical area. The seller should treat the amount allocable to the covenant as ordinary income, and the buyer should treat such payment as deductible over the term of the covenant. Conversely, payments for goodwill would be treated as proceeds from the sale of a capital asset, yielding capital gain to the seller. The buyer's investment in goodwill, however, would not be amortizable because of the lack of a determinable life.

The adverse interests of the seller and the buyer regarding the allocation and the need for tax advice by both parties are apparent in negotiations for the sale of a going business. Perhaps if all such negotiations were conducted at arm's length, and the parties were fully aware of the tax consequences, a recital that an amount was allocated to the covenant not to compete normally would be the end of the matter. However, as the Tax Court observed in Lazisky v. Commissioner,[139] there is a:

> [G]reat body of litigation revolving around the question of whether, in any particular case, a proper, or at least tax-enforceable, allocation between a covenant not to compete ... and goodwill has been made. The reports are replete with cases in which one or both parties have resorted to the courts in their effort to be held to a contract other than the one they made, or prove the contract that they would have made had they thought of it.[140]

It added that:

> [P]ulled in opposite directions by two powerful axioms of law, (1) that a person should be free to contract and that once made, contracts should be enforced as made (absent certain enumerated exceptions), and (2) that in the tax law, substance must prevail over form, the courts have tended to base their decisions on theories incorporating elements of both these principles.[141]

---

139. 72 T.C. 495 (1979). See also Jorgl v. Commissioner, T.C. Memo. 2000–10; Joseph P. Jaconetta, Purchase Price Allocations to Covenants not to Compete Under the Internal Revenue Code of 1986, 44 Tax Law. 217, 241 (1990).

140. 72 T.C. at 500.

141. Id.

Chapter 11

TAX ISSUES RELATED TO
LITIGATION RECOVERIES
AND SETTLEMENTS

Table of Sections

§ 11.01 INTRODUCTION

The receipt of damages[1] for personal physical injuries or physical sickness is governed by section 104(a)(2), which is discussed in detail below.[2] The receipt of all other damages is governed by common law, which generally provides that the tax consequences of the receipt of damages depends entirely on the origin of the claim.[3]

Under the origin of the claim doctrine, the pertinent inquiry is: "In lieu of what were the damages awarded?"[4] This rule holds true whether the damages are received as the result of an award by a judge, jury, or arbitration panel, or whether they are received in settlement of an action brought to recover damages, whether they are received without the need for any action or threat thereof, and whether they are received from a third party or from the taxpayer's own insurance carrier. The rule also holds true whether the taxpayer receives more, less than, or an amount exactly equal to what she initially requested.

[1] TAXABLE RECOVERIES

Hence, if damages are awarded in lieu of income which is otherwise taxable (such as wages), the resulting damages are also generally taxable.[5]

Moreover, the taxpayer who recovers lost profits for breach of contract is taxed on the damages just as she would have been taxed on the profits themselves had they been earned under the contract.[6] Beyond mere inclusion in (or exclusion from) income, the taxpayer who recovers damages will also look to what the damages are in lieu of in order to determine the character of any income recognized.

For example, damages that represent lost profits for the breach of a contract to compensate the taxpayer for the performance of services will

§ 11.01

1. For tax purposes it is irrelevant whether a claim is settled by a judgment (resulting in damages) or by compromise (resulting in a settlement). See Longino Estate v. Commissioner, 32 T.C. 904 (1959) (settlement); Levens v. Commissioner, 10 T.C.M. 1083 (1951) (arbitration award). See also Sager Glove Corp. v. Commissioner, 36 T.C. 1173 (1961), aff'd, 311 F.2d 210 (7th Cir.1962). For convenience, most of the remainder of this chapter address tax issues related to damages, but this guidance is equally applicable to settlement payments.

2. See § 104(a)(2).

3. Hort v. Commissioner, 313 U.S. 28, 61 S.Ct. 757, 85 L.Ed. 1168 (1941); United States v. Gilmore, 372 U.S. 39, 83 S.Ct. 623, 9 L.Ed.2d 570 (1963); United States v. Patrick, 372 U.S. 53, 83 S.Ct. 618, 9 L.Ed.2d 580 (1963); Lyeth v. Hoey, 305 U.S. 188, 59 S.Ct. 155, 83 L.Ed. 119 (1938).

4. Raytheon Production Corp. v. Commissioner, 144 F.2d 110 (1st Cir. 1944), cert. denied, 323 U.S. 779, 65 S.Ct. 192, 89 L.Ed. 622 (1944).

5. See, e.g., Knuckles v. Commissioner, 349 F.2d 610 (10th Cir. 1965); Glynn v. Commissioner, 76 T.C. 116 (1981), aff'd without published opinion, 676 F.2d 682 (1st Cir. 1982). Notwithstanding the foregoing, all damages (including those which would otherwise be taxable such as wages) which are paid on account of personal physical injury or physical sickness are excludable from gross income. See § 104(a)(2).

6. See Nahey v. Commissioner, 196 F.3d 866 (7th Cir. 1999), cert. denied, 531 U.S. 812, 121 S.Ct. 45, 148 L.Ed.2d 15 (2000); OKC Corp. and Subsidiaries v. Commissioner, 82 T.C. 638 (1984).

be taxed as if the taxpayer had received payment for the actual perform-ance of services.[7] This is the case whether the taxpayer recovers for services actually performed or for the loss of anticipated profits from intended fulfillment of her own obligations under the contract.

Similarly, the taxpayer who receives damages for interest due and owing on an underlying obligation will be taxed as if she had received actual interest.[8]

If the taxpayer receives damages that are not in lieu of anything that the taxpayer would have otherwise received, such as punitive damages awarded to punish a defendant's bad conduct rather than to compensate the plaintiff for any loss, such damages are generally taxable as any other "windfall."[9]

[2] EXCLUDABLE RECOVERIES

Along the same lines, if the taxpayer receives damages in lieu of some other receipt that would have been exempt from tax, the damages are similarly tax exempt. For example, if T sues X's estate, asserting that she should recover under X's will, any damages awarded will be treated as if she in fact did receive a distribution from the estate pursuant to the will.[10] If T sues X's estate by challenging the validity of the will and asserting that she should recover under intestacy, any damages will be treated as if recovered by way of such intestate succession.[11] Since inheritance by way of a will and by intestate succession are both excluded from gross income, either case would result in the exclusion from income of the amounts the taxpayer recovered.[12]

Similarly, the taxpayer who recovers damages in lieu of receiving tax-exempt interest owed to her will be treated as if she received that tax exempt interest, so that the damages will be excluded from tax.[13]

[3] RECOVERIES RELATED TO PROPERTY

If a taxpayer receives damages related to property, the tax conse-quences related to these damages depend on in lieu of what the damages are paid.[14] Damages received for the improper or uncompensated *use* of property are treated (and taxable) as any other amounts received for the

---

7. See, e.g., Stocks v. Commissioner, 98 T.C. 1 (1992); Byrne v. Commissioner, 90 T.C. 1000 (1988); Glynn v. Commissioner, 76 T.C. 116 (1981); LeFleur v. Commission-er, T.C. Memo 1997–312.

8. See § 61(a)(4).

9. See Commissioner v. Glenshaw Glass Co., 348 U.S. 426, 75 S.Ct. 473, 99 L.Ed. 483 (1955); Greene v. Commissioner, 47 T.C.M. 190 (1983). See also O'Gilvie v. United States, 519 U.S. 79, 117 S.Ct. 452, 136 L.Ed.2d 454 (1996).

10. Amounts received pursuant to a will are generally excludable from gross in-come under § 102(a) which provides:

"Gross income does not include the value of property acquired by gift, bequest, devise, or inheritance."

11. See § 102(a).

12. Id.

13. See § 103 (generally excluding from gross income any interested paid on qualified state and local bonds).

14. Raytheon Production Corp. v. Commissioner, 144 F.2d 110 (1st Cir. 1944), cert. denied, 323 U.S. 779, 65 S.Ct. 192, 89 L.Ed. 622 (1944).

use of property—that is, as rent.[15] Similarly, amounts received for the conversion or destruction of property are treated as amounts received in exchange for the damaged or destroyed property.[16]

To see how even amounts received for the destruction or conversion of property can be taxed in very different ways, assume that T owns land held as an investment, and the land has a basis for T of $10,000 and is worth $50,000. D is negligent and causes $2,000 worth of damage to land belonging to T, and T recovers $2,000 of damages. The recovery will be treated as a nontaxable return of capital, reducing T's basis in the land to $8,000 but generating no taxable income.[17] One might suggest that if T recovers $2,000 for the destruction of $\frac{1}{25}$ (by value) of her land, she ought to be taxed on the excess of $2,000 (her amount realized) over $400 ($\frac{1}{25}$ of her total basis in the land). If such were the case, T would be taxed on a gain of $1,600 on receipt of the damages. As is the case with part sales, part gifts, however, T is allowed to treat all damages received as recovery of capital up to the amount of her entire basis in the damaged property.

If, instead, D causes $12,000 of damage to the land, and T recovers that $12,000, the first $10,000 of damages will be treated as a nontaxable return of capital. But the $2,000 received in excess of T's basis in the land represents gain (because it is an amount received in excess of basis) and is taxable as such. Since T held the land as a capital asset, the gain realized will, if recognized, be treated as capital gain.[18]

Thus, such amounts may ultimately be treated as a mere return of capital, as ordinary income, as capital gain, or as a combination of two or more of the foregoing.[19]

If a recovery relates to a capital asset, it is tax-free to the extent of the taxpayer's basis, and thereafter any additional recovery is taxed at favorable capital gain rates.[20] The rationale for this result is simple—to

---

15. See § 61(a)(5).

16. See Commissioner v. Speyer, 77 F.2d 824 (2d Cir. 1935), cert. denied, 296 U.S. 631, 56 S.Ct. 155, 80 L.Ed. 449 (1935); Commissioner v. Ulman, 77 F.2d 827 (2d Cir. 1935), cert. denied, 296 U.S. 631, 56 S.Ct. 155, 80 L.Ed. 449 (1935); Helvering v. Drier, 79 F.2d 501 (4th Cir. 1935).

17. Id.

18. See discussion of capital gain and losses in Chapter 10, *Capital Gains and Losses*. To take this a step further, assume that T's property was equipment held as an investment rather than land, that T had initially purchased the equipment for $22,000 and had taken $12,000 of depreciation which reduced the property's adjusted basis to $10,000. Finally, assume that D caused $40,000 worth of damage to the equipment and T recovered $40,000 of damages. The first $10,000 of damages would be

treated as return of capital, bringing T's adjusted basis to $0. The next $12,000 of damages would be treated as recapture of depreciation under § 1245, and the remaining $18,000 of damages would be treated as § 1231 gain.

19. Any amounts received as damage for the destruction or other involuntary conversion of the taxpayer's property into money or other property may avoid current taxation if the taxpayer reinvests the proceeds in property that is similar or related in service or use to the property so converted under § 1033. For a complete discussion of § 1033, see § 9.03.

20. Raytheon Production Corp. v. Commissioner, 1 T.C. 952 (1943), aff'd 144 F.2d 110 (1st Cir. 1944), cert. denied, 323 U.S. 779, 65 S.Ct. 192, 89 L.Ed. 622 (1944); Rev. Rul. 68–378, 1968–2 C.B. 335; Rev. Rul. 81–227, 1981–2 C.B. 14.

the extent the taxpayer received nothing in excess of his basis in the asset he has no economic gain and therefore should not be taxed.[21]

§ 11.02 DEDUCTIBILITY OF ATTORNEYS FEES AND JUDGMENT OR SETTLEMENT PAYMENTS

[1] DEDUCTIBILITY UNDER SECTION 162 OR SECTION 212

As difficult as it may be to believe, nowhere does the Internal Revenue Code provide for the express deductibility of attorneys fees or for the deduction of judgment or settlement payments. Even so, attorneys fees (as well as payments made in settlement or judgment) are generally deductible under section 162 if they constitute an ordinary and necessary business expense, under section 212(1) if encountered in the production of income, or under 212(3) if encountered "in connection with the determination, collection, or refund of any tax."

Deductions under section 162 ultimately turn out to be worth far more in eventual tax savings than deductions under section 212. Because section 212 deductions are properly characterized as miscellaneous itemized deductions, they are subject to a 2% of adjusted gross income floor.[1] That is to say that section 212 litigation expenses (as well as any other miscellaneous itemized deductions a taxpayer may have) cannot be deducted unless they exceed 2% of the taxpayer's adjusted gross income. Additionally, the deductibility of section 212 litigation expenses may be subject to phase-out for certain high-income taxpayers.[2] But by far and above the biggest disadvantage of section 212 litigation expenses (instead of section 162 litigation expenses) is the fact that they are entirely disallowed for purposes of computing the alternative minimum tax.[3]

[2] NO DEDUCTION PERMITTED FOR PERSONAL LEGAL FEES OR LITIGATION PAYMENTS

Of course, as a general rule attorneys fees (as well as the amount of any underlying settlement or judgment) which are personal in nature are not deductible.[4] Hence, if a taxpayer gets divorced, his legal fees (and the amount of any settlement of judgment) are generally not deductible.[5] Even so, any portion of a taxpayer's legal fees (and the amount of any settlement of judgment) relating to his divorce which can be accurately characterized as relating to tax issues are deductible under section 213(3) as an expense encountered in determination of a tax.

Because of the general prohibition on the deduction of personal legal expenses (as well as personal settlements and judgments), frequently

---

21. Rev. Rul. 81–277, 81–2 C.B. 14.

§ 11.02

1. See § 67(a) and (b).

2. See § 68(a) and (c).

3. See § 56(b)(1)(A)(i)

4. See § 262(a).

5. United States v. Gilmore, 372 U.S. 39, 83 S.Ct. 623, 9 L.Ed.2d 570 (1963); § 262(a).

taxpayers have attempted to relate the payment of attorneys fees (and the amount of any settlement or judgment) to some trade or business or investment activity.

[3] IMPORTANCE OF ORIGIN OF THE CLAIM

In United States v. Gilmore[6] the taxpayer owned the controlling interests in three corporations that held automobile franchises. His wife sued for divorce and claimed a community property interest in the taxpayer's stock by virtue of the corporations' accumulated earnings that were allegedly due to the taxpayer's personal efforts, and hence they constituted community property under California law. The taxpayer counterclaimed for divorce and expended $40,000 in legal fees for a judgment in which his wife received nothing. Against the government's position that the legal expenses were personal, the Court of Claims allowed 80% under section 212, which it said was attributable to the conservation of the taxpayer's property. The Supreme Court reversed and held that the expenses were not deductible under section 212.

The Court, found the deductibility of the legal fees (as well as the amount of any underlying settlement of judgment) turn upon the "origin and nature" of the claim; in this case the origin of the claim was personal (divorce) and the legal fees were therefore found not to be deductible.

[4] LEGAL FEES INCURRED FOR THE DEFENSE OR PERFECTION OF TITLE

The regulations seem clear about the treatment of legal expenses in connection with the acquisition of title to property. For section 263 they state that the cost of defending or perfecting title to property is an example of a nondeductible capital expenditure,[7] and for section 212 they state that expenses in defending or perfecting title to property "constitute a part of the cost of the property and are not deductible."[8] Difficulty has occurred, however, in determining the character of such outlays in certain instances.

In BHA Enterprises, Inc. v. Commissioner[9] the taxpayer operated two radio stations, and it was allowed a deduction for legal expenses incurred in proceedings commenced by the FCC to revoke its broadcast licenses. Relying on the "origin" test, the Tax Court found that the proceedings were the result of the taxpayer's business activities rather than in defense of title to the radio licenses, which were admittedly capital assets. While the taxpayer's right to the assets was at stake, it was not a contested aspect of the proceedings. Rather, revocation of title was only a sanction imposed upon a finding that the taxpayer's business was engaged in violative activities.

---

6. 372 U.S. 39, 83 S.Ct. 623, 9 L.Ed.2d 570 (1963).

7. Treas. Reg. § 1.263(a)–2.

8. Treas. Reg. § 1.212–1(k).

9. 74 T.C. 593 (1980), acq., 1982–2 C.B.

1.

In BHA Enterprises Inc. the Tax Court cited Revenue Ruling 78–389,[10] which gives three examples of legal expenses incurred in challenging the actions of a municipality that adversely affected the conduct of a taxpayer's business. In the first example, which was cited in BHA enterprises, the taxpayer incurred the expenses in successfully invalidating a municipal ordinance that would have prohibited the operation of a business. Because the suit arose out of the taxpayer's business and did not result in the acquisition or disposition of a capital asset, the Service concluded that the expenses were deductible under section 162. In the second example, the taxpayer contested the denial of a permit for an equipment acquisition as part of the expansion of the business. The legal expenses were determined to be incurred "as a result of the taxpayer's expansion of an ongoing business and had their origin in the acquisition of permanent improvements." Consequently, the Service concluded that the expenses had to be capitalized under section 263. In the third example the taxpayer unsuccessfully challenged the establishment of a building line across its business property. The building line adversely affected the value of the taxpayer's property. Since the legal expenses arose out of the taxpayer's ownership of the property, the Service concluded they were nondeductible capital expenditures under section 263. In sum, legal expenses related to the production of income are currently deductible, while those pertaining to title to property are capitalized as part of the cost of the property.[11]

Defense or perfection of title proceedings in which legal expenses must be capitalized include not only contests regarding ownership of title, but also those involving condemnation proceedings. For example, in Madden v. Commissioner[12] the taxpayer operated an orchard that was the subject of a condemnation proceeding by a county public utility district. The taxpayers unsuccessfully attempted to limit condemnation

---

10. 1978–2 C.B. 126. See also FSA 199925012.

11. In Boagni v. Commissioner, 59 T.C. 708 (1973), the taxpayer initiated legal proceedings for a determination of his royalty interest in mineral rights and for payment of past royalties, the amount of accrued royalties being dependent upon the determination of the taxpayer's interest. While recognizing that "almost every contest over income derived from real property has a question of title," the Tax Court held that the legal expenses related to the determination of the royalty interest were capital in nature but that the legal expenses related to the collection of past royalties were currently deductible. The court relied on the language in Treas. Reg. § 1.212–1(k) that considers expenses incurred in determining title to property as capital in nature, while those incurred in recovering income from investment property (for example, accrued rents) as deductible. In Von Hafften v. Commissioner, 76 T.C. 831 (1981), the tax-

payer entered into negotiations for the sale of rental property but then declined to sell. The taxpayer was sued for specific performance, breach of contract, promissory estoppel, and fraud. The Tax Court held that the litigation costs were capital expenditures since the suit arose out of a purported sale of the property and not the taxpayer's business conducted on the property.

12. 514 F.2d 1149 (9th Cir. 1975), rev'g 57 T.C. 513 (1972), cert. denied, 424 U.S. 912, 96 S.Ct. 1108, 47 L.Ed.2d 316 (1976); accord Soelling v. Commissioner, 70 T.C. 1052 (1978), in which the taxpayer was denied a deduction under § 212. See also Edward J. Schnee and Nancy J. Stara, The Origin of the Claim Test: A Search for Objectivity, 13 Akron Tax J. 97, 127 (1997); Legal Fees Incurred in Litigation Involving Title to Assets—Allocation Between Deductible Ordinary Expenses and Non–Deductible Capital Expenditures, 126 U. Pa. L. Rev. 1100 (1978).

to the taking of an easement rather than a fee simple interest. In reversing the Tax Court, which had applied a purpose of the litigation test, the Ninth Circuit applied the origin of the claim test and concluded the taxpayer's legal expenses did not arise out of the taxpayer's business, but, instead, they arose out of a public need for the taxpayer's land. The court observed that the government was attempting to appropriate the land and that the taxpayer was resisting that attempt. "Such a controversy is inherently related to the sale and acquisition of land, even though the ultimate sale, if one is made, is a forced sale."

Ownership of the property does not have to be at issue in the litigation for legal expenses to be capitalized. If the suit originated in a transaction by which property was acquired, the purpose of the taxpayer's defense will be regarded as protection of title. For example, in Redwood Empire Savings & Loan Association v. Commissioner[13] the taxpayer was sued for monetary damages as a result of alleged fraudulent conduct in a series of transactions involving its acquisition of property. The complaint did not allege any adverse claims to the property. The taxpayer settled the suit and deducted its legal expenses under section 162, claiming it settled to avoid liability for exemplary damages. However, because the fraud claim arose out of the sale of the property, the settlement amount was for the balance of the purchase price, and it was paid to clear title to the property, the arrangement was merely a part of the purchase of the property. Hence, the legal expenses were part of the capital transaction.

In Clark Oil & Refining Corp. v. United States[14] the taxpayer operated a refinery that was hazardous to an adjoining property owner. The taxpayer made several attempts to purchase the adjoining property, but a price could not be agreed upon. The taxpayer then became the subject of a nuisance action seeking damages and injunctive relief. The taxpayer settled by agreeing to purchase the property being infringed upon by its activities. As in Redwood, the taxpayer claimed the purpose of the settlement was not to effect a purchase of the property, but to avoid liability that would be damaging to its business. However, the court found the dispute was based upon the use of the adjoining property. It reasoned the hazardous nature of the taxpayer's activities precluded the adjoining owner from using the property, and the nuisance action was commenced only to seek a determination of the price to be paid for the property. Because the taxpayer's acquisition of the property "was at the heart of the dispute," the expenses were nondeductible capital expenditures.

While expenses incident to the acquisition of corporate stock are generally capital in nature and therefore nondeductible,[15] in Newark

---

13. 68 T.C. 960 (1977), aff'd, 628 F.2d 516 (9th Cir. 1980).

14. 473 F.2d 1217 (7th Cir. 1973).

15. An analogous situation to Clark Oil relating to the acquisition of corporate stock arose in Dower v. United States, 668 F.2d 264 (7th Cir. 1981). In Dower the taxpayer was the subject of both a shareholder derivative suit for alleged mismanagement and a separate action for specific performance of a stock purchase agreement.

Morning Ledger Co. v. United States[16] litigation costs incident to settlement of a stock purchase were held deductible under section 162. There the taxpayer purchased the majority interest in a newspaper. Later, the taxpayer initiated two shareholder derivative actions. The complaints alleged that management was siphoning off earnings into employee pension funds. The suits were subsequently dismissed in exchange for the purchase by the taxpayer of the remaining stock interest in the newspaper. The court found that the purchase of the minority interest was merely the means for satisfying the obligation to restore diverted earnings. The court concluded that no nexus existed between the origin of the litigation and the acquisition of the stock and the expenses incurred to recover diverted revenue and to prevent further diversion of earnings. Consequently, the expenses were not capital in nature.

§ 11.03 PERSONAL PHYSICAL INJURIES OR PHYSICAL SICKNESS

Section 104 excludes from income "the amount of any damages (other than punitive damages) received (whether by suit or agreement and whether as lump sums or as periodic payments) on account of personal physical injuries or physical sickness."[1]

Determining whether damages fall under this exclusion involves answering three separate questions:

(1) Is the legal action brought to recover the damages a "personal injury" action?

(2) Is the personal injury or sickness "physical?" and

(3) Are the specific damages received "on account of" personal injuries or sickness?

[1] NECESSITY OF TORT OR TORT–TYPE RIGHTS

In Commissioner v. Schleier,[2] the Supreme Court determined that in order for a recovery to qualify for exclusion on section 104(a)(2) it must be: (1) a recovery based on tort or tort-type rights; and (2) received "on account of personal injuries or sickness."[3] Since section 104(a)(2) was amended in 1996 to require personal physical injuries or physical sickness (rather than mere personal injuries or sickness) the rule of Schleier

---

A settlement was reached in which payment was based upon the number of shares under the purchase agreement. Because the corporation received no payment, which it would have been entitled to under the shareholder derivative action, the settlement being distributed solely among the parties to the specific performance agreement, the court held that the settlement was merely a buyout of claims to the ownership of the stock and the related litigation expenses were capital in nature.

16. 539 F.2d 929 (3d Cir. 1976).

§ 11.03

1. Amounts attributable to deductions previously allowed under § 213 (medical expenses) are not excluded. See discussion at § 11.04[2].

2. 515 U.S. 323, 115 S.Ct. 2159, 132 L.Ed.2d 294 (1995).

3. 515 U.S. at 334.

has been consistently modified to require that any injuries or sickness be physical in nature.[4]

[2] PHYSICAL INJURY OR PHYSICAL SICKNESS REQUIREMENT

The specifics of the distinction between tort and non-tort type statutory rights have become less important since 1996. The 1996 amendments to section 104 inserted the term "physical" immediately prior to "personal injury," and by doing so limited not only the types of injuries that could lead to tax-free recoveries but also much of the tax-related litigation that previously surrounded section 104. Prior to 1996, plaintiffs who recovered damages for discrimination, violation of laws relating to the workplace, or sexual harassment contended that any damages they received should be exempt from taxation under section 104 because they were received on account of "personal injury," and in many cases the Service fought those claims by asserting the rights violated were not sufficiently "tort like" to fall under section 104(a)(2)'s exclusion of "personal injury" damages which existed at that time. Section 104(a)(2)'s current exclusion only of damages received on account of "personal *physical* injury or *physical* sickness" makes it unnecessary to examine whether actions brought to remedy discrimination, harassment or indeed virtually any other kinds of rights are "personal injury" actions; the mere fact that the actions are not brought to remedy "physical injuries or physical sickness" is enough to take them out of the bailiwick of section 104(a)(2).

Section 104(a)(2) does not define the term "personal physical injury or physical sickness," in part because in most cases the term is self-defining. Nevertheless, section 104(a) makes it clear, that "emotional distress shall not be treated as a physical injury or sickness."[5] The fact that recent developments in brain science reveal that various forms of emotional distress correlate with physical changes in the brain does not convert that distress into "physical injury or physical sickness." Indeed, even where the emotional distress *results* in obvious physical symptoms, such as rashes, the mere existence or compensation for those symptoms does not bring damages within section 104 unless the claim itself is *based* on the physical injuries or the physical sickness that resulted. At the very least, physical injury or sickness requires some direct physical contact between the "injured" party and some person, object or germ, and the damages must be awarded because that *contact* caused actual physical injury or physical sickness.[6]

---

4. Venable v. Commissioner, T.C. Memo 2003–240; Schaltz v. Commissioner, T.C. Memo 2003–173; Henderson v. Commissioner, T.C. Memo 2003–168, 104 Fed. Appx. 47 (9th Cir. 2004); Prasil v. Commissioner, T.C. Memo 2003–100.

5. § 104(a) (flush language).

6. See, e.g., Murphy v. Commissioner, 493 F.3d 170, 174–175 (D.C. Cir. 2007) (citations omitted):

Murphy points both to her psychologist's testimony that she had experienced "somatic" and "body" injuries "as a result of NYANG's blacklisting [her]," and to the American Heritage Dictionary, which defines "somatic" as

At least in a few letter rulings, the Service has stated that "we believe that direct unwanted or uninvited physical contacts *resulting in observable bodily harms such as bruises, cuts, swelling, and bleeding* are personal physical injuries under section 104(a)(2)."[7] In most cases, there is no need to specify the need for some "observable bodily harm." If there is no such harm, there are no damages to be recovered, and therefore there is nothing to be excluded from gross income under section 104(a)(2). There are a few kinds of cases where the issue is less clear, however, and as a result somewhat more controversial. As discussed below, the lack of clarity in those cases, to the extent it actually exists, is related not so much to whether physical contact resulted in any observable bodily harm, but to whether the damages were received "on account" of personal physical injury or physical sickness.

[3] MEDICAL EXPENSES

Although Congress did not want taxpayers to be able to exclude damages received as compensation for nonphysical injuries or sickness, it did not seek to go so far as to require taxpayers to include in income reimbursements for the taxpayer's actual costs of medical treatment. Section 104 itself does not make the exclusion of medical costs clear. Nevertheless, it does provide that the phrase "emotional distress shall not be treated as a physical injury or physical sickness" for purposes of 104(a)(2).

Standing alone, this suggests that if a taxpayer recovers damages for a personal nonphysical injury that produces emotional distress, then those damages will be excluded to the extent they are reimbursements for (nondeducted) medical expenses. The legislative history seems to go a bit beyond this, however. The legislative history suggests that to the extent that a taxpayer recovers as damages nondeducted medical expenses actually incurred, she need not include the recovered medical expenses in income.

The Service has not questioned this interpretation, and it has allowed taxpayers to exclude all recoveries of medical expenses actually incurred (and not previously deducted), regardless of the nature of the injury or recovery.

"relating to, or affecting the body, especially as distinguished from a body part, the mind, or the environment." Murphy further argues the dental records she submitted to the IRS proved she has suffered permanent damage to her teeth … Murphy contends that "substantial physical problems caused by emotional distress are considered physical injuries or physical sickness. . . ."

In O'Gilvie v. United States, 519 U.S. 79, 117 S.Ct. 452, 136 L.Ed.2d 454 (1996), the Supreme Court read that phrase to require a "strong causal connection," thereby making § 104(a)(2) "applicable only to those personal injury lawsuit damages that were awarded by reason of, or because of, the personal injuries." The Court specifically rejected a "but-for" formulation in favor of a "stronger causal connection."

7.   PLR 200041022 (emphasis added).

[4] DAMAGES RECEIVED "ON ACCOUNT OF" PERSONAL PHYSICAL INJURIES OR PHYSICAL SICKNESS

If the taxpayer recovers pursuant to a claim based on physical injury or physical sickness, and the claim is in tort or is sufficiently "tort like," then *any* damages recovered (other than punitive damages and previously deducted medical expenses) are excludable under section 104(a)(2).

To see the extent of the section 104(a)(2) exclusion, assume that T is injured in a car accident, and as a result T sustains a broken leg. If T sues and recovers, she can exclude, under section 104(a)(2), any of the following damages received: pain and suffering; emotional distress caused by the accident; medical expenses incurred by the accident; medical expenses resulting from the emotional distress caused by the accident; lost wages incurred as a result of the accident; and damages to compensate for any other financial hardship incurred as a result of the accident.

So long as recovery is brought pursuant to a claim based on physical injury (or physical sickness) and is in tort or is sufficiently tort like, damages can be excluded under section 104(a)(2) even if the plaintiff is not the one injured. For example, if T's spouse is injured in an auto accident and T recovers in a separate tort claim based on loss of consortium that is the result of the personal physical injury to the spouse (or its accompanying emotional distress to the spouse), T's recovery, as well as the tort recoveries of T's spouse, is excludable under section 104(a)(2).

Similarly, if T's spouse or child is killed in an accident and T sues and recovers damages under a wrongful death claim founded on the accident that killed her loved one, her recoveries, including for her own emotional distress, will be excluded under section 104(a)(2). In other words, if the taxpayer's recovery is founded on the right type of claim, the type of damages received under that claim is irrelevant—all recoveries (other than punitive damages and previously deducted medical expenses) founded on the claim are excluded under section 104(a)(2).

On the other hand, if the taxpayer's claim and the resultant damages are based on harm not brought about by some personal physical injury (or physical sickness), the exclusion provided by section 104 will be denied. For example, assume that Boss sexually harasses Employee by verbally abusing her. It is clear that any damages collected by Employee as a result of the harassment are on account of the violation of her workplace rights, and not on account of personal physical injury; accordingly, the damages are not excludible under section 104(a)(2). On the other hand, if, in the course of harassing Employee, Boss pushes her against a desk and breaks her arm, damages recovered for *battery* (the pushing and arm-breaking) will obviously *be* excluded under section 104(a)(2).

Somewhere between these two kinds of cases, Boss may assault and batter Employee by kissing or touching her inappropriately, thereby inflicting unwanted physical battery which leads to significant emotional harm in addition to violation of Employee's rights to be free from sexual harassment on the job. If Employee brings actions to recover for these harms, both as violations of her right to be free from sexual harassment at the workplace under Title VII and as tortious assault and battery, any recovery she receives will not be excluded from income under section 104(a)(2). As explained by the Supreme Court in Burke, any recoveries under Title VII will not be governed by section 104 because such actions are not based on tort-type rights.[8]

More significantly, no recoveries, even those awarded on the claim of the tort of assault and battery, will be excluded, because none of the damages awarded are received on account of "personal physical injury or physical sickness." Put simply, physical *contact* alone cannot turn Employee's stress and distress into the kind of physical injury or physical sickness required by section 104(a)(2).

[5] PERIODIC PAYMENTS

Section 104(a) provides for the exclusion of damages received "whether as lump sums or as periodic payments." The exclusion of periodic payments was intended to help taxpayers who suffered long-term disability and need care for long periods of time (such as for life). Often such taxpayers enter into structured settlements that provided for equal annual payments over a long term, and if the interest element of such payments were taxed, a substantial portion of these payments would be lost to taxes.

Like any other provision that benefits taxpayers, section 104's exclusion of periodic payments can be abused. The plaintiff who receives damages on account of personal physical injuries and receives a single lump sum can, of course, invest that lump sum payment. Any investment income earned on that amount will be taxable in full. Instead of receiving that lump sum and then earning taxable interest or other income on the investment of that amount, thought, the taxpayer can negotiate to receive periodic payments rather than a single lump sum. The longer those payments extend to the future, the higher is the proportion of those payments that represent (otherwise taxable) return on the initial damages.

Nonetheless, all of the payments, whenever received, are tax-free. It is possible that if the "periodic payments" are arranged in a way that makes the taxpayer's abuse too obvious (for example, one payment to be received at the end of 10 years and a second payment to be received at the end of 20 years), the Service could potentially assert that the payments are not "periodic payments" but instead are simply deferred payments of principal plus interest. So far, though, the Service has accepted the periodic payments it has seen. Perhaps the fact that the

---

8. Commissioner v. Schleier, 515 U.S. 323, 336, 115 S.Ct. 2159, 132 L.Ed.2d 294 (1995).

defendant's deduction of such payments is dependent on the plaintiff's receipt has kept abuse in check.

§ 11.04   DAMAGES EXCEPTED FROM SECTION 104

[1]   PUNITIVE DAMAGES

While section 104(a)(2)'s exclusion of damages resulting from a tort or tort-like claim based on personal physical injury or physical sickness is wide-ranging, it is not all-encompassing. First, section 104(a)(2) specifically excludes from its application (and thus includes in income) punitive damages.[1] Historically, punitive damages have been awarded not because of the plaintiff's personal physical injuries or physical sickness; instead, punitive are typically award with the intent of punishing the defendant.

While the exclusion or taxation of damages is governed by the federal tax laws, the award of damages is governed by relevant state tort laws. Under some such laws, some states limit wrongful death recoveries to "punitive damages." The wrongful death recoveries under such state laws were similar to recoveries in wrongful death actions in other states (and were actually compensatory rather than punitive in nature), but the plaintiffs seeking such recoveries were required to allege that the damages they were seeking were "punitive." In order to ensure that wrongful death recoveries in those states were not included in the plaintiff's income while the same recoveries were excluded from income in all other states, Congress, in section 104(c), provided that the exception from 104 of punitive damages shall not apply to damages awarded in a civil action in which there was a wrongful death and with respect to which state law provided (beginning prior to 1995) that only "punitive damages" may be awarded in such an action.

What is the tax result if a taxpayer lives in a state which requires that a portion of any punitive damage recovery must be paid to the state? Is the taxpayer taxed on the portion of the punitive damages paid to the state? Because the punitive damages in these cases are paid to the state by operation of law the IRS has taken the position that the taxpayer is taxable sole on the portion of the punitive damages it receives, and not on the portion of the punitive damages paid to the state.[2]

[2]   AMOUNTS ATTRIBUTABLE TO DEDUCTIONS ALLOWED UNDER SECTION 213

Section 104(a) begins by excepting from any of its exclusions "amounts attributable to (and not in excess of) deductions allowed under

§ 11.04

1. See also See also O'Gilvie v. United States, 519 U.S. 79, 117 S.Ct. 452, 136 L.Ed.2d 454 (1996).

2. See CCA 200246003.

section 213 [relating to medical, etc., expenses] for any prior taxable year." This exception is both limited and sensible. To begin with, section 213 allows a deduction only for those medical expenses or healthcare costs "not compensated for by insurance or otherwise." As a result, T would have been allowed a deduction for medical expenses only on the assumption that those expenses would not be reimbursed. When actual reimbursement reveals the underlying assumption was incorrect, it is entirely reasonable to take away the benefit of the deduction that was based on that assumption. Since the deduction was proper when taken, the simplest way to take away its benefit is to include the reimbursement in T's income in the year received.

[3] PREJUDGMENT AND POST–JUDGMENT INTEREST

Not surprisingly, any amounts paid as pre-judgment[3] or post-judgment[4] interest are taxable to the recipient,[5] since they do not represent damages on account of personal physical injury, but instead represent damages based on the plaintiff's failure to promptly pay what is owed to the plaintiff. The inclusion of interest in income, though, does not subject to taxation any part of periodic payments not specified as interest, despite the fact that a significant amount of such payment may represent the time value of money.

§ 11.05 ALLOCATING DAMAGES AND SETTLEMENT PAYMENTS

As in all cases, it is the taxpayer who bears the initial burden of showing her receipts are not gross income; so it is the taxpayer who bears the burden of showing that any damages received are excluded under section 104.[1] Often plaintiffs may bring suit against the same defendant for more than a single claim for damages. A plaintiff may sue for personal physical injury damages and for damages for violation of statutory or constitutional rights arising out of the same incident but unrelated to, or at least not based on, the fact of the plaintiff's personal physical injuries or sickness. In such cases, any damages received on account of the claim based upon the personal physical injuries or sickness will be excluded under section 104, but any damages received on account of the other claims will be taxable.

In addition, a plaintiff who brings even a single claim based upon a personal physical injury will be entitled to exclude most damages re-

3. See Rozpad v. Commissioner, 154 F.3d 1 (1st Cir. 1998); Brabson v. United States, 73 F.3d 1040 (10th Cir. 1996), cert. denied, 519 U.S. 1039, 117 S.Ct. 607, 136 L.Ed.2d 533 (1996); Kovacs v. Commissioner, 100 T.C. 124 (1993), aff'd, 25 F.3d 1048 (6th Cir. 1994); Chamberlain v. United States, 286 F.Supp.2d 764 (E.D. La. 2003), aff'd, 401 F.3d 335 (5th Cir. 2005). Note: Pre-judgment interest payments of $600 or more must be reported on IRS Form 1099–INT.

4. See Bagley v. Commissioner, 105 T.C. 396 (1995); Srivastava v. Commissioner, T.C. Memo 1998–362, rev'd on other grounds 220 F.3d 353 (5th Cir. 2000).

5. See § 61(a)(4) (expressly including interest in gross income).

§ 11.05

1. See Welch v. Helvering, 290 U.S. 111, 54 S.Ct. 8, 78 L.Ed. 212 (1933).

ceived, but the plaintiff will generally be required to include in income any punitive damages as well as any reimbursed medical expenses that were previously deducted. In all of these cases, the taxpayer has no way of knowing the exact amount of damages to be excluded without knowing either the claim for which those damages were received, or the specific type of damages awarded, or both.

If the plaintiff brings more than a single claim, or seeks more than a single type of damages, only some of which are excluded under section 104, any award granted by a judge or jury that specifies the claim for which damages are awarded and the specific types of damages awarded under that claim will obviously determine the taxation of the award.[2]

If the judge or jury awards a single lump sum without allocating the award among the various claims, or among various types (that is, taxable and nontaxable) of damages sought, things may become somewhat more difficult. In such cases, the Service typically looks to the plaintiff's complaint to characterize the awards made. Most likely, the Service will allocate a lump sum award made according to the damages requested in the complaint. Thus, if T asks for $500,000 damages for pain and suffering and $500,000 punitive damages and receives a single award of $300,000, then without any more information the Service is likely to characterize 50% of the award as tax-exempt personal injury damages and the other 50% as taxable punitive damages.[3]

The vast majority of personal physical injury claims are settled, so there is typically no judge or jury award. In these cases, as in all settlements, the initial question to determine the ultimate taxability of payments remains, "for what were the payments received?" If the payments were received as compensation for personal physical injury (including emotional distress recoveries), they are excludable; if they were received for punitive damages, or based on a claim for a nonphysical or non-personal injury, or for contract breach, etc., they are gross income when received. What the payments were received for depends, in turn, on the intent of the parties to the agreement.[4] Absent any other evidence, the Service will likely look to the complaint to make that determination.

Well advised plaintiffs will not simply leave a settlement agreement to provide for a single amount; instead, a savvy plaintiff will take advantage of the settlement process to allocate payments among the various claims. If the parties negotiate at arm's length and in good faith, any allocation of payments (among various claims and, within claims,

---

2. The judge or jury cannot, of course, characterize awards as taxable or not taxable. That determination is made by the IRS by applying the Internal Revenue Code. The judge or jury, though, can specify what claims it is awarding judgment under and what types of damages it is awarding. Once that determination has been made, the taxability of the award should be clear.

3. Rev. Rul. 85–98, 1985–2 C.B. 51

4. See Robinson v. Commissioner, 102 T.C. 116, 126 (1994), aff'd in part rev'd in part, 70 F.3d 34(5th Cir.1995), cert. denied, 519 U.S. 824, 117 S.Ct. 83, 136 L.Ed.2d 40(1996).

among various types of damages sought) agreed to by the parties will likely be respected.[5]

Unfortunately for taxpayers, the Service may well question the arm's length and good faith of settlement agreements that allocate payments in ways that characterize all or a disproportionate percentage of payments as nontaxable damages under section 104.[6] To the extent the defendant is unconcerned about the characterization of payments while the plaintiff will benefit by characterizing payments as damages for a personal physical injury claim, the Service may look to facts beyond the settlement agreement to characterize the payments.[7] In its efforts to determine the "intent of the parties" (with more attention to the intent of the payor than to the intent of the recipient), the Service will likely look at the damages asked for in the complaint, rather than simply the stipulation of the type of damages made in a settlement agreement between non-adversarial parties. Of course, to the extent the taxpayer can show that the defendant had adversarial positions with respect to the characterization of damages, as well as with respect to the total amount of such damages, the allocation in the settlement agreement is more likely to be respected.

§ 11.06   ACCIDENT OR HEALTH INSURANCE PAYMENTS

Under section 104(a)(3), amounts received under the taxpayer's accident or health insurance (other than some payments made by certain employer-paid policies) are generally excluded from gross income. This exclusion applies regardless of whether the taxpayer suffers physical injury or physical sickness, or merely emotional distress, and it applies regardless of fault. When enacted, section 104(a)(3) was entirely consistent with 104(a)(2)'s exclusion of damages. At that time, 104(a) was not limited to physical injuries or sickness, so the absence of any such limit in 104(a)(3) was unremarkable. In addition, since no accident or health insurance pay "punitive" awards, there was no need to exclude any such payments from 104(a)(3).

The fact that 104(a)(3) was not amended to apply only to payments received on account of personal physical injuries when section 104(a)(2) was so amended speaks simply to the lack of any apparent need to amend section 104(a)(3). Even as amended, section 104(a)(2) allows taxpayers to exclude any amounts recovered (even for nonphysical injury or for nonpersonal injury) to the extent they simply reimburse nondeducted medical expenses, and the taxpayer's health and/or medical insurance is not likely to reimburse the taxpayer for anything other than those expenses. While taxpayers might like to imagine their insurance policies will reimburse them for their own pain and suffering, the

5. Id.   **7.** Id.
6. See Hess v. Commissioner, T.C. Memo 1998–240.

absence of any medical insurance policies that do so obviates the need to tax any part of the proceeds paid by the taxpayer's own medical insurance.

§ 11.07 EMPLOYMENT INJURIES AND OTHER EMPLOYER–PROVIDED PAYMENTS FOR INJURY

Rather than receiving "damages" for personal injury or sickness, individuals injured in the course of employment are generally entitled to some form of workers compensation for job-related injuries or sickness under state law in each of the fifty states. Section 104(a)(1) excludes from income "amounts received under workmen's compensation acts as compensation for personal injuries or sickness."

The regulations make it clear the exclusion applies to awards in the nature of workers compensation for injuries or sickness incurred in the course of employment, even if the statute that provides for the award is not so titled under state law.[1] Just as the title of a state law will not take an award out of section 104(a)(1) if the award is actually in the nature of worker's compensation, nor will the state's characterization of an award as being worker's compensation bring within section 104(a)(1)'s exclusion payments that are actually not in the nature of worker's compensation. Instead, the regulations provide that section 104(a)(1) does not exclude any "retirement pension or annuity to the extent it is determined by reference to the employee's age or length of service, or the employee's prior contributions, even though the employee's retirement is occasioned by an occupational injury or sickness."[2]

Unlike section 104(a)(2), the exclusion of worker's compensation awards is not limited to payments for only physical injuries or physical sickness. As a result, if a taxpayer receives an award for incidents that resulted in emotional distress, but not physical injuries or physical sickness, the amounts received may nonetheless be excludable.

Of course, employers may provide health insurance to employees for injuries or illness beyond those incurred in the course of employment. Section 105(b) allows individuals to exclude from income any amounts paid by employer-provided insurance to reimburse the employee for amounts actually spent on health care for herself or her dependents (other than reimbursement for medical expenses previously deducted by the taxpayer).

In addition to excluding amounts paid to cover medical expenses, section 105(c) excludes from an employee's gross income any amounts paid by employer-provided insurance to the extent that such amounts constitute payment for loss, or loss of use of, a member or function of the body or permanent disfigurement of the taxpayer or her dependents, so

§ 11.07

1. Treas. Reg. § 1.104–1(b).

2. Id.

long as the amounts paid are determined by the nature of the injury rather than the period of the taxpayer's absence from work.

§ 11.08 TAXATION OF CONTINGENT ATTORNEY'S FEES

[1] HISTORICAL DEVELOPMENT

In delivering its decision in Cotnam v. Commissioner,[1] the Firth Circuit Court of Appeals could never have envisioned the great debate which would later ensue as a result of its decision. Cotnam resulted from an oral agreement between Mr. Hunter and Ms. Cotnam; essentially Mr. Hunter orally agreed to give Ms. Cotnam twenty percent of his estate if she would care for him during the waning years of his life. Unfortunately for Ms. Cotnam, Mr. Hunter died without a will, and the executor of his estate repudiated the oral agreement between Ms. Cotnam and Mr. Hunter.

Ms. Cotnam sued Mr. Hunter's estate, and she was awarded $120,000, *inclusive* of attorney's fees. In accounting for her recovery, Ms. Cotnam alleged that the entire $120,000 recovery constituted a non-taxable gift pursuant to section 102. Alternatively, the IRS asserted that the entire recovery, including the portion of the $120,000 which represented recovered attorney's fees, was taxable as income from the performance of services. At the Tax Court level, the government prevailed.[2]

Undeterred, Ms. Cotnam appealed to the Fifth Circuit Court of Appeals.[3] The Fifth Circuit Court of Appeals reversed the Tax Court with respect to the inclusion of the attorney's fees in Ms. Cotnam's gross income. The Fifth Circuit held that the applicable attorney's lien law was so strong that it resulted in a portion of Ms. Cotnam's claims being transferred to her attorneys. According to the Fifth Circuit, this portion of the recovery was accordingly taxable solely to the attorneys who labored to earn these fees. With this opening salvo, the great attorney's fee debate was born.

[2] SPLIT IN THE CIRCUIT COURTS OF APPEALS

The Circuit Courts of Appeals failed to reach a consensus in this area of the tax law. In fact, the resulting decisions are anything but uniform. The First, Second, Third, Fourth, Seventh, Eighth, Ninth, Tenth, and Federal Circuits have held that recovered contingent attorneys fees represent gross income to the recovering plaintiff.[4] The Fifth,

---

§ 11.08

1. 263 F.2d 119 (5th Cir. 1959).

2. Cotnam, 28 T.C. 947 (1957).

3. Cotnam, 263 F.2d 119 (5th Cir. 1959).

4. See Alexander v. Commissioner, 72 F.3d 938 (1st Cir. 1995); Raymond v. United States, 355 F.3d 107 (2d Cir. 2004),

petition for cert. filed, 72 USLW 3659 (Apr. 09, 2004) (NO. 03–1415); O'Brien v. Commissioner, 319 F.2d 532 (3d Cir. 1963), cert. den. 375 U.S. 931, 84 S.Ct. 331, 11 L.Ed.2d 263 (1963); Young v. Commissioner, 240 F.3d 369 (4th Cir. 2001); Kenseth v. Commissioner, 259 F.3d 881 (7th Cir. 2001); Bagley v. Commissioner, 121 F.3d 393 (8th Cir. 1997), reh'g en banc den.; Benci–Wood-

Sixth, Ninth, and Eleventh Circuits have held that recovered contingent attorneys fees do not result in gross income to the recovering plaintiff.[5] For some years now, commentators have frequently written about the inequities in this area the tax law.[6] For that matter for some years now the Supreme Court had sat on the sidelines while the Circuit Courts of Appeal arrived at horribly inconsistent decisions.[7] That all changed on in 2004, when the Supreme Court granted *certiorari* in Banks and Banaitis.[8] As discussed below, in 2005, the Supreme Court handed down its decision in Banks, but it is clear this decision will not be the final word on the attorneys fee issue.

[3] IMPORTANCE OF ABOVE–THE–LINE VS. BELOW–THE–LINE DEDUCTION

Just a few months before the Supreme Court's decision in Banks, in October, 2004, the President signed into law the American Jobs Creation Act of 2004.[9] Believe it or not, the Act was originally intended to rescind the exclusion for extraterritorial income, which the World Trade Organization determined to be an unlawful export subsidy. Notwithstanding the foregoing, by the time it was all said and done, the Act contained sweeping changes to the tax law. Most notably, the Act provides for the above-the-line deduction of attorney's fees and costs paid in a variety of cases.

While there are multiple causes to the inequity in this area of the tax law, the primary culprit is the alternative minimum tax (or AMT). As hard as it is to believe, there have even been cases where taxpayers have ended up out-of-pocket after ostensibly winning a lawsuit.[10] This preposterous result can be traced directly to the AMT.

ward v. Commissioner, 219 F.3d 941 (9th Cir. 2000), cert. den. 531 U.S. 1112, 121 S.Ct. 855, 148 L.Ed.2d 770; Coady v. Commissioner, 213 F.3d 1187 (9th Cir. 2000), cert. den. 532 U.S. 972, 121 S.Ct. 1604, 149 L.Ed.2d 470; Hukkanen–Campbell v. Commissioner, 274 F.3d 1312 (10th Cir. 2001), cert. den. 535 U.S. 1056, 122 S.Ct. 1915, 152 L.Ed.2d 824; Baylin v. United States, 43 F.3d 1451 (Fed. Cir. 1995). Compare Banaitis v. Commissioner, 340 F.3d 1074 (9th Cir. 2003) (holding that under Oregon law, recovered attorney's fees are not gross income to the plaintiff) with Benci–Woodward v. Commissioner, *supra*, and Sinyard v. Commissioner, 268 F.3d 756 (9th Cir. 2001), aff'g TCM 1998–364.

5. See Srivastava v. Commissioner, 220 F.3d 353 (5th Cir. 2000); Estate of Clarks v. Commissioner, 202 F.3d 854 (6th Cir. 2000); Banks v. Commissioner, 345 F.3d 373 (6th Cir. 2003), cert. granted, 541 U.S. 958, 124 S.Ct. 1712, 158 L.Ed.2d 398 (2004); Davis v. Commissioner, 210 F.3d 1346 (11th Cir. 2000); Banaitis v. Commissioner, 340 F.3d 1074 (9th Cir. 2003).

6. See e.g., "Shop Talk: Debunking The Crop–Share Analogy To Contingent Attorney's Fee Arrangements," 97 J. Tax'n 320 (Nov. 2002); "Shop Talk: Whipsaw On Lawsuit Settlements: The Courts Still Can't Agree," 93 J. Tax'n 188 (Sept. 2000); "Sixth Circuit Reverses Tax Court And Excludes Contingent Attorney's Fees," 99 J. Tax'n 259 (Nov. 2003).

7. See Benci–Woodward, *supra*; Coady, *supra*; Hukkanen–Campbell, *supra*; and Sinyard, *supra*.

8. Banks, *supra* and Banaitis, *supra*. Note: Banks and Banaitis were consolidated by the Supreme Court into a single case, Commissioner v. Banks, 543 U.S. 426, 125 S.Ct. 826, 160 L.Ed.2d 859 (2005).

9. Hereinafter the American Jobs Creation Act of 2004 is sometimes referred to as the "Act".

10. See Spina v. Forest Preserve District of Cook County, 207 F. Supp.2d 764 (N.D. Ill. 2002) (plaintiff won a sex discrimination suit against her former employer and ended up paying $99,000 more in federal income tax than she recovered).

Before ratification of the Act, deductions for legal fees were generally treated as miscellaneous itemized deductions and were disallowed entirely for AMT purposes.[11] What impact did this have? This query is best answered by way of example. Assume a plaintiff in a wrongful termination action recovers $5 million in a settlement, inclusive of attorney fees. Assume further that the recovery is not excludable from gross income under section 104 or otherwise.

If the plaintiff lived in a majority jurisdiction, he would have previously been required to book the entire $5 million recovery into income. Prior to the ratification of the Act, the plaintiff would have been entitled to a miscellaneous itemized deduction for any recovered attorney's fees. Assume that the amount of recovered attorneys fees in this case is $4 million. Under this scenario, this deduction was treated as a miscellaneous itemized deduction, and it was disallowed entirely for AMT purposes.[12]

Based on these facts, the plaintiff would end with almost a $1.4 million federal income tax liability as a result of winning this lawsuit. A vast majority of this tax liability stems from the AMT. The appalling result here is that the plaintiff actually ended up out-of-pocket almost $400,000 after "winning" this lawsuit. Under this scenario, the plaintiff only receives $1 million as his net recovery. When this is netted with a tax liability of almost $1.4 million, the plaintiff ends up out-of-pocket $400,000. This result certainly does not seem equitable. In fact, this result is nothing short of egregious. Thankfully the Act puts an end to this inequity in many, buy not all, cases.

[4] THE AMERICAN JOBS CREATION ACT OF 2004

The American Jobs Creation Act of 2004 provides the cure for the attorney's fee problem in some situations by modifying the Internal Revenue Code so as to provide for an above-the-line deduction of legal fees in certain circumstances. What impact does this have on the attorney's fee issue? Because legal fees in these situations are no longer considered to be miscellaneous itemized deductions, they are no longer subject to phase-out for AMT purposes. Moreover, these recovered legal fees are not subject to a two-percent of AGI floor and phase-out for high-income taxpayers. Under the terms of the Act, Internal Revenue Code sections 62(a)(19) and 62(e) were amended to provide that attorneys fees and costs relating to the following causes of action may be deducted on an above-the-line basis:

(1) Section 302 of the Civil Rights Act of 1991;[13]

(2) Section 201, 202, 203, 204, 205, 206, or 207 of the Congressional Accountability Act of 1995;[14]

---

11. § 56(b)(1)(A)(i).

12. Id.

13. 2 U.S.C. 1202.

14. 2 U.S.C. 1311, 1312, 1313, 1314, 1315, 1316, or 1317.

(3) The National Labor Relations Act;[15]

(4) The Fair Labor Standards Act of 1938;[16]

(5) Section 4 or 15 of the Age Discrimination in Employment Act of 1967;[17]

(6) Section 501 or 504 of the Rehabilitation Act of 1973;[18]

(7) Section 510 of the Employee Retirement Income Security Act of 1974;[19]

(8) Title IX of the Education Amendments of 1972;[20]

(9) The Employee Polygraph Protection Act of 1988;[21]

(10) The Worker Adjustment and Retraining Notification Act;[22]

(11) Section 105 of the Family and Medical Leave Act of 1993;[23]

(12) Chapter 43 of title 38, United States Code;[24]

(13) Section 1977, 1979, or 1980 of the Revised Statutes;[25]

(14) Section 703, 704, or 717 of the Civil Rights Act of 1964;[26]

(15) Section 804, 805, 806, 808, or 818 of the Fair Housing Act;[27]

(16) Section 102, 202, 302, or 503 of the Americans with Disabilities Act of 1990;[28]

(17) Any provision of Federal law prohibiting the discharge of an employee, the discrimination against an employee, or any other form of retaliation or reprisal against an employee for asserting rights or taking other actions permitted under Federal law;

(18) Any provision of Federal, State, or local law, or common law claims permitted under Federal, State, or local law—

   (i) providing for the enforcement of civil rights, or

   (ii) regulating any aspect of the employment relationship, including claims for wages, compensation, or benefits, or prohibiting the discharge of an employee, the discrimination against an employee, or any other form of retaliation or reprisal against an employee for asserting rights or taking other actions permitted by law.

15. 29 U.S.C. 151 et seq.

16. 29 U.S.C. 201 et seq.

17. 29 U.S.C. 623 or 633a.

18. 29 U.S.C. 791 or 794.

19. 29 U.S.C. 1140.

20. 20 U.S.C. 1681 et seq.

21. 29 U.S.C. 2001 et seq.

22. 29 U.S.C. 2102 et seq.

23. 29 U.S.C. 2615.

24. 38 U.S.C. 4301 et seq. (relating to employment and reemployment rights of members of the uniformed services).

25. 42 U.S.C.1981, 1983, or 1985.

26. 42 U.S.C. 2000e–2, 2000e–3, or 2000e–16.

27. 42 U.S.C. 3604, 3605, 3606, 3608, or 3617.

28. 42 U.S.C. 12112, 12132, 12182, or 12203.

[5] EQUITY AND FAIRNESS CONSIDERATIONS

Ultimately, this laundry list of protected recoveries basically boils down two types of cases, employment cases and False Claims Act cases. What about other types tort claims? Why were claims outside of the employment context not addressed by the Act? If a taxpayer recovers for deformation of character, or intentional infliction of emotional distress outside of the employment arena this recovery does not fall within the bailiwick of the Act.

It is just sound tax policy to for similarly situated individuals to pay a similar amount of taxes. It is ridiculous that the Act only applies to the aforementioned limited types of claims.

Accordingly, if a taxpayer is wrongfully imprisoned by his employer he would be allowed to net the attorney's fees from his recovery, but if he were wrongfully imprisoned by a department store (assuming he were not employed by the department store), he would taxed on his entire gross recovery, including the amount paid to his attorneys. This reeks of inequity to such an extent some might question its constitutionality. How is it two individuals who have suffered the exact same harm, are taxed at substantially different rates because one occurred in an employment context and the other did not?

Many decades ago the Supreme Court noted the significance of avoiding inequities in the administration of federal tax laws.[29] The inequity and unfairness of the attorney's fee issue is staggering.

As practical matter what happens when a taxpayer brings a lawsuit with multiple counts, some of which are covered by the Act, and some of which are not? Does the taxpayer allocate the recovered attorneys fees by simply dividing the amount by the number of claims? Perhaps it is more appropriate to allocate the recovered attorneys fees on a pro-rata basis? It is anyone's guess how the IRS will seek to allocate recovered attorneys fees in these types of cases. These types of tangential issues are exactly the types of issues which will make for future Tax Court cases. It really would have been nice if Congress had obviated this entire issue by either solving the attorneys fee issue for all recoveries or providing for some standard type of allocation formula.

[6] IMPORTANCE OF COMMISSIONER v. BANKS

The Supreme Court's ruling in Banks[30] lacks clarity. The Court held that, "As a general rule, when a litigant's recovery constitutes income, the litigant's income includes the portion of the recovery paid to the attorney as a contingent fee.[31]" Not only did the Court reach what is arguably the wrong result, its holding is overly broad. Wherever "general rules" exist, exceptions to those general rules are almost always found to also exist.

29. Commissioner v. Sunnen, 333 U.S. 591, 599, 68 S.Ct. 715, 92 L.Ed. 898 (1948).

30. 543 U.S. 426, 125 S.Ct. 826, 160 L.Ed.2d 859 (2005) (This is a consolidated decision which consolidates Banks, *supra* and Banaitis, *supra*).

31. 543 U.S. at 430.

The Court hints that if a taxpayer could find a way to fundamentally change the usual attorney-client relationship that you might find yourself outside the boundaries of Banks.[32] Most states have laws on the books which prohibit fee splitting between attorneys and non-attorneys. But the question becomes what if a taxpayer had a case where a maritime attorney formed a partnership with a litigator for the purposes of splitting any recovery relating to a false imprisonment cause of action which occurred outside the employment context.[33] Can these two lawyers form an actual partnership and thereby avoid the application of Banks? It would appear that there is a substantial possibility that this course of action may well be successful in circumventing the inequitable result of Banks. This is just one of many examples of how the Supreme Court's Banks leaves a lot of unanswered questions.

It is somewhat ironic that during oral argument Justices O'Connor, Breyer, and Ginsberg raised serious doubts as to the constitutionality of taxing recovered attorney's fees to litigants; apparently they had a change of heart between the time of oral argument and the time Justice Kennedy issued a unanimous decision for the government.

This result is more than a little suspect. What has changed to alleviate the constitutionality concerns raised by Justices O'Connor, Breyer, and Ginsberg during oral argument? Taxing litigants on fees paid to their attorneys is unfair, inequitable, and smacks of an unconstitutional confiscatory taking. It is hardly sporting to tax a fellow on money which was never intended to be paid to him. That is the difference between the attorney's fee situation and the classic assignment of income cases such as Helvering v. Horst[34] and Lucas v. Earl;[35] the litigant in the attorney's fee situation never had an unfettered right to ultimately keep the attorney's fees. On the other hand, the taxpayers in Earl and Horst had the right and wherewithal to do whatever they wanted with their funds. Admittedly, the difference is somewhat subtle.

---

32. Id. at 433.

33. As noted previously, because the false imprisonment cause of action arose outside of the employment context the taxpayer will not be able to take advantage the netting provisions which the Act added to section 62.

34. 311 U.S. 112, 61 S.Ct. 144, 85 L.Ed. 75 (1940).

35. 281 U.S. 111, 50 S.Ct. 241, 74 L.Ed. 731 (1930).

Chapter 12

LOSSES ON BUSINESS OR INVESTMENT PROPERTY

Table of Sections

§ 12.01 INTRODUCTION

[1] USES OF THE TERM "LOSS"

The term "loss" has many different meanings for federal income tax purposes. The particular meaning which is discussed in this chapter is the use of the term "loss" to mean the excess of a taxpayer's adjusted basis over his amount realized in a property transaction.[1] Before proceeding into a detailed review of this meaning of the term "loss," it is worthwhile to briefly look at some of the other meanings of the term "loss" and some of the many limitations on the deductibility of losses.

[2] GENERAL LOSS LIMITATIONS

For tax purposes, the term "loss" is often also used to refer to the excess of deductions over income, whether it is for a certain period of time, with respect to a specific activity, or with respect to the disposition of certain kinds of property. Often, the references in the Code to various kinds of losses are there specifically in order to limit their deductibility.

A taxpayer whose total personal deductions for the year exceed her income may be said to have a loss for the year; even so, losses such as this one are generally not recognized for federal income tax purposes. A taxpayer whose business deductions for a year exceed her business income, though, may well have a net operating loss, which she may be able to carry either forward or backwards in time and deduct against net income in a different year.[2]

Many of the limitations on the deductibility of losses are more specific. For example, section 465, which encompasses the "at risk rules," limits the taxpayer's ability to deduct as a loss against other income any excess of deductions over income from certain individual "activities" to the extent the taxpayer is at risk in that activity.[3]

There are other Code sections that limit losses (again, for this purpose defined as the excess of deductions over income) from certain *kinds* of activities. A good example is section 469, which limits a taxpayer's losses from "passive activities" to the extent of net income from other passive activities, at least until the particular activity is disposed of by the taxpayer.[4] Another example is section 165(g), which limits the deductibility of gambling losses to the amount of any gambling winnings for the year in question.

Still other loss limitations refer to the character of the loss generated. For example, section 1211, basically limits the deductibility of capital

---

§ 12.01

1. See § 1001(a).

2. See § 172.

3. For a complete discussion of the "at risk rules," see § 14.04.

4. For a complete discussion of the "passive activity loss rules" see § 14.05.

gains to the extent of the taxpayer's capital gains.[5]

The remainder of this chapter is devoted to the allowance and restrictions on losses incurred in specific, individual, transactions.

§ 12.02 LOSSES FROM BUSINESS OR INVESTMENT ACTIVITIES

Section 165(a) appears to allow taxpayers to deduct "any loss sustained during the taxable year and not compensated for by insurance or otherwise." In actuality, the deductibility of losses is not nearly that simple or generous. The basic limit on the deductibility of losses appears in section 165(c), which provides that in the case of an individual taxpayer, only certain specified losses are allowed. Section 165(c) allows the deduction of: (1) losses incurred in a trade or business and (2) losses incurred in a transaction entered into for profit, though not connected with a trade or business. Sections 165(c)(1) and 165(c)(2) are in line with the basic idea that only profit-seeking expenditures are deductible. In restricting deductible losses to those incurred in a trade or business or in a transaction entered into for profit, they closely resemble the similar limitations inherent in sections 162 and 212, relating to the deductibility of expenses.

Section 165(c)(3) allows the deduction of "losses of property not connected with a trade or business or a transaction entered into for profit, if such losses arise from fire, storm, shipwreck, or other casualty, or from theft." Although this appears in the same Code section as the deduction of losses incurred in profit-seeking activities, it is in fact a "personal" deduction, similar to the deduction for certain medical expenses under section 213.[1]

In order for a taxpayer to sustain a loss deductible under section 165(c)(1), that loss must be sustained in a trade or business. This means, at a minimum, that the taxpayer must be operating a trade or business at the time the loss is sustained, and the loss must arise out of that trade or business. Whether a taxpayer's pursuits constitute a "trade or business" for tax purposes depends, in turn, on several factors. These factors are explored at length with respect to section 162, and really need no further elaboration with respect to section 165; they include determinations with respect to the taxpayer's intent to make a profit, the extent of activity involved, and, if there is, at some point, a "trade or business," whether that business is ongoing at the time the loss is sustained.

Obviously, it is not sufficient for the taxpayer seeking to deduct a loss under section 165(c)(1) to establish that a particular loss was sustained while she was carrying on a trade or business; she must also

---

5. In the case of a taxpayer other than a corporation, capital losses are generally deductible to the extent of capital gains plus up to $3,000 annually. See § 1211(b).

§ 12.02

1. See Chapter 4, *Deductions*, for a complete discussion of the deduction of personal casualty and theft losses as well as medical expenses.

establish that the loss was sustained *within* the trade or business. While the determination of this factor is usually simple, it can become significantly more complicated when: (1) the taxpayer has mixed uses for a single asset, or has mixed motives with respect to his use of a particular asset; or (2) the taxpayer changes motives with respect to an asset.

If the taxpayer is not engaged in a trade or business, either because there is not sufficient activity to make his enterprise into a business, or because the activity, though extensive, has not yet begun when the taxpayer incurs the loss (or because an activity that once constituted a trade or business has since ceased), she may nonetheless be able to deduct losses incurred under section 165(c)(2), if the losses arise out of a "transaction entered into for profit."[2]

The existence of a requisite profit motive to qualify for deduction of losses under section 165(c)(2) is similar to that required to qualify for deduction of expenses under section 212.[3] Similar to deductions permit-

---

2. While such losses are deductible under § 165(c)(2), the deduction is treated less favorably than losses incurred in a trade or business in several ways: (1) these losses cannot contribute to a net operating loss of an individual (§ 172(d)(4)(C)); these losses may not be deductible for AMT purposes (§ 56(b)(1)(A) and § 67(b)); and (3) these losses are itemized deductions subject to the limits of §§ 67 and 68 as well and other limits.

3. As discussed in conjunction with § 212, to qualify a transaction as one entered into for profit, the taxpayer need not establish that his *only* purpose for obtaining the asset was for profit, but he must establish, not surprisingly, that his *primary* purpose for engaging in the transaction was to make a profit. Taxpayers' motivations for even a single transaction are often mixed. Taxpayers may purchase property or make an expenditure with the intention of making a profit on its sale, but in the mean time the taxpayer may have the intention of enjoying its use (or enabling people close to them to enjoy its use), fulfilling a moral obligation, or enhancing their personal reputations through use of the property. In such cases, the IRS and the courts (and the taxpayer, of course) must determine which intention or motivation predominates. As might be expected in such an issue, there are no bright lines, but only hints and general inferences, to guide the determination process. To the extent that guidance has been put together, it appears in the regulations enacted under § 183. Those regulations state, *inter alia*, that:

> In determining whether an activity is engaged in for profit, all facts and circumstances with respect to the activity are to be taken into account. No one

factor is determinative in making this determination. In addition, it is not intended that only the factors described in this paragraph are to be taken into account in making the determination, or that a determination is to be made on the basis that the number of factors (whether or not listed in this paragraph) indicating a lack of profit objective exceeds the number of factors indicating a profit objective, or vice versa.

Treas. Reg. § 1.183–2(b). Indeed, perhaps the most telling part of the regulation is its explanation that none of the listed factors is determinative. Nonetheless, the regulation describes nine potentially significant, if not determinative, factors:

(1) Manner in which the taxpayer carries on the activity. The fact that the taxpayer carries on the activity in a businesslike manner and maintains complete and accurate books and records may indicate that the activity is engaged in for profit. Similarly, where an activity is carried on in a manner substantially similar to other activities of the same nature which are profitable, a profit motive may be indicated. A change of operating methods, adoption of new techniques or abandonment of unprofitable methods in a manner consistent with an intent to improve profitability may also indicate a profit motive.

(2) The expertise of the taxpayer or his advisors. Preparation for the activity by extensive study of its accepted business, economic, and scientific practices, or consultation with those who are expert therein, may indicate that the taxpayer has a profit motive where the taxpayer

ted under section 212, losses under section 165(c)(2) need not be incurred in transactions in which the taxpayer's primary profit motive was related to a profit on *disposition* of the asset. Motivation to earn a net profit by way of receipt of a current income stream is quite sufficient. As with section 212, the determination of the taxpayer's profit motive is one of fact, and the fact at issue (i.e., the taxpayer's state of mind) is not one that can always be easily assessed. The taxpayer's predominate, or primary motive (i.e., profit-seeking or personal use), determines whether the loss is deductible in full or not at all.[4]

carries on the activity in accordance with such practices. ...

(3) The time and effort expended by the taxpayer in carrying on the activity. The fact that the taxpayer devotes much of his personal time and effort to carrying on an activity, particularly if the activity does not have substantial personal or recreational aspects, may indicate an intention to derive a profit.... The fact that the taxpayer devotes a limited amount of time to an activity does not necessarily indicate a lack of profit motive where the taxpayer employs competent and qualified persons to carry on such activity.

(4) Expectation that assets used in activity may appreciate in value....

(5) The success of the taxpayer in carrying on other similar or dissimilar activities. The fact that the taxpayer has engaged in similar activities in the past and converted them from unprofitable to profitable enterprises may indicate that he is engaged in the present activity for profit, even though the activity is presently unprofitable.

(6) The taxpayer's history of income or losses with respect to the activity. A series of losses during the initial or start-up stage of an activity may not necessarily be an indication that the activity is not engaged in for profit. However, where losses continue to be sustained beyond the period which customarily is necessary to bring the operation to profitable status such continued losses, if not explainable, as due to customary business risks or reverses, may be indicative that the activity is not being engaged in for Profit....

(7) The amount of occasional profits, if any, which are earned. The amount of profits in relation to the amount of losses incurred, and in relation to the amount of the taxpayer's investment and the value of the assets used in the activity, may provide useful criteria in determining the taxpayer's intent....

(8) The financial status of the taxpayer. The fact that the taxpayer does not have substantial income or capital from sources other than the activity may indicate that an activity is engaged in for profit. Substantial income from sources other than the activity (particularly if the losses from the activity generate substantial tax benefits) may indicate that the activity is not engaged in for profit especially if there are personal or recreational elements involved.

(9) Elements of personal pleasure or recreation. The presence of personal motives in carrying on of an activity may indicate that the activity is not engaged in for profit, especially where there are recreational or personal elements involved. On the other hand, a profit motivation may be indicated where an activity lacks any appeal other than profit. It is not, however, necessary that an activity be engaged in with the exclusive intention of deriving a profit or with the intention of maximizing profits. For example, the availability of other investments which would yield a higher return, or which would be more likely to be profitable, is not evidence that an activity is not engaged in for profit. An activity will not be treated as not engaged in for profit merely because the taxpayer has purposes or motivations other than solely to make a profit. Also, the fact that the taxpayer derives personal pleasure from engaging in the activity is not sufficient to cause the activity to be classified as not engaged in for profit if the activity is in fact engaged in for profit as evidenced by other factors whether or not listed in this paragraph.

Treas. Reg. § 1.183–2(b)(1)-(9).

4. Ewing v. Commissioner, 213 F.2d 438 (2d Cir. 1954); Tyler v. Commissioner, 6 T.C.M. 275 (1947). E.g., Arata v. Commissioner, 277 F.2d 576, 579 (2d Cir. 1960) (voluntary payments made because of "feeling of obligation" primarily personal); Lewis v. Commissioner, 253 F.2d 821, 825 (2d

One obvious factor courts and the Service look to in order to determine whether the requisite profit-seeking motive exists is the extent to which the property in question is likely to be used for consumption. For example, intangible investment assets such as stocks or bonds that do not lend themselves to personal or consumption-type use, so that acquisition is very likely for the purpose of making a profit.[5] On the other hand, purchases of property typically consumed are likely to generate much closer scrutiny if the taxpayer sells them at a loss and attempts to deduct that loss.[6] Many kinds of property that may be used both in business and for personal use are simply deemed by the IRS or the courts as primarily personal, resulting in no loss being allowed on their full or partial disposition other than as a result of a casualty or theft deductible under 165(c)(3).[7]

[1] MIXED USE PROPERTY

If a taxpayer uses property in a business or in a transaction entered into for profit, but also separately uses the same property for personal use, she will generally be entitled to a deduction for any loss sustained on the property while it is being used for business or other profit-seeking enterprises.[8] However, unless the property is actually damaged by a casualty while being used in business or for the production of income, it will be impossible for the taxpayer to prove what portion of the reduction in value of the property was incurred in the business or other profit-seeking use rather than in the personal use by the taxpayer. Instead, any loss on the disposition of property used partly in business and partly for personal use (other than casualties or thefts that occur during one of the specific uses) will be apportioned between the deductible "business use"

Cir. 1958) (author's expenditures to defend suits to have him declared insane primarily personal).

5. It is possible to use even these assets to assist someone else rather than to make a profit. For example, if T purchases stock for the sole purpose of pledging that stock as security for an obligation of T's child so as to allow his child to borrow funds she otherwise cannot, T has not purchased that stock in an effort to make a profit, and any loss on the sale of the stock will not be deductible under § 165(c)(2).

6. E.g., clothes, food, housing, cars, and listed property. Anticipated or hoped for *tax* savings do not equate to a "profit" motive. As a result, the taxpayer who enters into a transaction for the primary purpose of avoiding taxes rather than for the primary purpose of making a before-tax profit (not taking into account tax savings) will not be allowed a deduction for any loss sustained in that transaction. See Chapter 14, *Tax Shelters and Tax Avoidance*. It is the taxpayer's motivation for the transac-

tion rather than the outcome that determines whether or not he engaged in the transaction for profit. Neither an actual profit, nor a likelihood of profit, are essential to prove the taxpayer's motivation. On the other hand, if the taxpayer *knew* that profit was impossible, it would be difficult, if not entirely impossible, to prove a profit motive, and evidence of continued losses may be taken as at least an indication that the taxpayer understood the unlikelihood of success.

7. Assets deemed personal, and on which a sustained loss would not be allowed, are also those with respect to which no § 162 deduction is allowed (for example, personal clothing and meals).

8. The loss, as other deductions with respect to the asset, would be bifurcated between that allocable to business and that part allocated to personal use. Rev. Rul. 72–111, 1972–1 C.B. 56.

and the nondeductible personal use according to the relative time the asset is used for each purpose.[9]

[2] CONVERSION FROM PERSONAL TO BUSINESS USE

Typically, the taxpayer's profit-seeking motivation exists at the time he acquires an asset for use in a business, and it lasts through the time of disposition. Even so, this is not always the case. As a result, the designation of property as being used either for personal use or for business use is not necessarily permanent. A taxpayer may use a single asset for personal use and then transfer that property into a business, or the taxpayer may just as easily use an asset in a trade or business and then use it for personal use.

The action that changes the taxpayer's holding of property from personal to business may take the form of transferring the property from an activity that is personal in nature to a different, business, activity,[10] or it may take the form of leaving the property in the same basic activity, but it may change the entire activity from a personal one to a business.[11] In either case, the property will not be found to have been converted to business use until it is so used. As explained below with respect to transactions entered into for profit, a mere change of "motive," without more, is not sufficient to convert property from personal to business use.

[3] CONVERSION FROM PERSONAL USE TO PROFIT–SEEK-ING USE

If the taxpayer is seeking to deduct a loss under section 165(c)(2) on an asset originally acquired or held for personal use and then held for profit-seeking use, but not used in a "trade or business," as required by section 165(c)(1), it is important to note the precise language of section 165(c)(2), which allows the deduction of "losses incurred in any *transaction entered into for profit*." Typically, the taxpayer's profit seeking motivation exists at the time she acquires the asset, and it lasts through the time of disposition. Hence, the purchase or other acquisition of the property is itself the "transaction entered into for profit." But where the taxpayer initially acquires property for personal use, the courts and Service typically require her to enter into some "transaction for profit" in order to be able to deduct any subsequent loss on the disposition of the property.

It is important to note that the standard for deducting a *loss* on the sale of property can be significantly different from the standard that is applied to determine whether the taxpayer who converts property from

---

9. Time that the asset is not in use for either purpose will be disregarded in making the allocation. Cf. § 280A.

10. For example, moving furniture from a personal residence into a business office or warehouse owned by the taxpayer would be sufficient to establish the profit-seeking use of the furniture.

11. For example, leaving furniture in a home, but no longer using the building as a home and instead and using it to house an actual business activity would be sufficient to establish the profit-seeking use of the furniture.

personal use to profit-seeking use can deduct depreciation, maintenance and other expenses incurred with respect to the same property under section 212. The taxpayer who previously held property for personal use and then holds that property for the production of income is entitled to deduct appropriate current expenses and depreciation with respect to that property as soon as she begins to "hold" the property for the production of income rather than for personal use. The sole question to be addressed under section 212 is one of intent. Did the taxpayer change the purpose for which she was holding the property from personal to profit-seeking? While actions and transactions entered into may be evidence of a changed intent, they are no more than evidence of intent (or the absence thereof). No actions or transactions are necessary to change the status of the property in the taxpayer's hands.[12]

The requirements under section 165 are different. Under section 165, if a taxpayer who has been using property for personal use merely decides, without more, to hold the property for appreciation and profit, and to no longer use it for pleasure, that mere change of mind is not a "transaction entered into for profit," and any subsequent loss is not likely to be deductible under 165(c)(2).[13] This is the case no matter how strong the evidence may be of the taxpayer's changed purpose.

A taxpayer can enter into a "transaction for profit" by leasing or renting out her home, but mere unsuccessful attempts to rent that never lead to rental income do not constitute a transaction entered into, and they are not sufficient to convert the property to the type of profit-seeking use that can result in a deductible loss on sale.[14]

If the asset being converted from personal use to profit-seeking use is something other than a personal residence, it is clear that the taxpayer must do *something* to convert it from personal use to profit-seeking use, but exactly what he must do is less certain. The Supreme Court long ago stated that:

> [T]he words 'any transaction' as used in [the predecessor to 165(c)(2)], are not a technical phrase, or one of art. They must therefore be taken in their usual sense, and, so taken, they are, we think, broad enough to embrace at least any action or business operation . . . by which property previously acquired is devoted exclusively to the production of taxable income.[15]

It is worth noting that mere receipt of property by gift or inheritance neither requires nor indicates any specific intent with regard to profit. In such cases, whether the taxpayer will be found to have acquired the property in a transaction for profit typically depends on what the taxpayer does with that property immediately after acquisition.[16] If she actually uses it for personal use, it is that personal use that

---

12. E.g., Lowry v. United States, 384 F.Supp. 257 (D.N.H. 1974).

13. Heiner v. Tindle, 276 U.S. 582, 48 S.Ct. 326, 327, 72 L.Ed. 714 (1928).

14. Horrmann v. Commissioner, 17 T.C. 903 (1951).

15. Heiner v. Tindle, 276 U.S. 582, 585 (1928).

16. The acquisition of property by in-

will be deemed to have motivated the acquisition, but if she immediately puts it to use in a profit-seeking enterprise, holds it for appreciation without personally using it, or immediately puts it on the market, any loss incurred will be deemed to have occurred in a transaction for profit.[17]

[4] BASIS LIMITATION ON CONVERTED USE PROPERTY

Basically, the loss that may be deducted upon the disposition of property that has been converted from personal use to profit-seeking use is only that part of the loss that has been incurred while the property was being used in business. Any decline in value of the property while it was serving the taxpayer's personal use is a non-deductible "personal, living or family expense,"[18] regardless of whether the decline in value was due to the taxpayer's actual physical use of the property or to market forces which decreased the property's value while the taxpayer was either using it or holding it for personal use. The regulations ensure that no reduction in value accrued while the property was being held for personal use can later be deducted by providing that the basis for loss (as well as the basis for depreciation) is the lesser of the taxpayer's actual basis or the fair market value of the property at the time the property was converted to business use.[19]

While this limitation of basis to the lesser of the taxpayer's actual adjusted basis or the fair market value of the property at the time of conversion ensures that any loss incurred on the property while it was being held for personal use cannot give rise to a subsequent deduction under 165(c)(2),[20] it also has a few other potential side effects. Among

---

heritance is a neutral fact. See Marx v. Commissioner, 5 T.C. 173 (1945); Campbell v. Commissioner, 5 T.C. 272 (1945); McBride v. Commissioner, 50 T.C. 1, 7 (1968).

17. See Campbell v. Commissioner, 5 T.C. 272 (1945); Estate of Assmann v. Commissioner, 16 T.C. 632 (1951); Crawford v. Commissioner, 16 T.C. 678 (1951). The tax status of inherited property was neutral at the moment of death, and the use the devisee thereafter made of the property determined its future tax status. This was the case even though the devisee had owned the property with the deceased as joint tenant or tenant by the entirety and had used the property for personal use prior to the spouse's death. In each case, inheritance of a different interest in the property was held to begin a new transaction, and the transaction was found to be one entered into for profit where no personal use was made of the property after inheritance.

18. § 262.

19. "The adjusted basis for determining loss (of property converted from person-

al to profit-seeking use) shall be the lesser of either . . . (i) the fair market value of the property at the time of conversion of the property to income-producing purposes, or (ii) the adjusted basis for loss . . . without reference to the fair market value." Treas. Reg. § 1.165–9(b)(2). Although Treas. Reg. § 1.165–9(b)(2) specifically refers only to a personal residence converted from personal to business use, the restriction applies as well to the conversion of other property previously held for personal use. If property is not converted to use in a trade or business, so that the taxpayer is seeking to deduct a loss under § 165(c)(2) rather than under § 165(c)(1), other restrictions apply to the conversion of the property. If property is subject to depreciation after being converted to business use, then the basis for determining a loss on a subsequent disposition is adjusted downwards for any depreciation allowed or allowable after conversion. See § 1016.

20. This is because the taxpayer's adjusted basis for loss will reflect only the reduced value of the property at the time of conversion to profit-seeking use.

them is that it does *not* guarantee that any actual losses incurred by the taxpayer while the property is being used in a business *will* be deductible.

For example, assume that T purchased a home for $1,000,000, and while T was using it for personal use, the home grew in value to $1,250,000. Assume further that T then converts the home to business use, and the property decreases in value to $1,000,000. Thereafter, T sells the property for $1,000,000. The property appreciated by $250,000 while T used it as a home, and it declined in value by $250,000 while T used it in business.[21] By simply limiting T's basis for loss to T's basis at the time of conversion, the regulations[22] ensure that T is neither taxed on his pre-conversion gain nor allowed to deduct her post-conversion loss. Where the gain and loss would be of the same character, the denial of both simply balances out.

If, though, the gain and loss would be subjected to different tax consequences, that balancing may not be so simple. For example, if T could have excluded the $250,000 gain that accrued while she lived in the home under section 121, but could have deducted, perhaps against ordinary income,[23] the $250,000 loss that accrued to the property while it was being used for business, the cancellation of both the gain and the loss puts T in a tax situation substantially different from what she would have been in had she been taxed separately on both the gain and the loss.[24]

Similar distortions can occur if T's property actually declined in value while she used it for personal use and then increased in value after it was converted to business use. For example, assume that T purchased a home for $1,000,000, and the property declined in value to $750,000 while T used it for personal use. T then converts the property into business use. The property becomes worth $1,000,000 while it is being so used, and T sells it for $1,000,000, realizing no gain and no loss. The net result is quite different from what it would be if T were treated as realizing a nondeductible personal loss of $250,000 and were taxed (at either capital gains rates or ordinary income rates) on a corresponding $250,000 gain.

[5] CONVERSION FROM PROFIT–SEEKING TO PERSONAL USE

If property is converted from business use to personal use prior to disposition, then at the time of disposition, the taxpayer is not sustaining a loss on property used in a trade or business; nor is the loss incurred in a transaction which was entered into for profit. As a result, any loss on

---

21. For the sake of simplicity, the example assumes that T's basis in the home was not decreased by allowable depreciation while T was using the property for business.

22. Treas. Reg. § 1.165–9(b)(2).

23. See § 10.07 for a complete discussion of Section 1231 property.

24. For similar kinds of distortions in partnership taxation, see Treas. Reg. § 1.704–3.

the disposition of the property is allowed under 165(c)(1),[25] regardless of when the loss was actually accrued.

§ 12.03   WHEN IS THERE A REALIZED LOSS?

[1] REALIZATION REVISITED

Section 165 allows a taxpayer to deduct losses "sustained during the taxable year...." Put most simply, a taxpayer "sustains" a loss by engaging in any realization event in which her amount realized is less than his adjusted basis.[1] Neither mere appreciation nor gradual decline in value of an asset results in realization of gain or loss.

For the most part, both gains and losses are realized when a taxpayer sells or exchanges an asset.[2] If the taxpayer's amount realized exceeds her basis, she realizes a gain, and if her basis exceeds her amount realized, she realizes a loss.[3] As made clear by the Supreme Court's decision in Cottage Savings,[4] so long as there is either a sale or an actual exchange of one property for a different property, there is a realization event so long as the "legal entitlements" represented by the two assets are not exactly the same. It is enough that the legal entitlements represented by the exchanged properties are different in either kind or extent.[5]

[2] REALIZATION EVENTS OTHER THAN SALES OR EXCHANGES

Obviously, the idea of realization is essentially the same for losses as it is for gains or income. In both cases, realization requires a specific identifiable occurrence, which more often than not is a sale or exchange of property. Nonetheless, there are some differences.

A taxpayer realizes income when she *gets* something she *did not have previously*. Conversely, a taxpayer realizes a loss when she *loses* or *disposes* of something she *did* have previously. As discussed at § 10.03, a taxpayer need not actually sell, exchange or dispose of an asset in order to realize gain; she may receive property in exchange for the performance of actual, anticipated or merely hoped for services, or for the use of property. In any case, the receipt of property the taxpayer did not have before is a realization event and results in taxable income.

On the loss side, the taxpayer cannot realize a loss without the *disposition* (in full or in part) of some property, but she need not actually

---

25. But the mere fact that a taxpayer made some use of business property for personal convenience does not without more convert an enterprise into a merely personal venture. Sinsheimer v. Commissioner, 7 B.T.A. 1099 (1927); Campe v. Commissioner 17 B.T.A. 575 (1929).

§ 12.03

1. Typically, basis refers to the taxpayer's cost for the asset. See § 1012.

2. See § 1001(c).

3. See § 1001(a).

4. Cottage Savings Assn. v. Commissioner, 499 U.S. 554, 111 S.Ct. 1503, 113 L.Ed.2d 589 (1991).

5. Id.

receive anything in exchange in order for a loss to be realized. In addition to realizing a loss upon the sale or exchange of property, a taxpayer may also realize a loss on property by simply losing or abandoning it; having the property stolen, condemned, or destroyed; or in some cases, damaged. What is important for purposes of realization of loss is simply that there is *some* specific identifiable closed and completed event or transaction that results in the disposition of all or part of a specific property.[6]

Not surprisingly, issues can arise with respect to determining whether and when some of the above events give rise to realization of losses. For example, "abandonment" of property can give rise to a deductible loss, but exactly when a taxpayer actually "abandons" property is not always clear. Abandonment means something more than simply discontinuing use on a temporary basis, but something less than physically disposing of the property. Discontinuing all use of a property on a permanent basis will suffice, but that proposition (i.e., that all use of the property, including its potential sale, is discontinued on a permanent basis) may be difficult to establish. Similar issues can arise with respect to when property becomes "obsolete" in a way that gives rise to a deductible loss.[7]

[3] CASUALTY DAMAGE TO PROPERTY

Another area which may give rise to disagreement as to whether or not a realization event has occurred is that of casualty losses. While some of the cases and rulings in this area may relate to losses of property held for personal, rather than profit seeking, use, the question of whether or not there has been a realization event relates to both. The primary difficulty in determining whether damage to property was caused by a casualty lies in distinguishing between normal wear and tear to property, which is progressive and is *not* a realization event, and the type of "casualty" that is a realization event.

In general, a "casualty" that gives rise to a realized loss is an identifiable event that is sudden and unexpected, such as a fire, storm or shipwreck, and as such it is distinguished from gradual wear and tear.[8] Unfortunately, though, this distinction is not always clear. For example, the Service has distinguished between termite damage, which occurs over a few months or more and therefore does not give rise to a realization event, and damage by certain kinds of beetles, which is very quick and therefore does give rise to a realized loss.[9]

---

6. The disposition of property is a necessary, but not sufficient, element of any loss deductible under 165(a). Although not every disposition of property in which the taxpayer's adjusted basis exceeds his amount realized results in a loss (gifts, bequests, and nonrecognition transactions such as §§ 351, 721, 1031, and 1092 are examples of dispositions that will not result in losses), no loss can ever be sustained unless there is some disposition by the taxpayer of all or part of an asset.

7. See Treas. Reg. § 1.165–2.

8. Rev. Rul. 72–592, 1972–2 C.B. 101.

9. See Rev. Rul. 79–174 (allows a casualty loss as a result of destruction by beetles); Rev. Rul. 63–232, 1963–2 C.B. 97 (disallowing a casualty loss in the case of termite destruction). See also Nelson v. Commissioner, T.C. Memo. 1968–35; Black v. Commissioner, T.C. Memo. 1977–337.

Indeed, even the same kind of event may give rise to a realization event in some cases but not in others. For example, gradual damage from exposure to the elements can be difficult to distinguish from sudden and unexpected damage from the same cause.

In some cases taxpayers have asserted they have realized losses with respect to assets because sudden and unexpected external events that would qualify as realization events decreased the value of property even though there was no actual physical damage to the taxpayer's property. Examples include fires or storms which damage neighboring properties and result in reduced a value of the taxpayer's undamaged property because it becomes unexpectedly situated in an undesirable neighborhood, or regulatory legislation that is enacted that significantly reduces the value or utility of the taxpayer's property. The Service and the courts have been consistent in denying that these types of events are realization events for the taxpayer whose property is not either physically damaged[10] or made completely worthless by the event. Even if these events are sudden and unexpected, they simply represent surrounding conditions that decrease the value of property, and in this respect they are similar to market fluctuations that may significantly decrease the value of the taxpayer's holdings, but such fluctuations give no rise to deductible losses until those holdings are sold, exchanged or otherwise disposed of in whole or in part.

[4] CASUALTY LOSSES V. ORDINARY REPAIRS

Losses deductible as casualties under section 165(a) must be distinguished from incidental repair costs that are deductible under section 162(a) as ordinary and necessary business expenses. If property is completely lost, destroyed, or abandoned as a result of a casualty or theft, the propriety of a loss deduction under section 165(a) is clear. On the other hand, if property suffers very minor damage in an event that would normally qualify as a realization event, small expenditures made to repair the property that do not permanently improve or better it or prolong its useful life may be treated as business expenses deductible under section 162(a).[11] Thus, the nature and extent of the damage may also be taken into account.

[5] POSSIBILITY OF REIMBURSEMENT

An additional factor that can arise in determining whether there has been a realization event is the possibility of reimbursement for any

---

10. The requirement that the taxpayer's loss be the result of damage to her own property rather than damage to other property that simply reduces the value of the taxpayer's property is in some ways akin to the notion that damages for personal physical injury (including amounts attributable to emotional distress) are excluded from income if they are the result of personal physical injury but not if they are the result only of emotional distress without any physical injury to the plaintiff. See Chapter 11, *Tax Issues Related to Litigation Recoveries and Settlements.*

11. Hensler v. Commissioner, 73 T.C. 168, 179 (1979). See also Hubinger v. Commissioner, 36 F.2d 724, 726 (2d Cir. 1929) (expenses resulting from "trifling accidental causes" are deductible only under § 162(a) and not under § 165(a)); Prop. Treas. Regs. § 1.263(a)–3(f)(iv).

damage caused. Section 165 provides deductions for losses not reimbursed by insurance or otherwise.[12] As long as the realistic possibility of reimbursement for the damage exists, whether by recourse to the taxpayer's insurance or by reimbursement from a tortfeasor, no deductible loss has been realized.[13] When it becomes clear to an objective observer that reimbursement will not be forthcoming, the loss becomes realized.[14]

Some taxpayers may forego an existing right to reimbursement for damage, out of business or personal concerns. For example, a taxpayer whose property is damaged by the negligence of a customer may choose to forego reimbursement in order to retain a beneficial working relationship. Technically in such cases the taxpayer has not suffered a deductible "loss" to her property, but the taxpayer has instead decided to forego reimbursement as a business decision.[15] Similarly, the taxpayer whose property is damaged by a family member and who decides not to seek reimbursement simply out of concern for the family member has likely made a gift to that family member of the foregone reimbursement, and he has not actually realized a deductible loss.[16]

Often, the taxpayer may have a right to reimbursement, but the amount of possible reimbursement is limited. To the extent that it is clear that at least some amount of an otherwise realized loss will not be reimbursed, that amount is currently deductible.[17]

[6] AMOUNT OF LOSS REALIZED AND THE IMPACT ON BASIS

[a] Complete Disposition

Section 165(b) provides that the basis for determining the amount of the deduction for any loss shall be the property's adjusted basis. Where property is sold or exchanged, this simply means that, as provided in section 1001(a), the loss realized is the excess of the taxpayer's adjusted basis over the amount realized for the property.

If property is completely disposed of in a realization event other than a sale or exchange, but the taxpayer nonetheless receives reimbursement by way of insurance or damages, the insurance and/or any other reimbursement is considered to be a part of the amount realized for the asset (along with any other cash, money or services received on

---

12. § 165(a)(1).

13. See Treas. Reg. § 1.165–1(d)(2)(i).

14. According to the regulations, no deduction is allowed for a loss if and to the extent there exists any claim for reimbursement with respect to which there is a reasonable prospect of recovery "until it can be ascertained with reasonable certainty whether or not such reimbursement will be received." Treas. Reg. § 1.165–1(d)(2)(i). Problems may arise with respect to claims for reimbursement that have not been adju-

dicated, paid or settled, nor affirmatively and finally denied to the taxpayer. Whether such claims present a reasonable prospect of recovery, and when a claim that initially presents a reasonable prospect of recovery ceases to do so, are questions of "fact to be determined upon an examination of all facts and circumstances." Id.

15. Treas. Reg. § 1.165–1(d)(2)(i).

16. Id.

17. Id.

the disposition, if any).[18] To the extent the amount realized falls short of the taxpayer's adjusted basis in the property disposed of or lost, the taxpayer realizes a potentially deductible loss.[19]

If property is completely disposed of in some other realization event that gives rise to a loss with *no* amount realized (for example, abandonment, loss, or total destruction of property without any reimbursement), the amount of the deductible loss is the entire adjusted basis in the disposed property. This result is consistent with section 1001, with the taxpayer's amount realized simply being $0.

[b] Partial Disposition, Sale or Exchange

If the taxpayer sells or exchanges only a *portion* of the asset and retains the remainder, then only a corresponding portion of the taxpayer's entire adjusted basis in the asset is allocated to the sale or exchange, and the taxpayer recognizes a loss only to the extent the proceeds fall short of that portion of the asset's adjusted basis.[20]

[c] Partial Disposition, Casualty

Very frequently, when a taxpayer incurs a loss as a result of casualty (or other unexpected and unwanted damage to an asset that is sufficiently sudden and unexpected so that it would constitute a realization event), the damage to the asset is less than total destruction. In such cases where no insurance or other reimbursement is received, the amount of damage done is generally determined by reference to the decline in fair market value (as determined by competent appraisal) of the property attributable to the casualty event.[21] The reasonable cost of repairs necessary to restore the damaged property to its pre-casualty condition is acceptable evidence of its decline in value.[22]

The Internal Revenue Code does not require allocation of basis between the damaged and intact parts of the property in casualties. Instead, when property is only partially damaged in a casualty or similar involuntary realization event, the taxpayer is directed to allocate the entire asset basis to the part of the asset destroyed.[23] As a result, the

---

18. See § 1001(b).

19. See § 1001(a). Of course if the taxpayer receives insurance or other reimbursement in *excess* of her basis in the property disposed of, the transaction results not in a loss, but in a realized and potentially recognized gain. Id.

20. If a taxpayer disposes of an asset in exchange for an amount less than its value in a part sale, part gift, the taxpayer may use the entire basis to offset the amount realized before reporting a gain, but no loss is deductible, even if the amount realized is less than a proportional part of the asset's basis. Treas. Reg. § 1.1001–1(e). See also Miller's Estate v. Commissioner, 27 T.C.M. 1140 (1968), aff'd per curiam, 421 F.2d 1405 (4th Cir.1970). The taxpayer who wishes to deduct a loss on such property could do so by making a separate sale of a part of the asset (on which she could deduct a loss to the extent her basis in the part sold exceeded her amount realized), and a separate gift of the remainder.

21. Treas. Reg. § 1.165–7(a)(2)(i).

22. Treas. Reg. § 1.165–7(a)(2)(ii). Not surprisingly, the costs of repairs that improve the damaged property rather than restore it merely to its pre-casualty condition are not currently deductible. Instead, the costs of such nondeductible repairs, if and when paid, go to increase the taxpayer's basis in the property.

23. Treas. Reg. § 1.165–1(c).

taxpayer may deduct as a loss the lesser of the amount of damage done[24] or the entire basis of the damaged property.[25]

For example, assume that T uses an asset in business with an adjusted basis of $8,000 and a fair market value of $20,000. Further assume that the asset suffers $5,000 of damage in a "casualty," leaving it with a fair market value of $15,000. T can deduct as a loss the entire $5,000 of damage.[26] Although only 25% of the asset's value was lost, up to 100% of the basis can be allocated to the destroyed part of the asset; hence, T can deduct the entire $5,000 of damage in this case. Because T has deducted, as a loss, $5,000 of his original $8,000 basis, T's basis in the asset (now worth $15,000) must be reduced by $5,000,[27] to $3,000.

To see how the loss deduction is limited by T's basis, and to see further how the deduction impacts basis, assume that T's asset (FMV $20,000, basis $8,000) suffers $10,000 of damage from a casualty, leaving it with a fair market value of $10,000. Since T cannot deduct an amount in excess of her entire basis in the asset, her loss deduction is limited to her basis of $8,000. After she deducts that $8,000, her remaining basis in the asset, now worth $10,000, is $0. Since she was allowed to deduct her entire basis, she has no basis remaining.

[d] Partial Disposition by Casualty, Accompanied by Reimbursement

In cases of destruction or damage by casualty, as in all other cases, the amount of any realized loss is limited in the first instance by any reimbursement received. As a result, since T, in the example above, has an asset with an adjusted basis of $8,000 and a value of $20,000, and a casualty results in $5,000 of damage, but T receives insurance payments of $5,000, no loss is sustained. T is entitled to no deduction because she has been fully compensated for any damage to the property.[28]

It is important to note that the receipt of insurance or other proceeds is not taxed to the extent it represents a mere return of capital rather than profit. As a result, to the extent that T receives reimbursement for casualty damage and the amount received goes untaxed, that receipt is treated as a return to T of her invested capital, and, as any return of capital, it reduces T's basis in the asset. In other words, T's pre-casualty basis of $8,000 in the damaged asset above represents her invested and not yet deducted (for example, as depreciation) capital in that property. When she receives $5,000 in insurance proceeds and does not include those proceeds in income, her total invested and undeducted

---

24. Basically, the deduction here is equal to the lesser of the decline in value of the property or the cost of restoring the property to its undamaged condition.

25. To the extent the taxpayer deducts a loss as a result of damage to or destruction of an asset, the taxpayer's basis in the asset is reduced by the amount deducted. Treas. Reg. § 1.165–1(c)(1); Treas. Reg. § 1.1011–1.

26. For the proper methods to determine the amount of the loss, see Treas. Reg. § 1.165–7(a)(2).

27. Treas. Reg. § 1.165–1(c); Treas. Reg. § 1.1011–1.

28. If the taxpayer's amount realized, including insurance or other reimbursement, exceeds her basis in the property, she will realize a gain. See § 1001(a).

capital in the asset is now only $3,000 ($8,000 less the $5,000 she has just received). T's asset basis is reduced by the $5,000 received and untaxed via insurance proceeds; this leaves her with a basis of $3,000.

Assume, instead, that T's property (basis $8,000, value $20,000) suffers $10,000 of casualty damage, and T receives insurance proceeds of only $3,000. The receipt of $3,000 of untaxed insurance proceeds reduces her basis by $3,000, to $5,000. T sustains net unreimbursed damage of $7,000, but she realizes a deductible loss of only $5,000. T's newly adjusted (for the untaxed insurance receipts) basis in the damaged property is $0. This is because T cannot deduct any loss in excess of her basis (as adjusted) in the damaged property. Accordingly the $5,000 loss deduction reduces T's adjusted asset basis by $5,000, to $0.

To hammer home the point, assume the asset suffers damage and T recovers insurance of $2,000. Regardless of the amount of damage done to the property, T can deduct a loss of not more than $6,000 (her $8,000 initial basis in the asset, reduced by the $2,000 in insurance proceeds received as a nontaxable return of capital).

Finally, and perhaps obviously, regardless of the amount of damage done, to the extent that the taxpayer receives insurance or other reimbursement in excess of her basis in the damaged property, she realizes a gain.[29]

[e] Repairs and Basis

It should be clear by now that the taxpayer's ending asset basis depends on both the reimbursement she receives and the amount of loss (or gain) realized by the taxpayer as a result of the casualty. The taxpayer's asset basis is reduced by any reimbursement. Only unreimbursed losses can result in a realized loss, and the amount of any unreimbursed loss is limited to the taxpayer's adjusted basis in the asset.

The decrease in the taxpayer's basis that results from the receipt of insurance or other proceeds, as well as the decrease in basis that results from a deductible loss, is often not the end of the story, however. If the taxpayer spends any amount on nondeductible repairs[30] of her damaged property, that amount expended and not deducted represents an additional investment in her property, and, accordingly, it increases her basis in the property.

Thus, while the taxpayer's basis in the damaged property is not directly impacted by how the taxpayer chooses to use the specific insurance or other reimbursement received on account of the casualty, her basis will be increased by any amounts she spends on nondeductible repairs to the damaged property, regardless of the source of funds.

---

29. § 1001(a). As to whether that gain is recognized, see discussion of § 1033 at § 9.03.

30. When a taxpayer properly deducts a casualty loss, any repairs done to restore the property after the casualty cannot be treated as ordinary and necessary repair costs. Any other rule would result in a double deduction. Prop. Treas. Reg. § 1.263(a)–3(f)(iv).

To see what this means, assume, once again, that T owns property with a basis of $8,000 and a value of $20,000, and the property suffers $7,000 of damage in a casualty. If T receives $5,000 in insurance proceeds, that receipt reduces her basis to $3,000. Accordingly, T realizes a loss of $2,000 (the amount of loss not reimbursed by insurance or otherwise). Her basis in the property is now decreased by the deductible loss, from $3,000 to $1,000. If T spends any nondeductible amount repairing the damage caused by the casualty, that amount will *increase* her basis in the damaged property. In other words, if T uses the entire $5,000 of insurance proceeds to repair some of the damage, her ending basis in the car will be $6,000. That is to say her ending basis is equal to T's initial $8,000 basis, reduced to $3,000 by the receipt of $5,000 in insurance proceeds, reduced to $1,000 by the $2,000 deductible loss, and *increased* back to $6,000 by the $5,000 spent on nondeductible repairs. If T spends less than the full $5,000 of insurance proceeds to repair the property, her basis will be increased from $1,000 by whatever amount she spends on the nondeductible repairs. If T spends *more* than $5,000, her basis in the property will be increased by whatever amount she spends on those nondeductible repairs, regardless of the source of the funds.

§ 12.04 LIMITATIONS ON LOSSES

[1] SUBSTANCE VERSUS FORM

The concept and application of the "substance versus form" doctrine and other similar doctrines is discussed at length elsewhere in this work.[1] Nonetheless, it is worth raising this issue in conjunction with losses under sections 165(c)(1) and (2) because these sections may provide particular incentives for taxpayers to manipulate transactions in order to obtain questionable deductions. Basically, a taxpayer who owns an asset that has declined in value may wish to realize the loss on that asset without really divesting herself of the property. There are certain specific statutory provisions that prevent taxpayers from taking deductions in some of these cases, but none of these specific statutory provisions can be applied as broadly or as flexibly as the "substance versus form" doctrine.[2]

Examples of how the substance versus form doctrine can be applied to prevent taxpayers from deducting losses are found in cases of sales and repurchases, sales with options to reacquire the property, and sales and leasebacks.[3] A taxpayer may "sell" an asset at a loss, seeking a deduction under section 165, but at the same time the taxpayer may seek to retain actual ownership of the sold property. In order to accomplish these apparently conflicting goals, the taxpayer may execute, along with the "sale," an agreement to repurchase or otherwise re-acquire that

---

§ 12.04

1. See § 14.06.

2. See § 14.06[1][b].

3. Also see discussion of the application of § 1031 to losses, at § 9.02.

same asset.[4] In general, if the taxpayer retains and subsequently exercises a legal right to reacquire the asset for an amount substantially equivalent to (or less than) the sales price, the Service and the courts are most likely to find that the taxpayer has not made a complete disposition of an asset.[5] This is likely to be the case whether the right retained by the taxpayer is a contractual right and obligation to repurchase the property, or merely an option to reacquire it at a favorable price. If the taxpayer reacquires the "sold" property at such a price soon after making the "sale," the initial sale may be disregarded even where the repurchase is not in the form of a legally binding agreement.[6] This is most likely to be the case if the purchaser-reseller is a related party, who can be relied upon by the "seller" to cooperate.[7]

The other area where the Service is most likely to question the substance of a purported sale of loss property is where the seller simultaneously leases back the sold property. A short-term leaseback will generally not lead the Service to question the sale, but a lease term that exceeds the likely useful life of the property "sold," so that the purchaser has no realistic possibility of obtaining any actual use or benefit from the seller, will likely be examined very closely by the Service.[8]

While the above examples are the most likely candidates to be restructured by the Service, this is by no means an exhaustive list. As in other areas, if the Service or the courts determine that any apparent disposition of property has no economic substance, or if they determine that the substance of a transaction is different from its form, the substance versus form doctrines may apply.[9]

In addition to applying the substance versus form doctrine to determine that an alleged sale never actually occurred, the Service or the courts may also use that doctrine to support a conclusion that while property was sold, the taxpayer realized no loss because either the taxpayer's basis or amount realized was actually different from what was reported.[10] In these cases, the determination of both basis and amount

---

4. See § 14.03 for a complete discussion of sale and leaseback transactions.

5. Robert Bosch Corp. v. Commissioner, T.C. Memo. 1989–655; Clark Equipment Co. & Consolidated Subsidiaries v. Commissioner, T.C. Memo. 1988–111.

6. See Shoenberg v. Commissioner, 77 F.2d 446 (8th Cir. 1935).

7. See e.g., Shoenberg v. Commissioner, 77 F.2d 446 (8th Cir. 1935). In addition to determining that what is structured as a sale is in reality merely a lease, or at least a "non-sale," the courts and the Service may at other times recharacterize what is structured to appear as a lease to in fact be a sale. For example, a taxpayer who "leases" property subject to an option for the lessee to purchase the property upon expiration of

the lease for an amount substantially less than the expected fair market value at the time of the option purchase may be found to have sold, rather than leased, the asset from the beginning of the transaction. If the "leased" property had declined in value in the hands of the "lessor," recharacterizing the transaction as a sale rather than as a lease with an option to purchase would result in a loss for the lessor/seller.

8. See e.g., Estate of Starr v. Commissioner, 30 T.C. 856 (1958), aff'd on this ground but rem'd on other issues, 274 F.2d 294 (9th Cir. 1959).

9. For a complete discussion of the substance versus form doctrine, see § 14.06[1][b].

10. Id.

realized is determined no differently than it is in other cases.[11] However, as in all cases, the taxpayer's amount realized includes the value of property, services, or anything else of value received,[12] and her basis in any property sold includes only the amount she actually paid for that property, and not any gifts or payments made for other property at the same time.[13]

[2] NONRECOGNITION AND SECTION 1031

Section 1031, which grants nonrecognition to realized gains and losses in certain exchanges of like-kind property, is discussed at length at § 9.02 . Nonetheless, section 1031 may in certain circumstances prevent taxpayers from deducting realized losses; hence it bears some discussion in this section as well. In particular, section 1031 may be applied to deny recognition to realized losses in two different kinds of cases: (1) where the taxpayer seeks to separate the trade-in of used property from the acquisition of new, like-kind, property from the same dealer, in order to avoid nonrecognition and instead recognize a realized loss on the property traded-in; and (2) where the taxpayer sells and leases back (for 30 years or more) the same real property, and the Service has argued that the sale and leaseback constitute a like-kind exchange under section 1031; hence, the taxpayer cannot deduct any loss realized on the sale of the property.

An example of the first of these kinds of cases is found in Redwing Carriers, Inc. v. Tomlinson.[14] In order to save taxes,[15] the taxpayer traded-in used trucks (plus cash) for new ones. Thereafter, the corporation argued that it had engaged in two separate exchanges, one a mere cash purchase of new trucks, and the other a (taxable) sale of the old ones. Quoting Revenue Ruling 61–119,[16] the court stated that:

> Where a taxpayer sells old equipment used in his trade or business to a dealer and purchases new equipment of like kind from the dealer under circumstances which indicate that the sale and the purchase are reciprocal and mutually dependent transactions, the sale and purchase is an exchange of property within the meaning of section 1031 . . . , even though the sale and purchase are accomplished by separately executed contracts and are treated as unrelated transactions by the taxpayer and the dealer for record keeping purposes.[17]

11. See § 1012; § 1001(b).

12. See § 1001(b).

13. See § 1012.

14. 399 F.2d 652, 659 (5th Cir. 1968).

15. In that case, the taxpayer did not seek to recognize a loss on the old trucks. Instead, it argued that the two transactions were separate so that it could have a higher basis in the new trucks. At the time the case arose, the taxpayer could have obtained capital gains treatment on the sale of the old trucks, while getting a higher basis, and thus more depreciation against ordinary income on the new ones. Since the enactment of § 1245 depreciation recapture in 1962, that particular reason for avoiding nonrecognition no longer survives, but taxpayer desire avoid § 1031 in order to recognize a realized loss remains strong.

16. 1961–1C.B. 395.

17. 399 F.2d at 659.

While this holding has provided ammunition for the Service in several cases, it provides significantly less benefit to taxpayers. In those cases where taxpayers have relied on the reasoning of Redwing in order to qualify as nonrecognition exchange transactions that they initially structured as separate, the courts have been much less willing to treat those separate sales as a single "exchange" that qualifies for nonrecognition under section 1031. Courts typically point out, in such cases, that they are simply not convinced on the facts that the apparently separate transactions were so mutually dependent they should be viewed as a single transaction.

Other occasions when the Service has applied section 1031 to prevent taxpayers from recognizing losses have involved sales and leasebacks of real property. In several cases where taxpayers sought to deduct losses accrued on real property while continuing to enjoy the use of that property, they have sold the property and leased it back for a period of 30 years or more.[18] As discussed above, the Service may assert, in such cases, that the taxpayer is not entitled to deduct a loss because there has simply been no real sale, but too often for the Service's liking, it is clear that there has been some kind of sale or exchange so that an argument that the entire transaction should be disregarded will fail. In these cases, the Service will instead assert that while some transaction has occurred, the substance of the transaction is an exchange of like-kind properties under section 1031; hence, it does not give rise to recognition of the taxpayer's loss.

The Service is able to assert nonrecognition in these sale and leaseback cases because under the applicable regulations, a leasehold interest of 30 years or more in real property is like-kind to all other real property.[19] As a result, the taxpayer who exchanges real property for cash or other property plus a continuing leasehold interest (of 30 years or more) in the property sold has engaged in a like-kind exchange.[20] Although section 1031 results in the complete nonrecognition of gain only if the taxpayer receives solely like-kind property and no boot, it provides for nonrecognition of all loss regardless of any boot, or non-like-kind property, received.

If the taxpayer can actually convince a reviewing court that any leasehold interest she acquired in the property she sold was obtained in a genuinely separate transaction, section 1031 will not apply. If the taxpayer receives, as consideration in exchange for real property, and as part of the same overall transaction, a leasehold interest of 30 years or more in the same (or, for that matter, any other) real property, the cases in this area have consistently held that there has been a section 1031 exchange, and the taxpayer can recognize none of her realized loss on the property exchanged.[21]

---

18. See also Treas. Reg. § 1.1031a–1(c).

19. Treas. Reg. § 1.1031a–1(c).

20. See Treas. Reg. § 1.1031a–1(c).

21. See also Treas. Reg. § 1.1031a–1(c).

If, however, the taxpayer is able to convince the reviewing court that the lease she signed, even as part of a single transaction, was not part of the consideration for the property transferred, she may be able to escape application of section 1031. In those cases where the taxpayer has successfully made this argument, it has been because she has convinced the court that she received full consideration for the real property in cash or other (non like-kind) property, and the leaseback, even though for more than 30 years, and even though signed as part of the same transaction, was not consideration for the property because it had no value at all.[22] The reasoning behind these cases is that if the lease had no value, it was not received "in exchange" for anything at all; hence section 1031 does not apply. Not surprisingly, the Service will often be unwilling to accept the proposition that the lease had no value. Even if in fact the lease has no value, though, the Service still holds to the position that even a leasehold interest that has no value at all constitutes "property" received in the exchange, and therefore the application of section 1031 is warranted.[23]

[3] WASH SALES AND SECTION 1091

Unlike section 1031, which provides a weapon the Service can use to prevent taxpayers from deducting losses, but which was actually enacted for very different reasons (primarily, to enable taxpayers to avoid recognition of certain gains), section 1091 was enacted specifically to prevent taxpayer-investors from being able to deduct certain losses.

[a] When Section 1091 Applies

Prior to the enactment of section 1091, a taxpayer who owned stock or other securities which had declined in value could quite easily obtain a loss deduction with respect to those shares, regardless of whether she had any real desire to terminate her investment. The taxpayer could simply call her broker to sell her loss shares, and a short while later she could call back the same (or a different) broker and ask to purchase the an identical number of identical shares in the same company. If the taxpayer did not want to be without the particular investment for even a day, she could purchase identical shares shortly *before* selling her loss shares, instead of purchasing them shortly after selling her original shares. Because the shares were sold and purchased over a stock exchange, the taxpayer was not buying back the same shares she sold; hence, it was difficult for the Service to convincingly argue that there was no sale. And, since section 1031 does not apply to intangibles such as stock or securities, the Service could not rely on that section to prevent a loss deduction.

Section 1091 was enacted specifically to prevent taxpayers from taking such risk-free and substance-free loss deductions.[24] Section 1091 provides that if a taxpayer (other than a dealer acting in the ordinary

---

22. See e.g., Leslie v. Commissioner, 539 F.2d 943 (3d Cir. 1976)

23. Rev. Rul. 60–43, 1960–1 C.B. 687.

24. Section 1091 has no application to shares sold at a gain.

course of business) who sells stock or securities at a loss either acquires or enters into a contract or option to acquire "substantially identical" stock or securities within 30 days before or after the sale, no deduction shall be allowed under section 165.[25] Stock or securities are substantially identical essentially only if they represent the same rights in the same corporation.[26] As a result, the investor who wishes to deduct a loss on stock or securities must be willing to actually divest herself of the stock or securities at issue for at least 30 days before and 30 days after the sale.

By providing that entering into an option or other contract to purchase replacement stock is treated the same as actual acquisition of the stock, section 1091(a) prevents the selling taxpayer from avoiding the 61 day limitation (30 days before the sale, 30 days after the sale, and the day of the sale) on reacquisition by simply entering into an option or other contract to acquire replacement stock.[27]

The clever taxpayer who realizes that entering into a contract to *purchase* stock in the future is treated as a current acquisition, though, might enter into a contract to *sell* the old stock in the future rather than to *purchase* the replacement stock in the future. To see how this might occur, assume that on April 15, T owns 100 shares of ABC Corp. common stock with a basis of $100,000 and a value of $70,000, and T wishes to deduct her $30,000 accrued loss while continuing to hold her investment in ABC Corp. If T sells the 100 shares of ABC Corp. and enters into a current contract to acquire the replacement stock at the end of 31 days, she will still be subject to section 1091; this is because for purposes of section 1091 entering into a the contract to acquire the stock in the future is treated as a current acquisition of the stock subject to that contract. Instead, T might currently *acquire* the replacement stock, but enter into an agreement to *sell* the old stock only after 31 days. By fixing the price of the old stock now, but delaying the actual sale until more than 30 days after the acquisition of the "replacement" stock, T might hope avoid section 1091 altogether. Unfortunately for T, though, this tactic also fails to avoid the reach of section 1091. The regulations provide that if a taxpayer currently owns the stock which she contracts to sell in the future, the sale date for purposes of section 1091 is the date on which the sale contract was entered into rather than the date on which it was closed.[28]

Finally along these lines, the regulations provide that the taxpayer who contracts to deliver shares which she does *not* own at the time of entering the contract is treated as making the sale only when she actually delivers those shares.[29] To see how this applies, assume that on

25. § 1091(a).

26. See § 1091(a). In addition, shares that do not actually embody the same rights but whose value changes in direct proportion to the value of the shares sold, so that they exactly mirror those shares may also be "substantially identical" to those shares.

27. See § 1091(a).

28. Treas. Reg. § 1.1091–1(g).

29. Treas. Reg. § 1.1091–1(g); Treas. Reg. § 1.1233–1.

January 1 ABC Corp. stock is trading for $100,000. On that date, T, who owns no ABC Corp. stock, contracts with Q to deliver 100 shares of ABC Corp. stock on December 31 for $100,000. If ABC Corp. is trading at $150,000 on December 31, T will be required to purchase 100 shares for $150,000 and deliver them to Q in exchange for only $100,000. T will realize a loss of $50,000 on this transaction (the sale of 100 shares of ABC Corp.). Moreover, if T purchases 100 additional shares of ABC Corp. stock within 30 days of December 31, section 1091 will apply to disallow the original loss.[30]

While this result seems in accord with the language of section 1091, it seems peculiarly out of place with the intent of section 1091. The intent behind section 1091 is to restrict a loss deduction if the taxpayer basically retains the same investment. In the above example, where T sold short stock that she did not in fact own, T's "investment" was in her guess that the value of ABC Corp. stock would go down, so that she could purchase for *less* than $100,000 the shares she would need to fulfill her obligation to Q, and then collect the full $100,000 from Q. T "lost" on her investment because her bet that ABC Corp. stock would go down turned out to be wrong. If after closing that transaction by purchasing Q stock for $150,000 and delivering it for only $100,000 T purchases additional ABC Corp. stock, she is in no way continuing her initial investment in her expectation that ABC would go down in value. Instead, she is reversing that investment, and now betting that ABC will go up in value. This does not seem to be anything like the kind of transaction that section 1091 was designed to attack.

[b] How Section 1091 Works

Section 1091 is actually a "disallowance" provision rather than a nonrecognition provision, in that it states that "no deduction shall be allowed under section 165" in the cases to which it applies.[31] Indeed, section 1091 could not easily have been drafted as a "nonrecognition" section; the primary reason for this result is that no one could be sure whether it applied at the time of the realized loss engendered by the sale of the loss securities. Since the selling taxpayer falls under section 1091 even if she does not acquire the substantially identical securities until as much as 29 days after the loss sale, section 1091 may apply not only in a different month, but even in a different taxable year than the initial sale. To go back in time to retroactively provide nonrecognition was more than Congress had hoped to accomplish by enacting section 1091.

Nonetheless, section 1091 functions as a nonrecognition section. While section 1091 prohibits the selling taxpayer from currently deducting her realized loss, it defers that loss rather than eliminating it, in the same manner as nonrecognition provisions. Section 1091(d) provides that the taxpayer's basis in the replacement shares is not a cost basis, but it is instead the taxpayer's basis in the shares sold, increased or decreased, as the case may be, by any difference between the price at

30. See § 1091(e).   **31.** § 1091(a).

which the loss shares were sold and the replacement shares are purchased. In other words, to the extent the taxpayer had to pay a net amount out-of-pocket for the replacement shares, her basis in those shares is increased. To the extent that the taxpayer was able to pocket any net difference between her selling price and her purchase price, her basis in the replacement shares is decreased. As with other nonrecognition provisions, any loss deferred (or, technically, "disallowed") by section 1091 is built into the replacement shares, and it will be recognized when those shares are sold. In addition, just as the taxpayer's basis in the replacement shares is determined by reference to her basis in the shares sold, her holding period for the replacement shares also includes the time during which she held the shares sold.

To see section 1091 in action, assume that T has owned 100 shares of ABC Corp. common stock for three years, and she has a basis of $100,000. On December 20, she sells those shares for their value of $70,000. On January 3 of the following year, she purchases another 100 shares of ABC Corp. common stock for $75,000. Because T has purchased substantially identical shares within 30 days of the loss sale, section 1091 applies to disallow the $30,000 realized loss on that sale. T's basis in the replacement shares is $105,000; this is simply her basis in the old shares ($100,000) increased by the extra $5,000 she paid for the replacement shares (because she received $70,000 for the old shares and paid $75,000 for the new shares, she has a net out-of-pocket cost of $5,000, which is added to her basis in the old shares in order to arrive at her basis in the replacement shares). If T sells the new shares for $50,000, she will recognize a loss of $55,000, which includes her deferred loss of $30,000 on the sale of the old shares, plus the $25,000 loss on the replacement shares (purchased for $75,000 and sold for $50,000). No matter when T sells the new shares, her loss will be long-term rather than short term; this is because she is treated as having held the replacement shares during the entire time she held the old shares.

If, in the above example, T paid only $65,000 for the replacement shares rather than $75,000 (because the stock went down, rather than up, in value between the time she sold her old shares and purchased the new ones), the original $30,000 loss would still be disallowed under section 1091. T's basis in the replacement shares would be $95,000 (her initial basis of $100,000 in the old shares, decreased by the $5,000 she was able to pocket because she sold the old shares for $70,000 and purchased the new ones for only $65,000). If she sells the replacement shares for $50,000, she can then deduct, as a long-term capital loss, $45,000, which represents the $30,000 disallowed loss plus the actual $15,000 loss on the replacement shares (purchased for $65,000 and sold for $50,000).

[4] SECTION 267: LOSSES ON SALES BETWEEN RELATED PARTIES

Another way that taxpayers have tried to deduct losses when they really had no interest in disposing of the loss property was to sell the property to family members or other closely related parties. If T had property with a basis of $400,000 and a value of $100,000 and had no desire to part with either the property or the perceived tax deduction that would be generated by a sale, she might sell the property to her spouse or children, or to her wholly-owned corporation. Prior to the enactment of Section 267, such a sale could generate a deductible loss while leaving the taxpayer with full access to and potentially full control over the property.

Section 267(a) responds to these situations by providing that "no deduction shall be allowed in respect of any loss from the sale or exchange of property" between certain related parties. Section 267(b) describes the relationships that invoke the section 267(a) restriction.

[a] Meaning of "Related Parties"

The relationships covered by section 267 include, but are not limited to, the taxpayer's family[32] (defined as siblings, spouse, ancestors and lineal descendants);[33] the taxpayer and a corporation (S corporation or C corporation) of which she owns more than 50% by value;[34] trusts and their fiduciaries and grantors;[35] and estates and their executors and beneficiaries[36] (other than a sale or exchange made by the estate in satisfaction of a pecuniary bequest).

Of course, if the rules were just that simple, sophisticated taxpayers could avoid the headaches of section 267 with relatively little work. Rather than sell loss property to the entities they control, or have those entities sell the loss property to them, individuals could arrange to have the entities they control, or persons they are otherwise closely related to (e.g., as grantor, fiduciary or beneficiary of a trust) sell or exchange loss properties between themselves. In order to prevent this, section 267(b) also includes certain relationships between corporations,[37] trusts (and their beneficiaries,[38] grantors[39] and fiduciaries[40]) subject to common ownership or other potential control or influence.[41]

[b] Attribution Rules of Section 267

Section 267(c) provides a fairly complicated set of attribution rules, under which taxpayers are *treated* as owning stock actually owned by others to whom they are closely related. Because these rules treat persons as owning only shares of stock that are in fact owned by other, closely related persons, they are relevant to determining the existence of "prohibited" relationships based on stock ownership, such as a shareholder and a corporation,[42] or two corporations under common control,[43]

---

32. § 267(b)(1).

33. § 267(c)(4).

34. § 267(b)(2).

35. § 267(b)(4) and (5).

36. § 267(b)(6) and (7).

37. § 267(b)(3), (11), (12). See also § 267(b)(10).

38. § 267(b)(6), (7).

39. § 267(b)(4), (7).

40. § 267(b)(4),(5),(6), (7), (8).

41. § 267(b).

42. § 267(b)(2).

43. § 267(b)(11), (12).

or a corporation and a partnership under common control.[44]

Under these attribution rules, owners of interests in entities (shareholders of corporations, partners in partnerships, and beneficiaries of estates and trusts, etc.) are treated as owning a proportionate share of any stock actually owned by those entities.[45] In other words, for purposes of determining the relationship between T and ABC Corp., if another corporation, for example X Corp., owns any shares of ABC Corp. and T owns any shares of X Corp., T will be treated as owning a proportion of the ABC shares owned by X Corp. So if T owns 10% of the outstanding shares of X Corp., and X Corp owns 6% of the shares of ABC Corp., T will be treated as owning 3% of the ABC shares in addition to any other shares she owns directly or indirectly. Any shares of a corporation (ABC Corporation, in this case) attributed to a person as a result of her ownership of shares of another corporation (X Corp., in this example), are treated as actually owned by the shareholder (T), and they may *then* be *again* attributed to still others under the section 267(c) attribution rules.[46]

In addition to the proportionate attribution from a corporation to a shareholder, section 267 includes two other attribution rules. An individual is treated as owning stock actually owned by members of her family,[47] as well as stock owned by any partners (that is, co-owners of a partnership) she has.[48] Shares treated as owned by a person (P) under either of these two rules will not be treated as owned by P for purposes of again attributing the shares from P to any other person, regardless of P's relationship with that other person.[49]

As a result of these rules, a taxpayer who sells property to a corporation may find that section 267 disallows a recognized loss on that sale even though she may directly own substantially less than 50% of the corporation's stock by value. For example, assume that T sells property (basis $100,000, value $70,000) to X Corp. Further assume that X Corp. is owned as follows: T's daughter—25%; T's partner (in an unrelated venture)—10%, and Y Corp.—40%. Finally assume that T's spouse owns 50% of the stock of Y Corp. Although T does not directly own any stock of X Corp., section 267 would nonetheless apply to deny T any loss on the sale. Under the attribution rules of section 267, T is treated as owning the 25% of X owned by her daughter, as well as the 10% owned by her partner. In addition, because T's spouse owns 50% of the stock of Y Corp., the spouse is treated as owning 50% of the stock actually owned by Y Corp. Since Y Corp. owns 40% of the stock of X Corp., T's spouse is treated as owning 50% of that 40%, or 20% of X Corp. Finally, because T is treated as owning all of the shares owned by her spouse, she is also treated as owning that 20% of X Corp. Altogether, T is treated as owning

44. § 267(b)(10).

45. § 267(c)(1).

46. § 267(c)(5).

47. § 267(c)(2). Family for purposes of § 267 includes siblings, spouse, ancestors and lineal descendents. § 267(c)(4).

48. § 267(c)(3).

49. § 267(c)(5).

55% of X Corp. (25% because it is owned by her daughter, 10% because it is owned by her partner, and 20% because it is attributed to her spouse under section 267(c)(1) and can then be reattributed to T under section 267(c)(2); accordingly section 267(a) would deny any loss on the sale from T to X.

Note that T's deemed ownership of more than 50% of the X stock might affect more than simply sales by T to X. Section 267 would also disallow a loss if property were sold to X Corp. not by T, but by a different corporation of which T was a more than 50% owner.[50]

[c] Indirect Sales

Not surprisingly, the taxpayer who uses an intermediary to sell property at a loss to a related party will be disallowed that loss, at least if the Service becomes aware of the entire transaction. The substance rather than the form of the transaction will govern the tax consequences, and if the substance is a sale to a related party, section 267 will apply regardless of the presence of an unrelated intermediary.[51]

More interesting than use of an intermediary to disguise a sale between related parties was the case of McWilliams v. Commissioner.[52] In that case, the taxpayer sold stock on a stock exchange and directed his broker to immediately buy an equal number of identical shares for his wife's account. The taxpayer argued, and the Supreme Court appeared to accept, that the sale and purchase did not constitute a "wash sale" made nondeductible by section 1091, because the taxpayer who sold the shares at a loss did not purchase replacement shares within the 61 day time period. After all, it was the taxpayer's wife, and not he, who made the purchase.

Nonetheless, the taxpayer failed to persuade the Supreme Court he ought to be allowed to deduct his loss on the initial sale; the Court determined that section 267(a) was more than sufficient to deny the sought-after loss deduction. The Court based its decision on the fact that section 267(a) disallows losses from the sale or exchange of property "directly or indirectly, between related parties." The Court looked to the legislative history of section 267, which strongly suggested that Congress wanted to put an end to loss deductions arising out of intra-family sales, regardless of the form those sales took. The fact that the taxpayer's wife ended up with different actual shares because all of the actual shares were sold and bought on a stock exchange was found to be on no consequence to the Court.

50. § 267(b)(3),(f); § 1563(a)(2). This impact would actually be the result of attribution rules contained in § 1563 rather than those of § 267, but the rules are similar in relevant part.

51. There is some question, though, of when a third party should be viewed as "an intermediary" facilitating a sale between related parties. In a few cases, loss property owned by the taxpayer has been seized and sold to pay an obligation, and the purchase has been a party related to the original owner. The courts are in some disagreement as to whether this combination of factors ought to be treated as a "sale, direct or indirect," subject to § 267.

52. 331 U.S. 694, 67 S.Ct. 1477, 91 L.Ed. 1750 (1947).

[d] Purchaser's Basis

Unlike nonrecognition provisions, section 267 does not merely defer the taxpayer's loss; instead, if applicable, it extinguishes any otherwise applicable losses. This is because the taxpayer is allowed no deduction for loss on the sale to the related party, and the purchaser's basis in the property is her cost for the property under section 1011 rather than the seller's basis. Ultimately, the loss is eliminated rather than simply deferred because after the sale to the related party, the taxpayer no longer owns the property. To build the disallowed loss into the property in the hands of the transferee would be to allow the taxpayer to essentially transfer to the related transferee whatever loss deduction was in the property. An owner of property that has declined in value cannot transfer that loss by giving a gift.[53] Section 267 is consistent in that it also prevents the taxpayer from selling a loss deduction to the related party.[54]

While section 267 does not permit the related purchaser to deduct the seller's disallowed loss, it does grant some relief for purchasers from related parties in some instances. Section 267(d) provides that if the purchaser of loss property from a related person later sells that property at a gain (because her amount realized exceeds her cost basis in the property), she will recognize no gain except and to the extent that her recognized gain on the sale exceeds the loss disallowed to related seller on the original transaction. In other words, assuming the property's basis does not otherwise change (as a result of depreciation, untaxed damage awards, or casualty losses, etc.) the related purchaser in a section 267 sale will recognize gain on a subsequent sale of the property only if and to the extent that she sells the property for an amount in excess of the original related party-seller's basis. This limitation on the amount of gain recognized on a subsequent sale applies only to a subsequent sale by the original purchaser of the loss property. If that related purchaser transfers the property to any other taxpayer, whether by sale, gift, or inter-spousal transfer, any gain realized on the sale will be recognized.

To see how these provisions apply, assume that T owns land (basis $400,000, value $100,000), which she sells to her sister S for $100,000. Because sisters are considered members of a family under section 267(c)(4), T's $300,000 realized loss is disallowed, and S takes the property with a cost basis of $100,000. If S sells the property for any amount less than $100,000, she will recognize a loss equal to the excess of $100,000 over her amount realized. If S sells the property for any amount in excess of $400,000 she will recognize a gain equal to the excess of her amount realized over $400,000. If S sells the property for

53. The donee's basis for loss is the lesser of the donor's basis or the fair market value at the time of transfer. § 1015.

54. While § 267 is consistent with § 1015, in that they do not allow taxpayers to transfer losses inherent in property to other taxpayers, both of these sections seem inconsistent with the fact that taxpayers can readily transfer appreciated property and built-in gains to whomever they want. See § 1015.

any amount equal to or greater than her own cost basis but not more than T's original basis of $400,000, she will recognize no loss (because her amount realized is greater than her cost basis), but she will also recognize no gain, because of section 267(d).[55] If S transfers the property as a gift, for example back to T, the donee will recognize a gain to the extent that her amount realized exceeds S's $100,000 cost basis. Neither T nor any other donee can take advantage of section 267(d).

[5] CAPITALIZATION AND SECTION 280B

As any other potential deductions, losses may be subject to the capitalization requirement. Of course when the taxpayer incurs a loss on the sale or exchange of property it is difficult to see how the loss could be capitalized, because the taxpayer has disposed of the property.

At one time, capitalization became an issue (now resolved) with respect to the demolition of buildings. Taxpayers contended that when they demolished a building, they suffered a deductible loss equal to their basis in the building. Taxpayers proffered that they had owned an asset, the asset was now gone, and, accordingly, there was a realization event. As result, these taxpayers' losses were realized, recognized and currently deductible.

Section 280B brought an end to these shenanigans. Congress determined that demolishing an existing structure is not a deductible loss with respect to the former structure. Instead, for tax purposes, it is part of the cost of obtaining vacant land, whether the taxpayer owns the land or is merely a tenant. Regardless of the cost of the building and regardless of the taxpayer's intent when she acquired the building, no deduction is available as a result of its demolition.[56] Section 280B makes this clear by stating that "in the case of the demolition of any structure, no deduction ... shall be allowed to the owner or lessee ... for any amount expended for such demolition, or any loss sustained on account of such demolition."[57] Instead, any expenses of demolition, as well as the taxpayer's basis in the demolished structure, must be capitalized as part of the cost to the taxpayer of the underlying land.[58]

---

55. Compare the determination of the donee's basis for loss under § 1015.

56. § 280B(a)(1) and (2).

57. Id.

58. § 280B(b).

Chapter 13

DEFERRED COMPENSATION

Table of Sections

§ 13.01 PURPOSE AND TYPES OF ARRANGEMENTS

The purpose of a deferred compensation arrangement is twofold. First, it provides an employee with income upon retirement. Second, such an arrangement defers income to a time when the recipient's tax rate may be lower.

Compensation may generally be deferred through three types of arrangements: (1) plans that are qualified under the Internal Revenue Code, (2) nonqualified deferred compensation plans, and (3) stock options. Each of the foregoing is discussed in this chapter.

§ 13.02 QUALIFIED PLANS

[1] IN GENERAL

A qualified plan[1] has several advantages. Contributions to a qualified plan on behalf of an employee are not taxable and neither is the income from the amounts that have been contributed.[2] The employee is not taxed until payment is received.[3] The employer, on the other hand, is entitled to a current deduction for a contribution.[4] These advantages of qualified plans are conditioned upon strict compliance with the requirements of the Internal Revenue Code, particularly section 401 which contains the plan qualification rules. Additionally, there are provisions applicable to both qualified and nonqualified plans in Title 29 of the United States Code; the Department of Labor administers these provisions.

§ 13.02

1. A qualified plan is one that meets the requirements of § 401(a). Treas. Reg. § 1.401–0(b)(1).

2. § 401(a)(1).

3. § 402(a).

4. §§ 404(a)(1), 404(a)(2), 404(a)(3), 404(a)(6). *Nota bene:* to be deductible, pension payments along with other compensation must meet the reasonableness requirement of § 162.

The legislative dichotomy of the qualified plan rules resulted from the enactment of the Employee Retirement Income Security Act (ERISA). "Congress enacted ERISA to protect working men and women from abuses in the administration and investment of private retirement plans and employee welfare plans."[5] These abuses included inept and corrupt management of pension funds and the exclusion of large numbers of employees, usually blue collar or clerical employees, from the benefits of their employers' pension plans; ERISA sought to remedy the abuses in a number of ways.[6]

First, ERISA limits an employer's ability to impose eligibility requirements, such as minimum or maximum age requirements or years of service requirements, that prevented an employee from participating in a qualified plan. Second, ERISA requires an employee to have a *nonforfeitable* right to accrued benefits after a certain number of years of participation in the plan. Third, ERISA imposes minimum funding standards to assure that a plan is financially sound. Fourth, ERISA imposes detailed fiduciary standards for those in charge of plan assets. Fifth, ERISA imposes strict reporting and disclosure requirements. Finally, ERISA established a system of plan insurance administered by a federal agency, the Pension Benefit Guaranty Corporation.

Although ERISA does not require employers to adopt pension plans, those who chose to do so are subject to the administrative restrictions established by the Department of Labor under Title I of ERISA. In addition, the plan must comply with the Internal Revenue Code if it is to qualify for tax-preferred status. Most plans are subject to both sets of restrictions.[7] However, a plan that is not intended to be tax qualified will nevertheless be subject to Title I of ERISA.

One of the purposes behind the qualified-plan provisions in the Internal Revenue Code is to foster a strong private pension system.[8] The tax benefits afforded qualified plans encourage their establishment.[9] However, the propensity of employers might be to establish plans benefiting only officers, shareholders, and highly compensated employees, leaving out rank-and-file employees. Thus, many, if not most, workers would not be covered by private pension plans. Congress realized this, and it therefore decided to require that any plan, in order to be qualified, must not discriminate in favor of officers, shareholders, or highly compensated employees.[10] The objective of encouraging a private pension system that covers most employees should not be forgotten in the study

5. Donovan v. Dillingham 688 F.2d 1367, 1370 (11th Cir. 1982). See also H.R. Rep. No. 93–533, 93d Cong. 2d Sess., reprinted in 1974 U.S. Code Cong. and Admin. News 4639.

6. H.R. Rep. No. 93–533, 93d Cong. 2d Sess., reprinted in 1974 U.S. Code Cong. and Admin. News 4639.

7. Much of Title I of ERISA is identical to the qualified-plan provisions of the Internal Revenue Code.

8. H.R. Rep. No. 93–533, 93d Cong. 2d Sess., reprinted in 1974 U.S. Code Cong. and Admin. News.

9. See Plucinski v. I.A.M. Nat'l Pension Fund, 875 F.2d 1052, 1058 (3d Cir. 1989).

10. See § 401(a)(4).

of the highly technical Internal Revenue Code provisions concerning qualified plans.

[2] COMMON TYPES OF QUALIFIED PLANS

Pension, profit-sharing, and stock-bonus plans must meet the requirements of section 401 in order to be qualified.[11] Qualified pension plans may be classified as either defined benefit or defined contribution plans. Under a defined benefit plan the amount a retired employee is entitled to receive is based on such factors as years of service or average compensation.[12] Accordingly, with a defined benefit plan, employer contributions are determined in a manner actuarially consistent with the minimum funding standards of section 412 and the limitations of section 415. Under a defined contribution plan each employee has an account and the employer makes contributions determined by a stipulated formula.[13] Hence with a defined contribution plan, a retired employee is entitled only to the account balance, consisting of the contributions plus investment income, rather than a predetermined amount.

[a] Profit–Sharing Plans

Regulation section 1.401–1(a)(2)(ii) describes a profit-sharing plan as enabling "employees ... to participate in the profits of the employer's trade or business ... pursuant to a definite formula for allocating contributions and for distributing the funds accumulated under the plan." A profit-sharing plan may provide incidental life, accident, or health insurance; its primary purpose, however, is to defer compensation.[14] The determination of whether a plan is a profit-sharing plan is made without regard to current or accumulated profits of the employer and without regard to whether the employer is a tax-exempt organization.[15]

The benefits from a profit-sharing plan may be distributed after a fixed number of years, the attainment of a certain age,[16] or the occurrence of a stated event such as death, disability, retirement, or severance of employment.[17] The Service has interpreted the words "fixed number of years" used in the regulations to mean that distributions may be made after as little as two years.[18]

[b] Stock–Bonus Plans

A stock-bonus plan provides benefits similar to a profit-sharing plan except that contributions and distributions are generally made in the

---

11. See § 401(a).

12. See § 414(j); 29 U.S.C. § 1002(35).

13. See § 414(i); 29 U.S.C. § 1002(34).

14. Treas. Reg. § 1.401–1(b)(1)(ii).

15. § 401(a)(27).

16. See Rev. Rul. 80–276, 1980–2 C.B. 131 (profit-sharing plan distributions made at age 55).

17. Treas. Reg. § 1.401–1(b)(1)(ii). Distributions before death, disability, or retirement are generally subject to a 10% excise tax. § 72(t).

18. Rev. Rul. 71–295, 1971–2 C.B. 184.

stock of the employer.[19] Distributions may be made in cash, but only if the requirements 409(h) and (o) are met.[20]

[c] Pension Plans

Regulation section 1.401–1(b)(1)(i) provides that a pension plan is "established ... primarily to provide systematically for the payment of definitely determinable benefits to ... employees over a period of years, usually for life, after retirement." Thus, a pension plan is generally prohibited from making distributions before retirement.[21] A pension plan may provide incidental medical benefits to a retired employee if the plan complies with the requirements of section 401(h).[22] Death benefits payable to a beneficiary upon the death of an employee must be incidental to the primary purpose of providing retirement benefits.[23]

[d] Target–Benefit Plans

A target-benefit pension plan is similar to both a defined contribution plan and a defined benefit plan.[24] A target-benefit plan is funded like a defined benefit plan in that the annual contribution is an actuarially determined amount designed to produce a defined benefit at retirement.[25] A target-benefit plan also resembles a defined contribution plan in that at retirement the employee is entitled only to the account balance.[26] Thus, the benefit at retirement is not defined; instead it is targeted and the actual account balance may be greater or lesser than the target.[27] For some purposes the Code treats target-benefit plans like defined contribution plans, and for other purposes the Code treats them like defined benefit plans.[28]

[e] Employee Stock Ownership Plans

An employee stock ownership plan (ESOP)[29] is a type of stock-bonus plan. Because of the potential for abuse and the risk involved, the ERISA fiduciary standards generally prohibit investment in securities of the employer and mandate diversification of the plan's investments.[30] An exception is provided, however, for plans that invest primarily in securities of the employer.[31] The alleged virtues of ESOPs include enhanced

---

19. Treas. Reg. § 1.401–1(b)(1)(iii).

20. § 401(a)(23).

21. See Treas. Reg. § 1.401–1(b)(i).

22. Id.

23. Id. Generally, the present value of payments to be made to the participant, as distinguished from beneficiaries, must be greater than 50% of the total present value of all payments. Rev. Rul. 72–241, 1972–1 C.B. 108

24. Rev. Rul. 76–464, 1976–2 C.B. 115.

25. Id.

26. Id.

27. Id.

28. See Hira & Perry, Target Benefit Plans: An Appealing Option for Small Employers, 18 Tax Adviser 330 (1987).

29. An ESOP is defined in § 4975(e)(7).

30. § 4975(a) and (b) imposes an excise tax on certain prohibited transactions such as those between a plan and the employer or fiduciary. ERISA, 29 U.S.C.A. § 1107, permits a profit-sharing plan to hold not more than 10% in value of qualifying employer securities.

31. See § 409(a)(2).

employee productivity and increased savings and investment.[32] Many special rules are applicable to ESOPs.[33]

[f] 401(k) Plans

Normally, an employee would be taxed on income if he had the choice of taking cash or deferring an amount.[34] Unless such an arrangement is qualified, the employee is currently taxed because he had control over the disposition of the money, and because there was no substantial risk of forfeiture.[35] However, under conditions specified in section 401(k) an employee may be given a choice between cash or deferral of funds into a profit-sharing or stock-bonus plan. Amounts that are deferred generally may not be distributed prior to retirement, death, disability, separation from service, or age 59½ (unless hardship can be shown).[36] The amounts deferred must also be nonforfeitable.[37] Furthermore, the deferral percentage for highly compensated employees may not be greater than 1.25 times the deferral percentage of other eligible employees or 2 times the deferral percentage of other eligible employees but not more than 2%.[38] Hence, section 401(k)(3)(ii) prevents plans from discriminating in favor of highly compensated employees. The amount that may be deferred under a section 401(k) or other elective deferral arrangement is limited to $15,000 a year for each employee.[39]

[g] Other Qualified Plans

A plan can be funded in a number of ways. One conventional way is for the employer to contribute funds to a trust for the benefit of employees.[40] The plan administrator then invests the trust funds.

Section 401(a) seems to limit qualified plans to funding through trusts. However section 401(f), supports an alternative interpretation. For example, a common method of funding is to invest in annuity contracts; i.e., contracts that pay a fixed sum over a period of years. Distributions under an annuity contract usually begin at retirement. A trust may purchase annuity contracts and pay the premiums. If the employer purchases the annuities and holds them without a trust, section 401(a) is not directly applicable because it refers only to trusts. However, under section 401(f) a nontrusteed annuity plan is treated like a section 401(a) trust so long as all other requirements for qualification are met except those specific to a trust. Moreover, section 403(a)(1)

32. For a critique of nontax benefits claimed by ESOP supporters, see Doernberg & Macey, 23 Harv. J. on Legis. 103, 121–43 (1986).

33. See § 409 for restrictions on ESOPs. Although § 409 on its face applies only to "tax-credit" ESOPs, § 4975(e)(7) makes certain requirements under § 409 applicable to ESOPs generally.

34. See generally § 61(a)(1).

35. See § 83(a).

36. § 401(k)(2)(B). Correlatively, amounts must not be distributable merely by reason of completion of a stated period of participation or lapse of a fixed number of years. Id.

37. § 401(k)(2)(C).

38. § 401(k)(3)(ii).

39. § 402(g)(1)(B).

40. A qualified trust is one that meets the requirements of § 401(a). Treas. Reg. § 1.401–0(b)(2).

provides that an employee is taxed under an annuity plan in the same manner as under a qualified trust,[41] and section 404(a)(2) provides that an employer's current deduction for the purchase of annuities is permitted so long as the plan meets the other qualification requirements.

[h] Individual Retirement Accounts

Section 219 permits a deduction of up to $5,000 a year for contributions to an individual retirement account (IRA),[42] and section 408(e)(1) exempts IRAs from tax. Moreover, IRA distributions are taxed in the same manner as other qualified-plan distributions under section 72.[43] The full deduction is allowable only if an individual is either not an active participant in a qualified plan or, if covered, has adjusted gross income not exceeding $50,000 if single and $80,000 if a joint return is filed.[44] The deduction is phased out for adjusted gross income above these amounts. Nondeductible contributions may, however, be made up to the contribution limit, allowing income to build up in the IRA tax-free.[45]

[i] Roth IRAs

Roth IRAs provide taxpayers with a vehicle to obtain retirement distributions which are entirely nontaxable.[46] However, unlike contributions to traditional IRAs, contributions to Roth IRAs are not deductible.[47] Contributions to Roth IRAs are limited to $5,000 per year.[48]

[j] Simplified Employee Pensions

The simplified employee pension (SEP) is provided for in section 408(j), (k), and (l). In effect, SEPs are IRAs to which an employer makes deductible contributions. The employer may make contributions using the limitation under section 415(c)(1)(A) for defined contribution plans.[49] Contributions to SEPs may not discriminate in favor of highly compensated employees[50] and must bear a uniform relationship, under a written formula, to total compensation not in excess of $225,000.[51] SEPs, unlike IRAs, have participation requirements. An employer must make contributions to a SEP for the taxable year for all employees who are: (1) over the age of 21, (2) have performed service for the employer for at least three of the immediately preceding five years, and (3) have received at

---

41. In addition to annuity plans there are tax-deferred annuities under section 403(b). These are available only to section 501(c)(3) charitable organizations, public schools, or state agencies. These employers may purchase annuities for their employees, and the employees are taxed as if covered under a qualified plan.

42. § 219(b)(5)(A).

43. § 408(d)(1). The rules for required distributions are similar to those in § 401(a)(9). § 408(a)(6).

44. § 219(g). The amount is $40,000 for a joint return and zero for a married individual filing separately.

45. § 408(o), (e)(1).

46. § 408A(d)(1)(A).

47. § 408A(c)(1).

48. § 408A(c)(2) (referencing § 219(b)(5)(A)).

49. § 408(j).

50. § 408(k)(3).

51. § 408(k)(3)(C), (5).

least $500 in compensation during the year.[52] A SEP may include a 401(k) plan if the employer has less than 25 employees and at least 50% of the employees actually participate.[53]

[3] REQUIREMENTS FOR QUALIFICATION

A plan may receive the benefits of qualification only if it meets the requirements of section 401(a). Before enumerating the substantive requirements, section 401(a)(1) sets forth five prerequisites. Under section 401(a) here must be: (1) a trust, (2) created or organized in the United States, (3) forming part of a stock bonus, pension, or profit-sharing plan, (4) of an employer, and (5) for the exclusive benefit of employees. Perhaps, the most important of these prerequisites is that of a "plan." Section 1.401–1(a)(2) of the regulations defines a "plan" as "a definite written program and arrangement which is communicated to the employees and which is established and maintained by an employer." The Tax Court interpreted the regulation in Engineered Timber Sales, Inc. v. Commissioner.[54]

In Engineered Timber Sales the Commissioner disallowed a deduction to a supposedly qualified profit-sharing plan because the plan had not come into existence. The taxpayer argued that the agreement by the Board of Directors to adopt a plan, execute a trust instrument, notify the employees, and deposit funds in the trust were sufficient to satisfy section 401(a). The Tax Court rejected the taxpayer's argument and held that creation of a plan requires affirmative intent and conduct in the form of a written, permanent, and specific program. No provisions were contained in the trust for plan eligibility requirements, participation requirements, or vesting schedules. In addition, no plan instrument was in existence, and no other writings contained any definite provisions. The Tax Court reasoned that Congress had endorsed the administrative position taken in the regulations because any plan with vague and tenuous provisions would make employee enforceability difficult.

Additionally, a plan must be established and maintained by the employer. In Times Publishing Company v. Commissioner[55] the court held that a plan established by the employees to which the employer contributed did not qualify.

The benefits in a defined benefit pension plan, the contributions in a money-purchase plan, and the allocation of contributions in a stock-bonus or profit-sharing plan must be specific. In pension plans the benefits must be "definitely determinable."[56] This means that the benefit in a defined benefit plan must be based on a formula using factors

---

52. § 408(k)(2).

53. § 408(k)(6).

54. 74 T.C. 808 (1980).

55. 13 T.C. 329 (1949), aff'd without opinion, 184 F.2d 376 (3d Cir. 1950).

56. Treas. Reg. § 1.401–1(b)(1)(i). See Rev. Rul. 71–24, 1971–1 C.B. 114 (benefits definitely determinable if participant may elect to have trustee invest funds at retirement); Rev. Rul. 80–122, 1980–1 C.B. 84 (benefits definitely determinable even if there is a suspension during which social security benefits are discontinued on account of employment after retirement because no employer discretion).

such as years of service and the amount of compensation.[57] For example, a plan may provide upon an employee's retirement an annuity of $500 a month for each year of service with the employer. Generally, any formula used must preclude employer discretion.[58] For a defined contribution pension plan, contributions must be fixed in order to be "definitely determinable."[59] For stock-bonus and profit-sharing plans a definite predetermined formula must be established to allocate the contributions among the participants.[60] The regulations use the example of allocating in proportion to the compensation of each participant.[61] Defined contribution pension, profit-sharing, and stock-bonus plans must keep individual accounts for each participant.

The plan must be permanent and must not be abandoned except for business necessity.[62] This can cause problems with respect to profit-sharing plans because contributions to such plans may be discretionary or contingent on profits. The regulations state that contributions to a profit-sharing plan must be recurring and substantial for the plan to be qualified.[63] Therefore, even though an employer may not have intended to terminate a profit-sharing plan, the consistent lack of substantial contributions to the plan, especially in profitable years, could cause a technical termination of the plan.[64]

In addition to the five prerequisites detailed heretofore, a plan must satisfy the substantive requirements set forth in the numerous paragraphs of section 401(a).

[a] Purpose

Under section 401(a)(1) a trust must be created by an employer for the purpose of making distributions to its employees or the employee's beneficiaries.

[b] No Diversion and Exclusive Benefit

Section 401(a)(2) requires that the trust instrument preclude the use or diversion of trust funds for any purpose other than the exclusive benefit of employees or their beneficiaries. This rule has two parts. First, the Code prohibits any diversion of trust funds. ERISA permits a contribution to be returned to the employer within one year if: (1) the contribution is made through a mistake of fact, (2) the contribution is conditioned on plan qualification and the plan does not qualify, or (3) the contribution is conditioned on deductibility.[65] The second part of section 401(a)(2) is the exclusive-benefit rule. It has been interpreted to mean

---

57. See Treas. Reg. § 1.401–1(b)(1)(i).

58. Id.

59. Rev. Rul. 80–155, 1980–1 C.B. 84 (plan assets must be valued and earnings credited to employee accounts at least yearly using a uniform method and time of valuation).

60. See Treas. Reg. § 1.401–1(b)(1)(ii) and (iii).

61. Treas. Reg. § 1.401–1(b)(1)(ii).

62. Treas. Reg. § 1.401–1(b)(2).

63. Id.

64. Plan terminations are discussed below.

65. 29 U.S.C.A. § 1103(c)(2).

that only employees or their beneficiaries benefit from the plan; i.e., the employer should receive no direct or indirect benefit.

[c] Participation

Section 401(a)(3) states that a plan must comply with the requirements of section 410. A plan will meet the requirements of section 410 if the plan satisfies the requirements on at least one day during each quarter of the taxable year.[66] Section 410 consists of the minimum-participation requirements of section 410(a) and the minimum-eligibility requirements of section 410(b).

Under section 410(a)(1)(A) a qualified plan may not require as a condition of participation a period of service beyond the later of the date the employee completes one year of service or the date the employee reaches age 21. However, a plan may provide a two-year-service requirement for participation if the employee is 100% vested in the accrued benefit after two years of service.[67] Additionally, section 410(a)(2) requires qualified plans to have no maximum age restrictions.

After the employee satisfies the requirement for the minimum period of service or minimum age, section 410(a)(4) requires that an employee begin participating in the plan no later than the earlier of the first day of the plan year beginning after the date the employee satisfied such requirement or the date six months after the employee satisfied such requirement.[68] If, however, the employee is separated from service before either of these two dates, no plan participation is required.[69]

In addition to the age or service requirement, eligibility to participate in the plan must be available on a nondiscriminatory basis.[70] Section 410(b) requires a plan to satisfy one of two numerical tests or a more subjective nondiscriminatory classification test.

Section 410(b)(1)(A) sets out the numerical eligibility tests. For purposes of the eligibility rules certain employees may be excluded from the numerical calculations.[71] For example, employees who have not satisfied the plan's minimum age or service conditions may be excluded.[72] Thus, the numerical tests are based on the number of employees after exclusions, not on the total number of employees.

The numerical tests in section 410(b)(1) provide that either (A) "The plan benefits at least 70 percent of employees who are not highly compensated employees"[73] or (B) "The plan benefits a percentage of employees who are not highly compensated employees which is at least 70 percent of the percentage of highly compensated employees benefiting under the plan."[74]

---

66. § 401(a)(6).

67. § 410(a)(1)(B).

68. See Rev. Rul. 80–360, 1980–2 C.B. 142, in which the Service interprets § 410(a)(4).

69. § 410(a)(4) (flush language).

70. See § 410(b).

71. See § 410(b)(3) and (4).

72. § 410(b)(4)(A).

73. § 410(b)(1)(A).

74. § 410(b)(1)(B).

Hence, in order to satisfy the requirements of section 410(b)(1), a plan must cover a fair cross section of all employees in all compensation ranges in order to meet the classification test. The regulations refer to a facts-and-circumstances test.[75] This test allows a reasonable difference between the ratio of prohibited group participants to all prohibited group employees compared with the ratio of other employee participants to all other employees.[76] The ratio test is only one of the factors to be considered. Under section 401(a)(5)(A) a classification is not discriminatory merely because it includes only salaried or clerical workers or because it excludes wage earners. However, such classification may be discriminatory if other factors are involved.

For purposes of section 410 a "highly compensated employee" is defined generally in section 414(q) as any employee who during the taxable year or preceding taxable year (1) was at any time a 5% owner[77] or (2) received compensation from the employer in excess of the applicable amount[78] and was in the top-paid group (generally top 20%) of all employees.[79]

Section 410(b) sets out three alternate coverage tests. Under the first test the plan must benefit 70% of all nonhighly compensated employees.[80] Under the second test the percentage of nonhighly compensated employees benefiting under the plan must be at least 70% of the percentage of highly compensated employees benefiting under the plan.[81] For example, if the plan benefits 90% of the highly compensated employees, at least 63% of the rank-and-file employees must benefit. The third test is an average-benefit-percentage test.[82] Under section 410(b)(2), the plan must benefit "such employees as qualify under a classification set up by the employer and found by the Secretary not to be discriminatory in favor of highly compensated employees,"[83] and the average benefit percentage for employees who are nonhighly compensated employees must be "at least 70 percent of the average benefit percentage for highly compensated employees."[84] The average benefit percentage with respect to any group refers to the average of the benefit percentages calculated separately for each employee in the group without regard to whether an employee is a participant in a plan.[85] Hence, if a rank-and-file employee does not participate, his benefit will be averaged in at zero.[86] If too many nonhighly compensated employees do not participate, the zeros averaged in will quickly drop the average benefit percentage for the rank-and-file.[87]

75. Treas. Reg. § 1.410(b)–1(d)(2).

76. Id.

77. § 414(q)(1)(A).

78. Note the amount listed in § 414(q)(1) is $80,000, but it is indexed for inflation. § 414(q)(1) (flush language).

79. § 410(b)(6)(A) (referring to § 414(q)).

80. § 410(b)(1)(A).

81. § 410(b)(1)(B)(i) and (ii).

82. See § 410(b)(2).

83. § 410(b)(2)(A)(i).

84. § 410(b)(2)(A)(ii).

85. § 410(b)(2)(B).

86. See § 410(b)(2)(B).

87. Id.

The minimum coverage rules of section 410(b) may be applied separately to each of an employer's separate lines of business.[88] Nevertheless, each plan covering employees in a separate line of business must meet a nondiscriminatory classification test.[89] A separate line of business is defined in section 414(r) as a separate line operated for bona fide business reasons and having at least 50 employees.[90] Additionally, the line of business must meet guidelines prescribed by the Service or receive a determination letter concerning the highly/nonhighly compensated makeup of the line or, alternatively, meet a safe-harbor test.[91] The safe harbor is met if the highly compensated employee percentage of the line of business is not less than half or more than twice the percentage for all employees of the employer.[92] This precludes separation of highly and nonhighly compensated employees through artificial separate lines of business.

Section 401(a)(26) provides that a trust must benefit the lesser of 50 employees[93] "the greater of 40% of all employees of the employer, or 2 employees (or if there is only 1 employee, such employee)."[94] This rule is designed to prohibit qualification if the plan, even though nondiscriminatory, does not benefit employees in general. Ultimately, if a trust is not exempt because it fails to meet the requirements of section 401(a)(26) (or section 410(b)), only highly compensated employees suffer the effects of nonexemption.[95]

[d] Discrimination

Section 401(a)(4) prohibits discrimination in contributions or benefits in favor of the prohibited group. The discrimination problems encountered under section 401(a)(4) are similar to the problems in section 410(b).[96] Nevertheless, a few differences exist. Section 410(b) compares non-covered employees with covered employees while section 401(a)(4) is concerned with discrimination among covered employees only.[97] In addition, a finding of discrimination under section 410(b) is more difficult to overturn than a finding under section 401(a)(4). Under section 410(b) a taxpayer must show that a finding was unreasonable, arbitrary, or an abuse of discretion. In E. F. Higgins & Company v.

88. § 414(b)(5).

89. § 414(b)(5)(A).

90. See § 410(b)(5)(A) (referring to § 414(r)).

91. § 414(r)(2)(C).

92. § 414(r)(3)(A)(i) and (ii).

93. § 401(a)(26)(A)(i).

94. § 401(a)(26)(A)(ii).

95. § 402(b)(4).

96. In Rev. Rul. 79–348, 1979–2 C.B. 161, the Service held that because a pension plan met the coverage requirements of § 410(b)(1)(A) the plan's failure to provide benefits for ineligible employees would not cause the plan to be discriminatory within the meaning of § 401(a)(4).

97. Contributions may discriminate in a defined benefit plan because of actuarial funding differences. Only the benefit need be nondiscriminatory. Rev. Rul. 74–142, 1974–1 C.B. 95. However, differences in distributions among the prohibited group and rank-and-file employees will cause the prohibited discrimination. Rev. Rul. 85–59, 1985–1 C.B. 135. Discrimination in availability of employer stock that participants may elect to have the trustee purchase for their accounts is not permitted. Rev. Rul. 71–93, 1971–1 C.B. 122.

Commissioner[98] the Tax Court stated that the statutory authority granted to the Service in section 410(b) to determine discriminatory classifications is lacking in section 401(a)(4) cases. Accordingly, the Service's findings merit less judicial deference in section 401(a)(4) cases.[99]

For purposes of section 401(a)(4) a "highly compensated employee" is defined generally in section 414(q) as any employee who during the taxable year or preceding taxable year (1) was at any time a 5% owner[100] or (2) received compensation from the employer in excess of the applicable amount[101] and was in the top-paid group (generally top 20%) of all employees.[102]

A companion provision to the nondiscrimination provision of section 401(a)(4) is section 401(a)(5). Section 401(a)(5) specifies some of the arrangements that are permitted, assuming other factors do not cause the plan to be found discriminatory. Section 401(a)(5)(B) provides that a plan will not be considered discriminatory merely because contributions or benefits bear a uniform relationship to total or basic compensation. Hence, section 401(a)(5)(B) permits individuals with larger salaries to receive large benefits without the plan being discriminatory. However, other factors may nevertheless cause a plan to be discriminatory. This problem is demonstrated in Auner v. United States.[103]

Auner involved a profit-sharing plan with a fixed allocation of contributions based on compensation, years of service, and experience. As a result, the contributions on behalf of 3 of 4 members of the prohibited group ranged from 12% to 20% of compensation. The contributions on behalf of the other employees were between 2% and 7% of compensation. The Seventh Circuit said that "a plan must be deemed to discriminate where the ratio of allocation to compensation is substantially higher for those named in section 401(a)(4) than for other employees."[104] The Seventh Circuit added that business objectives, such as attracting competent personnel and creating an incentive for further education, would not prevent a plan from being found to discriminate in favor of the prohibited group.

---

98. 74 T.C. 1029 (1980), aff'd without opinion, 661 F.2d 914 (3d Cir. 1981). See also Federal Land Bank Ass'n of Asheville v. Commissioner, 74 T.C. 1106 (1980); Michael W. Melton, Making the Nondiscrimination Rules of Tax–Qualified Retirement Plans More Effective, 71 B.U. L. Rev. 47, 130 (1991); Bruce Wolk, Discrimination Rules for Qualified Retirement Plans: Good Intentions Confront Economic Reality, 70 Va. L. Rev. 419, 471 (1984).

99. See E. F. Higgins & Company v. Commissioner, 74 T.C. 1029 (1980), aff'd without opinion, 661 F.2d 914 (3d Cir. 1981). See also Federal Land Bank Ass'n of Asheville v. Commissioner, 74 T.C. 1106 (1980); Michael W. Melton, Making the Nondiscrimination Rules of Tax–Qualified Retirement Plans More Effective, 71 B.U.

L. Rev. 47, 130 (1991); Bruce Wolk, Discrimination Rules for Qualified Retirement Plans: Good Intentions Confront Economic Reality, 70 Va. L. Rev. 419, 471 (1984).

100. § 414(q)(1)(A).

101. Note the amount listed in § 414(q)(1) is $80,000, but it is indexed for inflation. § 414(q)(1) (flush language).

102. § 401(a)(4) (referring to § 414(q)).

103. 440 F.2d 516 (7th Cir. 1971); see also Michael W. Melton, Making the Nondiscrimination Rules of Tax–Qualified Retirement Plans More Effective, 71 B.U. L. Rev. 47, 130 (1991).

104. 440 F.2d 516, 519 (7th Cir. 1971).

Section 414(s) defines the term "compensation;" it includes compensation for services currently includible in gross income.[105] Thus, deferred compensation is generally not counted.[106] Section 414(s)(3) states that the regulations "shall ... provide for alternative methods of determining compensation" if an employer may not discriminate in favor of the prohibited group.

[e] Vesting

Under section 401(a)(7) a plan must comply with the minimum vesting requirements of section 411 to be a qualified plan. Plan benefits vest in a participant when he has a nonforfeitable right to the benefits. Before ERISA it was common for employees to receive nothing upon retirement because of a plan's inordinately long vesting requirements; section 411 remedies this problem.

Section 411(a) deals with the timing of vesting. First, an employee must have a nonforfeitable right to his normal retirement benefit upon reaching normal retirement age. Second, an employee must always be 100% vested in his own contributions.[107] Third, a plan must meet or exceed one of the statutory vesting schedules for employer contributions.[108]

Section 411(a) states that an employee must have a nonforfeitable right to the normal retirement benefit at normal retirement age. According to section 411(a)(8) normal retirement age is the earlier of (1) normal retirement age under the plan,[109] or (2) the later of the participant's 65th birthday[110] or the participant's 5th anniversary of plan participation.[111] Section 411(a)(9) defines the term "normal retirement benefit" as the greater of the early retirement benefit, if any, under the plan or the normal retirement benefit using actuarial equivalencies. Normal retirement benefits do not include medical and certain disability benefits.[112]

Section 411(a)(1) provides that an employee must always be fully vested in the accrued benefit derived from his contributions. Section 411(a)(7)(A) defines the term "accrued benefit" for defined benefit plans as the annual benefit commencing at normal retirement age, and for all other plans the term means the employee's account balance. Section 411(c) provides for the allocation of accrued benefits between employer and employee contributions.

Section 411(a)(2) provides that a plan must meet the vesting requirements by complying with one of two standards.

In the case of defined benefit plans, "A plan satisfies the requirements of this clause [section 411(a)(2)] if an employee who has completed at least 5 years of service has a nonforfeitable right to 100 percent of

---

105. § 414(s)(1) (referring to § 415(c)(3)).

106. See § 414(s)(1)(referring to § 415(c)(3)).

107. § 411(a)(1).

108. See § 411(a)(2)(A) and (B).

109. § 411(a)(8)(A).

110. § 411(a)(8)(B)(i).

111. § 411(a)(8)(B)(ii).

112. § 411(a)(9)(A) and (B).

the employee's accrued benefit derived from employer contributions."[113] Alternatively, a defined benefit plan may satisfy the requirements of section 411(a)(2), "if an employee has a nonforfeitable right to a percentage of the employee's accrued benefit derived from employer contributions determined under the following table:"[114]

Years of Service	The Nonforfeitable Percentage is:
3	20%
4	40%
5	60%
6	80%
7 or more	100%[115]

In the case of defined contribution plans, "A plan satisfies the requirements of this clause [section 411(a)(2)] if an employee who has completed at least 3 years of service has a nonforfeitable right to 100 percent of the employee's accrued benefit derived from employer contributions."[116] Alternatively, a defined benefit plan may satisfy the requirements of section 411(a)(2), "if an employee has a nonforfeitable right to a percentage of the employee's accrued benefit derived from employer contributions determined under the following table:"[117]

Years of Service	The Nonforfeitable Percentage is:
3	20%
4	40%
5	60%
6	80%
7 or more	100%[118]

The foregoing vesting standards would be meaningless if the employer could, for example, provide a benefit equal to an annuity of $10 a year for each year of service up to 7 years and $100,000 a year for each year of service thereafter. This technique is called backloading, and it is prohibited by the accrued benefit requirements of section 411(b).[119] The backloading rules only apply to defined benefit plans.[120] To satisfy them, a plan must provide an accrued benefit that is at least equal to the benefit computed by the 3% method,[121] the 133 1/3% rule,[122] or the fractional rule.[123] Generally, under the 3% method a plan must provide in each year of participation an accrued benefit that is not less than 3% of the normal retirement benefit to which the participant would be entitled

113. § 411(a)(2)(A)(ii).

114. § 411(a)(2)(A)(iii).

115. This table is adopted from § 411(a)(2)(A)(iii).

116. § 411(a)(2)(B)(ii).

117. § 411(a)(2)(B)(iii).

118. This table is adopted from § 411(a)(2)(B)(iii).

119. See § 411(b)(1)(A)-(C).

120. See § 411(b)(1).

121. § 411(b)(1)(A).

122. § 411(b)(1)(B).

123. § 411(b)(1)(C).

if he had commenced participation at the earliest possible entry age and worked until normal retirement age;[124] under this method compensation is imputed until retirement. Under the 133 1/3% rule the rate of accrual for later plan years cannot be more than 133 1/3% of the annual rate for earlier plan years.[125] The fractional rule requires that a participant's accrued benefit may not be less than a fraction of the participant's annual benefit at normal retirement age.[126] The fraction cannot exceed 1, and it is determined by adding the number of years of plan participation at the time of separation and dividing by the number of years an employee would have participated in the plan if he had worked until normal retirement age.[127] Again, compensation is imputed until retirement.[128]

A plan that satisfies the vesting requirements is treated as satisfying the nondiscrimination requirement of section 401(a)(4) unless there has been a pattern of abuse, such as dismissal before vesting, or there is a reason to believe that benefits will accrue resulting in discrimination in favor of the prohibited group.

[f] Forfeitures

Under section 401(a)(8) forfeitures under a defined benefit plan may not be reallocated to the remaining participants. The forfeitures may, however, be used to reduce future employer contributions.[129]

Under section 411(a)(3)(A) forfeiture of a participant's accrued benefit of employer contributions is permitted if the participant dies. Forfeiture is not permitted, however, for a survivor annuity payable under section 401(a)(11).

[g] Commencement and Duration of Benefits

Section 401(a)(9) and (14) set forth requirements for the payment of benefits. Payments must commence by the starting date in section 401(a)(9) or (14), whichever is earlier. Under section 401(a)(9)(A) distributions generally must start not later than the "required beginning date;" this term means the later of April 1 of the calendar year following the calendar year in which the employee attains age 70½ or retires.[130] Under section 401(a)(14) distributions must begin, unless the participant elects otherwise, no later than the 60th day after the latest of the close of the plan year in which (1) the participant attains the earlier of age 65 or normal retirement age,[131] (2) the participant completes 10 years of plan participation,[132] or (3) the participant terminates service.[133]

Section 401(a)(9) also deals with the duration of benefits. The plan must provide that the entire interest of each employee be distributed

---

124. See § 411(b)(1)(A).

125. See § 411(b)(1)(B).

126. See § 411(b)(1)(C).

127. Id.

128. Id.

129. Treas. Reg. § 1.401–7(a).

130. § 401(a)(9)(C)(i)(I) and (II).

131. § 401(a)(14)(A).

132. § 401(a)(14)(B).

133. § 401(a)(14)(C).

over the life of the employee or the lives of the employee and a designated beneficiary or over a period not extending beyond the life expectancy of the employee or the life expectancy of the employee and a designated beneficiary.[134]

If the employee dies after distributions have commenced, the remainder of the interest must be distributed at least as quickly as before his death.[135] If the employee dies before distributions have commenced, generally the interest must be paid out within five years.[136]

If a plan retains an amount required to be distributed, section 4974 imposes a tax of 50% on the difference between the minimum required distribution and the actual distribution.[137] The tax may be waived if the shortfall was due to reasonable error and steps are taken to remedy it.[138]

[h] Owner–Employee and Top–Heavy Rules

Under section 401(a)(10) the plan must also comply with the owner-employee rules of section 401(c) and (d) and the top-heavy rules of section 416. These rules are discussed below.

[i] Joint-and-Survivor Annuity

Section 401(a)(11) requires benefits to be paid in the form of a qualified joint-and-survivor annuity and that prior to retirement a plan must provide a qualified pre-retirement survivor annuity. Section 401(a)(11) applies to any defined benefit plan and to any defined contribution plan that is subject to the funding standards of section 412. However, section 417(a)(1) and (2) provides that the qualified joint-and-survivor annuity or the qualified pre-retirement survivor annuity is not required if the participant and the participant's spouse elect to waive it. Such election is valid only if the spouse is informed of the consequences of such an election.[139]

[j] Merger or Consolidation

For a merger or consolidation of plans or transfer of assets or liabilities to another plan, a participant must receive a benefit at least equal to the benefit under the prior plan.[140]

[k] Alienation and Assignment

Section 401(a)(13) states that a qualified plan must prohibit the assignment or alienation of accrued benefits. An exception exists for loans to a plan participant that are secured by his accrued benefit.[141] In addition, an exception is provided for a qualified domestic relations order (QUADRO).[142] A QUADRO is defined in section 414(p) as an order pursuant to state domestic relations law relating to child support,

134. § 401(a)(9)(A)(ii).

135. § 401(a)(9)(B)(i).

136. § 401(a)(9)(B)(ii).

137. § 4974(a).

138. § 4974(d).

139. § 417(a)(2)(A)(i).

140. § 401(a)(12).

141. See § 401(a)(13)(A).

142. See § 401(a)(13)(B).

alimony, or similar matters that creates or recognizes the existence of a right to payment with respect to qualified plan benefits. QUADROs recognize that a pension is often an important marital asset that should be divisible upon dissolution of marriage.

[l] Benefit and Contribution Limitations

Under section 401(a)(16) a plan may not exceed the benefit or contribution limits of section 415.[143] For purposes of the limitation all defined contribution plans and all defined benefit plans of the same employer are treated as one defined contribution or one defined benefit plan.[144]

The general limitation under a defined benefit plan is that plan benefits may not exceed the lesser of the applicable amount or 100% of the average compensation for the employee's highest three years expressed as a single life annuity.[145] Adjustment must be made for payment in a form other than a single life annuity or for early retirement benefits.[146] A pro rata reduction is made in the limitation if the participant has completed less than 10 years of service.[147] In addition, a minimum benefit of $10,000 is permitted.[148]

The contribution limitation for a defined contribution plan is an annual addition to the account of a participant of the lesser of the applicable amount[149] or 100% of the participants compensation.[150] The term "annual addition" is defined as employer contributions and forfeitures allocated to the participant's account.[151] The annual addition does not include tax-free rollovers.[152] All plans of the same type with the same employer are aggregated for purposes of the limitation.[153]

[m] Compensation

The annual compensation of each employee taken into account under the plan may not exceed the applicable amount;[154] this amount is adjusted for cost-of-living increases.[155]

[n] Withdrawal and Forfeiture

Under section 401(a)(19) a participant's accrued benefit attributable to employer contributions may not be forfeited if a participant who is at least 50% vested withdraws his mandatory employee contributions.

---

143. Section 415(d) permits adjustments in the limitation figures for changes in the cost of living.

144. § 415(f)(1)(A) and (B).

145. § 415(b)(1)(A) and (B). *Nota bene:* the amount listed in § 415(b)(1)(A) is $160,000; however, it is adjusted annually for inflation.

146. § 415(b)(2)(B).

147. § 415(b)(5)(A).

148. See § 414(b)(4).

149. § 415(c)(1)(A).

150. § 415(c)(1)(B). *Nota bene:* the amount listed in § 415(c)(1)(B) is $40,000; however, it is adjusted annually for inflation.

151. § 415(c)(2).

152. § 415(c)(2) (flush language).

153. § 415(f)(1)(B).

154. § 401(a)(17).

155. § 401(a)(17)(B).

[o] Actuarial Assumptions

Section 401(a)(25) provides that a defined benefit plan does not have definitely determinable benefits unless the actuarial assumptions are specified in a manner that precludes employer discretion.

[p] Determination Letter Procedure

Because of the critical importance of plan qualification, most employers want assurances that the plan is qualified, at least on its face. For this reason, the Service issues determination letters that are similar to private letter rulings. A determination letter may be sought at the initial adoption of a qualified plan and is often sought in connection with amendment or termination of a plan. A plan that has received a favorable determination letter may still be disqualified if, for example, the plan is discriminatory in operation. For initial qualification, ERISA requires interested parties, usually the employees, to receive notice before a favorable determination letter is issued.[156]

Section 7476(a) permits a declaratory judgment action challenging a determination letter or the failure of the Service to make a determination. This, however, only relates to initial plan qualification and not to qualification of a plan in operation.

[4] EMPLOYEE–SERVICE RULES

A qualified plan must be maintained exclusively for the benefit of employees or their beneficiaries.[157] The Code provides rules for counting an employee's years of service for purposes of participation and vesting.

The initial determination is whether an individual is an employee. The issue is a factual one and state law controls. In Azad v. United States[158] the Eighth Circuit stated that "[t]he authorities seem to be in general agreement that an employer's right to control the manner in which the work is performed is an important if not the master test to be considered in determining the existence of an employer-employee relationship."[159] In Azad the Eighth Circuit held that a radiologist was not an employee of a hospital because he was not subject to any supervision, required to work certain hours, required to account for any absence from work, or otherwise regarded as in an employment relationship with the hospital.

Once an employment relationship is determined to exist, years of service must be counted. This is most important for the coverage and vesting requirements. The provisions for counting years of service under sections 410 and 411 are similar. The general rule is that all years of service with the employer must be taken into account for purposes of participation and vesting. However, for purposes of section 411 only, an employer may exclude, among others, years of service before age 18,

---

156. ERISA § 3001(a), 29 U.S.C.A. § 1201(a).

157. § 401(a).

158. 388 F.2d 74 (8th Cir. 1968). See also Hathaway v. Commissioner, T.C. Memo. 1996–389; TAM 9808001;

159. 388 F.2d 74, 76 (8th Cir. 1968).

years of service when the employee failed to make mandatory contributions, and years of service prior to the existence of a plan.

A year of service for purposes of both section 410 and section 411 is a calendar year or other consecutive 12–month period designated by the plan during which the participant has at least 1,000 hours of service.[160] Special rules apply for defining and counting hours of service.

An employee's service prior to a one-year break in service need not be taken into account until the employee has returned to work and completed a year of service.[161] A one-year break in service is a one-year period during which an employee has not completed more than 500 hours of service.[162] For a nonvested participant any years of service before any period of consecutive one-year breaks are not required to be counted if the number of years of breaks equals or exceeds the greater of five or the aggregate number of years of service before such period.[163]

[5] SPECIAL RULES

[a] Aggregation

Through its requirement of plan aggregation, section 415 prevents an employer from circumventing the benefit limits by setting up multiple plans.[164] Similarly, an employer may not circumvent the coverage rules by setting up multiple organizations so that certain individuals are no longer employees for purposes of an organization's plan.[165] Section 414 prevents this and other schemes.

An employer might set up two corporations and two plans to circumvent the antidiscrimination and coverage provisions. One plan would be for prohibited-group employees and the other plan would be for rank-and-file employees. Under section 414(b), for purposes of sections 401, 408(k), 410, 411, 415, and 416, all employees that are employed by a controlled group of corporations[166] are treated as employed by a single employer. Groups that meet the specified ownership percentage are treated as owned by one employer. In addition, multiple plans of the employer must be comparable or face the threat of disqualification. In Fujinon Optical, Inc. v. Commissioner[167] a plan was disqualified for failing to meet the coverage requirements even though the company that administered the plan was in a separate business from the controlled group, and there was no manipulative purpose. Under section 414(c) all employees of trades or businesses under common control, whether incorporated or not, are treated as employees of a single employer.

---

160. §§ 410(a)(3)(A), 411(a)(5)(A).

161. §§ 410(a)(5)(C), 411(a)(6)(B).

162. § 411(a)(6)(A).

163. § 410(a)(5)(D).

164. See § 415(f).

165. See § 415(g).

166. See § 1563(a). This section governs parent-subsidiary groups, brother-sister groups, and combinations of these groups.

167. 76 T.C. 499 (1981). See also Sheldon P. Barr, P.C. v. Commissioner, T.C. Memo. 1992–552.

In Sutherland v. Commissioner[168] the Tax Court refused to apply section 414(c) and did not include employees from two of three commonly controlled businesses when testing coverage under section 410. The excluded businesses were losing money, and at the time of trial they had been discontinued. Thus, although employees of businesses in imminent danger of failure were excluded, the remaining plans continued to be qualified. Hence, the congressional purpose of encouraging the establishment of employee pension plans was furthered.[169]

Two or more employers might transfer their employees to another business in an attempt to circumvent the common control rules, but section 414(m) prohibits this. Section 414(m) treats employees of affiliated service groups as employees of a single employer. An affiliated service group has a first service organization (FSO) and one or more of the following: (1) any service organization (A–ORG) that (a) is a shareholder or partner in the FSO and (b) regularly performs services for the FSO or is regularly associated with the FSO in performing services for third persons and (2) any other organization (B–ORG), if (a) a significant portion of the business of the B–ORG is the performance of services for the FSO or A–ORG of a type historically performed in the service field of the FSO or A–ORG by employees and (b) 10% or more of the interest in the B–ORG is held by persons who are in the prohibited group of the FSO or A–ORG.[170] An affiliated service group also includes an organization performing management functions for related organizations.[171]

A similar abuse, employee leasing, is treated in section 414(n). This subsection is aimed at attempts to circumvent the coverage rules by leasing employees from third parties. Section 414(n) provides that for certain of the qualified plan rules an individual who performs services for another person pursuant to a lease agreement between the lessee and the lessor is treated as an employee of the lessee.[172] A "safe harbor" is provided if the lessor has a plan for the leased employees that meets the requirements of section 414(n)(5).

[b] Plans for Self–Employed Individuals and Top–Heavy Plans

Special rules apply to plans benefiting self-employed individuals, owner-employees, and plans that accrue a significant percentage of benefits for prohibited-group employees. Even though plans for such persons must comply with the antidiscrimination requirements, additional rules are imposed.

Section 401(c)(1) provides that the term "employee" includes a self-employed individual.[173] Income from self-employment is net earnings

---

168. 78 T.C. 395 (1982).

169. See H.R. Rep. No. 93–533, 93d Cong. 2d Sess., reprinted in 1974 U.S. Code Cong. and Admin. News.

170. § 414(m)(2). See Rev. Rul. 81–105, 1981–1 C.B. 256, for examples of the application of § 414(m).

171. § 414(m)(5).

172. See § 414(n)(1).

173. Plans for self-employed individuals are called Keogh plans. Treas. Reg. § 1.401(e)–1(a).

after deductions are taken under sections 404 and 405(c), including a deduction for contributions to a qualified plan in which personal services of the taxpayer are a material income-producing factor. Because Keogh plans benefit owner-employees, defined in section 401(c)(3) as sole proprietors or 10% partners, section 401(a)(10)(A) requires compliance with section 401(d) which provides:

> A trust forming part of a pension or profit-sharing plan which provides contributions or benefits for employees some or all of whom are owner-employees shall constitute a qualified trust under this section only if, in addition to meeting the requirements of subsection (a), the plan provides that contributions on behalf of any owner-employee may be made only with respect to the earned income of such owner-employee which is derived from the trade or business with respect to which such plan is established.

If a plan is considered top heavy, section 401(a)(10)(B) mandates compliance with section 416. A top-heavy plan is one in which 60% or more of the benefits or contributions are accrued on behalf of key employees.[174] A key employee is (1) an officer with compensation over the applicable amount,[175] (2) a 5% owner,[176] or (3) a 1% owner with compensation over $150,000.[177]

Top-heavy plans must vest more rapidly and must provide a minimum benefit for employees who are not key employees without integrating the benefit with Social Security. Top-heavy plans must have 3–year 100% vesting[178] or graded 6–year vesting that provides 20% vesting after two years and increasing 20% each year thereafter until the employee is 100% vested.[179] The minimum benefit provided by top-heavy defined benefit plans is an annual benefit expressed as an applicable percentage of the employee's average compensation for the highest five years.[180] The applicable percentage is the lesser of 2% times the number of years of service or 20%.[181] For defined contribution plans the employer must contribute 3% of each participant's compensation.[182] However, if 3% is lower than the highest percentage contribution on behalf of any key employee, then the key employee's percentage must be used.[183]

[6] DEDUCTIBILITY OF CONTRIBUTIONS

Section 404 governs the deductibility of employer contributions to deferred compensation plans.[184] Under section 404(a)(5) employer contributions to nonqualified plans are deductible in the year the employees include the contribution in gross income.[185] Section 404(a)(5) is a major

174. § 416(g)(1)(A).

175. § 416(i)(1)(A)(i). *Nota bene*: the amount listed in § 416(i)(1)(A)(i) is $130,000; however it is indexed annually for inflation.

176. § 416(i)(1)(A)(ii).

177. § 416(i)(1)(A)(iii).

178. § 416(b)(1)(A).

179. § 416(b)(1)(B).

180. § 416(c)(1)(D).

181. § 416(c)(1)(B).

182. § 416(c)(2)(A).

183. § 416(c)(2)(B).

184. See generally § 404(a).

185. If more than one employee participates, separate accounts must be kept; otherwise no deduction will be allowed. § 404(a)(5). A plan includes any arrange-

disadvantage of nonqualified arrangements; because of it employers usually cannot deduct contributions for at least several years. Qualified plans, on the other hand, permit employers to take immediate deductions while allowing employees to defer income.[186]

Section 404(a) is the exclusive provision for deduction of contributions to deferred compensation arrangements. Section 404(a) precludes deduction under sections 162 or 212. However, contributions must satisfy the requirements of section 162 or 212 in order to be deductible under section 404(a).[187]

Contributions to a qualified plan are deductible when made to the plan. Thus, an accrual method taxpayer may not deduct an accrued pension liability until payment is made.[188] Nevertheless, section 404(a)(6) permits a contribution to be made before the due date for filing a return, including extensions; the payment is treated as being made on the last day of the preceding taxable year. Thus, a calendar year taxpayer may make deductible contributions until April 15, or later if an extension is permitted.[189]

Current deductibility is also dependent upon plan qualification. No deduction is allowed for a year in which a plan is not qualified. Even if a plan was qualified in the past, no deduction is permitted for any year the plan is not qualified.

Pension plans are subject to section 404(a)(1). The amount deductible may be computed under one of three methods referred to in section 404(a)(1)(A): minimum-funding,[190] level-cost,[191] and normal-cost.[192] According to the last sentence of section 404(a)(1)(A) the funding method and actuarial assumptions must be the same as those used under section 412, and the deduction may not be in excess of the section 412 full-funding limitation.[193]

The purpose of section 412 is to keep plans on an actuarially sound basis by imposing a minimum funding standard. However, violation of the minimum funding standard does not result in disqualification; instead, section 4971 imposes a penalty tax on the accumulated-funding deficiency.[194] To determine the deficiency section 412 establishes a minimum funding standard account for each plan.[195]

The Service may waive the minimum funding standard when there is substantial business hardship.[196] To determine whether substantial business hardship exists the following questions are considered: Is the

---

ment that has the effect of deferral of compensation. § 404(b)(1).

186. § 404(a).

187. § 404(a).

188. Cf. Don E. Williams Co. v. Commissioner, 429 U.S. 569, 97 S.Ct. 850, 51 L.Ed.2d 48 (1977), in which the Supreme Court disallowed a deduction for a contribution of a promissory note by the employer.

189. See § 404(a)(6).

190. § 404(a)(1)(A)(i).

191. § 404(a)(1)(A)(ii).

192. § 404(a)(1)(A)(iii).

193. § 404(a)(1)(A) (referring to § 431, which refers to § 412).

194. See § 4971(a) and (b).

195. See § 412(a)(2).

196. § 412(c)(1).

employer operating at a loss?[197] Is there substantial unemployment in the industry?[198] Are industry sales and profits declining?[199] Is the plan able to continue only if the waiver from the minimum funding standard is granted?[200]

Because of the tax-exempt status of the plan, an employer might be tempted to make contributions in excess of the deductible amount. Section 4972 imposes a 10% tax on excess contributions, unless they are returned within the taxable year to the employer.[201] Under section 4973 a 6% tax is imposed on excess contributions to IRAs and section 403(b) annuities.[202] Moreover, section 4979 imposes a 10% tax on excess contributions under cash or deferred arrangements and under employee contribution or employer matching contribution arrangements.[203]

[7] DISTRIBUTIONS FROM QUALIFIED PLANS

[a] Tax on Early Distributions

As a preliminary matter, distributions from qualified plans encompass the receipt of property by participants, the purchase of life insurance for participants, or the receipt of loans by participants from the plan. Because the primary purpose of a pension plan is to provide retirement income,[204] distributions are usually deferred until participants retire. Profit-sharing and stock-bonus plans, however, require only a minimum period of deferral before distributions can be made.[205]

In addition to any regular tax that may be imposed, section 72(t) imposes upon the recipient a 10% additional tax for early distributions. The additional tax does not apply to distributions made after the employee attains age 59½, dies, becomes disabled, or retires early after attaining age 55.

[b] Life Insurance

A qualified plan may provide death benefits through insurance or other programs.[206] However, for pension plans these benefits may be only incidental. If a plan purchases life insurance for a participant, that individual is currently benefited through this protection. Thus, the

---

197. See § 412(c)(2)(A).

198. See § 412(c)(2)(B).

199. See § 412(c)(2)(C).

200. See § 412(c)(2)(D).

201. § 4972(a).

202. § 4973(a).

203. § 4979(a).

204. See Treas. Reg. § 1.401–1(b)(1)(i).

205. See Treas. Reg. § 1.401–1(b)(1)(ii), (iii).

206. Profit-sharing and stock-bonus plans must defer distributions for at least two years, according to Rev. Rul. 71–295, 1971–2 C.B. 184. Thus, a distribution of funds accumulated for at least two years, including the purchase of life insurance, is permitted. The Service takes the position that 25% of nonaccumulated funds (funds accumulated for less than two years) may be used to purchase term life insurance and 50% to purchase ordinary life insurance because of the cash surrender value. Rev. Rul. 61–164, 1961–2 C.B. 99. For money-purchase pension plans the 25% and 50% figures are used, except the percentages are of total contributions. Rev. Rul. 70–611, 1970–2 C.B. 89, modified by Rev. Rul. 85–15, 1985–1 C.B. 132. For defined benefit plans the pre-retirement death benefit may not exceed 100 times the anticipated monthly retirement benefit. Rev. Rul. 60–83, 1960–1 C.B. 157.

individual is taxed on the plan's purchase of life insurance. Section 402 governs the taxation of distributions and indicates that the tax is imposed in the year of the distribution under section 72.[207] If a plan purchases life insurance and the proceeds are payable directly or indirectly to the participant, under section 72(m)(3) deductible employer contributions used to purchase such insurance are included in the participant's income in the year of the contribution.

[c] Loans

Because of potential abuses, certain loans are treated as distributions under section 72(p). However, if loans are made in a nondiscriminatory manner and are generally repaid, no abuse results.

According to section 72(p)(2)(A) a loan is not treated as a distribution if it:

[D]oes not exceed the lesser of:—(i) $50,000, reduced by the excess (if any) of—(I) the highest outstanding balance of loans from the plan during the 1–year period ending on the day before the date on which such loan was made, over (II) the outstanding balance of loans from the plan on the date on which such loan was made, or (ii) the greater of (I) one-half of the present value of the nonforfeitable accrued benefit of the employee under the plan, or (II) $10,000.

Apart from a loan used to acquire a principal residence, a loan must be repaid within five years for the employee to avoid distribution treatment.[208]

[d] The Annuity Rules

Section 402(a)(1) provides that distributions from qualified plans are taxed under the annuity rules of section 72. Section 72(a) provides that as a general rule gross income includes any amount received as an annuity. However, under section 72(b) the product of the annuity payment multiplied by the exclusion ratio is not included in gross income. The exclusion ratio is the employee's investment in the contract divided by the expected return. The employee's investment in the annuity contract usually includes employee contributions.[209] Also included in the investment in the contract are amounts previously included in income when the plan was not qualified, principal repayments if a loan was treated as a distribution,[210] and amounts included in the employee's income when the plan purchased life insurance.

The following example describes how the annuity rules work when both the employee and the employer have contributed to the plan. Employee X contributed $10,000, and her employer contributed $40,000 to a qualified defined contribution pension plan. The plan provides for a

---

207. § 402(b)(2).

208. § 72(p)(2)(B)(i) and (ii).

209. If the contributions have been made only by the employer, the employee usually has no investment to recover so that the entire amount of each payment received by the employee is included in gross income.

210. § 72(p).

$10,250 a year life annuity upon retirement payable in monthly install-ments of a little more than $854. After 30 years of employment, X's account balance at retirement is $111,000 because of the earnings on plan assets. X's investment in the contract is her contribution of $10,000. The expected return is computed using actuarial tables in the regulations. If X is 65, the multiple is 20.0 for a single life annuity. This is multiplied by the annual benefit ($10,250) to find the expected return of $205,000. The exclusion ratio is the employee's total investment divided by the total expected return, $10,000/$205,000 or almost 5%. Hence, $500 of the annual $10,250 benefit is excluded from gross income; $9,750 is included in gross income each year. This is the normal method of taxation. Adjustments must be made for payments in the form of a joint-and-survivor annuity or for an annuity with a certain number of guaranteed payments.

[e] Lump Sum Distributions

Section 72 provides for the general treatment of distributions. However, special treatment is provided in section 402 for a lump sum distribution, the distribution of an employee's benefit in a lump sum upon the occurrence of a specified event.[211]

The term "lump sum distribution" is defined in section 402(e)(4)(D)(i) as a distribution or payment made within one taxable year of the account balance of an employee that becomes payable because of the employee's death,[212] attainment of age 59 ½,[213] separation from service,[214] or disability.[215]

[8] MISCELLANEOUS

[a] Exemption of Trust From Taxation

Section 501(a) exempts from taxation an organization described in section 401(a). Therefore, the trust forming part of a qualified plan is exempt from taxation. Nevertheless, like all exempt entities, trusts exempt under section 501(a) are taxed under sections 511–514 on unre-lated business taxable income. The purpose of this tax is to discourage unrelated business activity and put such activity of exempt organizations on an even basis with their profit-oriented taxable competitors.

[b] Fiduciary Standards and Prohibited Transactions

One of the reasons for the enactment of ERISA was to protect plan participants from mismanagement and corruption. For qualified plans and plans that involve interstate commerce, ERISA prescribes fiduciary standards while both ERISA and the Internal Revenue Code cover prohibited transactions between plans and parties in interest.[216]

---

211. § 402(e)(4)(B).

212. § 402(e)(4)(D)(i)(I).

213. § 402(e)(4)(D)(i)(II).

214. § 402(e)(4)(D)(i)(III).

215. § 402(e)(4)(D)(i)(IV).

216. Crawford, Prudent Investments for Plan Fiduciaries and Plan Administra-tors, 40 N.Y.U. Inst. Fed. Tax'n ERISA Supplement Ch. 5 (1982); Note, Fiduciary

The fiduciary standards are set forth in section 404 of ERISA.[217] Section 404 of ERISA provides that "a fiduciary shall discharge his duties ... solely in the interest of the participants and beneficiaries" (1) for the exclusive purpose of providing benefits to participants and defraying reasonable expenses of the plan (2) with the care and skill of a prudent man under like circumstances (3) by diversifying plan investments to avoid the risk of large losses. In Marshall v. Glass/Metal Association and Glaziers and Glassworkers Pension Plan[218] the Secretary of Labor successfully brought an action to enjoin a plan from investing 23% of plan assets in a real estate venture that had already failed once.

Both ERISA and the Internal Revenue Code identify prohibited transactions.[219] Participation in prohibited transactions subjects the offender to an excise tax of up to 100% under the Internal Revenue Code if the violation goes unremedied and to civil liability under the Labor Title of the United States Code.[220] Prohibited transactions are those engaged in by a disqualified person or as the Labor Title states, "a party in interest." Such persons include, among others, the employer, certain employees, and fiduciaries.[221]

In Marshall v. Kelly[222] a plan's sole shareholder who was also a plan fiduciary caused the plan to make a number of improperly secured loans to the plan's sponsor, to himself, and to others. Some of the loans were at below-market rates. The shareholder also paid himself a commission on the sale of plan property. The court removed the shareholder as a fiduciary, replaced him with disinterested trustees, and required repayment of the loans to the plan.

Certain transactions are statutorily exempted from characterization as prohibited transactions, including plan loans to participants on a nondiscriminatory basis.[223] In addition, the Labor Department and Treasury Department may jointly exempt certain transactions if they are administratively feasible, if the transactions protect the rights of the participants and beneficiaries, and if adequate notice is given to interested parties.[224]

[c] Plan Amendments

A qualified plan may be amended and will remain qualified so long as certain requirements are met. Indeed, section 401(b) permits an

---

Standards and the Prudent Man Rule Under the Employee Retirement Income Security Act of 1974, 88 Harv. L. Rev. 960 (1975).

217. 29 U.S.C.A. 1104(a)(1)(A)-(C). "Fiduciary," defined broadly in ERISA, has also been given a broad meaning by the courts.

218. 507 F.Supp. 378 (D. Hawaii 1980). See also Donovan v. Bierwirth, 680 F.2d 263 (2d Cir. 1982), cert. denied, 459 U.S. 1069, 103 S.Ct. 488, 74 L.Ed.2d 631 (1982) (a plan's purchase of employer stock to deter a tender offer was a breach of

fiduciary duty, especially because the tender offer inflated the price).

219. ERISA § 406, 29 U.S.C.A. § 1106; § 4975(c)(1).

220. § 4975(a), (b); ERISA § 502(i), 29 U.S.C.A. § 1132(i).

221. See § 4975(e)(2).

222. 465 F.Supp. 341 (W.D.Okl. 1978).

223. § 4975(d)(1); ERISA § 408(b), 29 U.S.C.A. § 1108(b).

224. ERISA § 408(a), 29 U.S.C.A. § 1108(a); § 4975(c)(2).

amendment to a plan that is retroactive to the plan's commencement. The amendment, however, must be made by the due date of the plan return[225] and must be expressly applicable to the prior period.[226]

It is implicit in the Code that a plan may be amended prospectively if the plan as amended would otherwise qualify, even if the amendment reduces future accrual of benefits. A change in vesting, however, will disqualify a plan if the nonforfeitable percentage of the accrued benefit as of the effective date of the amendment is less than the nonforfeitable percentage after the amendment.[227] Furthermore, an employee with three years of service must be allowed to elect to retain the former vesting schedule.[228] A plan also may be amended retroactively under section 412(d)(2) if the amendment is made within 2 ½ months of the close of the plan year, and it does not reduce the accrued benefit of any employee.

[d] Plan Terminations

If a plan is qualified while in operation and through its termination, the benefits of qualified plan status continue. A plan that does not qualify at termination risks retroactive disqualification and loss of any previous benefits of qualification.

Pursuant to Title IV of ERISA the Pension Benefit Guaranty Corporation (PBGC) provides a plan termination insurance program. Premiums are paid to the PBGC for participants.[229] The PBGC is also the supervisor of plan terminations. Not only does the PBGC provide a plan termination insurance program, but it also has authority to collect from the sponsor of a terminated plan the lesser of the amount of any deficit necessary to fund accrued benefits up to termination or one-third of the sponsor's net worth.[230] The PBGC may recapture certain distributions paid prior to termination to protect plan participants.[231]

A plan may be terminated either voluntarily or involuntarily. The PGBC may institute proceedings to involuntarily terminate a plan if the plan has not met the minimum-funding standards, will be unable to pay benefits when due, or makes certain distributions to a substantial owner causing accrued benefits to go unfunded.[232] Involuntary termination proceedings may also be instituted if long-run losses of the PGBC are likely to increase unreasonably if the plan is not terminated. Plan administrators are required to notify the PGBC of "reportable events."[233]

225. See Rev. Rul. 82–66, 1982–1 C.B. 61, in which the Service allowed retroactive amendments after the remedial amendment period expired if the employer applied for a determination letter prior to the expiration of the remedial period and if the amendment was retroactive to the date of the defect.

226. § 401(b).

227. § 411(a)(10)(A).

228. § 401(a)(10)(B).

229. ERISA § 4007, 29 U.S.C.A. § 1307.

230. ERISA § 4062, 29 U.S.C.A. § 1362.

231. ERISA § 4045, 29 U.S.C.A. § 1345.

232. ERISA § 4042, 29 U.S.C.A. § 1342.

233. ERISA § 4043, 29 U.S.C.A. § 1343.

Section 411(d)(3) provides that a plan will not qualify unless the rights of affected employees to accrued benefits is nonforfeitable upon a plan's termination. Thus, employees must be 100% vested in their accrued benefits upon termination.

A plan may be voluntarily terminated only if advance notice is provided to "affected parties" and the PBGC is notified.[234] After receiving notice of termination, the PBGC must determine whether the plan has sufficient assets to meet its obligations.[235] If the assets are not sufficient, the PBGC must make up the deficit by methods that include taking action against the employer.

A plan may also be partially terminated. A partial termination is determined by a facts-and-circumstances test. Pertinent facts and circumstances include plan amendments severing a previously covered group of employees and amendments adversely affecting vesting.[236]

§ 13.03   NONQUALIFIED PLANS

[1]   IN GENERAL

In some situations a nonqualified deferred compensation plan may serve the needs of both the employer and the employee better than a qualified plan. Nonqualified plans have been used to provide key employees with deferred compensation benefits in excess of the those allowed by qualified plans. This has been especially true for employees whose contributions or benefits have reached the section 415 limitations. The purpose of most nonqualified arrangements has been to provide incentives and tax advantages to top-level personnel. A nonqualified plan may defer employee income.[1] However, an employer's deduction is usually postponed until the amount is included in the employee's gross income.[2]

In general, ERISA covers plans established or maintained by employers engaged in interstate commerce,[3] and provisions of the Internal Revenue Code govern nonqualified plans. However, ERISA expressly exempts any unfunded plan that is "primarily" for "a select group of management or highly compensated employees" from the participation, vesting, funding, and fiduciary responsibility portions of ERISA.[4] In

---

234. ERISA § 4041, 29 U.S.C.A. § 1341.

235. See LLC Corp. v. PBGC, 703 F.2d 301 (8th Cir. 1983), in which the Eighth Circuit allowed a reversion of a plan that provided for employee contributions after it was shown that no part of the residue could be attributed to employee contributions.

236. In Ehm v. Phillips Petroleum Co., 583 F.Supp. 1113 (D.Kan. 1984), termination of 415 plan participants, approximately 2.5% of the total, did not constitute a partial termination. For an example of a partial termination, see Rev. Rul. 81–27, 1981–1 C.B. 228 (95 of 165 plan partici-

pants discharged in connection with dissolution of one division of employer's business).

§ 13.03

1. See § 83.

2. See § 404(a)(5).

3. ERISA § 4(a), 29 U.S.C.A. § 1003(a)

4. ERISA §§ 201(2), 301(a)(3), 401(a)(1); 29 U.S.C.A. §§ 1051(2), 1081(a)(3), 1101(a)(1). See e.g., Belka v. Rowe Furniture Corp., 571 F.Supp. 1249 (D.Md. 1983), in which the court held that a plan covering 4.6% of the employee's work

addition, unfunded excess benefit plans that provide benefits in excess of the section 415 limits are exempt from ERISA.[5]

In general, an employer may provide income deferral for employees in the form of distributions of restricted property (property subject to a substantial risk of forfeiture) through unfunded plans and deferred compensation contracts.

[2] SECTION 83 AND RESTRICTED PROPERTY

As a general rule, the form of receipt is immaterial for tax purposes. Thus, if an employee receives compensation in the form of property, the property's fair market value is subject to tax at the time of receipt.[6] Suppose, however, an employee receives compensation in the form of stock of the employer that is not transferable and is subject to a substantial risk of forfeiture. In such a situation the stock is not includible in gross income when it is received,[7] and under section 83(h) the employer is not entitled to a compensation expense deduction under section 162 until such time when the stock is actually included in the employee's gross income.

Section 83(a) states that if property is transferred in connection with the performance of services, the difference between the fair market value of the property and the price paid, if any, is includible in the gross income of the person performing the services when the property is "transferable" or is "not subject to a substantial risk of forfeiture."[8]

The following rules are also applicable: (1) recipients may elect to include in gross income the face amount of the bargain element at the time of receipt of the property even though the restrictions are in force;[9] (2) employee trust beneficiaries are taxed on employer contributions to nonqualified pension and profit-sharing trusts and annuities;[10] and (3) employers may deduct transfers and contributions when the amounts are includible in gross income, and employers may deduct contributions

force with an average annual salary of $55,000 (rank-and-file averaged about $16,000) was not covered by ERISA. Although most of the highly compensated employees were salesmen, the court noted the "or" between "select group of management" and "highly compensated" and that "primarily" does not mean exclusively.

5. ERISA § 4(b)(5); 29 U.S.C.A. § 1003(b)(5). See Dependahl v. Falstaff Brewing Corp., 653 F.2d 1208 (8th Cir. 1981), cert. denied, 454 U.S. 968, 102 S.Ct. 512, 70 L.Ed.2d 384 (1981), in which the Eighth Circuit held that corporate ownership of whole life insurance policies benefitting certain employees were funded plans not exempt from ERISA.

6. § 83(a)(1).

7. Id.

8. Treas. Reg. § 1.83–3(c)-(d).

For purposes of section 83 and the regulations thereunder, whether a risk of forfeiture is substantial or not depends upon the facts and circumstances. A substantial risk of forfeiture exists where rights in property that are transferred are conditioned, directly or indirectly, upon the future performance (or refraining from performance) of substantial services by any person, or the occurrence of a condition related to a purpose of the transfer, and the possibility of forfeiture is substantial if such condition is not satisfied.
Id.

9. § 83(b).

10. §§ 402(b), 403(c).

to multi-employee plans if separate accounts are maintained for each person.[11]

Section 83 deals with the transfer of property in connection with the performance of services. The term "property" includes both real and personal property except money or an unfunded unsecured promise to pay money or property in the future.[12] Consequently, section 83 has no application to unfunded nonqualified plans. These include "shadow" or "phantom" stock plans in which an employee may be credited with deferred compensation units that are adjusted by changes in stock value but without the issuance of stock.

Thus, with an unfunded deferred compensation plan, an employee will not be subject to tax merely because amounts are credited to an account. Actual or constructive receipt, discussed in the following section, is required to subject such amounts to taxation.[13] Section 404(a)(5) restricts an employer's deduction under a nonqualified plan to the time of inclusion in the employee's gross income, Section 162(a) may provide the authority for an ordinary and necessary business expense deduction if section 404 does not apply.[14]

[3] DEFERRED COMPENSATION CONTRACTS

A typical executive deferred compensation contract may provide for payments during retirement if the individual has been employed for a specified number of years, does not work for a competitor, and is available for consultation after retirement. Generally, there is no funding of the employer's obligation; the employee merely believes in the employer's ability in the future to make the payments. Under such an arrangement the employee is not deemed to be in constructive receipt at the time of making the contract unless certain conditions are satisfied. Generally, the employee is taxed only as payments are received. The courts have not treated the employer's unsecured promise as having an ascertainable value. Moreover, the employer deducts the payments when paid or accrued.

In Goldsmith v. United States[15] a physician decided to forego some of his current fees in exchange for a contractual deferred compensation arrangement with a hospital. The hospital agreed to the plan arranged by the taxpayer that involved the purchase of life insurance by the hospital. Because the taxpayer had no right to the withheld sums, either against the hospital or the insurance company, there was no funding or

11. §§ 83(h), 404(a)(5).

12. Treas. Reg. § 1.83–3(e).

13. See, e.g., Rev. Rul. 71–419, 1971–2 C.B. 220, in which the Service concluded that deferred directors' fees under an unfunded deferred compensation plan were not taxable until actually paid or otherwise made available to the directors.

14. See Greensboro Pathology Assocs. v. United States, 698 F.2d 1196 (Fed.Cir. 1982), in which the court held that an edu-

cational benefit plan was not governed by § 404 and that contributions were currently deductible under § 162. In response to Greenboro Pathology, § 419 was added in 1984 to restrict certain deductions for funded welfare-benefit plans. Section 419(f) applies to arrangements that have the effect of a plan as well as to actual plans.

15. 218 Ct.Cl. 387, 586 F.2d 810 (1978).

security interest. Thus, the taxpayer was not in constructive receipt of the income. The court held, however, that a portion of the sums withheld for pre-retirement death and disability benefits was taxable to the taxpayer under the economic benefit doctrine.

If a trust or escrow arrangement is used, the employee has gross income under the doctrine of constructive receipt or economic benefit when the trust or escrow is established and funded. In E. T. Sproull v. Commissioner[16] a trust was established in 1945 by a corporate employer to pay the employee a bonus of $10,500, half in 1946 and half in 1947. The court held that the $10,500 was income to the employee in 1945, the year the corporation paid over $10,500 to the trustee. Even though the taxpayer had only an equitable interest in the trust, the court reasoned "that such an interest had a value equivalent to the amount paid over for his benefit, and that this beneficial interest could have been assigned or otherwise alienated."

A popular nonqualified arrangement is known as a rabbi trust, named after a rabbi who received the first favorable ruling for the arrangement.[17] Under such an arrangement the employer establishes an irrevocable trust to which the employer contributes. The employee receives the employer's unsecured promise to pay benefits upon retirement, death, or severance from employment without cause. In the rabbi trust ruling the Service held that because the trust was subject to the claims of the employer's creditors, and because no payments were made to or made available to the employee, the employee did not have to include any benefits in income.

An employer may use deferred annuity contracts to guarantee a source of funds to pay deferred compensation. However, section 72(u) generally taxes the income on such contracts if held by persons other than individuals.

Under what circumstances is an employee regarded as receiving a taxable benefit? To provide a measure of guidance in this area, the Service stated its position in Revenue Ruling 60–31,[18] which, as modified, provides examples of deferred compensation arrangements.

The first example involves an executive employment contract. The second example involves an unfunded profit-sharing plan for key employ-

---

16. 16 T.C. 244 (1951), aff'd *per curiam*, 194 F.2d 541 (6th Cir. 1952).

17. Priv. Ltr. Rul. 8113107 (Dec. 31, 1980).

18. 1960–1 C.B. 174, modified by Rev. Rul. 64–279, 1964–2 C.B. 121, and Rev. Rul. 70–435, 1970–2 C.B. 100, provides a substitute fifth example discussed in the text; see also Rev. Rul. 69–649, 1969–2 C.B. 106 (stock bonuses awarded to employees under unfunded incentive plan not taxable until received or made available); Rev. Rul. 69–650, 1969–2 C.B. 106 (deferral of elective portion of employee's salary until retire-ment under unfunded arrangement; accrual method employer limited to deduction under § 404(a)(5) at time of actual payment to extent it constituted ordinary and necessary business expense under § 162); Rev. Proc. 71–19, 1971–1 C.B. 698 (requirements prescribed to secure advance rulings for deferred compensation arrangements); and Rev. Rul. 80–300, 1980–2 C.B. 165 (exclusion of income for phantom-stock plan permitted because risk of forfeiture existed on future appreciation), amplified by Rev. Rul. 82–121, 1982–1 C.B. 79.

ees. The third example involves a deferred compensation agreement to defer royalty income of an author-publisher. In the revenue ruling the Service accepts the case law and states that a mere promise to pay not evidenced by a note or otherwise secured is not regarded as receipt of income by a cash method taxpayer.

In the fourth example a bonus received by a professional football player upon signing a contract with a team was deposited for deferral with an escrow agent designated by the player. The Service held that the player realized income in the year the club unconditionally paid the bonus to the escrow agent.

The fifth example concerns a contract between an actor and a producer. Under the contract the parties agreed to share profits and losses from the production of a play. The contract required the producer to provide the financing and the actor to play the leading role and to direct the play. The contract also limited the payment of the actor's share of the profits to 25% annually during the run of the play and payment of the balance on a deferred basis over the four years after the close of the play. The Service held that because the arrangement qualified as a joint venture, which is taxed as a partnership, the actor could not qualify as an employee. As a partner the actor could not defer income because a partner's share of partnership profits is taxed at the close of the partnership's tax year.

The preceding example replaced one that used a similar partnership theory. The original example, however, was between a fighter and a promoter and was designed to fortify the Service's position in a controversy with a taxpayer at the administrative level.

§ 13.04   STOCK OPTIONS

[1]   IN GENERAL

To attract and keep key personnel, a corporation may grant employees options to purchase stock in the corporation. For tax purposes options may be classified as qualified and nonqualified. Most nonqualified options are governed by section 83. Qualified options are dealt with in section 422A (incentive stock options) and section 423 (employee stock purchase plans).

[2]   NONQUALIFIED STOCK OPTIONS

Section 83 applies to nonqualified options that have a readily ascertainable market value. An option generally has a readily ascertainable value if it is traded on an established market.[1] For nonqualified options whose value is readily ascertainable, the person who performs services realizes income at the time the option is granted.[2] If the option has no

---

§ 13.04   **2.**   See § 83(a); Treas. Reg. § 1.83–7(a).
1.   Treas. Reg. § 1.83–7(b)(1).

readily ascertainable market value, it is not taxable when granted; section 83 applies when the option is disposed of or exercised.[3]

In Commissioner v. LoBue[4] the Supreme Court rejected the argument that stock options designed to provide an employee with a proprietary interest in the corporation were not taxable. The Court also held that the employee realized gain when he purchased the stock, not when the options were granted. The options were not transferable and the employee's right to buy the stock under the options was contingent upon his remaining an employee of the corporation until they were exercised.

[3] INCENTIVE STOCK OPTIONS

Section 422 governs incentive stock options (ISOs). ISOs must be granted pursuant to a stockholder approved plan designating the number of shares that may be issued and the employees eligible to receive the options.[5] Moreover, the stockholders must approve the plan within one year before or after it is adopted.[6] Although there is no antidiscrimination requirement, several other requirements must be satisfied. The options must be granted within 10 years from the earlier of the date the plan is adopted or the date the plan is approved by the stockholders.[7] The options must not be exercisable later than 10 years following the date of the grant.[8] The option price must equal or exceed the fair market value of the stock when the options are granted.[9] The options must not be transferable except at death.[10] At the time the options are granted the individual may not be a 10% stockholder of the employer or of a parent or subsidiary corporation.[11]

An individual is limited to $100,000 on the value of stock covered by options that are exercisable for the first time during any calendar year. The options may be granted to an individual "for any reason connected with his employment."[12]

Section 422(a) directs that section 421(a) apply to shares transferred to an individual who exercised an ISO if: (1) no disposition of the shares is made within two years of the grant of the option nor within one year of the transfer of the shares to the individual[13] and (2) the individual is an employee of the corporation that granted the option or of a parent or subsidiary corporation from the date the option is granted until three months[14] before the option is exercised.[15] No income is recognized at the time of the grant of the option because section 83(e)(1) specifically exempts options that are provided for in section 421. Under section 421(a)(1) no income results from a qualifying transfer of shares at the

---

3. Id.

4. 351 U.S. 243, 76 S.Ct. 800, 100 L.Ed. 1142 (1956).

5. § 422(b)(1).

6. Id.

7. § 422(b)(2).

8. § 422(b)(3).

9. § 422(b)(4).

10. § 422(b)(5).

11. § 422(b)(6).

12. § 422(b).

13. § 422(a)(1).

14. The period is one year for an employee who is disabled. § 422(c)(6).

15. § 422(a)(2).

time of the exercise of the option. Also, section 421(a)(2) states that no deduction under section 162 is allowed when the shares are transferred pursuant to the exercise of the option.

[4] EMPLOYEE STOCK PURCHASE PLANS

Section 423 provides for another type of qualified option, employee stock purchase plans. Section 423 options are designed for rank-and-file employees. Generally, the plan must include all employees, although top-level employees, part-time employees, and employees with less than two years of service may be excluded.[16]

Section 423 options are subject to rules that are similar to those governing incentive stock options (ISOs), and the method of taxation upon disposition of the stock is similar. Also, section 423 options require the following: (1) a shareholder approved[17] plan that is limited to employees[18] owning 5% or less of the employer's stock[19] and that does not discriminate in favor of highly compensated employees (as defined in section 414(q)), (2) an option price of at least 85% of the fair market value at the time of the grant of the option or the exercise of the option,[20] (3) a holding period of 27 months (or 5 years if the 85% rule applies at the time of exercise),[21] and (4) an annual ceiling of $25,000 for each employee, valued at the time the option is granted, on the amount of stock available for purchase.[22]

16. § 423(b)(4).
17. § 423(b)(2).
18. § 423(b)(1).
19. § 423(b)(3).

20. § 423(b)(6).
21. § 423(b)(7).
22. § 423(b)(8).

Chapter 14

TAX SHELTERS AND
TAX AVOIDANCE

Table of Sections

§ 14.01   PROLOGUE ON TAX SHELTERS

During the heyday of tax shelters, a high-income individual taxpayer might significantly reduce her tax liability by doing little more than going to her tax professional, explaining she wanted a tax shelter, and writing a check. In return for that check and a signature, the taxpayer would receive papers explaining her right to substantial tax deductions and/or credits whose value far exceeded the amount of the check she had written.

At the most basic level, those who put together and marketed tax shelters sought to assemble transactions that allowed taxpayers to get current deductions: (1) for amounts they would have to pay only years later, if at all, (2) to avoid current taxation on income they could use now, (3) to convert ordinary income to capital gains, or (4) to put together some combination of all three—acceleration of deductions, deferral of income, and conversion of ordinary income to capital gains.

[1]   TAX SHELTER BASICS

The most simple tax shelters involved basic tax concepts. For the most part, tax shelter promoters simply purchased property and leased it out to those individuals looking to shelter their income from taxation. Consider, for example, the results if a taxpayer, T, purchases a commercial airplane (three year recovery property) for $10,000,000 by paying $1,000,000 cash and taking out a $9,000,000 nonrecourse loan (secured by the airplane) to finance the acquisition. Assume, for simplicity, the interest rate is 10%, so each year T must pay interest of $900,000 on the loan, and principal of $9,000,000 is due at the end of 10 years. Assume further that T does not really want any involvement in the airline business, but wants only a tax shelter, so that T has no interest in operating or maintaining the airplane. Instead, she leases the plane to Operator for a net rent of $900,000 per year for 10 years.

The obvious non-tax results of this transaction for T are that:

1.   T pays $1,000,000 in year one;

2.   In years one through 10, T receives $900,000 rent from Operator and pays $900,000 interest on the nonrecourse loan used to finance the airplane; and

3.   At the end of year 10, T must pay the $900,000 due and owing on the nonrecourse loan, or else the lender will foreclose on the airplane which secures that loan.

[2]   BASIS AND DEPRECIATION

Taxes aside, then, this is clearly a losing proposition for T, as she never recoups the $1,000,000 cash she pays in year one. Not surprisingly, what makes this "tax shelter" work for T, though, are the tax consequences; perhaps most importantly it is worth noting that: (a) T's cost for the plane is $10,000,000 (which includes both the $1,000,000 cash down-payment and the $9,000,000 nonrecourse loan;[1] and (b) the plane is three year recovery property). As a result of T's high basis and accelerated depreciation, T's depreciation deductions are as follows:[2]

Year 1: $3,333,000 (33.33% of $10,000)

Year 2: $4,445,000 (44.45% of $10,000)

Year 3: $1,481,000 (14.81% of $10,000,000)

Year 4: $741,000 (7.41% of $10,000)

Accordingly, since T's rental income each year equals her interest deduction every year for ten years, the net tax consequences for T each year are a net loss equal to the amount of depreciation to which she is entitled each year. If T has a 40% marginal tax rate,[3] her tax savings from the purchase and lease equal 40% of the amount of her net loss deduction, as follows:

Year one tax savings: $1,333,200 (40% of $3,333,000)

Year two tax savings: $1,778,000 (40% of $4,445,000)

Year three tax savings: $592,400 (40% of $1,481,000)

Year four tax savings: $296,400 (40% of $741,000)

To put this all together, in year one, T pays $1,000,000 and receives tax savings of $1,333,200, for an immediate *profit* of $332,200. In year two, T pays nothing and receives tax savings (profit) of $1,778,000. In year three T pays nothing and receives tax savings (profit) of $592,000, and in year four T pays nothing and receives tax savings of $296,000.

These benefits result primarily from the fact that T's basis, which can be depreciated (deducted) beginning in year one, includes the $9,000,000 borrowed on a nonrecourse basis that T will pay, if at all (because the loan is nonrecourse), only at the end of 10 years. The high basis, in turn, is a direct result of the holdings in cases such as Crane v. Commissioner[4] and its progeny. In addition, the investment is made even more attractive because accelerated depreciation enables T to deduct higher losses earlier on than would otherwise be the case.

[3] CLOSING OUT THE TAX SHELTER

The only catch for T in this example comes at the end of ten years, when payment of $9,000,000 becomes due on the nonrecourse note. At

---

§ 14.01

1. See Black's Law Dictionary (8th ed. 2004) which defines "nonrecourse loan" as "A secured loan that allows the lender to attach only the collateral, not the borrower's personal assets, if the loan is not repaid."

2. See Rev. Proc. 87–57 at § 8.02 (Table 1).

3. Keep in mind that at the time these tax shelters became popular, the top tax bracket was 70%, and taxpayers typically owed state income tax of up to 10%, putting many high-income taxpayers in combined brackets of up to 80% and thereby doubling the value of the tax savings.

4. 331 U.S. 1, 67 S.Ct. 1047, 91 L.Ed. 1301 (1947) (holding that a taxpayer who sold property encumbered by a nonrecourse mortgage that was less than the property's fair market value had to include the unpaid balance of the mortgage in the computation of the amount the taxpayer realized on the sale).

that time, T can choose to pay the $9,000,000 (if the airplane has substantially retained its value or increased in value), or she can choose to *not* pay (the note is, after all, nonrecourse). Of course, if she does not pay the note when it becomes due, the lender will foreclose on the note, and T will no longer own the airplane. But, since T has already made a profit of well over $4,000,000 in tax savings, she will likely be happy to sacrifice the airplane.

Most tax shelter investors in T's position were sanguine about losing the airplane in year ten, when they failed to pay the note, but they were often less comfortable with the tax consequences that occurred on the lender's foreclosure. The problem is that, just as nonrecourse debt borrowed to purchase property and nonrecourse debt to which property is subject at the time of purchase are part of the purchaser's cost basis for the property, nonrecourse debt to which property is subject at the time of sale or exchange (including foreclosure) is part of the seller's (or mortgagor's, in the case of foreclosure) amount realized on disposition of the property. As a result, when the lender forecloses in year 10, T's amount realized will include $9,000,000 debt relief. Since T's adjusted basis in the property has been reduced to 0 because of depreciation, T will realize and recognize a gain of $900,000 at the time of foreclosure in year 10. If T is still in the 40% tax bracket at that time, she will be liable for tax of $3,600,000![5]

Many tax shelter investors ignored the potential problems in closing out the tax shelter in year 10 because they realized that all that would happen in year 10 would be that they would have lots of income, and all they would need to do to avoid paying tax on that income would be to invest in another tax shelter in year 10. Those taxpayers who were more risk averse, however, may well have performed a present value analysis of the original investment, taking into account the impending year 10 liability, prior to investing. To do so, T might initially set out the net receipt or payment, after-taxes, for each year, and its present value, as follows:

Net Receipt/payment	Present Value (discounted at 10% rate)
Year 1: + $333,200	+ $333,200
Year 2: + $1,778,000	+ $1,616,202
Year 3: + $592,400	+ $489,332
Year 4: + $296,400	+ $222,596
Year 10: − $3,600,000	− $1,526,400
Net present value:	**+ $1,134,930**

What all of this means is that this tax shelter presents an opportunity for an immediate return of an amount in excess of T's investment, and over 10 years it provides a risk-free, capital-investment-free return with a present value of $1,134,930.

5. If the property subject to the depreciation is real estate, note that in addition to the benefit of deferral of the gain, the taxpayer will likely recognize only capital gain rather than ordinary income (from recapture) on the sale.

§ 14.02   TAX SHELTERS AND LIMITED PARTNERSHIPS

Not surprisingly, most taxpayers interested in sheltering income were not eager to purchase an airplane or any other depreciable property in order to obtain tax benefits. Finding the asset to purchase, obtaining financing, finding a lessee, entering into an appropriate lease agreement, and overseeing the lease agreement are potentially time consuming and difficult. In addition, taxpayers could not often find a particular asset at exactly the right price to provide just the amount of deductions they needed. What taxpayers wanted, and what tax shelter promoters gave them, was the ability to simply determine the deductions they wanted, make out a check, and get the deductions.

To give taxpayers what they sought, promoters would (for an appropriate fee) do all the groundwork of finding the asset, securing financing, obtaining the lessee, and overseeing the transaction. Rather than attempting to enter into a separate transaction for each taxpayer, promoters would put together a single large transaction, and then allow taxpayers to each take a "piece" sufficient to provide them the deductions they sought.

To see how this might work, let us return to the original example from above, which involves a cash payment of $1,000,000 in year one in return for tax savings of $1,333,200 in year one, $1,778,000 in year two, $592,400 in year three and $296,400 in year four. Assume that T does not wish to pay $1,000,000 cash and does not need millions of dollars in tax savings, but, instead, T wants to pay only $50,000 ($\frac{1}{20}$ of the total $1,000,000 down-payment) and will be happy with $\frac{1}{20}$ of the total tax savings. In other words, T would like to do nothing other than walk into the tax shelter promoter's office, make out a check for $50,000, and save $66,600 in year one, $88,900 in year two, etc.

Partnerships, but not corporations, provide for pass-through taxation.[1] As a result, the taxpayer who acquired a $\frac{1}{20}$ interest in the tax shelter partnership discussed above could do exactly as she wanted and get exactly the results she wanted.[2] The partnership, rather than any individual, would incur losses in year one through four, and each partner would be permitted to deduct her proportionate share of the partnership's net loss.

§ 14.02

1. See § 701 which provides, "A partnership as such shall not be subject to the income tax imposed by this chapter. Persons carrying on business as partners shall be liable for income tax only in their separate or individual capacities." See also § 11 which provides, "A tax is hereby imposed for each taxable year on the taxable income of every corporation." *Nota bene:* although S corporations (those corporations making an affirmative election under § 1361(a)) provide flow-through taxation similar to a partnership, they nevertheless do not make very attractive tax shelter vehicles since S corporations cannot utilize leverage in the same manner as a limited partnership can to artificially enhance basis for depreciation purposes.

2. Indeed, results could be even better because of special allocations. See 704(b).

Of course, tax shelter investors had no interest in either managing the partnership or incurring the potential liability that goes along with being a general partner in a partnership. Hence, limited partnerships (rather than general partnerships) proved to be the optimal vehicle for tax shelters. The common scenario of the day involved a tax shelter promoter who was the general partner and various passive limited partners with a tax appetite. As limited partners, their potential liability for partnership obligations was limited to their actual cash payment, and unlike general partners, limited partners can typically freely sell or exchange their interests.

§ 14.03 SALES AND LEASEBACKS

Shortly after-taxpayers discovered the potential of tax shelters, several of them attempted in a single stroke to both simplify the mechanics of the transactions and enhance their tax benefits. To see how they did so, consider the possibility that T, who wants a tax shelter, contacts P, who owns an airplane worth $10,000,000 which she intends to continue to use in her business. T agrees to purchase P's plane for $20,000,000 (twice its actual value) on the terms delineated hereafter. T will pay P $1,000,000 cash and purchase the plane subject to a $19,000,000 nonrecourse loan (extended by P). The loan is an interest only loan for 10 years, so that each year T must pay to P interest of $1,900,000. Since P seeks to continue to use the plane, and T has no interest in the actual plane, T will lease the plane back to P for 10 years for annual rent of $1,900,000.

As a result, the net economics (absent tax consequences) of the transaction are that T pays $1,000,000 to P in year one. Thereafter P continues to operate the plane in her business for 10 years (during which time the interest T must pay to P and the rent P must pay to T cancel each other out). At the end of 10 years, T will likely not pay the nonrecourse debt when it becomes due, and P will foreclose and continue to own and to operate the property. Thus, the net cash result, as in the previous example, is a single payment of $1,000,000 from T to P in year one.

The tax consequences of this transaction for T (if it works as planned) are that each year the interest T pays and the rent T receives cancel each other out, again leaving T with a depreciation deduction and a net tax loss double what it was in the above transaction (because T's basis is now $20,000,000 rather than $10,000,000). The only difference for T from the above example is that T doubles her tax savings.

As to P, she receives $1,000,000 in year one and continues to be able to use her property without interruption. While T may be required to pay tax on some gain in year one, she can defer reporting 95% of her gain until she receives payments, under the installment sale rules.[1] Since it is likely that she will never receive additional payments, because T

§ 14.03

1. See § 453.

likely will never pay off the nonrecourse $19,000,000 debt, it is likely that P will never pay additional tax on the gain.[2]

Estate of Franklin[3] involved a transaction similar to the foregoing scenario. Franklin concerned the sale and leaseback of a motel. In Franklin, the purchase price was paid secured by a nonrecourse note and paid over a ten year period, with a balloon payment in year ten. As in the example above, the annual rental payments from the motel operator equaled the annual installment obligation from the purchaser. Accordingly, despite the fact that no cash actually changed hands, the purchaser purported to be entitled to massive depreciation and interest deductions.

In Franklin, the Ninth Circuit followed the rule of Crane v. Commissioner,[4] which held that a taxpayer who sold property encumbered by a nonrecourse mortgage that was less than the property's fair market value had to include the unpaid balance of the mortgage in the computation of the amount the taxpayer realized on the sale. As a corollary to Crane, the Ninth Circuit also followed the rule of Commissioner v. Tufts[5] where the Supreme Court concluded that the rule of Crane applies, even if the unpaid amount of the nonrecourse mortgage exceeds the value of the property. Hence, the Supreme Court said in Tufts that the fair market value of the property is irrelevant to the calculation of the amount realized.[6]

Accordingly, in Franklin, the court found that the taxpayer was entitled to no depreciation or interest deductions on the property because there was no equity in the property by nature of the fact that the amount of the nonrecourse debt involved in the transaction far-outweighed the fair market value of the property.[7]

While the holding in Franklin may well have put an end to some of the most abusive tax shelters, it did little to curb the run-of-the-mill shelter. While perhaps taxpayers could no longer artificially inflate the price of property in order to garner excess deductions, taxpayers were still free to purchase property for an amount not obviously in excess of its value; to finance the purchase with nonrecourse debt; and to shelter almost unlimited amounts of income from tax.

§ 14.04 THE "AT RISK" RULES

Section 465 generally limits a taxpayer's deduction to the amount "at risk" of otherwise allowable items for a trade or business or the

2. If P had taken depreciation on the plane prior to the sale, the amount of any gain that represented depreciation recapture would be ineligible for installment sale treatment. See § 453(i)(1) and (2).

3. 544 F.2d 1045 (9th Cir. 1976).

4. Crane v. Commissioner, 331 U.S. 1, 67 S.Ct. 1047, 91 L.Ed. 1301 (1947) (holding that a taxpayer who sold property encumbered by a nonrecourse mortgage that was less than the property's fair market value had to include the unpaid balance of

the mortgage in the computation of the amount the taxpayer realized on the sale).

5. 461 U.S. 300, 103 S.Ct. 1826, 75 L.Ed.2d 863 (1983).

6. See also Treas. Reg. § 1.1001–2(b), stating that the fair market value of property that secures a liability is not relevant for determining the amount realized.

7. Estate of Franklin v. Commissioner, 544 F.2d 1045, 1049 (9th Cir. 1976) (quoting Mayerson v. Commissioner, 47 T.C. 340, 350 (1966)).

production of income.[1] Specifically, section 465(a) provides that "losses" from impacted activities "shall be allowed only to the extent of the aggregate amount with respect to which the taxpayer is at risk." For purposes of section 465, the term "loss" is defined by section 465(d) as the excess of deductions otherwise allowed over the income from an activity. Thus, section 465 is aimed at preventing deduction of amounts in excess of the taxpayer's *economic* investment in an activity; i.e., section 465 is designed to prevent the taxpayer from taking deductions in excess of what the taxpayer could actually lose if the venture failed. Amounts considered at risk are defined in section 465(b); in general, the term encompasses the cash and other property the taxpayer has contributed to the activity as well as the proceeds from loans on which the taxpayer is personally liable[2] or for which property has been pledged but not contributed to the activity.[3]

To see how the at risk rules work, let us return to the original example, where T purchases a commercial airplane (three year recovery property) for $10,000,000 by paying $1,000,000 cash and taking out a $9,000,000 nonrecourse loan (secured by the airplane). Each year T must pay interest of $900,000 on the loan, and the principal is due at the end of 10 years. T also leases the plane to Operator for a net rent of $900,000 per year for 10 years. As above, this activity will result in a net loss for T of $3,333,000 in year one, $4,445,000 in year two, $1,481,000 in year three, and $741,000 in year four.

Section 465 allows T to deduct her year one loss only to the extent that she is at risk with respect to this activity. Since T contributed $1,000,000 cash, she is at risk only to the extent of $1,000,000, so can deduct only $1,000,000 of her year one loss of $3,333,000.

Losses limited by section 465 are treated as deductions incurred in the same activity in the following year.[4] As a result, in year two, T has a loss not of $4,445,000, but of $6,778,000 ($4,445,000 plus the carryover deduction of $2,333,000). Because T was at risk only to the extent of $1,000,000, and because she deducted $1,000,000 of her year one loss, though, none of her year two loss is deductible.[5]

[1] AMOUNT AT RISK

Basically, the "at risk" amount is a running account which is increased by the amounts the taxpayer invests in the activity or for which the taxpayer is personally liable with respect to the activity (and by the net income (if any) generated by the activity), and is decreased by

---

§ 14.04

1. See § 465(a).

2. *Nota bene:* because taxpayers are not personally liable for nonrecourse debt, it is generally not properly includable in

calculating the amount at risk under § 465(b).

3. See § 465(b).

4. See § 465(a)(2).

5. Id.

net losses from the activity deducted against other income and cash withdrawn from the activity. If T wished to increase the loss she was permitted to deduct in year one (for example so that she could deduct her entire year one loss of $3,333,000), she could increase the amount for which she is at risk by the end of year one by either contributing additional cash to the activity (for example, by paying off $2,333,000 of the loan), by contributing property to the activity (in which case her amount at risk would be increased by her adjusted basis in the contributed property), or by simply becoming personally liable on $2,333,000 of the loan. As a result, she can still deduct amounts that she will not pay for ten years, so long as it is clear that she will in fact pay those amounts when they become due.

While most tax shelters do not produce tax profits, to the extent that a tax shelter does produce net income for a given year and the taxpayer does not withdraw that income from the activity, that income represents tax profits which, if left in the activity, represent additional amounts at risk.

[2] LIMITATIONS OF SECTION 465

While section 465 might have been a good start in congressional regulation of tax shelters, it has two significant loopholes that allow such shelters to continue to prosper: (1) taxpayers can become personally liable for debt rather than borrowing on a nonrecourse basis, and (2) there are exceptions for real estate.

[3] PERSONAL LIABILITY

It is true that section 465 generally prevents taxpayers from deducting, by way of depreciation, amounts which they will likely never pay (because the liability that has given rise to basis is nonrecourse), but it is equally true that section 465 makes no effort to prevent taxpayers from deducting, by way of depreciation, amounts that they will pay in the future (because the liability is one for which the taxpayer is personally liable), despite the fact that payment may not be due for some time. As a result, the time value of money benefits offered by tax shelters remain unaffected by section 465.

[4] REAL ESTATE

Probably the most important escape from the limitations of section 465 lies in the fact that where financing of real estate is provided from outside lending institutions, such as banks, qualified nonrecourse liabilities secured by the real property are treated as amounts for which the taxpayer is "at risk."[6] Accordingly, with respect to real property, the classic tax shelter model discussed above is alive and well so long as you are able to obtain your nonrecourse financing from a financial institution.

---

6. § 465(b)(6).

Even so, because real property is not subject to the same rapid acceleration as is most other property (because it lasts longer), the benefits of tax shelters based on real property may be somewhat less than those based on personal property.

§ 14.05 THE PASSIVE ACTIVITY LOSS RULES

[1] IN GENERAL

The most significant congressional restriction on tax shelters has been the enactment of section 469, generally known as the passive loss rules. The passive activity loss rules apply to individuals, estates, trusts, closely-held C corporations, and personal service corporations.[1] The general idea of section 469 is that losses from tax shelters can be deducted only against income from other tax shelters, but tax shelter losses (in the aggregate) cannot be deducted against any other kind of income.[2] Excess losses are carried forward and treated as deductions and credits from tax shelters in future years.[3] Of course, since tax shelters are put together for the purpose of generating tax *losses* rather than taxable income, this means that, for the most part, tax shelters are now essentially useless. Indeed, about the only time that tax shelters produce taxable income is when the taxpayer disposes of his entire interest in a tax shelter, and excess losses from the activity are allowed in full (whether or not the disposition actually generates any taxable income or gain) only upon such disposition.

Additionally, credits from tax shelters generally are limited to the tax allocable to other tax shelters. Any excess is carried forward and treated as a credit from tax shelters in future years, but any excess credits from one activity are not allowed upon disposition of the activity (unless, of course, the taxpayer has sufficient tax liability from other tax shelters to enable use of the credits).[4]

[2] ARE ALL PASSIVE ACTIVITIES TAX SHELTERS?

While the idea behind section 469 was to create a "basket" into which only income and losses from tax shelters had to be put (so that tax shelter losses could offset only tax shelter income), Congress realized that it could not simply single out "tax shelters" for this limitation; no taxpayer would ever acknowledge that any investment was a "tax shelter." Instead, Congress created and defined the term "passive activity" so as to include most tax shelters (so that most tax shelters would be limited) and to exclude most other investments or sources of income (so that taxpayers could not offset income from these investments by using tax shelters); hence, this is why the "passive activity" loss rules exist today.

§ 14.05

1. See § 469(a)(2).

2. See § 469(a).

3. See § 469(b).

4. See § 469(b).

Perhaps the best way to approach the definition of a passive activity is to begin with an explanation of what Congress did *not* mean to include within the bailiwick of section 469. Obviously, any expenditure by a taxpayer for recreational rather than profit-seeking purposes is not deductible in any event, and there is no need to have section 469 limit expenditures of this type.[5] Hence, passive activities include only profit-seeking investments. In addition, any trade or business to which the taxpayer devotes substantial effort is likely to constitute a legitimate business of the taxpayer, and represents an effort to make money rather than to get tax deductions; as a result, a "passive activity" is defined generally in section 469(c) as a trade or business activity in which the taxpayer does not materially participate.[6]

Since an individual may participate in numerous genuine profit-seeking efforts or in none at all, any taxpayer may materially participate in no trade or business activity, or in more than one trade or business activity. "Material participation" in any activity requires that the individual's involvement must relate to operations and the individual must be involved on a "regular, continuous, and substantial basis."[7]

The regulations elaborate on and explain the definition of material participation.[8] Factors that are considered in determining whether the material participation requirement is satisfied include: (1) whether and how regularly the taxpayer is present at the site or sites of the principal operations of the activity, (2) whether the taxpayer's participation in management is merely formal and nominal rather than a genuine exercise of independent discretion and judgment, and (3) whether the taxpayer has little or no knowledge or experience regarding the business.[9] An individual who works full-time in a line of business consisting of one or more business activities is generally treated as materially participating in those activities. The provision of legal, tax, or accounting services as an independent contractor do not constitute material participation in an activity, other than the activity of providing such specialized services to the public.[10]

While the definition of passive activity in section 469(c) works to exclude from section 469 any trade or business in which the taxpayer is sufficiently active, that definition alone is also both too narrow and too broad to be effective. It is too narrow in that it does not include many kinds of typical tax shelters, and it is too broad in that it does include numerous investments that are not tax shelters. In order to ensure that the vast majority of tax shelters are included in the definition of passive

---

5. See § 469(c)(1)(A) (which provides that § 469 only applies to the conduct of an activity which constitutes a trade or business). Of course, if a taxpayer is engaged in a trade or business by definition he has a profit motive.

6. § 469(c)(1).

7. 469(h)(1). Estates and trusts are treated as materially participating if the executor or fiduciary acting in that capacity is materially participating.

8. Treas. Reg. § 1.469–5T.

9. See Treas. Reg. § 1.469–5T(a)(1)-(7).

10. See Treas. Reg. § 1.469–5T(a)(6) and (d).

activity, Congress examined tax common shelter schemes. Since many tax shelters (and all of the ones used as examples in this work) involved the purchase and leasing out of property, Congress enacted section 469(c)(2) to ensure that these and similar transactions were brought within the scope of 469 by directly providing that "the term 'passive activity' includes any rental activity."[11]

Additionally, since so many tax shelters took the form of limited partnerships, Congress was careful to ensure that such interest would be restricted by section 469 by providing, in section 469(h)(2), that except as provided in regulations, no limited partnership interest shall be treated as an interest with respect to which the taxpayer materially participates.[12]

With the additions set forth above, section 469 was broad enough to include as passive activities almost all types of tax shelter investments, but without further exclusions, it would have also included as "passive activities" almost all sources of portfolio income such as income from stocks and bonds. Had Congress left the statute like that, it would have meant that those who *work* for money could not use tax shelters to offset their earned income (because "passive activity" losses can be used only to offset income from "passive activities"), but those whose income took the form of interest, dividends and capital gains could use tax shelters (because interest, dividends and capital gains represent income from activities in which the taxpayer does not materially participate, so would be left in the "passive activity" basket). In order to ensure that taxpayers could not use tax shelters to offset portfolio income (by excluding such investments from the definition of "passive activities"), Congress enacted section 469(e) to directly address the issue by excluding such portfolio income from passive activity status.

[3] DEFINITION OF "ACTIVITY"

If two or more undertakings are separate activities, the taxpayer must establish material participation separately for each.[13] If they are part of the same "activity," the taxpayer need only establish material participation with respect to the activity as a whole.[14] In addition, when there is a disposition of interest in some passive activity, it is crucial to know the scope of the activity, to determine whether the taxpayer has disposed of his entire interest in the activity, which would make any deferred losses from that activity currently deductible in full.[15] The legislative history states that "[t]he determination of what constitutes a separate activity is ... to be made in a realistic economic sense" and that the factors enumerated in the regulations for section 183 are

---

11. Interestingly, if a taxpayer has a working interest in an oil or gas property, such interest generally *is* treated as active even though the taxpayer does *not* materially participate. § 469(c)(3).

12. See generally § 469(m)(2); but see also § 469 (c)(7) (which provides a limited

exception from the rule of § 469(m)(2) for certain real estate professionals).

13. See § 469(c)(1)(B).

14. Id.

15. See § 469(g).

relevant in ascertaining the scope of an activity.[16] In determining whether two or more undertakings are part of a single activity, normal commercial practices are considered probative,[17] and any limited partnership interest is treated as inherently including no more than one activity.

[4] TREATMENT OF LOSSES AND CREDITS

Passive activity losses generally are deductible only against passive activity income.[18] Suspended passive activity losses cannot be carried back, but they can be carried forward indefinitely and are allowed in subsequent taxable years to be netted against passive activity income.[19] Moreover, suspended losses from an activity are allowed in full upon a taxable disposition.[20]

Passive activity credits generally are treated in the same manner as passive activity deductions;[21] they may be used to offset only tax attributable to passive income.[22] To determine the amount of tax attributable to net passive income, one must compare the amount the taxpayer would pay with regard to all income with the amount that would be paid with regard to taxable income other than net passive income (disregarding credits in both situations).

It should be noted that closely-held C corporations (other than personal service corporations) may offset passive losses and credits against active business income but not against portfolio income.[23]

[5] OFFSET FOR REAL ESTATE ACTIVITIES

In some circumstances, taxpayers may deduct up to $25,000[24] of passive activity losses (and credits in a deduction-equivalent sense)[25] attributable to rental real estate activities against other (non-passive) income. To qualify for this limited benefit, an individual must be able to show that while she does not "materially" participate in the activity, she does "actively participate" in the rental real estate activity.[26] "Active participation" in turn requires significantly less involvement than does "material participation," and it is generally satisfied so long as the taxpayer owns, either directly or as a general partner, a sufficiently substantial (more than 10%) interest in the building.[27] The allowance is phased out ratably as the taxpayer's adjusted gross income (determined without regard to passive activity losses) increases from $100,000 to

---

16. Rep. No. 313, 99th Cong., 2d Sess. 739 (1986). There are certain elections available for real estate professionals. See § 469(c)(7).

17. See Treas. Reg. § 1.469T–5(a)(7).

18. See § 469(a).

19. See § 469(b).

20. See § 469(g).

21. See § 468(d)(1) and (2).

22. See § 469(a)(1)(B).

23. See § 469(e)(2).

24. For spouses filing separate returns the limit is $12,500. 469(i)(5)

25. The deduction equivalent of credits is the amount that, if allowed as a deduction, would reduce tax by an amount equal to the amount of the credit. § 469(j)(5).

26. § 469(i)(1) and (2).

27. § 469(i)(6).

$150,000, and it is simply unavailable to any taxpayer with an adjusted gross income in excess of $150,000.[28]

[6]   DISPOSITIONS

If there is a fully taxable disposition of the taxpayer's entire interest in the activity, any overall loss from the activity is currently deductible against any other income the taxpayer has, whether active or passive.[29] However, a transaction that is a sale in form only and not treated as a taxable disposition under general tax principles, for example, a wash sale or sham transaction, does not give rise to the allowance of suspended deductions. In addition, if a taxpayer, in an otherwise fully taxable transaction, disposes of his interest in a passive activity to a related party,[30] the suspended losses will not be allowed; instead they will remain with the taxpayer.[31] Such suspended losses may be offset by the taxpayer's income from passive activities.

When a taxpayer makes a gift of his entire interest, the donee's basis is increased by the amount of any suspended losses. If the donee later sells at a loss, the donee's basis is limited to the fair market value of the interest at the time of the gift.[32] If a limited partnership conducting two or more separate activities disposes of one of the activities, the limited partners are not treated as having made a disposition so that suspended losses are allowed.[33] Accordingly, a limited partner must dispose of his entire limited partnership interest in order to potentially utilize any suspended losses.[34]

§ 14.06   SYSTEMATIC RESPONSES TO TAX AVOIDANCE

The basic structure of our tax system appears to be here to stay, and the problems of mismeasurement, unintended motivation of taxpayers, and some imprecision in the definition of transactions are all, to some extent, inherent in that structure. These problems are, in very real ways, interdependent and mutually compounding: a system that accurately measured economic income and other significant statuses would not unintentionally influence taxpayer behavior; a system that relied on transactions that could be described only with some minimal imprecision would not be subjected to manipulation if different characterizations did not dramatically alter taxable income; and a transaction-based system that was not full of taxpayers seeking both to act and to characterize their actions in ways that minimize tax liability would provide a more trustworthy measurement of each person's taxable income. Clearly, it is the compounding of these different problems that makes them as signifi-

28.   § 469(i)(3)(A).

29.   § 469(g)(1).

30.   Within the meaning of § 267(b) or § 707(b)(1).

31.   § 469(g)(1)(B).

32.   § 469(j)(6).

33.   See § 469(c)(7)(ii).

34.   See § 469(g) and (c)(7)(ii).

cant as they are; as a result, current tax jurisprudence uniformly addresses each of these issues in conjunction with one another.

Even though the three problems raised above are mutually compounding in *effect*, they are at their *sources* entirely separate problems. Current judicial approaches to the problems have failed to acknowledge they are indeed separate and, as a result, they have never satisfactorily addressed any of them. In addition, because courts have been unable to *segregate* the issues that arise, they have been uniformly unable to devise remedies that tend to *deal* with those issues. Problems actually generated by inherent imprecision have been "solved" not by acknowledging, but by denying, that imprecision, and problems of taxpayer motivation have been "solved" by asserting that the problems were *not* motivation but imprecision.

Only when these problems are segregated as separate issues can they be addressed in a meaningful way. To segregate these issues ultimately requires acknowledgement that any transaction-based system is flawed (it is necessarily inaccurate, imprecise) and improperly normative, but to acknowledge these inherent flaws is the only way to begin to address them.

[1]   CURRENT DOCTRINES

Essentially, while many doctrines have grown around both unclear characterization of actions and tax-motivated behavior, these doctrines have never really been very clearly articulated or classified. Instead, the Internal Revenue Service and the courts are more likely simply to cite, rather than explain, one or more of these doctrines to justify withholding various tax benefits. When more than one doctrine is cited, a court may view them as alternative justifications for its decision, or as merely alternative names for a single rationale. Against such a background, the summary that follows necessarily will not conform with all of the different uses of the relevant terms which have been adopted; however, it should provide insight into the scope and variety of rationales and will explain generally how each "works."

[a]   The Sham Transaction Doctrine

The "sham transaction" label has long been a popular one, and its popularity in part appears to stem from its flexibility. At one time or another it has been used to describe actions that fit into all of the categories that follow.[1] Simply for the sake of categorization, it is used here to connote its most narrow legal construction and the one that most closely resembles its general usage outside of tax law. So defined, a "sham transaction" is one that never occurred. If tax consequences depend on representations regarding changes in legal rights and if those changes simply did not occur, the reported "transaction" is a sham.

---

§ 14.06

1. See e.g., Gregory v. Helvering, 293 U.S. 465, 55 S.Ct. 266, 79 L.Ed. 596 (1935); Knetsch v. United States, 364 U.S. 361, 365 (1960); Rice's Toyota World, Inc. v. Commissioner, 81 T.C. 184, 207 (1983), modified, 752 F.2d 89 (4th Cir. 1985).

Since most "shams," in this sense of the word, are nothing less than tax fraud, they (as opposed to what penalties should be imposed for them) are not often seriously litigated,[2] and, accordingly, they will not be discussed in depth herein.

[b] Substance Versus Form

As with "sham," references to substance versus form have been parts of a wide range of cases and have been imbued with numerous different meanings. Because of the flexibility which courts have shown in applying this expression, it cannot seriously be contended that there is a single "correct" application of the doctrine. The assignment of the words to the transactions that follow is admittedly for the purpose of identifying and labeling a specific kind of approach taken by some courts rather than for the purpose of either fully describing all the situations in which courts have applied the "substance versus form" terminology, or suggesting that one of those applications is more "correct" than the others. That said, the substance versus form doctrine will be used here to describe the situation where: (1) there is no factual dispute as to the significant legal and economic interactions and relationships (*i.e.*, the rights and liabilities of the parties) involved;[3] and (2) there are at least two alternative tax transactions which can describe those interactions. Examples of this type of substance versus form question are less common than might be expected, in part because it is fairly rare that the significant legal and economic relationships upon which characterization depends are clearly established. Typical of these are questions regarding whether certain kinds of property transactions are sales, leases, or simply mortgages.

2. The most widely known example of this kind of "sham" is the case of Goodstein v. Commissioner, 267 F.2d 127 (1st Cir. 1959), aff'g. 30 T.C. 1178 (1958). In that case, the purported (and reported) transaction was as follows: Goodstein borrowed $10,000,000 from Lender. Goodstein transferred this money, plus $15,000 of his own funds, to Broker. Broker took a $15,000 commission and used the remaining $10,000,000 to buy bonds from Seller. The bonds were pledged with Lender to secure Goodstein's $10,000,000 obligation. Goodstein then borrowed more from Lender to pay the (deductible) interest owed to Lender on the first loan. When it was time for repayment to Lender, Lender would merely foreclose on the pledged bonds. The tax consequences to Goodstein were substantial current interest deductions and complete deferral of income accruing on the pledged bonds. The "legal" transaction was quite different. Broker actually purchased the bonds from Seller out of its own funds. Goodstein paid $15,000 to Broker. Lender, which had no funds, asked Broker to sell

the pledged bonds. One half hour after Broker had purchased the bonds from Seller, it sold them back at the same price. It was over the next year and a half that Goodstein purported to pay deductible "interest" to Lender.

The Tax Court determined that Goodstein was entitled to no deduction because the series of transactions was pursuant to a preconceived plan that lacked economic substance and should be ignored for tax purposes. 30 T.C. at 1188. On appeal, the First Circuit did not comment upon the asserted lack of economic substance and instead decided that the legal relationship that existed between Goodstein and Lender was not that of borrower and lender, so that payments from one to the other could not be interest. See 267 F.2d at 131. It is just this lack of a purported legal relationship that defines what is here referred to as a "sham."

3. Or, if there *was* a factual dispute as to these rights and liabilities, the questions of fact have been resolved.

[c] Business Purpose

Like the sham and substance versus form approaches, considerations of "business purpose," or a taxpayer's lack thereof, have appeared in numerous cases and for numerous reasons,[4] and the business purpose test is indeed often seen as a synonym for sham or substance versus form.

As used here, and as most commonly used by tax lawyers, the test means something quite different from these other doctrines: certain transactions defined in the Code carry with them a requirement not specifically mentioned therein, and that requirement is that the exchanges be engaged in for some legitimate business purpose.[5] As commonly used, the business purpose doctrine is nothing more than a nonstatutory element of the definition of certain transactions.

[d] The Step Transaction Doctrine

Each of the above doctrines, when applied to a given exchange, may change the tax consequences sought by the taxpayer entering into that exchange. None of the doctrines can be applied without first determining the exchange(s) to which its application is to be made. In other words, an essential prerequisite to characterizing taxpayer actions is a description of the specific actions to be characterized. The step transaction doctrine is the tool by which the courts determine what *actions* make up a single *transaction*.

Sometimes explicitly, and sometimes by implication, this doctrine permeates the tax field. Often courts specifically describe their holdings as applications of the doctrine,[6] but just as significantly, many courts which do not view themselves as applying the doctrine base their decisions on an assumption that the actions to be characterized (e.g., for purposes of applying the substance versus form doctrine) are not the actions isolated for characterization by the taxpayer.[7] Because the step transaction doctrine determines only what actions are to be looked at together to determine the "substance" of the transaction, its application is necessarily (but, again, not always explicitly) followed by application of

---

4. For a general history of the beginnings of the business purpose requirement, see Spear, "Corporate Business Purpose" in Reorganization, 3 Tax L. Rev. 225 (1947); Michaelson, "Business Purpose" and Tax Free Reorganization, 61 Yale L.J. 14 (1952).

5. The most widely used example of this concept originates in corporate reorganizations where the courts and the Internal Revenue Service have often held that exchanges seemingly meeting the reorganization definitions of § 368(a) are not reorganizations because they lack a "business purpose."

6. Many of the thousands of these cases are described in Mintz & Plumb, Step Transactions in Corporate Reorganizations, 12 N.Y.U. Inst. on Fed. Tax'n. 247 (1954);

Note, Step Transactions, 24 U. Miami L. Rev. 60 (1969); Hobbet, The Step Transaction Doctrine and Its Effect on Corporate Transactions, 19 Tul. Tax Inst. 102 (1970).

7. See e.g., Knetsch v. United States, 364 U.S. 361, 81 S.Ct. 132, 5 L.Ed.2d 128 (1960). In Knetsch, the taxpayer purportedly borrowed money to purchase an annuity. He pledged the annuity as security for the loan and consistently borrowed against any appreciation in the annuity. In holding that the "substance" was not a loan, the Court referred to the "transaction" as the entire series of events rather than the borrowing alone; but nowhere does it appear that the Court considered itself to be actually applying the step transaction doctrine.

the substance versus form doctrine, in that courts must determine the appropriate tax characterization of the redefined exchanges.

[2]   Problems With the Responses to Tax Avoidance

Rather than counteract the problems caused by the system's transaction-based focus, the above doctrines have been consistently applied in a manner which is so colored by that focus that they might be said to have exacerbated rather than solved the system's problems. Despite some appearance of reasonableness and consistency, none of the doctrines have any coherent application. What follows is an in-depth analysis of the history and application of these doctrines.

[a]   Business Purpose

The business purpose test originated in Gregory v. Helvering.[8] Ms. Gregory owned all the stock of United Mortgage Company, which in turn owned, *inter alia*, 1,000 shares of Monitor Securities Corporation. Gregory sought to have the Monitor shares sold and to have the proceeds of the sale inure to her personal account. To accomplish these results with a minimum of tax liability, Gregory caused United Mortgage to transfer the Monitor shares to a newly formed subsidiary (Averill) which was distributed to Gregory and then immediately liquidated, leaving Gregory in possession of the Monitor shares, which she then sold. Gregory contended that the formation of Averill and the subsequent distribution of the Averill stock to her was a tax-free reorganization, and the only tax-significant transaction was the liquidation of Averill, which resulted in a relatively small capital gains tax to Gregory.

Despite the fact that the transfer of Averill appeared to meet the statutory language defining a reorganization,[9] the Court held the distribution of Averill was *not* a reorganization, and that Gregory should be taxed as if she had instead received a dividend taxable at the substantially higher ordinary income rates (which were applicable to dividends at that time). The Court explained that the reorganization provision, which speaks of a transfer of assets by one corporation to another, refers only to a transfer made "in pursuance of a plan of reorganization of corporate business; and not a transfer of assets by one corporation to another in pursuance of a plan having no relation to the business of either.... "[10] It went on to state that the transaction which had occurred was "simply an operation having no business or corporate purpose" and as such "the transaction upon its face lies outside the plain intent of the statute."[11] The apparent instruction to be gained from the Court's language is that

---

8. 293 U.S. 465, 55 S.Ct. 266, 79 L.Ed. 596 (1935).

9. The pertinent statutory language the Gregory court relied upon defined a tax-free reorganization to include "a transfer by a corporation of all or a part of its assets to another corporation if immediately after the transfer the transferor or its stockhold-

ers or both are in control of the corporation to which the assets are transferred.... " 293 U.S. at 468 (quoting § 112(g)(1)(i)(B) of the Revenue Act of 1928).

10. 293 U.S. at 469.

11. 293 U.S. at 469.

a transaction which has no business or corporate purpose is not a "reorganization."[12]

The same business purpose test has been integrated by the Treasury not only as a requirement of other corporate reorganization provisions,[13] but also as a requirement to achieve tax-free status on the formation of corporations,[14] and cases have found the business purpose requirement to apply as well to dividends,[15] and to a broad array of other kinds of transactions. Indeed, Judge Learned Hand explained that Gregory generally has been taken to mean that "in construing words of a tax statute which describes *any* commercial or industrial transaction we are to understand them to refer to transactions entered upon for commercial or industrial purposes and not to include transactions entered upon for no other motive but to escape taxation."[16] Indeed, Gregory has been broadened even further, and a form of the test which purported to require business reasons for commercial transactions has been applied to admittedly *noncommercial* transactions.[17]

Before further exploring what the doctrine *does* mean, it is important to emphasize what it does *not* mean. In order to avoid application of the doctrine, a taxpayer need not show that the transaction engaged in is one which she would have entered into in a tax-free world.[18] Indeed, if

12. Some commentators have suggested that, in fact, the Court's opinion means only that corporations must carry on some business to be recognized as corporations for tax purposes. See e.g., Gunn, Tax Avoidance, 76 MICH. L. REV. 733, 739 n.21 (1978). This view would seem to be dispelled by the Court's assertion in Gregory that "No doubt, a new and valid corporation was created." 293 U.S. at 469.

13. See Treas. Reg. § 1.368–1(b) (which describes reorganizations as relating to "readjustments . . . required by business exigencies"). See also Treas. Reg. § 1.368–1(c) (which excludes from its definition of a plan of reorganization "a mere device that puts on the form of a corporate reorganization as a disguise for concealing its real character . . . the object . . . of which is the consummation of a preconceived plan having no business or corporate purpose . . .").

14. See Rev. Proc. 73–10, 1973–1 C.B. 760, 762.

15. See Basic Inc. v. United States, 549 F.2d 740 (Ct. Cl. 1977).

16. Commissioner v. Transport Trading & Terminal Corp., 176 F.2d 570, 572 (2d Cir. 1949), cert. denied, 338 U.S. 955, 70 S.Ct. 493, 94 L.Ed. 589 (1950).

17. See e.g., Goldstein v. Commissioner, 364 F.2d 734 (2d Cir. 1966), cert. denied, 385 U.S. 1005, 87 S.Ct. 708, 17 L.Ed.2d 543 (1967). In Goldstein, the taxpayer borrowed funds at 4% interest, prepaid the interest, and invested the same funds at less than 2%, solely to lower her taxes for the year in which she prepaid the interest. The court held the business purpose test sufficient to deny the sought-after interest deduction "when it objectively appears that a taxpayer has borrowed funds in order to engage in a transaction that has no substance or purpose aside from the taxpayer's desire to obtain the tax benefit of an interest deduction. . . ." 364 F.2d at 741–42.

18. It is only appropriate to note some of the well-known comments that courts seem to recite in almost every case decided against the would-be tax-avoiding citizen:

> [A] transaction, otherwise within an exception of the tax law, does not lose its immunity, because it is actuated by a desire to avoid, or, if one choose, to evade, taxation. Any one [sic] may so arrange his affairs that his taxes shall be as low as possible; he is not bound to choose that pattern which will best pay the Treasury; there is not even a patriotic duty to increase ones taxes.

Helvering v. Gregory, 69 F.2d 809, 810 (2d Cir. 1934), aff'd., 293 U.S. 465, 55 S.Ct. 266, 79 L.Ed. 596 (1935).

> Over and over again courts have said that there is nothing sinister in so arranging ones affairs as to keep taxes as low as possible. Everybody does so, rich or poor; and all do right, for nobody

such were the case, it is likely that very few tax-free exchanges could satisfy the test, because many of these exchanges have both substantive and technical requirements which few transactions would meet without intentional advance planning. For example, a fairly simple and straight-forward transaction which might not be entered into in a tax-free world could be the kind of reorganization defined in section 368(a)(1)(B). That section grants nonrecognition to shareholders of a company (T) who exchange their shares for shares of an acquiring company (P) if immedi-ately after the exchange P has more than 80% control of T and if in the exchange P acquires the T stock solely for P voting stock. Assume that (1) P, a publicly held company, offers cash to the T shareholders in exchange for all of the stock and that, tax consequences aside, the T shareholders would prefer cash to P stock; (2) nonetheless, simply in order to avoid the imposition of tax on the exchange, the T shareholders decide to sell to P only if P acquires the T stock solely for P voting stock. The transaction will qualify as a tax-free "B" reorganization despite the fact that it was engineered solely for tax savings.

Rather than applying when the taxpayer structures an exchange in a certain way in order to achieve tax benefits, the business purpose doctrine has been said to apply only when there is no business reason at all for engaging in a particular transaction—"[a] transaction ... lacks business purpose if its *raison d'être* is tax reduction."[19] But despite the wide array of cases which cite to the business purpose doctrine for support, there are very few sales, exchanges or other tax-significant transactions which could reasonably be said to exist entirely for tax savings, and of those that do exist, none has yet been subjected to a "business purpose" analysis.

The easiest way to avoid taxation of accrued appreciation in proper-ty is to hold the property. Because simply failing to engage in any transaction with respect to an appreciated asset will result in a zero rate of tax; it would appear that a transaction might exist *solely* for tax purposes only if that transaction produces a rate of tax which is less than zero. The most obvious single transaction that produces a rate of tax below zero is the sale of property which has *declined* in value. If A has investment property with a basis of $100 and a value of $10, sale of that property will result in a $90 tax deduction, while retention of the property will produce no tax consequences. A might sell the property solely in order to recognize that $90 loss, and indeed A might be so tempted even at a price below market value, because the tax savings would likely outweigh the economic loss. Assuming a marginal tax rate of 30%, the savings would be 30% of $90, or $27. Nonetheless, no one has

owes any public duty to pay more than the law demands: taxes are enforced ex-actions, not voluntary contributions. To demand more in the name of morals is mere cant.

Commissioner v. Newman, 159 F.2d 848, 850–51 (2d Cir. 1947) (Hand, J., dissenting),

cert. denied, 331 U.S. 859, 67 S.Ct. 1755, 91 L.Ed. 1866 (1947).

19. Bittker, What is "Business Pur-pose" in Reorganization?, 8 N.Y.U. Inst. on Fed. Tax'n. 134, 137 (1950).

ever suggested the business purpose doctrine should be applied so as to convert that sale into a "nonsale."

In addition to a sale, *purchase* of property can, in some circumstances, also produce a tax rate below zero. As difficult as it may be to believe, between 1981 and 1984, the combination of accelerated cost recovery and the investment tax credit available to the purchaser of equipment could produce tax savings which, in present value terms, exceeded the tax that would be imposed on the income generated by the equipment. The result was, in effect, a negative rate of tax on income earned on certain investments.[20] Despite the fact that taxpayers might purchase property that was an admittedly uneconomic investment and that might be expected to produce a pretax return of zero or less, never did the Internal Revenue Service or a court assert that such an investment lacked a "business purpose" and was therefore not a "purchase" for tax purposes.[21]

Even today, there are several exchanges which, because of the application of more than a single kind of tax benefit, can offer tax savings sufficient to motivate action without any corresponding economic (nontax) benefit. While the act of engaging in a tax-free incorporation does not reduce the taxpayer's taxes, the effect is to allow continued operation of a business, but in a form which can potentially be subject to lower rates of tax. As a result, an incorporation may well be entered into for no reason other than to reduce taxes.[22] Nonetheless, the courts have not seen fit to require a taxpayer to demonstrate that he had a business purpose or a profit motive in order to receive nonrecognition for an incorporation transaction.

It would appear from the above that business purpose is generally *not* a requirement for the tax characterization of many commercial transactions described in the Code. In fact, in many situations, to hold otherwise might lead to results which could be not just unwarranted, but completely absurd. For example, one of the reasons for the enactment of what is now section 351, which grants nonrecognition to individuals who form a corporation, was to "increase the revenue by preventing taxpayers from taking colorable losses in wash sales and other fictitious exchanges."[23] Prior to section 351's existence one could imagine two

---

20. See Steines, Income Tax Allowances for Cost Recovery, 40 Tax L. Rev. 483, 506–07, 540 (1985).

21. Often the Internal Revenue Service and courts attacked such investments when the property was acquired with borrowed funds and was leased back to the seller. See e.g., Estate of Franklin v. Commissioner, 544 F.2d 1045 (9th Cir. 1976); cf. Swift Dodge v. Commissioner, 692 F.2d 651 (9th Cir. 1982) (taxpayer, an automobile dealer, borrowed funds to purchase cars for lease; court held arrangement to be a conditional sale). In these cases, however, the courts were careful to point out that it was not merely the acquisition of the property, but the combination of the borrowing, purchase, and lease, that caused the taxpayer to lose purported tax benefits. In any event, the taxpayer who spent $100 cash to buy property which he intended to rent out for amounts with a total present value of $99 would, after-taxes, have a positive return on his investment only because of tax savings. That taxpayer's rights to deductions were never questioned on "business purpose" grounds.

22. Compare § 11 with § 1.

23. S. Rep. No. 275, 67th Cong., 1st Sess., 11–12 (1921).

taxpayers, each of whom owned depreciated property of equal value. They could arguably simply transfer their properties to a new corporation in exchange for one half of the shares of that corporation. A taxable sale or exchange would have occurred, and each taxpayer would enjoy a deductible loss on the transfer of his depreciated property to the newly formed company.

Section 351 was enacted partially to combat this technique by providing that on such exchanges no gain or loss is recognized to the contributing shareholder(s). To read a business purpose requirement into the section would be to prevent taxpayers from deducting realized losses on the formation of a corporation *only* when they had some business purpose for establishing that corporation, and to *allow* the deduction of such losses *only* where the taxpayers incorporated for the sole purpose of deducting the losses (because in such a case, the taxpayers would have no "business purpose" for incorporating and would therefore fail to satisfy that implicit requirement for the application of section 351).

A similarly counter-intuitive result could arise from across-the-board application of the business purpose test in the very area in which the test was born—corporate reorganizations. In Survaunt v. Commissioner,[24] the taxpayer was a 50% shareholder of a corporation. Several steps were taken in order for the shareholders to pay off certain personal obligations: (1) the corporation was liquidated; (2) a new corporation, owned by the same shareholders in the same proportions, was formed; (3) the shareholders each contributed to the new corporation all but $30,000 worth of the assets received upon liquidation of the old corporation; and (4) the shareholders sold to the new corporation the remaining $30,000 worth of the assets received on liquidation of the old company.

The Internal Revenue Service argued that the entire series of events constituted a reorganization, with the result, under the provisions applicable to corporate reorganizations, that the shareholder should be taxed as if he had received a $30,000 dividend.[25] The shareholder's response was that the entire transaction had no business purpose and was instead motivated by his own desire to receive $30,000 from his corporation without incurring any tax liability.[26]

Since Gregory v. Helvering[27] appeared to make it clear that one of the essential elements of classification as a corporate reorganization was a business purpose, it was claimed that the transaction at issue, lacking that essential purpose, could not be so characterized. The court rejected

24. 162 F.2d 753 (8th Cir. 1947), modifying 5 T.C. 665 (1945).

25. 162 F.2d at 755.

26. The taxpayer asserted that: (1) the liquidation was tax-free to the old corporation and resulted in a capital loss to the shareholder (because his basis in the stock surrendered exceeded his amount realized); (2) the formation of the new corporation was tax-free; (3) the contribution of property to the new corporation was tax-free to all parties; and (4) the sale of $30,000 worth of property to the new corporation, though a taxable sale, resulted in no gain because the shareholder's basis in the assets sold equaled his amount realized. 162 F.2d at 756.

27. 293 U.S. 465, 55 S.Ct. 266, 79 L.Ed. 596 (1935).

this contention,[28] holding that the only relevant question raised by Gregory was *what* was done rather than *why* anything was done, and that what was done in this case qualified as a reorganization.

The net result of these cases is that a doctrine which originated as an implicit requirement of statutory provisions describing corporate reorganizations has in some ways grown well beyond that role, so that courts feel comfortable imposing a "business purpose" requirement as an adjunct to almost *any* kind of transaction. On the other hand, the same requirement is at other times dysfunctional, and it is disregarded, in the characterization of transactions including the very ones (corporate reorganizations) that gave birth to the doctrine. As a result, the doctrine is often not applied to so-called commercial transactions totally lacking in business purpose;[29] yet it is not only alive but also growing in a wide array of different kinds of cases.

This inconsistency and apparent random application of the business purpose doctrine is an unavoidable consequence of viewing the doctrine as a requirement for classification of a given exchange as a specific type of transaction. The doctrine is fundamentally premised on an unspoken assumption that at least certain kinds of tax-motivated behavior (as opposed to business-motivated behavior) ought not to be rewarded, and it proceeds from that assumption to a conclusion that certain transactions require a business purpose. Unfortunately, for every tax-motivated taxpayer who would be *hindered* by classification of an exchange as other than some specific kind of transaction, there is another taxpayer who would *benefit* by that same classification. As a result, the doctrine as originally explained must be either arbitrarily applied or self-defeating.

To the extent that there may be consistency in the application of the business purpose doctrine in all of the situations discussed above, it simply does not lie in a view of the doctrine as an extra-statutory requirement of certain transactions otherwise defined in the Code, as suggested by Judge Hand. Instead, the doctrine seems to have consistent meaning only when seen as a test for application of the step transaction doctrine. The results of the cases purporting to deny tax benefits because of a lack of a business purpose seem reconcilable if one takes the business purpose test to mean that if an action has no business purpose, then that action is not entitled to be taxed as a distinct exchange, but it is deemed to be part of a larger transaction. In other words, the business purpose test is no part of the definition of any commercial *transaction* described in the Code, but it is a part of the determination of what *facts* should be considered as having occurred together. Viewed this way, the test, whether or not it is appropriate, at least produces results consistent with many of the relevant court decisions.

When the business purpose doctrine as so interpreted is applied to Gregory, the absence of business purpose for the formation of Averill

---

28. Survaunt, 162 F.2d at 757.

29. See e.g., Moline Properties, Inc. v. Commissioner, 319 U.S. 436, 63 S.Ct. 1132, 87 L.Ed. 1499 (1943).

becomes a reason for treating the formation, distribution, and immediate liquidation as a single integrated transaction. The substance versus form doctrine can then be applied, resulting in treatment of the transaction as a taxable distribution.[30]

Similarly, while the broader business purpose test fails to account for apparently contradictory results in simple incorporation transactions and in reorganization cases such as Survaunt, application of the business purpose doctrine *qua* step transaction doctrine generates results which are, if nothing else, at least consistent. For example, despite a reference in certain rulings to a business purpose as a necessary prerequisite to the grant of tax-free status to a corporate formation,[31] courts have declined to apply a business purpose test to a straightforward incorporation. One might instead suggest that application of the business purpose test to corporate formation followed only by operation of the corporation could result in viewing the formation and operation as an integrated series of events, but because application of the substance versus form doctrine to that series of events would nonetheless result in characterization of the events as nothing other than an incorporation followed by the conduct of corporate business, the doctrine, though in fact applicable, does not change the tax consequences.

In Survaunt, where the taxpayer argued that a liquidation followed by an incorporation could not be classified as a reorganization because the series of exchanges lacked a business purpose, application of this reformulated business purpose test results in the apparently more appropriate conclusion that the liquidation and subsequent reincorporation should be viewed as part of a single transaction—that transaction being, as the court found, a reorganization.

This view of the role of the business purpose test is consistent with other facets of its current use as well. Generally, where some purported transaction is found to have no business purpose, the transaction will be held to be *not* what it is purported to be. However, the business purpose test alone does not purport to provide a way to determine exactly what the transaction *is*, as opposed to what it is not. Whether a purportedly tax-free exchange is simply characterized as a nontax-free exchange or whether it is characterized as some different kind of transaction by application of the substance versus form doctrine seems not to have been discussed in the cases, but if the business purpose doctrine is something other than a version of the test for application of the step transaction doctrine, then its precise meaning is unclear.

30. Somewhat at odds with this conclusion are regulations which explain that, regardless of the sequence of events, the kind of reorganization attempted in Gregory will not be found to have occurred unless carried out for real and substantial nontax reasons common to the business of the corporations. See Treas. Reg. § 1.355–2(c). The regulation is essentially an attempt to incorporate what Treasury saw as the holding of Gregory. The cases and rulings tend to point out the kind of reasons that meet the requirement.

31. Rev. Proc. 73–10, 1973–1 C.B. 760, 762 (requires a statement of the business reasons for a tax-free incorporation as a prerequisite to receipt of a favorable ruling with respect to qualification for tax-free incorporation under § 351).

[b]   The Step Transaction Doctrine

[i]   Step Transaction Doctrine Iterations

While perhaps encompassing some sort of business purpose test, the step transaction doctrine at least *appears* to focus on the opposite side of the coin from that given attention by the "business purpose" analysis. Rather than a nonstatutory element of the definition of certain tax-favored transactions, the step transaction doctrine is one which purports to be applied to certain *facts* prior to and independent of the application of a specific transactional label to those facts. The doctrine is simply a way to determine "what was done;" the thing found to have been done then awaits characterization through application of a substance versus form analysis.

Nonetheless, the doctrine can still trace its roots to the same opinion which gave birth to the business purpose test. In discussing Ms. Gregory's predicament in Gregory v. Helvering, the Court explained that it was doing no more than "putting aside ... the question of motive in respect of taxation altogether, and fixing the character of the proceeding by what actually occurred."[32] This determination that what actually occurred can be different from what is represented to have occurred is the essence of the step transaction doctrine.

A fairly typical application of the step transaction doctrine can serve as an example. Assume that T owns several low basis assets that she has been using in an ongoing sole proprietorship, and Publicly Held Company seeks to acquire the entire business. If T trades her business to Publicly Held in exchange for either cash or Publicly Held stock, the exchange will be fully taxable.[33] However, T might be tempted to suggest a somewhat more complex, but nonetheless apparently less taxing arrangement. If T exchanges her business for all of the shares of newly formed Newco, the transaction would appear to qualify as a tax-free incorporation.[34] If Publicly Held then acquires all of the assets of Newco in exchange for Publicly Held stock, and Newco liquidates, distributing the Publicly Held stock to T, that exchange would appear to qualify as a tax-free reorganization under section 368(a)(1)(C). If the separate actions are respected, T will have converted a single taxable exchange (assets for Publicly Held stock) into two separate nontaxable exchanges. In such a situation, the step transaction doctrine will be applied, and the "transaction" will be defined as a taxable exchange by T of her business assets for Publicly Held stock.[35]

The utility of some sort of objective determination of the facts of a transaction seems apparent. Nor does this need arise merely from the possibility of a transaction in which the documentation retained by the taxpayer or submitted to the Internal Revenue Service does not represent the actual legal rights and liabilities of the parties to the transac-

---

32.   293 U.S. at 469.

33.   See § 1001.

34.   See § 351(a).

35.   See e.g., West Coast Mktg. Corp. v. Commissioner, 46 T.C. 32 (1966); Rev. Rul. 70–140, 1970–1 C.B. 73.

tion. Such cases fall clearly within the confines of the "sham" transaction principles. Instead, the step transaction doctrine is applied where the written documentation accurately reflects the legal rights and liabilities of the signatories thereto, but those legal rights do not fully reflect the underlying economic realities or the expectations of the parties.

The substantial difference which can exist between legal rights and economic expectations, and the occasional relative insignificance of legal rights when compared to the underlying economics, is apparent in situations such as the one described heretofore. If, after receiving an offer from Publicly Held, *T* transfers her business to Newco in exchange for all of the Newco stock in contemplation of Newco's transfer of those same assets to Publicly Held, the transfer of those assets to Newco in exchange for Newco stock clearly has independent legal significance.[36] There was a legal obligation on the part of *T* to transfer assets, in consideration of which there was a corresponding obligation on the part of Newco to transfer stock. The obligations were legally interdependent on each other and independent of any other rights or obligations of either party. The problem is that where there is an identity of interest between *T* and Newco, the very concept of legally binding commitments seems irrelevant—if legal commitments exist they can be mutually abrogated, and if they do not, *T* can still just as easily see that her goals are accomplished.

While the problem caused by focusing on legal commitments is most *obvious* in situations where there is an identity of interests between the parties, it is by no means limited to such situations. It is not within the province of the tax laws to enforce legal agreements made among taxpayers, but only to use those agreements to evaluate the relationships and exchanges of the taxpayers. Thus, it is arguable that legal relationships ought to have significance within the tax system only to the extent they describe relationships or exchanges more accurately than do non-legal descriptions.

To say that an exchange of assets for stock has independent legal consequences is to say nothing more than that if one party fails to perform its contractual obligations, the aggrieved party may seek redress in a court of law (or, perhaps, equity) upon proof of the existence and breach of the legally binding agreement. Essentially, legal rights merely give one party the ability to incur some expenses (i.e., legal fees and court costs) in order either to compel the other party to act in accordance with the agreement (in those few situations where injunctive relief might be available), or to punish the other party (and reap some financial reward for itself) for failing to act accordingly.

Without demeaning the judicial system, it must be acknowledged that in many situations the free marketplace provides the economically powerful and astute actor with the same kinds of ability to provoke or to

---

36. This statement assumes that at the time of the incorporation T is not legally obligated to see to it that the assets are transferred, directly or indirectly, to Publicly Held.

prevent actions of others. Especially within the context of ongoing economic (and, often, social) relationships, one party can enforce its will by the threat of cutting off or somehow altering a relationship that has previously proved mutually productive. While such enforcement may involve costs to the enforcing party, such as requiring it to seek another outlet or source of supply for goods, these costs are not necessarily always greater than the costs involved in prosecuting a legal action, and in many situations the actual cost of producing behavioral changes by way of economic, rather than judicial, force is nothing more than that involved in merely *threatening* to take, rather than taking, any action. To the extent the federal income tax system is attempting to measure the relatedness and interdependence of purportedly separate exchanges, the economic power of one party over another would appear no less significant than potential resort to judicial enforcement.

If reliance on *legal* relationships is not a prerequisite to accurate measurement of actual economic relationships, the question then becomes by what means *can* the interrelationship of purportedly separate exchanges be determined? Because the step transaction doctrine is neither a method of statutory interpretation nor a non-statutory requirement of certain Code provisions, but merely a means of determining the *facts* to which the Code should be applied, it would seem that the method arrived at for determining those facts ought to be of general applicability and should not be subject to variation dependent on the law to be applied to those facts.

The courts have generally set forth three different tests for determining whether several exchanges should be treated as a single transaction: (1) the binding commitment test; (2) the end result, or intention test; and (3) the interdependence test.[37] Each term is basically self-descriptive. Under the binding commitment test, different actions by a taxpayer are not treated as a single transaction on his part unless at the time he takes the first step he is under a binding commitment to proceed with the next step.[38] The end result, or intention test, links actions together if they are "component parts of a single transaction intended from the outset to be taken for the purpose of reaching the ultimate result."[39] Finally, the interdependence test will unify actions for tax purposes if the steps "are so interdependent that the legal relations created by one transaction would have been fruitless without a completion of the series."[40] As will be seen, each of these three tests will often

---

37. See Mintz & Plumb, Step Transactions in Corporate Reorganizations, 12 N.Y.U. Inst. on Fed. Tax'n. 247 (1954); Note, Step Transactions, 24 U. Miami L. Rev. 60 (1969); Hobbet, The Step Transaction Doctrine and its Effect on Corporate Transactions, 19 Tul. Tax Inst. 102 (1970).

38. Commissioner v. Gordon, 391 U.S. 83, 96, 88 S.Ct. 1517, 20 L.Ed.2d 448 (1968).

39. King Enters., Inc. v. United States, 418 F.2d 511, 516 (Ct. Cl. 1969).

40. Redding v. Commissioner, 630 F.2d 1169, 1177 (7th Cir. 1980), cert. denied, 450 U.S. 913, 101 S.Ct. 1353, 67 L.Ed.2d 338 (1981).

lead to the intuitively correct result. But, because none of these tests has a valid conceptual foundation, none of them will *always* do so.

The first of these tests, which joins actions if they are taken pursuant to a binding commitment, is the most straightforward and the least followed. The Supreme Court first applied the test in Commissioner v. Gordon.[41] There, a corporation distributed to its shareholders in 1961 about 57% of the stock of a wholly owned subsidiary. At the time, the corporation notified its shareholders that it expected to distribute the remainder of the subsidiary stock within about three years. The remaining 43% of the subsidiary stock was distributed about two years later, in 1963. The taxpayer claimed that receipt of his share of the initial distribution in 1961 was tax-free because that distribution was merely one of a series of steps which, taken together, qualified as a nontaxable distribution pursuant to section 355, which grants tax-free status to certain distributions of the stock of a subsidiary if the amount of stock distributed exceeds 80% of all outstanding shares of the subsidiary.[42]

If the 1961 and 1963 distributions had been treated as a single transaction, that transaction would have qualified for nonrecognition. The Court held that the step transaction doctrine did not apply, however, and that instead there was a taxable distribution in 1961 and a second, separate, taxable distribution in 1963. In so holding, the Court expressed concern that if it held otherwise, the Internal Revenue Service and the courts could have been required to wait for an indefinite period to determine the tax consequences arising out of the 1961 distribution. It refused to apply the step transaction doctrine when to do so would mean that "the essential character of a transaction, and its tax impact, should remain not only undeterminable but unfixed for an indefinite and unlimited period in the future, awaiting events that might or might not happen."[43] The Court concluded that "this requirement that the character of a transaction be determinable does not mean that the entire divestiture must necessarily occur within a single tax year. It does, however, mean that if one transaction is to be characterized as a 'first step' there must be a binding commitment to take the later steps."[44]

Essentially, because federal income tax must be determined and imposed each year, the Internal Revenue Service and the courts must be able to judge the "substance" of a transaction at the time it occurs. Similarly, because taxation depends on the occurrence of classifiable and discrete events, the "substance" of an event or exchange must exist at the time the event occurs. The problem raised in Gordon was that neither the Internal Revenue Service nor the trial court was able to know, in the year of the first distribution, the "real" relationship between that distribution and a subsequent transaction.

The problem caused by uncertainty regarding the relationship among several events in a system dependent upon characterizing trans-

41. 391 U.S. 83, 88 S.Ct. 1517, 20 L.Ed.2d 448 (1968).

42. See § 355(a)(1)(D).

43. 391 U.S. at 96.

44. 391 U.S. at 96.

actions *based* on the interrelatedness of those events is not new. Including the approach taken in Gordon, the Internal Revenue Service and the courts have traveled along at least three different avenues in addressing it: (1) if we are uncertain of the facts, take our best guess; if we are subsequently proven wrong, take steps in that subsequent year to redress that previous wrong;[45] (2) if we are unsure of the facts at the actual time of the transaction, wait till the facts become clear before characterizing the transaction;[46] and (3) if we are unsure of the facts, rule against the taxpayer. This last approach is the one chosen in Gordon.

The Gordon Court's concern with establishing the taxability of an event in the year it occurs rather than waiting to see what happens in subsequent years is warranted. Unfortunately, however, this concern is fundamentally different from the previously enunciated concerns which have given rise to the step transaction doctrine, and the result in Gordon is necessarily of limited applicability.

Whatever else can be said for or against the particular approach to the problems of unknown future events which was adopted in Gordon, it is clear that the Court was describing a way to deal with cases where the facts could not be known at the time of the supposed "transaction." Whether the rule which it adopted gains in administrative convenience what it may sacrifice in fairness or accuracy is not as significant as the fact that the rule adopted *was* one of administrative and judicial convenience. Rather than propose a method for determining what the "facts" *were*, the Court explained that where the facts could *not* be known they should be held against the taxpayer. While the Court and scholars have looked at the opinion as a test for application of the step transaction doctrine, to the extent the doctrine represents a way of determining *what* the significant facts were, rather than a way of determining what to do when the significant facts are unknown, the "binding commitment" test is simply not relevant.

Indeed, although often failing to explain their grounds for doing so, courts, commentators, and the Internal Revenue Service have generally rejected the use of the binding commitment test. While courts and commentators often list it as an alternative formulation for application of the step transaction doctrine,[47] after such listing they generally proceed to explain either that it does not apply to the case at hand,[48] that it is only one "factor to consider,"[49] that it applies only to the specific facts of Gordon, or that it applies only when the taxpayer rather than

---

45. This approach has its foundation in the Court's opinion in Burnet v. Sanford & Brooks Co., 282 U.S. 359, 51 S.Ct. 150, 75 L.Ed. 383 (1931).

46. See Burnet v. Logan, 283 U.S. 404, 51 S.Ct. 550, 75 L.Ed. 1143 (1931).

47. See e.g., McDonald's Restaurants v. Commissioner, 688 F.2d 520, 530 (7th Cir. 1982).

48. See McDonald's Restaurants, 688 F.2d 520, 531 (7th Cir. 1982).

49. Redding v. Commissioner, 630 F.2d 1169, 1178 (7th Cir. 1980), cert. denied, 450 U.S. 913, 101 S.Ct. 1353, 67 L.Ed.2d 338 (1981).

the Internal Revenue Service is attempting to integrate several steps into a single transaction. In any event, few if any individuals subscribe to the binding commitment test as worthy of general application.

A more commonly applied test for implementation of the step transaction doctrine is the "end result" or "intention" test, pursuant to which legally independent actions will be linked together if they are parts of a single scheme or plan taken for the purpose of reaching a given end result. As applied to the taxpayer discussed above, who incorporates assets in order to exchange them indirectly, and tax-free, for stock of Publicly Held Company, this test would treat the legally separate exchanges as a single transaction—an exchange of assets for Publicly Held stock—because the exchanges were part of a preconceived plan to reach that result.[50]

A problem with this test is that while it provides a ready means to support an allegation that two legally independent exchanges are actually parts of a single, integrated transaction, it provides almost no basis whatsoever to support an allegation that two actions are ever separate. If all that is required to join two separate exchanges together is that at the time the first is engaged in, the taxpayer also intends to engage in the second, this test could treat as a "transaction" every single exchange intended by a taxpayer at the time he engages in any other, seemingly unrelated, exchange. For example, imagine that *A* forms a corporation in 2007. At the time, *A* intends to make the corporation successful and to have it go public in 2010. *A* also intends to purchase Treasury bonds in 2008 and to sell short some stock in an unrelated enterprise in 2007. All of these purchases and sales are planned to maximize *A*'s profit potential and to minimize his risk; yet to suggest that these events are a single "transaction" would be absurd.

One could suggest that all of the above exchanges, though planned and intended simultaneously, are not part of a plan to reach a *single* intended result and thus should not be integrated under the end result test (*i.e.*, because each exchange has its own independently anticipated economic result). To suggest this, however, is to do no more than to suggest that there is some *other* means to determine when a taxpayer's plans and intentions are separate and when they are part of a single plan. If there is a means to make that determination, then that means, rather than the taxpayer's intention or plan, must be the appropriate test for application of the step transaction doctrine. No such test has been proposed.

A test which has become more popular than either binding commitment or intent is the "interdependent" test. This test essentially converts the business purpose doctrine into a test for application of the step transaction doctrine. Elsewhere described as asking whether "the initial steps would be fruitless in the context of the taxpayer's particular purpose without completing the plan,"[51] this test incorporates the busi-

---

50. See King Enters., Inc. v. United States, 418 F.2d 511, 517 (Ct. Cl. 1969).

51. Hobbet, The Step Transaction Doctrine and its Effect on Corporate Transactions, 19 Tul. Tax Inst. 102, 111 (1970).

ness purpose doctrine by segregating actions where each step was motivated by a business purpose existing independent of the other contemplated steps, and integrating steps where several "unnecessary" steps were taken only in contemplation of the others and without any independent business purpose.[52]

Essentially, this test views certain transactions as having at least two effects: (1) changing the taxpayer's legal rights and liabilities; and (2) changing the taxpayer's tax status. When the purpose of the exchange is only to affect the taxpayer's tax status, and the economic effects are undone or redone by way of another contemplated exchange, the steps will be integrated.

This interdependence test has been popular in large part because it can be used to integrate transactions in the absence of a binding commitment, but, unlike the intent test, it provides a basis for *segregation* of intuitively separate actions as well as for integration of intuitively connected ones. Applying the test to some of the cases discussed earlier reveals results in line with those reached by the courts and the Internal Revenue Service. Indeed, in Gregory the Court apparently did no more than apply the step transaction doctrine to integrate the formation of, a distribution by, and subsequent liquidation of, a corporation because none of the transactions had an independent business purpose. The act of incorporation was engaged in only as a prelude to the corporation's own undoing by way of liquidation, and, as a result, the actions, being self-cancelling, were ignored.

In another application of the test, if a taxpayer incorporates assets in order to operate a business as a corporation, whether or not operation as a corporation is chosen because of its tax benefits, that incorporation is recognized as a separate transaction for tax purposes because it has a lasting impact on the taxpayer's legal rights. On the other hand, if the taxpayer incorporates assets solely for the purpose of being able to transfer those assets to some other company in a tax-free reorganization, the incorporation, having no independent business purpose and no lasting effect on the taxpayer's legal rights, is not treated as separate and the incorporation and purported reorganization will be taxed as a single unified exchange.

This interdependence test, unlike the other tests for application of the step transaction doctrine, even has a degree of internal consistency and reasonableness. If an action viewed independently achieves some purpose, be it a change in economic circumstances or even a tax savings, that action is independently motivated and ought to be independently taxed. If an action, when viewed independently, serves no taxpayer purpose, either that action will not be taken at all, or, if taken, it must not be independent.

52. See e.g., Knetsch v. United States, 364 U.S. 361, 81 S.Ct. 132, 5 L.Ed.2d 128 (1960).

Application of this test to nonrecognition exchanges is fairly straightforward. Most exchanges, and almost all nonrecognition transactions, generate no tax savings. A nonrecognition exchange merely results in no current taxation of accrued appreciation in the exchanged assets, a result identical to that imposed upon simple retention of the asset. As a result, the tax savings generated by a single nonrecognition transaction could never entirely motivate that transaction. The taxpayer must either have some business purpose (i.e., the desire to exchange assets), some other tax goal which will be accomplished by the nonrecognition exchange,[53] or some tax purpose which can be accomplished only by combining the first nonrecognition exchange with a second exchange. In the last case, the two (or more) exchanges necessary to achieve the single tax purpose will be integrated and treated as a single transaction.

Despite the frequent utility of the interdependent test, it will not work in all scenarios. Instead, there are a great many cases in which this test will not work at all, and the problem with the test is not lessened by the fact that its failures are balanced. Sometimes exchanges can be *unified* despite the *existence* of separate business purposes, and other times they can be *separated* despite the *lack* of such independent purposes.

There are numerous examples of unified characterization of multiple exchanges having independent purposes. The shareholder who has some of her stock redeemed and plans to and does shortly thereafter sell the remaining shares will be entitled to treat the two exchanges as a single transaction resulting in a complete termination of her stock interest (and therefore taxable at capital gains rates). Neither cases nor rulings imply this tax benefit could be denied if it could be established the taxpayer would have redeemed the shares even absent a later sale of the remaining stock. As long as that subsequent sale is part of a unified "plan," the benefits of integration of the planned exchanges are available.

Similarly, the corporation that acquires stock of another corporation solely in exchange for its voting stock over a relatively short time, such as twelve months, will be entitled to treat all of the stock so acquired as obtained in a single transaction for purposes of qualifying the series of exchanges as a tax-free reorganization.[54] Evidence that the acquiring company would have made the initial stock acquisitions even absent the later acquisitions would show that the series of exchanges were not mutually interdependent; it would not, however, cause those exchanges to be separated for tax purposes.

On the other hand are cases in which different exchanges would not have been made but for the taxpayer's expectation of undoing them, but which are nonetheless treated as separate, despite their interdependency

---

53. For example, the taxpayer in a 33% marginal tax bracket might incorporate assets in order to take advantage of lower corporate rates on the first $50,000 of the corporation's taxable income (assuming the corporation would not be a personal service corporation, see § 11(b)(1)).

54. Treas. Reg. § 1.368–2(c).

and lack of separate business purpose. The corporation that sells stock with the hope of reacquiring that same stock in a subsequent reorganization may be entitled to treat the sale and reacquisition as separate exchanges even if the sale is made for no purpose other than to allow the reacquisition to qualify as a tax-free exchange.[55] And, indeed it appears that the taxpayer who sells stock at a loss only in order to be able to deduct that loss and only because he will "undo" the sale by a later repurchase of the same stock is entitled to treat the sale and repurchase as separate despite the lack of any independent motive, so long as he waits long enough before making the repurchase.[56] Similar separation of interdependent exchanges is allowed for taxpayers who sell (or purchase) stock in a liquidating corporation solely for the purpose of reducing (or increasing) their stockholdings prior to liquidation and solely in order to qualify for favorable treatment on that liquidation.[57] In all of these cases, mutual interdependence of the series of exchanges seems to give way to the fact that the taxpayer is taking a "risk" which justifies separation of the exchanges.

Indeed, it should not be surprising that the business purpose, or interdependence, test does not provide a satisfactory measuring rod for determining the "true" facts of a series of exchanges. The very enunciation of the test is enough to reveal that its focus lies not on determining "what" happened, but on determining "why" it happened—what was the taxpayer's motive for entering into a given exchange? While an examination of motive may have relevance for purposes of determining how a taxpayer should be treated, it provides no more than an explanation of *why* she did what was done, and it cannot logically be a tool for determining *what* it was that was done.

[ii]   Summary of Step Transaction Doctrine Iterations

None of the three tests which are generally used to determine what exchanges ought to be treated as unified are capable of doing so: one test is nothing more than an allocation of burden of proof; the second is incapable of ever separating any concurrently contemplated transactions, no matter how separate legally or functionally; and the third examines the taxpayer's *purpose* for doing what he did rather than explaining what it *was* that was done.

The result is compromise: sometimes courts use the binding commitment test; sometimes they use versions of the intent test; and sometimes they use the interdependent/business purpose test. While reasoned compromise is certainly worthwhile, there is at least some question regarding the reasoning behind this compromise. Acceptable grounds for choos-

---

55. Cf. Chapman v. Commissioner, 618 F.2d 856 (1st Cir. 1980).

56. See § 1091(a) (disallowing the loss on the first such sale if the repurchase is made within 30 days before or after the sale).

57. See, e.g., George L. Riggs, Inc. v. Commissioner, 64 T.C. 474 (1975), acq.

1976–2 C.B. 2 (minority shareholder sold to majority shareholder in order to allow majority shareholder to reach 80% ownership and qualify for tax-free liquidation under § 332); Rev. Rul. 75–521, 1975–2 C.B. 120 (same).

ing different tests at different times might include: (1) different courts take different approaches; (2) different statutes suggest different levels of necessary integration; or (3) different relationships require various tests to determine objective facts. Unfortunately, none of these possible bases for differentiating among the different tests offers an adequate explanation of what has been done.

First of all, the existence of three different tests for application of the step transaction doctrine is clearly not the result of mere disagreement among different courts as to which of the tests represents the single proper standard. The Supreme Court has led the way by using all three of the tests without ever explicitly overruling one or the other; instead, the Court's opinions reflect the unspoken assumption that sometimes one standard is appropriate and at other times another standard "works" better.[58] This pattern of choosing a different test for different cases seems to be generally followed by the Internal Revenue Service as well as lower courts.

Indeed, one would be hard pressed to find even an implicit acknowledgment that different statutory provisions require different standards for integration. In interpreting a single Code section (the reorganization provisions of section 368) the courts and the Internal Revenue Service have at times used each of the three different tests: in determining whether a series of acquisitions is a single "B" reorganization, the intent test is generally applied;[59] at other times, determination of whether a purportedly separate "B" reorganization should be so treated has seemed to warrant application of the interdependent/business purpose test;[60] and at still other times, determining whether a "B" reorganization has occurred has apparently mandated application of the binding commitment test.[61] The Supreme Court has at times applied the binding commitment test and the interdependent/business purpose test to the same kind of reorganization.[62]

Nor do the courts choose a specific test based upon the relationship of the parties involved. Gregory applied the business purpose test to related parties; Gordon applied the binding commitment test to related

---

58. In Commissioner v. Gordon, 391 U.S. 83, 96 (1968), the Court enunciated the "binding commitment" test. In Gregory v. Helvering, 293 U.S. 465, 55 S.Ct. 266, 79 L.Ed. 596 (1935), the same Court applied the "business purpose" test. In McWilliams v. Commissioner, 331 U.S. 694, 697–702 (1947), the Court appeared to apply the "intent" test. In none of the cases did the Court feel a need to differentiate the case before it from the other situations. The Internal Revenue Service agreed with the Court in all three cases and continues to use the three different tests without explaining its choices.

59. Treas. Reg. § 1.368–2(c).

60. See Weikel v. Commissioner, 51 T.C.M. (CCH) 432 (1986); West Coast Mktg.

v. Commissioner, 46 T.C. 32 (1966) (§ 351 transfer followed by purported "B" reorganization held taxable because there was no independent business purpose for incorporation).

61. Rev. Rul. 72–354, 1972–2 C.B. 216 (sale of target stock followed by reacquisition as part of "B" reorganization separate transactions because purchaser not under binding commitment to retransfer).

62. Commissioner v. Gordon, 391 U.S. 83, 88 S.Ct. 1517, 20 L.Ed.2d 448, and Gregory v. Helvering, 293 U.S. 465, 55 S.Ct. 266, 79 L.Ed. 596, both involved tax-free "spin-offs," now described in § 355.

parties; and in other situations the intent test has been applied to related parties.[63] In sum, the step transaction doctrine simply provides no consistent method for determining the "facts" of a specific exchange.

A closer look at what the doctrine purports to do reveals why *no* test can serve its purpose. The transaction-based nature of the tax system requires correlating each receipt with one or more specific payments. Only when each payment is linked to a particular receipt and each receipt to a particular payment can the two (or more) events be treated as an "exchange," which can then be characterized as a particular type of "transaction," depending on other circumstances surrounding the exchange. If "what was done" means something other than a determination of the purely legal rights and liabilities that existed, it would appear that it must mean "what was exchanged for what?" Unfortunately, as suggested earlier, that question is one which simply cannot be answered.

But the fact that the kind of reciprocal causation which the step transaction doctrine seeks to identify often does not exist is only one of the problems with application of the doctrine. Even where such reciprocal causation *does* exist, the doctrine attempts to go further and to provide a means for determining when reciprocal exchanges should be separated and when they should be treated as part of some still *larger* reciprocal "exchange."

For example, assume that *A* transfers her business assets to Newco in exchange for all of the Newco stock, and that *A* does so for the purpose (and with the intention) of transferring the Newco stock to Publicly Held in exchange for Publicly Held stock in a tax-free "B" reorganization.[64] One might suggest that there are two reciprocal exchanges: assets for Newco stock, and Newco stock for Publicly Held stock. Using the tests applied by the courts, the facts of these exchanges may be proved by each party's purpose, intentions or binding legal commitments: *A*'s purpose in transferring the assets was to receive the Newco stock, which *A* wanted so that she could trade with Publicly Held; Newco's purpose, intention, and legal commitment in transferring its stock to *A* was to receive *A*'s assets. *A*'s purpose, intention, and obligation in transferring the Newco stock is to receive Publicly Held stock; and Publicly Held acts to receive *A*'s Newco stock. Each party in turn makes its transfer for the purpose of receiving the property it gets; and mutually interdependent purposes, expectations, and obligations establish reciprocal causation.

Unfortunately, the step transaction doctrine is *not* used to establish exchanges such as the ones above, but it instead provides a rationale for explaining that in "reality" those two exchanges did *not* occur—that there was only a single exchange in which *A* transferred assets to Newco and Publicly Held transferred stock to *A*. The result is that when the traditional step transaction tests of intent and purpose do have a

---

63. For example, in Rev. Rul. 85–139, 1985–2 C.B. 123, acquisitions by a parent and its subsidiary were integrated because of their combined intent. See also Rev. Rul. 85–138, 1985–2 C.B. 122.

64. See § 368(a)(1)(B).

legitimate role in determining reciprocal causation, the exchanges which they describe are *not* the exchanges found by the courts.

The problem is that there are innumerable levels of reciprocal effect: *A*'s action can affect *B*, whose resultant action can affect *C*, whose action can affect *D*, whose action can in turn affect *C, B*, and eventually *A*. That one might choose to describe each relationship as independent or all as parts of a whole "transaction" seems clear. It may be that the further away the two ends of the defined transaction, the less primary are the reciprocal causes, but the difference in primacy of causation is only one of degree, and the relationship between *A* and *D* will in some cases be stronger than the relationship between *A* and *B* in others.

If one chooses to look beyond each individual "exchange," the more appropriate issue is the basis for doing so. Taxpayer intention or purpose may serve to establish a connection between *A* and *D*, but it does not establish a basis for determining when *that* connection should be more significant than the connection between *A* and *B*. Perhaps the *degree* of reciprocal effect between actions might establish a basis for determining when to integrate those purportedly separate actions, but no test for determining the degree of reciprocal effect has ever been suggested. In any event, it is difficult to imagine *any* situation where the reciprocal effect between more distant actions could be stronger than that between the direct "intermediary" exchanges, but at the same time it is easy to imagine *several* transactions where the degree of reciprocal causation in even a *single* direct exchange is minimal.

Another problem with the doctrine and the way it has been applied is that to the extent that the traditional tests of intent or purpose are relevant, they are relevant because they tend to establish reciprocal causation. However, when intent or purpose is referred to in application of the doctrine, it is *not* reciprocal causation, but the intention or purpose of a single party that seems to carry the day. How a single party's intent or purpose could establish a reciprocal "exchange" beyond the legal one reported by the parties is unclear.

Given the impossibility of any consistent standard for application of the step transaction doctrine, it would appear that while the doctrine may serve some purpose, that purpose is something other than determining "what was exchanged for what." Use of three different standards, each to be applied where "appropriate," has the same effect as would administration of any other single test with a series of standards which can be applied by the test administrator as he sees fit. It allows the test administrator to discriminate among the test-takers by using some other, unexpressed, subjective criteria.

For example, assume that *A, B*, and *C* each take a test, and *A* gets a grade of 60, *B* gets a grade of 70, and *C* gets an 80. Further assume that a passing grade is sometimes a 50%, sometimes 75%, and sometimes 90%, depending on which standard the administrator applies. To suggest that whether or not one of the takers passes the test is a determination of the "facts" with respect to that person, rather than a determination of whether the administrator made a predetermination of whether that person should pass, and then chose to apply the standard which brought about the desired result, is simply naive. Similarly, to suggest that the step transaction doctrine represents a method to determine the "facts" of an exchange, rather than an *ex post* rationale for decisions made on some other ground, is simply wrong.

[c] Substance Versus Form

[i] Step Transaction Cases

Even were there a principled rationale for determining when a series of exchanges ought to be treated as a single, integrated exchange, classification of that exchange as a particular transaction requires one more step. That step, of determining the "substance" of the redefined exchange, generally replaces some inappropriate transactional label with a different one that more accurately describes the facts surrounding a given exchange or series of exchanges.

At the heart of the substance versus form doctrine is the search for some label that can appropriately account for the economic consequences which result from a given set of exchanges. As applied to step transaction cases, the doctrine would ideally be applied to whatever "steps" make up the completed "transaction" and would label that transaction as one that accurately describes the economic impact on every party thereto. Unfortunately, there are three problems with the application of the substance versus form doctrine to these cases: (1) there is often no single transactional label that accurately describes the "exchange" from even one party's point of view (instead, steps that have been "integrated" by application of the step transaction doctrine must, as often as not, be immediately disintegrated by the substance versus form doctrine in order to permit accurate description of the economic consequences for the parties involved); (2) where some label does accurately describe the economic consequences to one party, that label is often inconsistent with the economic results to the other parties to the same exchange; and (3) in those cases where labels can be found that accurately describe the series of exchanges, there is generally a *variety* of applicable labels, each with different tax consequences, and no apparent basis for choosing any one label over the others.

Several cases have made it clear that the system depends on the "discovery" of a *single* transactional label that accurately describes an exchange from *all* viewpoints, rather than on different labels for different parties. In McDonald's Restaurants v. Commissioner[65] the taxpayer transferred its newly-issued stock to the shareholders of X, and X was merged into McDonald's. Shortly after the merger, the X shareholders, who had indicated a desire for cash, sold their McDonald's stock. The court held that the step transaction doctrine should be applied and that the merger and the subsequent sale of the McDonald's stock should be

---

65. 688 F.2d 520 (7th Cir. 1982).

treated as an integrated series of exchanges. As a result, the substance of the exchange did not qualify as a tax-free reorganization because the *X* shareholders did not have the type of continuing interest in McDonald's (because of their stock sale) required for such characterization.[66]

What makes this decision interesting is that the *X* shareholders, whose actions and intentions served to disqualify the transaction from nonrecognition treatment, were not before the court and were unaffected by the outcome of the case. Instead, it was McDonald's which was before the court, arguing that the transaction was not a reorganization and its basis in the acquired assets was therefore its cost for those assets[67] rather than a transferred basis.[68] Indeed, the result to the *X* shareholders would have remained unchanged regardless of the characterization of the transaction.[69] Not only did the court search for a single transactionally consistent label for the exchange, but it was only this requirement of transactional consistency that allowed McDonald's even to raise the question of application of the step transaction doctrine in the first place.

Even a cursory review of the cases reveals, however, that often there simply is no transaction which accurately describes a given set of exchanges for all parties involved.

For example, if *A* transfers assets to Newco for stock, in contemplation of trading the Newco stock to Publicly Held for Publicly Held stock, and the series of exchanges is integrated, the "exchange" will be treated as one involving *A*'s assets for Publicly Held stock. If Newco is liquidated by Publicly Held prior to engaging in any economic transactions, its transitory existence will have had no long-term economic effect and can easily be ignored. However, if Publicly Held decides not to liquidate Newco upon its acquisition, the single "exchange" (as characterized by the step transaction doctrine) will have had effects on at least three different entities: *A* will have "exchanged" assets for Publicly Held stock; Newco will have "exchanged" its newly issued stock for assets; and Publicly Held will have "exchanged" its stock for the stock of Newco. If one looks at any one of the taxpayers individually, characterization of its exchange seems apparent: *A* has engaged in a taxable exchange of assets for Publicly Held stock; Newco has engaged in a tax-free exchange of stock for assets;[70] and Publicly Held has engaged in a

---

66. In so holding, the court noted that Internal Revenue Service's ruling that the continuity of shareholder interest requirement would not be met if the shareholders receiving stock in the purported reorganization had a "plan or intention ... to [reduce their new holdings] to a number of shares having, in the aggregate, a value of less than 50 percent of the total value of the acquired stock outstanding immediately prior to the proposed transaction." 688 F.2d at 528

67. See § 1011.

68. See § 362.

69. If the transaction had been a reorganization, the reorganization would have been tax-free (§ 354), but the shareholders would have been taxed on the subsequent sale of the McDonald's stock (which would have first taken a basis equal to the shareholders basis in the exchanged X Corp. stock under § 358). If the exchange were instead a taxable sale, the shareholders would have been taxed at the time of that exchange, but would have taken a cost basis in the McDonald's stock, so that no further tax would have been imposed on their sale of that stock.

70. See §§ 351 and 1032.

tax-free exchange of stock for stock.[71] However, if tax consequences are based on characterization of the actions of *all* parties to a single transaction, it is not enough to state that, for example, A transferred assets and received Publicly Held stock. Instead, determination of A's tax consequences would seem to require explanation of the entire transaction in which A engaged—to whom did A transfer assets, and what did that person transfer to A in exchange for those assets? In our example, A has transferred assets to Newco and received stock from Publicly Held; there is no such transaction described in the Code.

There have generally been two kinds of responses to this problem. Courts have either: (1) recharacterized step transactions by defining them *not* as a single, integrated exchange, but as a series of separate exchanges whose net economic effect mirrors the actual impact on the parties involved; or (2) recharacterized transactions differently with respect to each of the different parties to the exchange. Neither of these actions is without its own problems.

One problem with redefining the substance of step transaction cases as a different *series* of exchanges rather than as a single transaction is that, while such treatment might allow consistent treatment of all parties to a series of exchanges, it would also undo exactly what the step transaction doctrine was supposed to have done in the first place. Why application of the step transaction doctrine to "integrate" a series of exchanges into a single transaction should be followed by application of the substance versus form doctrine to resegregate those exchanges into a different series of transactions is unclear and perhaps nonsensical. It is not, however, without precedent. In Commissioner v. Court Holding Co.,[72] Court Holding had discussed the sale of its only asset to Purchaser. Prior to signing a contract of sale, however, the company realized it could save taxes by distributing its asset to its two shareholders in complete liquidation, and having them then sell the asset to Purchaser. The company proceeded to liquidate, and the shareholders then sold the asset to Purchaser. The Court determined the series of steps should be treated as a single transaction. Surprisingly, its next step was to impose tax as if the company had sold the asset, and then in a separate exchange, distributed the sales proceeds in liquidation.

Similarly, in Idol v. Commissioner,[73] the taxpayer sold some of the stock of his otherwise wholly owned corporation to Purchaser, and it subsequently caused the corporation to distribute some assets to Purchaser in redemption of that stock. After concluding that the exchanges should be integrated and that the same net result could have been reached (with greater tax liability) by the corporation's first selling some assets to Purchaser and then distributing the cash to Idol, the Tax Court decided to tax the exchanges as if they had occurred in the latter order.

---

71. See § 1032.

72. 324 U.S. 331, 65 S.Ct. 707, 89 L.Ed. 981 (1945).

73. 38 T.C. 444 (1962), aff'd., 319 F.2d 647 (8th Cir. 1963).

Finally the Tax Court seems to have realized the folly inherent in integrating steps only to resegregate them in reverse order. In Esmark, Inc. v. Commissioner,[74] Purchaser acquired approximately 50% of the outstanding stock of Esmark, and Esmark subsequently distributed the stock of Subsidiary to Purchaser in redemption of Purchaser's newly acquired Esmark stock. In refusing to adopt the Internal Revenue Service's argument that Esmark should be taxed as if it had first sold the Subsidiary stock to Purchaser for cash and then used the cash to redeem its own shares, the Tax Court stated that "this proposed recharacterization does not simply combine steps; it invents new ones. Courts have refused to apply the step-transaction doctrine in this manner."[75]

What is perhaps more surprising than the court's belated acknowledgement of this inconsistency in the application of the step transaction doctrine is the ease with which the court was able to reconcile its insight with previous cases in which it had done exactly what it found so offensive in Esmark. Indeed, even in the very case in which it voiced its antipathy to the concept of inventing new steps, the court appeared to reconfirm its holding in Idol,[76] where it had done exactly that. Rather than overrule Idol, the Esmark court merely found it "factually distinguishable"[77] because in Idol the percentage of shares redeemed was smaller. If the implication is that a court can invent new steps only in certain kinds of cases and not in others, then the court was somewhat lax in its explanation of what separates those different kinds of cases. If the court simply decided to proceed slowly along a more rational path, then there are many steps along the path of irrationality that eventually need to be undone.

Aside from its own inherent inconsistency, another problem with this integration-reverse-disintegration approach is that reversing the order of exchanges would appear to have sometimes significant effects on other parties to the redefined transaction.

In Kimbell–Diamond Milling Co. v. Commissioner,[78] the taxpayer-corporation sought to acquire the assets of Seller. Rather than simply purchase the assets, Kimbell–Diamond decided to purchase the stock of Seller and immediately liquidate the company because that sequence of events would leave it with a higher basis in the newly acquired assets.[79] The court, realizing that the stock purchase and liquidation were parts of a single pre-arranged plan by Kimbell–Diamond, decided to treat the actions as a unified exchange. It determined that Kimbell–Diamond paid to acquire the assets and should be treated as if it had acquired those assets directly. Essentially, Kimbell–Diamond was taxed as if the liqui-

---

74. 90 T.C. 171 (1988).

75. 90 T.C. at 196.

76. 38 T.C. at 444.

77. 90 T.C. at 190.

78. 14 T.C. 74 (1950), aff'd., 187 F.2d 718 (5th Cir. 1951), cert. denied, 342 U.S. 827, 72 S.Ct. 50, 96 L.Ed. 626 (1951).

79. A corporation owning at least 80% of the stock of a subsidiary could assume the subsidiary's asset basis upon its liquidation under former §§ 332–334(b)(1) (now § 337). Because Seller's asset basis exceed the value of those assets, Kimbell–Diamond hoped to have the assets retain that high basis.

dation of Seller had preceded, rather than followed, the taxpayer's purchase.

As a result, the court disallowed Kimbell–Diamond's planned transferred basis and determined that the company's asset basis was simply its cost for each asset. Seller was not before the court in that case, but the court's opinion clearly implied that its presence would not have changed the result and, moreover, that the result did not change the consequences to Seller. In other words, the court looked only to Kimbell–Diamond's actions to determine whether to treat the purchase-liquidation as a direct purchase, and it was satisfied with simply changing the consequences to that taxpayer.

The implication, then, is that the substance versus form analysis may provide a method for re-determining the tax consequences to one party to a multiparty exchange without affecting the other parties. Aside from the obvious and direct conflict between this single party approach and cases such as McDonald's,[80] which appear specially to require interparty transactional consistency, neither the courts nor the Internal Revenue Service would be likely to be content with this approach for several other reasons.

Some of the problems with inconsistent treatment of the parties to an exchange can be made apparent by putting Kimbell–Diamond in a post-Tax Reform Act of 1986 setting. In the original case, the court (and the Internal Revenue Service) disregarded the tax consequences of its own liquidation to Seller. Since at that time, liquidation carried no tax consequences to the liquidating corporation, and the tax consequences of a liquidation to the owner of the "liquidated" company would not have differed from those of a stock sale, disregarding the consequences to Seller was not problematic.[81] Under current law, liquidation of a corporation results in recognition by that company of all gain inherent in all of its assets.[82] It is doubtful either the Internal Revenue Service or any court would now be content to allow Seller's gain to go unrecognized simply because the liquidation occurred immediately after the acquisition of its stock and as part of the purchaser's plan to acquire its assets.

Another case that illustrates the same problem in Basic Inc. v. United States.[83] In Basic, Parent company owned Child company, which in turn owned Grandchild company. Purchaser sought to acquire the assets of Child and Grandchild. Prior to the sale, Child distributed all of the Grandchild stock to Parent, which then sold the stock of both companies to Purchaser. Parent reported its receipt of the Grandchild stock from Child as a dividend. This characterization was essentially tax-free to all parties and gave Parent a basis in the Grandchild stock which served to reduce Parent's gain on the sale to Purchaser. The court, referring to its actions as being based upon a "business purpose" or "substance versus form" approach, treated the distribution and sale as a

80. 688 F.2d 520 (7th Cir. 1982).

81. See 14 T.C. at 79.

82. See § 336.

83. 549 F.2d 740 (Ct. Cl. 1977).

single transaction, and then it held that the "substance" of the distribution was not a dividend. Instead, it explained that "the whole transaction was a foregone conclusion that might just as well have been carried out in reverse order without changing the attendant risks or final result to the slightest degree."[84] Apparently, the court believed that this justified disintegrating the "whole" transaction and treating it *as if* it had been carried out in reverse order. Parent was taxed as if it had not received any distribution but had sold the Child stock while Child still owned the stock of Grandchild.

To complete the picture, Purchaser acquired stock of two companies, Child and Grandchild. If the "real" facts were that Parent sold the stock of Child, which, at the time of sale, owned the stock of Grandchild, it would appear that subsequent to the sale, Child must have distributed the stock of Grandchild to Purchaser. In basic, Purchaser was not before the court, so that Purchaser's tax consequences were not at issue. Nonetheless, it would not be exaggerating to suggest that Purchaser might have been surprised to learn, after purchasing the stock of two separate corporations, that it had *really* purchased only the stock of Child and that Child distributed the Grandchild stock as a dividend immediately after the purchase.

In fact, the court treated the seller as if there had been no pre-sale dividend without any apparent need to treat Purchaser as if there had been a post-sale dividend, with the result that the distribution of the Grandchild stock was essentially ignored. At the time the case arose, the tax result of the distribution, had it not been ignored, would have been simply to increase Parent's basis in the stock it sold, thereby reducing its taxable gain. Under current law, however, a dividend distribution by Child could result in that company recognizing as gain all the accrued appreciation on its Grandchild stock.[85] A transactionally inconsistent recharacterization of the exchanges which disregarded the dividend would allow substantial and unwarranted tax savings, and it is highly unlikely that taxpayers who sought that savings could find it by simply making the dividend distribution without any business purpose and as part of a broader plan of tax avoidance.[86]

The conclusions to be drawn from analysis of the above cases are that: (1) sometimes inter-party transactional consistency is crucial to a determination of whether and how an integrated series of exchanges will be recharacterized; (2) other times such consistency is irrelevant; and (3) no basis has ever been enunciated for distinguishing between the two possibilities or for determining which aspect (importance or irrelevance) will rule in any particular case.

There are many substance versus form cases, however, where inter-party consistency is not a problem. Courts can often simply ignore self-

84.   549 F.2d at 746.

85.   See § 311.

86.   See also Waterman S.S. Corp. v. Commissioner, 430 F.2d 1185 (5th Cir.

1970), cert. denied, 401 U.S. 939, 91 S.Ct. 936, 28 L.Ed.2d 219 (1971).

cancelling steps or telescope two or more steps into a single, less complex, transaction;[87] in these cases, deciding that the "substance" of the exchanges differs from the characterization chosen by the taxpayer seems more straightforward. Even these seemingly straightforward cases leave room for concern, however. They necessarily advance from a determination that a series of exchanges should be integrated to a conclusion that integration means characterization as a single transaction—or, in the case of self-cancelling steps, characterization as a "nontransaction"—is a more appropriate description of the "substance" of the exchanges. The problem is that when the "substance" of an exchange is so defined, all that can be meant by "substance" is "a more convenient way of achieving a given result." Unfortunately, in most areas of tax law, a more convenient way of doing something is only a more convenient way of doing something; it is not necessarily the "substance" of actions that are done less conveniently.

The difference between "convenience" and "substance" is well established. For example, tax-free reorganizations are only those exchanges which meet certain statutory requirements.[88] If X acquires all of the stock of Y in exchange solely for X voting stock, the exchange would qualify as a reorganization.[89] If X does not want reorganization treatment, it could intentionally fail to meet some of the statutory requirements, perhaps by acquiring some of the stock for cash or for X nonvoting stock. Similarly, if X had wanted to acquire some of the Y stock for cash, but went to the trouble of issuing X voting stock instead, it could qualify the exchange as a reorganization. In either case, X could manipulate the status of the transaction (as a tax-free reorganization or as a taxable sale) by simply acting in a somewhat less convenient way than it had at first anticipated.

One might be tempted to point out that in the above context, unlike in other substance versus form cases, characterization as a reorganization or a sale is dependent on real economic distinctions—the quality of consideration (some cash or all equity) makes for a substantive economic difference, which in turn governs the tax characterization of the exchange. The point, while superficially appearing persuasive, is irrelevant. The Code is full of other provisions which make tax characterization wholly independent of economic substance. Nonetheless, no court has been tempted to hold the "substance" of these actions to be different from their form. Even more telling, the Code often makes determination of the tax "substance" of transactions *explicitly* dependent on nothing more than the taxpayer's own stated choice of form.[90]

On the other hand, there often *is* economic effect to actions which *are* disregarded in even the most straightforward cases. When a taxpayer simply takes two steps to achieve a single result, there often is some

---

87. See e.g., Battelstein v. Commissioner, 611 F.2d 1033 (5th Cir. 1980).

88. See § 368.

89. See § 368(a)(1)(B).

90. See e.g., § 71(b)(1)(B) (treatment of alimony payments); § 152(e)(2) (determination of which parent gets personal exemption for dependent).

effect on legal rights during the interim between the two steps. If *A* lends *B* $100 on Monday and forgives the debt on Tuesday, the "transaction" puts *A* and *B* in a different legal and economic position for 24 hours than had *A* simply given *B* $100 on Monday (or on Tuesday). While in cases such as this the economic consequences of two steps may differ only minutely from what would have been the case if only a single step had been taken, the *degree* of economic consequence would appear to be of little concern. Indeed, the economic consequences of a corporation paying $1,000 to a single shareholder (in addition to transferring, say $1,000,000 worth of its voting stock to other shareholders) to avoid characterization of a stock acquisition as a "B" reorganization, or the consequences of a taxpayer waiting two days (until the next tax year) to sell an asset in a fixed market, are themselves almost meaningless.

In addition to some perhaps insignificant economic consequence inherent in almost all step transaction and substance versus form cases, many such cases which are found to have a substance different from their form can actually involve *substantial* economic consequences which are simply disregarded. For example, in Knetsch v. United States,[91] the Supreme Court collapsed a loan and transfer of the same proceeds into essentially a non-transaction, despite the taxpayer's out-of-pocket costs of over $90,000.

The problem with attempting to redefine the substance of a transaction based upon its ultimate economic effect is that transactions are simply not defined by reference to their economic effect, but by reference to facts such as the items exchanged and other similar attributes. While the substance of a series of exchanges might be seen as the overall change in economic status of the taxpayer involved, tax transactions are always defined by reference to the *means* (*i.e.*, exchanges) used to reach the ends (economic changes) rather than by the ends themselves.[92]

When courts do tax individuals by looking to the change in their overall economic circumstances and determining what transaction(s) *might* have achieved those economic results, their actions do not seem unreasonable, but the problem in most cases is simply that there is *not* just a single transaction that could have achieved the actual economic results. Instead, there are usually *several* different kinds of transactions by which those results could have been reached: for some, the formal statutory requirements have been met; for others, they have not. Typically, in these cases, the court will choose only the *latter* as accurately describing the "substance" of the transaction.

Indeed, in those few situations where there *is* a single economic substance that appears more accurate than other choices; courts never-

---

91. 364 U.S. 361, 81 S.Ct. 132, 5 L.Ed.2d 128 (1960).

92. One consequence of looking to economic result, rather than the means of achieving that result, to define a transaction is that often the "substance" of the redefined exchange is held to be a transac-

tion defined by the Code as consisting of one or more specific exchanges when those exchanges which define the transaction have, quite simply, not occurred. See e.g., Davant v. Commissioner, 366 F.2d 874 (5th Cir.), cert. denied, 386 U.S. 1022, 87 S.Ct. 1370, 18 L.Ed.2d 460 (1967).

theless will frequently characterize the situations as constituting a transaction that, according to the Code, has requirements that are unmet by the exchange, even as recast, and that also *fails* to reflect the economic substance of the exchange. For example, in Higgins v. Smith,[93] a shareholder sold property to his wholly owned company, and the Court simply disregarded the sale, despite the fact that property previously owned by the shareholder was afterwards owned by the corporation. Similarly, in Revenue Ruling 60–133[94] the taxpayer transferred stock of one wholly owned corporation (*X*) to another wholly owned corporation (*Y*) just prior to *X*'s payment of a dividend. The Internal Revenue Service simply ignored the transfer and treated the taxpayer as if he had personally received the dividend. Again, the recharacterized transaction was further from the economic substance (and from its statutory definition) than was the taxpayer's original characterization of the exchange.[95]

[ii] Summary of Substance Versus Form in Step Transaction Cases

To the extent that the "substance" of a series of exchanges for a single taxpayer can be determined, that substance represents an overall change in the taxpayer's economic position. For example, she may have begun with stock of *X* and may end up with stock of *Y*, which owns the former operating assets of *X*, so that the "substance" from her point of view is an exchange of *X* stock for *Y* stock. This change in substantive rights might have been accomplished by some tax-free transaction, but it might also have been accomplished by a fully taxable exchange. The problem is that the Code does not impose taxes based on changes in economic rights; it imposes taxes based on certain *transactions*. And, transactions are not defined as any actions which work certain changes in economic rights; they are defined as very specific sets of *exchanges*.

While it would not be wrong to impose tax on net economic "substance" rather than on the objective determinants listed in the Code, the substance versus form doctrine provides no framework for determining either when or how such should be done. Even were there guidelines for determining *when* substance should rule over form, because the Code specifies transactions only by reference to formal characteristics, there often is no true substance that describes a taxpayer's exchanges, but only a choice of potentially applicable forms, one of which was chosen by the taxpayer accurately, and a different one of which may be chosen by a court. Finally, even if a single transaction could be said to describe the substance of the actions of one taxpayer accurately, it is just as likely as not that that transaction would not truthfully represent the actions of all the other parties to the exchange.

The overwhelming contradictions in both the theory and the application of substance versus form analysis to step transaction cases can be

---

93. 308 U.S. 473, 60 S.Ct. 355, 84 L.Ed. 406 (1940).

94. 1960–1 C.B. 189.

95. See also Reef Corp. v. Commissioner, 368 F.2d 125 (5th Cir. 1966), cert. denied, 386 U.S. 1018, 87 S.Ct. 1371, 18 L.Ed.2d 454 (1967).

understood only when it is also understood that the doctrine is simply not what it purports to be. When it is acknowledged that the doctrine is aimed at preventing tax-motivated behavior, a court's conclusion that the parties *could* have achieved their goals by different means, so they should be taxed *as if* they did so becomes understandable. All of a sudden, questions such as whether and when transactional consistency should be required and *which* sequence of exchanges more "accurately" reflects the substance become readily answerable. Unfortunately, at the same time, any appearance of judicial honesty disappears.

[iii]   Substance Versus Form in Defining Relationships

In some cases, the substance versus form issue appears to have a fundamentally different role from that discussed above: rather than seeking to re-characterize transactions by focusing on the order of exchanges or by defining transactions by reference to their economic effect, the issue raised by these cases has to do initially with characterizing ongoing *relationships*. If A simply sells property to B, the exchange is obviously a sale. But what if A transfers some, but less than all, of his rights in that property? Depending on the extent of the rights transferred, the exchange may be characterized as a sale, a lease, a financing agreement, or any of numerous other transactions. Proper characterization, it seems, depends on the relationship between A and B and the property. If B "owns" the property after the exchange, the exchange is a sale. If A "owns" the property, then whatever the transaction is, it is not a sale. Essentially, rather than attempting to redefine what rights are exchanged for what other rights, these cases focus on defining the *relationship* caused by transfers which are acknowledged to have occurred. Unlike transactions, relationships *do* vary based on actual economic substance, so that an analysis of the substance seems not only possible, but appropriate. Analysis of these cases reveals interesting results.

In Helvering v. F. & R. Lazarus & Co.[96] the taxpayer transferred legal title in some buildings to a bank as trustee for land-trust certificate holders. Pursuant to the same contract, the taxpayer leased the buildings for 99 years with an option to repurchase. The annual rental was five percent of the amount that had been paid to the taxpayer by the bank. The agreement provided for additional payments that would, over 49 years, equal the principal amount paid by the bank. Upon completion of those payments, the taxpayer could retain possession of the building without further cost. The Court explained that "in the field of taxation, administrators of the laws, and the courts, are concerned with substance and realities, and formal written documents are not rigidly binding."[97] It held that the substance of the agreement was more like a mortgage than a sale and leaseback, and that the taxpayer should be treated as the tax "owner" of the buildings.

96. 308 U.S. 252, 60 S.Ct. 209, 84   **97.** 308 U.S. at 255.
L.Ed. 226 (1939).

In Frank Lyon Co. v. United States[98] Worthen Bank & Trust Co. owned land on which it wanted to build an office building. State and federal banking laws made that direct course impossible. Instead, Frank Lyon Co. leased the land from Worthen for 76 years, at an annual rent of $50 for the first 26 years, and higher amounts in later years. Lyon purchased the building from Worthen piece by piece as it was constructed, but the building was leased back to Worthen under a net lease. Worthen's rent to Lyon equaled Lyon's mortgage payments on the building. At all times, Worthen could acquire ownership of the building by paying to Lyon an amount equal to Lyon's original down payment plus 6% interest, in addition to the unpaid balance of Lyon's mortgage. The government argued that the transaction was not a sale and lease-back, but that in substance Worthen continued to be the owner of the building and Lyon was simply a conduit for Worthen's own mortgage payments. The Court treated Lyon as the owner of the property, stating that:

> Where, as here, there is a genuine multiple-party transaction with economic substance which is compelled or encouraged by business or regulatory realities, is imbued with tax-independent considerations, and is not shaped solely by tax-avoidance features that have meaningless labels attached, the Government should honor the allocation of rights and duties effectuated by the parties.[99]

Lyon has been often cited, but for different propositions by different courts. In fact, the Tax Court has found it to stand for "the principle that, in a sale-leaseback context, a nonuser-owner recipient of tax benefits must prove that his entry into the transaction was motivated by a business purpose sufficient to justify the form of the transaction."[100] While the court did not hold that business purpose alone is *sufficient* to determine whether a specific party is the owner of property, it implied that if the form of a business transaction does *not* meet a minimum threshold of business purpose or economic objective, ownership of property may be determined according to what an objective observer may determine to be its substance.

One principle clearly established by Lyon, then, is that the same rights may be deemed ownership in one case and mere tenancy in another, depending on the presence of business purpose. In these cases, no party is "the owner ... in any simple sense."[101] Each of the parties has some rights; none of the parties has all; and looking to a business purpose at least avoids requiring a weighing of these rights against one another in all cases.

Unfortunately, focusing on whether parties had a business purpose for structuring a transaction a certain way in order to determine the

---

98. 435 U.S. 561, 98 S.Ct. 1291, 55 L.Ed.2d 550 (1978).

99. 435 U.S. at 583–84.

100. Rice's Toyota World, Inc. v. Commissioner, 81 T.C. 184, 201 (1983), aff'd. in part, rev'd. in part, 752 F.2d 89 (4th Cir. 1985).

101. 435 U.S. at 581.

substance of the relationships created thereby does create some problems. If nothing else, the focus suggested by the Court makes the parties' relative economic rights and liabilities of only secondary importance. The crux of Justice Stevens' lone dissent in Lyon is apparent in his first sentence: "In my judgment the controlling issue in this case is the economic relationship between [the parties];"[102] and the majority opinion itself explained that generally "in applying this doctrine of substance over form we have looked to the objective economic realities of a transaction rather than to the particular form the parties employed."[103] Nonetheless, when the Lyon majority looked at the "economic realities," those to which it gave the most significance were the objective legal factors that mandated the *choice* of a specific form rather than the economic rights which arose out of the arrangement between the parties. The implication is that the transaction has the "substance" assigned to it by the taxpayer because it was engaged in for some nontax reasons (business purpose). Thus, in one of the few situations where there may be ongoing economic relationships which may be characterized by terms (owner or lessee) which actually reflect different economic relationships, those economic relationships would seem to become irrelevant (or only marginally relevant).

Another problem with Lyon is that it gives little guidance for determining how ownership should be determined in the *absence* of a business purpose for the structure adopted by the parties. If parties are free to structure a transaction as either a sale-leaseback or as a financing transaction, and can achieve identical economic results from either structure, when will the parties' chosen form be respected for tax purposes? Unless Lyon also means that lack of business purpose is enough to justify *rejecting* the taxpayer's form (which would *completely* eliminate economic relationships from the equation), there must be some way to evaluate objectively the economic relationships growing out of a transaction so that one of the parties can be labeled "owner." Unfortunately, no one has yet been able to enunciate exactly how that determination can be made. Some suggest that ownership means a "realistic hope of profit."[104] Others believe that it means a realistic possibility of loss. Most simply acknowledge that there is no accurate test.

This inability to articulate a means of determining the "substance" of ownership says more about the shortcomings of ownership as a concept than it does about any shortcomings of tax attorneys. The problem is that the cases are generally concerned with determining which of two (or more) parties is the "owner" of a specific depreciable asset. To the extent the concept of ownership has any real meaning (outside of tax law), it relates not to an asset as a whole, but to certain rights to act with respect to that asset. While people often casually refer to "ownership" of property, what one owns is properly *not* the asset, but rather certain rights with respect to the asset, such as current or future

---

102. 435 U.S. at 584.

103. 435 U.S. at 573.

104. See Dunlap v. Commissioner, 74 T.C. 1377 (1980), rev'd. and remanded on other grounds, 670 F.2d 785 (8th Cir. 1982).

possession or use of the asset. At least under commonly accepted principles of property law, "one having a lesser estate such as tenancy may be an owner, and, indeed, there may be different estates in the same property, vested in different persons, and each be an owner thereof."[105]

Where one of the parties is the owner of certain property, in the sense that she owns *all* of the possible rights to possession and enjoyment of that property, no court will be asked to determine ownership; when a court *is* asked to determine "ownership" of a particular asset, no such thing exists. To the extent that courts are attempting to ascribe to one party a relationship (ownership of the *asset*) that does not exist in the cases before them, it is understandable that they have a hard time getting it right.

Another common situation in which tax consequences explicitly depend on characterization of the relationships created by an exchange, rather than on identification of the items exchanged, arises when courts and the Internal Revenue Service attempt to define corporate obligations as debt or equity. If the obligations represent ownership of the corporation (equity), corresponding corporate payments are either dividends[106] or stock redemptions.[107] Neither is deductible by the paying corporation. If the obligations are debt instruments, payments are either interest (deductible to the payor under section 163(a)) or tax-free payments of principal. Significant tax consequences thus depend on whether the relationship established by the shareholder's transfer is ownership of the corporation.

Generally, the difference between debt and equity is that equity represents an investment in the company, while the return on debt is more secure and not dependent on the company's performance. In those cases hard enough to attract attention, the obligations sought to be characterized have significant elements of both debt and equity but all of the elements of neither. Sometimes the obligations on their face have more risk (perhaps because they may be subordinated to other creditors or because the corporation is thinly capitalized) and more upside potential (perhaps because of high interest conditioned on the company's performance) than "debt," but they have less risk (because of priority over other shareholders and because payment is dependent not on profits but on simply avoiding bankruptcy) and upside potential than equity. Other times obligations appear to be straight debt, but the relationship between the corporation and the shareholder is such that the parties are unlikely to treat it as such.[108]

105. Baltimore & Ohio R.R. v. Walker, 45 Ohio St. 577, 16 N.E. 475, 480 (1888).

106. See §§ 301, 316.

107. See § 302.

108. For example, a sole shareholder is unlikely to enforce the terms of a debt instrument against her own corporation. See, e.g., Gooding Amusement Co. v. Commissioner, 23 T.C. 408 (1954), aff'd., 236 F.2d 159 (6th Cir. 1956), cert. denied, 352 U.S. 1031, 77 S.Ct. 595, 1 L.Ed.2d 599 (1957) (notes were not debt because controlling shareholder would not enforce them to corporation's detriment).

Another example of the same problem involves determining whether transfers from one person to another are gifts or compensation. The answer depends on whether the payments are compensation for past or future services by the recipient (or someone else), or whether they are made out of detached and disinterested generosity.[109] But in fact, when cases come up, the truth lies somewhere in the middle. Similarly, whether payments from a corporation to a shareholder are dividends or compensation for services depends on establishing which extreme is the case when the reality is simply somewhere between the two.

The result is that when there are easy cases, description of the substance is simple. When there are hard cases, all available descriptions of the substance are simply wrong.

[d] The Real Basis for the Doctrines

At this point, one might question the validity of much of the judicial analyses of tax cases. "Business purpose" is supposedly a requirement of certain *statutes*, but it appears to be relevant only as a means of determining whether the *facts* of a case are different from those alleged by the taxpayer. The relevant facts must be determined so that the appropriate law can be applied, but there is no way to determine what those facts (the "real" exchanges) are, so that a court's view of the "facts" depends more on what law it wants to apply than on any kind of objective observation of facts. Transactions are to be characterized as those which reflect the "substance" of the facts, but the facts often have different substance for the different taxpayers involved. Other times *none* of the potentially applicable characterizations accurately reflect the substance from *anyone's* point of view. Still other times, several *different* provisions, with very different tax consequences, can describe a single exchange equally well. Citizens may do whatever they wish to avoid taxes; but if actions are seen as motivated by tax avoidance rather than by a business purpose, the desired tax consequences may not be available. Then again, maybe they will be.

All of these inconsistencies flow from the same basic systemic flaws: (1) the federal income tax system attempts to force precise transactional definitions on imprecise relationships; (2) even where the facts of a case accurately reflect the precise statutory requirements for certain tax-favored exchanges, they may *not* reflect the behavior that Congress sought to encourage (or to avoid discouraging) because the statutory *requirements* simply do not mirror the statutory *objectives*; and (3) in any system where a person's taxable income and ultimate liability depend on his transactions rather than on accurate measurement of economic income, taxpayers will be encouraged to engage in tax-favored transactions rather than in the most economically productive activities. As a result, the federal income tax system is inherently inaccurate both in defining transactions and in defining income by way of transactions.

109. See Commissioner v. Duberstein, 363 U.S. 278, 80 S.Ct. 1190, 4 L.Ed.2d 1218 (1960).

Left unchecked, these problems would allow taxpayers to avoid taxes through economically meaningless (or worse) activity.

Those charged with administering and enforcing the tax law have responded to the flaws caused by the system's transaction focus by enunciating and applying all of the doctrines discussed above—business purpose, step transaction, and substance versus form. None of these doctrines adequately addresses the problems, however, because these doctrines are progeny of the same system that created the problems. The problems are the result of basing taxation on transactions. The purported solutions are all simply *ex post* justifications for re-characterizing one transaction as some different one, resulting in neither accuracy nor consistency.

While courts have made a point of explaining that tax minimization is not "bad,"[110] the truth is that some tax minimization *is* bad and *is* condemned by the courts. All of the above doctrines were designed essentially to combat it. The problem is that when doctrines address tax minimization only within the context of determining whether some implicit statutory requirement is met (business purpose), whether the "facts" are different from those embodied in legal contracts (step transactions), or whether the "substance" of a transaction is different from its form, the response seems to be simply that tax minimization becomes "bad" only when the taxpayer's exchanges can somehow be recharacterized as a different transaction from that posited by the taxpayer. In the law of tax avoidance, the remedy determines the rights. Sometimes courts will hold that the "facts" are different from those alleged by the taxpayer; other times they will instead hold that the substance of the exchange is different from its form. In either case, the unexpressed reasoning behind the decision is the same. If the transaction can be recharacterized, tax minimization becomes tax avoidance and is bad. If the taxpayer was motivated by tax avoidance, but there is no other label we can readily put on her exchanges, her behavior is only tax minimization and is good.

Viewing these doctrines as mere devices to combat tax avoidance when the recharacterization remedy is available also serves to explain why the business purpose test for either doctrine does not always "work." If the doctrines are nothing more than justifications for punishing certain transactions fraught with tax avoidance, it would make sense that when taxpayers engage in transactions that have a legitimate business purpose and are not motivated by tax avoidance those taxpayers should not be punished. It should not be surprising that the business purpose test does not "work" only in those cases in which its application might do something *other* than punish tax avoidance. In cases such as Zenz v. Quinlivan[111] and Revenue Ruling 83–142[112] the taxpayer *had* a

110. "[A] man's motive to avoid taxation will not establish his liability if the transaction does not do so without it." Chisholm v. Commissioner, 79 F.2d 14, 15

(2d Cir. 1935), cert. denied, 296 U.S. 641, 56 S.Ct. 174, 80 L.Ed. 456 (1935).

111.   213 F.2d 914 (6th Cir. 1954).

112.   1983–2 C.B. 68.

business purpose for his actions, but those actions were nonetheless integrated *for the taxpayer's benefit*. If viewed as exceptions to a general rule that determines "facts" by reference to business purpose, these cases do not make sense. When viewed from the perspective of a doctrine which is addressed to punishing tax avoidance and rewarding economically motivated behavior, they make perfect sense.[113]

Use of these doctrines to combat tax avoidance does have some benefits. It allows the courts and the Internal Revenue Service to counter abuses, and it allows them to do so in a manner that appears (to some) to be consistent with the system and with the rule of law. Rather than stating that tax avoidance is wrong but our weapons against it are weak, it should be recognized that tax minimization is not tax avoidance and is not therefore wrong. Courts and the Internal Revenue Service can enforce equity under the guise of determining "facts" or "substance," thus protecting the image of precision while fighting some of its untoward consequences.

But use of the business purpose, step transaction, and substance versus form rationales for punishing tax avoidance does have some flaws. Essentially, there are three problems with this approach: (1) it is misunderstood; (2) it is inaccurate; and (3) it is misdirected.

If the courts and Internal Revenue Service acknowledged the true role of the step transaction and substance versus form doctrines as *ex post* justifications for punishing tax avoidance when the facts are close enough to some other transaction so that either the "facts" or the "substance" of the exchange can be said to be described by that other transaction, at least everyone would understand both the principles to be applied and the relevant facts. Because the doctrines are instead supposed to be objective observations of fact or law, however, their roles are often fundamentally misconceived. Courts may be convinced they are reaching an objective determination of an exchange when there is no such thing. While tort scholars long ago realized that proximate cause is merely identifying circumstances where the law should impose liability and that liability must therefore be rooted in fairness at least as much as in causation, tax lawyers and courts are still attempting to figure out objective causation—a task which is not only fruitless but also misleading. As a result, a court may cling to a test such as business purpose, intent, or binding commitment, or to a concept such as transactional consistency, because that court, or one by whose decision it is bound, used that test in a previous decision. By so doing, it may reach an inappropriate result in the case before it, because it fails to understand that *really* the proper test is a function of the desired result rather than vice versa.

---

113. See e.g., Selfe v. United States, 778 F.2d 769 (11th Cir. 1985) (taxpayer was obligor of debt in substance, even though in form her corporation was debtor).

Appendix

RESEARCHING FEDERAL TAXATION ON WESTLAW

Section 1. Introduction

The Law of Federal Income Taxation provides a strong base for analyzing even the most complex problem involving issues related to federal taxation. Whether your research requires examination of statutes, case law, administrative materials, or expert commentary, West books and Westlaw are excellent sources of information.

To keep you informed of current developments, Westlaw provides frequently updated databases. With Westlaw, you have unparalleled legal research resources at your fingertips.

Additional Resources

If you have not previously used Westlaw or if you have questions not covered in this appendix, call the West Reference Attorneys at 1–800–REF-ATTY (1–800–733–2889). The West Reference Attorneys are trained, licensed attorneys, available 24 hours a day to assist you with your Westlaw search questions. To subscribe to Westlaw, call 1–800–344–5008 or access **www.westlaw.com**.

Section 2. Westlaw Databases

Each database on Westlaw is assigned an abbreviation called an *identifier*, which you can use to access the database. You can find identifiers for Westlaw databases in the online Westlaw Directory and in the printed *Westlaw Database Directory*. When you need to know more detailed information about a database, use Scope. Scope contains coverage information, lists of related databases, and valuable search tips.

The following chart lists selected Westlaw databases that contain information pertaining to federal taxation. For a complete list of federal tax databases, see the online Westlaw Directory or the printed *Westlaw Database Directory*. Because new information is continually being added to Westlaw, you should also check the online Westlaw Directory for new database information.

Selected Federal Income Tax Law Databases on Westlaw

Database	Identifier	Coverage
Combined Federal Materials		
Federal Taxation–Combined Tax Materials	FTX–ALL	Varies by source
Federal Taxation–Cases and Releases	FTX–CSRELS	Varies by source
Federal Taxation–Code and Regulations	FTX–CODREG	Varies by source

Selected Federal Income Tax Law Databases on Westlaw

Database	Identifier	Coverage
Federal Case Law		
American Federal Tax Reports (AFTR)	RIA–AFTR	Begins with 1880
Federal Taxation–Cases	FTX–CS	Begins with 1789
Federal Taxation–Supreme Court Cases	FTX–SCT	Begins with 1790
Federal Taxation–Courts of Appeals Cases	FTX–CTA	Begins with 1891
Federal Taxation–District Courts Cases	FTX–DCT	Begins with 1789
Federal Taxation–Court of Federal Claims	FTX–FEDCL	Begins with 1856
Federal Taxation–Tax Court Cases	FTX–TCT	Decisions begins with 1924; memorandum decisions begins with 1928; summary opinions begins with 2001
Federal Taxation–Tax Court Decisions	FTX–TC	Begins with 1924
Federal Taxation–Tax Court Memorandum Decisions	FTX–TCM	Begins with 1928
Federal Taxation–Tax Court Summary Opinions	FTX–TCSO	Begins with 2001
RIA® Federal Tax Citator Second	RIA–CITE	Begins with 1954
Briefs, Pleadings, and Other Court Documents		
Federal Taxation Briefs	FTX–BRIEF	Begins with 1963
Federal Taxation–Tax Court Briefs and Petitions	FTX–TCBRIEF	Briefs begins with 1999; petitions begins with 2004
Taxation Trial Filings	TAX–FILING	Begins with 2000
Taxation Trial Motions	TAX–MOTIONS	Begins with 2000
Taxation Trial Pleadings	TAX–PLEADINGS	Begins with 2000
Federal Statutes, Legislative Materials, and Rules		
Federal Taxation–U.S. Code Annotated	FTX–USCA	Current data

Selected Federal Income Tax Law Databases on Westlaw

Database	Identifier	Coverage
Internal Revenue Code of 1954	FTX–IRC54	August 16, 1954–October 21, 1986
1939 Internal Revenue Code	FTX–IRC39	January 2, 1939–August 15, 1954
Federal Taxation–Congressional Record	FTX–CR	Begins with the First Session of the 99th Congress (1985)
Federal Taxation–General Accounting Office Reports	FTX–GAO	Begins with January 1994
Federal Taxation–Joint Committee on Taxation's General Explanation of Tax Legislation (the Blue Books)	FTX–BLUEBOOKS	1976, 1981, 1982, 1986, 1991, 1993, 1996–1998, 2001, 2003, 2005, 2007
Federal Taxation–Public Laws	FTX–PL	Begins with 1973
Federal Taxation–Congressional Bills	FTX–BILLTXT	Begins with 104th Congress (1995–1996)
Federal Taxation–Congressional Research Service	FTX–CRS	Begins with 1989
Federal Taxation–Legislative History	FTX–LH	Begins with 1948
Federal Taxation–Materials on the Tax Reform Act of 1986	FTX–TRA86	Begins with 1986
RIA Internal Revenue Code	RIA–IRC	Current data
RIA Internal Revenue Code Historical Notes	RIA–HN	Begins with 1954
RIA United States Tax Reporter–Committee Reports	RIA–USTR–LH	Current data
RIA United States Tax Reporter–Estate Committee Reports	RIA–USTREST–LH	Current data
RIA United States Tax Reporter–Excise Committee Reports	RIA–USTREXC–LH	Current data
Federal Taxation–Rules	FTX–RULES	Current data

Federal Administrative Materials

Federal Taxation–Combines FTX–GCM,	FTX–MEMOS	Varies by source

Selected Federal Income Tax Law Databases on Westlaw

Database	Identifier	Coverage
FTX–AOD, FTX–TM, FTX–LB, and FTX–LGM		
Federal Taxation–Combines FTX–WD, FTX–CB, and FTX–NR	FTX–CBWD	Varies by source
Federal Taxation–Circular 230	FTX–CIRC230	Current data
Federal Taxation–Code of Federal Regulations	FTX–CFR	Current data
Federal Taxation–Delegation Orders	FTX–DO	Begins with 1954
Federal Taxation–Executive Orders	FTX–EO	Begins with 1954
Federal Taxation–Exemption Rulings and Publication 78	FTX–EXEMPT–ALL	Exemption rulings begins with January 1994; Publication 78 current data
Federal Taxation–Federal Register	FTX–FR	Begins with January 1981
Federal Taxation–Final, Temporary, and Proposed Regulations	FTX–REG	Varies by source
Federal Taxation–Industry Specialization Program	FTX–ISP	Begins with 1992
Federal Taxation–IRS Actions on Decisions	FTX–AOD	Begins with 1967
Federal Taxation–IRS Announcements and Notices	FTX–ANN	Announcements begins with 1988; notices begins with 1980
Federal Taxation–IRS Chief Counsel Advice	FTX–CCA	Begins with 1999
Federal Taxation–IRS Combined Releases	FTX–RELS	Varies by source
Federal Taxation–IRS Cumulative Bulletins	FTX–CB	Varies by source
Federal Taxation–IRS Exempt Organizations CPE Technical Instruction Program	FTX–EOTIP	Begins with 1999

Selected Federal Income Tax Law Databases on Westlaw

Database	Identifier	Coverage
Federal Taxation–IRS Exemption Rulings	FTX–EXEMPT	Begins with January 1994
Federal Taxation–IRS Field Service Advice	FTX–FSA	Begins with 1992
Federal Taxation–IRS General Counsel Memoranda	FTX–GCM	Begins with 1962
Federal Taxation–IRS Information Letters	FTX–INFO	Begins with 2000
Federal Taxation–IRS Litigation Bulletins	FTX–LB	Begins with 1986
Federal Taxation–IRS Litigation Guideline Memoranda	FTX–LGM	Begins with 1986
Federal Taxation–IRS Market Segment Specialization Program	FTX–MSSP	Begins with 1993
Federal Taxation–IRS Miscellaneous Documents	FTX–IRSMISC	Begins with 2002
Federal Taxation–IRS News Releases	FTX–NR	Begins with January 1981
Federal Taxation–IRS Private Letter Rulings	FTX–PLR	Begins with 1954
Federal Taxation–IRS Publications	FTX–IRSPUBS	2006
Federal Taxation–IRS Publications (Retired)	FTX–IRSPUBS–OLD	1984–2005
Federal Taxation–IRS Service Center Advice	FTX–SCA	Begins with 1999
Federal Taxation–IRS Technical Advice Memoranda	FTX–TAM	Begins with 1954
Federal Taxation–IRS Technical Memoranda	FTX–TM	Begins with 1967
Federal Taxation–IRS Written Determinations (Combined Materials)	FTX–WD	Varies by source
Federal Taxation–Revenue Procedures	FTX–RP	Begins with 1954

Selected Federal Income Tax Law Databases on Westlaw

Database	Identifier	Coverage
Federal Taxation–Revenue Rulings	FTX–RR	Begins with 1954
Federal Taxation–Treasury Decisions	FTX–TD	Begins with 1954
Federal Taxation–Treasury Department Orders	FTX–TDO	Begins with 1954
Federal Taxation–U.S. Treaties and Conventions	FTX–TREATIES	Begins with 1844
Internal Revenue Manual–Manual Transmittals	FTX–IRMMT	Begins with March 2001
IRS Chief Counsel Attorney Memoranda	FTX–AM	Begins with 2006
IRS Publication 78–Cumulative List of Organizations	FTX–PUB78IRS	Current data
RIA Federal Final and Temporary Tax Regulations	RIA–FTREGS	Current data
RIA Federal Proposed Tax Regulations with Preambles	RIA–PREGS	Current data
RIA Federal Tax Citator Second	RIA–CITE	Begins with 1954
RIA Federal Tax Regulations	RIA–REGS	Current data
RIA Internal Revenue Manual	RIA–IRM	Current data
Statements of Federal Financial Accounting Concepts and Standards	FAS–SFFAC	Current data
Public Records		
Dockets–Federal Taxation	DOCK–FTX	Full docket records begins with January 2000; index records begins with 1990
Dockets–U.S. Tax Court	DOCK–USTAXC-OURT	Begins with January 2000
Journals and Law Reviews		
Taxation–Law Reviews, Texts, and Bar Journals	TX–TP	Varies by publication

Selected Federal Income Tax Law Databases on Westlaw

Database	Identifier	Coverage
Journals and Law Reviews	JLR	Varies by publication
Akron Tax Journal	AKRONTJ	Selected coverage begins with 1987 (vol. 4); full coverage begins with 1993 (vol. 10).
Business Entities	WGL–BUSENT	Full coverage begins with 1985 (vol. 1)
Corporate Taxation	WGL–CTAX	Full coverage begins with 2000 (vol. 27)
Estate Planning	WGL–ESTPLN	Full coverage begins with 1985 (vol. 12)
Fordham Journal of Corporate and Financial Law	FDMJCFL	Full coverage begins with 1997 (vol. 2)
Houston Business and Tax Law Journal	HOUBTXLJ	Full coverage begins with 2001 (vol. 1)
Journal of Taxation	WGL–JTAX	Full coverage begins with 1985 (vol. 62)
Pittsburgh Tax Review	PTTAXR	Full coverage begins with 2003 (vol. 1)
Practical Tax Lawyer	PRACTXL	Full coverage begins with 1999 (vol. 14)
Practical Tax Strategies	WGL–PRACTXST	Full coverage begins with 1985 (vol. 34)
Real Estate Taxation	WGL–RETAX	Full coverage begins with 1985 (vol. 12)
Taxation of Exempts	WGL–TXNEXEMPT	Full coverage begins with 1999 (vol. 11, no. 2)
Tax Law Review	TAXLR	Full coverage begins with 1988 (vol. 44)
Tax Lawyer	TAXL	Selected coverage begins with 1982 (vol. 35)
Tax Management Journals: All (Multi-base)	TM–ALLJNL	Varies by publication
Valuation Strategies	WGL–VALST	Full coverage begins with 1997
Virginia Tax Review	VATXR	Selected coverage begins with 1987 (vol. 7); full coverage begins with 1993 (vol. 13)

Selected Federal Income Tax Law Databases on Westlaw

Database	Identifier	Coverage
Warren Gorham Lamont Tax Journals	WGL–TAXJ	Varies by publication
Legal Texts and Practice Materials		
Taxation–Law Reviews, Texts, and Bar Journals	TX–TP	Varies by publication
706/709 Deskbook	PPC–706DB	11th edition
990 Deskbook	PPC–990DB	13th edition
1040 Deskbook	PPC–1040DB	18th edition
1041 Deskbook	PPC–1041DB	14th edition
1065 Deskbook	PPC–1065DB	16th edition
1120 Deskbook	PPC–1120DB	15th edition
1120S Deskbook	PPC–1120S	15th edition
5500 Deskbook	PPC–5500DB	14th edition
Am Jur® Legal Forms 2d–Federal Tax Guide to Legal Forms	AMJUR–TGLF	Current data
Bennett, Bradley, Kaiser, Northwood, and Sharpe: Taxation of Distribution from Qualified Plans	WGL–QUALIFPL	Current edition
Bishop and Kleinberger: Limited Liability Companies	WGL–LLC	Current edition
Bittker and Lokken: Federal Taxation of Income, Estates, and Gifts	WGL–IEG	Current edition
Bittker, McMahon, and Zelenak: Federal Income Taxation of Individuals	WGL–INDV	Current edition
Comisky, Feld, and Harris: Tax Fraud and Evasion	WGL–FRAUD	Current edition
Corpus Juris Secundum®: Internal Revenue	CJS–FTX	Current data
Creamer and McMahon: Tax Planning for Transfers of Business Interests	WGL–DISPOS	Current edition

Selected Federal Income Tax Law Databases on Westlaw

Database	Identifier	Coverage
Esperti and Peterson: Irrevocable Trusts: Analysis with Forms	WGL–IRREVTR	Current edition
Federal Limitations on State and Local Taxation 2d	FLSALT	Current data
Federal Tax Practice (Casey)	CASEY	Current data
Handling Federal Estate and Gift Taxes 6th	HFEGTAX	Current data
Harrington, Plaine, and Zaritsky: Generation–Skipping Transfer Tax	WGL–GENSKIP	Current edition
Henkel: Estate Planning and Wealth Preservation: Strategies and Solutions	WGL–WEALTH	Current edition
Hill and Mancino: Taxation of Exempt Organizations	WGL–TEO	Current data
Income Taxation of Estates and Trusts	PLIREF–TXTR	Current edition
Internal Revenue Manual–Abridged and Annotated	IRM–AA	Current edition
Internal Revenue Service Practice and Procedure Deskbook	PLIREF–IRS	Third edition
Inventory Tax Accounting and Uniform Capitalization	INVTA	Current data
Lathrope: Alternative Minimum Tax	WGL–AMT	Current edition
Law of Federal Income Taxation (Mertens)	MERTENS	Current data
McGaffey Legal Forms with Tax Analysis	MG–LF	Current data
Model Documents: Tax	MODELDOC–TAX	Begins with 2000
Payroll Deskbook	PPC–PAYROLL	12th edition

Selected Federal Income Tax Law Databases on Westlaw

Database	Identifier	Coverage
Perdue: Qualified Pension and Profit Sharing Plans	WGL–PENPLAN	Current edition
PLI Tax Law Treatise Multibase	PLIREF–TAX	Current data
Pond: Personal Financial Planning Handbook	WGL–FINPLAN	Current edition
Real Estate Investment Trusts Handbook	SECREITHB	Current data
Real Estate Professional's Tax Guide	REPROFTAX	Current data
Real Estate Transactions–Tax Planning and Consequences	REALETAXPL	2007 edition
Representation Before the Appeals Division of the IRS	IRS–REPAP	Current data
Representation Before the Collection Division of the IRS	IRS–REPCOL	Current data
Representation Before the United States Tax Court	IRS–REPTXCT	Current data
Representing Nonprofit Organizations	IRS–REPNPO	Current data
Representing the Audited Taxpayer Before the IRS	IRS–REPAUD	Current data
Representing the Bankrupt Taxpayer	IRS–REPBNK	Current data
RIA Complete Analysis of the Tax Act–Current	RIA–CATA	Current data
RIA Estate Checklists	RIA–ESTC	Current data
RIA Estate Client Letters	RIA–ESTCL	Current data
RIA Estate Filled In Forms	RIA–ESTF	Current data
RIA Estate IRS Sample Correspondence	RIA–ESTIRS	Current data
RIA Estate Planning	RIA–ESTP	Current data
RIA Estate Planning Analysis	RIA–ESTA	Current data

Selected Federal Income Tax Law Databases on Westlaw

Database	Identifier	Coverage
RIA Estate Planning Collection Complete	RIA–EST	Current data
RIA Federal Tax Coordinator 2d	RIA–FTC	Current data
RIA Tax Advisors Planning System	RIA–TAPS	Current data
RIA United States Tax Reporter Reporter	RIA–USTR	Current data
Robinson: Federal Income Taxation of Real Estate	WGL–REALEST	Current edition
Robinson: Real Estate Forms: Tax Analysis and Checklists	WGL–REFORMS	Current edition
Rosenberg and Daher: The Law of Federal Income Taxation	FEDTAX–HB	Current edition
Saltzman: IRS Practice and Procedure	WGL–IRSPRAC	Current edition
Tax and Estate Planning with Real Estate, Partnerships and LLCs	PLIREF–TAXREL	Current data
Tax Aspects of Marital Dissolution	GABINET	Second edition
Tax Aspects of Real Estate Investments	TAREI	Current data
Tax Penalties and Interest	IRS–TXPINT	Current data
Tax Planning for Real Estate Transactions	IRS–TPRET	Current data
West Federal Taxation–Corporations, Partnerships, Estates, and Trusts	WFT–CPET	2007 edition
West Federal Taxation–Individual Income Taxes	WFT–INDIV	2007 edition
West's Federal Forms–U.S. Tax Court	FEDFORMS–TCT	Current data
Willis, Pennell, and Postlewaite: Partnership Taxation	WGL–PARTTAX	Current edition
Zaritsky and Lane: Federal Income Taxation of Estates and Trusts	WGL–TAXET	Current edition

Selected Federal Income Tax Law Databases on Westlaw

Database	Identifier	Coverage
Zaritsky: Tax Planning for Family Wealth Transfers: Analysis with Forms	WGL–FAMTRAN	Current edition

Legal Newsletters, Current Awareness Materials, and Directories

RIA Federal Taxes Weekly Alert	RIA–FTWA	Begins with June 1995
WG & L® Internal Auditing Report	WGL–INTAREP	Begins with January 1995
Westlaw Topical Highlights–Taxation	WTH–TAX	Current data
West Legal Directory®–Taxation	WLD–TAX	Current data
West's® Tax Law Dictionary	DITAXWTDB	Current data

Section 3. Retrieving a Document with a Citation: Find and Hypertext Links

3.1 Find

Find is a Westlaw service that allows you to retrieve a document by entering its citation. Find allows you to retrieve documents from anywhere on Westlaw without accessing or changing databases. Find is available for many documents, including case law (state and federal), the *United States Code Annotated®* (USCA®), state statutes, administrative materials, and texts and periodicals.

To use Find, simply type the citation in the *Find this document by citation* text box at the tabbed Westlaw page and click **Go**. The following list provides some examples:

To find this document:	Access Find and type:
United States v. Hill 113 S. Ct. 941 (1993)	**113 sct 941**
26 U.S.C.A. § 61	**26 usca 61**
26 C.F.R. 1.61–12	**26 cfr 1.61–12**
Tax Ct. R. 31	**tax ct rule 31**
Rev. Rul. 2008–5	**rev rul 2008–5**

For a complete list of publications that can be retrieved with Find and their abbreviations, click **Find & Print** at the top of any Westlaw page and then click **Publications List** in the left frame.

3.2   Hypertext Links

Use hypertext links to move from one location to another on Westlaw. For example, use hypertext links to go directly from the statute, case, or law review article you are viewing to a cited statute, case, or article; from a headnote to the corresponding text in the opinion; or from an entry in a statutes index to the full text of the statute.

Section 4. Searching with Natural Language

Overview: With Natural Language, you can retrieve documents by simply describing your issue in plain English. If you are a relatively new Westlaw user, Natural Language searching can make it easier for you to retrieve cases that are on point. If you are an experienced Westlaw user, Natural Language gives you a valuable alternative search method to the Terms and Connectors search method described in Section 5.

When you enter a Natural Language description, Westlaw automatically identifies legal phrases, removes common words, and generates variations of terms in your description. Westlaw then searches for the concepts in your description. Concepts may include significant terms, phrases, legal citations, or topic and key numbers. Westlaw retrieves the documents that most closely match the concepts in your description, beginning with the document most likely to match.

4.1   Natural Language Search

Access a database such as the Federal Taxation–Cases database (FTX–CS). Click the **Natural Language** tab if it is not already selected and type a description such as the following in the *Search* text box. Then click **Search Westlaw**.

definition of a tax home

4.2   Browsing Search Results

Best Mode: To display the best portion (the portion that most closely matches your description) of each document in a Natural Language search result, click the **Best** arrows at the bottom of the right frame.

Term Mode: **To display portions of the document that contain your search terms, click the** Term **arrows at the bottom of the right frame.**

Previous/Next Document: To view the previous or the next document in the search result, click the left or right **Doc** arrow at the bottom of the right frame.

Section 5. Searching with Terms and Connectors

Overview: With Terms and Connectors searching, you enter a query consisting of key terms from your issue and connectors specifying the relationship between these terms.

Terms and Connectors searching is useful when you want to retrieve a document for which you know specific details, such as the title or the fact situation. Terms and Connectors searching is also useful when you want to retrieve all documents containing specific terms.

5.1 Terms

Plurals and Possessives: Plurals are automatically retrieved when you enter the singular form of a term. This is true for both regular and irregular plurals (e.g., **child** retrieves *children*). If you enter the plural form of a term, you will not retrieve the singular form.

If you enter the nonpossessive form of a term, Westlaw automatically retrieves the possessive form as well. However, if you enter the possessive form, only the possessive form is retrieved.

Compound Words and Abbreviations: When a compound word is one of your search terms, use a hyphen to retrieve all forms of the word. For example, the term **stand-by** retrieves *stand-by, standby,* and *stand by.*

When using an abbreviation as a search term, place a period after each of the letters to retrieve any of its forms. For example, the term **i.r.s.** retrieves *IRS, I.R.S., I R S,* and *I. R. S.* Note: The abbreviation does not retrieve the phrase *Internal Revenue Service,* so remember to add additional alternative terms such as **"internal revenue service"** to your query.

The Root Expander and the Universal Character: When you use the Terms and Connectors search method, placing the root expander (!) at the end of a root term generates all other terms with that root. For example, adding the ! to the root *deduct* in the query

deduct! /s income

instructs Westlaw to retrieve such terms as *deduct, deducted, deducting, deductible,* and *deduction.*

The universal character (*) stands for one character and can be inserted in the middle or at the end of a term. For example, the term

withdr*w

will retrieve *withdraw* and *withdrew.* Adding three asterisks to the root *elect*

elect* * *

instructs Westlaw to retrieve all forms of the root with up to three additional characters. Terms such as *elected* or *election* are retrieved by this query. However, terms with more than three letters following the root, such as *electronic,* are not retrieved. Plurals are always retrieved, even if the plural form of the term has more than three letters following the root.

Phrase Searching: To search for an exact phrase, place it within quotation marks. For example, to search for references to *alternative minimum tax,* type **"alternative minimum tax"**. When you are using the Terms and Connectors search method, you should use phrase searching only if you are certain that the terms in the phrase will not appear in any other order.

5.2 Alternative Terms

After selecting the terms for your query, consider which alternative terms are necessary. For example, if you are searching for the term *admissible*, you might also want to search for the term *inadmissible*. You should consider both synonyms and antonyms as alternative terms. You can also use the Westlaw thesaurus to add alternative terms to your query.

5.3 Connectors

After selecting terms and alternative terms for your query, use connectors to specify the relationship that must exist between search terms in your retrieved documents. The connectors are described below:

Type:	To retrieve documents with:	Example:
& (and)	both search terms	**deprecia! & property**
a space (or)	either search term or both search terms	**i.r.a. "individual retirement account"**
/p	search terms in the same paragraph	**farm! /p loss**
/s	search terms in the same sentence	**assign! /s income**
+s	the first search term preceding the second within the same sentence	**burden +s prov! proof**
/n	search terms within *n* terms of each other (where *n* is a number from 1 to 255)	**flat /5 rate**
+n	the first search term preceding the second by *n* terms (where *n* is a number from 1 to 255)	**statute +3 limitation**
" "	search terms appearing in the same order as in the quotation marks	**"de minimis"**

Type:	To exclude documents with:	Example:
% (but not)	terms following the YMBOL	**fraud 'statute of frauds"**

5.4 Field Restrictions

Overview: Documents in each Westlaw database consist of several segments, or *fields*. One field may contain the citation, another the title, another the synopsis, and so forth. Not all databases contain the same fields. Also depending on the database, fields with the same name may contain different types of information.

To view a list of fields and their contents for a specific database, see Scope for that database. Note that in some databases not every field is available for every document.

To retrieve only those documents containing your search terms in a specific field, restrict your search to that field. To restrict your search to a specific field, type the field name or abbreviation followed by your search terms enclosed in parentheses. For example, to retrieve the U.S. court of appeals case titled *United States v. Sabino*, access the Federal Taxation–Courts of Appeals Cases database (FTX–CTA). Click the **Terms and Connectors** tab if it is not already selected and type the following query in the *Search* text box, restricting your search to the title field (ti). Then click **Search Westlaw**.

ti(u.s. "united states" & sabino)

The fields discussed below are available in Westlaw case law databases you might use for researching issues related to federal taxation.

Digest and Synopsis Fields: The digest (di) and synopsis (sy) fields summarize the main points of a case. The synopsis field contains a brief description of a case. The digest field contains the topic and headnote fields and includes the complete hierarchy of concepts used by West's editors to classify the headnotes to specific West digest topic and key numbers. Restricting your search to the synopsis and digest fields limits your result to cases in which your terms are related to a major issue in the case.

Consider restricting your search to one or both of these fields if

- you are searching for common terms or terms with more than one meaning, and you need to narrow your search; or

- you cannot narrow your search by using a smaller database.

For example, to retrieve federal courts of appeals cases that discuss deduction of meal expenses, access the FTX–CTA database and type the following query:

sy,di(deduct! /p meal /p expense)

Headnote Field: The headnote field (he) is part of the digest field but does not contain the topic names or numbers, hierarchical classification information, or key numbers. The headnote field contains a one-sentence summary for each point of law in a case and any supporting citations given by the author of the opinion. A headnote field restriction is useful when you are searching for specific sections. For example, to retrieve headnotes from federal district court cases that cite 26 U.S.C.A. § 7433, access the Federal Taxation–District Courts Cases database (FTX–DCT) and type the following query:

he(26 +s 7433)

Topic Field: The topic field (to) is also part of the digest field. It contains the hierarchical classification information, including the West digest topic names and numbers and the key numbers. You should restrict search terms to the topic field in a case law database if

- a digest field search retrieves too many documents; or

- you want to retrieve cases with digest paragraphs classified under more than one topic.

For example, the topic Internal Revenue has the topic number 220. To retrieve federal district court cases with headnotes classified under Internal Revenue that discuss the accrual of liability for estate taxes, access the FTX–DCT database and type a query like the following:

to(220) /p liab! /p accru! /p estate /3 tax!

To retrieve cases with headnotes that may be classified under more than one topic and key number, search for your terms in the topic field. For example, to retrieve federal courts of appeals cases with headnotes discussing deductions, which may be classified to such topics as Bankruptcy (51), Internal Revenue (220), or Taxation (371), among other topics, access the FTX–CTA database and type a query like the following:

to(deduct!)

For a complete list of West digest topics and their corresponding topic numbers, access the West Key Number Digest (also known as the Custom Digest) by clicking **Key Numbers** at the top of any page. Then click **West Key Number Digest Outline** under *Browse Key Numbers*. Alternatively, click **Custom Digest** at a case law database Search page.

> *Note*: Slip opinions and cases from topical services do not contain the West digest, headnote, and topic fields.

Prelim and Caption Fields: When searching in a database containing statutes, rules, or regulations, restrict your search to the prelim (pr) and caption (ca) fields to retrieve documents in which your terms are important enough to appear in a section name or heading. For example, to retrieve federal statutes relating to depreciation, access the Federal Taxation–U.S. Code Annotated database (FTX–USCA) and type the following query:

pr,ca(deprecia!)

5.5 Date Restrictions

You can use Westlaw to retrieve documents *decided* or *issued* before, after, or on a specified date, as well as within a range of dates. The following sample queries contain date restrictions:

da(2008) & capital /5 gain

da(aft 1998) & capital /5 gain

da(11/30/1994) & capital /5 gain

You can also search for documents *added to a database* on or after a specified date, as well as within a range of dates, which is useful for updating your research. The following sample queries contain added-date restrictions:

ad(aft 2004) & capital /5 gain

ad(aft 3/15/2005 & bef 4/15/2005) & capital /5 gain

Section 6. Searching with Topic and Key Numbers

To retrieve cases that address a specific point of law, use topic and key numbers as your search terms. If you have an on-point case, run a search using the topic and key number from the relevant headnote in an appropriate database to find other cases containing headnotes classified to that topic and key number. For example, to search for federal cases containing headnotes classified under topic 220 (Internal Revenue) and key number 3114 (Net Income), access the FTX–CS database and type the following query:

220k3114

For a complete list of West digest topics and their corresponding topic numbers, access the West Key Number Digest by clicking **Key Numbers** at the top of any page. Then click **West Key Number Digest Outline** under *Browse Key Numbers*. Alternatively, click **Custom Digest** at a case law database Search page.

> *Note*: Slip opinions and cases from topical services do not contain West topic and key numbers.

6.1 West Key Number Digest

The West Key Number Digest, also known as the Custom Digest, contains the complete topic and key number outline used by West attorney-editors to classify headnotes. You can use the West Key Number Digest to obtain a single document containing all case law headnotes from a specific jurisdiction that are classified under a particular topic and key number.

Access the West Key Number Digest by clicking **Key Numbers** at the top of any page. Then click **West Key Number Digest Outline** under *Browse Key Numbers*. Alternatively, click **Custom Digest** at a case law database Search page. Select up to 10 topics and key numbers from the easy-to-browse outline and click **Search selected**. Then follow the displayed instructions.

For example, to research issues involving taxation, scroll down the list of topics until topic *371 Taxation* is displayed. Click the plus symbols (+) to display key number information. Select the check box next to each key number you want to include in your search, then click **Search selected**. Select the jurisdiction from which you want to retrieve headnotes and, if desired, type additional search terms and select a date restriction. Click **Search**.

6.2   KeySearch

KeySearch is a research tool that helps you find cases and secondary sources in a specific area of the law. KeySearch guides you through the selection of terms from a classification system based on the West Key Number System® and then uses the key numbers and their underlying concepts to provide a query for you.

To access KeySearch, click **Key Numbers** at the top of any page. Then click **KeySearch** under *Browse Key Numbers*. Browse the list of topics and subtopics and select a topic or subtopic to search by clicking the hypertext links. For example, to search for sources that discuss the accrual method of accounting, click **Taxation–Federal** at the first KeySearch page. Then click **Accounting** and **Accrual Basis** at the next two pages, respectively. Select the source from which you want to retrieve documents and, if desired, type additional search terms. Click **Search**.

Section 7. Verifying Your Research with KeyCite

Overview: The KeyCite citation research service is a tool that helps you ensure that your cases, statutes, regulations, and administrative decisions are good law; retrieve cases, legislation, articles, or other documents that cite them; and verify the spelling and format of your citations.

7.1   KeyCite for Cases

KeyCite for cases covers case law on Westlaw, including unpublished opinions. KeyCite for cases provides the following:

- direct appellate history of a case, including related references, which are opinions involving the same parties and facts but resolving different issues

- negative citing references for a case, which consist of cases outside the direct appellate line that may have a negative impact on its precedential value

- the title, parallel citations, court of decision, docket number, and filing date of a case

- citations to cases, administrative decisions, secondary sources, and briefs and other court documents on Westlaw that have cited a case

- complete integration with the West Key Number System so you can track legal issues discussed in a case

7.2   KeyCite for Statutes and Regulations

KeyCite for statutes and regulations covers the USCA, the *Code of Federal Regulations* (CFR), statutes from all 50 states, and regulations from selected states. KeyCite for statutes and regulations provides

- links to session laws or rules amending or repealing a statute or regulation

- statutory credits and historical notes

- citations to proposed legislation affecting a statute

- citations to all drafts of bills proposed before the statute was enacted

- citations to reports, journals, *Congressional Record* documents, presidential or executive messages, and testimony relevant to the statute

- citations to cases, administrative decisions, secondary sources, and briefs and other court documents that have cited a statute or regulation

7.3 KeyCite for Administrative Materials

KeyCite for administrative materials includes materials such as the following:

- Board of Contract Appeals decisions

- Board of Immigration Appeals decisions

- Comptroller General decisions

- Environmental Protection Agency decisions

- Federal Communications Commission decisions

- Federal Energy Regulatory Commission (Federal Power Commission) decisions

- Internal Revenue Service revenue rulings, revenue procedures, private letter rulings, and technical advice memoranda

- National Labor Relations Board decisions

- *Public Utilities Reports*

- U.S. Merit Systems Protection Board decisions

- U.S. Patent and Trademark Office decisions

- U.S. patents

- U.S. Tax Court (Board of Tax Appeals) decisions

7.4 KeyCite Alert

KeyCite Alert monitors the status of your cases, statutes, regulations, and administrative decisions and automatically sends you updates at the frequency you specify when their KeyCite information changes.

Section 8. Researching with Westlaw: Examples

8.1 Retrieving Law Review Articles

Recent law review articles are often a good place to begin researching a legal issue because law review articles serve as an excellent introduction to a new topic or review for an old one, providing terminology to help you formulate a query; as a finding tool for pertinent primary authority, such as cases, statutes, and rules; and in some instances, as persuasive secondary authority.

Suppose you need to gain background information on the factors the federal courts have considered in determining whether punitive damage awards are taxable.

Solution

- To retrieve law review articles relevant to your issue, access the Journals and Law Reviews database (JLR). Using the Natural Language search method, type a description like the following:

are punitive damages awards taxable

- If you have a citation to an article in a specific publication, use Find to retrieve it. (For more information on Find, see Section 3.1 of this appendix.) For example, to retrieve the article found at 71 Notre Dame L. Rev. 913, access Find and type

71 notre dame l rev 913

- If you know the title of an article but not the journal in which it was published, access the JLR database and search for key terms in the title field. For example, to retrieve the article "From Injury to Income: The Taxation of Punitive Damages 'On Account of' United States v. Schleier," type the following Terms and Connectors query:

ti(taxation & punitive & schleier)

8.2 Retrieving Administrative Law

Suppose you need to retrieve IRS revenue rulings addressing the deductibility of medical expenses.

Solution

- Access the Federal Taxation–Revenue Rulings database (FTX–RR). Type a Terms and Connectors query such as the following:

deduct! /p medical

- When you know the citation for a specific revenue ruling, use Find to retrieve it. For example, to retrieve Rev. Rul. 2007–72, access Find and type

rev rul 2007–72

8.3 Retrieving Case Law

Suppose you need to retrieve U.S. Supreme Court cases discussing transfers of property of like kind.

Solution

- Access the Federal Taxation–Supreme Court Cases database (FTX–SCT). Type a Terms and Connectors query such as the following:

transfer! exchang! /s property /s like-kind in-kind

- When you know the citation for a specific case, use Find to retrieve it. For example, to retrieve ***Cottage Sav. Ass'n v. Comm'r,*** 111 S. Ct. 1503 (1991), access Find and type

111 sct 1503

- If you find a topic and key number that is on point, run a search using that topic and key number to retrieve other cases discussing that point of law. For example, to retrieve federal cases containing headnotes classified under topic 220 (Internal Revenue) and key number 3184 (Exchange of Property), access the FTX–CS database and type a query like the following:

220k3184

- To retrieve opinions written by a particular judge, add a judge field (ju) restriction to your query. For example, to retrieve opinions written by Judge Hug of the U.S. Court of Appeals for the Ninth Circuit that contain headnotes classified under topic 220 (Internal Revenue), access the FTX–CTA database and type the following query:

ju(hug) & to(220)

- You can also use KeySearch and the West Key Number Digest to retrieve cases and headnotes that discuss the issue you are researching.

8.4 Retrieving Statutes and Regulations

Suppose you want to retrieve federal regulations concerning notice of qualification as executor of a decedent's estate.

Solution

- Access the Federal Taxation–Code of Federal Regulations database (FTX–CFR). Search for your terms in the prelim (pr) and caption (ca) fields using the Terms and Connectors search method:

pr,ca(estate & executor /s qualif!)

- When you know the citation for a specific regulation, use Find to retrieve it. For example, to retrieve 26 C.F.R. § 20.6036, access Find and type

26 cfr 20.6036

- To look at surrounding sections, use the Table of Contents service. Click **Table of Contents** on the Links tab in the left frame. To display a section listed in the table of contents, click its hypertext link.

8.5 Using KeyCite

Suppose one of the cases you retrieve in your case law research is *United States v. Burke*, 112 S. Ct. 1867 (1992). You want to make sure it is good law and retrieve a list of citing references.

Solution

- Use KeyCite to retrieve direct history and negative citing references for *Burke*. Access KeyCite and type **112 sct 1867**.

- Use KeyCite to display citing references for *Burke*. Click **Citing References** on the Links tab in the left frame.

8.6   Following Recent Developments

If you are researching issues related to taxation, it is important to keep up with recent developments. How can you do this efficiently?

Solution

One of the easiest ways to follow recent developments in taxation is to access the Westlaw Topical Highlights–Taxation database (WTH–TAX). The WTH–TAX database contains summaries of recent legal developments, including court decisions, legislation, and materials released by administrative agencies. When you access WTH–TAX, you automatically retrieve a list of documents added to the database in the last two weeks.

You can also use the WestClip® clipping service to stay informed of recent developments of interest to you. WestClip will run your Terms and Connectors queries on a regular basis and deliver the results to you automatically. You can run WestClip queries in legal and news and information databases.

Table of Cases

*

Table of Internal Revenue Code Sections

641

UNITED STATES CODE ANNOTATED

26 U.S.C.A.—Internal Revenue Code

Sec.	This Work Sec.	Note
465(a)(2)	14.04	4
465(b)	14.04	
465(b)	14.04	2
465(b)	14.04	3
465(b)(6)	14.04	6
465(d)	14.04	
468(d)(1)	14.05	21
468(d)(2)	14.05	21
469	12.01	
469	14.05	
469	14.05	5
469(a)	14.05	2
469(a)	14.05	18
469(a)(1)(B)	14.05	22
469(a)(2)	14.05	1
469(b)	14.05	3
469(b)	14.05	4
469(b)	14.05	19
469(c)	14.05	
469(c)(1)	14.05	6
469(c)(1)(A)	14.05	5
469(c)(1)(B)	14.05	13
469(c)(2)	14.05	
469(c)(3)	14.05	11
469(c)(7)	14.05	12
469(c)(7)	14.05	16
469(c)(7)(ii)	14.05	33
469(c)(7)(ii)	14.05	34
469(e)	14.05	
469(e)(2)	14.05	23
469(g)	14.05	15
469(g)	14.05	20
469(g)	14.05	34
469(g)(1)	14.05	29
469(g)(1)(B)	14.05	31
469(h)(1)	14.05	7
469(h)(2)	14.05	
469(i)(1)	14.05	26
469(i)(2)	14.05	26
469(i)(3)(A)	14.05	28
469(i)(5)	14.05	24
469(i)(6)	14.05	27
469(j)(5)	14.05	25
469(j)(6)	14.05	32
469(m)(2)	14.05	12
471	5.08	
471	10.11	
471(a)	5.08	2
472	5.08	
481(a)	5.09	
481(a)	5.09	2
481(a)	5.09	3
481(b)	5.09	2
482	10.11	114
483	8.05	
483	10.11	
483	10.11	31
483	10.11	103
483(a)	10.11	29
483(a)(1)	10.11	30

UNITED STATES CODE ANNOTATED

26 U.S.C.A.—Internal Revenue Code

Sec.	This Work Sec.	Note
501(a)	13.02	
501(c)(3)	13.02	41
509(a)(2)	4.19	
509(a)(2)	4.19	111
509(a)(3)	4.19	
509(a)(3)	4.19	111
510	1.06	29
511—514	13.02	
529	1.06	35
529	3.06	
529	3.06	27
529	3.06	34
529	3.06	40
529(a)	3.06	
529(a)	3.06	23
529(a)	3.06	26
529(a)	3.06	27
529(b)(1)(A)	3.06	44
529(b)(2)	3.06	28
529(b)(4)	3.06	29
529(b)(5)	3.06	31
529(b)(6)	3.06	30
529(c)	3.06	
529(c)(3)	3.06	
529(c)(3)(A)	3.06	35
529(c)(3)(A)	3.06	36
529(c)(3)(B)(i)	3.06	32
529(c)(3)(B)(i)	3.06	33
529(c)(3)(B)(iv)	3.06	40
529(c)(3)(B)(v)	3.06	34
529(c)(3)(B)(vi)	3.06	34
529(c)(3)(C)	3.06	38
529(c)(6)	3.06	37
529(e)(2)	3.06	39
529(e)(3)(A)	3.06	24
529(e)(3)(B)	3.06	24
529(e)(5)	3.06	
529(e)(5)	3.06	25
530	3.06	
530	3.06	40
530(a)	3.06	41
530(b)(1)	3.06	45
530(b)(3)(A)(i)	3.06	44
530(c)	3.06	42
530(c)	3.06	43
530(d)(4)	3.06	37
611	4.18	
611	10.11	108
611—613A	4.18	
611—613A	4.18	4
611(a)	4.18	
611(b)	4.18	
611(b)(1)	4.18	37
611(b)(2)	4.18	36
611(b)(3)	4.18	35
611(b)(4)	4.18	38
612	4.18	
613	10.11	108
613(a)	4.18	
613(a)	4.18	49

UNITED STATES CODE ANNOTATED

26 U.S.C.A.—Internal Revenue Code

Sec.	This Work Sec.	Note
1234	10.11	37
1234(a)	10.11	
1234(a)(3)	10.11	
1234(a)(3)(A)	10.11	36
1234(a)(3)(B)	10.11	37
1234(a)(3)(C)	10.11	38
1234(b)	10.11	
1234(b)(2)(A)	10.11	40
1234(b)(3)	10.11	39
1234A	10.11	
1234A(1)	10.11	
1234A(1)	10.11	43
1234A(2)	10.11	44
1235	10.11	
1235	10.11	115
1235	10.11	121
1235	10.11	122
1235(a)	10.11	116
1235(a)	10.11	122
1235(a)	10.11	124
1235(a)(1)	10.11	119
1235(a)(2)	10.11	119
1235(b)	10.11	
1235(d)	10.11	
1236	10.11	
1236(a)	10.11	12
1236(b)	10.11	12
1237	10.11	4
1239	10.09	
1239(a)	10.09	1
1239(c)(1)(A)—(c)(1)(C)	10.09	2
1241	10.11	
1242—1244	10.11	
1244	4.17	13
1244	10.11	
1244(b)(1)	10.11	52
1244(b)(2)	10.11	53
1244(c)(1)(B)	10.11	54
1244(c)(1)(C)	10.11	56
1244(c)(3)	10.11	51
1244(c)(3)(A)	10.11	57
1245	4.18	
1245	8.05	
1245	8.05	39
1245	9.02	
1245	10.10	
1245	11.01	18
1245	12.04	15
1245(a)(1)	9.02	53
1245(a)(1)	9.02	55
1245(a)(1)	10.10	3
1245(a)(1)	10.10	7
1245(a)(1)	10.10	10
1245(a)(1)(A)	10.10	9
1245(a)(1)(B)	10.10	9
1245(a)(2)	9.02	53
1245(a)(2)(A)	9.02	54
1245(a)(2)(A)	10.10	8
1245(a)(3)	10.10	1
1245(b)	10.10	5

UNITED STATES CODE ANNOTATED

26 U.S.C.A.—Internal Revenue Code

Sec.	This Work Sec.	Note
1245(d)	10.10	
1250	8.05	
1250	10.10	
1250(a)(1)	10.10	4
1250(a)(1)(A)	10.10	12
1250(c)	10.10	2
1250(d)	10.10	5
1250(h)	10.10	
1252	10.11	
1252(a)(3)	10.11	95
1253	10.11	
1253(a)	10.11	
1253(a)	10.11	84
1253(b)(2)	10.11	
1253(b)(2)(A)	10.11	85
1253(b)(2)(A)—(b)(2)(F)	10.11	84
1253(b)(2)(B)	10.11	86
1253(b)(2)(C)	10.11	87
1253(b)(2)(D)	10.11	88
1253(b)(2)(E)	10.11	89
1253(b)(2)(F)	10.11	90
1253(c)	10.11	
1253(d)	10.11	
1256	2.03	3
1256	7.04	12
1256	10.11	
1256(a)(3)(A)	10.11	47
1256(a)(3)(B)	10.11	47
1256(e)(3)(B)	5.04	3
1256(g)	10.11	45
1271—1288	10.11	
1272	2.03	3
1272	10.11	
1272 et seq.	7.04	11
1272 et seq.	8.02	
1272 et seq.	8.02	9
1272 et seq.	8.03	8
1272 et seq.	8.05	51
1272(a)(1)	8.02	
1272(a)(1)	8.02	16
1272(a)(1)	10.11	28
1272(a)(2)(A)	8.02	17
1272(a)(2)(B)	8.02	18
1272(a)(2)(E)	8.02	19
1272(a)(3)	8.02	
1272(a)(4)	8.02	12
1273(a)	8.02	15
1273(a)(1)	8.02	13
1273(a)(1)	10.11	23
1273(a)(2)	8.02	13
1273(a)(2)	10.11	23
1273(b)	10.11	23
1274	8.05	
1274(a)(1)	8.02	11
1274(a)(1)	8.05	56
1274(a)(2)	8.05	53
1274(a)(2)	8.05	57
1274(b)	8.05	54
1274(c)(3)	8.05	52
1274(d)	2.02	22

*

Table of Treasury Regulations

TREASURY REGULATIONS

Table of Revenue Rulings

---

*

Table of Revenue Procedures

*

Table of Articles and Books Cited

by Accrual Method Taxpayers: The All Events Test and Economic Performance, 49 Ohio St. L.J. 1439 (1989)—§ **5.05, n. 37.**

Dubinsky, The Minnesota Mandatory Seat Belt Law: No Right to be Reckless?, 10 Hamline L. Rev. 229 (1987)—§ **1.02, n. 21.**

Dubroff, The Claim of Right Doctrine, 40 Tax L. Rev. 729 (1985)—§ **5.10, n. 1.**

Edwards, Interest–Free Loans Are Held To Be Gifts in Supreme Court's Recent Dickman Decision, 60 J. Tax'n 266 (1984)—§ **2.02, n. 23.**

Ekonomon, Constructive Receipt of Income Baxter v. Commissioner, 5 Akron Tax J. 241 (1988)—§ **5.04, n. 27.**

Englebrecht & Windlinger, Justifying Reasonable Compensation for Executives of Closely Held Corporations, 31 Tax Executive 321 (1978)—§ **4.09, n. 1.**

Evans, The Condition of the Tax Legislative Process, 39 Tax Notes 151 (1988)— § **1.05, n. 1.**

Exclusive Business Use Distinguishes Deductible Home Office, 74 Prac. Tax Strategies 240 (2005)—§ **4.14, n. 1.**

Fenton & Davis, The Economic Interest Concept: An Illusion?, 33 Oil & Gas Tax. Q. 259 (1984)—§ **4.18, n. 34.**

Ferguson, Hickman & Lubick, Reexamining the Nature and Role of Tax Legislative History in Light of the Changing Realities of the Process, 67 Taxes 804 (1989)—§ **1.02, n. 8; § 1.05, n. 1.**

Ford & Page, Reasonable Compensation: Continuous Controversy, J. Corp. Tax'n 307 (1979)—§ **4.09, n. 1.**

Forney, Appellate Review of Dealer Status in Realty Sales under § 1221, 45 U. Pitt. L. Rev. 847 (1984)—§ **10.11, n. 58.**

Fredenburg, Legal Issues Presented by Motor Vehicle Restraint Systems, 17 Akron L. Rev. 781 (1984)—§ **1.02, n. 19.**

Friedlander, "To Customers:" The Forgotten Element in the Characterization of Gains on Sales of Real Property, 39 Tax L. Rev. 31 (1983)—§ **10.11, n. 58.**

Gadarian & Dezart, The Trade or Business Requirement Under Sec. 174 After Green, 16 Tax Advisor 348 (1985)— § **4.07, n. 18.**

Gaffney, Davis, Weber & Smith–Gaffney, Advance Payments: Rev. Proc. 2004–34 Expands Rev. Proc. 71–21 and Provides Needed Clarity, 101 J. Tax'n 84 (2004)— § **5.05, n. 35.**

Gallagher, The Tax Legislative Process, 3 Rev. Tax'n Individuals 203 (1979)— § **1.05, n. 1.**

Garrison, Help Clients Take Advantage of Tax Breaks for the Disabled, 78 Prac. Tax Strategies 34 (2007)—§ **4.19, n. 54.**

Glassman, "It's Not a Lie if You Believe it:" Tax Shelters and the Economic Substance Doctrine, 58 Fla. L. Rev. 665 (2006)—§ **7.03, n. 100.**

Goldberg, Open Transaction Treatment for Deferred Payment Sales After the Installment Sales Act of 1980, 34 Tax. Lawyer 605 (1981)—§ **7.03, n. 80.**

GOP Senators Attach Comments on Tax Freedom Day to Policy Committee Release, Tax Notes Today, 96 TNT 96–35 (May 15, 1996)—§ **1.02, n. 7.**

Graetz, Paint-by-Numbers Tax Lawmaking, 95 Colum. L. Rev. 609, 612–13 (1995)— § **1.02, n. 14, 15.**

Greenbaum, The Basis of Property Shall Be the Cost of Such Property: How Is Cost Defined?, 3 Tax L. Rev. 351 (1948)— § **7.03, n. 20.**

Gunn, Tax Avoidance, 76 Mich. L. Rev. 733 (1978)—§ **14.06, n. 12.**

Gunn, The Requirement That a Capital Expenditure Create or Enhance an Asset, 15 B.C. Ind. & Comm. L. Rev. 443 (1974)—§ **4.07, n. 2.**

Haig, The Concept of Income–Economic and Legal Aspects, in The Federal Income Tax 1 (Robert Murray Haig ed., 1921)—§ **1.06, n. 6.**

Halperin, Business Deductions for Personal Living Expenses: A Uniform Approach to an Unsolved Problem, 122 U. Pa. L. Rev. 859 (1974)—§ **4.05, n. 3.**

Hammond, The Amortization of Intangible Assets: § 197 of the Internal Revenue Code Settles the Confusion, 27 Conn. L. Rev. 915 (1995)—§ **4.18, n. 16, 17.**

Hariton, When and How Should the Economic Substance Doctrine be Applied?, 60 Tax L. Rev. 29 (2006)—§ **4.18, n. 13; § 4.19, n. 28.**

Harris, Selling or Disposing of Professional Practices, C472 ALI–ABA 37 (1990)— § **10.11, n. 138.**

Hartigan, From Dean and Crown to the Tax Reform Act of 1984: Taxation of Interest–Free Loans, 60 Notre Dame L. Rev. 31 (1984)—§ **2.02, n. 23.**

Hellwig, The Supreme Court's Casual Use of the Assignment of Income Doctrine, 2006 U. Ill. L. Rev. 751 (2006)—§ **6.02, n. 28.**

Heyde, Transfers of Technology: The Appropriateness of Capital Gain Treatment, 64 Taxes 3 (1986)—§ **10.11, n. 113.**

Lee & Murphy, Capital Expenditures: A Result in Search of a Rationale, 1 U. Rich. L. Rev. 443 (1981)—§ **4.07, n. 2.**

Legal Fees Incurred in Litigation Involving Title to Assets—Allocation Between Deductible Ordinary Expenses and Non-Deductible Capital Expenditures, 126 U. Pa. L. Rev. 1100 (1978)—§ **11.02, n. 12.**

Leonard, Perspectives on the Tax Legislative Process, 38 Tax Notes 969 (1988)— § **1.05, n. 1.**

Lester, The "Casualty" to Taxpayers From a Misapplied Application of Internal Revenue Code Section 165(c)(3): The Need for an Objective Approach, 48 S.D. L. Rev. 52 (2003)—§ **4.16, n. 11, 23.**

Lewis, Exploring Section 1015 and Related Topics, 43 Tax Law. 241 (1990)—§ **7.03, n. 33, 35.**

Lieber, Interest–Free Loans, 23 Duq. L. Rev. 1019 (1985)—§ **2.02, n. 23.**

Lipman, Anatomy of a Disaster Under the Internal Revenue Code, 75. 6 Fla. Tax Rev. 953 (2005)—§ **4.16, n. 1.**

Lipton, New Tax Shelter Decisions Present Further Problems for the IRS, 102 J. Tax'n 211 (2005)—§ **4.19, n. 26.**

Luke, Beating the "Wrap:" The Agency Effort to Control Wraparound Insurance Tax Shelters, 25 VA Tax Rev. 129 (2005)—§ **5.04, n. 32.**

Lurie, Crane's Ghost Not Laid to Rest: Still a Work in Progress, According to Owen, 27 J. Real Est. Tax'n 257 (2000)— § **7.03, n. 88.**

Lurie, How Tax Shelters Evolved: The Road From Crane Has Been Paved With Bad Contentions, 100 J. Tax'n 274 (2004)— § **7.03, n. 68, 84.**

Lynch, Income Tax Statute of Limitations: Sixty Years of Mitigation–Enough, Already!!, 51 S.C. L. Rev. 62 (1999)— § **5.12, n. 24.**

Lynch, Travel Expense Deductions Under I.R.C. § 162(a)(2)—What Part of "Home" Don't You Understand?, 57 Baylor L. Rev. 705 (2005)—§ **4.10, n. 13, 17, 21.**

Maloy, Public Policy—Who Should Make it in America's Oligarchy?, 1998 Det. C.L. Mich. St. U. L. Rev. 1147 (1998)— § **4.04, n. 8.**

Malveaux, Statutes of Limitations: A Policy Analysis in the Context of Reparations Litigation, 74 Geo. Wash. L. Rev. 68 (2005)—§ **5.12, n. 10.**

Marroni, Zarin v. Commissioner: Does a Gambler Have Income From the Cancellation of a Casino Debt, 27 New Eng. L. Rev. 993 (Summer 1993)—§ **3.04, n. 13.**

Marsico, Chopping Down The Fruit Tree: Caruth Corp. v. United States Applies Assignment of Income Doctrine to Gift

of Stock Between Declaration and Record Dates, 40 Depaul L. Rev. 845 (1991)—§ **6.02, n. 24; § 6.03, n. 9.**

Massin & McGuire, Death of a Loophole: Recent Legislation and Case Law Dealing with Taxation of Interest–Free and Low–Interest Loans, 24 Am. Bus. L.J. 105 (1986)—§ **2.02, n. 23.**

Masters, et al., Behavior Therapy 245–46 (3d ed. 1987)—§ **1.02, n. 13.**

Maydew, Mitigation Offers Escape from Expired Limitations Period, 65 Prac. Tax Strategies 153 (2000)—§ **5.12, n. 24, 25.**

McCaffery, Cognitive Theory and Tax, 41 UCLA L. Rev. 1861 (1994)—§ **1.02, n. 5, 6.**

McCue & Brosterhous, Interest–Free and Below–Market Loans After Dickman and the Tax Reform Act of 1984, 62 Taxes 1010 (1984)—§ **2.02, n. 23.**

McDaniel, Federal Income Tax Simplification: The Political Process, 34 Tax L. Rev. 27 (1977)—§ **1.05, n. 1.**

McIntyre, An Inquiry into the Special Status of Interest Payments, 1981 Duke L.J. 765—§ **4.19, n. 4.**

Mckee, Income Tax Consequences of Dispositions of Development Rights in Property, 97 J. Tax'n 347 (2002)—§ **7.03, n. 13.**

McMahon, Random Thoughts on Applying Judicial Doctrines to Interpret The Internal Revenue Code, 54 SMU L. Rev. 195 (2001)—§ **6.02, n. 11.**

Melton, Making the Nondiscrimination Rules of Tax–Qualified Retirement Plans More Effective, 71 B.U. L. Rev. 47 (1991)—§ **13.02, n. 98, 99, 103.**

Michaelson, "Business Purpose" and Tax Free Reorganization, 61 Yale L.J. 14 (1952)—§ **14.06, n. 4.**

Miller, Taxpayers' Ability to Avoid Tax Ownership: Current Law and Future Prospects, 51 Tax Law. 279 (1998)— § **6.02, n. 28.**

Mintz & Plumb, Step Transactions in Corporate Reorganizations, 12 N.Y.U. Inst. on Fed. Tax'n. 247 (1954)—§ **14.06, n. 6, 37.**

Moore, Religious Tax Exemption and the "Charitable Scrutiny" Test, 15 Regent U. L. Rev. 295 (2003)—§ **4.19, n. 78.**

Murawski & Schooner, Communicating Governance: Will Plain English Drafting Improve Regulation?, 70 Geo. Wash. L. Rev. 163 (2002)—§ **1.02, n. 25.**

Must Show Year Debt Goes Bad to Claim Bad Debt Deduction, 74 Prac. Tax Strategies 111 (2005)—§ **4.17, n. 9.**

Nasner, The Unexpected Tax Consequences of "Extreme Makeover: Home Edition," 40 Gonz. L. Rev. 481 (2004/2005)— § **4.14, n. 4.**

Newman, Of Taxes and Other Casualties, 34 Hastings L.J. 941 (1983)—§ **4.16, n. 7.**

Newman, On the Tax Meaning of "Ordinary:" How the Ills of Welch Could be Cured Through Christian Science, 22 Ariz. St. L.J. 231 (1990)—§ **4.05, n. 1.**

No Sale, No Exchange—No Capital Gains Treatment, 62 Prac. Tax Strategies 54 (1999)—§ **10.04, n. 9.**

Note, Fiduciary Standards and the Prudent Man Rule Under the Employee Retirement Income Security Act of 1974, 88 Harv. L. Rev. 960 (1975)—§ **13.02, n. 216.**

Note, Sale of Future Income Successful in Accelerating Income into Taxable Year to Fully Utilize a Personal Deduction, 20 Wayne L. Rev. 933 (1974)—§ **6.02, n. 29.**

Note, Section 162(a)(2): Resolving the Tax Home Dispute, 2 Va. Tax Rev. 153 (1982)—§ **4.10, n. 5.**

Note, Step Transactions, 24 U. Miami L. Rev. 60 (1969)—§ **14.06, n. 6, 37.**

Note, The Tax Home Doctrine: Fifty–Five Years of Confusion, 34 Maine L. Rev. 141 (1982)—§ **4.10, n. 5.**

Olson, Federal Income Taxation of Patent and Know–How Transfers, 28 St. Louis U.L.J. 537 (1984)—§ **10.11, n. 113.**

"Ordinary and Necessary" Business Expenses for Entertainers: What's Reasonable?, 87 J. Tax'n 63 (1997)—§ **4.03, n. 14.**

Ordower, Seeking Consistency in Relating Capital to Current Expenditures, 24 Va. Tax Rev. 263 (2004)—§ **4.07, n. 1.**

Palermo, Assault on Crime Criticized, Las Vegas Rev.-J., Oct. 13, 1996—§ **1.02, n. 17.**

Paul, Another Uneasy Compromise: The Treatment of Hedging in a Realization Income Tax, 3 Fla. Tax Rev. 1 (1996)—§ **7.04, n. 20.**

Pearle, Interest–Free and Below–Market Gift Loans, 26 Tax Mgmt. Mem. 3 (1985)—§ **2.02, n. 23.**

Pease, Stephens v. Commissioner and the Continuing Confusion Surrounding the Public Policy Doctrine of the Internal Revenue Code, 11 J.L. & Com. 105 (1991)—§ **4.04, n. 5.**

Pechman, Federal Tax Policy 37–51 (4th ed. 1983)—§ **1.05, n. 1.**

Peschel & Spurgeon, Federal Taxation of Trusts, Grantors & Beneficiaries (RIA 2007)—§ **1.06, n. 21.**

Polito, Constitutional Law: Seatbelt Laws and the Right to Privacy, 10 Harv. J.L. & Pub. Pol'y 752 (1987)—§ **1.02, n. 21.**

Rands, The Closely Held Corporation: Its Capital Structure and the Federal Tax Laws, 90 W. Va. L. Rev. 1009 (1988)— § **4.17, n. 26.**

Rao, Section 266 Carrying Charges: Tax Planning Opportunities, 58 Taxes 787 (1980)—§ **4.07, n. 9.**

Raskolnikov, Contextual Analysis of Tax Ownership, 85 B.U. L. Rev. 431 (2005)— § **4.07, n. 6;** § **4.18, n. 9;** § **5.05, n. 5;** § **10.06, n. 3;** § **10.11, n. 15.**

Reese, The Politics of Taxation (1980)— § **1.05, n. 1.**

Renshaw, Federal Taxation–Timing of Deductions–Deduction by Accrual Basis Taxpayer of its Liability for Medical Services Received by Employees for Which Claims Have not Been Filed Disallowed—§ **5.05, n. 37.**

Repetti, Commentary It's All About Valuation, 53 Tax L. Rev. 607 (Summer 2000)—§ **2.02, n. 49.**

Rice, The Corporate Tax Gap: Evidence on Tax Compliance by Small Corporations, in Why People Pay Taxes 125 (Joel S. Slemrod ed., 1992)—§ **1.02, n. 3.**

Rice, When and How Will the Courts Apply the Mitigation Provisions?, 69 J. Tax'n 106 (1988)—§ **5.12, n. 15.**

Richardson, Maximizing Tax Benefits to Farmers and Ranchers Implementing Conservation and Environmental Plans, 48 Okla. L. Rev. 449 (1995)—§ **4.07, n. 13.**

Rieser, Hitt & Aromatorio, Obtaining an Abandonment or Worthlessness Deduction for a Partnership Interest, 15 JPTAX 42 (1998)—§ **7.04, n. 25.**

Rigney, Zarin v. Commissioner: The Continuing Validity of Case Law Exceptions to Discharge of Indebtedness Income, 28 San Diego L. Rev. 981 (1991)—§ **3.04, n. 13.**

Roberts, Allocation of Costs of Common Improvement to Bases of Benefited Properties Disallowed Under Section 1016(a) (1): Norwest v. Commissioner, 52 Tax Law. 425 (1999)—§ **7.02, n. 6.**

Roche, Jr., Lease Cancellation Payments are Capital Gain? Yes! The TRA '97 Change to 1234A Overturned Hort, 102 J. Tax'n 364 (June 2005)—§ **10.11, n. 80.**

Rohrbach, The Disposition of Properties Secured by Recourse and Nonrecourse Debt, 41 Baylor L. Rev. 231 (1989)— § **7.03, n. 95.**

Root, The Commissioner's Clear Reflection of Income Power Under § 446(b) and the Abuse of Discretion Standard of Review: Where Has the Rule of Law Gone, and Can We Get it Back?, 15 Akron Tax J. 69 (2000)—**§ 5.01, n. 2.**

Rosenberg, The Psychology of Mediation, The Recorder ADR Special Supplement, Spring 1994—**§ 1.02, n. 11.**

Ross, When Did the "Switch In Time" Actually Occur?: Re–Discovering The Supreme Court's "Forgotten" Decisions of 1936–1937, 37 Ariz. St. L.J. 1153 (2005)—**§ 6.02, n. 10.**

Salyer, Lawyers Going Back to School: It's All Tax Deductible, 7 Me. B.J. 40 (1992)—**§ 4.06, n. 13.**

Schenk, A Positive Account of the Realization Rule, 57 Tax L. Rev. 355 (2004)—**§ 7.04, n. 6.**

Schnee & Stara, The Origin of the Claim Test: A Search for Objectivity, 13 Akron Tax J. 97 (1997)—**§ 11.02, n. 12.**

Schneider & Solomon, New Uniform Capitalization and Long–Term Contract Rules, 65 J. Tax'n 424 (1986)—**§ 4.07, n. 4.**

Seago, Do Advance Trade Discounts Represent a Liability or Income?, 105 J. Tax'n 144 (2006)—**§ 5.05, n. 25.**

Seftenberg, Kiss Your Crown (Loan) Goodbye: Below–Market Rate Loans After the Tax Reform Act of 1984, 74 Ill. B.J. 34 (1985)—**§ 2.02, n. 23.**

Seto, Inside Zarin, 59 SMU L. Rev. 1761 (2006)—**§ 3.04, n. 13.**

Shaheen, Tax Planning for the Transfer of Franchises, Trademarks, and Trade Names, 28 J. Corp. Tax'n 11 (2001)—**§ 4.07, n. 37.**

"Shop Talk: Debunking The Crop–Share Analogy To Contingent Attorney's Fee Arrangements," 97 J. Tax'n 320 (Nov. 2002)—**§ 11.08, n. 6.**

"Shop Talk: Whipsaw On Lawsuit Settlements: The Courts Still Can't Agree," 93 J. Tax'n 188 (Sept. 2000)—**§ 11.08, n. 6.**

Siegel & Ballou, The "Primarily for Sale" Provisions of Sections 1221 and 1231 of the Internal Revenue Code as Related to Timber Transactions, 39 Ark. L. Rev. 73 (1985)—**§ 10.11, n. 96.**

Simmons, An Essay on Federal Income Taxation and Campaign Finance Reform, 54 Fla. L. Rev. 1 (2002)—**§ 4.04, n. 33.**

Simons, Personal Income Taxation: The Definition of Income as a Problem of Fiscal Policy 50 (1938)—**§ 1.06, n. 6.**

"Sixth Circuit Reverses Tax Court and Excludes Contingent Attorney's Fees," 99 J. Tax'n 259 (Nov. 2003)—**§ 11.08, n. 6.**

Slemrod, Why People Pay Taxes: Introduction, in Why People Pay Taxes 1 (Joel S. Slemrod ed., 1992)—**§ 1.02, n. 4.**

Spear, "Corporate Business Purpose" in Reorganization, 3 Tax L. Rev. 225 (1947)—**§ 14.06, n. 4.**

Steines, Income Tax Allowances for Cost Recovery, 40 Tax L. Rev. 483 (1985)—**§ 14.06, n. 20.**

Stephan, Federal Income Taxation and Human Capital, 70 Va. L. Rev. 1357 (1984)—**§ 6.03, n. 9.**

Stolworthy, No M.B.A. Left Behind: Professional Education as a Business Expense in Allemeier v. Commissioner, 59 Tax Law. 927 (2006)—**§ 4.06, n. 27, 31.**

Strupp & Binder, Psychotherapy in a New Key, A Guide to Time–Limited Dynamic Psychotherapy 38 (1984)—**§ 1.02, n. 11.**

Stumpff, The Reasonable Compensation Rule, 19 Va. Tax Rev. 371 (1999)—**§ 4.09, n. 9.**

Surrey, The Congress and the Tax Lobbyist—How Special Tax Provisions Get Enacted, 70 Harv. L. Rev. 1145 (1957)—**§ 1.02, n. 8.**

Tax Cheats Called Out of Control, N.Y. Times, August 1, 2006—**§ 1.02, n. 2.**

Thomas, The Art of Abandoning Securities and Taking an Ordinary Loss, 104 JTAX 22 (2006)—**§ 7.04, n. 25.**

Thomas, Freedom to be Foolish? L.B. 496: The Mandatory Seatbelt Law, 19 Creighton L. Rev. 743 (1986)—**§ 1.02, n. 21.**

Thompson & Serrett, Shore–Up Tax Breaks for Weather–Related Casualty Losses, 74 Prac. Tax Strategies 68 (2005)—**§ 4.16, n. 7.**

Tison, Amending the Sentencing Guidelines for Cocaine Offenses: The 100–to–1 Ratio is not as "Cracked" up as Some Suggest, 27 S. Ill. U. L.J. 413 (2003)—**§ 1.02, n. 18.**

Toemo, Slot Machine Player was not a "Professional Gambler," so no "Business Loss," 17–Sep J. Multistate Tax'n 38 (2007)—**§ 4.02, n. 8.**

Watson, Equitable Recoupment: Revisiting an old and Inconsistent Remedy, 65 Fordham L. Rev. 691 (1996)—**§ 5.12, n. 4, 11.**

Weber & Outslay, A House is Not Necessarily a Tax Home: An Examination of the Deductibility of Away-from-Home Expenses, 65 Taxes 275 (1987)—**§ 4.10, n. 1.**

Weidner, Synthetic Leases: Structured Finance, Financial Accounting and Tax Ownership, 25 J. Corp. L. 445 (2000)—**§ 4.18, n. 12.**

Wells & Caplan, Achieving Capital Gains Treatment on Predevelopment Real

Index

References are to Sections

†